H.W. Smith N.Y.

Andrew Johnson

THE

GREAT REBELLION;

A HISTORY OF THE

Civil War in the United States.

BY J. T. HEADLEY,

AUTHOR OF "NAPOLEON AND HIS MARSHALS," "WASHINGTON AND HIS GENERALS," "SACRED MOUNTAINS," ETC., ETC.

WITH NUMEROUS FINE STEEL ENGRAVINGS.

In Two Volumes:
Volume II.

Hartford, Conn.
AMERICAN PUBLISHING COMPANY,
BRANCH OFFICE, COLUMBUS, OHIO.
R. C. TREAT, CHICAGO, ILL.
SOLD BY SUBSCRIPTION ONLY.
1866.

PUBLISHERS' NOTICE.

It is with no ordinary satisfaction and confidence that we issue this Second Volume of the History of the Great Rebellion. No other History of this mighty and memorable conflict, has won so large a favor from the American people. Mr. Headley's genius has here found a subject worthy of, and demanding its amplest resources; and he has successfully risen to the height of the great occasion. He here completes a historic record, that will be read with amazement and the deepest interest by present and future generations—the record of the sacrifices and successes of a people, sacredly cherishing the traditions and legacies of the Fathers and Founders of their Republic, and shrinking from no cost of treasure and blood necessary to subdue the most causeless and criminal insurrection against human rights and human freedom, that ever challenged a nation to the bitter and bloody arbitration of the battle field.

Ours is no dry and dreary compilation, which, even if read, can be of little profit, save to a few minds. It is not the speculations of the political theorist or philosopher, upon the causes and obscure agencies culminating in this atrocious conspiracy against the best human Government. But, it is the vivid and faithful portraiture—by an author of surpassing genius for historic delineation—of all the important events in our Civil War. From it may be got the clearest and most adequate idea of the spirit of the nation, and of the sweep and shock of its armies during these four eventful years of heroism and glory. It is a splendid and faithful panorama of a great people in arms, inspired with a sublime enthusiasm for Law and Liberty. It shows the prominent actors in the Tragedy which has held the gaze of the civilized world—some of them incompetent or unfaithful and disappearing in defeat or dishonor—others grand, heroic, moving to victory or honorable death, blessed with the prayers and love of all true patriots, and crowned with their gratitude and homage.

The delay in the completion of the work, though a pecuniary detriment to us, will however be compensated by important advantages to our subscribers. If it had been issued at the close of the conflict, it must have been written, as were some other Histories, without the aid of the official reports of Generals Grant and Sherman—the only reliable sources of information respecting the last, great and decisive campaigns of the War.

No History can possess perfect accuracy. Authorities of apparently equal claims for credence often differ, and time not infrequently makes disclosures that modify statements and judgments once regarded correct. Special effort has been made to authenticate the statements of this work by a comparison with every accessible authority, and we are confident that it has no superior, and, we think, no equal in fidelity of historical narration.

We have employed the very best Artists in the production of the fine steel engravings which embellish this volume, and though these have been executed during the period of high prices, no expense has been spared to secure in them the highest degree of excellence. The engravings of the two volumes taken together constitute a series of elegant and varied illustrations unequaled in any other History of the War.

In view of its size, its valuable portraits and other illustrations, its elegant typography, and the general excellence of its mechanical execution, we are conscious of having more than fulfilled the pledges made to our subscribers, and in anticipation of their entire satisfaction, send forth this work.

AMERICAN PUBLISHING COMPANY.

LIST OF ILLUSTRATIONS.

VOLUME II.

CONTENTS.

VOLUME II.

CHAPTER I.

JUNE–JULY, 1862.

CHAPTER II.

JULY—AUGUST, 1862.

CHAPTER III.

SEPTEMBER, 1862.

CHAPTER IV.

JULY--AUGUST--SEPTEMBER, 1862.

CHAPTER V.

SEPTEMBER—OCTOBER, 1862.

CHAPTER VI.

OCTOBER, 1862.

CHAPTER VII.

OCTOBER—DECEMBER, 1862.

CHAPTER VIII.

OCTOBER—DECEMBER, 1862.

CHAPTER IX.

DECEMBER, 1862—JANUARY, 1863.

CHAPTER X.

JANUARY, 1863.

CHAPTER XI.

APRIL—MAY, 1863.

CHAPTER XII.

MAY—JULY, 1863.

CHAPTER XIII.

JANUARY—APRIL, 1863.

CHAPTER XIV.

APRIL—JUNE, 1863.

CHAPTER XV.

JULY, 1863.

CHAPTER XVI.

JULY, 1863.

CHAPTER XVII.

AUGUST, 1863.

CHAPTER XVIII.

JULY—AUGUST, 1863.

CHAPTER XIX.

SEPTEMBER, 1863.

CHAPTER XX.

SEPTEMBER—NOVEMBER, 1863.

CHAPTER XXI.

OCTOBER—DECEMBER, 1863.

CHAPTER XXII.

JANUARY—APRIL, 1864.

CHAPTER XXIII.

MARCH—APRIL, 1864.

CHAPTER XXIV.

MAY–JULY, 1864.

CHAPTER XXV.

JULY–SEPTEMBER, 1864.

CHAPTER XXVI.

APRIL–JULY, 1864.

CHAPTER XXVII.

MAY, 1864.

CHAPTER XXVIII

MAY—JUNE, 1864.

CHAPTER XXIX.

JUNE, 1864.

CHAPTER XXX.

JUNE, 1864.

CHAPTER XXXI.

JULY, 1864.

CHAPTER XXXII.

JULY—AUGUST, 1864.

CHAPTER XXXIII.

AUGUST, 1864.

CHAPTER XXXIV.

AUGUST–SEPTEMBER, 1864.

CHAPTER XXXV.

SEPTEMBER, 1864.

CHAPTER XXXVI.

SEPTEMBER—OCTOBER, 1864.

CHAPTER XXXVII.

NOVEMBER—DECEMBER, 1864.

CHAPTER XXXVIII.

NOVEMBER—DECEMBER, 1864.

CHAPTER XXXIX.

JANUARY, 1865.

CHAPTER XL.

JANUARY—FEBRUARY, 1865.

CHAPTER XLI.

FEBRUARY---APRIL, 1865.

CHAPTER XLII

APRIL–MAY, 1865.

Eng^d by H. W. Smith, N.Y.

THE GREAT REBELLION.

CHAPTER I.

JUNE–JULY, 1863.

THE SEVEN DAYS' CONTEST—REMARKABLE FORESIGHT—POSITION OF OUR ARMY—LEE'S PLAN—THE MOVEMENT COMMENCED—BATTLE OF GAINES' MILL—SEVERE LETTER TO THE SECRETARY OF WAR—DESTRUCTION OF PROPERTY—A TRAIN CUT ADRIFT—THE RETREAT—ARMY TRAIN—BATTLE OF SAVAGE STATION—BATTLE OF NELSON'S FARM AND GLENDALE—BATTLE OF MALVERN HILL—RETREAT TO HARRISON'S LANDING—FEELINGS OF THE PEOPLE—LETTER OF THANKS FROM THE PRESIDENT—MC CLELLAN'S LETTER TO THE PRESIDENT ON THE POLICY THAT SHOULD BE ADOPTED IN PROSECUTING THE WAR—EFFECT OF IT ON HIMSELF.

BEFORE McClellan had fully determined that retreat would be necessary, he had decided in what direction it should be, when it became inevitable, viz., to James River, and not back to the base of his supplies at the White House.

With a foresight that seems almost like a divine premonition, he sent to Fortress Monroe to have transports carry up supplies to Harrison's Landing on James River, to be ready for his exhausted troops when they should arrive there, and with them gunboats, to co-operate with his land forces as circumstances might direct. These precautions saved him from annihilation. Having thus done all that human sagacity or foresight could accomplish, he anxiously waited the decisive movements of the enemy, which should settle at once his course of action.

To understand the exact position of our army at this time, it is necessary only to remember that the Richmond and York River railroad, running east to the White House, (the base of supplies,) and the Chickahominy River, form the two sides of a letter V—Bottom's bridge being at the point. The right arm of the V looking north is the river, which our forces occupied up to Mechanicsville north of Richmond, and the left arm is the railroad, running directly towards Richmond. The Williamsburg stage road ran alongside of the railroad, and not far from it. On the railroad, directly in front of the rebel capital, stood our intrenchments.

Here, and between the river and rebel fortifications, extending northward from the city, lay eight divisions of our army. On the opposite side of the river was General Porter, with two divisions, and the regular reserves, to guard against a flank movement from the north, which *should* have been taken care of by McDowell. The other flank, south of the railroad and turnpike, was protected by the White Oak Swamp.

This was McClellan's position; and in case of retreat, two courses lay open to him—either to fall back along the route by which he had advanced, to the White House on York River, or cross the White Oak Swamp southward, and reach the James River, where he still would be in striking distance of the rebel capital.

The various roads by which the enemy, from his central position at Richmond, could advance on the Union army, stretching from White Oak Swamp nearly to Mechanicsville, may be understood, by standing with the face toward it in Richmond and placing the right hand spread out, on the map. The thumb would represent the space between the Central railroad and Mechanicsville turnpike—the forefinger, the road to the New Bridge—the middle finger, the York

River railroad and Williamsburg turnpike running near each other—the space between this and the third finger, the White Oak Swamp—the finger itself, the Charles City turnpike south of it, and the little finger the Derbytown road, still nearer the James River. By these two latter roads, the rebels could swarm from Richmond, and fall on the heads of columns as they emerged from White Oak Swamp, should McClellan attempt to retreat towards the James River.

As soon as Lee ascertained that McDowell was not to advance to the aid of McClellan, and the country was clear around the right flank of the latter, he called in all his troops from the northern part of Virginia, including Stonewall Jackson, till he had a force in hand nearly double that of the Union army. With this, he resolved at once to fall on McClellan, and utterly destroy his whole army. The plan he adopted was a very simple one, and almost certain of success. It was to send an entire army beyond the Chickahominy, and with a single blow, crush the comparatively small force there, and keeping down its banks, get between McClellan and the White House, and thus cut off supplies and starve him into a surrender, or crush him between the two armies in front and rear—each equal to his entire force.

If in this dilemma, he should attempt to move off towards James River, through White Oak Swamp, he was to be received beyond it, by heavy columns from Richmond, which occupying all the roads, should hem him in in that direction, so that no supplies could reach him from any quarter. It was a gigantic scheme, and complete in every part, while the means were at hand to carry it into successful execution. Nothing but the most consummate generalship, and the steadiest troops, could extricate the American commander from the terrible position in which it would inevitably place him.

The main Union army, it will be remembered, was between the Chickahominy and Richmond. Fitz John Porter, however, with the fifth corps, was on the north side—his communication with it preserved by numerous bridges. The first object of the enemy was to sweep this force away, and then keep down the river in our rear. At the same time he was to attack in front, to prevent reinforcements from being sent to Porter.

The storm which had been slowly gathering, at length, on the 26th of June, burst in all its fury on the devoted army. The day was clear and warm, and at about three o'clock in the afternoon, Jackson moved from Ashland down the Chickahominy. Driving our advanced pickets before him, he uncovered the bridge at Brook turnpike, and General Branch, who was on the opposite side, crossed over, and wheeling to the right, kept down the north bank a little in the rear of Jackson, who gradually worked off towards the Pamunkey. The two divisions kept on till they reached Meadow Bridge, from which they also swept all obstacles, and A. P. Hill, on the other side, crossed over and joined Branch. The three columns now moved down towards Mechanicsville—Jackson in advance, stretching off towards the Pamunkey to get in flank and rear, Branch next, and Hill last, resting his right on the Chickahominy. Thus moving *en echelon*, they advanced on the Union batteries and a fierce artillery action commenced, which shook the shores of the stream, and rolled in heavy thunder peals over the city of Richmond. But our troops were in a strong position along the left bank of Beaver Dam Creek, the left resting on the Chickahominy, and the right on a thick piece of woods. Seymour's brigade held the left, reaching from the river to a little beyond Ellison's Mills—woods and open ground alternating—and Reynolds the right, mostly in the woods. Felled timbers and rifle pits strengthened the position, and the creek could be crossed by artillery, only on two roads, along which the fight chiefly raged. Our batteries swept the ground beyond the creek, yet in face of their murderous fire, the enemy advanced intrepidly towards the stream, making his most desperate effort along the upper road, where Reynolds was posted. The struggle was fierce but short, and the rebel host surged back. Determined, however, to carry the position at whatever cost, the rebel leaders, under a fierce artillery fire along their whole line, massed their troops for another attack. With shouts and yells that rose over the roar of cannon, they again advanced, only to be mowed down with terrible slaughter from the steady murderous fire poured in from Seymour's brigade. The battle raged for six hours, or until nine o'clock at night, when the enemy retired.

McClellan now ascertained that Jackson was moving rapidly down on his communications, far to the right of Porter, and directed him to fall back, while the heavy guns and wagons were sent across the river.

BATTLE OF GAINES' MILL.

At Gaines' Mill a second position was taken, so as to cover the bridges, while Stoneman, who had been in command of a flying column to protect Porter's flank, was sent off towards the White House, to prevent its being cut off by Jackson.

The new position was the arc of a circle, and opposite the army of McClellan, on the other side of the stream. Morell's division held the left of this line, which extended about a mile and a half, its extremity resting on the slope that descended to the stream, and commanded by Butterfield. Martindale came next, and then Griffin, who touched the left of Sykes' division, which extended to the rear of Cold Harbor. Each brigade had two regiments in reserve.

McCall's division, which had been heavily engaged the day before, formed a second line in rear, with Meade's brigade on the left, near the Chickahominy, and Reynold's on the right. Seymour was held in reserve in the rear. The artillery was posted on the elevations around, and in the spaces between the divisions and brigades.

This was the position of that portion of the army which was on the north side of the stream at noon, on the 27th of June. The enemy, relying on his superior numbers, advanced with such determination upon our line of battle, that by two o'clock, Porter sent to McClellan for reinforcements and more axes, to complete his defences. General Barnard, by whom the order was sent, never delivered it,—an act of disobedience or neglect, meriting the severest condemnation, —and by three o'clock, Porter was so fiercely pushed, that the entire second line and the reserves had to be ordered forward to support the first. An half hour later, Slocum's division reached him, having been hurried across the bridges by McClellan as soon as he heard of Porter's sore need. When it came into action, Porter's whole force numbered about thirty-five thousand men, while that of the enemy was full sixty thousand, if not more. With his overwhelming numbers, he dashed now on one portion of the line, and now on another, each time repulsed with terrible slaughter. But our troops, most of which had been severely tasked by the previous day's fighting, were rapidly becoming exhausted, and at five o'clock an officer dashed into McClellan's headquarters, with an urgent demand for more reinforcements, as the day was going against them. McClellan had already sent all that he felt he could spare, for an overwhelming force was on his side of the river also, ready to swoop down on him, the moment his exhausted numbers gave them the opportunity. And yet so pressing was the danger, that he sent over French's and Meagher's brigades.

The scene which the battle field presented at this moment was one of imposing grandeur. Thirty-five thousand exhausted, beleagured men, enveloped in the smoke of their own guns, stood bravely battling against twice their number, that darkened all the surrounding country with their moving masses. The last of our reserves are in, and have been for some time, and now the enemy is moving up his own for a final assault. The thunder of artillery, which has been breaking along the whole line for four long hours, is redoubled, while the crash of musketry, fierce, rapid and incessant, tells the Commander-in-chief, that the final hour has come. Oh for but ten thousand of those forty thousand of McDowell's, fatally held back in this hour of terrible need, and the victory would be sure. But alas, they are lounging idly in their camps on the banks of the Rappahannock, while their brave comrades here, are falling thick as autumn leaves, in a vain effort to uphold the honor of the flag.

The summer sun was sinking in the western sky, which, without a cloud, looked like a sea of blood through the smoke of battle that filled all the air. In the valley, the long lines of lancers might be seen, their pennons fluttering in the breeze, waiting the pealing bugle note that shall send them headlong on the heavy battalions,—their sabre-points sending long lines of light over the green fields, dotted with groves on every side, while the gentle stream, reflecting the crimson light, murmurs gently along as though its sweet music was not drowned in the wild uproar that shakes its banks. It is a placid summer evening, and a beautiful landscape spreads away on every side, but the eye of the commander sees naught of this. His swelling heart is ready to burst, as he sees the ever-increasing flood of the enemy, and no troops with which to stem it. Oh for night to come! was his mental exclamation. But it is all in vain. The heavy reserves are steadily pressing back Porter's left, and it begins to crumble, until the disorder reaches the very centre of the Federal lines. "There is no panic, the men do not fly in the wild excitement of fear; but deaf to every appeal, they march off deliberately, as if success were impossible." In vain the officers fling themselves in front of the troops, and shout to them to stand by their flag—in vain they offer to lead them back on the foe. On foot, his horse having been shot under him, Butterfield, surrounded by his falling staff, plants a flag and calls on his men to rally around it,—but in vain. With sword in hand, aids dash amid the broken ranks with stirring appeals, in vain. Amid the storm of shot and shell, the gallant leaders move and fall, in vain. The battle is lost, and nothing now remains but to save it from becoming a rout. Then came the order for the cavalry to charge. The bugles rang out over the horrible din and uproar, and with sabres shaking over their heads, the Fifth cavalry, shouting as they rode, dashed fiercely on the dense battalions. But they might as well have dashed on a rock. Broken into fragments by the shock, they galloped wildly back through the artillery and flying infantry, sending up a cloud of dust in their headlong passage, and increasing tenfold the hopeless disorder. Borne back for a mile, the shattered army came upon the fresh brigades of Meagher and French, standing like a wall of iron, on the field. Undismayed by the frightful wreck that came heaving wildly down upon them, they maintained their firm formation, and hurled it scornfully back, and sent up a loud hurrah that rose over the tumult and told the enemy that fresh troops were on the field. Advancing boldly to the front, they arrested the confident and on rushing enemy, and gave time for our troops to rally. Twilight had now settled over the landscape, and the enemy, having exhausted all his reserves, and weary with his long and desperate conflict, paused in his victorious career, and fell back, and the bloody day was ended. The slaughter had been fearful on both sides, and the trampled green sward and dusty roads were crimson with the blood of brave men, and sprinkled thickly with the dead and wounded. Twenty-three guns were left in the enemy's hands as trophies, and many prisoners, among them the gallant General Reynolds.

It was while smarting under this defeat and slaughter of his brave troops, that McClellan used the following strong and stinging language to the Secretary of War:—

"I know that a few thousand more men would have changed this battle from a defeat to a victory. As it is, the government must not, and cannot, hold me responsible for the result.

"I feel too earnestly to-night. I have seen too many dead and wounded comrades to feel otherwise than that the government has not sustained this army. If you do not do so now, the game is lost.

"If I save this army now, I tell you plainly, that I owe no thanks to you, or to any other persons in Washington.

"You have done your best to sacrifice this army."

This was a terrible accusation to come from a General-in-chief on the field of battle, but it is one from which the Secretary of War has never yet successfully vindicated himself. That night the entire army was transferred to the other side of the river, preparatory to the movement of the whole force to the James River. All the wagons, heavy guns, etc., were also gathered there, and General Keyes, with his corps, sent across the White Oak Swamp to seize strong positions on the opposite side, so as to cover the passage of the trains and the army. Orders were also sent to embark all the troops and stores at the White House, and destroy what could not be removed. This was done, and a whole loaded train that could not be saved, was afterwards sent adrift, with a full head of steam on, which, rushing unguided along the track, plunged headlong into the stream, the bridge over it having been destroyed. Huge fires, caused by the burning material collected on the route to the White House, lightened the midnight heavens, leaving no fragment of the rich spoils which the enemy had fondly hoped to seize. The bridges over which our troops had passed were also destroyed, so that when morning dawned, the Army of the Potomac was all on the Richmond side of the Chickahominy, while more than half of the Confederate forces were on the opposite side, and the bridges broken down between. This was a complete surprise to the enemy, and compelled him for awhile to rest—powerless to do mischief. This result had been planned by McClellan, for he needed the time it gave him, to get his immense trains across the swamp, before his army began to móve. Tangled up between his corps, it would throw every thing into comfusion. Only a single road crossed the swamp, along which five thousand wagons, twenty-five hundred cattle,his immense siege train,and various war material had to be transported. It required nice calculation and prompt, rapid movements to accomplish all this before the overwhelming force of the enemy would be on his rear, and rushing down, at right angles, on his line of march along the roads leading from Richmond beyond the swamp.

The 28th was a quiet day to both armies, so far as hostilities were concerned; but the Army of the Potomac was stripping itself for the race and the struggle before it. The distance to the James River was only seventeen miles, so that along that single line of road, scarcely half of the immense train would have entered the swamp when its head would be on James River. All day long it was winding, like a mighty serpent, its tedious length through the forest, whose gloomy recesses resounded with the rumbling of wheels, the lowing of cattle, and the shouts and curses of men, as they urged on their teams. Time pressed, and the huge caravan was crowded along the hot and narrow way to its utmost speed. Wounded men lay bleeding in the wagons, or limped along beside them, while every ear was turned to catch the thunder of cannon from the pursuing foe. It was oppressively hot, yet all day and night the vast throng of wagons kept hurrying forward to give room for the army, for the peril to which it was exposed increased with every hour's delay. The moon rose over the dark forest about nine o'clock, and revealed a strange, confused, wild spectacle; but its light was dimmed by a thunder cloud, that pushing up the heavens, sent peal after peal like the roar of artillery over the alarmed multitude.

The next day was the Sabbath, but not a day of rest to that imperilled army. Early in the morning McClellan broke up his head-quarters at Savage Station, and moved across the swamp, to examine the ground beyond, for the disposition of the corps, and make sure his communication with the gunboats, without which all would be lost. He sent Slocum also across, to relieve Keyes, so that the latter could move on to James River. Porter was to follow, to make the communication sure. The whole army now began to move. Sumner, who was at Fair Oaks, started at daylight towards Savage Station, but before he reached it was attacked at Allen's field. With Richardson's and Sedgwick's divisions he succeeded however in holding the rebels at bay for three hours. In the meantime, the enemy, having repaired the bridges, began to cross the Chickahominy and were now advancing towards Savage Station.

Franklin hearing of it, sent word to Sumner, who pushed on to that point and assumed chief command. It was plain that a battle must be fought here to cover the retreat.

BATTLE OF SAVAGE STATION.

Sumner, Franklin and Heintzelman were here—on whom the Commander-in-chief could rely, and he told them to hold that position till dark, and right gallantly was the order obeyed. The public property which had accumulated here was first destroyed, so as not to fall into the hands of the enemy, and then they prepared for a stubborn resistance.

In vain did the enemy move upon this noble rear guard, determined to break through to the trains beyond. It knew the mighty trust which had been reposed in it, and that it held the destiny of the army in its hands. Sumner and Franklin's commands were drawn up in line of battle, in an open field, the right stretching down the road, and the left resting on a piece of woods held by Brooks' brigade. About four o'clock the rebels, in overpowering masses, came moving down the Williamsburg road, and fell with savage fury on Burns' brigade. They could not have selected a worse point of attack, for a more gallant and stubborn commander never led troops to battle than he. Rooted to the ground —his hat pierced with balls, and bleeding from a wound in his face, he beat back the hostile battalions with a stern courage that elicited the highest praise from even the cautious Sedgwick. Hazzard'sand Pettit's batteries covered themselves with glory. The battle raged for five hours, or until nearly nine o'clock—the thunder of the guns breaking in successive crashes over the forest, and sending consternation through the struggling trains far ahead, and urging them on to still greater speed.

As soon as the battle was over, Sumner received orders to fall back across the swamp. He obeyed reluctantly, for his blood was up, and he wished to punish still further the presumptuous foe. But the columns were quickly put in motion, and by midnight were all on the road to White Oak Swamp, General French bringing up the rear. All night long the brave but weary columns toiled on through the forest, and just as the rays of the sun were tipping the tree tops, the last regiment crossed White Oak Swamp bridge, and then the bridge itself was destroyed.

One of the most difficult steps of the perilous feat which McClellan had attempted to perform was now accomplished. His trains were well on towards James River; the enemy in the rear were arrested in their pursuit, and he had now chiefly the forces sent down from Richmond to contend with, which were designed to fall on him in flank and cut his army in two. The enemy on the Chickahominy had two sides of a triangle to traverse to reach him by this route, while he had but one, so that though he had to delay his march till his immense trains got away, he was able to have heavy forces guarding the roads leading from Richmond on the farther side of the swamp.

In the meantime, as soon as daylight revealed to the enemy that Sumner had abandoned Savage Station, and fallen back through the swamp, he started in pursuit, but on finding the bridge destroyed was compelled to halt on the banks of the stream. Here, planting his batteries, he opened a furious artillery fire on Franklin, who with his division had been left to defend the crossing. But Keyes handled his artillery with a skill that baffled all his efforts.

BATTLE OF NELSON'S FARM AND GLENDALE.

But while Franklin was thus keeping back the enemy that had followed through the swamp from Savage Station, a fierce battle was raging farther on towards the James River, with a rebel army under A. P. Hill which had moved down from Richmond, between the swamp and river. The first road that intersected our line of march after crossing the White Oak Swamp was the Charles City road, and this Slocum was left to guard. Farther on towards the James, was the Newmarket road. McCall was posted on this, with Meade's brigade on his right, and Seymour's on his left; the batteries of Randall, Kern, Cooper, Diedrich and Kanahan all posted in front of the infantry line. The country was open in front, leaving a clean sweep for the artillery.

About three o'clock the enemy was seen moving in heavy force upon this position, and at the same time coming down the Charles City road on Slocum. Checked here by the artillery, they, a little later, fell with desperate fury on McCall's division. Right in the face of the death-dealing batteries they advanced with grand, heroic courage, and though swept by the storm of grape and canister, closed up their rent columns and still faced the fiery sleet without flinching. The slaughter was frightful, but making good the losses with fresh troops, the rebel leaders pressed this devoted division with such fury that at length it was compelled to fall back. The gallant, fiery leaders, Hooker and Kearney, were hurried to the rescue, and falling with their weary, heroic columns on the shouting, victorious enemy, hurled him back stunned and astonished. The battle lasted till after dark, and again the Union troops had showed their indomitable valor. Here Burns again distinguished himself, and here the Sixty-third Pennsylvania, under Colonel Hays, and the Thirty-seventh New York Volunteers covered themselves with glory, for by their rapid volleys and desperate charge, they repelled the third attack, though made by overwhelming numbers. There was fighting everywhere to-day. The rebel artillery was thundering on our rear guard at White Oak Swamp bridge; where the roads crossed at right angles our line of march, a fierce battle was raging; while, at the same time the enemy came down on Porter already on the James, to help whom, the gunboats opened with their ponderous guns, sending their awful missiles of death through the astonished hostile lines. The latter, maddened that the foe was about to escape them, resolved at whatever sacrifice of life to break through our long line at some point, and thundered on it from the middle of the swamp to the James River with frightful energy. The whole country was dark with his moving masses, and the summer sun went down in an ocean of rolling smoke, that heaved and rifted before the deafening explosions which made the earth tremble. Our wearied, hungry troops moved amid this carnival of death with a heroism that mocked at numbers, and made that last day of June one long to be remembered. The burdened earth turned red with the blood of the slain, but still our flag floated triumphantly over the field. McCall fell into the hands of the enemy, and Heintzelman, who was in chief command of the troops, began at midnight to fall back towards the James, on the banks of which our trains were now rapidly gathering. Franklin also retired, and McClellan ordered the whole army to fall back to Malvern Hill. He had selected this as the key to his position. Although he had given General Barnard, Engineer-in-chief, special orders as to the location of the troops as fast as they arrived, he on the morning of the first of July, made the entire circuit of the position himself with some of his general officers, to see that no mistake should occur.

BATTLE OF MALVERN HILL.

McClellan had been for the last three days fighting at fearful disadvantages, for his army lay scattered all the way from White Oak Swamp to the James River,—a line too long to be held throughout by his enfeebled army, and yet which could not be shortened without peril. The communication with the river must be kept up on account of his transports, the trains be protected, the enemy in the rear held back, and all the roads coming down from Richmond strongly guarded; hence, when the enemy appeared in overwhelming numbers at any given point, the wearied troops guarding it were compelled to hold it till reinforcements could be hurried up from some other point. But now all this was changed. He had his noble army once more well in hand, and concentrated where it could strike its powerful blows like a single engine. But the rebels had also concentrated their forces, outnumbering his own, two to one, and was preparing to make one last great effort to wring victory from the hand of adverse fate.

Malvern Hill, on which McClellan had drawn up his wearied but unconquerable host, is a plateau about a mile and a half long, and three-quarters of a mile wide, with several roads, converging to a single point, running over it. On the side towards the river, the slope ended in a deep ravine, which stretched to the shore. Here Porter was posted, with one brigade in the plain, to check any flanking movement; and here, too, in the stream, were stationed the gunboats, under Commodore Rodgers, for the purpose of hurling their ponderous shells into the advancing columns of the enemy. In front were several ravines, furnishing natural obstacles to an approaching enemy, while the ground sloped away, giving a clean sweep for the artillery. On this plateau McClellan massed his splendid artillery, at least three hundred guns, frowning, like a brow of wrath, on the plain below, while on the highest point, dominating all, Col. Tyler had planted ten of his heavy siege guns. This officer had made almost superhuman efforts to save his unwieldy siege train amid the struggling mass that crowded the road through White Oak Swamp, and had succeeded with the loss of only three guns, which had broken down, and so could not be brought off. Justly proud of his achievement, he now determined they should no longer remain useless burdens, and dragged these ten pieces to the top of the hill, that their voices should first speak in the coming conflict.

McClellan had not enough men to make his whole line of battle strong as it ought to be, and so he massed his main force to the north and east, conjecturing the weight of attack would come from that quarter—against his left wing. The pursuing force coming from White Oak Swamp, and that rushing down from Richmond, he thought, would make the attack in that direction, instead of losing time by swinging round down stream to the right wing, which would endanger their own communication with the Capital.

In front of Porter's division, the artillery was so posted that the tremendous fire of sixty cannon could be concentrated on any single point, and made that grim chieftain feel that the troops which could reach him must be something more than flesh and blood. Sykes commanded his left, and Morell, his right divisions; Couch came next, and after him, Kearney and Hooker, then Sedgwick and Richardson, Smith and Slocum, strong leaders every one, on whom their chieftain could in that last trying hour rely with unbounded trust. A portion of Keyes' Corps finished the line, that curved back nearly to the river again below, in a huge semicircle. The shattered, mutilated Pennsylvania reserve corps was stationed behind Porter and Couch as a reserve.

Thus stood the immortal army of the Potomac on the first of July. When all was completed, McClellan, with his brilliant Staff, galloped along the mighty line, followed by the deafening cheers of his devoted battalions, who felt that they were to fight once more under his immediate eye. Seeing, at a glance, that the fury of the storm, as he had conjectured, was to burst on his left, he took his station there.

The infantry was posted down the hill, so that the artillery had a clean sweep over their heads. The scene was one of imposing grandeur, and as the bright sun looked down upon it, his rays flashed along the triple lines of steel that girdled the hill with light, while the steady ranks belted it with long dark lines—soon to be lines of fire. As far as the eye could see, banners drooped in the still air, while groups of horsemen here and there told where the respective commanders awaited the coming shock. It seemed downright madness for any troops to advance on such an infernal fire as, it was plain, could at any moment open from that plateau. But Magruder, commanding the rebel forces, relying on his overwhelming numbers, determined to carry it. Skirmishing in the plain below commenced between nine and ten in the morning, but the enemy seemed in no haste to enter on the desperate undertaking before him. At length, however, about two o'clock, a dark mass emerged on the plain and moved steadily forward on Couch's division. The artillery opened on both sides, and though ugly rents were made at every step in the enemy's ranks, they closed firmly up, and kept unfalteringly on. An ominous silence rested on Couch's division, which lay motionless on the ground. Still, on swept the hostile column, till within close musket range, when at the word of command, the division sprung to its feet and poured in one deadly volley. Before it, that compact mass was rent like a cloud, torn with an explosion in its own bosom, and was driven in shattered fragments over the field. About four o'clock the firing ceased all along the line, and the hill that for two hours had groaned on its firm foundations, under the heavy crack of artillery, lapsed into silence again. Two hours more passed by, but, about six o'clock, the plain below suddenly opened like a volcano with the fierce fire of all the rebel artillery, and, under its cover. were seen advancing the heavy columns of the enemy. In a moment the hill was in a blaze of light, and from three hundred cannon rained a horrible tempest of shot and shell. Seeing that nothing could long stand before it, the rebel leaders ordered the troops on the double quick, to carry the hill in one impetuous rush. Brigade after brigade, emerging from the distant woods, dashed on a run across the intervening space, and swept up, in one black overwhelming tide, towards the batteries. But when they came within reach of the musketry, the volleys were too murderous for flesh and blood to withstand. The reeling lines shrivelled up before it and disappeared from sight. Still, bent on victory, the rebel leaders reformed their broken battalions; and, bringing forward fresh troops, sent them forward with drums beating and banners flying, in the same all-engulfing fire. More desperate courage was never displayed by any troops on any field than they evinced in these successive charges. Again and again, they crossed the whole line of fire of our batteries, breasting the storm of grape and canister without flinching, till close upon our line of battle, when their shouts of victory arose within short pistol shot of the coolly awaiting ranks. Then the hill side would seem to gap and shoot forth flame. One volley, and instantly the shouting troops were on them with the bayonet, sending them like scattered sheep to their cover, leaving the slope carpeted with their dead. It seemed that each repulse must be the last, and that no troops on earth could be made to advance again, on such certain destruction. But in a few moments the reformed columns would be seen emerging from the sulphurous cloud that canopied the field, and moving swiftly upon the batteries. They advanced, however, only to vanish again when they came within reach of the volleys of the infantry. In the midst of the horrible din and uproar, and this terrible slaughter, ever and anon came the deep boom of the one hundred pounders on board the gunboats, followed by a shrieking mass rushing through the clouds of smoke—the next second to explode, like a clap of thunder, amid the ranks of the astonished foe.

The fiery sun went down on this strange scene,—his beams struggling dimly through the murky atmosphere, but still the work of death went on. As twilight deepened over the field, the puffs of smoke that shot out over the plain were illuminated with flame,—while blazing shells crossed and re-crossed each other in every direction, weaving a fiery net-work over the struggling armies. Into the midst of this pandemonium, every few minutes, fell one of the ponderous shells from the gunboats, bursting with a sound that shook the earth, and sent terror into the rebel ranks. Darkness at length closed the scene, and the shattered, bleeding host of the enemy withdrew in despair. The last blow had been struck and failed, and a loud shout rolled along the Union lines. But what a field it was! The ploughed and trampled earth, the shattered trees and buildings, and the fields strewn with dead horses, broken artillery wagons, muskets and men, looked as if all the forces of heaven and earth had been striving to see what a fearful wreck could be made.

Commodore Rodgers, of the gunboats, in a consultation with McClellan, had said that the southern shore of the river was so near at this point that should the enemy occupy it, it would be impossible to get up the supplies for the army, and as Harrison's Landing was the nearest point of safety, it had been resolved, two days previous, to fall back there. Hence, all day long, while the earth was shaking to the uproar of battle on Malvern Hill, the immense trains were hurrying forward towards Harrison's Landing. To the same point McClellan now directed the army to be moved. This was a delicate operation in the presence of the enemy, especially as the rear of the trains still blocked the road. General Keyes, with his corps, was appointed to cover the manœuvre, and nobly did he fulfill the trust reposed in him. Colonel Averill, with his cavalry, who had done good service in the advance beyond White Oak Swamp, covered the withdrawal of the left wing under Porter, and so skillfully did he manage, that, with only his regiment and Lieut. Colonel Buchanan's brigade of regular infantry, and one battery, he so deceived the enemy, that they allowed him to hold the battle-field unmolested all the next day. General Keyes, by the way in which he took advantage of every formation of ground, and kept the trains closed up, and the army disencumbered of the countless wagons and vehicles of every description that thronged the single road over which he was compelled to move, showed executive ability equal to the management of a great battle, and won the highest praise of his Commander.

The army was at last safe, and the terrible struggle that had been kept up since the 26th of June, was over. Pressed by overwhelming numbers, allowed no rest, scarcely time to snatch a morsel of food, bleeding at every step, and leaving its dead and wounded on almost every foot of ground it had traversed, this gallant army had fought its way triumphantly out of the very jaws of destruction, and now drew up along the banks of the James River, proud and defiant as ever. The mighty effort put forth by the rebel government had failed of success. At an immense sacrifice of life, it had succeded only in compelling McClellan to adopt a better base, from which he could advance surely on Richmond. It is true he had lost 15,000 men in the terrible struggles of the last seven days, but the enemy had suffered still more heavily, and the rebel Capital was crowded with the wounded and dying.

The whole movement had taken the country by surprise. Though every newspaper correspondent had said that unless the army was reinforced, its overthrow or defeat was certain, and although the people wondered and clamored because McDowell, with nearly 40,000 men, was kept idle at Fredericksburg, and cursed the Secretary of War for keeping a part of the army from McClellan, it still would not admit defeat to be possible. It had resolved that Richmond should fall, and that the fourth of July should celebrate its overthrow. Hence, when the first news of the retreat of the army was received, it was confidently believed that it was an advance on Richmond. When the whole truth burst upon the country, it was stunned at the danger it had escaped, and filled with admiration at the valor of the army and skill of its leader, which had not merely kept at bay, but rolled back the overwhelming numbers of the enemy, even in defeat—its last blow, the greatest and most fearful of all. Murmurs and complaints were in every body's mouth, and rage and disappointment filled the land, while Richmond was ablaze with illuminations.

McClellan issued a spirited address to his soldiers, promising soon to lead them into Richmond. The President thanked him in a letter, saying, "I am satisfied that yourself, officers and men, have done the best you could. * * * Ten thousand thanks for it." Two days after, when the full accounts had been received, he wrote again: "Be assured the heroism and skill of yourself, officers and men is, and forever will be, appreciated." McClellan now asked for reinforcements, which the Government at Washington declared itself unable to furnish.

In this crisis of affairs he wrote a letter to the President, dated the 4th of July, in which he sketched out the policy which he thought should be adopted. This letter had an important influence on his destiny, for although it was not made public for more than a year, it was the cause of his removal from the command of the army. The main features of the policy he recommended, were, no confiscation—no emancipation act by the Government—hoping thus to bring about a reaction on the part of the South. These views made him the leader of the Opposition, who immediately named him as the future candidate for the Presidency.

CHAPTER II.

JULY—AUGUST, 1862.

POPE'S CAMPAIGN—POPE CALLED TO THE ARMY OF VIRGINIA—HIS ORDERS—CONCENTRATION OF HIS ARMY—HALLECK MADE GENERAL-IN-CHIEF—HIS PLAN OF OPERATIONS—MC CLELLAN RECALLED FROM THE PENINSULA—HIS LETTER OF REMONSTRANCE—LEE TAKES ADVANTAGE OF THE BLUNDER OF HALLECK—BATTLE OF CEDAR MOUNTAIN—LEE'S GREAT MOVEMENT BEGUN—ACCOUNT OF SUBSEQUENT OPERATIONS—BATTLE OF BULL RUN—BATTLE OF GROVETON—THE LAST DAY'S BATTLE—THE ARMY FALLS BACK TO THE FORTS—LEE MOVES TOWARDS THE POTOMAC—MC CLELLAN'S TELEGRAM TO HALLECK ASKING PERMISSION TO JOIN THE ARMY—PLACED ONCE MORE AT THE HEAD OF THE ARMY—POPE'S FAILURE—REVIEW OF THE CAMPAIGN.

WHILE these momentous events were passing in front of Richmond, great changes were being introduced into the army around Washington. The President and the country, had had enough of the military strategy of the Secretary of War, and it became imperatively necessary to have some other head, to direct the corps of McDowell, Banks and Fremont, which had been taken away from the General-in-chief. General Pope was, therefore, called from the West, to take command of these, to be called the Army of Virginia, and also of all the troops, in garrison, around Washington. He entered on his duties the 26th of June, the very day on which commenced the seven days' struggle before Richmond. He began his career by issuing two orders, in which he ridiculed the idea of bases of operations and of "securing lines of retreat," declaring that he should leave that for the enemy to do. This was regarded as an indirect stab at the General-in-chief, and hence excited a great deal of ill will against him throughout the country.

Thoughtful men looked upon it as a bad omen, that he should, at the outset of the campaign, avow that he meant to disregard the soundest military maxims, and, like the First Napoleon, revolutionize the science of war.

The "Army of Virginia" numbered, at this time, about fifty thousand men fit for the field, with which Pope was to protect Washington, and co-operate, in some way, with the Army of the Potomac. This force was scattered all along, from Fredericksburg to Winchester, and his first object was to get it together. Adopting the theory, that if the enemy should attempt to advance on Washington by way of the Shenandoah Valley, it would be better, instead of meeting him there, to be more in front of Washington, so as to cut his force in two while on the march, he therefore, began to concentrate his army, in and about Sperryville. By occupying this position, he hoped to be able also, to operate on the enemy's line of communication, in the direction of Gordonsville and Charlottesville, so as to draw off a part of the army arrayed against McClellan. It has been seen, however, that the movement was too late to effect the latter object. In the meantime the President began to see that to have two distinct armies operating against the same point, and yet entirely independent of each other, with no common head but the Secretary of War whose incapacity to direct movements in the field, had been tested to his satisfaction, would only complicate the difficulties of the situation instead of removing them, sent for General Halleck to assume the chief command. This officer, who had never fought a battle, and never conducted a campaign in person, except the extraordinary one against Corinth, was, on the 12th day of July, placed at the head of the American armies, to control all the campaigns, and push the war to a speedy issue. He at once adopted a plan of campaign in accordance with the President's original policy, which was to move on Richmond overland from Washington. Of course, it became necessary to recall the Army of the Potomac, and abandon the peninsula route altogether; and, on the 3d of August, Halleck sent an order to McClellan to withdraw his army at once, and come up to Acquia Creek, covering his movements the best way he could. McClellan was astonished at this unexpected order, saying in reply, that "it had caused him the greatest pain he ever experienced." He sent in a strong remonstrance against it, demonstrating, in the clearest manner, that it was a suicidal policy, and closing with these remarkable words: "clear in my convictions of right, strong in the consciousness that I ever have been, and still am, actuated solely by the love of my country, knowing that no ambitious or selfish motives have influenced me from the commencement of this war, I do now what I never did in my life before, I entreat that this order may be rescinded." The appeal was in vain. Halleck would not rescind the order, and McClellan, at once, began to obey it, and withdraw his army, in such a way as to save it from being cut up in its retreat. But he was not molested. Such a huge blunder, as the General-in-chief had now committed, was sure not to escape the keen watchfulness of a man of Lee's sagacity. Richmond being so unexpectedly relieved from all danger, he determined to throw his army rapidly across the country, overwhelm Pope, before the Army of the Potomac could reach him, and move boldly upon Washington.

BATTLE OF CEDAR MOUNTAIN.

General Pope, being informed that Jackson was rapidly approaching the Rapidan, ordered Banks, commanding the Second Corps, nominally thirteen, but really only about eight thousand strong, to move to Culpepper Court House, where the whole army was being rapidly concentrated. On the

9th of August, he directed him to move forward towards Cedar Mountain, and take up a strong position, where he could resist the advance of Jackson, until the other corps could be brought up. Jackson, in the mean time, had already crossed the Rapidan, and occupied the sides of Cedar Mountain, in force. Banks, as he approached the mountain, about four o'clock in the afternoon, heard desultory firing from Bayard's cavalry, which was disputing the progress of the enemy, and from Crawford, who was engaged with his artillery. It was a warm August day, and the green trees that covered the mountain sides, effectually concealed the force of the enemy. From his masked batteries, Jackson immediately poured in a destructive fire on our advancing columns. Banks did not believe the enemy was in any considerable force, so, after suffering severely for a while, from the rebel batteries, he determined to charge those nearest him. General Williams held the right, and Augur the left, of the line of battle. General Prince, of the latter division, advanced his brigade from this part of the field, supported by General Geary, who moved nearly in a line with him. They swept past our artillery, entered a corn field in beautiful order, and moved steadily forward towards the hostile batteries, that all the while played fast and furiously into their exposed ranks. The brave men took the desolating fire with astonishing firmness, and, with their eyes bent on the deadly guns, kept grandly, devotedly on. But suddenly a heavy mass of infantry, till then concealed behind a low swell, rose before them and poured a fearful volley into their very faces. This unexpected fire, combined with that of the batteries, was too much for them, and they were compelled to fall back, though not till they had left nearly two-thirds of their entire number on the field. Prince, while gallantly holding his men to their murderous work, was surrounded and taken prisoner, and Geary was borne back severely wounded. Crawford and Gordon, in a piece of woods on the extreme right, contended with equal gallantry against the same hopeless odds; but were also compelled to fall back. The battle proper, lasted scarcely more than thirty minutes, and yet, in that short space of time, General Gordon lost one-fourth of his entire brigade, and the One Hundred and Ninth Pennsylvania and One Hundred and Second New York regiments, left half their number behind them. Pope, hearing the cannonade at Culpepper, hurried forward with McDowell's Corps, to the rescue. Sigel was also ordered to close up with all possible despatch, and every preparation was made for a great battle. Darkness settled over the summer landscape; yet, all along that mountain side, occasional spots of flame would flash out, as a battery, now and then, sent its heavy shot and shell into the valley below—but before Pope could get his forces up, Jackson had retired across the Rapidan. He had accomplished his purpose—decoyed Banks into a trap, and shattered his corps into fragments, that could unite no more, till that campaign was ended; for nearly one-fourth of his entire force was killed, wounded, and missing, at the close of that short desperate struggle.

Pope blamed Banks for bringing on this disastrous battle, saying that his orders were to stand on the defensive, until he could move up his main body, and that his neglecting to do so, not only caused a useless slaughter, but saved Jackson from total annihilation. What the ultimate result of the campaign would have been, had Banks obeyed orders, it is impossible to say. We only know it was a sad beginning of a sad campaign. Pope, finding that it was impossible to hold his advanced position, on which the enemy was moving in overwhelming force, resolved to abandon it, and on the 18th and 19th, safely moving his entire army across the Rappahannock, for several days succeeded in holding the fords against the repeated attempts of the enemy to cross. These demonstrations of Lee, however, in front, were not very determined, and evidently made to mask his grand movement, which was to turn the right wing of Pope's army. The situation was fast becoming one, that might well fill the latter with anxiety. It would not do to uncover Fredericksburg, yet to extend his lines so as to keep pace with the rebel movement to the right, rendered it so thin as to be easily forced at almost any point. A sudden freshet raising the river, so that there were but few points where it could be crossed, relieved him for a while. On the 25th only seven thousand men, the Pennsylvania reserves under Reynolds and Kearney's division, had reached him from the Army of the Potomac. But receiving word that thirty thousand more were on their way to join him, he determined to let go his hold on the lower fords of the Rappahannock, and concentrate his forces between Warrenton and Gainesville, and give the enemy battle. On the 26th he ascertained that Jackson, having passed around his right, was moving swiftly through Thorough Fare Gap, to cut off his communication with Washington. Pope had directed the approaching reinforcements to take certain positions as they arrived, which, he felt confident, would enable him to checkmate any such attempt. But he was disappointed. In fact, the whole movement of Jackson was a surprise to him. So rapid and secret had his march of nearly fifty miles, in forty-eight hours been, that his sudden appearance at Bristow Station, on the Orange and Alexandria railroad, was like an apparition. Without wagons or provisions, feeding his army on the standing corn, which the soldiers picked and roasted on the way, he had moved with the celerity of cavalry, and was now thundering in the rear of the puzzled American Commander, breaking up his head-quarters, and capturing his papers. Burning railway trains at Bristow, the enemy moved up to Manassas Junction, Ewell's division bringing up the rear. Destroying here, Quarter-Masters' and Commissary stores, and sutlers' depots, the ragged, famished soldiers, rioted, for a while, in luxury and drinking, and satiated themselves with the finest wines. But Jackson was now in a perilous position, being between Alexandria and Warrenton, and between Pope's army and that of McClellan. Turning night into day, by the immense conflagrations he kindled here, the enemy moved off to Centreville, and crossed the famous Bull Run, pursued by Pope. Jackson would hardly have dared to make this audacious movement, had he not entertained a thorough contempt for his adversary. Pope thought he had him in a trap, and telegraphed to Washington that he could not escape. In fact, he had him secure two or three times, yet the latter always managed to get off, but in every case, through somebody's criminal neglect, or almost equally criminal blunders. The misfortune at Bristow, was owing to the refusal, on the part of Porter, to obey orders, and the dilatoriness of Sigel, who commanded McDowell's advance. So too, if McDowell had "moved forward as directed, and at the time specified, they would have intercepted Jackson's retreat towards Centreville," and cut him up badly. But, after all these mishaps, Jackson was still in his toils, as he believed. Surrounded by an overwhelming force, his only way of escape was through Thorough Fare Gap, or north to Leesburgh. But McDowell, with twenty-five thousand men, was between him and the Gap, while Kearney was pressing him so closely, that the latter alternative would be impracticable. This was the state of things on the night of the 28th. From Pope's point of view, it did seem a desperate case for Jackson. Between him and the Gap, lay twenty-five thousand men—behind him, ready to fall on him in the morning, were twenty-five thousand more, while the rebel leader could not have had more than twenty thousand men all told. But here again, "some one blundered." Ricketts, according to Pope, made a false movement, causing King to withdraw his troops, leaving Thorough Fare Gap open, towards which Jackson was steadily falling back, and through which Longstreet was about to pour his division to succor him Of course, a new disposition of the forces became necessary. Sigel was directed to attack the enemy at daylight, and bring him to bay. He did so and the battle of Groveton followed. It was a bloody action, and at first, seemed doubtful, but the arrival of Hooker and Kearney soon changed the aspect of affairs. The battle raged all day, and the fields and woods were thickly strewn with the dead; but, at five o'clock, Heintzelman and Reno made a furious charge on the enemy's left, which doubled it up, and forced it back, so that, when darkness put an end to the strife, we were masters of the field, but nothing more. In the attack on the enemy's left, Grover's brigade, of Hooker's division, greatly distinguished itself by a bayonet charge, which shivered the first and second lines of the enemy, and was checked only by the third.

But while Jackson was compelled to fall back, Longstreet's troops were seen pouring through Thorough Fare Gap to his relief.

Our loss in this engagement was estimated at nearly eight thousand. Again, Pope saw his enemy elude his grasp, but this time, Porter was to blame; for, if he had come up in season, Pope "would have crushed or captured" (he said) "the larger portion of Jackson's force."

The next morning, Pope again gave battle, in the last desperate hope of breaking the enemy's left. The conflict was long and sanguinary, extending on into the night. As in the battle of the day before, no decisive advantage seemed to have been gained by the enemy, yet, at its close, Pope ordered the whole army to fall back to the fortifications around Washington, for protection. He had ridiculed the idea of securing lines of retreat, and the country had scoffed at the veteran Scott, and afterwards at McClellan, for building those elaborate works before venturing an advance movement; but now, the former was glad to take advantage of the refuge he had affected to despise, and the latter heaved a sigh of relief, that military science had not yielded to popular ignorance and conceit. Halleck, at last, discovered the bold plan of Lee, which, the constant fighting, and even the last two days' battles, had not for a moment arrested. Steadily sweeping on towards the Shenandoah Valley, all the battles he had fought, were for the purpose of clearing his line of communications, and forcing our army back into its fortifications, exhausted, bleeding, humbled, so that he could cross the Potomac into Maryland, and threaten the national Capital from the rear.

All this time, McClellan, stripped of his command, was in camp near Alexandria, a prey to the keenest anxiety. The army that he had created, and which had become endeared to him by common perils and a common destiny, was struggling in mortal combat near him—the sound of cannon constantly borne to his ears, and the earth trembling under the heavy explosions, and yet, he was not allowed to be with it. His brave troops were being mowed down, as he believed, a sacrifice to incompetency, yet he could do nothing, but send on fresh men as fast as they arrived, till he had nothing left, but the guard around his camp, and this, at last, was ordered forward also. Never was a Commander placed in a more painful position. Stripped of all command, he walked his solitary camp, borne down with grief. At last he could bear it no longer, and just before midnight, on the last day of the battle, he telegraphed to Gen. Halleck, at Washington: "I cannot express to you the pain and mortification I have experienced to-day, in listening to the distant sound of the firing of my men. As I can be of no further use here, I respectfully ask, that if there is a probability of the conflict being renewed to-morrow, I may be permitted to go to the scene of battle with my Staff, merely to be with my own men, if nothing more. They will fight none the worse for my being with them. If it is not deemed best to intrust me with the command of my own army, I simply ask to be permitted to share their fate on the field of battle. Please reply to this to-night." To this he received no answer.

Such an appeal was enough to move a heart of stone. Though disgraced from his high command, he did not yield to resentment, and stand aloof in scornful anger, but, from a heart wrung with anguish for his brave troops, he prayed simply that he might fly to the battle-field and share their fate. If, however, he had wished for revenge, he would have been satisfied the next day, when the terrified General-in-Chief, whose treatment of him had been so extraordinary, sent to him the following telegram: "*I beg of you to assist me in this crisis, with your ability and experience. I am entirely tired out.*" Cæsar was, at length, compelled to cry, "Help me, Cassius, or I sink." The President, too, who had hoped to the last for success, at length yielded to alarm, for he was suddenly aroused at the sight of the Capital in imminent peril, and sending for McClellan, placed him once more at the head of the army. The country, at last, awoke to the humiliating fact, that Pope's campaign had been a lamentable failure. A few friends, however, endeavored to break his fall, by asserting that he failed through the willful neglect of some of the commanders, to aid him—chief among whom was Porter. Certainly, if Pope's statements are to be received as true, he was the most injured and abused Commander of his time. In the first place, at the outset, General Hatch failed to obey orders and take Gordonsville. Afterwards, he neglected to march to Charlottesville and destroy the railroad between that place and Lynchburg, for which he was removed from the command of the cavalry of General Banks' Corps. On the top of this misfortune, came the calamitous battle of Cedar Mountain, which Pope declares was fought contrary to his orders. In the third place, when Jackson was retreating from Manassas Junction towards Centreville, Pope says, "if the whole force under General McDowell, had moved forward as directed, and at the time specified, they would have intercepted Jackson's retreat;" and he adds, "I do not believe it would have been possible for him to cross Bull Run without heavy loss." Again, directly after, when he "felt sure there was no escape for Jackson, to his great disappointment the plan all fell through," because "King's division had fallen back, leaving open the road to Thorough Fare Gap." Again, on the 29th, he would have achieved a signal victory over Jackson, but for the "strange failure" of Gen. Porter to move as he was directed. And finally, on the 30th, he says "he began to feel discouraged and nearly hopeless of any successful issue" to his operations, on account of a letter he received from General McClellan, informing him that "rations and forage were at Alexandria, waiting a cavalry escort." Beginning with a commander of cavalry, and being kept up by three corps commanders, two of whom were in the regular army, this constant disobedience to orders worked the disastrous issues over which the country mourned. If all this was true, he certainly was an injured man, and the wrongs done him received their climax, when the Administration virtually withdrew him from the field, and sent him to the Northwest, to conduct a campaign against the Sioux Indians, who had risen and massacred several hundred of the inhabitants of Minnesota. The campaign, however, needs no elaborate criticism. Recalling the army from the James River was a great blunder. The removal of McClellan did not necessitate the removal of the army, for there were Generals in it besides him, who, from that point, with proper reinforcements, could have carried it into Richmond. Pope, also, was no match for Lee, least of all in a country so thoroughly known by the latter, and of which he was almost wholly ignorant. Pope comprehended neither the campaign nor the country, and the General-in-chief, at Washington, was no wiser. The former, by looking at his map, could see points, where a proper force might thwart the movements of his adversary, and hence ordered them there, without taking into consideration the probabilities, and sometimes the possibilities, of their getting up in time to carry out his plans. If the army had been endowed with wings, his campaign might have been a very successful one, but, as it was, it turned out a miserable failure, the blame of which fell wholly on him, while it should be divided between him and General Halleck.

CHAPTER III.

SEPTEMBER—1862.

ALARM AT WASHINGTON—ANTIETAM—MC CLELLAN TAKES THE FIELD—BATTLE OF SOUTH MOUNTAIN—SURRENDER OF HARPER'S FERRY—BATTLE OF ANTIETAM—HOOKER'S STRUGGLE—FATAL DELAY OF BURNSIDE—LEE'S RETREAT—PUBLIC DISAPPOINTMENT—THE ARMY RESTS—EMANCIPATION PROCLAMATION—SUSPENSION OF HABEAS CORPUS—ITS EFFECTS—ITS DANGERS.

THE terror inspired at Washington, by the unfortunate turn of events, was not generally known to the country. Lee was throwing his mighty columns across the Potomac, in the vicinity of Hagerstown, but whether for the purpose of moving down upon Washington on the Maryland side, or of invading Pennsylvania, or with the design to draw our troops in that direction, and then suddenly recross the river, and come down on the Capital on the Virginia side, no one knew.

Reorganizing the army, as by magic, McClellan at once took the field, moving cautiously up the Potomac, on the Maryland side. His gallant army, though foot sore and worn, were, however, full of spirit and courage, because their beloved Commander rode at their head, and were eager to meet the exultant foe, before whom they had been so reluctantly compelled to retire.

With his left wing resting on the Potomac, and his right extending far out into the country, he moved by five different parallel roads, slowly and cautiously up the river, anxiously watching the development of the rebel plans. On the thirteenth, he had reached Fredericksburg, still in ignorance of the exact whereabouts of the rebel army. But, during the day, an order of General Lee, fell into McClellan's hands, which fully disclosed the plans of the former. This was all the latter had been waiting for. He was now no longer compelled to feel his way, and immediately gave orders for the entire army to move rapidly forward. Harper's Ferry, on the Virginia side of the river, was, at this time, held by Colonel Miles, with a large garrison, which, for some unexplained reason, was not allowed, at the first, to be under McClellan's charge, though being directly in the field of his operations. Before he left Washington, he had requested that the garrison be withdrawn, either to the Maryland Heights, which could be easily held, or sent to aid in covering the Cumberland Valley. This advice was unheeded, and the place kept from his control, until Jackson, with a heavy force, was already advancing against it. Two days after McClellan was informed that the place was under his command, he received a verbal report from Colonel Miles, that he had abandoned Maryland Heights, the key to the position, but that he could hold out two days longer. McClellan sent couriers back, by three different routes, to inform him that he was forcing the pass on the Hagerstown road, over the Blue Ridge, and that he would certainly soon relieve him. "Hold to the last extremity," was his urgent command. In the mean time the

BATTLE OF SOUTH MOUNTAIN.

was raging. The rebels occupied the sides and tops of the mountain, on both sides of the road, at a point called Frog's Gap. The lofty slopes were steep, broken, and wooded, furnishing a strong position for defense, and which commanded every approach to the base of the ridge. The battle commenced at seven o'clock in the morning, by the advance of Cox's division of Reno's Corps. A heavy artillery duel followed, the enemy pouring their shot and shell down from the sides of the mountains, and our batteries replying from the plain below. About noon, a short, severe conflict occurred between the infantry, over some pieces abandoned by our troops in a panic, in which the rebels were beaten. About two o'clock, the head of Hooker's column, coming to reinforce Reno, was seen moving along the turnpike. Sweeping off in a road that turned to the right, it steadily approached the foot of the mountain, amid the prolonged cheers of Reno's troops. An hour later, the line of battle was formed at the base of the ridge — Rickett's brigade on the extreme right, and Reno's on the left—and the order to advance given. The enemy opened on it with artillery, but it steadily advanced, and, at length, began to ascend the rugged slope. In a short time the whole rebel force was encountered, and then the wooded steep became wrapped in flame and smoke. For three hours, it thundered and flamed without a moment's interval, along the breast of the mountain, but nothing could stay the steady upward sweep of that magnificent line, and as the last rays of the sun were gilding the summit, our victorious flag was planted upon it, and the shout of triumph rolled down the farther side, after the fleeing enemy. Our total loss, in killed and wounded, was two thousand three hundred and twenty-five —that of the enemy was unknown. Among our dead was the gallant Reno.

The next day, the garrison at Harper's Ferry surrendered, numbering eleven thousand five hundred and eighty-three men, with nearly fifty pieces of artillery. The cavalry, about two thousand in number, under Colonel Davis, escaped previously, capturing Longstreet's train, and a hundred prisoners on its way. The unnecessary fall of this place, awakened the deepest indignation, and the blame was laid, now on Halleck, and now on Miles, and again on McClellan.

Colonel Ford, who commanded the Heights, also came in for his share of the blame. The disgraceful affair, however, is surrounded with no difficulties. Colonel Miles was not a fit man to command the place, as had been fully shown in his conduct at the first battle of Bull Run, and should not have been put there. His death, after he had hoisted the white flag, saved him from further disgrace.

The second blunder was in not putting it under McClellan's command at the first, as it was inclosed in the field of his military operations. His advice, at least, should have been taken. General Franklin was within a few miles of Harper's Ferry, to relieve it, when it surrendered. A proper officer could have held the place, though in itself it was of no consequence, in the campaign; for, if McClellan was beaten, we could not hold it, and if he drove the enemy out of Maryland, it was necessarily ours, for the latter would not attempt to retain it, as the sequel proved. The misfortune consisted in losing, at this critical period, so many men whom McClellan could have put to a useful purpose. The latter was blamed for not relieving it, at the last moment. But it fell within three days after it was placed under his command, and while his relieving columns were almost within cannon shot of it.

Although, as before stated, Harper's Ferry, as a military post, had no important bearing on McClellan's plan of the campaign, the loss of so many troops at this juncture, was a serious matter, and, in case of disaster, might increase it indefinitely. Still, no change was made in the Commander's purpose, and no delay permitted in the movement of the army. He had ascertained definitely, Lee's whereabouts and designs, and he was resolved at once to give him battle. Pushing his army rapidly forward, he, on the 15th, came upon the rebel host, drawn up in line of battle, on a row of heights that stretched along the west side of Antietam Creek.

BATTLE OF ANTIETAM.

Antietam is a sluggish stream, emptying into the Potomac, with but a few fords, and those difficult ones; near these the enemy had taken his position. Four stone bridges crossed within the distance of about seven miles—the last one being near its mouth. The creek entering the Potomac at a sharp angle, brought the two streams so near together at Sharpsburg, that Lee's position actually stretched from one to the other—thus protecting both his flanks and his rear. The rebel leader had chosen his position admirably, for a stronger one could not well be found. Not only was he protected by these two streams, but the heights on which he was planted, were not composed of a single line of hills, which, if once carried, the battle was won, but of a succession of hills—those in rear commanding those in front. The hollows between, successfully concealed the number and movements of the hostile troops. A direct advance in front was plainly out of the question, and McClellan, having thoroughly reconnoitered the ground, resolved to attack by both flanks. Hooker and Mansfield, supported by Sumner, were to attempt to turn the enemy's left, while Burnside, at the proper moment, was to carry the lower bridge, near the mouth of the creek, and crush the enemy's right, and then sweep along the heights towards the centre, which was then to advance and complete the victory. In accordance with this plan, Hooker, with his corps, composed of Rickett's, Meade's, and Doubleday's divisions, was ordered, on the afternoon of the 16th, to cross Antietam Creek by the upper bridge and a ford near it, attack the enemy's left, and fix himself firmly there, while Mansfield was to cross during the night, and Sumner early next morning. The passage of the stream was effected without difficulty, and the corps moved cau-

BATTLE OF ANTIETAM—TAKING OF THE BRIDGE ON ANTIETAM CREEK.

tiously down on the enemy's flank, on the further side. More or less skirmishing followed, but the firing ceased at dark, when Hooker found himself, breast to breast, with the hostile lines. The autumn night fell peacefully along the heights, but it was evident that the morning's dawn would witness the most fearful battle, thus far, of the war, and, in all human probability, settle the fate of Washington. It was clear, too, that the heaviest fighting was to be where Hooker commanded. Porter, holding the centre with Sykes, massed his troops, in a hollow, so as to be used as the exigencies of the battle might require, while his batteries above, played on the enemy.

The morning of the 17th broke somber and slow, over the heights, behind which slumbered the two great armies; for dull, heavy clouds wrapped the sky, giving a deeper gloom to the still forests around. But, in the early light, Hooker with his accustomed energy moved boldly on the foe. The men had scarcely swallowed their hasty breakfast, when the rapid shots of the Pennsylvania skirmishers announced that the fight had begun. The whole corps was soon engaged, and for half an hour it stormed and thundered miles away to the right, as though the main battle was being fought there at the outset. The contest was in an open space, made by a plowed field and a cornfield, and both armies stood up resolutely to their work. But at length, the enemy began to give way, when, "Forward!" ran along the line, and it sprang forward with a ringing cheer. Though at first retiring slowly, the rebels at this wild rush, fled precipitately, and were borne furiously back over the field, across the road beyond, and still back, till a piece of thick woods received them. Meade and his Pennsylvanians, whose blood was now up, followed fiercely after, and with a wild hurrah, dashed full on the cover. The next moment, those dark woods became a sheet of flame, bursting on those brave men.

Rent, shattered and torn before it, they reeled and staggered back. The next moment, like successive waves of the sea, the hostile lines swept out into view, cheering as they came, and carried the field like a storm. Hooker, seeing the danger, threw a brigade in the path of the foe, but it went down like frostwork, before the on-sweeping mass. "Give me," said he to Doubleday, "your best brigade." Down, on the run, came the best brigade, and reckless of shot and shell, moved straight up to the crest of the hill that crowned the cornfield, and forming in full view of the enemy, began to pour in their rapid, deadly volleys. Hartsuff, commanding, fell severely wounded; but that noble brigade held its own for half an hour, and then, finding no support coming up, dashed alone into the cornfield, and swept it with one gallant rush. Ricketts, holding the left of the line, was hard pressed, and Mansfield was ordered to his relief, but the gallant white-haired General fell in the onset. For a mile and a half, the battle raged furiously, all along Hooker's front; but at length, getting his two flanks safe, which the rebels had made almost superhuman efforts to turn, he determined to advance and end the struggle. To the right of the cornfield, was a piece of woods running out to a point which commanded the field, and he determined to take and hold it. Advancing to an eminence to reconnoiter the ground, he was struck in the foot with a bullet, and compelled to leave the field. Sumner immediately took command, and the advance commenced, the gallant Sedgwick leading; Crawford and Gordon stoutly battling in the woods; but the former, however, was compelled to give way, and his disordered troops poured like a torrent through Sedgwick's brigade, hurling it back broken and confused. The enemy, seeing his advantage, pressed fiercely on, with shouts that rose over the crash of artillery. Sedgwick, vainly striving to rally his troops under the rebel fire, was three times wounded, but refused to leave the field, till he saw the attempt was hopeless. His Adjutant-General, Major Sedgwick, threw himself among the broken ranks in vain, and fell mortally wounded. Howard now assumed command, but his efforts were equally fruitless. Sumner undertook to reform the line, but to no purpose, and the division fell back, leaving the cornfield to the enemy. It was now noon, and at this crisis, Franklin came up and was sent to the right. He at once ordered Slocum and Smith, commanding the two divisions, to sweep the field. The latter, moving with the rapidity and resistlessness of a whirlwind, in ten minutes, cleared it of all but the rebel dead. The enemy now gave it up, and a lull in the conflict followed.

Hooker's attack had not been as successful as McClellan had anticipated. The bulk of our army had been massed on that flank, and yet the most it had been able to do, was to fix itself on the left of the enemy, while the heavy loss in officers and men, and the protracted, exhausting fighting, had left it unable to make any further forward movement.

The advance of Burnside on the left, over the bridge, which was designed to be simultaneous with that on the right, had been weak and undecided—thus allowing the enemy, with his shorter lines, to throw the weight of his force against Hooker. This delay was fatal to the success of McClellan's plan. At eight o'clock he sent an order to Burnside to carry the bridge, gain the heights beyond, and move along their crest to the enemy's rear. He himself occupied an eminence about midway between the two wings, and anxiously swept the field with his glass. Although the earthquake crash of artillery on the extreme right, showed that the heroic Hooker was throwing himself with terrible force on the enemy there, the firing on the left indicated that Burnside had not closed resolutely with the foe, and

McClellan, becoming filled with anxiety, hurried off another aid to Burnside, who dashed up to him, with the order to carry the bridge in his front, at all hazards. The aid returning with the report that the enemy still held the bridge, McClellan, now thoroughly aroused to the danger that threatened him, sent his Inspector-General, Col. Sackett, with the peremptory order to Burnside, to push forward without a moment's delay, and carry the bridge at the point of the bayonet. If he hesitated, Sackett himself was directed to stay and see it done. At last, at one o'clock, the Fifty-first regiments of the New-York and Pennsylvania volunteers, in a gallant burst, carried it with triumphant shouts. Burnside then moved across, other troops, and the enemy fell back to the heights. Hours, golden hours, big with the fate of the army and the nation, had been allowed to slip by; yet, even now, a vigorous and daring advance might save the day. Instead of this, however, Burnside, acting on his judgment, ordered a halt, and began to plant his artillery. Hearing of this, McClellan dispatched Col. Key, with orders to him to push on and carry the heights—that success was impossible unless he did—that he must not stop to calculate losses. Three o'clock came, and still the heights were not carried. Again McClellan hurried off Key, with orders to storm the heights at all hazards. At last the order was obeyed—the enemy were driven from their guns by our gallant troops, that now pushed forward with loud hurrahs, some of them even reaching the outskirts of Sharpsburg. But the advantage came too late, for heavy rebel reinforcements, that had been hurrying forward all day from Harper's Ferry, arriving at this critical moment on the field, turned the scale against Burnside, and compelled him to fall back. Seeing himself suddenly threatened with overthrow, he sent to McClellan for help. "McClellan's glass, for the last half-hour, has seldom been turned away from the left. He sees clearly enough that Burnside is pressed—needs no messenger to tell him that. His face grows dark with anxious thought. Looking down into the valley, where fifteen thousand men are lying, he turns a half-questioning look on Fitz John Porter, who stands by his side, gravely scanning the field. They are Porter's troops below; are fresh, and only impatient to share in the fight. But Porter slowly shakes his head, and one may believe that the same thought is passing through the minds of both generals. McClellan remounts his horse, and, with Porter and a dozen of his Staff, rides away to the left, in Burnside's direction. Sykes meets them on the road—a good soldier, whose opinion is worth taking. The three soldiers talk briefly together. It is easy to see that the moment has come, when everything may turn on an order given or withheld—when the history of the battle is only to be written in thoughts, and purposes, and words, of the General."

"Burnside's messenger rides up. His message is, 'I want troops and guns. If you do not send them, I cannot hold my position a half an hour.' McClellan's only answer is a glance at the western sky. Then he turns and speaks, very slowly: 'Tell General Burnside, this is the battle of the war. He must hold his ground till dark, at any cost. I will send him Miller's battery. I can do nothing more. I have no infantry.' Then, as the messenger was riding away, he called him back:—'Tell him if he *cannot* hold his ground, then the bridge, to the last man—*always the bridge.* If the bridge is lost, all is lost.'"* The bridge was held—darkness soon covered the field, and the great battle was over. If Burnside had commenced his movement two hours sooner, there is scarcely a doubt, that night would have seen the rebel army fleeing across the Potomac. As it was, the two tired hosts lay down, front to front, along the slug-

* George N. Smalley, correspondent of the Tribune.

gish Antietam, waiting for the morning, to renew the conflict. Twelve thousand had fallen on our side, and a much larger number of the enemy—a ghastly throng—covering those wooded heights, and choking the hollows. We had taken six thousand prisoners, and thirteen guns.

The next morning, McClellan determined to renew the fight, but he found his heavy batteries were nearly out of ammunition—ten thousand stragglers were scattered among the hills—supplies were to be brought up, while fourteen thousand fresh troops were on the march to join him. He, therefore, deemed it prudent to delay the attack till the next day, and spent the 18th in caring for the wounded, burying the dead, and gathering up his energies for the last decisive blow. Everything being completed, the orders were issued to commence the attack at daylight, but the enemy during the night had retreated, placing the Potomac between himself and our victorious army.

The nation was exultant over the victory. The feeling of triumph was dashed, however, because Lee's army had escaped. From the commencement of the war, certain cries, taken up by a portion of the press, had become, for a time, popular, and, like all clamors, furious and unreasonable. The first, was derision of fortifications, as though it were impossible to suppose we should ever need them. Then, there came an unthinking demand, that a retreating army, no matter whether it was ten, or a hundred thousand strong, should always be "bagged" by an equal number, though operating in a country covered with forests, crossed by rugged heights, and seamed with rivers. Next, came the outcry against siege operations, and the adoption of the motto, "to move at once upon the enemy's works." One after another, they were abandoned, as they always must be, and the operations in the field, left to those who understood their business. Thus, the next year, the public saw, without one word of complaint, Meade's victorious army, with all its reinforcements up, sit down idly for a week on this very spot, and let Lee construct scows, and ferry his army, guns and supplies and all, over the Potomac, that seemed swollen with rains on purpose to secure the overthrow of the enemy. So, too, the clamor against the comparatively short siege of Yorktown, was changed to plaudits over the tedious sieges of Port Hudson and Vicksburg.

McClellan did not undertake to move his army at once, across the Potomac, for, he knew, if the enemy chose to retreat, he could do so without serious molestation; and if he risked another battle, it would have to be accepted under great disadvantages, and with the river, which was liable to be swollen at any time so as to be unfordable, between him and his base of supplies. On the night of the 19th, however, General Griffin, with a part of two brigades, crossed the river and carried the enemy's batteries, capturing several prisoners, and driving the rebel supports back a half a mile. He reported, on his return, that appearances indicated the retreat of Lee towards Winchester. To ascertain whether this was actually so, Porter, in the morning, sent over a detachment which advanced about a mile, when it fell into an ambush, and was driven back with great slaughter.

The balance of the month was spent in resting the overtasked troops, bringing up supplies and ammunition, and in vain attempts to get the soldiers properly clothed, so that an onward movement could be resumed with some prospect of success. While the first month of Autumn was thus drawing to a close, the two armies still confronting each other on the upper Potomac, two proclamations were issued by the President, which had an important bearing on the future prospects of the war. One appeared on the 22d, abolishing slavery in all the States that should be in rebellion on the 1st day of January. 1863. The President had long been urged to do this, both by politicians and ecclesiastical bodies, but he had stubbornly refused, not only on the ground of its doubtful constitutionality, but its uselessness, saying, facetiously, that it would be like the "Pope's bull against the comet." The armies freed the slaves, only as far as they advanced, and it seemed to him idle to suppose that a proclamation could achieve more than the bayonets of the soldiers. It would be time, he thought, to settle this vexed question when the rebel armies had been conquered. With these views, he had struggled hard to secure an Emancipation Act, which would allow compensation to the owners of slaves. In his preceding message, therefore, he had recommended the adoption of the following resolutions:—

"*Resolved by the Senate and House of Representatives of the United States of America in Congress assembled*, (two thirds of both Houses concurring.) That the following articles be proposed to the Legislatures (or Conventions) of the several States, as amendments to the Constitution of the United States, all or any of which articles, when ratified by three-fourths of the said Legislatures (or Conventions,) to be valid as part or parts of the said Constitution, namely:

ARTICLE —. Every State, wherein slavery now exists, which shall abolish the same therein, at any time, or times, before the first day of January, in the year of our Lord one thousand nine humdred, shall receive compensation from the United States, as follows, to wit:

The President of the United States shall deliver to every such State, bonds of the United States, bearing interest at the rate of ——— per cent. per annum, to an amount equal to the aggregate sum of ——— for each slave shown to have been therein, by the eighth census of the United States, said bonds to be delivered to such States by instalments, or in one parcel, at the completion of the abolishment, accordingly as the same shall have been gradual, or at one time, within such State; and interest shall begin to run upon any such bond only from the proper time of its delivery as aforesaid. Any State having received bonds as aforesaid, and afterwards reintroducing or tolerating slavery therein, shall refund to the United States, the bonds so received, or the value thereof, and all interest paid thereon.

ARTICLE —. All slaves who shall have enjoyed actual freedom by the chances of the war, at any time before the end of the rebellion, shall be forever free; but all owners of such, who shall not have been disloyal, shall be compensated for them, at the same rates as is provided for States adopting abolishment of slavery, but in such way that no slave shall be twice accounted for.

ARTICLE —. Congress may appropriate money, and otherwise provide for colonizing free colored persons, with their own consent, at any place or places without the United States."

He argued these resolutions at length, closing the message with the following eloquent, earnest language:

"This plan is recommended as a means, not in exclusion of, but additional to all others, for restoring and preserving the national authority throughout the Union. The subject is presented exclusively in its economical aspect. The plan would, I am confident, secure peace more speedily, and maintain it more permanently, than can be done by force alone; while all it would cost, considering amounts, and manner of payment, and times of payment, would be easier paid, than will be the additional cost of the war, if we rely solely upon force. It is much, very much, that it would cost no blood at all.

The plan is proposed as permanent constitutional law. It cannot become such, without the concurrence of, first, two-thirds of Congress, and afterwards, three-fourths of the States. The requisite three-fourths of the States will necessarily include seven of the slave States. Their concurrence, if obtained, will give assurance of their severally adopting emancipation at no very distant day, upon the new constitutional terms. This assurance would end the struggle now, and save the Union forever.

I do not forget the gravity which should characterize a paper addressed to the Congress of the nation, by the Chief Magistrate of the nation. Nor do I forget that some of you are my seniors, nor that many of you have more experience than I, in the conduct of public affairs. Yet I trust, that in view of the great responsibility resting upon me, you will perceive no want of respect to yourselves, in any undue earnestness I may seem to display.

Is it doubted, then, that the plan I propose, if adopted, would shorten the war, and thus lessen its expenditure of money and of blood? Is it doubted that it would restore the national authority and national prosperity, and perpetuate both indefinitely? Is it doubted that we here—Congress and Executive—can secure its adoption? Will not the good people respond to a united and earnest appeal from us? Can we, can they, by any other means, so certainly or so speedily assure these vital objects? We can succeed only by concert. It is not 'can *any* of us *imagine* better?' but, 'can we *all* do better?' Object whatsoever is possible, still the question recurs, 'can we do better?' The dogmas of the quiet past, are inadequate to the stormy present. The occasion is piled high with difficulty, and we must rise with the occasion. As our case is new, so we must think anew and act anew. We must disenthrall ourselves, and then we shall save our country.

Fellow-citizens, *we* cannot escape history. We, of this Congress and this Administration, will be remembered in spite of ourselves. No personal significance, or insignificance, can spare one or another of us. The fiery trial through which we pass, will light us down, in honor or dishonor, to the latest generation. We *say* we are for the Union. The world will not forget that we say this. We know how to save the Union. The world knows we do know how to save it. We—even we here—hold the power and bear the responsibility. In giving freedom to the slave, we assure freedom to the free—honorable alike in what we give, and what we preserve. We shall nobly save, or meanly lose, the last, best hope of earth. Other means may succeed; this could not fail. The way is plain, peaceful, generous, just—a way which, if followed, the world will forever applaud, and God must forever bless.

ABRAHAM LINCOLN."

This plan not having been tried, we can only conjecture how it would have worked, and what the final result would have been. But whatever differences of opinion may be entertained of these views, no one can doubt the sincerity, or the lofty patriotism from which they sprung. Their straightforward honesty must command the respect of all, while the feeling with which they are urged, cannot fail to awaken the deepest sympathy for their unselfish author. They were not coincided in by Congress—and the President seeing no alternative, issued the following proclamation:

"I, Abraham Lincoln, President of the United States of America, and Commander-in-Chief of the army and navy thereof, do hereby proclaim and declare that hereafter, as heretofore, the war will be prosecuted for the object of practically restoring the constitutional relation between the United States and the people thereof in those States in which that relation is, or may be, suspended or disturbed; that it is my purpose, upon the next meeting of Congress, to again recommend the adoption of a practical measure tendering pecuniary aid to the free acceptance or rejection of all the Slave States, so-called, the people whereof may not then be in rebellion against the United States, and which States may then have voluntarily adopted, or thereafter may voluntarily adopt, the immediate or gradual abolishment of slavery within their respective limits; and that the efforts to colonize persons of African descent, with their consent, upon the continent or elsewhere, with the previously obtained consent of the governments existing there, will be continued; that on the first day of January, in the year of our Lord one thousand eight hundred and sixty-three, all persons held as slaves within any State or any designated part of a State, the people whereof shall then be in rebellion against the United States, shall be then, thenceforward, and forever free; and the Executive Government of the United States, including the military and naval authority thereof, will recognize and maintain the freedom of such persons, and will do no act or acts to repress such persons, or any of them, in any efforts they may make for their actual freedom.

That the Executive will, on the first day of January aforesaid, by proclamation, designate the States and parts of States, if any, in which the people thereof, respectively, shall then be in rebellion against the United States; and the fact that any State, or people thereof, shall on that day be, in good faith, represented in the Congress of the United States, by members chosen thereto at elections, wherein a majority of the qualified voters of such State shall have participated, shall, in the absence of strong countervailing testimony, be deemed conclusive evidence that such State, and the people thereof, are not in rebellion against the United States.

That attention is hereby called to an Act of Congress entitled 'An Act to make an additional article of war,' approved March 13, 1862, and which Act is in the words and figures following:

'*Be it enacted by the Senate and House of Representatives of the United States of America in Congress assembled*, That hereafter, the following shall be promulgated as an additional article of war, for the government of the army of the United States, and shall be observed and obeyed as such:

'ARTICLE —. All officers or persons in the military or naval service of the United States are prohibited from employing any of the forces under their respective commands, for the purpose of returning fugitives from service or labor, who may have escaped from any person to whom such service or labor is claimed to be due, and any officer who shall be found guilty by a court-martial of violating this article, shall be dismissed from the service.

'SEC. 2. *And be it further enacted*, That this act shall take effect from and after its passage.'

Also to the ninth and tenth sections of an Act entitled 'An Act to suppress insurrection, to punish treason and rebellion, to seize and confiscate property of rebels, and for other purposes,' approved July 17, 1862, and which sections are in the words and figures following:

'SEC. 9. *And be it further enacted*, That all slaves, of persons who shall hereafter be engaged in rebellion against the Government of the United States, or who shall in any way give aid or comfort thereto, escaping from such persons and taking refuge within the lines of the army; and all slaves captured from such persons or deserted by them, and coming under the control of the Government of the United States; and all slaves of such persons, found on [or being within] any place occupied by rebel forces, and afterwards occupied by the forces of the United States, shall be deemed captives of war, and shall be forever free of their servitude, and not again held as slaves.

'SEC. 10. *And be it further enacted*, That no slave escaping into any State, Territory, or the District of Columbia, from any other State, shall be delivered up, or in any way impeded or hindered of his liberty, except for crime, or some offense against the laws, unless the person claiming said fugitive, shall first make oath that the person to whom the labor or service of such fugitive is alleged to be due is his lawful owner, and has not been in arms against the United States in the present rebellion, nor in any way given aid and comfort thereto; and no person engaged in the military or naval service of the United States shall, under any pretence whatever, assume to decide on the validity of the claim of any person, to the service or labor of any other person, or surrender up any such person to the claimant, on pain of being dismissed from the service.'

And I do hereby enjoin upon and order all persons engaged in the military and naval service of the United States to observe, obey, and enforce, within their respective spheres of service, the act and sections above recited.

And the Executive will in due time recommend that all citizens of the United States, who shall have remained loyal thereto throughout the rebellion, shall, (upon the restoration of the constitutional relation between the United States and their respective States and people, if the relation shall have been suspended or disturbed,) be compensated for all losses by acts of the United States, including the loss of slaves.

In witness whereof, I have hereunto set my hand, and caused the seal of the United States to be affixed.

Done at the City of Washington, this twenty-second day of September in the year of our Lord one thousand eight hundred and sixty-two, and of the Independence of the United States the eighty-seventh.

ABRAHAM LINCOLN.

By the President:

WILLIAM H. SEWARD, *Secretary of State.*"

It is not to be supposed that the President ever regarded the question with indifference, or one to be disposed of by a joke; but with his eminently practical mind, he saw that the motives which influenced many, were based altogether on erroneous views, and the effect which they predicted would follow such a Proclamation, wholly chimerical. Notwithstanding all that has been said on this subject, we doubt very much whether the President, to the last, ever expected, such an edict would have any favorable effect on the war, so far as the South was concerned—on the contrary, we think he foresaw what actually occurred, that it would unite its population more firmly than ever, and give Davis more complete and absolute power. He doubtless anticipated some effect on foreign governments, which was realized; but the great object with him seemed to be, to get rid of the monstrous evil of Slavery. The madness of the South had brought it within the reach of the General Government, and if he could make its fate and that of the Rebellion one, he would, he believed, achieve the greatest and most beneficent triumph of this century. Still, with these views and wishes, constitutional and other objections interposed in his mind, which made him long hesitate. It was a very self-complacent conclusion that many ardent immediate-emancipationists came to, that Mr. Lincoln was a man of excellent motives, but had not yet grown to their stature and completeness—and that when these were attained, he then issued his Proclamation. To him, it was a momentous step to take, and one he determined not to be forced into hastily; nor, with all his philanthropic desire to see Slavery extinguished, would he have assailed it, so long as he thought the attempt would imperil the Union.

There is no evidence that he ever departed from the purpose he expressed in his letter to Horace Greeley—the Union first and foremost—Slavery afterward. When, at length, he saw that to withhold action longer would not help the Union, and when, as Commander of the armies, and not as a civil magistrate, he could, as a war measure, strike Slavery, he did, and, on the 1st of January, 1863, issued the following final Proclamation:

" *Whereas*, on the twenty-second day of September, in the year of our Lord one thousand eight hundred and sixty-two, a proclamation was issued by the President of the United States, containing among other things, the following, to wit:

'That on the first day of January, in the year of our Lord one thousand eight hundred and sixty-three, all persons held as slaves within any State or designated part of a State, the people whereof shall then be in rebellion against the United States, shall be then, thenceforward, and forever, free; and the Executive Government of the United States, including the military and naval authority thereof, will recognize and maintain the freedom of such persons, and will do no act or acts to repress such persons, or any of them, in any efforts they may make for their actual freedom.

'That the Executive will, on the first day of January aforesaid, by proclamation, designate the States and parts of States, if any, in which the people thereof, respectively, shall then be in rebellion against the United States; and the fact that any State, or the people thereof, shall on that day be, in good faith, represented in the Congress of the United States, by members chosen thereto at elections, wherein a majority of the qualified voters of such States shall have participated, shall, in the absence of strong countervailing testimony, be deemed conclusive evidence that such State, and the people thereof, are not then in rebellion against the United States.'

Now, therefore, I, Abraham Lincoln, President of the United States, by virtue of the power in me vested as Commander-in-Chief of the Army and Navy of the United States, in time of actual armed rebellion against the authority and Government of the United States, and as a fit and necessary war measure for suppressing said rebellion, do, on this first day of January, in the year of our Lord one thousand eight hundred and sixty-three, and in accordance with my purpose so to do, publicly proclaimed for the full period of one hundred days, from the day first above-mentioned, order and designate as the States and parts of States wherein the people thereof, respectively, are this day in rebellion against the United States, the following, to wit:

Arkansas, Texas, Louisiana, (except the parishes of St. Bernard, Plaquemines, Jefferson, St. John, St. Charles, St. James, Ascension, Assumption, Terre Bonne, Lafourche, St. Mary, St. Martin, and Orleans, including the city of New Orleans,) Mississippi, Alabama, Florida, Georgia, South Carolina North Carolina, and Virginia, (except the forty-eight counties designated as West Virginia, and also the counties of Berkeley, Accomac, Northampton, Elizabeth City, York, Princess Ann, and Norfolk, including the cities of Norfolk and Portsmouth,) and which excepted parts are for the present, left precisely as if this proclamation were not issued.

And by virtue of the power and for the purpose aforesaid, I do order and declare, that all persons held as slaves within said designated States and parts of States are, and henceforward shall be, free; and that the Executive Government of the United States, including the military and naval authorities thereof, will recognize and maintain the freedom of said persons.

And I hereby enjoin upon the people so declared to be free, to abstain from all violence, unless in necessary self-defense; and I recommend to them that in all cases, when allowed, they labor faithfully for reasonable wages.

And I further declare and make known, that such persons, of suitable condition, will be received into the armed service of the United States to garrison forts, positions, stations, and other places, and to man vessels of all sorts in said service.

And upon this act, sincerely believed to be an act of justice, warranted by the Constitution upon military necessity, I invoke the considerate judgment of mankind and the gracious favor of Almighty God.

In witness whereof, I have hereunto set my hand, and caused the seal of the United States to be affixed.

Done at the City of Washington this first day of January, in the year of our Lord one thousand eight hundred and sixty-three, and of the Independence of the United States of America the eighty-seventh.

ABRAHAM LINCOLN.

By the President:

WILLIAM H. SEWARD, *Secretary of State*."

Thus was consummated the greatest event of the Nineteenth Century—the one that will forever be the distinguishing feature of this memorable war. What the final effect on the African race or the country may be, is yet an unsolved problem. But one thing is settled, Slavery is forever abolished in this free country, and the great blot on our national escutcheon removed.

The other proclamation, issued two days after, suspended the writ of *habeas corpus* throughout the land, and required all persons accused of disloyal practices, to be tried by court-martial. This last was received with a storm of indignation, and the courts of some of the States denounced it as unconstitutional. The right of trial by jury is the most sacred of all political rights, and when that is finally stricken down, liberty is dead. The opposition declared that to override thus the civil courts of a land, is the highest act of tyranny known to despotism. That civil courts must be disregarded in States in rebellion, and martial law be supreme there, was conceded by all, for it would be a farce to try a rebel in rebel courts. Having repudiated the authority of the Government, they could not act under it; and until that authority was re-established, none but military courts could exist. But to assert that the courts of New England, New York, Ohio, and the other States, in which not a band of organized rebels existed, or could exist openly for an hour, were not qualified to try every citizen accused of crime, it was argued was an insult to them. Good men, on the other hand, denied the allegation, on the ground that anything was allowable, which had for its object the overthrow of the rebellion—that extraordinary crises demanded extraordinary measures—that in the disturbed and distracted state of public feeling, it was absurd to expect that men of treasonable speech and action would receive justice in the ordinary courts. But that which excited the deepest indignation, and brought out the angry remonstrance of the Governors of New Jersey and New York, was the adoption of the system of arbitrary arrests, and imprisonment without accusation or trial, either by court-martial or otherwise. Provost-marshals, vested with almost unlimited power, acted as spies on the people, and on suspicion hurried men to prison, there to lie till the Secretary of State or Secretary of War saw fit to release them. That the abuse of this authority by the Secretaries was very great, is evident from the fact that scarcely one of these victims, after weeks or months of confinement, was ever tried for any crime whatever. The exercise of such a power was a most hazardous course on the part of the Government, and but for the President's interference with the free use of it, and the universal faith in the purity of his motives, it might, and probably would have worked incalculable evil. He was denounced as a tyrant and despot, on every hand, by his enemies, and crimination and recrimination took the place of calm discussion and argument. The ablest papers friendly to the Administration, and the soundest thinkers, deprecated these arbitrary arrests, and feared for the result, but still repudiated the charge of tyranny and despotism, as all felt that there was not a man in the land who loved liberty more, or who would make greater sacrifices for constitutional freedom, than the President. Such papers as *The Evening Post* and *New York Tribune* condemned them, not so much on the ground of personal injustice or hardship, but because no more dangerous principle can be introduced into a republican government, than that its citizens can be deprived of liberty at the mere dictum of those in power, and for no other reason than that in their judgment the public safety requires it. It is the fundamental law of the Constitution of the United States, and of the Constitution of every State, that "*no person shall be deprived of life and liberty without due process of law;*" and all history proves that no danger to a republic is so great, as the violation of this law. To override it on the plea of public necessity, is to adopt the policy of all despotic governments. It ought never to have been discussed or treated as a party measure, for every citizen, of whatever political faith, is equally interested in the principle involved.

CHAPTER IV.

JULY–AUGUST–SEPTEMBER.

OPERATIONS WEST—VICKSBURG—RAM ARKANSAS—MITCHELL'S GALLANT EXPLOIT—CURTIS CROSSES THE STATE OF ARKANSAS—BUELL'S CAMPAIGN—BRAGG INVADES TENNESSEE AND KENTUCKY—RETREAT OF BUELL TO LOUISVILLE—IS SUPERSEDED BY THOMAS—KIRBY SMITH ADVANCES AGAINST CINCINNATI—LANE IN KANSAS—NEW-ORLEANS—BATTLE OF BATON ROUGE—DEATH OF GENERAL WILLIAMS—PORTER, WITH THE ESSEX, DESTROYS THE REBEL RAM ARKANSAS—ROSECRANS AT CORINTH.

WHILE such momentous events were passing on the Atlantic seaboard, the military movements at the West were not crowned with that success, which our previous victories had led the public to expect. The capture of Memphis brought our victorious fleet to Vicksburg, the fall of which would open the Mississippi to New Orleans. But this place, situated on a high bluff, bid defiance to our gunboats; so that, while it was hoped that we had reached the end of our labors, it was found that they had only begun.

In the middle of July, the rebel ram Arkansas, an iron-plated vessel, came down the Yazoo, and, passing triumphantly through our surprised fleet, safely anchored under the guns of Vicksburg. Flag-officers Farragut and Davis, with Porter, now held a consultation as to the best mode of destroying this powerful antagonist at its moorings. It was determined to make the attempt at four o'clock on the 22nd, by Farragut attacking the lower batteries and Davis the upper, while W. D. Porter, in the Essex, should move boldly and swiftly down on the steamer and crush it with one deadly blow. Reckless of the fire of the batteries, Porter dashed full on the astonished rebel. The blow glanced from the mailed sides, and the Essex was carried by her momentum, high up on the river bank, where she lay for two hours or more, under the fire of seventy heavy guns in battery and twenty field pieces, besides the guns of the ram. Yet, strange to say, she eventually got off, and, passing down stream, anchored under the protection of the lower fleet of Farragut. A few days after, Col. Ellet went up the Yazoo and destroyed the rebel gunboats Van Dorn, Polk and Livingston.

On land, but little was accomplished. In Arkansas, Missouri and Louisiana, fights occurred between small forces, but having no important bearing on the main movements of the armies. The army of Curtis, which, after the battle of Pea Ridge the Spring before, attempted to cross the State of Arkansas to the Mississippi, arrived at Helena safe on the 12th of July, to the great relief of the country. It had been a long, most difficult and painful march; the cavalry, twenty-five hundred strong, on one occasion, marching sixty-five miles in twenty-four hours.

The great movement, however, at the West, during this month, was that of the army under Major-Gen. Buell, the object of which was to seize Chattanooga. His force consisted of about twenty-five thousand men, with some sixteen thousand more, scattered through Middle Tennessee and Northern Alabama, mostly under the command of the gallant Mitchell. His first great object was to repair the railroad running north to Nashville, which he foresaw, contrary to Halleck's opinion, must be his base of supplies. While this herculean task was being accomplished by the force under Mitchell, he with his army marched rapidly towards Chattanooga. All this time, Morgan was on a grand raid in Kentucky. Forrest, also, with a formidable force, suddenly appeared before Murfreesboro' on the 13th, surprised and captured the garrison, consisting of fourteen hundred men, and broke up the railroad to Nashville, which had only been completed the day before. This was a serious drawback, and Buell was blamed at the time, for the catastrophe. But the truth was, a sufficient force had not been given him to protect his front, three hundred miles long, reaching from Corinth to Cumberland Gap; he was also lamentably deficient in cavalry, though he had urged upon the Government the great necessity of his being supplied. It was plain to him, and ought to have been plain to Halleck, that the force was too small to hold the country, even if he should conquer it, to say nothing of the long line of communication to Nashville, which must be kept open. Morgan interrupted this so constantly, threatening even Nashville, that Buell sent Major-General Nelson there to take charge of affairs. In the meantime, Bragg was concentrating an army of sixty thousand men at and near Chattanooga, preparatory to an invasion of Middle Tennessee. Buell was aware of the approaching storm, and divided his inadequate force, so as to protect the most important points the best way he could. On the 20th of August, hearing that Bragg had commenced his march, and was crossing the Tennessee at Chattanooga and other points, he began to concentrate his forces at Altamont. But his supplies were getting short, when the startling news was received, that Kirby Smith, with a large army, had poured through the gaps of the Cumberland Mountains, and was invading Kentucky—having beaten Nelson and routed his army at Richmond. Even this stern and self-reliant Commander, who had never turned his back on the foe, began to be filled with anxiety at the perils that surrounded him, and to see clearly, that instead of conquering East Tennessee, it would tax his utmost skill and energy to save Middle Tennessee and Kentucky. He immediately concentrated his troops at Murfreesboro'. It was now September, and he at once marched out in search of the enemy, who retired as he advanced, first from Glasgow, and then from Munfordsville from which he withdrew on the 20th. Buell now determined to fall back to Louisville, which was seriously threatened by Kirby Smith. He accomplished the long, tedious march without the loss of a wagon. The citizens of the place were in great trepidation, and when the tread of his advance columns sounded through the street, at midnight, the shout of "Buell has come! Buell has come!" went up, as it did on the banks of the Tennessee, at Pittsburg Landing, from our shattered, beaten forces, when they saw his trained legions sweeping to their relief. He immediately reorganized his army, and prepared to march forth against the enemy, but an order was received from Washington suspending him from chief command, and appointing Thomas in his place.

All this time, General George Morgan was grimly holding Cumberland Gap, against overwhelming odds.

While military affairs were assuming an alarming aspect in Tennessee and Kentucky—the bold advance of Smith threatening even Cincinnati, causing consternation among its inhabitants and sending them forth to the defense of the city—along the Mississippi, but little was accomplished, for Vicksburg still held out against the Federal fleet. Farther west, General Lane, having been appointed by the Government to raise an army in Kansas, issued his proclamation in August, calling on the inhabitants of Nebraska, Colorado and Dacotah to rally to his standard. Affairs remained unchanged at New Orleans under Butler's rigorous sway. He issued an order this month, assessing the inhabitants who had subscribed to the rebel defense fund, three hundred and forty-two thousand dollars. Colonel McNeil and General Blunt were dealing the guerrillas and organized bands some severe blows in Missouri; but the only battle that occurred in the West during the month was at Baton Rouge, which was attacked on the 5th by a heavy force under Breckenridge. General Williams, commanding our troops there, formed his line of battle the night before, some distance outside of the town. But, though he was prepared to receive the expected attack, the enemy, taking advantage of a dense fog, came down at early daylight so suddenly upon him that a portion of his line gave way, and some guns were captured. He, however, rallied his troops, and gallantly led them in person against the advancing, shouting battalions, hurling them back with resistless fury. But he fell in the charge, and was borne back, mortally wounded, to the rear. The battle raged, with varied fortunes, for five hours, when the enemy fell back. The gunboats Essex and Sumter shelled the woods during the action; and after our lines were drawn in, as ordered by General Williams before he fell, two other gunboats added their fire, deterring the enemy from making another advance. The ram Arkansas, and the gunboats Webb and Music, had designed to take part in the combat, but the former, becoming disabled, was compelled to lie by. So, the next morning, Porter, in the Essex, went in search of the monster, and met it coming down to attack him. The former at once opened his guns on the formidable foe. The engine of the ram becoming disabled, it was compelled to run ashore, where it continued the combat. Porter, choosing his position, now poured a terrible fire into his adversary. The boat was soon in flames, and, deserted by her crew, drifted down stream till her magazine caught fire, when she blew up with a tremendous explosion. Thus ignobly perished this much-dreaded vessel.

Sherman at this time commanded at Memphis under Grant, who was over the Department of West Tennessee. His army lay comparatively idle during the month; but the next month, September, it seemed to rouse from its inexplicable inaction. Grant's head-quarters were at Corinth, where he was confronted by Van Dorn and Price, who the Winter before had been beaten at Pea Ridge by Curtis.

Rosecrans, who in the middle of the preceding May had been ordered to join Halleck before Corinth, was, after the latter's elevation to the chief command, and Pope's transfer to Virginia, placed at the head of the Army of the Mississippi, as it was termed, under Grant. During the Summer he was active in the field, but accomplished nothing of importance. At this time he was established in Corinth. Suddenly he was informed that Price had advanced and taken possession of Iuka.

CHAPTER V.

SEPTEMBER—OCTOBER.

BATTLE OF IUKA—GALLANTRY OF GENERAL HAMILTON—FAILURE OF GRANT—ATTEMPT OF THE ENEMY TO CUT GRANT'S LINE OF SUPPLIES—BATTLE OF CORINTH—A GALLANT TEXAN—TERRIFIC SLAUGHTER OF THE ENEMY—THE VICTORY—ARRIVAL OF MC PHERSON—THE PURSUIT—THE BATTLE-FIELD—ROSECRANS PLACED AT THE HEAD OF THE DEPARTMENT OF THE CUMBERLAND.

ROSECRANS knew that this movement was merely preparatory to an attack on Corinth itself, and, with his usual promptitude, determined at once to retake the place, and proposed to Grant to advance by one road, while he, marching by way of Jacinto, should get in rear, and prevent the force there from retreating southward. This was agreed to, and Rosecrans, having concentrated the troops of his two divisions, started on the morning of the 19th, and marching eighteen miles and a half, came within a little over a mile of Iuka. Price did not wait for his attack, but immediately marched forth to meet him. One division, Hamilton's, numbering less than three thousand men, and with but one battery, was in advance, and on this, Price with eleven thousand men suddenly moved. Hamilton had reached the brow of a hill, which fell off abruptly on both sides, when the enemy, hid in a ravine below, broke cover with a shout, and poured in a sudden volley of musketry. The woods were so dense that Hamilton could not deploy his men, and, marching them by either flank, from the only road that ran through the woods, and planting his single battery so as to command this road, received the shock. It was fortunate for him that his position was so cramped, for it lessened the numerical advantage of the enemy, and left the contest to be decided, very much by the comparative strength of the heads of columns. The movements of the regiments into their assigned places were made with great steadiness, though under a withering fire the whole time. Each colonel had his orders to hold his ground at all hazards. It was a square, stand-up fight. The rebel onslaught was terrific. In dense masses, regiment closing in on regiment, like successive waves of the sea, they bore down on our thin line, with a desperation that threatened to sweep it to quick destruction. At this juncture, Sullivan arrived with his division, and, though no more troops could be used in front, his timely arrival prevented Hamilton from being outflanked by the overwhelming numbers of the enemy. He believed he could stand pounding longest, and his brave division stood like a wall of adamant across the road. The woods on either side of it, were alive with the rolling volleys, and echoed to the shouts and yells of the combatants. The rebels, determined to force our line, moved into the desolating fire that met them, with unfaltering resolution. As they came within close range, that single battery, the Eleventh Ohio, opened on them with grape and canister. The guns were worked with great rapidity, and at each discharge, gaps opened in the dense ranks, but they closed up again, and the hostile line swept steadily forward over all obstructions. At length, the Forty-eighth Indiana, pressed by three times its number—its gallant Commander cut down—fell back in disorder. This left the death-dealing battery exposed, and with an exultant shout the enemy sprang upon it. Receiving without flinching the load of canister and grape that met them, they swept over it and captured it; but not till every officer, and nearly every gunner was killed or wounded, and scarcely a horse left standing. At this juncture, Sullivan, by a great effort, rallied a part of the right wing, and flung it like a loosened cliff on the shouting, triumphant captors, and sent them astounded back to cover. Maddened to fury by their loss, the rebels rallied, and with yells precipitated themselves upon Sullivan's diminished band, and recovered the battery. Around its guns, the battle raged with awful fury. Every flank movement of the enemy being promptly stopped, he was compelled to fight it out in front, and from five o'clock till dark, the Fifth Iowa, and Eleventh and Twenty-sixth Missouri, held that single road, with a stubbornness that scoffed at numbers. Rooted to their places—a line of fire running incessantly along their front, they stood unconquerable as fate. Three times did the Fifth Iowa, when about to be swallowed up by the ever-increasing masses, leap forward with the bayonet, and send them broken and discomfited back. When their ammunition was at last exhausted, they slowly retired, but with their faces to the foe. All this time Rosecrans listened, with intense anxiety, to hear the sound of Grant's guns on the other road, but it came not, and darkness at length closed the bloody contest. Those two brave, shattered divisions, lay down on their arms, on the ground they had crimsoned with their blood, to wait for the morning light to renew the unequal struggle. But the enemy, under cover of the darkness, stole away; and when the morning dawned, Iuka was found deserted. Rosecrans immediately started in pursuit with his cavalry, but being only three companies strong it could do little more than harass the rebel rear, and after going twenty-five miles, gave up the chase. About eleven o'clock, Grant marched into Iuka, where he should have been long before. Some unfortunate mistake had caused the delay, and thus saved the enemy from total destruction. Rosecrans, in alluding to it, said, "The unexpected accident which alone prevented cutting off the retreat of Price, and capturing him and his army, only shows how much, success depends upon Him in whose hands are the accidents, as well as the laws of life." The total loss in this battle, was six hundred and eighty, or nearly a quarter of the whole force engaged.

Rosecrans immediately fell back on Corinth, where he again took up his head-quarters. He soon discovered that the enemy was concentrating on that place, or some other point, which would cut off his communications and compel him to evacuate it. Price, Van Dorn, and Lovell, had in fact united their entire forces, for the purpose of crushing his comparatively small army, before he could receive reinforcements. The latter, calling in all his troops from the adjacent posts, watched with the deepest solicitude the development of the hostile plan. At length, discovering that the rebels had marched around him to the eastward, and were moving down on Corinth from the north and north-east, he formed his plan, and disposing his troops to the best possible advantage, calmly awaited the attack. He knew he was outnumbered by two to one, but he relied on the strength of his position, and the indomitable character of his troops. McKean commanded the left, Davies the centre, and the gallant Hamilton the right, where Rosecrans supposed the weight of the struggle would fall. The old fortifications, thrown up by Beauregard, were too extensive for his little army to hold, and so he erected works within them.

This was on the third of October. Rosecrans' plan was to advance on the enemy, as he approached, in order to compel him to develop his lines, and then retire behind his own works, so that his batteries could sweep the rebels, as they emerged into the open ground in front. In carrying it out, more or less fighting occurred, and night found our army back in the town, and the rebel lines drawn closely around it. Much uneasiness was felt among the soldiers, because they had been so easily driven back into the place, where the enemy's shells could reach them, but they were not aware of the motives which governed their Commander.

This was not lessened by the sound of the enemy at work all night, planting batteries within close range. At length, the long wished for, yet dreaded dawn, streaked the eastern sky, and the roll of the drum and the pealing bugle, awoke the morning echoes, and were answered by those of the enemy in the dark forests beyond.

The rebel force was massed in the angle, formed by the Memphis and Columbus railroads. The left of our army rested on the batteries extending west from Fort Robinette—the centre on a slight ridge north of the houses, and the right on the high ground which covered the Pittsburg and Purdy roads, that led away towards the old battle ground of Pittsburg Landing. The rebel plan was to move at once, with overwhelming numbers, on our batteries, and sweep them with the rush of a torrent. The sacrifice, they knew, would be great, but they were ready to make it. Four redoubts covered all the approaches, while batteries were in every place where guns could be advantageously posted, so that the whole open space in front of our lines, could be swept with a hail-storm of fire.

With daylight, skirmishing commenced, and the heavy boom of cannon, here and there, shook the field; but, as yet, the enemy's lines were invisible. They were forming in the roads running through the forest, a half a mile or more in front, and every eye was strained to catch the heads of the columns as they moved out for the final advance. The very mystery that shrouded the rebel host, hidden in those stirless woods, added impressiveness to the scene. At length, a little after nine o'clock, the fearful suspense ended, for the heads of the dense columns began to issue from their leafy covering. In columns of division, the whole host moved in splendid order up the Bolivar road, straight towards the murderous batteries. Long lines of glittering steel, crested the gray formations below, as, with steady step and closed ranks, they swept forward. Like a great wedge, the mighty mass at first advanced, and then slowly unfolded like two expanding wings, and swooped down on Corinth, that lay glittering in the mellow sun-light. Price on the left, and Van Dorn on the right, moved on together, but the latter, meeting with unexpected obstacles, lost a little time, and Price first caught the full fury of the storm. Right up a turfy slope, the steady columns pressed, swept by our whole line of batteries, the shot and shell tearing through them every moment with awful desolation. Like clouds, rent before the incessant flashes of lightning, those gray formations everywhere parted, showing great ragged openings that closed as quickly as made. The dead and dying darkened all the ground, but the living never faltered. With heads bent, and leaning forms, like those who breast a driving sleet, they pressed sternly forward, making straight for Rosecrans' centre. When they came within musket range, death traversed their ranks with still more frightful rapidity; yet they never faltered. The earth groaned and shook under them, and the air seemed to flow with fire around them, yet they heeded it not. Still onward and upward they came, like the march of fate. At last they reached the crest of the hill, and Davies' division gave way in disorder. Rosecrans, whose eye has never for a moment left this onrolling mass, starts at this sudden great disaster, and dashing amid the broken ranks, heedless of the raining shot and shell, rallies them in person. But the rebels, seeing their advantage, spring forward with a shout, and Rosecrans' headquarters are inundated with the hostile troops, and the next moment their fire is pouring into the public square of the town itself. Under this sudden change of fortune, Hamilton's division of veterans is compelled to fall back, and instantly, with a shout of victory, the rebels rush on Fort Richardson, the key of the position. A single sheet of flame bursts from its sides, and when the smoke rises, the space where they stood is clear of living men; only the dead and bleeding are left. But those brave men have not trodden Death's highway so far, to yield now, when their hands are grasping victory; and once more rallying, they precipitate themselves forward with the fury and clamor of demons. Richardson, from whom the battery was named, sinks amid his guns, and the next moment, the rebels are leaping over them. Suddenly, as if rising out of the earth, the Fifty-sixth Illinois, hid in a ravine near it, spring to their feet, and pouring in one close deliberate volley, dash across the plateau, and into the fort, and almost lift the rebels bodily out of it, so sudden and desperate and wild is their charge. Hamilton sees the charge, and "*Forward*" runs along his glorious line. Sweeping forward with terrible front, he completes the overthrow. The rebel host is at last broken. Human endurance had finally reached its limit—despair at once took the place of courage, and, flinging away their useless arms, they broke wildly for the woods. And then such a shout of victory went up, as those who heard it, will never forget to their latest day. It rolled down the line, and Van Dorn, on the left, heard it with a sinking heart. Struggling through a ravine and thickets and abattis, he was a moment too late, to have his blow fall simultaneously with that of Price, else the issue might have been different. He was now in front of Fort Robinette, within a hundred and fifty yards of which, stood Fort Williams. These had poured a deadly enfilading fire through his ranks, as he advanced, and now the former, with its ten pound Parrotts, stood right in his path. Over this he must go, or turn back over the field, gained at such horrible sacrifice. The shout of victory borne to him from the left, sounded like the knell of doom. Price had failed at Fort Richardson, and now alone and unaided, he must carry the works before him, or all be lost. It was a mighty task, and he might well pause, before he undertook it. But instead of shrinking from it, he summoned all his energies for one desperate effort. Two brigades, one supporting the other, at close distance, and led by Colonel Rogers, of Texas, swiftly advanced straight on the fort. Instantly its guns, and those of Fort Williams, opened their fire, and shot and shell went tearing through the dense columns. But they had braced themselves up to the fearful work, they knew to be before them, and breasted the iron storm with sublime devotion. As they came within close range, and the infantry opened fire, the havoc was awful. The solid formations caved before it, as the sandbank before the torrent, but closing up compact as iron, the diminished numbers, with their eyes bent sternly on the prize before them, kept on their terrible way. Rogers, striding at their head, seemed to bear a charmed life, and "*Forward*—FORWARD," rang clear and strong from his lips, rising even above the roar of cannon. Struggling through the fallen timber, they fell and were caught amid the branches, presenting a ghastly spectacle. Still the living never faltered—with their eyes fixed on their heroic leader, they let the volleys crash, and the devastating fire burn along their ranks, with a heroic indifference. At last they reached the ditch, and for one fearful moment paused. Rogers, still towering in front unhurt, waved the rebel flag with his left hand, holding a revolver in his right, and, still shouting "*Forward*," with one bound cleared the ditch. Springing up the slope, he planted his standard on the ramparts. The next moment he fell, banner and all, into the ditch, a corpse.

Five brave Texans, that never left their leader's side, at the same instant pitched heavily forward into the fort, sharing his fate. The Ohio brigade, commanded by Colonel Fuller, had lain flat on their faces just over the ridge, and now in close range, rose and delivered six swift volleys, and the front was clear of rebels. The supporting rebel brigade now advanced into the same volcano, bent on the same hopeless errand. Taking the close and swift volleys into their bosoms without shrinking, they kept on, till maddened into desperation, they made one wild rush on the Sixty-third Ohio, that crossed their path. But the brave fellows stood like a rock in their places, and in a moment, friend and foe were locked in a hand to hand death-struggle. Bayonets, clubbed muskets, and, when these failed, clenched fists were used. The fight was brief but awful, and the shouts and yells, and oaths and curses that rose, seemed wrenched from the throats of demons. At length the rebels gave way, when the Eleventh Missouri and Twenty-seventh Ohio sprang forward and chased them swiftly to cover.

The battle was over. No second charge could be made, for the victory was won, but at a fearful cost. Of the two hundred and fifty of the Sixty-third Ohio, one-half lay dead or bleeding, on the spot where they had fought. The shout that rocked the field, when Price recoiled, shattered and broken, from Fort Richardson, now went up from around Fort Robinette, and rolling like the waves of the sea, along the whole line of battle, swelled back into Corinth, where it was again caught up and prolonged, till the heavens shook with the loud and joyous acclaim. There had been no long battle. The whole struggle lasted scarcely more than an hour and a half. It was a whirlwind—a hurricane——then a great wild thunder crash—and all was over. And yet, in the brief struggle, what awful destruction had been wrought. Over two thousand of our own soldiers had fallen, while over six thousand rebels had been piled on that bloody field. Death had moved through the thick-set ranks of the foe with a rapid footstep.

Forty thousand, it was estimated, composed the rebel force, while Rosecrans had but little over twenty thousand behind his works.

In front of Fort Robinette, the rebel dead lay in heaps. Fifty-six were buried in one ditch, but the brave Rogers was given a grave by himself—those stern Western men smoothing over and marking his last resting-place, with the tender care they would give the grave of a companion-in-arms. It was but a little to do; yet it was such a testimonial as the brave love to give to the brave, on whatever field they fall.

Two thousand two hundred and forty-eight prisoners fell into our hands, together with two pieces of artillery, fourteen stand of colors, and over three thousand small arms.

Rosecrans immediately rode along the whole line of battle, greeted with thundering cheers as he passed. He told his brave troops, that although they had been two days marching and preparing for battle, and had passed two sleepless nights, and endured two days' fighting, he wanted them to fill their cartridge-boxes, haversacks and stomachs, take an early sleep, and at daylight press after the flying foe.

McPherson, having arrived in the meantime at Corinth, with a fresh brigade, was immediately started in pursuit, and the roll of cannon died away in the distance, as he pressed fiercely after the retiring columns. The roads and fields were strewed with the wrecks of the fight. The rebels narrowly escaped destruction in the forks of the Hatchie, but finally got off.

The fields around Corinth presented a frightful spectacle, and for weeks after the battle, the place of slaughter could be scented miles away, by the traveler. It was a great victory, and people began to regard Rosecrans as invincible. Victory followed his standard wherever he moved, and the soldiers, with that fondness for nicknames which always characterizes them, christened him "Old Rosy."

Rosecrans believed that if Grant had supported him, as he requested him to do, he could easily have entered Vicksburg and saved the after sacrifice of men and money.

Having returned from the pursuit, he established his headquarters at Corinth, where he remained till the 25th of October. In the meantime, the Government having created the Department of the Cumberland, and the Fourteenth Army Corps, he was placed at the head of it, and departed for Louisville, where he arrived on the 30th.

With Buell's splendid army under his command, it was thought that he would immediately move on Bragg, and inflict that punishment on him, which he failed to receive at the hand of the former.

Repairing to Nashville, he took a survey of his position, and began to lay his plans for the future. Bragg, in the meantime, had assembled his army at Murfreesboro', and was strongly fortifying himself, preparatory to winter quarters.

CHAPTER VI.

OCTOBER.

BUELL RESTORED TO COMMAND—MOVES OUT OF LOUISVILLE—BATTLE OF PERRYVILLE—RETREAT OF BRAGG—PURSUIT—REMOVED FROM COMMAND—MORGAN AT CUMBERLAND GAP—GALLANT DEFENSE OF—CALL FOR REINFORCEMENTS—IS SURROUNDED BY A HUNDRED THOUSAND MEN—HIS EXTREME PERIL—GALLANT RESOLVE TO MAKE A FORCED MARCH OF TWO HUNDRED MILES TO THE OHIO—BLOWS UP THE MOUNTAIN—DESTROYS HIS SIEGE GUNS—BURNS UP EVERYTHING—FEARFUL CONFLAGRATION AND EXPLOSION—TERRIFIC SCENE—MIDNIGHT MARCH—THE RACE FOR LIFE—SUFFERINGS OF THE ARMY—ITS DELIGHT AT SIGHT OF THE OHIO—HALLECK'S TREATMENT OF MORGAN—EXTRAORDINARY STATEMENTS.

WHILE Rosecrans was thus crowning the Federal arms with success, in the neighborhood of the Mississippi, and Butler was trying to bring order out of chaos in New Orleans, and Galveston in Texas was surrendered (October 9th) to Renshaw, Commander of our fleet there, important events were occurring in Kentucky and East Tennessee. Buell's sudden removal from the head of the army at Louisville, arrested his march against Bragg, which he designed to commence the next day. Thomas, however, telegraphed to Washington, entreating the authorities there to reconsider their action, and retain Buell in the command, as the proper person to be at the head of the army. They acceded to his request, and Buell at once addressed himself to the task of driving Bragg out of Kentucky; and on the 1st of October moved out of Louisville, in five columns. Bragg, though constantly skirmishing, began to retire, with the evident intention of forming a junction with Kirby Smith, who had fallen back from his threatened attack on Cincinnati, though he had carried the rebel flag within seven miles of the city. Buell overtook the enemy at Perryville on the 7th. A partial engagement followed, which was renewed with great severity the next morning, by the enemy suddenly falling on McCook's brigade. Repulsed at first, he repeated the attack at noon, in which the whole left corps became engaged, and was terribly pressed till night fell, when the battle ended. Terrill's brigade was driven back in a rout, and he was killed, as well as Jackson, who commanded the division. The brave, heroic Rousseau, commanding the third division, bore the chief weight of the battle, and saved the left corps from total defeat. A charge by Sheridan, at night-fall, closed the fight. This partial disaster was attributed by Buell to the neglect of McCook to send him word that he was pressed with an overwhelming force, until it was too late to reach him before night with the other wing of the army, which was separated by a distance of five miles.

Our loss in this engagement was about four thousand, leaving Buell but fifty-four thousand men with which to pursue Bragg, whose army numbered over sixty thousand. But the nature of the country was such that he could not force him to a battle, though he pressed him with unrelenting severity. At Crab Orchard, where the country suddenly changed, being barren and cut up into defiles, so that a small force could protect the retreating army, he stopped his pursuit, having captured in all, four or five thousand prisoners.

But though he had driven Bragg out of Kentucky, and thus relieved the State, the Administration pretended to be dissatisfied at his not having destroyed the rebel army, and therefore removed him from his command. Whether Halleck, and the Secretary of War, really believed that Buell had not done all that could reasonably have been expected of him, or whether it was necessary, as usual, to have some scape goat for their own military blunders, is left to conjecture.

Cumberland Gap, which General Morgan, as before stated, had captured in the Spring, by a flank movement through Rogers' Gap, and immediately fortified, preparatory to a movement on Knoxville, was evacuated this September. The advance of Bragg into Kentucky, which compelled Buell to fall back rapidly to Nashville, left the enemy at liberty to push across the Cumberland Mountains, by various routes, and effectually cut Morgan off from his base of supplies, thus leaving him alone, to save himself as best he might. Strong in his position, he felt able to hold it against all odds, if he could be kept from starvation. He contested every foot of the advance of the enemy, and foraged the country in every direction that his forces could penetrate. In the meantime, he sent to Halleck, and General Wright of Ohio, for supplies, saying that if his communications could be kept open, he would hold the Gap against the whole rebel army. At different times he sent out five expeditions, in which he killed and captured seven hundred of the enemy, with a loss to himself of only forty men. For more than two months, he saw the storm gathering thicker and darker around him, for as Buell fell back towards Nashville, the rebel flood poured like a deluge into Kentucky, so that by the 21st of August, Morgan found Kirby Smith on the north side, and Stevenson on the south side of the Gap. Still, he kept buoyant and cheerful. Not a desponding word escaped him—he always wrote in a confident tone, but said that his supplies were getting shorter and shorter, and that even his animals were failing for want of forage. He would not stir from his position, he declared, though he had to kill his mules for food, if he could see any movement set on foot to open his communications. The country became alarmed for his safety. The very stubbornness with which he held the grim fortress, only ensured his destruction, if no relief should reach him. He at length put his army on half-rations, and still clung to his position, though he knew a hundred thousand men environed him, and held the entire country from the Gap to the Ohio.

Thus, for thirty days, his brave soldiers were kept on half-rations; a great part of the time without bread, rice, flour or potatoes. The overwhelming enemy continued to draw closer and closer around him, every day narrowing his field for forage, until at length, starvation began to stare him in the face. What now was to be done? He could hear of no movement for his relief, and he staid, waiting for it, until every known avenue of escape was closed against him. The rebel General telegraphed to Richmond, that Morgan's army might be considered prisoners of war, for its fate was sealed. True, one route was still left open—the wild, desolate region stretching for two hundred miles directly to the north—but this was reported by the engineers impossible for any army with artillery, if indeed it were possible for an army of ten thousand men, to be supported there at all, in the length of time it would take to traverse such a country. Yet the rebels seemed to think, that a man who had dragged siege guns up and over the cliffs of Cumberland Mountains, might attempt to escape by this route; and so Humphrey Marshall was sent to block it up, and, early in September, was making his difficult way through the sterile region to the north-east. In this painful dilemma, Morgan called a council of war, in which it was decided that the only alternative was an immediate evacuation or an unconditional surrender. This being decided upon, Morgan determined to make a desperate effort to save both his army and artillery, all but the siege guns, which he resolved to destroy. It was a dreary prospect at best—that frightful march of two hundred miles, with ten times ten thousand men before, behind and on every side of him. But he had tried his officers and men, and knew they would do anything short of a miracle, while he himself resolved to be annihilated, before he would surrender. Sending out officers to buy provisions along another route by way of Mount Sterling, who were purposely taken prisoners, he completely deceived the enemy as to his intentions. In the meantime, preparations were rapidly made to leave. The mountain was mined so as to tumble the cliffs upon the road in his rear, the heavy siege guns were destroyed, and, on the 16th, a large train started for Manchester. All that night, and the next day, the work went on. At evening, the pickets were quietly withdrawn, and Lieutenant-Colonel Gallup, with two hundred chosen men, was directed to hold the enemy in check, and, if he attempted to follow, to give the alarm by blowing up the magazine. Before he should finally leave the Gap, he was ordered to fire the military storehouse, commissary's and quartermasters' buildings, and tents, and then spring the mine that would unseat the cliffs, and hurl them into the road behind the retreating army. Five picked men were stationed at each magazine, to which the trains were already laid, and five more at a pit in which were piled several thousand stand of arms, mostly loaded, who at a given signal were to apply the torch, and set the volcano in motion. Gallup, having stationed his pickets, went forward with a flag of truce, and by adroit management effectually deceived the enemy respecting Morgan's designs. When he knew, by certain signs, that the army was well in motion, he took his leave, saying that he would call in the morning and get the answer to his flag of truce. He then visited his pickets, telling them to dispute every inch of ground, and repaired to Baird's head-quarters, where he found Morgan sitting on his horse, and with a serious, anxious face, watching his retiring columns. It was now ten o'clock at night, and the crisis of the fate of the army was fast approaching. Turning to Gallup, Morgan said: "You have a highly important duty to perform; this ammunition and these arms and military stores must not fall into the hands of the enemy. I hope you will not be captured." "Farewell," he added, and bowing, rode off into the gloom. The night wore on, and Gallup, sending off his small force to a place of safety, directed three men—Markham, O'Brien and Thad. Reynolds as he was called—the boldest scout and spy in the army—to kindle the conflagration. As the flames rolled heavenward, he gave the signal to fire the trains. To his astonishment, no answering explosion followed, and waiting a sufficient time, he put spurs to his horse and galloped to the spot. Not a soul was to be found—all had gone forward to the main column. Seizing some burning fagots, he fired the trains with his own hands, and mounting his horse, dashed down the Gap. He had barely reached a safe distance, when the first explosion followed, sending the huge rocks in every direction. The conflagration in the valley below was now in full headway, and the scene became indescribably grand. The savage precipices reddened like fire in the sudden illumination, and the whole midnight gorge shone brighter than at noon-day. Gallup, sitting on his horse, that glowed like a fiery steed in the intense glare of the flames, gazed with silent awe on the wild work his hands had wrought. Said he: "Every fissure and opening in the cliffs around me, was visible. The trees and rocks upon their sides, at any time picturesque and interesting, were now grand in their beauty. It was a scene more like enchantment than reality. I gazed, lost in admiration. But suddenly the scene changed. The large magazine, with its rich stores of powder and fixed ammunition, exploded. The explosion shook the mountains like a toy in the hands of a monster. The air was filled with dense smoke, so that I could scarcely breathe. Huge masses of rock, cartridge-boxes, barrels of powder, and other materials, were blown to an indescribable height, and went whirling through the air in wild confusion, falling, in some instances, more than a mile from the exploding magazine. A moment after, the burning roof of a building a hundred and eighty feet long, used as a store-house on the mountain, fell in, and set fire to the shells stored there." Before the blazing embers that shot in a fiery shower heavenward had descended to the earth again, the explosion took place, sounding like a thousand cannon let off there at once, in the trembling gorge. Lighted on its way by such a sea of flame, and keeping step to such stern and awful music, did that gallant army move off into the night, and turn its face towards the distant Ohio.

But the terrific fusilade made by the discharging guns and bursting shells, was kept up there among the solitary crags until noon. The rebels beyond the ridge were filled with consternation, as they gazed on the lurid sky, and felt the earthquake shock, and knew not what the strange uproar meant. When, at last, they were informed, by an inhabitant of the region, that Morgan had evacuated the Gap, they dared not approach it till three o'clock the next day, for fear of exploding shells and mines. When they did venture near, they gazed around in blank astonishment. Silence and desolation reigned throughout the gorge, while the rocks lay piled along it, in one wild wreck, heaved there by the exploding mines.

Morgan had done his work thoroughly and well, but the mighty task before him was only just commenced. Two hundred miles of such a country as lay before him, were never before marched over, by ten thousand men, with artillery and no supplies, while a vast army was closing in upon them on every side. As if to cloud the beginning of his great endeavor with increasing gloom, towards morning a pelting rain set in, accompanied with fierce gusts of wind that swept mournfully over the swiftly advancing columns. Ten ladies,

EVACUATION OF CUMBERLAND GAP.

the wives and daughters of officers, were with the army, to share its perils and its fortunes.

Morgan marched by two parallel roads, and so rapidly, that by morning his advance brigade was at Flat Lick, twenty miles from the Gap, which he had left the night before. By evening, the army was at Manchester. Here Morgan halted a day, to complete the organization of his forces, and gird himself for the long and doubtful race before him. Before he was ready to start, the enemy's bugles were sounding in his rear, while the scouts brought in the tidings that a brigade of cavalry, under the notorious Morgan, was hovering around his line of march. He learned also that Humphrey Marshall was moving to cut his line of march to the north. In fact, so perilous was his condition, that Gen. Jones, afterwards taken prisoner by us, confessed, that had Morgan delayed his retreat but a single day, his last avenue of escape would have been closed.

The storm was rapidly gathering, on every side of him, and nothing but swift marching could save him. A single inefficient or negligent officer might work his ruin; but a truer set of subordinates, or a more devoted body of soldiers, never closed around a brave Commander. Generals Spears, Carter and Baird, and Colonel De Coucy, led their respective commands, with a skill that won the admiration and praise of all. It was fortunate that he had, as topographical engineer with him, Captain Sidney Lyons, who, as State Geologist of Kentucky, had surveyed this whole region. He knew it so well, that he told Morgan that he doubted, even if he could succeed in getting his artillery trains over the terrible roads he must travel, whether he could subsist the army in such a country, during the short time it would take to traverse it.

It is impossible to give a detailed account of this extraordinary retreat. The army moved in a lengthened line, winding over the rocky, broken, sterile region like a huge serpent; the heavy rumbling of the trains and guns, the only music of the march. When it came to a cross-road, it would rapidly concentrate, to prevent flank attacks of the enemy's cavalry, and as soon as the dangerous point was passed, unwind again, and press forward. The streams were all dry, mocking with their stony beds the thirst of the weary soldiers. Sometimes, water could be got only by pulling it up from crevices in the cliffs, eighty or a hundred feet deep; and one day, the army was compelled to march thirty-four miles in order to reach water. So constantly and dreadfully did the soldiers suffer for want of it, that they began to talk of the distant Ohio, as the end of all human desires. They suffered, too, from want of food, as the enemy destroyed everything before them on which they could lay their hands. Even the officers and women grew faint as they marched along, gnawed by the pangs of hunger. One day, all that Morgan had to sustain life was a single ear of parched corn, and on another day, all that he and his staff together had, was a dozen potatoes. Occasionally, a field of standing corn was passed, which sufficed to keep them from starvation. On one occasion, as Morgan was riding along the column, he passed the wife of one of his colonels, sitting on a log, looking faint and pale. Stopping a moment, he said: "I hope you are not ill." "Oh, no," she replied, "I am well, General." "But," she added, with a wan smile, "I have eaten but once in forty-eight hours." Famine was staring him and his gallant army in the face, but there was no murmuring, no complaint. The roads were blockaded with fallen trees and rocks, which had to be removed, or a new road cut around them; and the crack of rifles from the thickets along their line of march, and from barricades in front, and the report of forces gathering in advance, kept them ever on the alert, and hard at work, and constantly moving. The usual September storm, even a little delay, would probably have sealed the fate of the army; but the bright autumnal weather enabled them to march steadily, and thus keep the advantage they had gained at the start, to the last. The rebel Morgan and Marshall were both in his front, and an overwhelming force in his rear, but the latter could not overtake him, while he moved so rapidly that the former had no time to concentrate a sufficient force to arrest his progress. Occasional conflicts with small bodies occurred, in which a few of his men fell, and were hastily buried in the sterile fields past which they marched.

Thus, day after day, for nearly a fortnight, this wonderful retreat was kept up, until at length, on the 3d of October, the advance brigade, as it reached a lofty swell, caught a glimpse of the lordly Ohio, rolling its glittering flood through the distant landscape. At the glad sight, a thrilling shout went up, and "The Ohio! The Ohio!" rolled like thunder down the excited line. Each regiment and brigade took it up in turn, till "The Ohio! The Ohio!" rose and fell in prolonged and jubilant acclamation for miles away, along the weary column. It recalled the time when the German army sent up in a wild shout, "The Rhine! The Rhine!" as they once more came in sight of their native stream, and joy and gladness filled every heart.

Morgan was at last safe. Right nobly had he won the race. By his foresight, energy and indomitable perseverance, he had escaped from the trap in which an inefficient General-in-Chief had allowed him to be caught. He had saved his entire train, and lost but eighty men since he moved out of the Gap. Instead, however, of congratulating him on his skill and success, in his report sent into Congress the following Winter, Halleck had the injustice to censure him for evacuating the Gap, saying that "an investigation had been ordered." No one, however, was deceived by it. The public had long known the situation of Morgan, and, that unless his communications were opened, and supplies sent him, he and his army were lost; and hence, instead of condemning him, felt unbounded gratitude, that he had outwitted the enemy, and saved his army and guns. But the General-in-Chief was guilty of deception, as well as injustice. When he said that "an investigation had been ordered," it had not only been ordered but finished, and the report laid on his table *six weeks* previous. He himself had directed Major-General Wright to make this investigation; and, in his report, the latter said he "did not see how, with starvation staring him (Morgan) in the face, and with no certainty of relief being afforded, he could have come to any other conclusion than the one he arrived at," &c. He stated also that it was unanimously decided, in a council of war, to be the only course left, if he would avoid a surrender of his army.

When Morgan, who was at Memphis, saw Halleck's report, stung by its gross injustice, he immediately wrote to him, demanding a court of inquiry or court-martial, at once, before which he could be heard. Halleck, in reply, said "that General Wright was directed some time since to investigate and report the facts concerning that affair, and if that report shall be satisfactory, no further proceedings will be required, and you will be relieved from all blame." Morgan immediately wrote to General Wright, and found to his astonishment, that he had sent in his report the October previous, exonerating him from all blame, and that this report was in Halleck's hands when he made out his own report. That the latter should be guilty of the gross injustice of casting censure on a brave officer, in order to cover up his own short-comings, is perhaps not surprising; but that he should put on record statements, which, placed side by side, present him in such a painful aspect to the public, is certainly very remarkable. The whole campaign as planned, was a palpable blunder, and it was natural that he should put the blame of failure upon some one else; but this mode of doing it admits of no excuse.

CHAPTER VII.

STATE OF AFFAIRS IN THE WEST—EAST TENNESSEE—ARKANSAS—BATTLE OF PRAIRIE GROVE—FORREST'S RAID IN KENTUCKY—SURRENDER OF HARTSVILLE, TENNESSEE—BUTLER'S DEPARTMENT—EXPEDITION AGAINST VICKSBURG—SURRENDER OF HOLLY SPRINGS—ASSAULT UPON VICKSBURG—GALLANTRY OF GENERAL BLAIR—SHERMAN SUPERSEDED BY MC CLERNAND—ARMY OF THE POTOMAC—MC CLELLAN DELAYS TO MOVE—CORRESPONDENCE BETWEEN HIM AND HALLECK—RAID OF STUART—MC CLELLAN ORDERED BY THE PRESIDENT TO MOVE—HIS ADVANCE—SUPERSEDED BY BURNSIDE—PARTING WITH THE ARMY—REVIEW OF MC CLELLAN'S CAMPAIGN AGAINST RICHMOND.

DURING this month, October, while East Tennessee had again fallen into the hands of the enemy, General Blunt, by a vigorous attack on the rebel Hindman, at Fort Wayne, Arkansas, had routed him, capturing his artillery, and thus relieved South-western Missouri from rebel depredations. In the latter part of the month, General Herron dispersed a large band of guerrillas, near Fayetteville, in Missouri. November passed without any battles of moment, though throughout the West, constant fighting was going on between detached forces. But in the last of this month, Gen. Blunt, who was fast rising into distinction, was pressing hard against the rebel forces under Hindman and Marmaduke in Arkansas. At Cane Hill, after a sharp contest, he forced the enemy to retreat. A few days after, however, learning that Hindman and Marmaduke, in conjunction, were moving from different points in heavy force to attack him, he immediately began to concentrate his troops, and on Friday, the 7th of December, gave him battle at Prairie Grove.

BATTLE OF PRAIRIE GROVE.

General Herron, who, in obedience to orders from General Blunt, endeavored to join him, was attacked by an overwhelming force, but, by the most gallant fighting, held his own until Blunt formed a junction with him. It was a beautiful day, and, the battle occurring in a comparatively open country, the scene it presented was picturesque and thrilling. It lasted till night-fall, apparently without any decisive results. But the next morning it was found that the enemy had retreated. Herron and Blunt had out-generaled the enemy and defeated him, though superior in numbers, in a fair field fight. Our loss was a little over a thousand, while that of the rebels must have been nearly three times as great. Soon after, hearing that Hindman was at Van Buren, Blunt pushed on and captured it.

In Kentucky, Forrest's great raid was the important event of the month of December. He seemed to go where he liked with his half-wild followers, sending consternation through the country. Elizabethtown was captured by Morgan on the 27th, and a large amount of property destroyed.

The shameful surrender of Hartsville, Tennessee, with some fifteen hundred men, this month, awakened the deepest indignation, and disgraced the troops left to hold it.

On the last day of the month, Forrest was defeated at Parker's Cross Roads by Sullivan, with a loss of a thousand men; but, on the whole, affairs in Kentucky and Tennessee at the close of the year, were in a very unsatisfactory condition.

The Department of New Orleans furnished nothing more important than the retirement of Butler, on the 15th of December, and the appointment of Banks in his place. The month previous, at Bayou Teche, fourteen miles from Brashear City, a fight occurred between five Union gunboats and a large rebel force, supported by the gunboat Cotton, which resulted in the retreat of the enemy and the escape of the gunboat.

Up the Mississippi, however, more important events were transpiring. Grant, in command, planned an expedition to take Vicksburg, which, though it proved a sad failure, was the beginning of the great measures to open that river to our fleet. The plan was, for Sherman with his army to move straight on the place, and attempt to carry it by assault, while Grant himself was to advance against Jackson City, and attack the enemy there, to keep him from sending troops to Vicksburg.

Sherman left Memphis on the 20th day of December, and the day after Christmas, entered the Yazoo, and ascended it nearly to Haines' Bluff. Here the army was disembarked, and moved down towards Vicksburg.

The gunboats had previously, on the 26th, assaulted the eight-gun battery on the bluff, but were unable to silence it.

In the meantime, disaster had overtaken Grant, so that his co-operation became impossible. Holly Springs, on which he partly relied for supplies, was attacked and disgracefully surrendered. This brought him to a halt, and the rebel forces, that he expected to keep back from Vicksburg were left free to reinforce the place.

Sherman, however, ignorant of all this, proceeded to carry out his part of the plan, and, on the 27th day of December, advanced with his accustomed rapidity against the city, and before night drove the enemy from his outer lines. For the next two days he continued to press the assault, and on the 29th, a series of charges was made with a fury amounting almost to desperation. "Blair's brigade, in the advance, emerging from the cover of a cypress forest, came upon an intricate abattis of young trees, felled about three feet from the ground, with the tops left interlacing each other in confusion. Beyond the abattis was a deep ditch, with quicksand at the bottom, and several feet of water over it. Beyond the ditch was a more impenetrable abattis of heavy timber. All this was swept by a murderous fire from the enemy's artillery. Yet, through and over it all, the brigade gallantly charged, and drove the enemy from his rifle pits at the base of the center hill, on which the city lay. Other brigades now came up in support, and the second line was carried; and still up the hill pressed the heroic advance."

But it was all in vain. The city was impregnable to so small a force, and reluctantly, the storming party yielded up their hardly earned conquests, Blair's brigade losing one-third of his men in the daring assault.*

Sherman now saw it was a hopeless task, and, under a flag of truce burying his men, re-embarked his army and proceeded to Young's Point. Here McClernand assumed command, and the army was divided into two corps, which were placed under Sherman and Morgan. In announcing the change of command, Sherman complimented his troops, adding: "Ours was but part of a combined movement in which others were to assist. We were in time; unforeseen contingencies must have delayed the others. We have destroyed the Shreveport road; we have attacked Vicksburg, and pushed the attack as far as prudence would justify, and, having found it too strong for our single column, we have drawn off in good order and good spirits, ready for any new move."

In the East, the year had closed disastrously to our arms. McClellan, after the Battle of Antietam, rested so long a time on the north side of the Potomac, that the President and his advisers became impatient, and urged an immediate advance

* Col. Bowman.

of the army. McClellan, in reply, stated that the troops were not in a fit condition to move, that they lacked clothing, supplies, horses, in short, could not march against the enemy, with any prospect of success. The correspondence between McClellan and Halleck at this time, is one of the most extraordinary developments of the war—the former repeating his needs, and urging that they be immediately supplied, and the latter, flatly contradicting him, affirming that he had clothing, horses, everything necessary. That the Commander of the army in the field, who had just saved Washington and won a great victory, should not know what his troops stood in want of—in fact, should be told, over and over again, that they had shoes, and clothing, and horses, right against the testimony of his own eyes, and the reports of his own officers—is a singular exhibition of want of harmony of action. The President seemed to think that Halleck was right, and, acting in accordance with the views of the latter, on the 6th of October, directed that the army move at once, while the roads were good. Four days after, the rebel Stuart crossed the Potomac with eighteen hundred men, on a raid into Pennsylvania, and so utterly was McClellan deficient in horses, that he could mount but eight hundred men to follow him—a sad comment on Halleck's assertions. It was on this account, that the rebel force, after penetrating to Chambersburg, some twenty miles in rear of the army, was able to make its way safely back to Virginia—having completed the entire circuit of the Federal forces. The successful return of this daring expedition was a cause of deep mortification, and kindled into greater strength the general desire that McClellan should move at once against the enemy.

At length, he put the army in motion, and on the 26th of October, began to cross the Potomac at Berlin, designing to move parallel with the Blue Ridge, holding each Gap as he advanced—Warrenton being the point of general direction.

By the 5th of November, he had planted his head-quarters at Warrenton—his army well in hand, and ready to close in a great struggle with the enemy—when he received a telegram from Washington, relieving him from the command of the army, and ordering him to turn it over to Burnside.

The announcement of this sudden change of leaders at this critical juncture, fell like a thunderbolt on the army and the nation, and awakened for a time the gravest fears as to its result. The reason given by Halleck—that it was done because McClellan disobeyed orders—if the true one, should have caused his removal a month before, when, directed to move at once across the Potomac, he had delayed until he thought he could do so with any prospect of success.

His parting with the army was a sad one to him and the troops, for it was the child of his creation, and common sufferings and dangers had endeared them to each other. None saw him leave, with keener regret, than Burnside himself, who did not wish to accept the position forced on him—openly declaring that McClellan was the only man fit to occupy it.

This terminated McClellan's connection with the army, and ended the first great chapter of the war. Public opinion will always be more or less divided as to his merits as a Commander, and the partisan character which the whole question at once assumed, rendered a just discussion of it impossible; and not, till the generation to which he belongs shall have passed away, will his conduct, during the two years and upwards that he was at the head of the Army of the Potomac, be judged simply by the rules of military criticism. But there are two great facts which do not admit of discussion. The first is, that the failure of the Peninsular campaign rendered a long and tedious war inevitable. The second is, that a great campaign cannot be successfully carried on, by a divided power and conflicting counsels.

CHAPTER VIII.

BURNSIDE ADVANCES ON FREDERICKSBURG—HIS DESIGN—IS DISAPPOINTED—RESOLVES TO CARRY THE HEIGHTS BY ASSAULT—TERRIFIC BOMBARDMENT OF THE PLACE—A STRIKING SCENE—GALLANTRY OF THE SEVENTH MICHIGAN—THE SHARPSHOOTERS—CROSSING OF THE RIVER—THE BATTLE—THE DEFEAT—THE ARMY RECROSSES THE RIVER—FEELING OF THE PEOPLE—BURNSIDE TAKES THE RESPONSIBILITY—REVIEW OF THE CAMPAIGN—SECOND ATTEMPT MADE AND ABANDONED—THE SOUTHERN DEPARTMENT—DEATH OF MITCHELL—FOSTER'S EXPEDITION INTO NORTH CAROLINA—CLOSE OF THE YEAR.

BATTLE OF FREDERICKSBURG.

TEN days after the removal of McClellan, Burnside broke up his head-quarters, and commenced a rapid march to Fredericksburg, with the design of capturing the place before Lee's main army could reach it, and thus to cut off his retreat towards Richmond, and compel him to a decisive battle in the field. But the pontoon trains, without which the army could not cross the river, did not arrive from Washington at the expected time. Consequently, it lay idly on the banks of the Rappahannock till nearly the middle of the next month. Ample time was therefore given to Lee to counteract the intended movement, and make that which at first seemed feasible, an impossibility. Still, Burnside did not abandon the project of taking the place, and, thinking that the most desperate movement would be never anticipated by the enemy—viz., a direct assault up an open slope, upon his intrenched positions, held by an ample force, with interior lines equally formidable—determined to hazard it. The country back of Fredericksburg rises in successive terraces, to the heights on which Lee's army lay intrenched.

This line of heights curves in towards the river, some three miles below the city, where it is wooded. Here the right of Lee's army rested. At this point also, Franklin, commanding our left wing, was directed to cross with his corps, and, if possible, turn the enemy's flank, while the main army was to cross directly at the city, and move in one grand assault up the heights. For two days before the battle, the banks of the Rappahannock presented a stirring spectacle. The moving of masses of troops, the far-echoing notes of the bugle, the heavy tramp of the marching columns, preparatory to the great "day of decision," the sullen thunder peals that rolled along the heights on either side of the river, dark with long rows of cannon—combined to make a scene at once grand and fearful. On Thursday, the place was bombarded, in order to drive out the sharpshooters who prevented the laying of the pontoons, and a hundred and seventy-nine guns opened at once on the town. At the commencement of this terrific cannonade, that shook the shores of the river like an earthquake, the city was enveloped in a dense fog—a spire here and there, piercing above the sleeping mass, alone revealing its locality. As the awful bombardment went on, dark columns of smoke, shooting fiercely through the white sea of mist, told where building after building was fired by the shells. About noon the, fog lifted, and, drifting gently away, revealed the city in flames. All day long, the deep reverberations shook the shore, and rolled heavily away over the trembling earth, and when the blood-red sun went down in the hazy sky, it shed a lurid light on field and river, and frowning heights, and miles of quiet tents. "As the air darkened, the red flashes of the guns gave a new effect to the scene—the roar of each report being preceded by a fierce dart of flame, while the explosion of each shell was announced by a gush of fire on the clouds. Towering between us and the western sky, which was *still* showing its faded scarlet lining, was the huge, somber pillar of grimy smoke that marked the burning of Fredericksburg. Ascending to a vast height, it bore away northward, shaped like a plume bowed in the wind."

The guns, however, could not be depressed enough to reach the houses on the bank of the river, in which the sharpshooters lay concealed. If these could be dislodged, the pontoons might be laid, for the river ran so deep between its banks, that Lee could not command it with his batteries.

To do this, the Seventh Michigan volunteered to cross over in boats, under the fire of the sharpshooters, and expel them with the bayonet. In ten boats, holding twenty-five or thirty men each, the regiment pushed off with a ringing cheer, and, pulling straight into and through the pattering balls, reached the opposite shore. The Nineteenth and Twentieth Massachusetts followed, and the rebels, popping up like rats from behind walls, rifle pits and heaps of rubbish, scampered off through the streets of the city, when three pontoon bridges were quickly laid, and soon shook to the tread of the mighty host.

By Saturday morning, the 13th, the army was across, including Franklin's Corps down the river. The fog lay heavy and still along the river and plain, and shrouded the batteries in gloom; yet heavy explosions incessantly shook its mysterious bosom, sounding the notes of preparation to the mighty columns, that, wrapped in its gray mantle, stood in battle array on the further side of the river. The battle, however, did not really commence till nearly noon, when the order to advance was given, and Couch's Corps moved forward into the fire. It is impossible to describe the din and carnage that followed. In three massive columns, our brave troops mounted the ascent, but, when they reached the second terrace, the rebel batteries, with a rapid and concentrated fire, rained shot and shell in a ceaseless, overwhelming storm on their uncovered ranks. Horses galloping furiously across the plain—brigades streaming on the double-quick through the fiery sleet, that made great gaps in them as they passed—swaying columns bravely endeavoring to breast the storm—the ragged front of battle wildly undulating along the slope—the ceaseless crash of cannon—all combined to make a scene of tumult and carnage inconceivable, indescribable. Said Col. Stevens, in his report to the Governor of New Hampshire: "For three-fourths of an hour, I stood in front of my regiment on the brow of the hill, and watched the fire of the rebel batteries, as they poured shot and shell from sixteen different points upon our devoted men on the plains below. It was a sight magnificently terrible. Every discharge of the enemy's artillery, and every explosion of his shells, was distinctly visible in the dusky twilight of that smoke-crowned hill. His direct and enfilading batteries, with the vividness, intensity, and almost the rapidity of lightning, hurled the messengers of death into the midst of our brave ranks, vainly struggling through the murderous fire to gain the hills and guns of the enemy." The dead and wounded were borne back in an incessant stream to the city; not a step in advance was gained; and still the troops were pressed to the devastating fire, and Death held high carnival in front of the rebel works. "*Forward, men—steady—close up!*" fell from firm-set lips that the next moment were sealed in death; and deeds of personal daring, and heroic sacrifices were made by regiments and brigades, that will ever render them immortal. But it was vain valor and vain sacrifice. Meagher's Irish brigade, of heroic renown, was almost annihilated. Below, down the river, the thunder of Franklin's guns could be heard, rolling up the banks, but, after his first advance, the heavy explosions came from the same spot, showing that he was making no progress towards accomplishing the task assigned him. Said the correspondent of the *Cincinnati Commercial*: "It was with a deep sense of relief, that I saw the sun go down, and felt that in a little while, darkness would put an end to the unequal combat. But, for a time, the fury of the fire on both sides redoubled, as the discovery was made by the combatants that their day's work was about done. For a half an hour the din was awful, and the smoke drifted through the streets as sometimes in a city, when there is a high wind and a great dust. * * * Franklin's and Jackson's guns throbbed heavily a few times on the left; and all was still on the north side of the river, save the rumbling of army wagons."

At length, silence rested along the crimson heights, and the battle was over. Not a battery had been taken; not a breastwork carried; not even the threshold of the enemy's works reached. Like men led out to execution, the brave battalions had been marched forth, only to be shot down. It was literally a "field of slaughter."

Burnside, instead of carrying the heights of Fredericksburg, by a splendid *coup-de-main*, had walked boldly, unsuspectingly, into a frightful trap, which closed on him with a swift, fatal spring. Though no impression whatever had been made on the enemy's works—showing that our frightful loss was a *dead* loss—that every life had been thrown away—yet Burnside wished, the next morning, to renew the attack, but was prevented by the remonstrance of some of his Generals.

He reported his loss at less than ten thousand, but it afterwards turned out to be double that number. Lee reported his entire loss to be only eighteen hundred.

The Sanitary Commission was promptly on the field, and again proved to the country what an admirable institution it was.

Sunday dawned warm and balmy as October, and the

birds sang along the banks of the Rappahannock, as merrily as though no scenes of death and carnage had made them as memorable as the shores of Trasymenus.

Some skirmishing and cannonading followed, but on Monday night, the wearied and bleeding army was secretly, silently transported across the river, the pontoons taken up—and the great campaign was ended.

The country was fearfully excited by this catastrophe, coming so quickly on the heels of McClellan's removal, and abuse was poured on the Government from every quarter, until Burnside publicly took the responsibility of the whole movement on himself.

Great complaint was made that the pontoons were not sent forward from Washington, in time to meet Burnside when he moved from Warrenton, so that he could have crossed at once, and taken possession of the heights, before the enemy had time to occupy them. Hooker, too, thought, if he could have had his own way, he might have seized and held them in advance. There are always supposed events after a defeat, which, had they occurred, would have made it a victory. But Lee was too good a General to allow his retreat to Richmond to be cut off by a sudden dash. He showed afterwards, when attacked by Hooker, and still later, when pressed by Grant with double his own force, that neither dash, great ability, nor overwhelming numbers, could accomplish this desired object. Still, deeply as the country was mortified at the defeat, but little condemnation of Burnside openly was heard. His unwillingness to take chief command, his modest appreciation of his own abilities, his known moral worth and true patriotism, warded off the blows, that afterwards fell fierce and fast on Hooker, who suffered a similar defeat near the same place.

Burnside soon after planned another advance movement, designed to retrieve his disasters, and had actually commenced it, but heavy rains set in, which turned the whole country into a sea of mud, and it was abandoned.

This practically closed the campaign in Virginia for the year. The rebels, some three thousand strong, crossed the Rappahannock above Burnside, and attacked Dumfries, but were repulsed.

Further south, but little was accomplished. General Mitchell, the celebrated astronomer, who had abandoned his quiet pursuits at the call of his country, and, under Buell, acquired the reputation of a skillful, energetic General, but was afterwards relieved from his command, under the insane charge of speculating in cotton, was sent, early in the Autumn, to the Southern Department to take the place of Hunter. He immediately infused energy and life into affairs, and great results were expected from his known force of character. But he was stricken down in the midst of his usefulness, by the yellow fever, and died at Beaufort on the 30th of October. A pure and noble man, he was at the outset, so ungenerously treated by the War Department, that, during Cameron's administration, he sent in his resignation, but it was not accepted. Afterwards, though he had filled the land with his deeds, he suffered under the charge of speculating, and at last was sent to Beaufort to die.

In North Carolina, only partial, isolated blows were struck, having no direct bearing on any of the great campaigns. The principal event which marked the closing year in this Department, was an expedition against Kinston, set on foot by Foster, with four brigades under General Wessels and commanded by Colonels Amory, Stevenson and Lee. He left Newbern on the 8th of December, and on the 14th, met the enemy in force, under General Evans, about a mile from Kinston, and gave him battle. The rebels were beaten, and retreated, abandoning the town, which Foster took possession of. He rendered useless two heavy guns which he could not bring off, and captured four field pieces. After destroying the quartermasters' stores, and burning the bridge, he proceeded to Whitehall. From thence, he continued his course, fighting as he advanced, till he came within eight miles of Goldsboro', which was only fifty miles from Raleigh, the Capital of the State. After burning trestle-work and cars, and tearing up railroad tracks, and, last of all, firing the bridge over the Neuse, under the shots of the enemy, he retraced his steps to Newbern—having advanced seventy or eighty miles into the heart of the State, and spread consternation wherever he went. Lieutenant George W. Graham applied the torch to the bridge, under the fire of the enemy's artillery and infantry, and then saved himself by jumping from it.

The total loss in the expedition, was five hundred and seventy-seven. Among the killed was Colonel Gray, of the Ninety-sixth New York regiment.

The sum total of the military operations for the year, was not satisfactory, and belied the promise of the Government, and the hopes of the people, that the war would be a short one.

But while in the East, the New Year came in gloomily, in the West, it was signaled by a battle that inaugurated a series of movements, which, in the end, were to have an important bearing on the war.

CHAPTER IX.

BATTLE OF MURFREESBORO', OR STONE RIVER—ROSECRANS AT NASHVILLE—HIS DELAY TO MOVE—THE COUNCIL OF WAR—ROSECRANS' PARTING WORDS—THE MARCH COMMENCED—THE ENEMY'S LINE OF BATTLE AT MURFREESBORO'—ROSECRANS' PLAN OF BATTLE—SCENES AND INCIDENTS—BRAGG'S PLAN OF ATTACK—MORNING OF THE BATTLE—ATTACK OF THE ENEMY—DESTRUCTION OF OUR RIGHT WING—ROSECRANS INCREDULOUS—HIS GALLANT CONDUCT WHEN INFORMED OF HIS DISASTER—HEROIC DEFENSE BY SHERIDAN—FORMING A NEW LINE OF BATTLE—STUBBORNNESS OF THE LEFT WING—SPLENDID BEHAVIOR OF HAZEN—THE CLOSE—APPEARANCE OF THE FIELD—OUR HEAVY LOSS—OPERATIONS OF THE FOLLOWING DAYS—LAST BATTLE—MURFREESBORO' EVACUATED—ROSECRANS CELEBRATES HIGH MASS—THE ARMY RESTS.

ROSECRANS, who had succeeded Buell in command of the Army of the Cumberland, had a high reputation for energy and skill, having never yet been beaten in a single battle. He took up his head-quarters at Nashville, and commenced the reorganization of the army.

Here he remained, apparently idle, for two months, and the country, ignorant of the circumstances that surrounded him, grew impatient. The usual pressure, which at the first had urged on McDowell, and which, like an evil genius, had followed every General since the war began, was brought to bear on him. But no power on earth could make him move till he was ready. They might supersede him, but could not force him to do that which his judgment condemned, if he was to be held responsible for the result.

At length, having settled matters somewhat to his satisfaction in Nashville—secured his communications, and accumulated thirty days' provisions, he determined to move. A consultation was held at head-quarters, on Christmas night, which broke up at midnight. The army was to march in the morning; and as Rosecrans, in parting, took each commander by the hand, he said: "Spread out your skirmishers far and wide! Expose their nests! *Keep fighting!* Good night."

The morning, so big with fate, dawned gloomily on the army—the clouds hung like a pall over the wintry landscape—great drifts of slowly moving mist lay along the valleys—while the rain came down in torrents, that gathered in pools in the road, or ran in yellow streams along the gullies. The reveille, as it rolled from camp to camp, had a muffled sound in the murky atmosphere, and everything conspired to shed a gloom over the army. But the soldiers seemed to forget the storm in the excitement of marching on the enemy, and soon the mighty host, nearly fifty thousand strong, was sweeping along the muddy roads and across the drenched fields. Thomas led the center, McCook the right, and Crittenden the left. About noon, the clouds broke away before a stiff north-west breeze, and the sun came out to lighten up the somber landscape. But already the dropping fire of musketry, and now and then the boom of a cannon, told that the rebel "nests" were being "stirred up." All day long, the steady columns toiled on over the broken country, and at night bivouacked in the wet fields. But with darkness came again the heavy rain-clouds, and the cold storm beat on the tired army. Through the darkness and storm, Rosecrans with his escort went dashing over the country, in search of McCook's head-quarters. Their horses' hoofs struck fire among the rocks, and they swung along at such a slashing pace that one of his escort finally exclaimed: "General, this way of going like h—l over the rocks will knock up the horses." "That's true," he replied; "walk." Moving on more slowly through the impenetrable blackness, he called an orderly and said, "Go back and tell that young man he must not be profane." Reaching McCook's head-quarters in the woods, the two entered a wagon, and sitting down on the bottom, with a candle between them, stuck in the socket of a bayonet, the point of which was driven into the floor, they consulted together of the movements for the morrow. "*Push them hard!*" were his last words as he arose to his feet. Emerging from the wagon between ten and eleven o'clock, he exclaimed, "We mount now, gentlemen." The blast of a bugle suddenly rung through the forest, rousing up the staff, some of whom, tired with being ten hours in the saddle, were dozing in their blankets, upon the rocks around. To the "Good night" of McCook, Rosecrans added, "God bless you!" and striking the spurs into his horse, dashed down the road, splashing the mud over himself, and those who pressed hard after him. Losing his way on his return, he "charged impatiently" through the woods, in the vain effort to find the right road. Amid bugle calls, and shouts, the escort got separated and confused, and lost their leader, who, with a part of his staff, wandered off alone, and at length, at one o'clock in the morning, reached his camp—having been in the saddle eighteen hours. The others did not arrive there till two hours later.*

The next day, Saturday, dawned in gloom, like the one before; the heavy clouds hung low, and a pall of mist wrapped the landscape. Slowly and uncertainly the columns felt their way on, but at one o'clock the fog lifted, and they moved off over the soft fields and along the muddy highways, driving the enemy's skirmishers before them. It was uncertain whether Bragg would make a decided stand before he reached Murfreesboro', or not, and the whole army was kept well in hand. The next day, Sunday, was a day of rest to the main army, for Rosecrans was averse to military operations on that day, unless they were absolutely necessary.

* W. D. B.'s "Rosecrans' Campaign with the Fourteenth Army Corps."

Monday morning, before sunrise, the army was again in motion, sweeping across the country in splendid order. About three o'clock in the afternoon, a signal message came from General Palmer, in front, stating that he was in sight of Murfreesboro', and that the enemy was in full flight. Rosecrans immediately sent an order to Crittenden to move a division into the town. But the report proved incorrect, and the order was revoked, yet not till Harker, with his brigade, had made a gallant dash forward, by which he was placed in a perilous position. He, however, succeeded in extricating himself from it without loss.

That night, it rained heavily—drenching the soldiers to their skins, and making the ground so soft that artillery carriages would sink, while crossing the fields, almost to their axles. The following day was dark, gloomy and depressing, and the soldiers stood shivering in their lines. Rosecrans was up at three o'clock in the morning, and the columns were pushed carefully over the broken ground, and through the cedar thickets, towards where the enemy was drawn up in line of battle. Crittenden moved forward about seven o'clock, when the enemy opened a sharp fire upon him. Rosecrans was standing, at the time, in front of his head-quarters, an orderly holding his horse near him, when a cannon ball struck in the road a short distance off, and bounded away—a second struck still nearer, and a third with a swift, rushing sound, swept past him almost in a line, taking off the head of an orderly in its flight. His head-quarters were evidently a target for some of the rebel gunners, and mounting, he rode up a slope a little way off, and halting under some trees near the road, remained there during the rest of the day. A shed was made by leaning some rails on a pole that rested in a couple of crotched sticks, and covering them with india rubber blankets. Here the staff, sheltered from the rain, wrote the orders as they were dictated by their Chief. The dark columns standing noiseless in the rain—the swift marching of others into position—bodies of horse galloping over the heavy fields—the dashing away of orderlies in different directions—the scattering fire of musketry now swelling into full volleys—the heavy boom of cannon in front—the bearing back of wounded officers on stretchers, and the certainty of a great battle at hand, combined to make those who clustered around the fire in front of that rude shelter, serious and thoughtful. Some, at least, were so, and among them the accomplished Garesche, Chief of the Staff, who sat apart, under a tree, reading "De Imitatione Christi," and pondering on his coming fate. As if instinctively to break the growing sadness of the scene, the Fourth Cavalry band struck up "The Star Spangled Banner," and as the soul-stirring strains arose, and swelled over the field, each eye grew brighter, and each heart kindled with the fire that ever warms the patriot's breast.

By evening, the different divisions were in their respective positions, though the right wing, under McCook, had suffered considerably from the determined resistance of the enemy.

The army now stood with its left resting on the Stone River, and its right stretching off into the country as far as the Franklin turnpike, making a line three miles long. The farthest brigade on the extreme right was Willich's, and was thrown back nearly at right angles to the main line, to be ready for any flank movement of the enemy. The main part of this right wing occupied a slight ridge, covered with woods, with open ground in front. At the foot of the ridge, between it and the enemy, stretched a valley, varying from forty to sixty rods in width, and covered with close cedar thickets and oak forests. The center, posted on a rolling slope, was a little in advance of the main line; while the left wing, starting in a piece of woods, crossed a broad cotton field, and ended in another piece of woods. The army, as it thus stood in line of battle, numbered forty-three thousand and four hundred men. Behind it were half-burned clearings, cedar thickets, cultivated fields, and patches of forest.

Parallel to our line, and distant about half a mile, lay the rebel army—its right resting on the river, which took a bend northward just below the point of junction, so as to keep nearly parallel with it. Being fordable at all points, the enemy, if forced to retreat, could fall back across it, and then make it a strong line of defense. Perhaps it would be more accurate to say, its actual right lay *across* the river, divided from the main army by the stream, for here, on an eminence, was posted Breckenridge's division, directly in front of Murfreesboro'. Rosecrans' design was to have McCook keep the enemy in front occupied, either by attack or defense, as circumstances might decide, so as to prevent reinforcements being sent to Breckenridge across the river, while he was to swing two divisions, under Van Cleve, over from his left, and crush Breckenridge by a sudden assault of superior numbers. Van Cleve was directed to plant his batteries, as soon as the heights were carried, so that they would sweep the enemy's whole line of battle, and take his works in reverse, compelling him to retreat to the south of Murfreesboro', which movement would probably prove fatal to him.

The plan was a skillful one, if the enemy would only give him time to execute it. But, unfortunately, Bragg had a similar one of his own, by which he hoped to double up his adversary's right by a secret concentration of a heavy force against it. All the later part of the day, he was moving his troops in this direction, and McCook, ascertaining this from one of the inhabitants whom he had captured, sent him at evening to Rosecrans with the information. On being interrogated, he mentioned the different rebel divisions that had moved, and their leaders. Rosecrans, however, instead of altering

MAJ. GEN. J. C. FREMONT
MAJ. GEN. W. S. ROSECRANS
MAJ. GEN. J. POPE
MAJ. GEN. N. P. BANKS
MAJ. GEN. O. M. MITCHEL
MAJ. GEN. J. HOOKER
MAJ. GEN. G. G. MEADE
UNION GENERALS
Entered according to Act of Congress, Dec.
by the American
Publishing Co. in the Clerk's Office of the District Court of Connecticut.

his plan, to checkmate this movement, resolved to anticipate it, and instead of strengthening his right wing, directed McCook simply to build large camp fires beyond its extremity, in order to give the impression to the enemy that a fresh division had been sent there. Whether this ruse was understood or not, it produced no change in the rebel plan.

This was the position of the two armies on the night of the 30th of December. It had rained all day, and the shivering soldiers lay on the cold ground, to snatch such rest as they could get, before commencing the terrible work of the morning.

The right wing was composed of three divisions, of which Johnson held the extreme right, Davis the center one, and Sheridan the last, which joined the center of the army. With the first streak of dawn, the roll of the drum and bugle blast swelled and echoed from hill to hill along the mighty line, bright with standards and glittering bayonets that swayed and shook for three miles in the morning light, and soon, General Van Cleve's division, which was to cross over on our left, and overwhelm Breckenridge, was in motion. Wood was to follow by another ford, and lapping on to his right, and closing with him as he advanced, storm the heights held by the rebel Commander.

In the meantime, Rosecrans had High Mass celebrated in his tent, and thus having committed himself and his army to the God of battles, he stepped forth into the open air. It was a cold, wintry morning, and the officers, with their overcoats on, gathered around the fires that had been kindled in the field. It was just before sunrise, and Rosecrans was listening anxiously to hear the artillery along the heights held by Breckenridge, when there suddenly came a strange, confused sound from the extreme right, like the fearful sweep of a distant hurricane rapidly approaching. At intervals, arose the dull, heavy roar of cannon. Nearer and nearer the noise came.

until distinct and plain the rattle of musketry was heard, sounding in the distance like the crackling of flames amid dry branches. The officers of the staff grew serious and alarmed, but Rosecrans only looked up, and went on talking. It was all going on as he expected. McCook was evidently stubbornly contesting the field, according to his instructions. Alas, McCook was not fighting, but retreating.*

Bragg's order was, that at daybreak the whole line, beginning at the extreme left, with Hardee's corps, and followed by Polk's, should swing forward on our extreme right, and bear it back, crumbling it in the retreat, till our army should stand with its rear to the river. Its communications with Nashville would thus be cut off, and its destruction sure. In double lines they came on, swift and terrible as in-rolling billows. The rebel General McCown first struck Johnson, on our extreme right, who was wholly unprepared for the sudden onset, and crushed him with a single blow—sweeping over his batteries with wild hurrahs. Cleburne followed him, and striking Davis' division, hurled it also back over the field. Like a swift succeeding wave, Withers came next, and fell with the same desperation on the last division of the right wing, which was Sheridan's. If this had given way, like the other two, no power on earth could have saved Rosecrans. His splendid army was trembling in the balance, but Sheridan, though left solitary and alone of all that right wing, stood fast. The wave that burst along that astonished line, dissolving it like frost work, here met a rock, and fell back in broken surges. There was no surprise here, as in Davis' division—every man was in his place, and every gunner at his piece, long before the shock came. Right in the face of one battery, vomiting forth death, and through a cross-fire of two more, the hostile column closed in mass, and, several regiments deep, came steadily on. Through

* W. B. F.

and through it, shot and shell tore with awful havoc, but the great ragged gaps closed swiftly up, and still this mass of living valor kept rolling on, until within pistol shot of Sill's brigade, when a sheet of fire burst in their very faces. Nobly did they attempt to bear up against it, but the head of each formation crumbled away ere it was completed, and at length the whole broke and fled. Sill then shouted the charge; and away went the brigade, with a thundering cheer, chasing the enemy to cover, but its gallant leader fell, mortally wounded.

But unless Sheridan could be dislodged, the overthrow of Johnson and Davis would be of no avail, and so the enemy, rallying again with fresh forces, came on more determined than ever. At the same time, the victorious columns that had crushed two of our divisions to fragments, now bore down on Sheridan's flank, and his overthrow by the double onslaught seemed certain. But instead of retreating, he moved up to Negley, and locking on to the center, faced his troops both south and west, thus presenting two slender fronts to the enemy. At the angle he placed most of his guns, and in this position awaited the onset of the overwhelming numbers. As they came on, those batteries ploughed long lanes through the dense masses, but they still advanced—pushing their artillery forward, until the guns played on each other, within close rifle shot. The slaughter now was horrible. Three times did the determined enemy advance, and as often was compelled to fall back. Said Polk, afterwards, of these awful charges, and their deadly effect on his troops: "The horse of every officer on the field and staff of Vaughn's brigade, except one, and the horses of all the field and staff of every regiment, except two, were killed. The brigade lost one-third of its force."

But Sheridan's ammunition now gave out, and no more could be got, for the train had been captured in the wild rout of the rest of the wing. Besides, the enemy was now all around him, in front, flank and rear, so that at last *he* also was compelled to retire, leaving nine guns, which he could not get through the dense cedar thickets, in the hands of the rebels. Still, not in panic or disorder did his brave, shattered division abandon the field—but, with even ranks, and colors flying, sullenly, savagely, fall back till it found ammunition.

The right wing was at last all gone, and the onset that had borne it backward now fell with unbroken fury on the center. But the heroic resistance of Sheridan had gained what was of vital importance—*time*. As he was retreating, thus uncovering the center, Rosecrans arrived on the field. He had staid at head-quarters after the first crowd of fugitives arrived from the battle-field with their story of defeat—not believing that any real disaster had occurred. But as the throng kept increasing, and the din swelled louder and louder, he strode backward and forward before his tent, with a disturbed, anxious look. At length, a staff officer from McCook dashed up to him, asking for help. "Tell General McCook," he shouted back, "to contest every inch of ground," and still continued his walk. Then came the tidings that Sill was killed, Willich killed or captured, and Kirk wounded. "*Never mind; we must win the battle*," was the stern reply. Another aid now dashed up on a gallop, asking that Rousseau be held in readiness. Rousseau commanded the reserves. This startled Rosecrans. What! reserves before the battle was fairly begun? At last, the frightful truth *must* be squarely met, crushing as it was, that the right wing was gone, and the center fighting a hopeless battle. "Tell General McCook I will help him!" he exclaimed, and almost the next instant, Rousseau's brave battalions were moving on the double-quick across the field. Another order flew to Van Cleve. to double-quick a brigade to the right. All now was hot haste—artillery went bounding across the field; swift riders galloped hither and thither with orders, and Rosecrans, exclaiming "*Mount, gentlemen,*" vaulted into the saddle, and striking the spurs into his steed, launched away like a thunderbolt. His face was like ashes, his lips closed like a vice, and a dangerous light burned in his flashing blue eye. His entire staff and escort pressed after him as he dashed forward into the fire. Horses and riders go down almost within reach of his sword—but, though his life at this fearful moment is worth twenty thousand men, he flings it without a moment's hesitation into the scale. The fugitives darken the fields, and the panic-stricken trains block the roads, but nothing can stay his course. Orders seem struck like fire from his lips. Down Harker's front of battle, shot and shell shrieking through his escort, he gallops, and mounting the only eminence near, draws rein on the top. Here, a sight appalling enough to daunt the stoutest heart, meets his eye. The smoke of battle rests in clouds over the valley below, rent ever and anon with terrific explosions—the dark cedar thickets are ablaze with volleys—the fields are black with his broken battalions, among which artillery wagons are plunging—and the chaos and wreck of a lost battle-field are all around him. Seeing a hostile battery playing with deadly effect on Harker's brigade, he shouted to the Chief of Artillery, "Silence that battery!" and planting the guns himself, again galloped off through a whirlwind of shot. He was skirting the edge of a thicket, when he met Sheridan leading back his diminished, but compact and heroic column. The gallant leader, as he met him, pointed back to it, saying, "Here is all that is left, General; we have no cartridges, and our guns are empty." Rosecrans himself directed him where to find ammunition, and in a few minutes the brave fellows were again facing the enemy.

By this time, the right wing of the center, under Negley, left exposed by Sheridan's retreat, was outflanked. An aid dashed up to Thomas with the startling intelligence that the enemy was in his rear. There was no alternative, and Thomas, in a bitter tone, replied, "Cut your way out." "Men, we must cut our way out," shouts Negley. The proud Stanley closes up his strong battalions—the other commanders catch the inspiration—the Eleventh Michigan and Nineteenth Illinois move forward with the bayonet, the Twenty-first Ohio does the same, and the victorious, exultant foe is rolled back in confusion. The rear is clear, and the division falls steadily back with its guns. What was left of the army was now swung round, and stood nearly at right angles to its former position. The left still clung to its position on the river, for when that should be yielded, all would be gone. Not like Sheridan must Palmer now fight, till his ammunition is exhausted, and then fall back, but fight and die where he stands. But with the falling back of Negley, the right brigade of this division also retired for a space, and Hazen, commanding the left extremity, alone held his ground. Rosecrans but little knew, at this moment, on what an apparently slender thread the fate of his army turned. But, luckily, Hazen embraced the whole danger of the condition of things. He knew, if it came to the worst, he must die there. It was not left to him to seek a new spot on which to fight. The enemy also knew that he held the key of the whole position, and fell upon him with tenfold fury, but he stood rooted rock-fast to the ground, and swept the deep on-coming columns with a wasting fire. But, at length, his ammunition gave out, and he sent off every staff officer for more. In the meantime, whether it came or not, he determined that his brigade should stand there and die, rather than yield. He ordered one regiment to fix bayonets, and another that had none, to club their muskets, and so meet the foe. At length, he received his ammunition, and what was needed just as much, reinforcements.

All this time, Rousseau and Sheridan had maintained a firm front. Opening their lines to let the fugitives pass through, they closed firmly again, and presented a solid wall on that broken, tumultuous field. In the meantime, Rosecrans, galloping from point to point, and followed furiously by his staff and escort, brought order out of confusion, and, infusing his own daring spirit into the troops, rapidly formed a new line of battle. He massed six batteries on the only commanding eminence near, which swept all the space over which the enemy must advance. The sun was shining brightly, and his beams revealed a waving forest of steel, as the long and glittering lines of the enemy, rank upon rank, came with awful splendor over the broken fields. The movement of the columns was swift but steady, and many a heart stood still, or trembled at what might be the issue in the coming shock. Rosecrans knew his army was at stake, but, wound up to that pitch of lofty daring which defies fate itself, he awaited it without change of countenance. As the enemy came on, in magnificent order, those six batteries opened like the very jaws of Hell, and out of them poured a wild torrent of fire and death on the astonished enemy. Rent and distorted, still the columns reeled forward, bent on victory. Rosecrans sat on his horse a moment, to watch the effect of this horrible fire, and then dashed down to Beatty's brigade, which lay on the ground in the plain below. Spurring up to the very edge of the line over which the shot were sweeping like a hail storm, he cried, "Now, let the whole line charge! *Charge home!*" Springing to their feet with a shout that rose over the wild din, they hurled themselves on the enemy. The staff officers, catching the enthusiasm of their Chief, flung themselves along the line, with loud cheers, and caps waving in the air. Before that fierce onset, the rebel line, as it struggles to bear up against it, halts, and shakes like a huge curtain over the field—then crumbles to pieces and disappears. "There they go," shouted Rosecrans; "now drive them home!" They did drive them home, leaving the earth piled with dead. This was the turning point of the battle, and the whole line at once advanced.

But, though repulsed, the enemy did not abandon the contest. Re-forming his lines, with every reserve brought up, he again advanced in imposing array; but Rosecrans had now completed his line of battle, and neither numbers nor reckless daring could force it. About four o'clock, Bragg made his last attempt, and this time it was chiefly directed against Palmer's division, on the river. But Hazen, with his immortal thirteen hundred, still held the ground to which they had clung with such marvelous tenacity during the day; and there, too, were the heroic Grose, Schaeffer, Hascall and Wagner, equally determined to hold that vital position to the last. Says Hazen, in his report: "About four o'clock, the enemy again advanced upon my front, in two lines. The battle had hushed, and the dreadful splendor of this advance can only be conceived, as all description must fall vastly short. His right was even with my left, and his left was lost in the distance." But this proud array had lost its strength; the confidence of victory was wanting, and at the first volley it wheeled and disappeared.

For a time, the heavy boom of cannon rolled over the field, and, here and there, volleys of musketry showed that detachments were still fighting; yet, at sunset, the battle was over. As the blazing orb sank to rest, his last look fell on a ghastly spectacle. The earth, torn, trampled and red, lay piled with thousands upon thousands—some, still and calm, as if in sleep, others mangled and blown into fragments, while bleeding arms and legs, without owners, lay scattered on every side. Dead horses and shattered gun-carriages helped to swell the frightful wreck, over which darkness, in mercy, soon drew its pall. Among the dead, was the young, accomplished, modest, yet lion-hearted Chief of the Staff, Garesche. He had never left the side of his Chief all day, wearing not merely a calm, but a gay and smiling air, through the wildest storm of battle. In the last attack, as Rosecrans dashed down the line, to throw the weight of his presence into the fight, a shell shrieking by him, in its flight struck Garesche in the head, carrying away all but the under jaw—and the spouting trunk, inclining gently from the saddle, fell headlong to the earth.

That night, there was a meeting of the Generals at head-quarters. All acknowledged that the prospect looked gloomy enough. The enemy was only arrested, not beaten. He still held two-thirds of the battle-field, and had in his hands one-fifth of all our artillery. Seven brigadier-generals, and twenty colonels and lieutenant-colonels, were killed or missing. The rebel cavalry had gained the rear, and it was uncertain if another pound of supplies or ammunition could reach the army; while seven thousand men, or one-sixth of the whole army, had disappeared from the field. The enemy, every one thought, would renew the attack in the morning. But Rosecrans, finding that he had ammunition enough on hand for another battle, made up his mind to fight it on that very spot. Mounting his horse, he rode to the rear to examine the country, and on returning, said, "*Gentlemen, we conquer or die right here!*" It was a clear, cold December night, but, about midnight, the heavens became overcast, and the bitter rain came pitilessly down on the weary ranks, and on the dead and wounded that burdened the field.

Making some slight changes in his line of battle, and falling back a short distance to a better position, Rosecrans waited the developments of the coming morning.

But the enemy had been too severely punished to risk another determined attack, though, during the latter part of the day, there was some heavy artillery firing. In the morning, Beatty had been sent across the river with two brigades of Van Cleve's division, and occupied a hill commanding the upper ford.

Bragg, seeing that delay only increased the difficulties before him, determined, on the next day to make another bold attempt to secure a complete victory. This time, his attack was directed against the left. About three o'clock in the afternoon, a double line of skirmishers was seen to advance from the woods in front of Breckenridge's position, and move across the fields. Behind them, came heavy columns of infantry, and it was evident the rebel right wing was bearing down on the small body of troops that had crossed the river the day before. It passed the open cotton fields in three heavy lines of battle—the first column, in three ranks, six men deep—the second supporting the first—and the reserve column last. Three batteries accompanied this imposing mass, as it came down in splendid order. White puffs of smoke soon shot out from the hill-side; our single battery responded, and the roar of guns shook the shores of the stream. At first, they came on with steady step and even front, and then, like a swollen torrent, flung themselves forward on that portion of Van Cleve's division which was across the river, and bore it back and over the stream to the main body. But Rosecrans was prepared for this movement—in fact, when it occurred, was about to execute his original plan, and swing his left against Breckenridge. He hastily massed fifty-eight cannon on an eminence, where they could completely enfilade the successive columns as they advanced. Their opening roar was terrific, and the crash of the iron storm, through the thick-set ranks, was overwhelming. It was madness to face it, yet the rebel columns closed up and pressed on; but, as they came within close range of our musketry, the line suddenly seemed to shrivel up like a piece of parchment, in the fire that met it. Yet, pushed on and cheered by the rear lines, the ranks endeavored to bear up against it and advance, but again halted; while officers, with waving caps and flashing swords, galloped along the lines, and still urged them on. They had now got so near that the men could be seen to topple over separately, before the volleys. A third and last time, they staggered forward, the foremost ranks reaching even to the water's edge. But here they stopped—it was like charging down the red mouth of a volcano. Balancing a moment on the edge of battle, they broke and fled. With a wild and thrilling shout, our troops sprung to their feet, and charged forward with the bayonet—dashing like madmen through the stream. They chased the flying foe for a half a mile, cheering as they charged, their cheers caught up by those on the other side of the river, and sent back with increased volume and power. Darkness ended the fight, and Crittenden's entire corps passed over, and, with Davis, occupied the ground so gallantly won.

That night, the rain again set in, and at daylight next morning, it was coming down in torrents, so that the camps and roads were soon one vast field of mud, rendering the movement of artillery impossible. Some sharp-shooting during the day, and a dash at night by two regiments from Rousseau's division, clearing the woods in front, comprised the fighting of Saturday.

That night, Bragg evacuated Murfreesboro, and next morning, Rosecrans spent an hour at "High Mass," giving glory to God for the victory. It was, however, dearly bought. He had lost, in killed and wounded, nearly nine thousand men, or a fifth of his entire army. He had lost, besides, fifty pieces of artillery, for which he had only a few captured pieces to show in return. He had gained the position, and that was all.

The army now settled down into camp life, and no attempt to follow up the enemy was made for nearly six months, or till the latter part of June. He then moved forward, Bragg retreating as he advanced, and abandoning the strong position of Tullahoma, rather than risk a battle. Detached portions of the army occasionally came in collision, in which the rebels were invariably worsted, losing many prisoners. Bragg finally took refuge in Chattanooga, a place immensely strong by nature, and made still more so by art.

CHAPTER X.

JANUARY.

CAPTURE OF ARKANSAS POST—GRANT COMMENCES HIS MOVEMENT AGAINST VICKSBURG—THE CANAL—A YEAR OF DISASTER—MISSOURI—ATTACK ON SPRINGFIELD—EXPEDITIONS UP WHITE AND RED RIVERS—LOSS OF THE QUEEN OF THE WEST—LOSS OF THE ARIEL—SINKING OF THE HATTERAS BY THE ALABAMA—DISASTER AT SABINE PASS—BANKS IN NEW ORLEANS—EXPEDITIONS—CAPTURE AND LOSS OF GALVESTON—THE HARRIET LANE—WESTFIELD LOST—DEATH OF BUCHANAN—GRAND EXPEDITION THROUGH THE STATE OF LOUISIANA—CAPTURE OF ALEXANDRIA, ON THE RED RIVER.

IMMEDIATELY after the failure of Sherman's attack on Vicksburg, McClernand, who, we have seen, assumed command of the army, on the 4th of January, at Milliken's Bend, set sail for Fort Hindman, or Arkansas Post, on the Arkansas River, which was considered the key to Little Rock, the Capital of the State, and to the extensive country from which hostile detachments were constantly sent to operate along the Mississippi River. Admiral Porter, with three iron-clads and a fleet of light-draft gunboats, accompanied the expedition, to co-operate with the land forces in the attack on the fort, which was known to be a strong one, and well garrisoned. The fleet reached the mouth of the White River on the 8th. Ascending this mere ribbon of water, enclosed by a dense, silent forest, from which the gray moss hung in huge festoons, it came at length to the "cut off," and passed into the Arkansas River. Slowly moving up this stream, with only here and there a wretched habitation, or a sunken scow, to break the solitude, the fleet cautiously approached the rebel position, which was hid from view by a bend in the river. Here it lay all night, flooded by the mild moonlight, while, inland, the air resounded with the ceaseless strokes of the axe, showing that the enemy were busy in obstructing all the roads that led to the place. At daylight, the troops began to disembark, and form on the high banks. The first line of rebel works was only a half a mile distant, and soon, the fire of the skirmishers echoed along the stream. The country was entirely unknown to McClernand, and all day, Saturday, was spent in marching and countermarching, to avoid impassable swamps and bayous; and so night found the army still struggling to get into position before the place. Part of the army passed most of the cold January night in moving forward, while the remainder dragged it out without fire or tents. Sunday morning, however, dawned bright and cheerful, and, by ten o'clock, both corps of the army were in position, having completely invested the place. At noon, McClernand sent word to Porter that he was ready to attack, and, an hour later, the gunboats gallantly moved up to within four hundred yards of the rebel works, and opened fire. The garrison replied, but the tremendous concentric fire from the river and land batteries gradually overwhelmed that of the fort, and, one by one, its guns grew silent, until, at length, they ceased to respond altogether. McClernand, who had fought his way steadily forward, now ordered a general assault along the whole line, but, before it could be effected, a white flag was raised, and the place was ours. Seven stand of colors, five thousand prisoners, seventeen pieces of cannon, besides small arms and munitions of war, were the fruits of this victory. Our total loss was a little under a thousand. Morgan was assigned to the command of the place, but immediately turned it over to General A. J. Smith, as an honor due to him, for the gallant manner in which his division had borne the brunt of the conflict. The brigade of Burbridge especially distinguished itself.

General Grant now assumed immediate command of all the forces in his Department, and began to work seriously for the reduction of Vicksburg. Being convinced, from the result of Sherman's operations, that it could not be taken from the north side, he determined to get below it, and advance from the south. For this purpose, he concentrated his entire army, on the last of the month, at Milliken's Bend, on the west shore, just above the place, and at Young's Point, a little further down, and opposite the city.

Vicksburg lies on the eastern shore of the Mississippi, on a high bluff, and near the point of a great bend in the river. General Williams had endeavored, the year before, to cut a canal across this bend, through which the boats could pass, and get below without coming under the fire of the batteries. A fleet could not come up from New Orleans, on account of Port Hudson, where the rebels had been allowed to erect strong fortifications, the previous year, though Porter had advised the Government of what was going on, and had urged the vital importance of putting a stop to it. He even offered, with a thousand men, to occupy the place himself, and hold it, with the aid of his gunboats. But the year 1862 was a year of blunders on the part of the War Department, and of great disasters in the field. The Army of the Potomac had been driven from Richmond, on the one hand, and from the Rapidan, on the other, and shattered into fragments on the heights of Fredericksburg; Buell had been forced back from Chattanooga to Nashville, and Morgan compelled to evacuate Cumberland Gap; and, to close up the sad record, Port Hudson had been allowed to become well-nigh impregnable.

Grant now sat down to the tedious work of completing this canal, and turning the Mississippi into it; and the spade and pick took the place of the musket and sword. For six weeks, his splendid army lay idle here, as if on purpose to bring the people to the stool of repentance, for having, in their pride, attempted to cast ridicule on the spade, as an instrument unworthy of the soldier. Week after week, the only report that greeted the country was, "Digging still."

While these events had been passing on the Mississippi, the rebels had made another advance into Missouri. On the 8th of January, Marmaduke, with a heavy force, attacked Springfield, occupied by General Brown, who commanded the South-west Department of Missouri. The forces of the latter were very much scattered, so that not over fifteen hundred men, at this time, held the place. The attack commenced at one o'clock, and was pressed with fierce determination for five hours, when the enemy fell back. General Brown, while gallantly charging at the head of his body-guard, to encourage a regiment that had given way, was severely wounded, and the command devolved on Colonel Crabbe, of the Nineteenth Iowa. Our total loss was one hundred and sixty-two—that of the enemy much larger.

General Brown, when he found himself menaced by a superior force, telegraphed to Major-General Curtis for help, and, on the 9th, a part of Warren's brigade, under Colonel Merrill, started from Houston on a forced march for Springfield. By eight o'clock that evening, they had reached Beaver Creek, twenty-two miles distant. Resting here for four hours, the gallant eight hundred again started, at midnight, reaching the vicinity of Hartsville just as the wintry morning was breaking. Starting again, in the afternoon, they pushed on as far as Wood's Creek, when, learning that the enemy was trying to get in their rear, the little force fell back to Hartsville. Here, the enemy, who had been foiled in their assault on Springfield, fell suddenly upon it, to overwhelm it before succor could arrive. But, though fearfully outnumbered, the little band gallantly held its ground, and at length forced the enemy to abandon his design. Very heavy marching was done by the men—the Twenty-first Iowa, under Lieutenant-Colonel Dunlap, having marched one hundred miles, through mud and rain, between Friday afternoon and Monday morning, and, in the meantime, fought two battles.

There were other engagements between small detachments in this State and Arkansas, during this and the following months, but no action of any importance occurred.

An expedition up the White River, under John G. Walker, captured some guns; and another, under Colonel Ellet, up the Red River, with the ram, Queen of the West, took three rebel transport steamers. But, on February 14th, the ram run aground, at Gordon's Landing, in full range of a rebel battery, which poured in so destructive a fire that it had to be abandoned. This was not the only naval disaster we met with in the South-west, in the latter part of this year, and the commencement of 1863. A Confederate steamer, fitted out in England, and called the Alabama, which had been destroying our commerce for some time, on the 7th of December, seized the California steamer Ariel, on her way to Aspinwall.

A sadder disaster still, befell the fleet under Commodore Bell, which was blockading the port of Galveston. On the 11th of January, in the afternoon, a strange sail was reported in the offing, and the steamer Hatteras, Lieutenant Blake commanding, was signaled, from the flag-ship Brooklyn, to give chase. After dark, he came up with the stranger, and hailed him, asking the name of the steamer. "Her Brittanic Majesty's ship Vixen," was the reply. Blake then said he would send a boat aboard. The next minute, however, even while the boatswain's whistle was ringing, came the shout, "We are the Confederate steamer Alabama," accompanied with a stunning broadside. Blake, who from the first had been suspicious that the stranger was the Alabama, was prepared for an attack, and immediately returned it. But he could throw but ninety-four pounds, to the rebel's three hundred and twenty-four. Knowing his vessel could not stand this unequal fire many minutes, he determined to close with his antagonist, and steamed straight towards her. But the rebel commander knew his advantage, and, avoiding the blow, poured in his terrific broadsides at the distance of thirty yards. Thus, within pistol shot, Blake was compelled to fight the unequal battle. Nothing daunted, however, he cried, "Give it to them, my boys, give it to them; the Stars and Stripes must never come down!"—to which, three hearty cheers responded. But what was such a frail thing as the Hatteras, before the one-hundred-pound shot and eight-inch shells of the privateer, delivered within thirty yards? In a few minutes, her engines were a wreck, and she was on fire in two different places. "Drown the magazine," was the quick order, but the enemy was doing that for her, for she had then seven feet of water in her hold. It was a short fight, and, in a few minutes, the Hatteras lay, a helpless wreck, on the water. Still, her gallant Commander fought on, hoping against hope, for he could not bear to strike his flag. But it was all in vain. The report came that the vessel was sinking, and he reluctantly gave the order to fire a lee gun, in token of surrender. In ten minutes after the crew were got aboard of the Alabama, the Hatteras, with one heavy lurch, went to the bottom. Blake lost his vessel, but not his honor, for a more gallant fight, against hopeless odds, was never waged on the water.

In the latter part of the month, the ship-of-war Morning Light, and the schooner Velocity, blockading the Sabine Pass, Texas, were surprised by two rebel steamers, and captured. These naval successes of the enemy, caused much chagrin and complaint.

The activity which characterized the opening year, along the valley of the Mississippi, extended also to the Department of the Gulf.

Banks, as before stated, was appointed to supersede Butler, in the command of the Department of the Gulf, in December. The duties devolving upon him were of a delicate nature, for both the people of Louisiana and the North were divided in their views respecting the course that should be adopted. The enemies of Butler expected a more conciliatory course than the one he had pursued, while his friends stood prepared to denounce the first act of leniency, as certain to produce disastrous results. Hence, Banks' conduct was closely watched, and, as the result, misrepresented on both sides. His old friends at the North began to denounce him, but he kept on in the even tenor of his way. The wisdom of his course, however, soon became apparent, for, while he allayed vindictive passions, he at the same time showed that he would hold the reins of government with a firm hand.

The troops under his command constituted the Nineteenth Army Corps, and much was expected of him from his known enterprise and energy. His first movement was to send Colonel Burrill, with a detachment of troops, into Texas, who, on the 24th of the month, took possession of Galveston. But, in a week, it was recaptured by the enemy, and Colonel Burrill and his two hundred and sixty men killed or taken prisoners. At the same time, the rebels sent three powerful rams against our vessels in the bay, and, after a short, fierce fight, captured the Harriet Lane, and compelled the Commander of the flag-ship, Westfield, to blow her up, in order to prevent her falling into their hands.

On the 11th of January, he sent General Weitzel, with a land force, across Berwick Bay to Bayou Teche, accompanied by gunboats commanded by Lieutenant Buchanan. The enemy stationed here was attacked, on the 14th, and the rebel gunboat Cotton so disabled that her Commander blew her up. The loss of the land force was about thirty, while several were killed on the gunboats, and among them the gallant Commander, Buchanan, who steamed to the front with his vessel, and fought with the greatest intrepidity.

In the Spring, while Grant was endeavoring to get below Vicksburg, Banks planned an extensive expedition into "The Attakapas Country," the garden of Louisiana, and which the rebels held in force. Berwick City, at the mouth of the Atchafalaya River, was selected as the starting point of the army, which was to move up the Teche River, strongly fortified, and protected by rebel gunboats. On the 11th of April, the main column, commanded by Banks in person, took up its line of march from Berwick City, while Grover, with his division, moved up the Atchafalaya in transports, for the purpose of passing into Grand Lake—which approached the Teche above the fortifications of the enemy—and thus cutting off his retreat. On Sunday, Banks came upon the rebel works, stretching along the shores on both sides of the river, and guarded by the gunboat Diana. A heavy artillery fight followed, which lasted till dark. It was renewed the next day, and soon the gunboat was compelled to retire up-stream. In the meantime, Grover was steadily moving around the rebels, to the east, who, finding themselves threatened in the rear, hastily retreated, leaving two thousand prisoners in our hands. Banks then resumed his march, and, on the 20th, reached Opelousas, a hundred and eighty miles from New Orleans, and only seventy-five from the Red River, the point at which he was aiming. Alexandria, an important and strongly fortified place upon it, was at length reached, on the 8th of May, but not until it had surrendered to Admiral Porter, who, acting in conjunction with Banks, had advanced against it with his gunboats. The latter immediately assumed command. Having marched two hundred miles, through the enemy's country, without meeting with a single repulse, after giving his army a short rest he moved down on Port Hudson from the north.

CHAPTER XI.

VICKSBURG CAMPAIGN—THE ATTEMPTS TO GET IN REAR OF HAINES' BLUFF—LAKE PROVIDENCE ROUTE—MOON LAKE ROUTE—STEELE'S BAYOU ROUTE—BOLD RESOLVE TO RUN THE BATTERIES—THE MARCH INLAND—THE BATTERIES RUN—DIFFICULTIES OF THE MARCH—NEW CARTHAGE—GRAND GULF—PORT GIBSON—GRAND RESOLVE OF GRANT—THE MARCH INLAND—BATTLES OF RAYMOND, JACKSON, CHAMPION'S HILL, BLACKWATER—VICKSBURG INVESTED—FIRST ASSAULT—SECOND ASSAULT—ACTION OF THE GUNBOATS.

WE left Grant, early in the Spring, attempting to get below Vicksburg, by means of the canal dug the year before, by General Williams. This scheme proving abortive, as sufficient water could not be got into the ditch, he started another project. About seventy miles above Vicksburg, and some five miles west of the Mississippi River, lies Lake Providence, which empties itself through a bayou, filled with snags, into Swan Lake; this in turn sends its waters southward, through a long, winding stream called the Tensas River, into the Black River, the last flowing on into the Red River, which effects a junction with the Mississippi below Natchez. The whole route was about a hundred and fifty miles in length. A canal five miles long had to be cut through a morass, the shallows to be dug out, the snags removed, and stumps cleared away, before the boats could be got out of the Mississippi, and sent through this long, crooked, inland course. As the work went on, predictions were uttered that a new channel for the Mississippi would be made, extending, perhaps, even to the Gulf.

The canal was at length opened, and a steamer and a few barges were got across into Lake Providence. But the Mississippi kept its old course, and, as the spring floods fell, the new channel became a shallow creek, so that the whole project had to be abandoned.

Grant, however, with his accustomed tenacity of purpose, determined not to abandon his design to get in the rear of Vicksburg, for it could be taken in no other way. He now made a third trial on the east side of the Mississippi. About a hundred and fifty miles, in a straight line, north from Vicksburg, there is a little lake, called Moon Lake, separated from the river only by a thin strip of land. From this lake, a narrow stream, called the Yazoo Pass, leads into the Coldwater River, which flows south into the Tallahatchie, that in turn unites with the Yazoo. If he could get into the latter river, he would be able to move down in the rear of Haines' Bluff, and thus effectually turn the fortifications there, which Sherman had failed to capture. The canal to the lake was quickly cut; the waters of the Mississippi poured through it, and the steamers floated into Moon Lake. Passing out of this, into the Coldwater and Tallahatchie Rivers, they slowly felt their tortuous way towards the navigable Yazoo. It was a strange spectacle, to see these armed vessels threading their way under overarching cypress trees, and plunging into apparently interminable swamps, where never before even a canoe had floated. It was like sailing through a flooded forest, made still more dangerous by the rapid flow of the swollen waters, which the Mississippi sent with headlong fury through this new channel. The paddle-wheels, instead of being used to propel the vessels, incessantly backed water, to prevent their too rapid descent among the gigantic trees, whose overhanging branches sometimes swept the decks. The solitude and gloom of this strange, winding route, oppressed the spirits, yet the men toiled patiently on—making, upon an average, less than a quarter of a mile an hour—till they reached the Yazoo. The heaviest part of the task now seemed accomplished, and a swift sail down to the rear of Vicksburg was anticipated. But the rebels had received information of the expedition, and, divining its object, erected, near the confluence of the streams, a fort which commanded the channel, and yet was so surrounded by bogs that the land force could not approach it. The frail wooden steamboats, of course, could not silence these batteries, and so this project, costing so much labor and time, also had to be abandoned.

Baffled, but not disheartened, Grant now made another attempt to get in the rear of the batteries on Haines' Bluff. About seven miles above where the Yazoo enters the Mississippi, Steele's Bayou is connected with the latter river. This, in turn, connects inland, north, with the Black Bayou, Rolling Fork and Sunflower Rivers, which, in their course, wind entirely around Haines' Bluff. On the 14th of March, Admiral Porter entered this bayou with a gunboat fleet, accompanied by a force of infantry under General Sherman. A portion of this, like each of the other routes which had been tried, was full of difficulties. One who accompanied the expedition, thus describes the Black Bayou: "Black Bayou, a narrow stream, heretofore navigable only by dug-outs, was made of the width of our steamers, with great labor, by felling trees and sawing stumps below the surface. Every foot of our way was cut and torn through a dense forest, never before traversed by steamers. I never witnessed a more exciting and picturesque scene than the transportation, on the last day, of the third brigade, by General Stuart. Crowded with men, the steamers, at the highest possible speed, pushed through overhanging trees and around short curves. Sometimes they were wedged fast between trees, then sailing along smoothly, a huge cypress would reach out an arm and sweep the whole length of the boats, tearing guards and chimneys from the decks. The last trip through the Black Bayou, was in a night, pitchy dark and rainy." Added to all this, the enemy, having been apprised of our design, filled the thickets along the banks with sharp-shooters, who swept the decks with their fire, at close range, and scattered the working parties. Large trees were felled across the stream, by negroes, in advance, to retard the boats and keep them under fire, and behind them, to prevent their return. Before the expedition reached Sunflower River, the peril of being caught there in the forest, permanently, with his boats, was so great, that Porter determined to return. This resolution was not taken a moment too soon, for, if he had pushed on a few hours longer, he would have been hemmed in beyond release.

When the expedition again reached the Mississippi, Grant saw that the last hope of getting in the rear of Vicksburg, inland, from the north, was gone. Still, he would not abandon the great object for which he had struggled so long and worked so patiently. Difficulties, instead of discouraging, roused him to greater efforts. Having exhausted all the plans that ingenuity could suggest, to avoid the direct fire of the rebel batteries, which lined the river for eight miles, he at last took the bold and apparently rash resolution of running them with his gunboats and transports. Preparatory to this, the army was marched inland, towards New Carthage, below Vicksburg, on the west side of the river. In this march, General McClernand led the advance, with the Eleventh Army Corps. The swampy country, however, soon became a vast mortar bed, in which the hubs of the artillery wheels would often entirely disappear from sight, and through which the army floundered, till further progress became impossible without constructing for itself a regular military road. Bridges had to be built over the sluggish streams, and corduroy causeways made across treacherous swamps, and, in the meantime, the levee carefully guarded, lest the enemy should cut it, and turn the swampy lowland into an impassable sea. The army thus worked its toilsome way, till at last it came in sight of New Carthage, the goal of its labors, but, alas! it was like an island in the sea, for the enemy had succeeded in cutting the levee near it, and flooding all the intervening country. Cut off from this point, McClernand resumed his march, striking the river twelve miles further down stream, making the whole distance from Milliken's Bend thirty-five miles. All the supplies and ordnance stores for the projected campaign on the other side of the river, had to be hauled over this miserable road.

This being accomplished, the next thing was to get the gunboats and transports past the Vicksburg batteries. The night of the 16th of April was fixed upon to make the attempt. Whether the frail transports could safely run the terrible gauntlet, was problematical, and it was resolved to try the experiment with only three—the Silver Wave, Forest Queen and Henry Clay. The plan was, for Porter to move down in single file, with his eight gunboats, and, planting them square abreast of the rebel batteries, engage them; while the transports, hugging the western shore, in their rear, covered by the smoke and darkness, were, with all steam on, to push swiftly below. A little before midnight, the gunboats, one after another, drifted out of the bend in which they lay concealed, and, showing no light from their chimneys, moved like great shadows down the noiseless current. Nearly an hour passed by, and not a sound broke the ominous stillness; and the listeners on the shore above began to think the boats had passed the batteries unseen, when suddenly there came a flash, followed by a crash that shook the shores. Lights danced along the heights of Vicksburg—soon, thunder answered thunder, and the flash of batteries, from land and water, rent the gloom, till the black midnight seemed turned into an element of fire. Still, the transports hoped to escape in the confusion, when, suddenly, a huge bonfire blazed forth on one of the hills near Vicksburg. The rebels were prepared for just such an attempt as this, and had collected a vast amount of combustibles, which, when lighted, would make the bosom of the Mississippi, in front of the batteries, bright as day. The poor transports were instantly flooded in light, and, as they swept along the ruddy stream, presented a fair target to the gunners. The enemy penetrated at a glance the design of Grant, and shot and shell fell and burst, in a horrible tempest, around the frail things. The commanders saw that the chances were against them, but they crowded on all steam, till the gleaming waters rolled away from their prows in a torrent of foam. Soon, a heavy shot tore through the timbers of the Forest Queen, and then another, and she drifted unmanageably on the current. A gunboat, seeing her distress, wheeled and took her in tow, and passed down the river, greeted, at every turn of its wheels, with shots from the batteries. The Henry Clay was struck by a shell which set her barricade of cotton bales on fire, and she soon flamed back to the beacon light on the shore. Blazing like a mighty torch, she sent her jets of flame, capped with angry wreaths of black, curling smoke, far up into the midnight heavens. The crew leaped from the glowing furnace into their boats, and took refuge on the western bank. The Silver Wave alone was untouched, and, bearing seemingly a charmed life, glided serenely through the horrible tempest, till the last battery was passed, and, with her fragile form unmarred, she floated gracefully on the water. The gunboats came through safely, with only one man killed and two wounded. For over an hour, they gallantly faced the heavy batteries, and though often struck, sustained no damage that was not speedily repaired. Still, but one transport was through, and this alone could be of no service to the army. More must be brought down, and Grant resolved, though but one out of three had escaped, to run the same fearful gauntlet with six more, slowly towing twelve barges. This was so hazardous an enterprise that the officers felt reluctant to order men to accompany the boats, and volunteers were called for. Immediately, enough stepped forward to man a fleet, and it had to be decided by lot, who the lucky ones should be. So eager were they to join in the desperate undertaking, that a boy, having drawn a successful number, was offered by a soldier a hundred dollars for his chance, which the spirited little fellow refused. He lived to tell of his share in the daring feat. With strange good fortune, the whole fleet, with the exception of the Tigress, and half the barges, passed in safety. She was struck below the water line, and being run ashore, sunk.

The army was now below Vicksburg, with transports to carry it across the river, and gunboats to protect it. And here, on the 29th of April, the Thirteenth Corps was embarked, and moved to the front of Grand Gulf, a fortified place, which Grant designed to capture and make his base. The gunboats at once engaged the batteries, and for five hours maintained a fierce fire, sometimes moving almost to within pistol shot of the enemy's guns. Grant witnessed the action from a tug, and saw with regret that the post could not be reduced from the water side, and that, from the position of things, no landing could be made near by, to take it from the shore. He therefore ordered the transports back to Hard Times, and, disembarking his troops, resumed his march down the river. At night, the gunboats again engaged the batteries, and, under cover of the fire, the transports ran past them, suffering but little damage. Grant's march through the forest had been unseen by the enemy, and, the next day, the army was ferried across the river to the eastern shore. With a patience and tenacity unparalleled, Grant had finally got his army south of Vicksburg, and over the river, and yet the mighty work he had assigned himself had only just begun—he had reached only the threshold of the perils it embraced.

He landed at Bruinsburgh, and immediately pushed forward McClernand's Corps to Port Gibson. About eight miles out, the latter met the enemy, and forced him back till dark. The next morning, he found him posted on two roads, about four miles from Port Gibson. The rebel position was admirably chosen, for the road ran mostly along high ridges, with impenetrable ravines on each side, to prevent any flank movements. McClernand, however, succeeded in pushing forward the divisions of Hovey, Carr and Smith, on the right, while Osterhaus advanced against the left. The latter was hard pressed by the enemy, but at length, being reinforced by Logan's division, he ordered a charge, and, leading it in person, fell in such fury on the rebel line, that it was shattered into fragments, and fell disorderly back. Three cannon were captured in this brilliant charge. The three divisions on the other flank, steadily forced the enemy back all day towards Port Gibson, until darkness closed the conflict. The fighting had been close and sharp, resulting in a loss on our side of some eight hundred and fifty, while we took a thousand prisoners, and five cannon. That night, the wearied troops slept on their arms. In the morning, it was found that the enemy had retreated across Bayou Pierre. A floating bridge was at once thrown across it, while McPherson pushed on eight miles to the northern fork of the bayou, which was also bridged, and the next morning, just as the sun was climbing the eastern hills, he marched with streaming banners across it.

On the 3rd, (May,) the enemy was closely pressed all day, and many prisoners taken. Grant was now in the rear of Grand Gulf, and, hearing that it was evacuated, he took an escort of cavalry, and galloped thither, fifteen miles distant, across the country, in order to make the necessary arrangements for changing his base of supplies from Bruinsburgh to that place.

When he started down the river, he left Sherman, with the Fifteenth Corps, to make a feint on Haines' Bluff, in order to keep the enemy from sending a heavy force to the assistance of Grand Gulf, before he arrived there. On the day that the Thirteenth Corps landed at Bruinsburgh, Admiral Porter opened a heavy fire against the rebel works at Haines' Bluff, and Sherman landed his troops as if about to carry them by storm. Pemberton, commanding at Vicksburg, was thus prevented from sending off troops south, and Sherman, having accomplished his object, re-embarked his corps, and pressed on after Grant from Milliken's Bend.

The latter did not design, when he crossed the Mississippi, to push on as he did, but expected to stop and concentrate his army at Grand Gulf, and effect a junction with Banks, which would give him an army strong enough to resist any force the enemy might bring against him. But he received a letter from the latter, informing him that he had projects of his own on foot, and could not join him. At the same time, he heard that Beauregard was about moving from the Southern cities, west to co-operate with Pemberton. To wait till the enemy, by the various railroads, could concentrate an immense force against him, would render his defeat almost certain. To advance with only a part of his army in hand, and his base of supplies not yet established, seemed equally perilous. With characteristic boldness, he determined, however, on the latter course, trusting to the country to furnish forage for his troops. The rebel hosts, he knew, were gathering on all sides, and his only chance of success lay in attacking and beating the several armies before they could effect a junction. His blows must fall, rapid and terrible as bolts from heaven, or he was ruined. With the daring of Napoleon, he determined to enact over again that great chieftain's famous Italian campaign, when, with fifty thousand men, he attacked in detail and beat an army of a hundred and fifty thousand, and killed and wounded, and took as prisoners, a number equal to his whole force. He knew that rapid marching and constant victories were indispensable to success in this daring movement, and the army was stripped like an athlete for the race before it. Delay was defeat; a single severe repulse, and the campaign was ended; but he did not falter a moment in his sublime determination. He set the example of self-sacrifice himself, by taking neither an orderly, camp chest, overcoat or blanket with him.

Thus cleared of every encumbrance, he ordered the advance, and his banners moved boldly inland. McPherson struck off to the north-east, while Sherman (who had arrived) and McClernand kept along the Black River—the three corps in supporting distance of each other. Grant, all the while, made demonstrations as if about to cross the Black River, and move directly to the rear of Vicksburg, which so confused Pemberton that he dared not march out to join the forces at Jackson.

McPherson, moving straight on the latter place, came, on the 12th, upon the enemy, strongly posted, near Raymond. No time could be spared, and the troops were pushed steadily forward, sweeping everything before them. Our loss here was four hundred and forty-two. The enemy fell back towards Jackson, losing heavily in prisoners. Grant now ordered Sherman and McClernand to bear off to the right, towards McPherson. On the night of the 13th, the rain fell in torrents, and continued the next day till noon, rendering the roads muddy and slippery; yet the troops, in close order, and with cheerful spirits, moved off through the deluge, making a wearisome march of fourteen miles, and at noon came upon the enemy, about two miles from the city.

Pressed in by McPherson, and threatened on the flank, the latter gave way, and left the Capital to its fate.

That evening, Grant learned that Johnston, who had been sent by Davis to take chief command of the rebel forces in this Department, had ordered Pemberton to march out from Vicksburg and attack his rear. He immediately faced about, and, leaving Sherman to destroy railroads, bridges, workshops, &c., in Jackson, moved the rest of his troops, by converging routes, west, towards Edwards' Station. The next morning at daylight, two men, who had been in the employ of the rebels, were brought to Grant, charged with important information. They had just passed through Pemberton's army, and gave the Union Commander the position of the rebel forces, and stated that they were twenty-five thousand strong. Grant immediately sent back a courier to Sherman, to leave Jackson at once, and hasten forward. Within an hour, after this prompt chieftain received the message, his troops were swiftly moving forward towards the point of rendezvous. Grant concentrated his army with wonderful rapidity. Trains, quarter-masters' stores, and everything, had to tumble out of the roads in hot haste, to give room for the marching columns. Soon, the enemy was encountered, strongly posted on a precipitous, narrow, wooded ridge, his left resting on a height, while below were open fields, in crossing which our troops would be exposed to the destructive fire of ten batteries of artillery. Hovey's division, and McPherson's Corps—all but Ransom's division, which did not arrive till the battle was over—were at once disposed in and to the right of the road leading to Vicksburg. But Grant delayed the order to attack, till he could hear from McClernand, with his four divisions, which, when they arrived, would complete his line of battle. But the skirmishing in front of Hovey's division, by eleven o'clock, swelled into a battle. In the meantime, Logan had worked around upon the left and rear of the rebels, and pressed them so vigorously that their superior numbers could no longer force Hovey back, and the latter, seeing his advantage, ordered a charge. The rebel line gave way before it, and disappeared in disorder over the ridge. A thousand prisoners, and two batteries, fell into our hands in this brilliant engagement, but the victory cost us nearly twenty-five hundred men. Grant was losing fast, and no reinforcements could be had. At daylight the next morning, the 17th, the pursuit was renewed—McClernand in the advance, who soon came upon the enemy strongly posted on both sides of the Black River. On the west, or further side, the shore rises abruptly into high bluffs, which were lined with heavy batteries. On the east side, a bayou, twenty feet wide and three feet deep, leaves the river, and sweeping in a semicircle, a mile in length, again enters the stream, inclosing a level space, on which the rebels had also planted heavy batteries, protected by a strong force of infantry. This bayou, or ditch, served as a natural rifle pit, behind which the enemy felt safe, while their guns swept the plains beyond, over which our troops would be compelled to pass. A railroad and turnpike bridge crossed both the bayou and river at this point, side by side, commanded by the hostile batteries beyond. McClernand opened a heavy artillery fire upon the position, to which the enemy vigorously responded. At almost the first fire, Osterhaus was wounded, and General A. L. Lee took his place. While the cannonade was going on, Lawler, of Carr's division, which held the right, under the protection of the river bank, succeeded in approaching near the rebel works in that direction, when the order to charge was given. Casting their blankets and knapsacks on the ground, the gallant fellows sprung forward, and, dashing across the open field on the double-quick, plunged into the muddy bayou, and, though shot and shell struck and burst

SIEGE OF VICKSBURG.

FIGHT IN THE CRATER MADE BY EXPLOSION OF A MINE UNDER A PORTION OF THE REBEL WORKS.

incessantly in their midst, struggled through, and with bayonets at charge, swept in headlong fury upon the rebel works. Taken by surprise at this sudden movement, the enemy at once raised the white flag, and the whole garrison, with seventeen pieces of artillery, was ours. The rebel army across the river, seeing the disaster, immediately set fire to the bridge—thus cutting off all chance of escape for any portion of their troops on the east bank—and retreated rapidly towards Vicksburg.

Sherman, in the meantime, had reached Bridgeport above, with the only pontoon train in the army, by which he effected a crossing of the river the next morning. McClernand and McPherson built floating bridges during the night, and on the 18th, the army was moving *en masse* on Vicksburg. Sherman, still holding the right, marched rapidly towards the Yazoo River, while McClernand, inclining to the south, closed in on the doomed garrison in that direction. The next day, Sherman's right rested on the Mississippi, within plain view of our gunboats, and Haines' Bluff was at once hastily evacuated by the enemy.

Vicksburg was now closely besieged, and Grant, finding his army eager for an assault, and believing the enemy to be demoralized by the staggering blows that had been dealt him, determined, desperate as the undertaking was, to attempt to carry the place by storm. The army moved gallantly to the assault, under a desolating fire, but the works were too strong to be carried. Only a portion of the army, the Fifteenth Corps, gained even a temporary advantage, and at night the troops were recalled.

The two following days were spent in bringing up supplies, and perfecting the communications, and giving a little rest to the troops, which had for twenty days been constantly marching and fighting, on short rations.

Everything being arranged, Grant determined to make another effort to carry this modern Gibraltar by assault.

Ten o'clock, on the morning of the 22nd, was the time appointed. The several corps commanders set their watches by Grant's, so that there should be perfect unity of movement, and at the appointed signal, the army, in splendid array and magnificent order, swept, awful as the ocean surge, full on the rebel works. Then commenced one of the wildest scenes of war. All along the frowning fortifications, there streamed an incessant sheet of fire, bursting through the thick smoke, on the brave, uncovered ranks below, that still pressed dauntlessly forward, heedless of the destruction that wasted them. They could see no enemy in front—only solid earthworks, clouds of rolling smoke, and waves of fire, confronted them. For two fearful hours, they struggled desperately to reach this blazing vortex, and quench its deadly fires, but struggled in vain. Just then, Grant received a dispatch from McClernand, stating that he had gained the intrenchments in front of him, at several points, and needed more troops. They were given, and the assault was pressed more vigorously than ever. McClernand, however, overestimated the amount of success gained, and the fresh attempt only helped to swell the slaughter, and the bleeding army was at length compelled to fall back, and abandon the struggle.*

Grant now gave up all attempts to take the place by storm, and sat down before it in regular siege. Porter, with his gunboats, kept watch and ward on the Mississippi, co-operating with the former by every means in his power. The gunboat Cincinnati was sunk by the rebel batteries, and fifteen men drowned, and twenty-five killed and wounded. The masts had all been shot away before she went down, yet she sunk with her flag flying—nailed to one of the stumps.

* Grant blamed McClernand for giving this false information, which provoked the latter to issue a general order, recapitulating the services of his corps, and also to defend himself in a letter to Governor Yates, which caused Grant to remove him from command, and put Ord in his place.

CHAPTER XII.

ASSAULT ON PORT HUDSON—THE SIEGE—SIEGE OF VICKSBURG—ITS SURRENDER—RESULTS OF THE VICTORY—SURRENDER OF PORT HUDSON—THE MISSISSIPPI OPENED—MINOR OPERATIONS WEST—ARREST OF VALLANDIGHAM—HIS BANISHMENT—EXASPERATED STATE OF PUBLIC FEELING.

THE very next day after this unsuccessful assault of Vicksburg, Banks arrived with his army, from Alexandria, before Port Hudson. Coming down the Red River, he had crossed the Mississippi above the place, hoping to find its defenses on that side much weaker than on the south.

Forming a junction with Augur's force, that came down from Baton Rouge, he immediately began to invest the place, but, unwilling to await the slow progress of a siege, made two unsuccessful assaults on its impregnable fortifications. The troops fought bravely, and Weitzel, Sherman and Augur maintained their old renown, and the colored regiments behaved with great gallantry; but it was a useless waste of life.

Banks now sat down before it in regular siege, and day by day, pushed his batteries nearer and nearer to the rebel works, until some of them were within three hundred yards. At length, after having dismounted several pieces of the rebel artillery, and silenced others with his sharpshooters, he determined to make another attempt to carry the place by assault. Sunday, the 14th of June, was the day fixed upon, and long before daylight the artillery opened all along the line, and the Sabbath morning was ushered in by a cannonading that shook the shores of the Mississippi.

Farragut, with his gunboats, was co-operating with Banks, and his heavy guns soon opened, and helped to swell the uproar that filled all the air.

The extreme north-east angle of the breastworks was selected as presenting the least formidable obstacles to success, for much of the artillery at this point had been, during the last week, dismounted or silenced. Still, almost insurmountable difficulties presented themselves, even here. At one point, a clear field, five or six hundred yards in width, swept up to the ramparts, crossed and recrossed with narrow, deep gullies, too small to afford protection and yet too broad to be easily passed, and covered also with fallen trees and vines, thus forming a trap for the advancing troops, who all the while would be exposed to a desolating fire.

In the dull, gray light of the early morning, the Seventy-fifth New York moved rapidly forward as skirmishers, followed by the Ninety-first New York, each soldier carrying a five-pound hand grenade, which was to be thrown over the breastworks to scatter the enemy. Next came the Twenty-fourth Connecticut, loaded with sand-bags filled with cotton, to fill up the ditch for the advancing stormers. The balance of Weitzel's brigade was to press close after, to be supported by other brigades under Colonel Birge. As soon as Weitzel should make a lodgment within the enemy's works, Paine was to follow, and then the two columns were to be quickly deployed in line of battle, and move swiftly on the town and the grand citadel itself. Grover commanded these two divisions, which were to do the chief work, while Augur and Dwight made feints on the rebel left.

The assaulting columns advanced with great intrepidity—brigade after brigade dashing forward under a heavy fire—but were compelled each time to fall back. A dense fog had lain along the river, giving a more somber hue to the gray twilight, but in the midst of the carnage, it suddenly lifted and rolled upward like a mighty curtain, and the bright sun lighted up the wild scene with noontide splendor. The assault was pressed with great valor and resolution, and the commanders held their troops to the deadly struggle till eleven o'clock, when such as could retire fell back; and the rest crouched in the gullies or hid behind trees and whatever could afford shelter, and waited for the darkness to cover the field, so that they could get out of the deadly range of the enemy's muskets. Col. Paine, being wounded, lay all day between two rows of earth, in an old cotton field, exposed to the blazing sun, and when at dark he was removed, his wounds were full of maggots. Many of the wounded soldiers lay exposed in the same way.

The loss in this assault was estimated at seven hundred and fifty. The Secretary of War's maxim, "to move at once upon the enemy's works," had now been tried quite enough, and the despised "spade" was resorted to again. Mathematical science and engineering skill, will always be found more worthy of trust than popular declamation or misguided bravery.

Banks now pressed the siege with great vigor, and being determined that Grant, around Vicksburg, should not get all the glory, planned another assault. But before it was attempted, the surrender of the latter place made further attempts to hold Port Hudson useless.

When Grant had completed his lines around Vicksburg, opening communication with the North by way of the Mississippi, so that supplies and reinforcements could be forwarded to him to any amount, the fall of the stronghold was evidently a mere question of time. Rumors, from time to time, were received, that Johnston was assembling a heavy army in his rear, to raise the siege; but the arrival of reinforcements allowed Grant to detach Sherman, with a large force, to watch the rebel leader. In the meantime, he pressed the siege with all the energy which distinguished him. Day by day, he dug his way towards the place, and at length reached positions where his shells could be dropped into the center of the city. These, crashing through the buildings, and bursting along the streets, forced the inhabitants to seek shelter in caves, dug in the earth. For six weeks, while the army was digging slowly onward, the batteries kept playing on the devoted citadel. Provisions became scarce, and the inhabitants grew wan and thin in their narrow dens. At length, the ammunition gave out, and Pemberton, whose only hope of deliverance lay in Johnston's ability to raise the siege, began to despair, and, seeing Grant about to carry the place by assault, he, on the 3rd of July, sent two officers with a flag of truce to the Federal lines, to arrange the terms of capitulation. Grant would listen to none but unconditional surrender. A personal interview then took place between the two Generals, who met midway between the lines, under a gigantic oak, while the two armies left their places of concealment and swarmed upon the ramparts, to witness this extraordinary scene. Pemberton was the first to speak, and asked Grant what terms he proposed. "Unconditional surrender," was the prompt reply. "Never," rejoined the haughty rebel, "so long as I have a man left me." "Then," said Grant, "you can continue the defense; my army was never in a better condition to continue the siege." After some further conversation, the interview terminated without coming to a definite result, Grant saying that he would confer with his officers. He did so, and sent a note saying that the entire surrender of the place and garrison would be required, but that the troops would be paroled, and allowed to march out of the lines—the officers taking with them their regimental clothing, and the staff and field and cavalry officers a horse each. The proposal was accepted, and on the morning of the 4th of July—our National Jubilee-day—the hostile flag came down, and the Stars and Stripes went up, over the rebel works, amid the enthusiastic shouts of the whole army.

When Johnston heard of the fall of the place, he immediately retraced his steps across the Big Black River, and Jackson once more fell into our hands.

"The result of the campaign," said Grant, "has been the defeat of the enemy in five battles outside of Vicksburg; the occupation of Jackson the Capital of Mississippi, and the capture of Vicksburg and its garrison and munitions of war—a loss to the enemy of thirty-seven thousand prisoners, among whom were fifteen general officers; at least ten thousand killed and wounded, and among the killed, Generals Tracy, Tilghman and Green, and hundreds and perhaps thousands of stragglers who can never be collected and reorganized. Arms and munitions of war for an army of sixty thousand men have fallen into our hands, besides a large amount of other public property, consisting of railroads, locomotives, cars, steamboats, cotton, etc., and much was destroyed to prevent our capturing it." His own total loss, in killed, wounded and missing, from the time he crossed the Mississippi, he estimated at eight thousand, five hundred and seventy-five.

Four days after the surrender of Vicksburg, Gardner, the Commander of Port Hudson, sent a flag of truce to Banks, asking a cessation of hostilities, for the purpose of settling the terms of capitulation. The latter would allow of no cessation, and commissioners were at once appointed, whose consultations ended in the surrender of the garrison as prisoners of war. To the stirring strains of "The Star-Spangled Banner," and "Yankee Doodle," the army entered the place in triumph, and marched proudly along the sullen, silent rebel line. The Union flag was run up on one of the highest bluffs, and, as its starry folds swung lazily out to the breeze, the artillery thundered forth a salute. About six thousand prisoners, fifty-one pieces of artillery, two steamers, besides a large quantity of small arms, ammunition, &c., fell into our hands.

It was a great victory, but the pleasure it was calculated to impart was marred by the reflection that but for the negligence of the Government such a fortified work would never, in the first place, have been in possession of the rebels; and, in the second place, the loss of life in securing it was wholly unnecessary, for the fall of Vicksburg, which was only a matter of time, involved the fall of this place also, without firing a gun.

But the number of guns, prisoners and materials of war captured were not the chief results obtained by these two campaigns. They opened the Mississippi in its entire length—an object which had been of paramount importance to the great North-west. It also bisected the Southern Confederacy, and cut off its large supplies of men and animals, which it had constantly received from the country west of the Mississippi. The nation was jubilant over it, for the people thought they now saw the end of the rebellion near. Grant advanced at once to the first place in general estimation, as a military leader, and deservedly so. He had, throughout this arduous, long campaign, exhibited a tenacity of purpose and a fertility of resource that few men possess, while the daring resolution to cut himself loose from supplies and reinforcements, and march boldly into the interior, depending solely on his celerity of movement to prevent a concentration of the enemy's forces, was the inspiration of true genius. The rapidity and power with which he dealt his blows, reminds one of Napoleon the Great.

As a part of this great campaign, Colonel B. H. Grierson's cavalry raid through Mississippi should be mentioned. It was planned to create a diversion in favor of the army operating against Vicksburg, as well as to destroy railroads and other public property. It was dispatched from La Grange, Tennessee, by General Hurlburt, on the 17th of April, and on the 2nd of May arrived at Baton Rouge, having traversed the whole State of Mississippi. Nothing like this raid, in boldness and extent, had as yet been attempted, and its success covered the young Commander with laurels. These great cavalry raids became for a time quite the rage with the people, but their effect on the war was greatly overestimated, and it is questionable whether the wear and tear, on horses and men, did not damage us quite as much as the destruction of property hurt the enemy.

The other operations in the West, during the Spring and early Summer, were of a minor character. Attacks were made by the rebels on Fort Donelson and Ship Island, and quite a heavy one by Van Dorn on Franklin, Tennessee—all of which were repulsed. In the latter part of March, Morgan and Wheeler were defeated by Colonel Hall, near Milton, Tennessee, and Pegram by General Gillmore, near Somerset, Kentucky; and in various parts of Missouri, Mississippi, Tennessee and Kentucky, conflicts were of frequent occurrence, between detached bodies of the Union and rebel troops, in most of which the former were successful. Cavalry raids, scouting expeditions, and guerrilla fights, kept these States in constant commotion, for independent parties and regiments, and bands of irregular forces, were constantly operating, outside of the main armies. These had but little bearing, however, on the great struggle, except to lay waste the country, exasperate the inhabitants, and cause great personal suffering among the people.

But no event caused greater excitement than the arrest of Clement L. Vallandigham, of Ohio, by order of Burnside, on the charge of contempt of his orders, and resistance to the Government in its measures to put down the rebellion. Seized at midnight in his own house, and dragged away to be tried by court-martial, his treatment was boldly denounced by the Democratic press. Indignant at these denunciations, Burnside caused the chief offender, in his Department, *The Chicago Times*, to be suppressed. This increased the excitement, and there was great danger, for a while, of an open outbreak in the West. The excitement was somewhat allayed by the President annulling the order of Burnside suppressing the *Times*. Still, the violent arrest of Vallandigham, and the refusal to grant him a trial by the civil courts, was denounced as an act of tyranny, by the opposition press East and West, and but little more was needed, at this time, to bring on a collision between the citizens and soldiers. His final trial, and sentence of banishment to the rebel lines, deepened the indignation. Congress had passed an Act the Winter before, covering just such cases as this, under which he could have been tried and punished in a manner becoming our republican notions, and without an apparent attempt to override the civil courts by the strong arm of military power.

CHAPTER XIII.

AFFAIRS EAST AT THE OPENING OF THE YEAR—THE PRESIDENT'S AFFIRMATIVE PROCLAMATION OF EMANCIPATION—HOOKER PLACED OVER THE ARMY OF THE POTOMAC—FIGHT AT SUFFOLK—ATTACK ON FORT MCALLISTER—DESTRUCTION OF THE NASHVILLE—THE FIRST COLORED REGIMENT—FIGHTS AT BLACKWATER AND KELLY'S FORD, VIRGINIA—WASHINGTON, NORTH CAROLINA, ATTACKED BY THE REBELS—ATTACK BY THE IRON-CLAD FLEET ON FORT SUMTER—DISAPPOINTMENT AT ITS FAILURE—INJUSTICE TO DU PONT.

EAST, the opening year was distinguished by the President's confirmatory Emancipation Proclamation, (previously noticed,) declaring the slaves, in certain States and parts of States, forever free. It was celebrated as a great event in many portions of the Northern States, and by the freedmen in Norfolk, Va., and Beaufort, South Carolina. The Richmond papers denounced it as the most "startling political crime, the most stupid political blunder, yet known in American history," and declared that servile insurrection was the sole object aimed at. It was also bitterly denounced by the opposition, who asserted that it would have no effect on the emancipation of the slaves; but, on the contrary, that it would effectually close the door against the long-cherished hope of a reaction at the South against the leaders of the rebellion. They said that if the army did not overthrow Slavery, no proclamation would; that it was to disappear under the tramp of our victorious battalions, or not at all.

On the 26th of January, Burnside was superseded by Hooker in command of the Army of the Potomac. By those unacquainted with military men and affairs, this was hailed with delight; and the most extravagant anticipations were entertained of the great results that the latter, with his brilliant fighting qualities, would accomplish.

The month closed, however, without any military operations of importance. A sharp fight took place near Suffolk, between a Union force under General Corcoran, and the rebels under General Roger A. Pryor, in which the latter, after a three-hours struggle, were compelled to retreat. An attack was also made on Fort McAllister, commanding the Savannah River, by Commander Worden, in the iron-clad Montauk, but it failed to produce any effect on the rebel works. On the 27th of February, however, he had the satisfaction of destroying, while aground, under the very guns of the fort, the troublesome rebel steamer Nashville. A few days after, March 3rd, Commander Drayton, with a fleet of monitors and mortar schooners, again attempted to reduce the fort, but, though a terrific bombardment, of eight hours' duration, was kept up, no material damage was done to the works.

The organization of the first colored regiment, at Beaufort, South Carolina, in the fore part of this year, caused a good deal of excitement. Under Colonel Higginson, a Unitarian clergyman, it made an expedition into the interior, and, though the blacks behaved with commendable gallantry, they afterward, under Colonel Montgomery, in an expedition to Darien, were a disgrace to the flag and to the nation.

Newbern was attacked on the 14th of March, by a rebel force under General Pettigrew, without any successful result; and Colonel Spear, on the 17th, assailed the rebel breastworks on the Blackwater, near Franklin, Virginia, but was repulsed. On the same day, a spirited cavalry fight occurred at Kelly's Ford, on the Rappahannock, between a force under General Averill, and Fitz-Hugh Lee, of the rebel service, which lasted for several hours, and finally resulted in the rout of the latter.

The month closed with a serious demonstration against Washington, North Carolina, garrisoned by two thousand National troops, under General Foster. The rebels, under Hill and Pettigrew, sat down before it, with strong force, and commenced throwing up fortifications.

In these minor combats, the months of January, February and March passed away, and the people waited anxiously for the settled weather of Spring to inaugurate those great movements which, it was believed, would break the power of the rebellion. In the West, as we have seen, things were at this time evidently drawing to a crisis, and corresponding movements were weekly looked for along the Atlantic slope and seaboard.

The first heavy blow of the war was struck at Fort Sumter, on the 7th of April, by Admiral Du Pont, who, with a fleet of monitors and iron-clads, endeavored to break down this barrier, which had so long kept the avenging hand from Charleston, the hot-bed of rebellion. An invention for the explosion of torpedoes, to be placed in front of the vessels, had been towed down from New York, with which, it was supposed, the iron-clads would be able to push through the obstructions opposite the fort; and the highest expectations were cherished, of a speedy downfall of the stronghold. Nine iron-clads and monitors were to make the attack, while a wooden squadron of five vessels was to lie in reserve, outside of the bar. Du Pont was not so sanguine of success as the Secretary of the Navy was known to be. As, through his glass, he surveyed the work before him, he saw that his little fleet was to be put to a test to which vessels had never before been subjected.

When it was announced that the fleet was under way, the steeples and roofs in and around Charleston became lined with spectators assembled to witness the approaching conflict.

As the eye swept around the harbor, it was cannon here, and there, and everywhere. In front, Sullivan's Island lay on the right, and Morris Island on the left—the two extreme points curving in towards each other, till they were separated by a channel only a mile wide. Midway in this channel, built on an artificial island, stood Fort Sumter. Opposite it, on Sullivan's Island, stood Fort Moultrie, while above and below it the shore was lined with formidable batteries. On the other side of the channel, flanking it, frowned Battery Bee, on Cummings' Point, while further up towards Charleston—should the fleet succeed in passing all these obstacles—battery succeeded battery, all the way to the city. Stretching down towards the fleet, batteries lined Morris Island, and among them Fort Wagner. The sight was enough to daunt the stoutest heart, for full three hundred cannon lay shotted and trained on the channel, ready to open their concentrated fire on the little fleet the moment it came within range.

Du Pont's plan was to push rapidly past the batteries, and get to the west and north-west side of Sumter, which was known to be less impregnable than the front face. This, he was aware, would be a desperate task, for piles, torpedoes, nets, and all sorts of obstructions, had been sunk in the channel between Sumter and the shores, to hold any vessels that might attempt to pass, under the horrible fire that commanded the spot. But it was hoped that the invention of Ericsson, previously mentioned, would be able to remove these.

At noon, the signal from the flag-ship to move to the attack, was seen, and the little fleet of low, black-looking objects steamed slowly forward. It was four miles to Sumter, and the batteries on Morris Island commanded the whole distance. It had hardly got under way, when the Weehawken, in the advance, with the torpedo machine attached to her bows, became tangled with the unwieldy thing, and lost an hour in clearing herself, when the fleet again moved forward. The spectators lining the shore looked on in breathless expectation—the rapid roll of the drum in Fort Sumter was heard beating to quarters, and all knew that the decisive moment had come.

The fleet moved steadily up, till opposite Fort Wagner, where, it was expected, the wild hurricane that awaited it would commence, but not a gun broke the calm of the slumbering bay. It kept on till opposite Battery Bee, and still not a cannon spoke; an ominous silence reigned over everything. This mysterious, death-like stillness foreboded mischief—still, the fleet kept undauntedly on, till it was under the guns of Sumter. As the Weehawken was rounding, to pass beyond into Charleston harbor, the crater of fire opened, and from Sumter and Moultrie, shot and shell fell thick as hail-stones from heaven. The Weehawken never stopped, but steamed steadily on, till she was suddenly brought up by an enormous hawser stretching from Sumter to Moultrie—supported by casks, and strung with nets, cables and torpedoes. The propeller got entangled in these, became unmanageable, and drifted about in the fiery tempest—her iron sides echoing under the blows of the heavy metal, that fell incessantly upon her. The other vessels, as they come up, see the danger, and sheer off to avoid it. Wheeling in the fire, they steer to the other side of the fort, to try the channel there. But here a row of piles, rising ten feet out of the water, meets their gaze, beyond which stretch other obstructions as far as the eye can reach—and beyond them still, rebel iron-clads lie ready for action. To make matters still worse, the Ironsides suddenly refuses to obey her rudder, and drifts on the heavy tide towards Fort Moultrie, getting foul of the Catskill and Nantucket.

Du Pont now clearly sees that his plan of action cannot be carried out, and he signals to the rest of the fleet to disregard his movements, which is a permission for each vessel to act as it deems best. To get *beyond* Sumter is now clearly impossible, and nothing remains but to see whether the fleet can stay long enough in the vortex of that horrible fire, to knock the fort to pieces. Tons of metal are falling, with the weight of descending rocks, upon those iron-clads; yet each gallant commander is determined to lay his vessel alongside the dark structure, and make a broadside engagement with it. The Keokuk is in advance, followed by the Catskill, Montauk and, further back, by the other vessels, till she is within rifle shot of the nearest batteries, when the conflict becomes awful. The gunners, stripped to their waists, work their ponderous guns with cool determination; and shot weighing four hundred and twenty pounds, strike, like heaven's own thunderbolts, the massive walls, sending the stones in fragments through the air. The din and uproar are so deafening that orders have to be shouted into the ear, while the thick smoke involves the shuddering sea and trembling land in impenetrable folds.

But scarcely thirty minutes had passed, when the Keokuk came limping out of the fire, and fast settling in the water. The Ironsides is pierced with red-hot shot—the Nahant gapes with thirty wounds—the turret of the Passaic is knocked to pieces so that it cannot revolve—the Nantucket can use but one gun—a rifled shot has pierced the Catskill, and five of the nine monitors must be reckoned out of the fight. All that thirty-two guns—the total number carried by the fleet—could do against three hundred, had now been done, and to keep up the contest with but fifteen or sixteen, would be downright madness. Besides, no land force was near to take possession of the fort, if silenced, and night was coming on. Du Pont therefore signaled the fleet to retire, and the strange conflict ended. The Keokuk had hardly got out of the fire, when she went to the bottom. A council of war was called the next morning, and it was decided that it would be unwise to renew the attack.

The result awakened deep mortification, and many were determined not to acknowledge that the failure was inevitable. Though Du Pont did all that man could do, and though every subordinate officer bore himself like a hero, and fought his ship with unequaled gallantry, the public and the Navy Department were dissatisfied, and this noble Commander had to suffer for not doing impossibilities, was removed from his command, and Admiral Foote put in his place. The sickness, and finally, the death of the latter, prevented him from entering on his duties, and Du Pont, in the meanwhile, retained his position. Difficulties, however, arose between him and the Navy Department, and one of the best and most popular commanders in the navy was laid aside, and Dahlgren ultimately put in command of the iron-clad fleet. History, however, will grant the former that justice which at the time he was denied, and place the blame where it belongs.

In the meantime, a good deal of interest was felt in the fate of General Foster, who, during this month, was for some time surrounded, at Washington, North Carolina, and cut off from supplies. General Peck, also, stationed at Suffolk, had some engagements with the enemy, who were evidently manœuvering to get possession of the place.

CHAPTER XIV.

CHANCELLORSVILLE—EXCITEMENT OF THE COUNTRY AT HOOKER'S ADVANCE—HIS CONFIDENT ADDRESS TO HIS TROOPS—PLAN OF THE BATTLE—THE CAVALRY SENT OFF TO SEVER LEE'S COMMUNICATIONS—ATTACK BY "STONEWALL" JACKSON ON HOWARD'S CORPS—ITS DEFEAT—DEATH OF JACKSON—SUBSEQUENT BATTLE—FREDERICKSBURG HEIGHTS CARRIED BY SEDGWICK—ATTACKED BY LEE, AND COMPELLED TO RE-CROSS THE RIVER—HOOKER WITHDRAWS HIS ARMY—DISAPPOINTMENT OF THE COUNTRY—FEINT ON THE REBEL CAPITAL FROM WEST POINT—KILPATRICK'S RIDE TO THE SUBURBS OF RICHMOND—SIEGE OF SUFFOLK—GALLANT DEFENSE OF PECK—LEE'S INVASION OF MARYLAND—SURRENDER OF WINCHESTER—HOOKER SUPERSEDED BY MEADE—FEELING OF THE PEOPLE.

BUT the great interest centered in the Army of the Potomac, which, it was expected, would move the moment the roads would permit. Still smarting with the sense of disgrace, in the slaughter and defeat at Fredericksburg, the country was impatient of delay; and when, at the latter end of the month, the news flew over the wires, that Hooker was crossing the Rappahannock, the most intense excitement prevailed. Those who had faith in his generalship felt that the remembrance of Fredericksburg was to be wiped out, and that McClellan's, Pope's and Burnside's failures to annihilate Lee's army and capture Richmond, were to be effaced by a victory that would astonish the world, and deal a death-blow to the rebellion. Those, on the other hand, who had no faith in him as a match for Lee, were almost equally excited, believing that a catastrophe would happen. This confidence on the one hand, and fear on the other, were deepened by the following address which General Hooker made to his army after he had safely crossed the Rappahannock: "It is with heartfelt satisfaction that the operations of the last three days have determined that our enemy must ingloriously fly, or come out from behind their defenses, and give us battle on our own ground, where certain destruction awaits him." To one class, this was the inspiration and confidence of genius—to the other, who remembered that to the question put to him by the War Investigating Committee, as to what the ill success of the Army of the Potomac was owing when in front of Richmond, he replied, "To the incompetency of its leader," his words seemed a rash boast, prophetic only of defeat.

The two great armies of the Union, West and East, were at the same time entering on movements of vital importance to the Union cause. Grant, as it has been seen, having thrown his army across the Mississippi, on the 1st of May attacked the enemy at Port Gibson, and commenced that series of extraordinary victories which brought him in the rear of Vicksburg, and insured its downfall. Hooker's army having crossed the Rappahannock, on the 2nd—the next day after the battle of Port Gibson—he fought the battle of Chancellorsville, which he had believed would force the enemy into a disastrous retreat to Richmond, and secure the conquest of that place. But the results of the two movements were widely different. The thunder of Grant's cannon, rolling up the Mississippi, proclaimed victory—the echoes of Hooker's, breaking across the Rappahannock, announced defeat and disgrace.

BATTLE OF CHANCELLORSVILLE.

The main plan of Hooker seems intelligible enough. He endeavored to confuse the enemy as to the intended point of crossing, and then suddenly throw his army over the river several miles above Fredericksburg, and fix himself in a position to compel Lee to attack him, or hastily retreat towards Richmond in order to save his communications with the rebel Capital. To threaten the latter still more, he stripped his army of its cavalry, and sent it, under Stoneman, to cut the railroads in rear of Lee. In the meantime, Sedgwick, with some twenty thousand men, was, at the proper time, to cross in front of Fredericksburg and carry the intrenched heights, and then co-operate with Hooker, as he drove the enemy before him. A part of the programme was successfully carried out. Stoneman got in the rear of Lee, and swept triumphantly on towards Richmond, tearing up the railroad as he advanced. Hooker succeeded, also, in throwing his army safely over the Rappahannock, and took up the position he desired, and began to intrench himself. He now felt that the most difficult part of his work was accomplished, and said, exultingly, that Lee's army was the "legitimate property of the Army of the Potomac."

On Saturday, May 2nd, his head-quarters were at Chancellorsville, which consisted of a single house, standing at the intersection of the Gordonsville plank-road and Orange County turnpike. This was a central point to his magnificent army of more than a hundred thousand men, and was five miles from the ford which he had successfully crossed. A small field lies in front of the house, but beyond and on every side, stretches away a tangled wilderness. Two miles out, on the plank-road, lay Howard's Corps—the Eleventh, composed in part of German troops—holding the extreme right. To prevent a flank movement, it was made to front three ways. Sickles was next to him. Slocum was stationed near the house, and Meade beyond him, with the Fifth Corps. Beyond these, completing the line on the left, Couch, with the Second Corps, lay, to prevent a movement in this direction on the United States Ford.

Thus matters stood, on Saturday afternoon. Lee, perfectly aware of our position, sent "Stonewall" Jackson to execute a grand flank movement on Hooker's extreme right, where Howard was stationed. This indomitable chieftain worked and cut his way through the tangled forest, till he overlapped Howard, and then, just at evening, fell on him like a bolt from heaven, shivering his corps, with one fierce blow, into a thousand fragments. His fierce battalions, shouting as they came, drove the panic-stricken fugitives, like a herd of frightened buffaloes, back towards the center of the army, and seemed about to get in Hooker's rear, and make an end of him, without the dignity, even, of a great battle. The latter saw his danger, and at once showed his true qualities as a Commander. A more terrible man, at the head of his own division, never trod a battle-field, and as such he must now save himself. Sickles had gallantly tried, but in vain, to make a successful stand. Howard, than whom a braver man never drew sword, galloped furiously among his broken columns, waving his empty sleeve as a banner to his men, in vain—his noble heart breaking at the disaster he was powerless to avert. A wilder wreck never strewed the ocean than that tumultuous field exhibited in the gloom of that night. In this perilous crisis, Hooker called on his old division, now Berry's, to stop this refluent tide of battle. Moving firmly into the breach, it presented a solid front, behind which Sickles, and Howard a little later, rallied a part of their troops, and arrested the further progress of the enemy. Thirty pieces of artillery were massed in front of Berry's position, and sent their terrific loads of canister without a moment's cessation, into the crowded ranks of the enemy, that pressed on, reckless of death. The moon shone brightly down on field and wood, over which rolled the white and sulphurous war clouds, like drifts of ocean mist along the trembling shore. Out of the deep shadows of the woods, and up from the open spaces flooded with moonlight, arose the shouts of men, the swift crash of musketry, and the confused noise of foes struggling in mortal combat. But, at midnight, Jackson's victorious charge was stopped, and a lull fell on the trampled field. Hooker had placed himself where, he said, the enemy must come out and attack him. The latter had done so, and, with one tremendous blow, doubled his army up.

Hooker now changed his position, so as to make his lines more compact and solid, and better able to resist the headlong charges of the rebels. What the object of the latter was, in not pressing the battle further that night, is not plain, for an event occurred after it was over, which doubtless had an important bearing on the operations of the next morning. Jackson, whose brilliant and overwhelming charge had so paralyzed Hooker, after the conflict rode with his staff over the ground in front of the skirmishers, to make observations, and decide where he should plant his next blow, and in returning, was fired on by his own men, through mistake, and mortally wounded. This disaster was almost equivalent to a victory for us. This indomitable chieftain, at the head of his veterans, pressing up the advantage he had gained the night before, could hardly have failed to affect the fortunes of the day. He himself is reported to have said, that had he not been struck down, he would have cut off Hooker's retreat to his pontoons.

The next morning, Sunday, at five o'clock, the enemy again moved to the attack, determined to finish what they had successfully commenced. They came along the turnpike from the west, and were met by Berry's and Birney's divisions, moving forward from both sides of the road, supported by Whipple and Williams. The artillery of the latter was posted so as to command all the approaches by the turnpike. Forty pieces, under Best, swept the ground in front, and when the rebels, in solid mass, came through the woods, opened their fire with appalling fierceness. "The advancing column was cut up and gashed, as if pierced, seamed and ploughed by invincible lightning. Companies and regiments melted away, yet still they came on. Berry and Birney advanced to meet them. They were terrible shocks. The living waves rolled against each other, as you have seen the billows on a stormy sea." Nothing, however, could resist the tremendous charges of the rebels, and Sickles' Corps was gradually forced back. They could not break our steadfast lines, but still, compelled them to yield the ground. For nearly six hours, the battle raged with fearful ferocity, and then the rebels withdrew. In the afternoon, they again advanced to the attack, but pressed it less vigorously, as if weakened by their own tremendous exertions.

On this same Sabbath day, Sedgwick had carried the heights of Fredericksburg—the "light brigade" winning immortal honor in the last brilliant assault—and prepared at once to co-operate with Hooker. Had the latter been able to carry out his part of the plan and advance, after the enemy had exhausted himself in a fruitless attack on his own defenses, doubtless a great victory would have been gained. But he had been beaten, though not routed, in his own chosen position—behind his defenses—and driven back. Under these circumstances, an advance was out of the question, and he began to look about anxiously, to see, not how he might beat the enemy, but save his army. Heavy rains had set in, and the river in his rear began to rise, and though Stoneman, with his fearless troopers, was in Lee's rear, and Sedgwick's gallant battalions were shouting on the heights of Fredericksburg, it all availed nothing. Humbled and mortified, he must swallow his boastings, and march back over the river, a defeated man. With an army variously estimated at one hundred and twenty and one hundred and fifty thousand men, he had been beaten by sixty thousand.

Seeing Hooker so badly punished, Lee sent an overwhelming force against Sedgwick, who, leaving a part of his force to hold the works of Fredericksburg, was with the main army advancing along the plank-road towards Chancellorsville, to co-operate with Hooker. After a severe fight, he compelled him to retreat across the river under the fire of his artillery, which threatened momentarily to break in pieces the frail bridge, that swayed and trembled under the weight of his swiftly marching columns. It was almost a miracle that this brave officer succeeded in saving his entire corps from utter destruction. The force left on the heights were also driven out of the works and over the Rappahannock, and the position, captured so gallantly, recovered by the rebels.

On Tuesday night, Hooker also recrossed the Rappahannock, without loss. Had Lee known of his movements, it could not have been done without serious disaster.

No battle of the war caused such fierce and angry discussion as this. Some asserted that Hooker retreated only because the sudden rise in the river threatened to carry away his pontoons, and cut off his communications. But if General Hooker made the important move he did, in the Spring of the year, without taking into account the probable rise of the Rappahannock, he committed a great blunder—in fact, an unpardonable one. No event was more likely to occur than this, at that season, and a movement made without anticipating it was a most unmilitary one.

Much was said of the skill and secrecy with which Hooker had thrown his army across the river at the point chosen—thus outwitting Lee; but it afterwards leaked out, through some private papers captured, that during the Winter previous, this very spot had been selected by the rebel Generals as the one where he would cross; and Chancellorsville, or its neighborhood, designated as the field where the next great battle would be fought. The truth is, Hooker escaped with less loss than he had a right to expect. If Jackson had not fallen, it is scarcely possible that the former would have been able to recross the river without discovery and attack. On the other hand, Sedgwick saved his corps by extraordinary skill. After their brilliant success, the rebels seemed to show a great lack of generalship or enterprise.

In conjunction with Hooker's endeavor to crush Lee's army, on the Rappahannock, a feint movement was made against Richmond, by way of West Point, under General Keyes, which many thought should have been a *real* one, as Richmond was so stripped of defenders, that its capture was considered an easy matter.

Colonel Kilpatrick, under Stoneman's command, had dashed down in rear of Lee's army, destroying depots, railroads and telegraph wires in his way—scattered the detachments that obstructed his path—galloped to the very suburbs of the rebel Capital, spreading terror and confusion wherever he went, and at length, on the 7th of May, he rode into our lines at Gloucester Point. He had been five days in the saddle, and, through rain and mud, marched two hundred miles—losing, in all, but one officer and thirty-seven men. In this bold march into the interior, Stoneman had destroyed bridges, culverts, ferries, wagons and trains, and captured horses and mules, with but little loss to himself; and the most that could be, was made of it, to compensate for the mortification of Hooker's defeat; but, aside from the boldness, and skill, and energy, with which it was conducted, there was little to console the people. It was a whirlwind sweeping through the country, terrible in appearance, yet producing no lasting or very serious results, for the defeat at Chancellorsville rendered the temporary destruction of Lee's communications of no value.

Another event occurred at this time, which excited but little attention, on account of the more stirring scenes passing on the Rappahannock. This was the raising the siege of Suffolk, by Longstreet. General Peck had been sent to command at this place, the September before, with an army of about thirteen thousand men, and for six months labored unweariedly to put it in a state of defense. It lies at the head of the Nansemond River, thirty miles above where it empties into the James River. A railroad, twenty miles long, connected it with Norfolk, from which Peck received his supplies. In April, Longstreet, with a force estimated at thirty or forty thousand men, advanced against Suffolk, designing to cut the railroad in rear of it, capture the army there, and march on Norfolk. In order to weaken the garrison, he sent a force to operate against Little Washington, which caused, as he anticipated, an order to be sent to Peck for reinforcements. He then crossed the Blackwater, and, in three heavy columns, moved confidently forward on Suffolk. Peck, advised of this movement, telegraphed to Admiral Lee, who sent up gunboats to operate in the Nansemond, and assist him in preventing this overwhelming force from crossing the stream. Longstreet, finding Peck prepared, at every point, to receive him, abandoned the attempt to take the place by surprise, and sat down before it in regular seige. Planting batteries along the stream, he first endeavored to drive the gunboats away or sink them. A fierce artillery fight followed, in which the gunboats were riddled with shot. Lieutenants Cushing and Lamson, who commanded the river fleet, clung to the enemy's batteries with a tenacity which nothing could shake loose. General Getty, commanding the third division of the Ninth Army Corps, held the line of the Nansemond, nine miles in length, and by his sleepless vigilance and skill, kept Longstreet's army from effecting a crossing. But, on the 18th of April, the enemy succeeded in establishing a battery at Hill's Point, six miles from Suffolk, which threatened to drive the gunboats off. But this strong earth-work was surprised and captured by a brilliant night attack, made by two hundred and eighty men of the Eighty-ninth New York and Eighth Connecticut volunteers. The garrison of one hundred and thirty-seven men, and five guns, were captured in this gallant assault. Longstreet now began to strengthen his defenses. Peck, with his small force, was compelled to overtask his men, yet he held his powerful foe grimly at bay, till the 3rd of May, when the events at Chancellorsville caused Longstreet to raise his siege of twenty-four days. The skill and courage of General Peck, in thus defeating the plans of Longstreet, called forth the highest encomiums of General Dix, who afterwards asked the Government to make a separate department of this section, and place Peck over it.

Longstreet was summoned, with his defeated army, to Fredericksburg, for Lee, now he had measured strength with Hooker, and tested satisfactorily his capacity, treated him with the same contempt he showed to Pope, and resolved to march some hundred and fifty miles around him, by the Shenandoah Valley, to the Potomac, and, crossing over into Maryland, complete the invasion which the year before had been brought to such a disastrous termination by the battle of Antietam. It was a bold move, but he seemed to think that he could give his antagonist thirty thousand men more than his own army, and yet beat him on any fair field.

The country was made to believe, that though Hooker was defeated, he had inflicted such a heavy blow on the enemy as to cripple him severely, and render him incapable of any serious movement for a long time to come. But the rumors that he was swinging his superb army around Washington, towards Harper's Ferry, effectually dispelled this illusion. His movements seemed wrapped in mystery, and the country was amazed that no blow was struck against his extended line. Lee actually moved clear around our army, as coolly and leisurely as though no enemy confronted him. By the last of the month, the people of Maryland were alarmed at the tidings that his advance troops were in the neighborhood of the Upper Potomac. On the 16th of June, Governor Bradford issued a proclamation, calling on the citizens to rally for their defense.

The first blow fell on General Milroy, at Winchester. He had been in command at this place since the last of December, the previous year, and had under him about seven thousand men, which was considered an ample force to hold the position against all the rebels known to be in the Valley. But, on the 11th of June, he received a telegram from Colonel Don Piatt, Chief of Staff, at Harper's Ferry, ordering him to fall back at once on the latter place. Milroy, instead of obeying, telegraphed to General Schenck, at Baltimore, his immediate Commander, expressing his regret at the order, and declaring that he could hold the post against all the force the "rebels could afford to bring against it." He received permission, in reply, to remain till further orders. But he soon ascertained, from his scouts, that Ewell and Longstreet, with an overwhelming force, were advancing swiftly against him, and he immediately called in all his outposts. Instead, however, of retreating, he still waited for further developments. On Sunday morning, four batteries suddenly opened on him, and ten thousand men precipitated themselves on the outwork commanding the approaches from the west, and swept it like a storm. But by the guns from the fort proper and the Baltimore battery, commanding this work, the enemy were soon driven out. An artillery fight then commenced, which lasted till eight o'clock in the evening. Milroy now called a council of war, in which it was decided to abandon the artillery and wagons, and fall back on Harper's Ferry. The troops marched out at one o'clock in the morning, and, proceeding by a ravine around the town, struck the Martinsburg road, and pressed swiftly forward. The column, however, soon found its way blocked by the enemy, who had got in front. In attempting to cut its way through, the army became divided, and hurried forward by different routes towards the Potomac. Milroy, with one column, took the road to Harper's Ferry, and arrived there safely the same afternoon. The other column, completely disorganized, crossed at Hancock, and finally assembled at Bloody Run, Pennsylvania, twenty-seven hundred strong. At first, it was supposed that Milroy had lost a third of his army, but, in the end, only a few hundred were found to be missing. The loss in artillery and trains, however, was felt to be a great disgrace, and Milroy was put under arrest, by order of Halleck. That he committed a great error, in not obeying at once the first order he received, is very clear. But Schenck, who gave him permission to remain till further orders, was still more culpable. His excuse was, that the original order, which he received from Halleck, contained no such peremptory command as Don Piatt had dispatched. This is true, and the guilt of this disgraceful surrender must be divided between the General-in-Chief, Milroy and Schenck. The only clear, prompt military mind engaged in the whole transaction, was Don Piatt.

Lee at once crossed the Potomac, occupied Hagerstown, and pushed on to Pennsylvania, causing the most intense excitement at Harrisburg, Philadelphia, Baltimore, Washington, and throughout the country. The President called on the several States for their militia, and New York had the honor of sending forward the first troops. Hooker followed Lee on his right flank, and, on the 27th of June, occupied Frederick City. Cavalry fights had occurred all along, at Beverly's Ford, Brandy Station, Berryville and Aldie, some of them very severe ones, but they had no effect on Lee's movements. He had occupied all the gaps of the Blue Ridge, through which he watched the movements of Hooker, ready at any moment to give him battle.

At Frederick, on the 28th, Hooker, by order of the War Department, relinquished the command of the army, and Major-General George G. Meade was put in his place. The announcement of this change, on the eve of a great and decisive battle, took the country by surprise, and awakened the deepest anxiety in every breast. Meade was but little known; besides, the time chosen to make this important change, was deemed ill-judged. More than this, it was currently reported that it was caused by a quarrel between Hooker, and Halleck the General-in-Chief. This disquieted the public mind, also, for everything seemed to go wrong with the noble army of the Potomac, whoever commanded it. Hence, when, soon after Meade had commenced his march, it was reported that he had cut telegraphic communication between himself and Washington, that he might not be interfered with, the whole country applauded the act. This fact is a bitter commentary on the management at Washington at that time, and shows how low in the estimation of the people, the military capacity of the Secretary of War and the General-in-Chief was held.

CHAPTER XV.

JULY.

CAMPAIGN OF GETTYSBURG—PURSUIT OF LEE—FIRST FIGHT AT GETTYSBURG—DEATH OF REYNOLDS—HOWARD ESTABLISHES HIMSELF ON CEMETERY HILL—HANCOCK SENT FORWARD TO SELECT A BATTLE-FIELD—THE SELECTION OF CEMETERY HILL—RAPID CONCENTRATION OF THE ARMY—THE PREPARATION—FIRST DAY'S BATTLE—GLOOMY PROSPECT FOR THE UNION ARMY—SECOND DAY'S BATTLE—THE GREAT, DECISIVE CHARGE—GALLANTRY OF FARNSWORTH—RETREAT OF LEE—BOTH ARMIES MARCH FOR THE POTOMAC—SUCCESS OF KILPATRICK—SERVICE OF THE CAVALRY—THE POTOMAC SWELLED BY THE RAINS—LEE HELD A WEEK ON THE NORTHERN BANK—STRANGE INACTION—THE REBEL ARMY ESCAPES—THE PURSUIT—CLOSE OF THE CAMPAIGN.

WHEN Meade took command of the army, Lee was well advanced into the interior, and he immediately followed after him. The latter was very anxious respecting his communications, and sent Ewell eastward from Chambersburg, to cross the South Mountain. Early's division moved east as far as York, on the inhabitants of which he levied a large sum of money, while the rest of the corps kept on to Carlisle. Lee now determined to move upon Harrisburg, but on the night of the 29th, hearing that Meade was well across the Potomac, and had advanced as far as the South Mountain, threatening his communications, he determined to concentrate his army east of the mountains, and Longstreet and Hill were directed to march from Chambersburg to Gettysburg, to which point, also, Ewell was ordered to hasten from Carlisle. The reports of these movements having reached Meade, he ordered Reynolds, with the First, Eleventh and Third Corps, to move forward and occupy the place. On the arrival of the latter, he found Buford's cavalry fighting fiercely with Hill, who was pouring his columns through the mountains, on the Cashtown road. Moving promptly around the town, he deployed his advance division, and marched steadily and sternly on the enemy, and at the same time sent back a courier to Howard, with the Eleventh Corps, to hurry forward. The conflict had hardly commenced, when Reynolds fell, mortally wounded, and the command of the First Corps devolved on Doubleday. In the meantime, at half-past eleven, Howard arrived on the field, and took chief command. The enemy were now pushed vigorously, and Doubleday handsomely entrapped and took prisoners an entire rebel brigade. The Eleventh Corps gallantly redeemed its fair fame lost at Chancellorsville, and Hill was getting severely punished, when, at two o'clock, the banners of Ewell's Corps were seen advancing to the field, along the York road, outflanking Howard's line of battle. The latter had, as he advanced to the attack, left Steinwehr's division, with its artillery, on Cemetery Ridge, in rear of the town, and when he found it necessary to fall back, with great forethought he sent to the same commanding position some more guns, and thus, almost by chance, and to protect himself from defeat, fixed the grand central point of the mighty battle that was to decide the campaign.

When the tidings of Reynolds' fall reached Meade, he immediately dispatched Hancock to represent him on the field, saying, as he departed, "If you find a good place to fight there, let me know." The latter arrived on the ground only to find the army in confused retreat, and Howard rallying his forces behind Cemetery Hill. The enemy poured tumultuously through Gettysburg in fierce pursuit, and captured some twenty-five hundred of our troops. But as they approached the ridge, they were met by a fierce artillery fire, and, after struggling a while to make head against it, fell back, and, night coming on, the conflict ended. Stuart, with his cavalry, which had been following Hooker in Virginia, when the latter crossed the Potomac, crossed further down, so that he was at this time between Meade, and Washington and Baltimore. His presence in this region created the wildest consternation, and the streets of the former place were barricaded, and the citizens summoned to defend the place. This isolated position of his, however, was of incalculable advantage to us, for had he been present with Ewell's corps on this day, the battle of Gettysburg, in all human probability, would never have been fought.

When Hancock reported the state of affairs to Meade, and the position which Howard had selected, he immediately resolved to give battle at that point, and, having dispatched swift riders to the different corps, with orders for them to march with the utmost speed to Gettysburg, he himself set out, and reached the place a little after midnight. Lee, all this eventful night, was also concentrating his army, but, being ignorant of Meade's movements, he advanced cautiously, and all too slowly for himself. One west, and the other east of the Cumberland Mountains which separated them, the mighty columns of the two armies pressed forward, all that warm July night, towards the great battle-field of the morrow. But how unequal were the prospects! Lee was hurrying on to find a place on which to fight; while Meade, not by his own foresight, but by the foresight of Providence, had selected his, which seemed by that same Providence made on purpose for the rebel host to break itself to pieces against. The defeat and retreat of the day had forced this position on us, which, if held by the rebels instead of us, would in all probability have reversed the fortunes of that great and vital campaign.

THE BATTLE OF GETTYSBURG.

The morning of the 2nd of July, lit up a strange and thrilling scene around that hitherto quiet inland town, the inhabitants of which, a few hours before, little thought that one of the mightiest battles of the war, and of the age, would be fought there. No teams of the farmer were moving that day. The swath in the harvest-field lay where it had fallen the evening before. The streets and the door-yards were filled with pale and anxious men and women, and all was expectation—save that the unconscious herds grazed quietly in the fields, and the summer birds sang merrily as ever among the green tree-tops. But these things were unheeded amid the mighty preparations on either side. The steady tramp, tramp, of the arriving columns, with streaming banners, and loud, defiant music—the heavy rumbling of artillery carriages, as they swept in long and ominous rows on the field—the pealing of bugles, the galloping of horsemen hither and thither, and all the fearful preparations necessary when two hundred thousand men are about to close in fierce and mortal combat, absorbed all minor interests, and made that July morning appear to those inhabitants solemn as the closing day of time.

As soon as daylight had revealed the landscape distinctly, Meade was in the saddle, and rode all over his position, to take in its capabilities, and arrange the location of his troops. His eye rested on the rebel army, marshaling in the distance, and ever and anon turned anxiously along the roads over which his own brave troops were coming. They were pressing forward at the top of their speed, brigade on brigade and division on division, till, by seven o'clock, the Second and Fifth Corps, and the balance of the Third, had reached the field, and at once marched to their appointed places. Far back, many a weary mile, panting over the dusty roads, was the gallant Sixth, with the noble Sedgwick at its head, straining every nerve to reach the point of danger. It had started at nine o'clock in the evening, and all night long swept forward as though on a race for life. Thirty-two miles lay between it and Gettysburg, to which the urgent order of Meade was hurrying it. It accomplished the whole distance by two o'clock in the afternoon.

Our line of battle, when completed, extended for nearly five miles along a row of heights which receded to the right and left from Cemetery Hill, that stood boldly out in front, overlooking Gettysburg, and field and woodland beyond. The line was in shape something like a horse-shoe. The right was strongly protected by Wolf's and Culp's hills, very steep and difficult of ascent, while Howard, with the Eleventh Corps, held the center. At his right, across the road, on another hill, was the First Corps. Next to him, completing the right, was the Twelfth Corps, under Slocum. On the left of Cemetery Hill, was Hancock's Second Corps; next to him, the Third Corps, under Sickles—forming the left, until the arrival, in the midst of the battle, of the Fifth Corps, under Sykes. Thus stood the Union army on Thursday afternoon.

In Lee's army, Ewell occupied the left, Hill the center, and Longstreet the right. He had not designed to give battle unless attacked, when he could choose his own position, but finding himself suddenly confronted by Meade, and doubtless encouraged by the previous day's success, he determined to try the issue in a bold assault on our strong position. His army was concentrated first, and had he moved earlier to the assault, before the arrival of the Fifth and Sixth Corps, he might, perhaps, have carried our position. But the "stars fought against him."

Thinking that if he could drive back our left, he could more easily assail the higher position of Cemetery Hill, he directed Longstreet, towards evening, to advance against it, while Hill threatened the center. Sickles, ignorant of the intention of the enemy, advanced his line a half a mile or more, when Meade rode up to post the Fifth Corps, which was rapidly approaching the field. Not liking the movement of Sickles, he began to explain to him the reasons, when the thunderbolt fell. The onset of Longstreet was tremendous. First came the crash of artillery, swelling and rolling along the whole line; and then, with firm and confident bearing, and deafening shouts, moved up the trained and steady battalions. Sickles, fighting bravely, was soon struck, and carried off the field; and the whole left wing was terribly shaken, and gradually fell back before the desperate charges of the enemy. Its fate was trembling in the balance, when the heads of Sykes' tired columns were seen approaching the field. At the welcome sight, a thrilling cheer went up. They came not a moment too soon, and the fight raged fiercer than ever. But heedless of the murderous discharges of artillery that swept their ranks, the enemy still pressed the left so desperately that it was pushed steadily back, and Meade had to order up the wearied Corps of Sedgwick, and part of the First Corps, to save himself from defeat. Met with these fresh forces, the rebels were arrested, and though refusing to abandon the struggle, could not break our line of battle. Hour after hour, the contest raged with fearful slaughter on both sides, till darkness closed over the field. The battle, however, was not over; for, later in the evening, a sudden, unexpected assault was made on our extreme right, and several rifle-pits were carried, which the enemy succeeded in holding.

That night, the prospect was gloomy enough. We had been pushed back on both wings, though all our reserves had been brought into action. The dead were piled everywhere—the army was weary, and had not been able to hold its own. What would the next day bring forth? was the anxious question of many a brave heart. Meade, however, resolved not to retreat, but to fight it out right there, at all hazards. No better position than that could be found, and if it should be yielded, a swift and disastrous retreat would be inevitable. True, he had been fearfully weakened; so had the enemy—his army was worn out with its long marches; so was the enemy's—and here he would stand, and let God help the right.

THE BATTLE OF FRIDAY.

Early next morning, the troops stood to their arms, while crashing volleys, all along the line, foretold another day of struggle and of slaughter. On our right, the battle raged furiously from early dawn. Ewell was determined to advance from the rifle-pits he had taken the night before, and Slocum was equally resolute to recover them. Geary and Birney here met the first assaults firmly. For six hours, the struggle was desperate on both sides. The rebels seemed to laugh at death, and again and again charged through the smoke of artillery, with shouts that swelled above the uproar. Wheaton's brigade, of the Sixth, was hurried up to the rescue; and our line, which had been forced back for a moment, again advanced. More troops were pushed forward—artillery brought up on a gallop, and posted so as to enfilade the hostile ranks; and though braver men never stood upon a battle-field to die, than did Ewell's veterans here, our right had become a wall of adamant, against which the heaviest surges broke in vain. At eleven o'clock, the enemy gave it up, and his shattered, bleeding battalions fell back in despair. Silence now rested on the field, and Lee, baffled in his first design, pondered what next to attempt. He had tried both wings, and failed to break them, and on the right had lost all he had gained the night before; while a line of earth-works had sprung up, as if by magic, all along our front. The weakest point still seemed to be the left, and he determined on a last desperate effort to crush it. For this purpose, he brought forward a hundred and twenty-seven cannon, and concentrated their terrific fire on our center and left. At two o'clock, they opened simultaneously, and there commenced one of the most awful cannonades ever witnessed on this continent. On Cemetery Hill, the storm fell with such fury that the earth was scattered in showers over the graves, and the tomb-stones shivered to atoms. Shot and shell fell and burst without a moment's cessation, and with a power that seemed able to start the very hills from their firm foundations. Our batteries responded, and, for three hours, more than three hundred cannon exploded on each other, with reverberations that shook the field, and wrapped it in white, rolling clouds, which tossed, and drifted, and settled between the contending lines, till they were hid from view, and the heavens were darkened as in an eclipse.

About four o'clock, Lee ordered a grand charge. In splendid order, and "with banners high advanced," and a courage that seemed to foretell success, the columns came steadily on. The chief attack was on the point occupied by the Second Corps. Moving forward with grand, imposing front and confident bearing, they entered the desolating fire, without flinching. It was a magnificent charge. A tempest of shot and shell, howling above their heads from the artillery in rear, swept the heights; and Hancock was soon borne wounded from the fight. Gibson succeeded to the command, and, walking along the lines, told the men to reserve their fire. On came the rebels, three lines deep, in perfect order, till within point-blank range, when the order to fire was heard. A sudden sheet of flame, a crash, and the first line disappeared like a wreath of mist. Undismayed, the second line swept on with a cheer. Up to the rifle-pits, and over them, and up to the guns, bayoneting the gunners beside their pieces, they pressed, waving their flags and shouting the victory. But the moment of their triumph was also the moment of their destruction. They had not seen that the guns on the western slope of Cemetery Hill enfiladed this spot. These now opened with grape and canister, on the uncovered ranks. The effect was awful. Nothing human could stand such a murderous fire, and the line swayed back in terror, and then crumbled into fragments. In an instant, our men were upon them, driving them like a herd of sheep. Whole regiments laid down their arms and surrendered. They seemed appalled—overwhelmed, by the frightful butchery, from which even flight could not save them. Other charges had been made, along the line, and gallantly repulsed; and our cavalry, though not performing any grand movement, came in for its share of the glory. Kilpatrick, having beaten Stuart at Hanover, and repulsed the rebel cavalry at Hunterstown, pressed forward to Gettysburg—which he reached Friday forenoon—and made a sudden dash on Lee's right. The enemy, finding his skirmishers driven in, took a strong position between two stone walls, surmounted by a rail fence. Kilpatrick was anxious to carry this position, for if he could, he would be able to reach Lee's ammunition train. General Farnsworth, with two regiments and a portion of a third, charged it with desperate fury. Leaping his horse over the first fence, sword in hand, he was followed by his gallant band. The space between the fences was covered by a fire from both flanks and the front, yet they dashed through it with a shout, and reached the second fence, where Farnsworth fell, pierced with five balls. Still on, over the second fence, the maddened riders went, "in a whirlpool of shot and shell," and pressed on through a horrible fire. They could not return, and so dashed on—what was left of them—for two miles, to the rebel rear, when they dispersed, and got back as they could.

But, the grand effort of the day having failed, the enemy slowly retired. No pursuit was attempted. Meade had no reserves, with which to follow up his advantage, and scarcely any ammunition. We were near defeat. Could Lee have commanded a few thousand fresh troops, even then, he might have won the day. But we had stood the pounding longest, and now a fresh corps on our part, could have driven him in disorder and rout from the field. As it was, both armies had done all they could. Lee had attacked, and failed; and now, with one-third of his forces killed, wounded or taken prisoners, his campaign was over, and nothing remained for him but to get back to Virginia with his shattered army.

On this very afternoon, what a different scene was taking place on the banks of the Mississippi! At the same hour in which the heights around Gettysburg were rocking to the thunder of cannon, and their slopes were reddening with the blood of brave men, Grant and Pemberton were quietly seated under a spreading oak, settling the terms of the capitulation of Vicksburg. While one army was being surrendered into our hands, another was retiring, beaten and humbled, from before our brave troops.

It had been a battle of the Giants—Antietam over again; and our loss amounted, in all, to twenty-three thousand and one hundred and eighty-six men. The field presented a sad wreck, and the slopes around Gettysburg were thickly covered with the dead—men of the same country and creed, and who should never have been foes.

The news of this great victory flew over the wires on the 4th, our National Jubilee-day, spreading joy and exultation, and swelling to a higher note the shouts of the people. To

BATTLE OF GETTYSBURG—FINAL CHARGE OF THE UNION FORCES AT CEMETERY HILL.

the army, however, it did not bring equal exultation, for it was not known whether another battle was yet to be fought. Lee still confronted our lines, but no general movements took place. But he had resolved on retreat, and by next morning his columns were retracing their steps, over the Cumberland Mountains, on their way back to the Potomac, leaving thirteen thousand, six hundred and twenty-one prisoners in our hands—so that if his loss in killed and wounded was no greater than ours, his total loss would have been over thirty thousand. But as the attacking party, unless successful, always suffers the most, a large number must be added to this, showing that Lee had good cause for retreating, without assigning, as he did, the lack of ammunition, and the strength of our position, as the reasons.

He saved his artillery, with the exception of two or three guns, though he left twenty-five thousand small arms strewn through the fields and woods. With his splendid army thus shivered into fragments, he recrossed the Cumberland Mountains, and pressed rapidly towards the Potomac. Sedgwick, with the Sixth Corps, was sent in pursuit, but on reaching Fairfield Pass, he found it so strongly held that he was compelled to abandon it, and then pressed towards the Potomac on the east side of the Cumberland Mountains, to intercept Lee's march. The cavalry, moving by different routes, harassed him continually, capturing trains and prisoners, and keeping the tired troops continually on the alert. A portion of the force, under General French, destroyed the enemy's pontoon train, at Falling Waters. Kilpatrick clung to the rebel army with a tenacity that did not allow it a moment's rest. At midnight, in a furious thunder storm, he charged down the mountain, through the darkness, with unparalleled boldness, and captured the entire train of Ewell's division, eight miles long. At Emmettsburg, Hagerstown, and other places, he smote the enemy with blow after blow. Buford, Gregg, Custis, and others, performed deeds which, but for the greater movements that occupied public attention, would have filled the land with shouts of admiration. In fact, the incessant, protracted labors of the cavalry, during this campaign, rendered it useless for some time. That it was so effective, was due to Hooker, who took great pains in its organization, when he assumed command of the Army of the Potomac.

Before Lee reached the Potomac, a heavy rain storm set in swelling the river so that all the fords were impassable. This seemed a special interposition of Providence, and the country looked to see Lee's army utterly destroyed or captured, before he could get across.

Meade, having spent the 5th and 6th in burying his dead and caring for the wounded, followed the enemy, by a flank movement, to Middletown, Md., and thence passed through South Mountain, and, on the 12th, was in front of Lee, drawn up on the heights of Marsh Run, near Williamsport. A whole week had thus been allowed to pass away, while Lee looked with anxious gaze on the turbulent waters of the Potomac, whose loud, monotonous roar seemed to scoff at his helpless condition. No sooner did the flood begin to subside, than another storm would set in, sending the water in torrents down the slopes of the Blue Ridge and the Alleghanies, and keeping the stream full to the top of its banks. It was a tantalizing condition for Lee, and seemed ominous of evil, for such a sustained freshet in July was a thing unheard of. It seemed sent on purpose to destroy him—just as the early and severe Winter, in Russia, came to overthrow the grand army of Napoleon. The whole country was kept in a state of the highest excitement, for a majority of the people believed that the escape of Lee, the year before, near the same place, after the battle of Antietam, was owing to the negligence or incapacity of McClellan.

Though Lee then got off, the first night after the battle, and under cover of the darkness, his escape seemed unpardonable. Hence, it was believed that if Meade should do his duty—swelled as his army was by reinforcements, and with ample time before him—Lee could not escape. But the latter was unmolested, and, gathering timber from the neighboring country, he constructed a bridge, and, the water at length falling, he transferred his entire army, trains, and munitions of war, safely into Virginia. The cavalry took some prisoners at Falling Waters, and Gregg's cavalry attacked and harassed the enemy at Charlestown and Shepherdstown; yet the latter escaped comparatively scathless—to the chagrin, disappointment, and ill-suppressed murmurings of the people.

Meade crossed the Potomac, and moved down the Loudon Valley on Lee's flank, hoping to cross his line of march somewhere; but the latter leisurely pursued his way to the Rapidan; and the Army of the Potomac, at the close of July, took up its position on the banks of the Rappahannock, and the campaign was over. It had been a grand success by our arms, marred only by the strange delays and inaction that allowed Lee to rest a week on the northern bank of the Potomac, and then get off without a blow being dealt him.

It would not be just to pass by this great battle without alluding to the efforts of the Sanitary Commission to relieve and care for the wounded. Never before was such a prodigality of expenditure in the way of charity, witnessed on a battle-field. Its agents, trains and supplies were everywhere. Clothing, medicines, food and luxuries were in profusion. Hospitals sprung up like magic on all sides, till it had nearly fifteen thousand wounded under its kind and generous protection. Its blessed charities, distributed alike to friend and foe, shed a benign radiance over the scene of slaughter, and rescued it from half its horrors.

CHAPTER XVI.

OPERATIONS IN CHARLESTON HARBOR—GILLMORE EFFECTS A LODGMENT ON MORRIS ISLAND—ATTEMPT TO TAKE FORT WAGNER BY SURPRISE—GRAND ASSAULT ON THE FORT—DEATH OF COLONEL SHAW—CRUELTY TO THE OFFICERS OF COLORED REGIMENTS—MOBS IN NEW YORK CITY—HOSTILITY TO THE DRAFT—ORDER OF THE PRESIDENT, RESPECTING THE TREATMENT OF COLORED SOLDIERS HELD AS PRISONERS BY THE REBELS—THE PRACTICAL SUPERIORITY OF THE PRESIDENT—CAUSES OF PUBLIC AGITATION—CONGRESS.

WHILE events of such magnitude were occurring on the banks of the Potomac, General Gillmore, who had superseded Hunter in command at Charleston, surprised, on the 10th of July, the rebels in the fortifications on the south end of Morris Island, in Charleston Harbor, and captured two hundred prisoners, eight single-gun batteries, and three mortars. General Strong, the next day, in command of the attacking party, advanced on Fort Wagner, and attempted to carry it by assault, but failed. It was a spirited affair, and is thus described by Captain Gray, the only one, of four captains, that was saved: "General Strong, with two thousand men, went up Folly River, in the Light-house Inlet, while over forty guns and mortars, in battery, which had been put in position on Folly Island, concealed by trees from the enemy's knowledge, were ready to open their unexpected fire at the right moment. The gunboats were to engage the rebel batteries on the opposite side of the island. The boats containing the troops arrived in good time, preceded by eight boat-howitzers from the gunboats. The first boat contained General Strong and Staff, and then came the battalion of the Seventh Connecticut volunteers.

"General Gillmore told Colonel Rodman that the General concluded that our battalion was the most reliable, and could be trusted, and was selected for that reason. The batteries opened at daylight, and in a short time the enemy discovered the boats, and threw shell and solid shot, trying to sink them. The shot and shell struck and burst all around us, but only one boat was struck, containing some of the Sixth Connecticut volunteers, killing one and wounding two or three." But the batteries of Gillmore are unmasked, and pour such a terrible fire on the astonished garrison, that they fly from their guns. "The General's boat had got two discharges of grape. Just at this moment, Lieutenant-Colonel Rodman said to the General, 'Let me land my command, and take that battery.' The General hesitated at first, and then said, 'Go.' Colonel Rodman stood up in the stern of his boat, and gave the command, 'Seventh Connecticut, man your oars and follow me!' At the order, we all headed for the shore, and as the boats struck, every man sprang, as if by instinct, and in an instant the men were in line. We advanced rapidly to the first line of rifle-works; our skirmishers cleared it with a bound, and advanced to the second line. Our main forces moved to the first line—the foe retired, firing." * * * "We bivouacked for the night under easy range of Fort Wagner. At about half-past two in the morning, General Strong came and called the Lieutenant-Colonel out. He soon returned, and said, 'Turn out; we have got a job on hand.' The men were soon out, and into line, but rather slow to time, as they were tired with the work of the day before.

"The programme was, to try to take Fort Wagner by assault. We were to take the lead, and to be supported by the Seventy-sixth Pennsylvania and Ninth Maine. Silently we moved up to the advance line of our pickets, our guns loaded and aimed, and bayonets fixed. We were then deployed into line of battle, (we had one hundred and ninety officers and men, all told,) reached and crossed the neck of land that approached the fort—our right resting on the beach. Our orders were, to move steadily forward until the pickets fired; then follow them close, and rush for the works; and we were promised ready support. General Strong gave the order, 'Aim low, and put your trust in God. Forward, the Seventh!' And forward we went—being not over five hundred yards from the fort when we started. We had not gone far, before the picket fired; and then we took the double-quick, and with a cheer rushed for the works. Before we reached the outer works, we got a murderous fire from the riflemen behind the works. A few fell—a check in the line. An encouraging word from the officers, and right gallantly we reached the outer works; over them, with a will, we went, down the opposite side—across the moat—there being about one foot of water in it—right up to the crest of the parapet; and there we lay, anxiously waiting for our support to come up so far as to make it a sure thing for us to rise up and go over with a bound—our men, in the meantime, busying themselves by picking off the sharp-shooters and gunners.

"As near as I can ascertain, we were in this position from ten to twenty minutes, when both of the regiments that were to support us broke and fled, leaving us to take care of ourselves as best we might." Of course, a retreat had to be ordered, the line of which, for a thousand yards, was swept by a murderous fire. Of the one hundred and ninety-one men, only eighty-eight—less than half—ever got back again. Of the mess of eleven officers of this gallant little band, only four were present at the next meeting. Fort Wagner was not taken, but a landing had been effected on Morris Island, and now it was generally believed that the fall of Charleston was a mere question of time. The rebels were greatly alarmed.

Seven days after, another more formidable assault was made, with similar results. Previous to making it, Gillmore had surrounded the fort with a semi-circle of batteries, about eighteen hundred yards distant. The land attack was to be assisted by the iron-clads, under Admiral Dahlgren. About half-past twelve, everything being ready, the signal was given, and, from land and water, a terrific bombardment was opened on the fort, and kept up all the afternoon. An incessant storm of shot and shell fell upon it, driving the gunners to cover. By night—no sound coming from the fort, except as our own shells exploded in and over it—it was supposed that the guns had been effectually silenced. For eight hours, this tremendous fire had been kept up; and as the sun went down, sinking in a mass of black and angry clouds, the artillery of heaven opened all along the western horizon, and the sheeted lightning cast a ghastly, fitful light over the barren waste of sand and the torn and ragged fort, that to all human appearance was garrisoned only by dead men. It was now resolved to carry it by assault, and Strong's brigade moved off to the perilous undertaking. This was composed of the Fifty-fourth Massachusetts (colored) regiment under Colonel Shaw, the Sixth Connecticut, Forty-eighth New York, Third New Hampshire, Seventy-sixth Pennsylvania and Ninth Maine. As soon as its dusky outline could be seen moving over the sand, the guns from distant Sumter and from Cummings' Point, and last of all from the hitherto silent Wagner, opened on it with terrible fury. Nothing daunted, the brigade sprung forward on the double-quick, and dashing swiftly through the iron storm, made straight for the fort, now lit up in the gloom by its own incessant fire. A part reached the ditch, crossed it, and mounted the parapet—led by Colonel Shaw, who fell there, waving on his men. But every foot of space was swept by the fire of the garrison, and in an incredibly short interval of time, Strong was wounded, and every commanding officer wounded or killed. The brigade, shattered, and torn into fragments, rushed wildly back into the darkness. The Second brigade, under Colonel Putnam, now advanced, and charging through the same desolating fire, mounted the ramparts, and, fighting hand to hand, actually got into a portion of the fort. But here it halted, shattered, exhausted, and powerless to advance another step. Putnam had fallen; and through the pitchy darkness, which was incessantly seamed with fire from bursting shells and exploding cannon, the broken, confused ranks—melting away as they fled—staggered, bleeding, back to their intrenchments; and the deep, silent, black midnight closed over the scene. The beach was strewed with the dead, whose dirge the waves sung as they rolled gently on the shore, while the wounded crawled away along the sand, sheltered by the darkness.

The presence of the colored troops in this assault, exasperated the garrison, and many acts of violence and cruelty were committed against their wounded officers. Colonel Shaw's body was pitched, with his negro soldiers, into the sand; and an exasperated feeling took possession of both armies. General Strong was wounded, and died soon after in New York. This repulse produced intense excitement all over the North, and charges against this or that person were made without much regard to justice. The colored regiment led the assault, and some laid the blame of defeat to this cause. It is very doubtful whether any other regiment would have succeeded better; still, placing it in this position was unwise, and cannot be justified on any military principle. To employ comparatively raw regiments—no matter whether colored or white—to do that which is regarded the hardest, most trying work the oldest veteran regiments are ever put to, is to tempt fortune and deserve defeat.

There was still another and sadder misfortune that marred the record of this month, made glorious by the capture of Vicksburg, the opening of the Mississippi, and the victory at Gettysburg. Collisions between the citizens and soldiery occurred in various parts of the North; and in New York city, they threatened, for a time, to bring back the bloody scenes of Paris in the time of the Bourbons. The offices of the Provost-Marshals were burned, telegraph wires cut, railroad tracks torn up, the Mayor's house sacked, the Colored Orphan Asylum burned, and many persons killed. The cause of these outrages was still more alarming—viz., the enforcement of the draft. A revolution at the North was far more to be dreaded than rebellion at the South, though backed by foreign intervention. Luckily, the mob lacked organization; and though, for two days, New York city seemed resting on the bosom of a volcano, whose earthquake throes extended to Albany and Boston, and even to the far West, the incipient outbreak was quelled, and the frightful chasm, that seemed opening beneath our feet, was closed. The ostensible ground of resistance, in New York, was the inequality of the draft, growing out of an erroneous enrollment. But various causes produced it. In the first place, such efforts had been made to get volunteers, that many people had come to believe that drafting was wrong. In the second place, the Government, ever since its organization, had always obtained troops by fixing the proper quota to each State, and then calling on its Governor to see that it was furnished. This policy had been accepted as the only constitutional way to raise an army. But the election of the previous Fall had given New York a Democratic Governor, and should the same state of political feeling exist in the coming Autumn, many other States might have Democratic Executives. The Administration feared that it might thus be balked in its demand for troops, just as Madison was, in the war of 1812, by Governor Strong of Massachusetts; and so, by one bold stroke, this power was taken out of the hands of the State Executives, and put in those of Provost-Marshals, who were scattered over the various Congressional Districts. This was a perilous innovation on a long-established rule. That it did not work untold mischief, was not owing to the wisdom of Congress, but to the patriotism of the people, of all parties. God, in his good providence, saved us from the evil effects of false impressions and bad legislation. That there is anything wrong, unjust or improper in a draft, is a miserable delusion. A Government that has no right to enforce one, does not deserve to exist. If the Government owes its subjects protection, the subjects owe it service, in return, and to that extent necessary for its self-preservation.

To prevent further troubles, Major-General Dix was called from the Department of Virginia to assume command of the Department of the East. This was a wise appointment, for men of all parties had the utmost confidence in his integrity, capacity and patriotism.

At the close of the month, the President issued the following order, which is memorable as the commencement of a series of measures which resulted in untold misery to our brave soldiers held as prisoners by the South:

"EXECUTIVE MANSION,
WASHINGTON, July 30, 1863.

It is the duty of every Government to give protection to its citizens, of whatever class, color, or condition, especially those who are duly organized as soldiers in the public service. The law of nations, and the usages and customs of war as carried on by civilized powers, permit no distinction as to color in the treatment of prisoners of war as public enemies. To sell or enslave any captured person, on account of his color, and for no offense against the laws of war, is a relapse into barbarism, and a crime against the civilization of the age.

The Government of the United States will give the same protection to all its soldiers; and if the enemy shall sell or enslave any one because of his color, the offense shall be punished by retaliation upon the enemy's prisoners in our possession.

It is therefore ordered that for every soldier of the United States killed in violation of the laws of war, a rebel soldier shall be executed; and for every one enslaved by the enemy or sold into slavery, a rebel soldier shall be placed at hard labor on the public works, and continued at such labor until the other shall be released and receive the treatment due to a prisoner of war.

ABRAHAM LINCOLN."

The employment of blacks as soldiers, many of whom were escaped slaves, exasperated the South, and the Confederate Government refused to regard them as prisoners of war. This, of course, necessitated action on the part of our Government; for there can be no plainer duty than that of every Government to protect its soldiers. This clear, explicit, just order, placed the matter on a right foundation; and had the Secretary of War been content to adopt it as the rule of his action, the colored soldiers would have been protected, and tens of thousands of brave men spared a horrible death. But, wishing to improve on it by a theory of his own, he broke up the cartel agreed on—which was working humanely—and filled Southern prisons with innocent victims. After a year of horrors, he was compelled to come back to the principle of this simple order, but all too late for an army of sufferers. This is but one of numerous instances which show how vastly superior the President—with his upright nature, freedom from passion, strong common sense, and clear appreciation of right—was, to the acutest lawyers and most accomplished diplomatists of the land. His practical mind seemed to seize by intuition the right course; and had he from the outset been followed, instead of pushed, we should have been saved many blunders and misfortunes.

Although this order disappeared from sight, in the long, learned discussion that followed, on the question of exchange, it reappeared at last, to vindicate the sagacity of its author.

The discussion of the Confiscation Act, and other legislative enactments having reference to the status of the slave and freedman, and the mode of carrying on the war, kept the North, during the Summer, in a state of turmoil, and furnished the Democratic party with the materials with which to organize an opposition, that they hoped might, in the coming year, overthrow the Administration, and institute a new order of things. McClellan—whose removal from the army was believed to be owing to his hostility to this kind of legislation, and to the President's Proclamation of Emancipation—was regarded as the man on whom these opposition elements would rally in the approaching struggle.

The heavy tax on incomes, necessary to meet the frightful expenses of the Government—swelled by the direct tax on property, to raise the enormous local bounties for volunteers—also caused great excitement. The public debt, in June, amounted, in round numbers, to ten hundred and ninety-eight millions of dollars—which practically, so far as the burden on the people was concerned, was swelled to an indefinite amount by local and State taxation. What the pressure of this mighty indebtedness would be, before the war could close, at the present rate of progress, men trembled to contemplate. The inability of Congress to grapple with this subject—the madness with which it persisted in spending the time, so pregnant with the fate of the country, in empty harangues or fierce partisan warfare—disgusted and discouraged all thoughtful men of both parties. It resolved that the war should go on, and yet seemed equally resolved that politics should keep pace with it—in fact, control it. All things considered, it was the darkest Summer of the war, notwithstanding the victories of Vicksburg and Gettysburg.

CHAPTER XVII.

CAVALRY ACTION OF GREGG—FOSTER'S EXPEDITION UP THE JAMES RIVER—FIGHT BETWEEN BUFORD AND STUART—AVERILL'S OPERATIONS IN VIRGINIA—GILLMORE'S SIEGE OF WAGNER AND SUMTER—HERCULEAN LABOR—"THE SWAMP ANGEL"—BOMBARDMENT OF SUMTER OVER THE TOP OF WAGNER—GREEK FIRE THROWN INTO CHARLESTON—REMONSTRANCE OF BEAUREGARD—ACTION OF THE FLEET—DEATH OF RODGERS—FRENCH OPINION OF THE SIEGE—STEADY APPROACHES TOWARDS WAGNER—ITS EVACUATION—EVACUATION OF FORT GREGG—MORRIS ISLAND OURS—BOMBARDMENT OF SUMTER—REFUSAL OF DAHLGREN TO ATTEMPT TO PASS IT—VINDICATION OF DU PONT—DESOLATION OF CHARLESTON—RETRIBUTION.

THOUGH the Summer campaign of the Army of the Potomac was ended, minor engagements, in Virginia, occasionally took place, and the guerrilla General Mosby caused a great deal of trouble. His conduct called forth a stringent order from Halleck.

In August, General Foster made an expedition up the James River, with four gunboats, and when about seven miles from Fort Darling, encountered a rebel battery, and at the same time, the Commodore Barney ran upon a torpedo, which exploded under her bows, lifting them ten feet out of water, and washing overboard fifteen of her crew. Foster was aboard at the time, but escaped injury.

On the Rappahannock, Buford had a sharp fight with Stuart's cavalry, reinforced by infantry, and, after an obstinate fight, drove him back, though with a loss to himself of a hundred and forty men, sixteen of whom were killed.

In the latter part of the month, General Averill returned from an expedition through several counties in the interior of Virginia, in which he burned some saltpetre works, and destroyed a quantity of arms and stores. He fought a superior force of the enemy, at White Sulphur Springs, and then retreated, with a loss of about a hundred men.

In the meantime, General Gillmore had pressed steadily towards Fort Sumter. After the failure of the assault on Fort Wagner, he sat down before it, in regular siege; but, while making his slow approaches towards it, he carried out the extraordinary plan of bombarding Fort Sumter over its top. There was between Morris and James Islands a marsh, covered with sea-weed, flags and rushes, which Beauregard had regarded as wholly untenable—as it was a mere bed of soft mud, in which a man would go down over his head—and so left it out, in completing the fortifications for the defense of Charleston. Yet Gillmore resolved to drive piles into this mortar-bed, and mount on them six two-hundred-pound Parrott guns, and one monster three-hundred-pounder. The timber for these piles had to be brought from Folly Island, a distance of ten miles, in rafts. To accomplish all this, without the enemy's knowledge, the work had all to be done in the night-time. The rafts were floated to their places, through the darkness, and before daylight covered with grass and sea-weed, that entirely disguised them, so that the enemy was kept in total ignorance of the work being done right under their eyes. In the night-time, also, the piles were driven into the mud. For two weeks, this strange work went on, without arousing the suspicion of the enemy. Ten thousand bags filled with sand, were carried two miles by the soldiers, to protect the guns. The monster gun broke down several trucks, before it was got into position, but by incredible labor it was finally mounted, and the "Swamp Angel," as it was called, was ready to open its fire. By the 16th of August, thirty-seven guns were in position on the artificial foundation laid in this mud-hole, within two miles and a half of Sumter, and but little over four from the city of Charleston. One can imagine the consternation of the enemy when these tremendous batteries were unmasked. It was a new creation—a volcanic island risen out of the sea.

On the 17th, they opened their fire on Sumter. In the meantime, Dahlgren, with the Ironsides and Monitor fleet, moved up opposite Fort Wagner, and engaged it, to keep it from concentrating its fire on this new position and distracting the gunners in their bombardment of Sumter. The fleet behaved gallantly; but almost at the outset, Captain George W. Rodgers, of the Catskill, who had boldly carried his vessel to within three hundred yards of Wagner, was killed, and the vessel, with a flag of distress flying, retired out of the fight. All day long, the terrific bombardment of Sumter was maintained. An immense wall of sand-bags had been built up on the outside and inside of the fort, fifteen feet thick—making the whole mass thirty-five feet thick. The sand-bags had first to be beaten down, before the wall itself could be reached; yet, so fierce was the fire, and so heavy the metal thrown, that on the second day the naked walls were exposed, and the work of demolition went on with greater rapidity. The barbette guns were soon dismounted, some of them toppling over into the sea. Day after day, the bombardment was kept up, till, at the end of the seventh day, Sumter was a heap of ruins. The rubbish, however, falling over some of the casemates, made them more invulnerable than ever, and a small garrison there still kept the rebel flag flying.

Gillmore now sent a flag of truce to Beauregard, demanding the surrender of Charleston, and threatening, in case of refusal, to shell the city. The demand and threat both seemed so preposterous, that Beauregard dismissed the officer without a reply. Gillmore then turned the "Swamp Angel" on the city, and shells were thrown into its very heart. The old "Greek fire" had been reproduced, and shells loaded with it were expected to burn the town. It, however, proved a failure. Still, the dropping of shells into the place aroused the indignation of Beauregard, who remonstrated against it as barbarous—saying that it was absurd to suppose that Charleston could be taken until the forts commanding the entrance to the harbor were in our possession.

The engineering skill displayed by Gillmore, and the tremendous range of his guns, astonished the civilized world. The idea of bombarding a city almost as far as it could be seen, was a novel one in carrying out siege operations. The French *Journal des Sciences Militaire* had a long article on it, which the *United States Service Magazine* published. It commences thus: "Prodigies of talent, audacity, intrepidity and perseverance are exhibited in the attack, as in the defense of this city, which will assign to the siege of Charleston an exceptional place in military annals. It is a duel 'to the death,' in which science calls to its aid, and puts in operation, all the modern discoveries to develop upon a gigantic scale the means of destruction and extermination. One is struck with amazement in reading, in the journals and letters from America, the details of this contest, in which the two adversaries ought to feel a mutual astonishment, as they rightfully astonish the entire world, by their daily proofs of superhuman heroism." * * * "Such a position," the writer adds, after describing Charleston Harbor, "defended by an engineer of transcendent merit—by soldiers who fear neither fatigue, suffering nor death—would seem to have been impregnable; and yet the besiegers, conducting their enterprise with incredible energy, make, day by day, slow progress, but with almost certain chances of ultimate success. It is the land artillery which plays the grand part in these brilliant and terrible operations. But what artillery, and what projectiles!—solid shot and shells, of two and three hundred pounds, describing *trajectories* of six and eight thousand metres, striking the mark with such precision and efficacy that they penetrate the earth-work to the distance of ten metres, and break in fragments works of brick and stone six and ten metres in thickness. It is a General, unknown one year ago, who directs this combat of artillery, which has no precedent hitherto in the history of sieges. Mahomet II, it is true, employed cannon of a monstrous caliber, which terrified the defenders of Byzantium, and finished the destruction of the Greek Empire; but the 'Balistique' of the Mohammedans produced only a *soothing* effect, in comparison with that of the Americans." He then goes on to describe the bombardment and assault of Fort Wagner.

The Journal containing this chapter, which thus places the siege of Charleston above all other siege operations in the history of the world, is the highest military authority throughout Europe.

By thus occupying a distant stand-point, and viewing Gillmore's engineering skill through the military mind of the Old World, we get some correct idea of the stupendous nature of the work done before Charleston. The want of success depreciated it in the popular mind, but it stands alone and without a parallel in military annals.

On the 1st of September, another engagement took place between our iron-clads and the forts, but, like the former, was barren of results. In it, Fleet Captain Oscar C. Badger—the successor of Rodgers—was wounded by a shell.

In the meantime, Gillmore pressed steadily towards Fort Wagner. If that could be taken, Fort Gregg, on the point opposite Sumter, must also fall, and then he could plant his batteries in point-blank range of the hated structure. He, however, had no intention of trying another assault. The spade and shovel, that had risen from their formerly despised position, were to do the work. "Day after day, our patient boys creep up, on hands and knees, to their dangerous toil, with shovel and gun rolling slowly in advance—for protection, the 'sap roller,' a round wicker-work filled with sticks. Gradually approaching parallels are thrown up, and each succeeding day brings our engineers nearer to the fort. They are digging their way, in spite of shot and shell, into Wagner. Although the distance from the first parallel to Fort Wagner is but six hundred yards, yet if the whole number dug were laid out in a straight line, they would reach ten miles." Through the long, hot Summer months, the troops worked, under the broiling sun, with unflagging courage, until the parallels were at last pushed so near to the fort, that, with a single bound, the assailants could be inside the ramparts. The preparations were all made for a final assault, when the enemy suddenly evacuated it, and streamed forward towards Fort Gregg. Our exultant troops followed after, and this also was evacuated, and we had Morris Island, for which we had struggled so long. Twenty-one guns were left in our possession. We were now in fair range of Fort Sumter, and its speedy fall was eagerly looked for. Fort Moultrie was also bombarded, and though Sumter soon became a still greater heap of ruins, and Gillmore pushed his operations with a skill and energy that deserved success, it soon became apparent that we were no nearer Charleston than ever.

Here, it is worthy of notice, that though both Forts Wagner and Gregg were reduced, and Sumter so demolished as to be able to mount but a few guns, Dahlgren never attempted to carry the iron-clads past it up to Charleston. The brave Du Pont was removed because, with all these forts in the enemy's possession, and thoroughly mounted with the most formidable cannon, he failed to make a second attempt to pass or destroy it; and yet Dahlgren, with but half the fire to encounter, did not even risk a trial. This single fact is all the testimony any just mind needs, to prove whose views were correct. Dahlgren saw plainly that Du Pont was right, and was too good an officer to risk his vessels where certain defeat awaited him.

Though Charleston was not taken, it was almost as desolate as Edom. A Southern paper thus described its condition: "Here and there, a pedestrian moves hurriedly along, and the rattle of a cart or a dray is alone heard for a whole square. The blinds are closed; vases of rare exotics droop and wither on the lonely window-sill, because there is no tender hand to twine or nourish them. The walk glistens with fragments of glass, rattled thither by the concussion of exploding shells; here, a cornice is knocked off; there, is a small round hole through the side of a building; beyond, a house in ruins, and, at remote intervals, the earth is torn where a shell exploded, and looks like the work of a giant in search of some hidden treasure; and little tufts of bright green grass are springing up along the pave, once vocal with the myriad tongues of busy trade."

What a picture this is, of the proud "cradle of secession!" Its destruction was never very important, in a military view; but, as the hot-bed of treason—the spot where the national flag was first fired upon, and compelled to come down at the bidding of traitors—its overthrow was an object of intense desire to the North; and yet, what fate could be worse than the one she actually suffered! Behold Charleston, rocking to the shouts of the excited multitude, and echoing to the joyful peal of bells, because the brave Anderson is compelled to haul down his flag! And behold that same city now, as drawn by the pen of one of her own people—desolate, dreary and mournful!—and who will say that she has not drank to the dregs the fearful cup she so madly mixed for herself?

CHAPTER XVIII.

JULY AND AUGUST.

EVENTS AT THE WEST DURING THE SUMMER—GRANT AT VICKSBURG—RAID OF PHILLIPS—ROSECRANS AT MURFREESBORO'—ADVANCE ON CHATTANOOGA—MORGAN'S RAID THROUGH OHIO—THE PURSUIT—ATTEMPTS TO CROSS INTO VIRGINIA—BATTLE OF BUFFINGTON'S ISLAND—ROUT OF THE BAND—CURIOUS ASPECT OF THE BATTLE-FIELD—QUANTRELL IN MISSOURI—RAID INTO KANSAS—MASSACRE AT LAWRENCE—THE PURSUIT—THE FLIGHT—HIS ESCAPE.

BUT while comparative quiet reigned around the Army of the Potomac, after the battle of Gettysburg, and but minor expeditions broke the monotony along the seaboard, and the tedious bombardment of Fort Sumter went on, events of great interest were transpiring in the West, some of which were to give direction to all future operations there, and eventually pierce the very heart of the Confederacy. After Grant had captured Vicksburg, and then turned and driven Johnston out of Jackson, he took up his head-quarters at the former place, and devoted himself to the business of his Department, while the army lay quiet in order to recover its strength for future operations. A successful raid was made into Central Mississippi, under the command of Lieutenant-Colonel Phillips, in which sixty-five locomotives and five hundred cars were destroyed, and the communications of the rebels sadly broken up. Besides this, little was done by Grant's army.

But, up at Murfreesboro', the Army of the Cumberland was in motion. Much complaint had been made against Rosecrans, its Commander, because he lay inactive while such important events were taking place around Vicksburg;

but he determined, when he advanced, to take no backward step. Bragg was in his front, with a powerful army, and Chattanooga was a strongly fortified place, and he knew that no easy task was before him.

When his preparations were complete, he put his army in motion, and, crossing the Cumberland Mountains by four different routes, pressed forward towards Chattanooga. But while he was thus pushing his victorious columns south, two events occurred, far back of him, which, though having no real effect on his campaign, or the war, produced the most intense excitement throughout the North. These were, Morgan's raid through Ohio, and the massacre at Lawrence.

In the latter part of June, Morgan, with a brigade, lay along the banks of the Cumberland River, evidently meditating some serious movement. A Union force was dispatched to the locality to watch him, and had several skirmishes with portions of his troops. But, on the 3d of July, it was found that he had crossed the river, the day before, at Burkesville. Captain Carter had a brush with his advance, in which he was severely wounded, and his command compelled to fall back. Reinforcements were immediately sent him, which arrived just before midnight in the vicinity of Columbia, then in possession of the enemy. An attack was at once ordered, but Morgan's force being much stronger than it had been reported, the Union troops were compelled to retreat to Jamestown, from which point Colonel Wolford dispatched a courier to Somerset, to General Carter commanding the United States troops there, stating that Morgan had crossed the Cumberland, and advanced north to Columbia. A proper force was immediately sent in pursuit, and all through the moon-lit night of the 4th of July, the excited pursuers pressed gaily forward, and reached the north bank of Green River about daylight Sunday morning. Taking a hurried breakfast, they pushed on all day, and that evening, just before dusk, were joined by the Second Tennessee mounted infantry.

Morgan, in the meantime, in his bold march, had captured Lebanon, though not until after a sharp fight, in which his brother Tom was killed. In revenge for his death, some twenty houses were burned, and the post office robbed. The Union troops captured here—numbering in all about three hundred—Morgan compelled to run on foot, in front of his mounted men, for twelve miles, to Springfield. A sergeant giving out, he was knocked on the head with the butt end of a musket, and his brains trampled out by the passing horsemen. At Springfield, the prisoners were robbed, and then paroled.

On the night of the 6th, the pursuing force was joined, at Bardstown, by General Hobson, with Shackleford's brigade, composed of the Third, Eighth, Ninth and Twelfth Kentucky cavalry, with two pieces of artillery. Hobson at once assumed command, and, pushing on to Shepherdsville, found that Morgan at that point had captured the mail train on the Louisville and Nashville railroad, and about twenty soldiers who were passengers in the cars. The horses here giving out, Hobson halted for a day, but at daylight, on the morning of the 8th, was again in motion, and followed the track of the rebel chieftain for thirty miles, by the letters which his band had taken from the mail-bags, and, after reading, had torn and scattered along the road. Morgan, in the meantime, had entered Elizabethtown, and, helping himself to what he wanted, struck for Brandenburg, and, by a sudden, skillful movement, captured the steamboats Alice Dean and J. T. McCoombs, by which he took his whole force across the Ohio River. Among all the bold and extraordinary movements of the war, none had been bolder or half so desperate as this. Right through the thickly settled State of Ohio, this fearless rider proposed to take his lawless band, and, after working incalculable evil, recross the Ohio, and rejoin the rebel army in Virginia or south of the Tennessee River.

As Hobson approached the Ohio, he saw the Alice Dean, wrapped in flame and smoke, burning on the opposite shore, and the rear guard of Morgan's force rapidly disappearing in the distance.

At Brandenburg, the Leavenworth home-guards showed fight, but were overpowered, and forty-five taken prisoners. The stores and houses were plundered and the raiders cumbered themselves with useless goods, which they soon had to throw away.

Morgan was now in the Free States, and his march henceforward assumed an importance which at once attracted the attention of the whole country.

Hobson was across the river on the morning of the 10th, and at once commenced a sharp pursuit. Morgan's path now began to be beset with ever-increasing difficulties; for a powerful force was pressing on his rear, while in front the country was rushing to arms.

At Corydon, the home-guards made a short stand, losing some fifteen in killed and wounded, and two hundred prisoners, which Morgan paroled.

Stealing all the horses he could find, and levying taxes where he did not destroy, he pushed on to Blue River, and, burning the bridge behind him, swept through Paris. Reaching Vernon, where a force of twelve hundred militia was assembled, he demanded the surrender of the place. "Come and take it," was Colonel Lowe's response. Morgan surrounded the town, but, contenting himself with burning some bridges, he moved around it to Versailles, where he robbed the County Treasurer of all his money, about five thousand dollars—saying, in grim jocoseness, that he was sorry the County was so very poor. Sacking the town, he sent out a detachment, which burned a bridge and captured a telegraph operator, while with the main column he kept on to Pierceville, burning all the bridges on the road. Near Wiseburgh, he had a skirmish with the home-guards, and at New-Ulsas, a German settlement, his soldiers captured a wagon-load of lager beer, which they carried along to drink by the way. The same night in which the pursuing force encamped at Harrison, with their horses thoroughly jaded out, Morgan's bugles were sounding north of Cincinnati. On his way, he at Miamiville turned over a railroad train, and burned fifty Government wagons. On the afternoon of the 15th, he entered Winchester, and robbed the mail and stole thirty-five thousand dollars' worth of property and fifty horses, while the soldiers tore up all the flags they could find, and tied the fragments to the tails of mules, which they drove, with shouts and laughter, through the streets.

Morgan now struck south-east, for the purpose of reaching the Ohio, and crossing into Virginia. The country was thoroughly aroused, and troops were concentrating from various quarters to head him off and intercept his retreat. Burning the bridge at Jacktown, he kept on to Wheat Ridge, where his force separated—a part going through Mount Olive. Six miles from Jackson, the citizens blockaded the road, which detained him two hours. Here and there shooting down a man who showed hostile intentions, and pillaging and destroying like a band of savages, the force pressed forward towards the Ohio. Arriving at Jackson, Morgan sent part of his forces up to Berlin, where three thousand militia were posted, who were quickly scattered by a single shell thrown into their midst. At the little town of Linesville, the home-guards tore up a bridge and blockaded the road, by which Morgan was detained another two hours—a great gain to the pursuers, who were straining every nerve to overtake him.

In the meantime, General Judah, with a strong force, was moving up the Ohio from Portsmouth, a town a hundred and fifteen miles above Cincinnati, while gunboats patrolled the stream. It was evident that Morgan would strike for the first fordable place on the river, and try to cross into Virginia, as he was becoming sorely pressed—for, although he could supply fresh horses on the way, his men were getting worn out by their long and rapid march.

Buffington Island lies about twenty miles below Blennerhassett Island; between them are a great many shoals, that make crossing comparatively easy. For this point, Morgan now struck, hoping to get across before his pursuers were up, or he was headed off by the force pressing up the river. On Friday night, the 17th, he was at Pomeroy, thirty-five miles below the island, and the next night encamped in some corn-fields nearly opposite it. At this point, a road, coming over a range of hills two miles distant, strikes the river road nearly at right angles. Three hundred yards above the former road, was a private one, leading into the corn-fields where Morgan lay. Judah came down the pike, and, there being a dense fog, almost run upon the rebels before he was aware of their position. Morgan immediately fired on the advance column, throwing it into confusion, and was about to follow up his success with a charge, when the gunboat Moose, in the river, opened on him, and at the same time Hobson's force came up in the rear. Our artillery was soon got in position, and the battle commenced. Finding himself between three fires, Morgan moved up-stream, to escape the shells of the gunboat; but she advanced, also—clinging to him with a tenacity that soon convinced him that in reaching the river, instead of finding safety he had actually run into the lion's mouth. Seeing that it was hopeless to make a stand here, he divided his force into two columns, and a rush was made by one for the river, at a point about a mile and a half above the island. But the gunboat, coming up, sent shot and shell into the mass floundering in the water—killing some, and turning others back, so that only about twenty succeeded in getting over.

In the meantime, Basil Duke, back from the shore, was so hard pressed that the men broke in despair—some surrendering themselves prisoners—among them Duke himself—and others taking refuge in flight. A running fight now ensued; the main body of the enemy, aiming for a point up the river, opposite Belleville, Virginia, on reaching it, plunged into the water, and began to push for the other shore. But the Moose soon came looming through the fog, and, pouring her shrapnel into the advance party, killed some, and stopped the remainder from attempting to cross. About twenty more, however, got over here. The remaining rebels now pushed on up the river fourteen miles further, to Hawkinsport, and again made an effort to cross; but the omnipresent gunboat was there, and they had to keep on in their headlong flight.

Scattering in detached bodies, the rebels now wandered hither and thither, striving in vain to break through the toils with which they were surrounded. Some two hundred succeeded in crossing at Readsville, while Morgan, with one portion, struck into Columbiana County, where his force surrendered to Colonel Shackleford.

Over two thousand were captured or killed, and all their guns, accouterments and plunder seized.

The battle-field, and line of retreat, presented one of the most curious spectacles ever seen in war. The ground was strewed, not only with guns, cartridge-boxes, &c., but with all sorts of hardware and dry-goods, and household articles, such as forks, spoons, calicoes, ribbons, and women's apparel, together with buggies, carriages, market-wagons, circus-wagons, and even quite a quantity of stationery. Such extraordinary spoils never before fell into the hands of warriors. It seemed as if a den of thieves, where their plunder was stored, had been broken up, and not that a reputed band of heroes were retreating, under the leadership of a noted captain. Altogether, this was one of the most remarkable raids of the war, though distinguished for nothing but foolhardiness.

Morgan crossed the Ohio a hundred and seventy miles below Cincinnati, and, passing clear around that city, attempted to recross the river about a hundred and seventy miles above it. For ten days, he marched through the heart of Ohio, plundering and destroying, with apparently no other object in view than simple retaliation. He must have moved, during this time, at the rate of at least fifty miles a day, and yet did not destroy property to the amount of more than fifty thousand dollars.

THE MASSACRE AT LAWRENCE.

War, from its very nature, is cruel, but in later days, among civilized nations, it has seldom been disgraced by such atrocities as the massacres at Lawrence and Fort Pillow. Men, fitted by nature to be leaders of banditti, took advantage of the war to follow the vocation for which they seemed designed, and, gathering around them a band of men, lawless and desperate as themselves, plundered and murdered, under the pretext of carrying on a war for independence. There were degrees of crime among even this abandoned class—some leaders having more control over their followers, and being more humane than others. Over all, however, Quantrell stands pre-eminent for his barbarities and depravity. His whole career during the war, was marked by crime and violence; but in the massacre at Lawrence, Kansas, he acquired a reputation that will make his name infamous to the end of time.

During the Summer, reports of intended raids on various

towns, constantly agitated the frontiers of Missouri and Kansas; but General Ewing, who commanded there, garrisoned the threatened places, and Quantrell's force, numbering some three hundred, was kept at bay. If disappointed in their intended attack on a particular place, they would break up into small predatory bands, and wreak their vengeance on isolated families or parties. Ewing scattered his force, which, in separate detachments, dogged these marauders from one haunt and locality to another. Missouri finally getting too hot for him, Quantrell determined, in August, to make a dash into Kansas. Selecting Blackwater, some fifty miles from the Kansas line, as the place of rendezvous, he, on the 19th, moved off with his mounted force, and passing through Chapel Hill, where he was joined by fifty more outlaws, pressed straight for Kansas.

Captain Pike, commanding two companies at Aubrey, forty-five miles from Lawrence, heard, on the evening of the 20th, that Quantrell had just passed five miles to the south of him; but instead of pushing on after him, he forwarded the information up and down the line, and to Ewing's headquarters. The latter at once sent forward a hundred men to Aubrey, thirty-five miles distant, with orders for the combined force to start at once in pursuit. At midnight, they mounted, and pressed rapidly forward. But Quantrell had struck across the open prairie, making it difficult to keep his track, so that they gained but little on him all night. With the start of several hours, he, by riding rapidly, reached Lawrence a little after daylight, and the tramp of his horses through the streets, and shouts of his men, aroused the terrified inhabitants to the sudden disaster that had overtaken them. The news spread like lightning through the town, and a few seized their guns and rushed forth to fight, but were shot down by the desperadoes, who had complete control of the place. Then commenced a scene of pillage and violence which in our history finds its parallel only in Indian atrocities. Houses and banks were broken into—women were stripped of their jewelry, and everything valuable that could be transported on horseback, was dragged forth and packed for removal on fresh horses gathered in the place. As fast as houses were pillaged, they were set on fire, and soon the crackling of flames mingled with the shouts and cries of the infuriated demons. "During all this time, citizens were being murdered everywhere. Germans and negroes, when caught, were shot immediately. Many persons were shot down after they had been taken prisoners and had been assured that they would not be hurt if they would surrender. Messrs. Trask and Baker, and two other citizens, were so taken, and while being marched towards the river as prisoners, were fired upon, and all four killed on the spot except Mr. Baker, who was not expected to live. Mr. Dix had been taken prisoner, and his house set on fire, when one of the fiends told him if he would give them his money he would not be killed; otherwise he would. Mr. Dix went into the burning house, and got a thousand dollars and handed it over. He was told to march towards the river, and had not proceeded twenty steps when he was shot dead from behind. Mr. Hampson, clerk of the Provost-Marshal had a revolver, and tried to defend the few things he had saved from the Johnson House. His wife interfered, and they told him if he would surrender he should be treated as a prisoner, and be safe from harm. He surrendered, and was immediately shot from behind—the ball entering near the spine, and coming out below the kidneys in front. In one instance, the wife and daughter of a man threw themselves over his body, begging for his life; but one of the murderers deliberately thrust his revolver down between the two women, and killed the man.

"Before ten o'clock, the main body of the guerrillas

departed with their plunder, leaving a guard over the prisoners in town, and a few stragglers. The few persons wounded, were wounded at this time by the passing fiends. In the earlier part of the day, most of the persons were fired at from very near, and killed instantly.

"One of the first persons out was Colonel Deitzler. Mr. Williamson and myself helped him carry off the dead. The sight that met us when coming out, I cannot describe. I have read of outrages committed in the so-called dark ages, and, horrible as they appeared to me, they sink into insignificance in comparison with what I was then compelled to witness. Well-known citizens were lying, completely roasted, in front of the spot where their stores and residences had been. The bodies were crisp, and nearly black. We thought, at first, they were all negroes, till we recognized some of them. In handling the dead bodies, pieces of roasted flesh would remain in our hands. Soon, our strength failed us, in this horrible and sickening work. Many could not help crying like children. Women and little children were all over town, hunting for their husbands and fathers, and sad indeed was the scene when they did finally find them among the corpses laid out for recognition. I cannot describe the horrors; language fails me, and the recollection of the scenes I witnessed, makes me sick when I am compelled to repeat them." *

These, however, are but few of the details. Twenty colored soldiers were shot in cold blood, a[illegible] in circumstances of fiendish atrocity. A hundred and forty unarmed men, in all, were murdered, and twenty-four wounded. The dead lined the streets everywhere, through which roamed weeping women and children, while the air was filled with the smoke and flames of a hundred and eighty-five burning buildings. Altogether, it was a scene one would never expect to see

* William Kempf, belonging to the Provost-Marshal's Office.

in the Nineteenth Century, in a civilized and Christian land. It rivaled in atrocity the massacre of the whites in Minnesota by the Sioux Indians, and shows what desperate bands of men infested our frontiers. General Lane was in the place at the time, and narrowly escaped capture by the desperadoes. Enraged at being unable to find him, they burned his house. Many heroic deeds were performed by the women in protecting the lives of the men, and it must be said to the honor of the wretches, that they refrained from committing violence on them.

After quietly taking a lunch amid the smouldering ruins of the town, Quantrell ordered his men to mount, and lifting his hat mockingly to the ladies, bowed politely, and said, "Ladies, I now bid you good morning; I hope when we meet again, it will be under more favorable circumstances." He then put spurs to his horse, and rode away, followed by his murderous gang. He took the precaution to collect all the fresh horses he could lay his hands on, so as to be able to elude pursuit.

The troops, under Major Plumb, reached the place only to find it in ruins, and the enemy gone. Although they had pressed rapidly forward, having made more than sixty-five miles, without rest or food, since the morning before—filled with rage at the sight which met their gaze, they immediately wheeled and started in pursuit. Lane, assembling a hundred and fifty of the citizens, joined them, and all day long they pressed on the flying track of the foe. Quantrell kept a hundred of his best-mounted men as a rear-guard, who the moment our men, scattered over the prairies, came in sight, would form in line of battle. This would compel a halt of the most advanced pursuers, and by the time the main body could get up, Quantrell's gang, with the booty, would be far ahead. The rear-guard, the moment Plumb was ready to commence an attack, would pour in one volley, then break into column and gallop off at a rate that defied pursuit. Thus the chase was kept up till eight o'clock at night, when the rear-guard made a stand, and a skirmish followed. The guerrillas, however, finding another force, under Lieut.-Colonel Clark, crossing their line of retreat, broke and scattered in the darkness, so that the trail could not be followed.

Quantrell, seeing that he had baffled his pursuers, halted to rest; but at midnight, a body of militia broke up his camp. Aided, however, by the darkness and the uneven surface of the prairie, he got safely off, and, continuing his flight, crossed the Kansas border, and at noon the next day reached the timber near the middle fork of the Grand River, Missouri, an hour in advance of his pursuers. Here, his forces scattered. About a hundred, with Quantrell at their head, moved down the river. Lieutenant-Colonel Lazear, with two hundred men, continued to press him so closely that he was compelled to abandon most of his horses and much of the plunder he had taken from the Lawrence stores.

There had been, in the pursuit, frequent engagements with detached parties, and Ewing reported about a hundred of the miscreants killed. Though the pursuers traveled a hundred miles in the first twenty-four hours—killing many of their horses by exhaustion, and some of the men themselves died from the effect of the sun, and want of rest—yet Quantrell, by desperate riding, succeeded in escaping. Never did bloodhounds hang more unflinchingly on the track of a poor fugitive, than did these gallant soldiers and enraged citizens on the flying footsteps of this desperado, until their horses gave out. No prisoners were captured—every man being shot remorselessly down when overtaken. The perfect knowledge of the fate that awaited him, imparted a desperation to Quantrell's efforts to elude his pursuers; and, mounted on the best horse the country could furnish, he pushed him to the limit of his endurance, and thus escaped a short shrift and a quick passage to the next world—to drag out a miserable life in this.

CHAPTER XIX.

SEPTEMBER.

ROSECRANS BEFORE CHATTANOOGA—RESOLVES TO FLANK IT—HAZEN LEFT TO GUARD THE RIVER—BRAGG EVACUATES CHATTANOOGA—ROSECRANS RESOLVES TO CUT OFF HIS RETREAT—SCATTERING OF HIS CORPS—BRAGG MARCHES BACK ON CHATTANOOGA—PERIL OF ROSECRANS—RAPID CONCENTRATION OF HIS ARMY—FIRST DAY'S BATTLE—SECOND DAY'S BATTLE—ROUT OF OUR ARMY—STEADFASTNESS OF THE LEFT WING—DESPERATE FIGHTING OF THOMAS—THE CRISIS—UNEXPECTED DELIVERANCE—THE GALLANT STEEDMAN—A DESPERATE CHARGE—THE BATTLE SAVED—THE ARMY FALLS BACK TO CHATTANOOGA—CAUSES OF DEFEAT.

WHILE these stirring events were occurring in Ohio and Kansas, Rosecrans, with his magnificent army well in hand, was pressing victoriously forward towards Chattanooga, and, the last week in August, drew up his columns on the banks of the Tennessee, in front of the place. It being a strong position by nature, and made more so by art, it was well-nigh impregnable against any direct attack. Rosecrans therefore determined to flank it by the west and south, and, if possible, get in Bragg's rear and cut him off from his base of supplies, so that if he did not retreat he would be forced to a decisive battle in the open field. In carrying out this plan, he took his main army over the Tennessee, a few miles below Chattanooga, and marched up the Lookout Valley, lying west of the Lookout Mountain. On the 3rd of September, he put the troops left behind—about seven thousand in number—under Brigadier-General Hazen, with orders to watch the movements of the enemy at all the crossings, and make Bragg believe that a large army was still on the north shore of the river. This force was scattered from Kingston to Williams' Island, a distance of seventy miles, and yet, so adroitly did Hazen manage it—causing the heads of strong columns to appear simultaneously at different fords—building camp-fires at prominent points, and beating calls all along the river—that Bragg was thoroughly deceived, until the main army was far to the south of him. When he discovered it, he saw at once that he must retreat, or be cut off from his base of supplies; and, hastily breaking up his camp, he evacuated Chattanooga. The news reached Rosecrans on the 8th, and he immediately started in pursuit.

To understand the positions of the armies at this time, it is necessary to remember that the Tennessee at this point runs nearly east and west in its general direction, and the Chickamauga Creek and the Lookout Mountain hang south from it, like two great pendants—the former above and the latter below Chattanooga. Bragg retreated along the valley formed by the Creek and Mountain. Over the Lookout Mountain, on the west side, lay the Lookout Valley, up which Rosecrans was marching. The Lookout Mountain, therefore, divided the two armies. But Rosecrans' army was very much scattered at the time he heard of Bragg's retreat. McCook's Corps was far up the Valley, forty-five miles south of Chattanooga; Thomas, commanding the center, was thirteen miles back of him, down the Valley; while Crittenden was on the river, and only some eight miles from Chattanooga—two of his divisions not yet being across. Rosecrans now immediately ordered Crittenden to move around the head of Lookout Mountain, and follow up Bragg's retiring columns as rapidly as possible, by crossing the Valley of Chickamauga in a south-easterly direction to Dalton. Had Crittenden done so, he would have been cut off; for Bragg, instead of striking the railroad, as Rosecrans supposed he would, had moved directly south, and now lay about half-way between Dalton and Lookout Mountain. Fortunately, Crittenden's movement was delayed, until Rosecrans ascertained where the enemy really was. The former was therefore ordered to follow up the Chickamauga Creek, and take position at Gordon's Mill, where the road from Lafayette to Chattanooga crossed. Rosecrans had supposed that Bragg was in full retreat, and that the chief effort should be to intercept him; but now, to his astonishment, he learned that the rebel General was not only not fleeing, but had faced about, and was preparing to march back on Chattanooga. His first, great object therefore was, to get his scattered army together, before Bragg should fall on Crittenden and cut him to pieces.

The Corps of the latter lay stretched along the Chickamauga, and extended up the Valley towards Crawfish Springs, in order to be near as possible to Thomas, who was directed to march with all haste over the mountain to his support. The latter must cross by way of Stevens' Gap, and Bragg, aware of it, ordered General Hindman to occupy and hold the Gap, while Polk should fall on Crittenden, isolated and away from all support. Had Hindman done as he was directed, Bragg would doubtless have won Chattanooga again, and hopelessly cut Rosecrans' line of communication. Why he neglected to do so, or why Polk did not attack Crittenden during the entire week he was alone in the Valley, does not appear. The double failure doubtless saved Rosecrans and the Army of the Cumberland.

Thomas, having sent forward Negley to hold the Gap, on the 8th and 9th hurried his columns across it, and, pushing down into the Valley, moved up to Crittenden's right.

McCook was over the Lookout Mountain, far to the south, when he received the order of Rosecrans to join Thomas, and at midnight put his columns in motion. Bragg was aware of his isolated position, and took measures to intercept him on the road which it was supposed he must take. McCook, however, instead of marching directly down to Thomas, recrossed Lookout Mountain, and, hurrying down Lookout Valley, crossed again at Stevens' Gap. He lost two or three days' march by this route, but saved his army.

But, while he was urging his columns down Lookout Valley, and over its rugged heights by Stevens' Gap, events were assuming an alarming aspect along the Chickamauga Creek. A race had already commenced between the two armies, that were moving in parallel lines back towards Chattanooga. Bragg, having received the reinforcements he had been waiting for, determined to get between our army and Chattanooga, and thus cut Rosecrans' line of communications, and force him into a dangerous retreat, or give him battle on ground of his own choosing.

Whether Rosecrans would have retreated to Chattanooga without risking a battle, had McCook arrived in time, would probably have depended on circumstances; but when the latter did at length form on Thomas' right, the line had been so prolonged that it was twelve miles in length, and still ten miles from Chattanooga.

On the 18th, two fords, on our extreme left, were fiercely assailed, and our forces there driven back—showing that the enemy, though manœuvering in front, designed to outflank Rosecrans, and thus force him to a decisive battle. On that night, therefore, Thomas was ordered to break off from the center and take position on the left, leaving McCook to close up and fill his place. Thus, on the morning of the 19th, he held the left, Crittenden the center, and McCook the right—the whole stretching along the Chickamauga Creek from Gordon's Mill towards Chattanooga. The army was still in motion on the morning of the 19th, closing up its line, for no portion of it was perfectly settled in position but the Corps of Thomas. Granger was at Rossville, four miles from the left, with a division in reserve.

Early in the morning, Wood, who was stationed at Gordon's Mill, saw low clouds of dust hovering along the roads that, beyond the Creek, run towards Chattanooga—showing that heavy columns were marching in that direction—and reported the fact to Rosecrans.

Brannan held the extreme left, Baird came next, and Reynolds next to him. Negley's division, belonging to Thomas, was holding Owen's Ford, two miles beyond Gordon's Mill. Palmer and Van Cleve, of Crittenden's Corps, held the center. Sheridan and Davis, of McCook's Corps, were marching swiftly up to close the right, when, about ten o'clock, the sudden explosion of artillery on the extreme left, told that the enemy had commenced the attack. Croxton's brigade, having been sent towards the river to reconnoiter, was furiously assailed, and the remainder of Brannan's division came to his succor. Thomas, hearing the rapid firing, rode forward to ascertain the nature of the attack, and finding the whole division hard pressed and slowly giving way, ordered Baird's division to move at once to its support. The enemy, to his surprise, was over the river, and all the advantage it was supposed to give as a line of defense was lost, and it might as well have never been chosen. No strong position was left to fall back upon, and ranks of living men and batteries, stretching for nearly four miles, through the fields and woods, stood face to face to each other. The storm that struck Brannan and Baird with such terrible fury, and rolled rapidly down the line from left to right, showed that Bragg, beginning with his extreme right, was swinging the rebel army against our whole line, with the intention, at some point, of breaking through it. Before the attack had reached the center, and while Reynolds and Johnson were struggling desperately to hold their ground, Thomas succeeded in rallying the broken divisions of Brannan and Baird, and hurled them once more on the enemy. The suddenness and energy of the assault, that had well-nigh driven his whole Corps from the field, thoroughly aroused him. His sturdy regulars had been rolled back in confusion, and Scribner's brigade saved from annihilation only by cutting its way through a horde of rebels; and, stung by the disaster, the moment his columns were once more in position, and presented a solid front, he ordered the whole line to advance. The troops now caught the high courage and resolution of their Commander, and the deep murmur that rolled along their terrible front, foretold a fearful onset. Not sudden and headlong, but grand and awful, like the mighty march of the ocean-tide, the firm-set battalions moved sternly, steadily forward. Longstreet's veterans, flushed with success, threw themselves in their way, but could not stay that determined march for a moment. The rebel batteries, forced back, wheeled into new positions, and hurled shot and shell into the close formations in vain. The leaders flung themselves along their yielding lines, with waving swords and fiery appeals, to no purpose. The head of each opposing column that advanced to stem the awful torrent, melted away; and on, on swept the unbroken line—over abandoned guns, caissons, everything—until the field was won, and the enemy borne back nearly a mile.

But while this victory was being gained on our left, Polk and Hill had thrown themselves with such resistless impetuosity on the center, that, though fighting manfully to hold its ground, it was forced back, and the rout was fast becoming complete, when Davis came up from the right, and stopped the progress of the enemy. It was but for a moment, however. Rapidly accumulating fresh troops on the weakened point, the rebel Generals threw them forward with resistless intrepidity. Hurling Davis to the right, and Van Cleve to the left, in their fierce onset, they boldly penetrated the gap they thus made, and for a moment the battle seemed lost. But Thomas, compelled, by the danger here, to pause and fall back, now came up; while Hazen, with twenty pieces of artillery massed at the threatened point, held the shouting enemy in check. At this juncture, too, Wilder's brigade of mounted infantry dashed up, and fell furiously on the advancing columns, forcing them back. But the rebel leaders, rallying their troops, and strengthened with reinforcements, again came on, each time swinging off and outflanking us to the right, so that Wilder was compelled to fall back. Sheridan then came up, and sending forward Bradley's brigade, restored the fight. But the attack, that had begun at our extreme left, kept drifting down our line so rapidly that Bradley in turn was nearly outflanked, and began to give way, when Negley and Wood came down the stream on the double-quick, and charging home, at once arrested the dangerous movement. Though at times on the point of complete success, the enemy had been stopped everywhere along the whole line, and the two armies now stood front to front, on ground that gave no advantage to either. Our troops had rallied everywhere with heroic determination, and the army stood in its place, immovable as a rock. Baffled in every attempt to break our line, Bragg at length, at night-fall, withdrew, and darkness closed over the trampled field, shrouding its multitude of mangled, bleeding victims from sight.

It had been a strange battle, and neither could claim a victory. The numbers engaged on either side were probably about equal. Bragg had not waited for the whole of Longstreet's Corps to arrive, nor for several thousand Georgia militia, on the way to reinforce him. The rapid concentration of our troops, made it necessary for him to attack at once, while the army was in motion. But the regular intervals between our columns, which threatened at first to be our ruin—and if they had been greater, would have been—saved us; for each time the enemy struck our flank, our columns, coming up, took his flank in turn—and so on, in succession, till Negley and Wood met and stopped the last attack, and closed the battle. On our part, it was a battle without a plan. The object with Rosecrans was, to concentrate his army, and secure his communications with Chattanooga. Attacked while doing this, he had to hold the enemy at bay as best he could, and nothing but the indomitable bravery of the troops saved him from total defeat. That Saturday night was one of much suffering to the army, for it was cold and chilly, and no fires were allowed to be kindled. The soldiers sunk down on the ground, to brood over the losses of the day, and ponder on the terrible struggle that they knew must take place in the morning. Their ranks had been dreadfully thinned; no impression had been made on the enemy, and no reinforcements were near. They had taken a few prisoners, and captured three more guns than the enemy, but had been driven from Chickamauga Creek, and were where no water could be obtained, except as it was brought a great distance, from springs. Weary and thirsty, they were compelled to lie down on the trampled earth, and weary and thirsty they must fight this battle over again in the morning.

During the night, Rosecrans made some changes in his line of battle. The strong position at Gordon's Mill being no longer of any use to him—as the enemy was over the creek—he withdrew his right, resting it on Missionary Ridge. This shortened his lines by nearly a mile, and made his army face more to the south.

That night, a consultation was held at head-quarters, and the following general dispositions made for the next day: Thomas, strengthened by Johnson's and Palmer's divisions, was to hold the position he occupied. McCook, after his pickets were driven in, was to close with his main line on Thomas' right; while Crittenden was to hold two divisions in reserve behind the point of junction, to be used as circumstances might require. Thus the army stood, on the early Sabbath morning, awaiting Bragg's attack, that all knew would not be long delayed. Suddenly, the thunder of cannon on the extreme left, announced the opening of the conflict, and the next moment, the storm broke with appalling fury on Thomas. With their usual tactics, the rebels did not feel their way into our position, but fell in one overwhelming charge upon it. The battle had hardly commenced, when its uproar became so awful, that the boldest all along the line held his breath. Along a part of his line, Thomas had thrown up a breastwork of logs and rails, in front of which ran an incessant stream of fire. Up against it the rebels moved with desperate valor. Line upon line, they came steadily on—each, as it entered that withering fire, crumbling to fragments; yet still, fresh ranks sternly advanced over the spot where the last had gone down. But all in vain did that devouring fire consume the devoted columns—in vain did it shrivel up and destroy the head of each formation. The rebel leaders kept pouring in fresh troops, determined to quench that volcano with human blood, and choke it with living victims. Rosecrans, seeing how fearfully Thomas was pressed, ordered Negley over to his help, and Wood, of Crittenden's division, to supply Negley's place; but even this did not arrest the ever-increasing flood of rebels. For awhile, Wood, in the center, was heavily pressed; but still, the weight of the attack fell on Thomas. Maddened by their repeated repulse, the rebel leaders rallied their troops for one last, decisive assault. Covered by a terrific fire of artillery, the massive columns moved steadily forward, and entering, without shrinking, the fiery sleet that swept the field, pressed straight for that glowing breastwork. Thomas, seeing the danger, poured in his volleys with increased rapidity, and the artillerists double-shotted their guns with canister; but still, that dark gray mass, wrapped in its sulphurous shroud, never faltered, and, though bleeding and lessening at every step, crept nearer and nearer, till at last our troops began to waver. The officers strove nobly to steady them, while Thomas rode fearlessly along the undulating lines to inspire them. But it was a vain effort. Division after division crumbled away, and at length the whole wing swung back in disorder. Thomas, however, aided by his gallant lieutenants, again rallied it in a new position; and, with his right resting on Missionary Ridge, and his left on an eminence by the Lafayette road, and his center a little advanced, he sent urgent request for more troops.

It was now about noon, and Rosecrans, seeing how hard Reynolds was pressed, ordered Wood to leave his position in the center and support him. Brannan was between him and Reynolds, and to do this he had to fall back and march to the rear of the former. This left a wide gap in the lines, which, the enemy perceiving, dashed into as quick as thought. We had broken our own center—lost our own battle. Davis, from the right, moved quickly up to close the fatal opening; but he came too late. The rebel flood, breaking with resistless fury through it, smote him with one terrible blow, swinging him back with such violence that he fell to pieces with the shock. Palmer and Van Cleve, on the other side, shared the same fate. Sheridan, left alone on the right, of course went with Davis; yet, scorning to fly, he rallied his men, and for awhile made a stand, against fearful odds. Gallant, fearless and terrible, even in a lost fight, it was pitiful to see him strive with such hopeless desperation to maintain his old renown, in that wild tumult. Rosecrans himself, whose head-quarters were directly in rear, and had been carried away in the rush, could not rally the troops; and though, with drawn sword, followed by his staff, he galloped amid the broken ranks, he, McCook and Crittenden were all borne backward in the refluent tide, and a scene of confusion and terror followed that beggars all description. Artillery and caissons, and wagons and horses, and a vast, excited multitude, with here and there only a fragmentary formation, heaved and struggled on towards the gap in the mountains, through which the road leads to Rossville. Here they became choked up, and the shouts and yells and curses, that rose in the troubled air, were more appalling than the roar of battle. For a moment, the conflict seemed over. The Commander-in-Chief was gone—the centre and right gone, and nought remained but the wearied, exhausted left wing, that had also been forced backward. Yet it alone must save the army, if it is to be saved. It was a mighty task that now devolved on Thomas, but with such division and brigade leaders as Baird, Brannan, Reynolds, Negley, Wood, Harker, Hazen, Scribner, Turchin, and others like them, he would do it, or make it the bloodiest field ever won by mortal foe. The enemy, having it all his own way in every other part of the field, and confident of complete success, now bore down with redoubled fury on this comparatively feeble band—full seventy thousand men against a few divisions. So stood the battle at noon. Thomas might well survey his desperate position with a dismayed heart. Still, he had no thought of retreating. Right there he would stand, and stand victorious or perish with the army. Gathering up his thinned and bleeding ranks, he lined the semicircular ridge, on which he stood, with a wall of fire, and set it blazing with artillery from one extremity to another. The rebels came on in overwhelming masses, but could not break through it. Battalion after battalion moved up in splendid order, only to scatter and melt away like mist. There was no shrinking now. A high, heroic purpose had taken possession of every man, and he stood there, a willing victim, in the great sacrifice that was demanded of him. Unable to force Thomas' front, the enemy then began to swing around his flanks. On the right of Thomas, a low ridge ran at right angles to the extremity of his line, with a gorge directly in his rear; and now the rebels were seen pouring in dark masses through it. The heart of Thomas stood still at the sight. He had no troops to oppose this force, for his moving calls for help had found no response from his Commander. His army, to all human appearance, was lost. A few minutes more, and the shouting foe would be in his rear, and then a swift butchery or surrender would close the scene. Turning his eye away to the left, he saw a vast cloud of dust rising over the tree-tops, and soon after, dark columns of men moving swiftly across the fields towards him. But were they friends or foes? Captain Johnson, of Negley's Staff, having in the fight become separated from his division, just then galloped up and reported himself for duty. "Find out," exclaimed his distressed Commander, "what troops those are, moving upon me." Away dashed Johnson to fulfill his perilous mission. Thomas, to whom the moments were now fraught with life and death, watched with painful anxiety the approaching force, with his glass. Nearer and nearer they came, with the long, swinging tread of trained battalions. It is—yes, it is the battle-flag of Granger that waves and flutters in the breeze! Oh, who can tell the load that rolled from his heart as he caught the welcome sight? The firm-set lip relaxed for an instant, and a sudden gleam flashed from his blue eye. "All is not yet lost." The old flag shall yet fly over the field, and the battle-shout still roll along his shattered lines! Granger had heard, at half-past ten, the roar of the fearful storm that was bursting on Thomas, and, as it swelled and deepened, he moved uneasily about, and turned his eye along the road to catch the form of some Staff-officer with orders to march. But none came, and being three miles distant, he was afraid when one should come it might be too late. Seized by a sudden inspiration, he called to horse, and started his columns for the scene of conflict. Leaving Colonel McCook to cover the Ringgold road, he took Mitchell's and Whittaker's brigades, under the command of Steedman, and moved swiftly forward. After going about two miles, he came upon the enemy, and halted. But quickly perceiving that it was a small force, he ordered Colonel McCook to take care of it, and pushed on to where the incessant crash and roar of artillery and musketry told him the decisive struggle was going on. He had not come a moment too soon. As his eye took in the perilous condition of Thomas, it needed no consultation to decide what was to be done. He saw the fearful danger at a glance, and moved at once to meet it. The gallant Steedman dashed forward, and seizing the regimental colors, spurred to the head of the two brigades, and waving them above him, shouted the charge. His troops were mostly new recruits, but, fired at the danger that menaced Thomas, they sent up a shout that rose over the din of battle. Where that flag went, they would go, even into the gates of death; and, sweeping swiftly forward, they met, breast to breast, the veterans of Hindman, pouring through the gorge and already shouting the victory. There was no halting, no wavering, no rallying. Right on into the desolating fire, they pressed, reckless of numbers and of death, with a loud and thrilling shout. Over the batteries, over the astounded battalions of Hindman, they went, in one wild wave. It was marvelous—the charge of those two immortal brigades. For one moment, they were lost in the smoke of battle—the next, their standards were waving along the ridge. Like a thunderbolt they had fallen on the columns pouring through the gorge, and shivered them to fragments—like a whirlwind they had swept the ridge, clearing it of the foe. Only twenty minutes had passed—and yet, in that brief time, the battle had been saved; and in the same short interval, a thousand men on our side, or nearly a third of those two heroic brigades, had fallen. A smile, such as heroes wear, lighted up the face of Thomas, when he saw our victorious banners waving where but a moment before the standards of the enemy were advancing to his certain destruction. Hindman, enraged to see the victory so suddenly snatched from his hands, rallied to retake the position, and Longstreet's veterans were sent against it. Though Steedman, by the fall of his horse in the charge, had been bruised severely, yet he still kept the field, and with scarce a dozen pieces of artillery in all, swept the enemy with such a terrific fire that he was forced to retire. But though driven back, he returned again and again to the attack; yet those two immortal brigades stood like a blazing citadel on the heights. Baffled here, the enemy advanced on the left. Thomas saw the heavy column approaching, and, pointing to it, told Reynolds to "go in there." This gallant Commander obeyed, and, facing his troops by the rear rank, to save time, ordered them to "charge bayonets." Springing forward at the double-quick, the weary, brave fellows walked straight over the column, capturing several hundred prisoners in their fierce passage. Night was now coming on, and Steedman's brigades, which all that Sabbath afternoon, though bleeding and lessening, had stood rock-fast, had exhausted all their own ammunition, and all they could gather from the dead and dying around them. In this fearful dilemma, Thomas saw the rebels rallying for a last assault. Casting his eye along his shattered line, standing stern and dark in the gathering gloom, he ordered it to "stand fast." Waiting till the shadowy mass came within striking distance, he shouted, "*Give them the cold steel!*" With bayonets at charge, they leaped forward at the double-quick, rending the gloom with their shout. As the rebels saw them advancing, and caught the faint sheen of their bayonets in the twilight, they turned and fled. The last blow had been struck, and a thrilling shout went up from the darkened field.

The struggle was over, and the enemy, exhausted and discouraged, sullenly withdrew. Never was a great battle more nearly lost, and then saved—not even that of Marengo. Thomas, and his brave commanders and troops, had covered themselves with glory; and Rosecrans sent him word to use his own judgment about attempting to hold his position. The former, seeing that his troops had been fearfully overtasked, and that ammunition, food and water were sadly wanting, concluded to fall back on Rossville, which place he reached in good order—the enemy hovering near, but afraid to risk another blow. A new line of battle was here formed, with the aid of McCook's and Crittenden's divisions, and the advance of the enemy awaited. But he had been too severely punished, however, to renew the attack, and the next night the whole army fell back to Chattanooga.

A bloodier Sabbath than that of the 20th of September, never closed over this land. Sixteen thousand, three hundred and fifty-one, or about a third of Rosecrans' splendid army, had disappeared, of which only five thousand were taken prisoners. Thirty-six guns, twenty caissons, and eight thousand, four hundred and fifty small arms, and other spoils, fell into the hands of the enemy; while we could show but two thousand prisoners to offset all these losses. The loss of the enemy in killed and wounded, however, was greater than ours; for, in their headlong advance on our batteries and positions, they had been mowed down with terrible slaughter. But, though they got the victory, it was to them a barren one, for they failed to recover Chattanooga. The possession of that was the chief object of the campaign, and we still held it, while the enemy, after two days of desperate fighting, had gained only a few miles of useless fields and roads.

Much criticism was passed on this battle, and on the movements that preceded it, and difference of opinion will probably exist forever. It is much easier to tell the causes of a failure, than to prevent it; still, there were some grave mistakes, that ought to have been better guarded against. If it was designed or supposed that Rosecrans, after he had taken Chattanooga, would advance further into the interior, the Government at Washington should have had supporting columns much nearer that place than it did have. A portion of Grant's army should have marched long before; for it was not to be expected that that stronghold would fall without a fierce struggle, and it might be at a sacrifice of a third of the army. Such a contingency ought to have been provided for, but was not; and when that loss actually occurred, it was by the narrowest chance that Chattanooga was saved.

Again, when the enemy evacuated Chattanooga, he did not destroy the supplies or bridges along the route, thus showing one of two things—either that he had fled in such haste that he could not do it, or that he expected to return and need them himself again very soon. Rosecrans adopted the former view, and therefore strained every nerve to cut off the retreat of a demoralized enemy. In doing this, he made so wide a separation of his corps that it was sure to provoke an attack if any fight whatever was left in the enemy. But the idea that Bragg had failed to destroy supplies and bridges through want of time, was preposterous —at all events, the circumstances were sufficiently suspicious to demand the greatest caution. The result showed it; for if the rebels had not committed a great blunder, the probabilities are, we should have lost Chattanooga.

C S A
GEN. STONEWALL JACKSON
GEN. MAGRUDER
GEN. P.S. EWELL
GEN. A.P. HILL
GEN. J. LONGSTREET
REBEL GENERALS.
Eng^d by H. Wright Smith

CHAPTER XX.

THE ARMY AT CHATTANOOGA—GRANT PLACED IN COMMAND OF THE MISSISSIPPI DIVISION—KNOXVILLE CAPTURED BY BURNSIDE—JOY OF THE PEOPLE—BESIEGED BY LONGSTREET—GRANT TAKES COMMAND AT CHATTANOOGA—SHERMAN ORDERED TO JOIN HIM—HOOKER EFFECTS A LODGMENT IN LOOKOUT VALLEY—HAZEN'S EXPLOIT—BATTLE OF WAUHATCHIE—SHERMAN'S ARRIVAL—THE ARMY TAKES UP ITS ASSIGNED POSITION—GRANT'S PLAN—CAPTURE OF LOOKOUT MOUNTAIN—BATTLE ABOVE THE CLOUDS—THE BATTLE OF MISSIONARY RIDGE—THE VICTORY—PURSUIT OF THE ENEMY—SHERMAN SENT TO RELIEVE BURNSIDE—LONGSTREET ABANDONS THE SIEGE—BANKS AT NEW ORLEANS—EXPEDITION TO SABINE CITY—EXPEDITION TO TEXAS—ITS FAILURE—THE DEPARTMENT.

ROSECRANS' position in Chattanooga soon became exceedingly precarious, though it was very strong—the flanks of the army resting on the Tennessee above and below the place. The enemy advanced against it, and occupied Missionary Ridge and Lookout Mountain, his line stretching across Chattanooga Valley. Our communications by way of Bridgeport, on the south bank of the river, were cut off, while the sharpshooters there effectually commanded the road on the opposite side. Supplies therefore had to be hauled for sixty miles by land, over mountain roads that soon, from the Fall rains, became almost impassable. A rebel raid, in the meantime, destroyed several hundred wagon-loads of provisions, and damaged the railroad between Stevenson and Nashville, rendering the subsistence of our army uncertain; and indeed, for a time, it was doubtful whether our communications would not be entirely destroyed, and thus a retreat become inevitable. This would be extremely perilous, for the artillery and war material would have to be abandoned. Chattanooga was the key to East Tennessee, and the army there at the same time threatened Atlanta, the grand focus of the net-work of railroads connecting the southern States of the Confederacy. If we were driven back from this place, the struggle in the Valley of the Mississippi would have to be gone over again. Hence, Grant sent a dispatch to Thomas, to hold on to the last extremity. The latter, in reply, assured him that he would keep the position at all hazards.

While affairs were in this precarious state, Rosecrans was relieved by Thomas; and in a few days, Grant, who had been placed in command of the Departments of the Ohio, of the Cumberland, and of the Tennessee—constituting the Military Division of the Mississippi—arrived in Chattanooga, and took charge in person. Hooker, with two corps from the East, had previously reached the vicinity of Bridgeport, thus increasing the difficulty of feeding the army.

In the meantime, however, a movement had been made which had an important bearing on Chattanooga. Burnside had, during the Summer, planned a campaign against Knoxville—the capture of which had been a great desideratum with the Government since the beginning of the war. His preparations being completed, he set his columns in motion in August. Buckner held the place with but a small force, and so secret had the movements of Burnside been kept, and so rapid was his march, that he encountered no opposition; and Colonel Foster, with the advance, entered the place on the 1st of September. Burnside himself proceeded to Kingston, where his scouts encountered the cavalry pickets of Rosecrans. The panic at Knoxville, at his sudden arrival, was great, and the rebel troops left behind them, in their flight, a considerable quantity of quartermaster-stores. The reception of our troops by the loyal East Tennesseans, who had almost begun to despair of ever seeing the old flag among them again, was most enthusiastic and touching.

They cooked everything they had for the soldiers, without ever dreaming of pay. Women stood by the roadside with pails of water, waving Union flags, and shouting, "Hurrah for the Union!"—and "Welcome, welcome, General Burnside, welcome to East Tennesse!" greeted the General, as he moved along with his Staff.

The rebel garrison at Cumberland Gap, two thousand strong, was cut off, and, on the 9th, surrendered to our forces. Burnside now occupied the East Tennessee railroad as far as Morristown, and a strong force proceeded down the road towards Chattanooga; and it was generally believed that the whole army would soon join that of Rosecrans. But the battle of Chickamauga, a few days after, and the shutting up of Rosecrans in Chattanooga, entirely changed the aspect of affairs, and it soon became evident that Burnside would have enough to do, to take care of himself—for Bragg, feeling that he was more than a match for the army at Chattanooga, sent Longstreet, with his division, to retake Knoxville. Being confident that we should be compelled to evacuate both places, the enemy expected to drive our armies back to the Ohio.

But, at this time, there was another important character moving to the scene of action. Before Grant was put over the army at Chattanooga, he, as soon as he heard of Rosecrans' disaster at Chickamauga, ordered Sherman—then on the Big Black River, twenty miles east of Vicksburg—to send a division to his aid. Sherman received this dispatch on the 22nd of September, and at four o'clock that day, Osterhaus, with his division, was on his way to Vicksburg, and the next day steaming towards Memphis. On the 23rd, Sherman received another order, to follow with his whole army. In four days, he was slowly steaming up towards Memphis. Fuel was scarce, and he was compelled to land troops to gather fence-rails and haul wood from the interior in wagons, to keep up steam. At Memphis, he got orders from Halleck to proceed to Athens, Alabama—repairing the railroad as he went, and depending on himself for supplies. The work was at once begun, and gangs were kept employed day and night; but Sherman soon saw—as Buell did, the year before, when marching to the same destination—that this would be too slow work, and he determined to take to the highways till he could clear his front. Having scattered the enemy, he again went to work repairing the railroad, in accordance with his first orders. But a dispatch from Grant, urging him forward, made him abandon again the unwelcome task, and push on in the manner which his judgment approved.

In the meantime, Grant was getting everything ready for his arrival, when he designed to make a general assault on the enemy's strong position.

All this time, the troops and animals were suffering for the want of provisions, which the obstruction of transportation rendered extremely scarce. As was stated previously, Missionary Ridge drops like a pendant, in a south-westerly direction, from the Tennessee River, above Chattanooga, and Lookout Mountain, in the same direction from the river, below the place. Chattanooga, lying in a bend of the river between the two mountains, was overlooked and commanded by both heights, and hence, both must be taken. Hooker was selected to operate against the latter mountain; but, in order to make a lodgment on the south side of the river, it was necessary to occupy Brown's Ferry, which was three miles below Lookout Mountain, by the river, and six from Chattanooga, yet, owing to the sharp bend of the stream that here runs back almost parallel to its course, was only a mile and a half from the latter place by land. The possession of this ferry would also lessen the distance of transportation to Bridgeport. The Chief-Engineer, General W. F. Smith, proposed a plan for seizing it, which, after a reconnoissance by Grant and Thomas, was adopted. Four thousand men being at once placed under his command, fifty pontoons, capable of holding twenty-five men apiece besides the oarsmen, and also two flatboats for carrying about a hundred more, were built, in which fifteen hundred picked men, under the gallant Hazen, were placed. It was, we have seen, six miles, by the tortuous river, to the Ferry—three miles of which were picketed by the enemy. On the night of the 27th of October, these pontoons—mere boxes—were quietly pushed off, and floated noiselessly down the current. It was very dark, and the drift of the current rendering the use of oars unnecessary, they passed unheeded by the pickets on shore. Down, around Moccasin Point, in front of Lookout Mountain, they rapidly floated, without being discovered. The landing was to be made at two different points, and here the alarm was given, and the flash of musketry lit up the darkness. This roused the neighboring camps of the enemy, but the Union troops jumped ashore, and quickly formed to repel an attack. The empty boats were then rowed swiftly across the river, to a point where stood the balance of the four thousand, who had secretly marched thither by land. These having been taken in, they were rowed back to the spot where the others had disembarked. A strong position was immediately secured, and intrenchments thrown up. The enemy, taken wholly by surprise, after a feeble resistance retreated up the Valley. The materials for a pontoon bridge, which had also been brought down by land, and concealed, were now brought out, and by noon a bridge, nine hundred feet long, spanned the river, by which supplies and reinforcements could be forwarded to our troops. The next day, the whole of the Eleventh Corps was across, and encamped in Lookout Valley. The enemy, alarmed at this demonstration, made an attempt to drive back our forces by a night attack.

BATTLE OF WAUHATCHIE.

Howard's Corps, at the time, was only a mile or so from Brown's Ferry. Geary, with his division, went into camp near Wauhatchie, three miles distant. Hooker, who was with Howard's Corps, was aroused about one o'clock in the morning, by the "muttering of heavy musketry" in the direction of Geary. The latter had been suddenly attacked by overwhelming numbers, and Hooker, anxious for his safety, ordered Howard to double-quick his nearest division, Shurz's, to his aid. "Forward to their relief, boys!" he shouted, as they streamed off on a run, through the gloom. They had not gone far, however, when suddenly there came a blaze of musketry from the hills near by, where no enemy was supposed to be. Tyndale's brigade was immediately detached, to charge the heights, while the other brigade kept on towards Geary. Steinwehr's division now came up, and the hill to the rear of Schurz, and along which the road ran, was also found to be occupied by the enemy. This, Orlan Smith's brigade was ordered to carry with the bayonet. It was bright moonlight; yet but little of the difficulties of the ascent could be seen. It was very steep, and covered with underbrush and seamed with gullies and ravines, and "almost inaccessible by daylight." Yet, right up this, two hundred feet high, in the face of a heavy fire, this skeleton brigade was ordered to charge bayonet. Flooded in the mellow light, silent as death, the Seventy-third Ohio and Thirty-third Massachusetts pressed up the slope, and at length reached the top, where they came upon rifle-pits, out of which suddenly burst a volley from nearly two thousand muskets. Overwhelmed by this awful fire, the brave fellows fell back in disorder to the foot of the hill. Though now fully aware of the difficulties before them, and that three times their number crowned the heights, these noble regiments re-formed their lines, and again sternly breasted the hill. Shouts, and yells, and taunts, were hurled down on them, and the crashing volleys tore through them; yet, without firing a shot—with set teeth and flashing eyes—they climbed steadily up to those blazing rifle-pits, and then with one bound cleared them. The bayonet did the whole work, and not a shot was fired till the enemy was in full retreat. One volley was poured after them, and then the shout of victory arose, wild and clear, in the night air. It was an astonishing charge. No wonder Hooker said, "No troops ever rendered more brilliant service," and that the reserved Thomas declared, "The bayonet charge of Howard's troops, made up the side of a steep and difficult hill over two hundred feet high, completely routing the enemy from his barricades on the top, * * * will rank among the most distinguished feats of arms of this war."

All this time, heavy and incessant volleys of musketry arose from the spot where Geary was struggling against overwhelming numbers. The fighting here was desperate, and several times he was nearly overborne; but, with that tenacity which has always distinguished him, he still clung to his position, and at length hurled the enemy back, compelling him to take refuge on Lookout Mountain. The Valley was now ours. Geary gained new honors in this hard-fought battle; but they were dearly won, for his son, a captain, was killed.

This fight by moonlight, after midnight, amid those wild hills—that blazed the while with musketry and exploding shells—presented a strange spectacle. Hooker himself was in the thickest of it, shouting on the men.

Our forces being firmly established here, steamboats could run up to Brown's Ferry, from which it was but a mile and a half to the upper bridge, opposite Chattanooga. The army was now relieved from the fear of starvation, unless the bridges should be carried away by rafts sent down by the enemy from above.

This was a great improvement in the condition of affairs; still, Grant felt too weak to assume the offensive against the strong works which confronted him, until Sherman should arrive.

The latter crossed the Tennessee in person, on the 1st of November, but there was no way by which to get his army over, and it had to take the long march by Fayetteville to Bridgeport. Sherman, in the meantime, pressing on, rode into Chattanooga on the 15th. Never was a man more welcome. Grant had received a summons from Bragg, to remove the non-combatants from Chattanooga, as he was about to bombard it, to which the former had returned no reply, but he now felt that he soon would be ready to send one, in the shape of his strong columns. Sherman's troops, after their long and wearisome march, needed rest sadly, and expected it, before entering on one of the most hazardous undertakings of the war. "But," said the gallant leader, "I saw enough of the condition of men and animals in Chattanooga, to inspire me with renewed energy." With a part of his command, he was directed to make a demonstration on Lookout Mountain, while, with the main army, he crossed the river and marched up above Chattanooga, opposite Missionary ridge. Returning to Bridgeport, he took a row-boat, and passed down the river, to hurry forward his weary, foot-sore divisions. Ewing's division was the force left to make the proposed demonstration on Lookout Mountain. The rest were hurried forward, but the roads were almost impassable—making the increased effort demanded at the end of such a long march, a terrible task to the soldiers. But they toiled cheerfully forward, in obedience to the orders of their beloved Commander, and, by the 23rd, were well up, and lay concealed behind the hills opposite the Chickamauga Creek, which, skirting the extremity of Missionary Ridge, here empties into the Tennessee. One division, however, was left behind—a delay caused by the breaking of the pontoon bridge at Brown's Ferry—and it was compelled to join Hooker's Corps, and operate with him in the battle that followed.

By a skillful manœuver, he, the same night, moved a small force silently along the river, capturing every guard of the enemy's pickets but one. The next thing was, to get his army across the Tennessee—here nearly thirteen hundred feet wide. About three miles above him, and on the same side, he found a stream emptying into the river. Thither, a hundred and sixteen boats were carried, by a concealed road, and launched, while three thousand men lay ready to embark in them. An hour after midnight, on the 24th, these boats silently floated down into the Tennessee, and, passing for three miles the enemy's pickets, landed the troops on both sides of the Chickamauga Creek, which emptied into the river opposite Sherman's army. Two divisions, with artillery, were soon ferried over, and a *tete-du-pont* established. In a few hours, a bridge fourteen hundred feet long was completed, and shaking to the tread of Sherman's mighty columns. Another bridge, two hundred feet long, was flung across the Chickamauga Creek. The extreme north point of Missionary Ridge was not occupied by the enemy—his right being further back, near the tunnel through which the railroad passed. This extremity, Sherman at once seized, thereby threatening Bragg's communications. A cavalry force, in the meantime, was sent off eastward towards Cleveland.

Grant now had Sherman's army above, and Hooker's below him, and both on the same side of the river; while Thomas lay in front of Chattanooga. Missionary Ridge, tending south-west from Sherman, passed in front of Chattanooga, where the center lay.

Bragg was amazed at this sudden apparition of a powerful army on his extreme right, and immediately made preparations to dislodge Sherman. In the meantime, Hooker, from below, moved against Lookout Mountain, and, by dark, carried the nose of it, and at once opened direct communications with Chattanooga. His advance up the steep sides of the mountain had been made with great celerity and skill. A thick fog for awhile concealed him, but, as it lifted before the sun, the cliffs above were seen crowded with the enemy, while cannon sent a plunging fire from the heights. Grant, far down in the mist-shrouded valley below, could hear the thunder of guns and crash of musketry high up in the clouds above, as though the gods were warring there. Says an eye-witness: "At this juncture, the scene became one of most exciting interest. The thick fog, which had heretofore rested in dense folds upon the sides of the mountain, concealing the combatants from view, suddenly lifted to the summit of the lofty ridge, revealing to the anxious gaze of thousands in the valleys and on the plains below, a scene such as is witnessed but once in a century. General Geary's columns, flushed with victory, grappled with the foe upon the rocky ledges, and drove him back with slaughter from his works. While the result was uncertain, the attention was breathless and painful; but when victory perched upon our standards, shout upon shout rent the air. The whole army, with one accord, broke out into joyous acclamations. The enthusiasm of the scene beggars description. Men were frantic with joy, and even General Thomas himself, who seldom exhibits his emotions, said involuntarily, 'I did not think it possible for men to accomplish so much.'" The day before, Thomas had made a strong reconnoissance in force, in his front, and, with but slight loss, had occupied Orchard Knob, and developed the lines of the enemy. Everything was therefore now ready for the grand assault upon the rebel position. Bragg had thought that Chattanooga was his beyond a doubt; but suddenly, to the right, in front, and left of him, he saw himself confronted by three armies. Still, he believed Missionary Ridge to be impregnable, and that no force could climb its steep and rugged sides, in the face of his powerful batteries.

Sherman, from his position, could glance across to Tunnell Hill, on which the rebel batteries were placed; and he looked grave, but determined, at the fearful task that had been assigned his brave troops. Before the great, decisive day (the 25th) had fairly dawned, he was in the saddle, and by the dim light that streaked the cloudy east betokening a stormy day, rode along his entire line. A deep valley lay between him and the steep hill beyond, which was partly covered with trees to the narrow, wooded top, across which was a breastwork of logs and earth, dark with men. Two guns enfiladed the narrow way that led to it. Further back, arose a still higher hill, lined with guns that could pour a plunging fire on the first hill if it should be taken. The depth and character of the gorge between, could not be ascertained. Just as the rising sun was tinging with red the murky rain-clouds, the bugles sounded "Forward!" and Corse, leading the advance, briskly descended the hill, crossed the valley under a heavy fire, began to ascend the opposite heights, and soon gained a foothold; but the spot where he stood was swept by the enemy's artillery.

BATTLE OF CHATTANOOGA.

The great battle had now fairly opened, and for more than an hour it swayed backward and forward in front of

Sherman. Bringing up brigade after brigade, this gallant Commander strove nobly, but in vain, to carry the lofty heights above him. By ten o'clock, it was one peal of thunder from top to base, while the smoke, in swift puffs and floating masses, draped it like a waving mantle. Corse, severely wounded, was borne to the rear; yet still the columns stubbornly held the ground. All the fornoon, the battle raged furiously at this point. This most northern and vital position must be held by the rebels at all hazards, for if once taken, their rear would be threatened, with all the stores at Chickamauga. Hence, Bragg massed his forces here, and at three o'clock, says Sherman, "column after column of the enemy was streaming toward me; gun after gun poured its concentric shot on us from every hill and spur that gave a view of any part of the ground." Once, he was partially forced back, but by a skillful move, he recovered his ground and drove the pursuing, shouting enemy to his cover. His men were sternly held to their terrible work; but Sherman was getting impatient for Grant to move on the center, as he told him the night before he would. From his elevated position, he could see the flags of Thomas' Corps waving in the murky atmosphere; but hour after hour passed away, and still they did not advance. The enemy was steadily accumulating his forces against him, and his troops, that had fought from early dawn, were getting weary. Grant had sat on his horse, listening to the thunder of artillery on his right, as Hooker came down like an avalanche from the heights of Lookout Mountain, and to the deafening uproar on his left, where his favorite lieutenant, Sherman, was hurling his brave columns on the batteries of the enemy; but still he did not move. Thinking, at one time, that Sherman was too hard pressed, he sent over a brigade to his help; but the latter, who had become thoroughly aroused at the resistance he met with, sent it back, saying he did not need it. And so, hour after hour, for six miles, it flamed and thundered along those rocky crests, until at last the decisive moment, looked for by Grant, had arrived. In front of him, the steep acclivity went sheer up four hundred feet. The base was encircled with a line of rifle-pits, while the summit was black with batteries. Between him and the foot of the mountain, was an open space a mile and a half wide, which the advancing columns would be compelled to cross. He saw that it would require no common effort, and no common bravery on the part of troops, to reach and climb that steep, in the face of such difficulties, and he therefore wished Sherman to push the rebel left till Bragg, in order to save the key of his position, would be compelled to weaken his center; and also till Hooker could come up, who was detained in building a bridge. The rebel Commander, not dreaming that Grant would attempt to advance up the steep face of the mountain in front, and evidently thinking that he meant at all hazards to crush his right, and thus threaten his rear, drew away his troops from the center, till the line here became comparatively weak. This was what Grant had been waiting for, though fearful that the day would be passed before it came. But it had come at last, and Hooker being well advanced, he, from his position on Indian Hill, ordered the signal for the "Forward!" to be given. These were, six cannon shots, to be fired at intervals of two seconds. Strong and steady the order rang out: "Number one, fire! Number two, fire! Number three, fire!" "It seemed to me," says an eye-witness, "like the tolling of the clock of destiny. And when, at 'Number six, fire!' the roar throbbed out with the flash, you should have seen the dead line, that had been lying behind the works all day, come to resurrection in the twinkling of an eye, and leap like a blade from its scabbard." Three divisions, under the command of Granger, composed the storming force, and as they moved off towards the frowning heights, the enemy seemed to regard it as a mere review. But, with a swift, steady motion, the glittering line swept on, and it was soon evident that desperate work was afoot. Suddenly, all along the crest of the ridge, the artillery opened, and the gallant line began to melt away. Still, it never faltered—the banners kept advancing, and at last that terrible mile and a half were past, and the columns stood face to face with the long line of rifle-pits at the base of the mountain. A sheet of fire ran along the summit, cutting with fearful mortality our exposed battalions. There was no time to stop here, for, great as was the obstacle that confronted them, it was only a barrier of mist, compared to the awful work that lay beyond; and so, with one wild cheer and a bound, they cleared it, and stood panting in the deserted ditch. And now for the ridge. "Take it if you can!" passed along the bleeding line, but it was already advancing. The brave fellows, casting one look up the steep, rocky sides, to the thirteen batteries flaming at the top, clutched their weapons with a firmer grasp, and began to mount the slope. Here can be no rush—no sudden charge. Step by step, like mountain goats, they must win their way upward. As the smoke lifted here and there, Grant saw, with inexpressible anxiety, the regimental flags, like mere crimson specks, fluttering slowly upward. Regardless of shot and shell, each vied with the other in the advance. Over their heads, from Forts Wood and Negley, and other batteries, our shot and shell flew with fearful precision, and fell crashing in the rebel works. Rocks and stones, and shells with lighted fuses, were rolled down on the torn line, and it now and then halted, under some projecting rocks, for breath. But "Forward!" again rung above the uproar, and each flag seemed to have a voice crying "EXCELSIOR." Oh! it was a thrilling sight. Shot and shell were doing their murderous work; but nothing short of annihilation could stop those noble battalions. Higher, and still higher, they crept, until at last, just as the sun was sinking in the west, they reached the summit, and then, as the gathered billow thunders and foams along and over the sunken ledges of the sea, they, with one wild shout and burst, swept over the deadly batteries. The next moment, cheer after cheer went up all along the smoking crest, and rolled down the crimson steep, till, to the right and left, and far below, the air trembled with glad echoes. Dismayed, and filled with consternation at the frightful calamity, Bragg, mounted on his gray horse, sped away to the rear, followed by his discomfited host. The army was now thrown forward in swift pursuit, which was kept up till late at night, and renewed next morning before daylight. As the columns swept on, wagons, guns, caissons, forage, stores, and all the wreck of a routed army, met them at every step. By night, the rear-guard of the enemy was reached, and a fight ensued, which lasted till darkness closed in. The next day, Hooker and Thomas joined in the pursuit, and the beaten enemy was smitten with blow upon blow, until further advance became impossible. In the meantime, Sherman detached Howard to move against the railroad between Dalton and Cleveland, to destroy it. This was done, and communication between Bragg and Longstreet cut off.

Our total loss in this battle, was about four thousand. We took six thousand prisoners, forty pieces of artillery, and five or six thousand small arms. The rebel killed and wounded was not known.

Sherman was now ordered to return to Chattanooga; but, receiving permission to make a circuit by the north, as far as Hiawassee, he did so, destroying railroads and capturing stores. "This," says Sherman, "was to have been the limit of our journey. Officers and men had brought no luggage or provisions, and the weather was bitter cold." But at this moment, Grant received a dispatch from Burnside, at Knoxville, saying that his supplies would not last a week longer, and asking for help. To reach him, nearly ninety miles distant, in that time, would require heavy marching; but Burnside and Knoxville must be saved, if human effort could do it. Grant at once ordered Granger to march; but finding that he would not have the necessary force, and, moreover, that he "moved with reluctance and complaint," he determined, "notwithstanding the fact that the two divisions of Sherman's forces had marched from Memphis, and had gone into battle immediately on their arrival at Chattanooga, to send him with his command," including Granger's. This was assigning him a fearful task, and the iron Commander, though shrinking from no effort where duty called, felt that it was asking a hard thing of his brave, exhausted men. The language he uses in regard to it, shows this, and also reveals the grand character of the man. "Seven days before," says he, "we had left our camps on the other side of the Tennessee, with two days' rations, without a change of clothing, stripped for the fight, with but a single blanket or coat per man,—from myself to the private included. Of course, we then had no provisions save what we gathered by the road, and were ill supplied for such a march. But we learned that twelve thousand of our fellow-soldiers were beleaguered in the mountain town of Knoxville, eighty-four miles distant; that they needed relief, and must have it in three days. *This was enough, and it had to be done.*" Noble words, from a noble man! His tired troops, though feeling that others could better make this long march, cheerfully consented to go, and that very night started forward. By daylight, they had made fifteen miles, and, on the 2nd of December, marched twenty-six, pushing the enemy, that attempted to delay their advance, before them.

In the meantime, Burnside was severely pressed. Having only some twelve thousand men, he had been obliged to fall back before Longstreet with his overwhelming force. Recrossing the Tennessee, which he had passed in his advance, and fighting as he retired, he was finally compelled to take refuge in Knoxville. Longstreet, confident of success, then sat down in regular siege before the place, knowing its reduction a certainty unless it should be relieved. Fearing its reinforcement, he made a desperate assault upon its strong works, but was repulsed with heavy loss. The near approach of Sherman now caused him to abandon his siege of twenty days. It was hoped that, being cut off from Bragg, his Corps would be captured or dispersed; but, passing around the stronghold that he could not capture, he retreated towards Virginia. Burnside pursued him, and an engagement took place at Beams' Station, but Longstreet succeeded in falling back without serious loss, and eventually opened up his communications with Richmond.

Sherman had pushed forward with great celerity. But the rebels burning the bridges in their retreat, he feared he might be delayed till Burnside would despair of succor, and he therefore ordered Colonel Long, commanding his cavalry brigade, to take his fleetest, strongest animals, and hurry forward, and be in Knoxville in twenty-four hours "*at whatever cost of life or horse-flesh.*" The distance was forty miles, and the roads horrible. But this gallant Commander accomplished the task assigned him, and the clatter of his horses' hoofs in the streets of Knoxville, on the night of the 3rd, sent joy to the hearts of the beleaguered little army. Sherman continued to advance till the night of the 5th, when a messenger arrived from Burnside, saying that Longstreet had raised the siege. Sending on Granger's two divisions to Knoxville, he then halted his army, for his work was done. He himself rode on to Knoxville, to see Burnside. He then leisurely returned, with his wearied army, to Chattanooga. The work it had done was chiefly of a character not to attract public attention, but it deserved higher encomiums than though it had won a victory. With short rations, poorly protected from the weather, sometimes barefooted, it had marched four hundred miles through the enemy's country, —without sleep for three successive nights—crossed the Tennessee, borne the brunt of the fight at Chattanooga, pursued the flying enemy into Georgia, then wheeled about and, by forced marches for nearly a hundred miles, compelled Longstreet to raise the siege of Knoxville, and then had marched back again.

East Tennessee was saved—in fact, a great part of the Valley of the Mississippi; for, had Knoxville and Chattanooga fallen, Grant could hardly have made a stand short of Nashville. And yet, the probabilities all were that these two places would fall. Grant knew that he could not long remain at Chattanooga with the rebel batteries crowning the heights that overlooked it; while, without help from him, Burnside must surrender. His only hope lay in the successful assault of the enemy's works. But this was a desperate measure, in which he knew the chances were against him. Still, it must be taken, or all be lost. Thanks to his brilliant strategy, and the bravery of his troops, he succeeded, and the turning point of the rebellion was gained.

While these momentous events were transpiring in East Tennessee, Banks, at New Orleans, was busy in his Department, and great results were expected from the army under his command, though no formidable rebel force confronted him.

In September, having been reinforced from Grant's army, he sent General Franklin to seize Sabine City, situated on the Sabine River. Commodore Bell, commanding the Gulf Squadron, detached four gunboats, under Lieutenant-Commanding Crocker, to co-operate with him, assisted by a hundred and eighty sharp-shooters from the army. The batteries, however, proved too powerful for the gunboats.

The Clifton and Sachem were disabled, and captured with all on board, and the expedition returned to Brashear City. The army afterward advanced, and, on the 21st of October, occupied Opelousas, and quite a severe fight occurred, Nov. 3d, near Bayou Bourbeaux—General Washburn commanding.

In September, Little Rock, Arkansas, was captured by General Steele.

In November, an important expedition was made into Texas. The garrison at Esperanza fled at our approach, after blowing up the magazine, and ten guns were captured. Brazos Island, Point Isabel and Brownsville were in Banks' hands on the 9th of November. From this point, the army marched north-east a hundred miles, to Aranzas, capturing three guns and a hundred prisoners. General A. J. Hamilton, of Texas, having been appointed Military Governor of the State, by the President, accompanied the army, and every one looked to the expulsion of Magruder—Commander of the rebel forces—and the speedy establishment of Federal authority. But not long after, the expedition was abandoned, and General Banks returned to New Orleans, followed by Hamilton. Washburn soon after left the army, and Major-General Dana was placed in chief command.

News of a projected movement against Mobile took the place of news from the army in Texas, and its failure there seemed to die out of mind. Festivities, balls and masquerades occupied the winter months in New Orleans, and military matters were kept in abeyance. Preparations were also made for an election to come off in February, and Banks devoted himself to the civil duties of his Department—not the least of which was the question of compensated labor. The large number of slaves made suddenly free must work, and to a great extent under their old masters, and therefore it was important that some just and equitable system be adopted, and power given to enforce it.

CHAPTER XXI.

ARMY OF THE POTOMAC—MEADE'S ADVANCE TO THE RAPIDAN—COMPELLED TO RETREAT—GALLANTRY OF KILPATRICK AND THE CAVALRY—BATTLE OF BRISTOW STATION—SUCCESSES AT KELLY'S FORD AND RAPPAHANNOCK STATION—MEADE'S SECOND ADVANCE TO THE RAPIDAN—THE RETREAT—WINTER QUARTERS—AVERILL'S RAID IN WESTERN VIRGINIA—NATIONAL CEMETERY AT GETTYSBURG—THE PRESIDENT'S PROCLAMATION OF AMNESTY—PROPOSITION TO ADMIT REBEL STATES INTO THE UNION—POLITICAL EXCITEMENT—CHANGE OF PLAN IN CARRYING ON THE WAR—GRANT MADE LIEUTENANT-GENERAL—SHERMAN'S GREAT MARCH THROUGH MISSISSIPPI.

IN the East, the Army of the Potomac had remained comparatively quiet, but, on the approach of Autumn, it again assumed offensive operations, for it was necessary to occupy the attention of Lee, as he was sending reinforcements to Bragg. A general advance of the army was therefore determined upon, about the middle of September. Pleasanton was directed first to cross the Rappahannock, and attack the rebel cavalry picketing the river in the neighborhood of Culpepper. Gregg crossed at Sulphur Springs, Buford at Rappahannock Bridge, and Kilpatrick at Kelly's Ford. These, moving on Culpepper, attacked Stuart, who held the town, and, after an obstinate fight, drove him out, capturing three guns. Meade now advanced, and crossing the river with his entire army, made the place his headquarters, with the cavalry guarding his flanks and rear. Lee, in the meantime, lay encamped near Orange Court House, and, though much inferior in numbers, boldly crossed the Rapidan on the 9th of October, and, by a skillful movement, completely outflanked Meade, which compelled the latter to break up his camp and retreat—losing some of his stores in his hasty retrogade movement. Pleasanton, with the cavalry, remained behind to watch the enemy, and then slowly retired toward the retreating army. Buford had been forced back more rapidly than Kilpatrick, whose command—with Davis over the right brigade, and Custer over the left—fell back more slowly. When the latter reached Brandy Station, he found that the former, ignorant of his movements, was far in advance, leaving his right entirely exposed. To make matters worse, Stuart had passed around his left, so that Kilpatrick, with whom was Pleasanton himself, was suddenly cut off. This gallant leader saw at a glance the peril of his position, and, riding to a slight eminence, took a hasty survey of the ground before him. He then gave his orders, and three thousand swords leaped from their scabbards, and a long, loud shout rolled over the field. With a heavy line of skirmishers thrown out, to protect his flanks and rear, he moved in three columns straight on the rebel host, that watched his coming. At first, the well-closed columns advanced on a walk, while the batteries of Remington and Elder played with fearful precision upon the hostile ranks. He thus kept on, till within a few hundred yards of the rebel lines, when the band struck up "Yankee Doodle." The next instant, a hundred bugles pealed the charge, and away, with gleaming sabres and a wild hurrah, went the clattering squadrons. As they came thundering on, the hostile lines parted and let them pass proudly through. Buford was soon overtaken, and a line of battle formed; for the rebels, enraged to think they had let Kilpatrick off so easily, reorganized, and now advanced to the attack. A fierce cavalry battle followed, lasting till after dark. Pleasanton, Buford, Kilpatrick, Custer and Davis again and again led charges in person. It seemed as if the leaders on both sides were determined to test, on the plains of Brandy Station, the question of superiority between the cavalry; for the charges, on both sides, were of the most gallant and desperate character. The dark masses would drive on each other, through the deepening gloom, with defiant yells, while the flashing sabres struck fire as they clashed and rung in the fierce conflict. At length, the rebels gave it up, and our cavalry, gathering up its dead and wounded, crossed the Rappahannock. The army fell back along the railroad, from Saturday night till Wednesday, without bringing on a general engagement. To the Second Corps, commanded by Warren, was assigned the difficult task of guarding its rear. At daylight on Wednesday, this Corps took up its march along the south side of the Orange and Alexandria railroad, and moved to Bristow Station, about three miles from Manassas Junction. As the advance, under General Webb, was crossing Broad Run, about noon, there suddenly came out of the woods north of the railroad, not more than a hundred yards distant, explosion after explosion of cannon, and the next moment, the heads of the rebel columns appeared in view. The attack was totally unexpected, and was designed to throw the Corps into confusion. But Warren, whose clear head no surprise could unsettle, at once, with that tactical skill for which he is so remarkable, threw his army into position along the railroad, and awaited the onset. Hurrying up his artillery, and planting it with consummate judgment, he soon rained a terrible fire on the rebel ranks. Scarce ten minutes had elapsed after the first sudden explosion of artillery, before our batteries were throwing their shells with fatal precision into those of the enemy. So horrible was the fire, that the rebels soon left their pieces in dismay, and fled to the woods. As the smoke lifted, and disclosed six of them standing deserted in the field, Warren detailed ten men from each regiment to bring them off. They bounded forward with a shout, and seizing them and wheeling them on the retreating foe, fired a parting salute, then dragged five of them back within their lines, amid the wildest cheering of their comrades. The rebel infantry now charged Warren's position, but were met with such a withering fire that they broke for the woods, to form again. After five hours of fighting, the rebel leaders gave it up, and retired to the woods, from which they kept up an irregular artillery fire till dark, when they fell back with a loss of some thirteen hundred in killed, wounded and prisoners, six pieces of artillery, and two battle-flags.

This was Warren's first battle as sole Commander, and the way he fought it showed the highest skill and capacity as a General. Meade, in his congratulatory order, said: "The skill and promptitude of Major-General Warren, and the gallantry and bearing of the officers and soldiers of the Second Corps, are entitled to high commendation."

Lee, having forced Meade to fall back to the line of Bull Run, destroyed the Orange and Alexandria railroad from the Rapidan to Manassas. He deserved a good deal of credit for this skillful movement, for, with an army much inferior to Meade's at the outset, he had sent off a large body to reinforce Bragg; then with his comparatively small force, had boldly assumed the offensive, and forced our army into a retreat.

On the 7th of the next month, Generals French and Sedgwick attacked a portion of the rebel army at Kelly's Ford, taking about five hundred prisoners. The Rappahannock Station was protected by several strong forts. On the north side was a fort and two redoubts, held by a force two thousand strong. Against these, French and Sedgwick next moved, with great rapidity, and, having cut off the enemy's retreat, stormed them—the Sixth Maine, Fifth Wisconsin and Fourteenth New York forming the assaulting force. As they dashed into the rifle-pits and forts, a short and bloody hand-to-hand fight followed—men actually grasping each other's bayonets, in the close death struggle. But in twenty minutes it was over, and then a loud and thrilling cheer went up. Over sixteen hundred men, four guns, and eight battle-flags, fell into our hands.

Lee now retired to his old position behind the Rapidan, not so jubilant as when he advanced across it to drive Meade back to the Rappahannock. The latter, stung at the audacious manner in which he had been driven, by an inferior force, from the Rapidan, now made preparations to advance again, and on the 26th of November, the day after the battle of Missionary Ridge, the Second Corps, under General Warren, marched to the Germania Ford, and crossed the river in the afternoon—many of the troops wading up to their necks in the icy water. Warren then moved forward, and next day, confronted the rebel army. But General French, on the right, and Sykes on the left, marching by different routes, had not been heard from—in fact, the former had lost his way—and hence, Warren could not make the attack he contemplated. But, at sundown, he advanced his skirmishers, and, by his brilliant manœuvering, made the enemy believe that he was about to attack him, and thus gained time for the other Corps to arrive. Just before dark, the First Corps, under Newton, came up, and at daylight next morning, the Sixth, under Sedgwick. The line of battle was at once formed, and advanced, but the enemy was gone, having decamped the night before. A pursuit was immediately started, and the rear-guard overtaken. But a heavy rain setting in, accompanied by a dense fog, it was impossible to obtain accurate knowledge of the rebel position, which was a very strong one, on the west bank of Mine Run. Warren, however, determined if possible to bring on a battle, and, with an escort, advanced and made a close personal reconnoissance of the enemy's fortifications. So perilous was this bold tour along the hostile lines, that twenty men were killed and wounded before it was completed. Warren having laid his plans, resolved to attack, and the next morning at daylight, his Corps was in motion. But the whole day was spent in manœuvering his forces, in the wooded, unknown country, to thwart the rebel attempt to get in his rear, and to obtain the required position. He reported to Meade that night, when it was resolved that a general assault on the enemy's fortifications should take place at eight o'clock the next morning. But Warren ascertained, at daylight, that the rebel lines had been entirely changed during the night, and that his force and position were such that it would be foolhardiness to make the attempt, when as yet the whole army was not up. Another plan was formed, but abandoned, and, on the night of the 1st of December, the army recrossed the Rapidan, and eventually retired to winter quarters.

Thus ended the third year of the history of the Army of the Potomac. Its last operations had not been successful, though Warren, the young and recently-made Major-General, had shown a generalship and capacity for command, which made him one of the most prominent leaders in it, and marked him out as one of the main pillars on which Grant was to rest in his great campaign.

During this month (December), a brilliant exploit was performed by General Averill, who was directed to destroy the East Tennessee and Virginia railroad. It cannot be described in fewer words than in his own language:

"I cut the Virginia and Tennessee railroad, at Salem, on the 16th instant, and arrived safely at this point (Edray, Pocahontas County, W. Va.,) with my command—consisting of the Second, Third and Eighth Virginia mounted infantry, Fourteenth Pennsylvania, Dobson's battalion of cavalry, and Ewing's battery at Salem.

"Three depots were destroyed, containing two thousand

barrels of flour, ten thousand bushels of wheat, one hundred thousand bushels of shelled corn, fifty thousand bushels of oats, two thousand barrels of meat, several cords of leather, one thousand sacks of salt, thirty-one boxes of clothing, twenty bales of cotton, a large amount of harness, shoes and saddles, equipments, tools, oil, tar, and various other stores, and one hundred wagons.

"The telegraph wire was cut, coiled and burned, for half a mile.

"The water-station, turn-table and three cars were burned, and the track torn up and rails heated and destroyed as much as possible in six hours. Five bridges, and several culverts, were destroyed, over an extent of fifteen miles.

"A large quantity of bridge-timber and repairing materials were also destroyed.

"My march was retarded occasionally by the tempest in the mountains, and the icy roads. I was obliged to swim my command, and drag my artillery with ropes, across Craig's Creek, seven times in twenty-four hours.

"On my return, I found six separate commands—under Generals Early, Jones, Fitz-Hugh Lee, Imboden, Jackson, Echols, and McCausland—arranged in a line extending from Staunton to Newport, upon all the available roads, to prevent my return. I captured a dispatch from General Jones to General Early, giving me the position and that of Jackson at Clifton Forge, and Covington was selected to carry.

"I marched from the front of Jones to that of Jackson, at night. His outposts were pressed in, at a gallop, by the Eighth Virginia mounted infantry, and the two bridges across Jackson's River were saved, although fagots had been piled ready to ignite.

"My column, about four miles long, hastened across, regardless of the enemy, until all but my ambulances, a few wagons, and one regiment, had passed, when a strong effort was made to retake the first bridge, in which they did not succeed.

"The ambulances and some sick men were lost, and, by the darkness and difficulties, the last regiment was detained upon the opposite side until morning. When it was ascertained that the enemy seemed determined to maintain his position up the cliffs which overlooked the bridges, I caused the bridges, which were long and high, to be destroyed, and the enemy immediately changed his position to the flank and rear of the detachment which was cut off. I sent orders to the remnants to destroy our wagons, and come to me across the river, or over the mountains.

"They swam the river, with the loss of only four men who were drowned, and joined me. In the meantime, forces of the enemy were concentrating upon me, at Callaghan's, over every available road but one, which was deemed impracticable, but by which I crossed over the top of the Alleghanies with my command, with the exception of four caissons, which were destroyed in order to increase the teams of the pieces. My loss is six men drowned, one officer and four men wounded, and four officers and ninety men missing.

"We captured about two hundred prisoners, but have retained but forty officers and eighty men, on account of their inability to walk. We took also about one hundred and fifty horses.

"My horses have subsisted entirely upon a very poor country, and the officers and men have suffered cold, hunger and fatigue with remarkable fortitude. My command has marched, climbed, slid and swum three hundred and fifty-five miles, since the 8th instant."

The public mind, East, had been kept in a state of excitement by other than military events. During November, the National Cemetery at Gettysburg, for the burial of the soldiers who fell there, was consecrated, with great ceremony—Edward Everett delivering the Address.

The most important event of December, however, was a proclamation of amnesty, by the President, and a proposition for the admission of rebel States back into the Union. A full pardon was granted to all who would take the following oath, except the class afterwards mentioned.

"I, —— ——, do solemnly swear, in presence of Almighty God, that I will henceforth faithfully support, protect and defend the Constitution of the United States, and the Union of the States thereunder; and that I will, in like manner, abide by and faithfully support all Acts of Congress passed during the existing rebellion with reference to slaves, so long and so far as not repealed, modified or held void by Congress, or by decision of the Supreme Court; and that I will, in like manner, abide by and faithfully support all proclamations of the President, made during the existing rebellion, having reference to slaves, so long and so far as not modified or declared void by decision of the Supreme Court. So help me, God."

The persons excepted from the benefits of the foregoing provisions, are: All who are, or shall have been, civil or diplomatic officers or agents of the so-called Confederate Government; all who have left judicial stations under the United States, to aid the rebellion; all who are, or shall have been, military or naval officers of said so-called Confederate Government, above the rank of Colonel in the Army, or of Lieutenant in the Navy; all who left seats in the United States Congress, to aid the rebellion; all who resigned commissions in the Army or Navy of the United States, and afterward aided the rebellion; and all who have engaged in any way in treating colored persons, or white persons in charge of such, otherwise than lawfully as prisoners of war, and which persons may have been found in the United States service as soldiers, seamen, or in any other capacity.

The following portion, relating to the re-establishment of the States in the Union, was met with a storm of denunciation by the opposition, as a high-handed attempt to secure electoral votes at the Presidential Election to take place the next Autumn:

"And I do further proclaim, declare, and make known, that whenever in any of the States of Arkansas, Texas, Louisiana, Mississippi, Tennessee, Alabama, Georgia, Virginia, Florida, South Carolina and North Carolina, a number of persons, not less than one-tenth in number of the votes cast in such State at the Presidential Election of the year of our Lord one thousand eight hundred and sixty, each having taken the oath aforesaid and not having since violated it, and being a qualified voter by the election law of the State existing immediately before the so-called Act of Secession, and excluding all others, shall re-establish a State Government which shall be republican, and in nowise contravening said oath, such shall be recognized as the true Government of the State, and the State shall receive thereunder the benefits of the Constitutional provision which declares that 'the United States shall guarantee to every State in this Union a republican form of government, and shall protect each of them against invasion, and, on application of the Legislature, or the Executive (when the Legislature cannot be convened), against domestic violence.'

And I do further proclaim, declare, and make known that any provision which may be adopted by such State Government in relation to the freed people of such State, which shall recognize and declare their permanent freedom, provide for their education, and which may yet be consistent, as a temporary arrangement, with their present condition as a laboring, landless and homeless class, will not be objected to by the National Executive. And it is suggested as not improper, that, in constructing a loyal State Government in any State, the name of the State, the boundary, the subdivisions, the Constitution, and the general code of laws, as before the rebellion, be maintained, subject only to the modifications made necessary by the conditions heretofore stated, and such others, if any, not contravening said conditions, and which may be deemed expedient by those framing the new State Government.

To avoid misunderstanding, it may be proper to say that this proclamation, so far as it relates to State Governments, has no reference to States wherein loyal State Governments have all the while been maintained. And, for the same reason, it may be proper to further say, that whether members sent to Congress from any State shall be admitted to seats, constitutionally rests exclusively with the respective Houses, and not to any extent with the Executive. And still further, that this proclamation is intended to present the people of the States wherein the National authority has been suspended, and loyal State Governments have been subverted, a mode in and by which the National and loyal State Governments may be re-established within said States, or in any of them; and, while the mode presented is the best the Executive can suggest, with his present impressions, it must not be understood that no other possible mode would be acceptable.

Given under my hand, at the City of Washington, the eighth day of December, A. D. one thousand eight hundred and sixty-three, and of the Independence of the United States of America the eighty-eighth.

ABRAHAM LINCOLN."

All during the Autumn, political matters agitated the public mind almost as much as events in the field. Schenck's military orders with regard to elections in Maryland and Delaware, were denounced as an attempt to control the polls with the bayonet; and all felt that the fierce party strife that was to be waged the coming year, would test the stability of our Government more than anything that had yet transpired—and trembled to contemplate it.

The Army of the Potomac, as we have noticed, went into winter quarters near Washington, confronted by the rebel army under Lee; and Grant's army did the same at Chattanooga, in front of Bragg. The calls, from time to time, for volunteers, had amounted to a prodigious number, and still the war seemed as far from being over as ever, and it became very evident that a radical change must be made in the mode of carrying it on. Scott's original plan was, to have two great armies move simultaneously—one down the Valley of the Mississippi, and another along the Eastern coast—and driving the enemy before them, finally crush him somewhere in the Southern States. McClellan's plan was the same; and the movements West commenced almost simultaneously with his. The recall of the army from before Richmond, broke up this plan, and ever since, in the East, the Government had been occupied in defending its own Capital. This course, it was plain, must be brought to a close, or the war never would be ended. Halleck was evidently unequal to the task of grasping and carrying out a great plan; and the Secretary of War was no better. Congress, had only made matters worse, by its interference, and resolved, at last, to abandon it, and compel the Cabinet to do the same, and so passed an Act creating the office of Lieutenant-General—evidently for the purpose of giving General Grant that rank. The President at once nominated him, and his confirmation took a heavy load from the public heart. A military man, with the power to grasp and the energy to carry out a great plan, and embrace the vast field of operations, was at last at the head of the national forces, and it was plain that the day of "quidnuncs" at Washington was over. The mighty power of the North, which had been hurled hither and thither with such blind energy, was to be held calmly in hand, and made to move like the steady, resistless tide of the ocean, on the rebel forces.

Previous, however, to the commencement of this new order of things, and as if designed by Providence as a preparation, a movement was made by Sherman into Central Mississippi. Placing a cavalry force of nearly eight thousand under General W. F. Smith, with orders to start on the 1st of February from Memphis, and to move toward Meridian, he himself, on the 3rd of February, with a force of about twenty thousand infantry and twelve hundred cavalry, and provisions for twenty days, took his departure from Vicksburg. His march was easterly, across the Big Black River, by way of Champion Hills, Clinton and Jackson. Moving rapidly eastward—scattering the astonished enemy as he advanced—by the middle of the month, he was at Meridian, the center of a network of railroads. Here he halted, and waited for Smith's cavalry, but it did not come. This officer did not start till the 11th, and had advanced only a little beyond Okalona, when he was met by the enemy. Ordering a retreat, he was attacked and defeated badly, and finally succeeded in reaching Memphis with his command completely disorganized. Sherman intended to cut off Mobile from Johnston, who had succeeded Bragg in the command of the Confederate army; confuse and cut up, as much as possible, Polk's army, that was confronting him; destroy military depots, supplies, &c.; and, if everything should work favorably, swoop down on Mobile, on which Farragut was pounding. But Smith's defeat put a stop to his movements. He did not dare to advance further without that cavalry force, and so he leisurely retraced his steps to Vicksburg, followed at a respectful distance by his cautious adversary.

This expedition was designed to be an important one, and the public expected great results from it; but the failure of the cavalry force to co-operate with it, converted it into a raid. Yet, in moving across the whole State of Mississippi, for a hundred and thirty miles, he had not merely caused great destruction, and terror among the inhabitants, but had tested practically the capacity of the country to feed an army, and doubtless obtained that knowledge which afterward made him attempt the bold and daring march across the State of Georgia.

E.W. Smith N.Y.

U. S. Grant

CHAPTER XXII.

GRANT AT THE HEAD OF ALL OUR ARMIES—SHERMAN APPOINTED OVER GRANT'S DEPARTMENT WEST—A SURVEY OF THE WHOLE FIELD—FARRAGUT AT MOBILE—CALL FOR FIVE HUNDRED THOUSAND MEN—BUTLER'S FAILURE BEFORE RICHMOND—THE EXPEDITION INTO FLORIDA UNDER GENERAL SEYMOUR—BATTLE OF OLUSTEE—KILPATRICK'S BOLD ATTEMPT TO LIBERATE OUR PRISONERS IN RICHMOND—DEATH OF COLONEL DAHLGREN—FORREST'S RAID IN KENTUCKY—SURRENDER OF UNION CITY—ATTACK ON PADUCAH—DASTARDLY CONDUCT OF THE REBELS—ATTACK ON FORT PILLOW—THE MASSACRE—THE REBELS ATTACK PLYMOUTH, NORTH CAROLINA—A REBEL IRON-CLAD ATTACKS THE MIAMI AND SOUTHFIELD, SINKING THE LATTER—EVACUATION OF PLYMOUTH—POPULAR INDIGNATION.

EVERYTHING now seemed ready for the great change that took place the next month, when Lieutenant-General Grant was put at the head of all the armies of the Union. The same order of the 12th of March, that gave him this high position, assigned to Sherman the command of the Department of the Mississippi—composed of the minor Departments of the Ohio, the Cumberland, the Tennessee, and Arkansas—in short, the command vacated by Grant. Under him, was a group of lieutenants rarely equaled, never surpassed, in any army—McPherson, Hooker, Thomas, Howard, Hurlbut, Logan and Schofield. It was a grand army, and grandly officered.

Grant, in Washington, at once went back to the original military plan of moving two armies simultaneously south—one east, and the other west of the Alleghanies. Richmond and Atlanta were the objective points, which, when once reached—the former the head, and the latter the heart of the Confederacy—the two mighty armies could steadily approach each other, crushing and grinding whatever lay between them. As Grant, from his high position, took a glance at the work before him, what a spectacle met his gaze! Never before had one Commander surveyed such a vast field of operations, and looked over such a mighty array, subject to his single control. From the Potomac to the Rio Grande, for five thousand miles, arose the smoke of camp-fires, and stood embattled hosts awaiting his bidding. To aid him in the gigantic task before him, six hundred vessels of war lined the rivers and darkened the coast for twenty-five hundred miles, while four thousand guns lay ready to send their stern summons into rebel defenses.

Soon, the effect of Grant's grand designs began to be felt, though scarcely seen by the public eye. Railways groaned under the weight of soldiers returning to their regiments; the rivers were black with transports bearing ordnance and supplies, and the entire North trembled under the tremendous preparations going forward. It was no single isolated battle that Grant contemplated, but mighty, unceasing blows to be dealt by the colossal force under his command. It was to be a final struggle between the North and South—the last fatal interlocking of the two giants in a death grapple.

We needed a practical head like his, over the Navy Department. If the naval power of the South had borne any proportion to its land forces, this want would have been felt in a deplorable manner. But our naval strength was so overwhelmingly preponderant, that great disasters were almost impossible. But the feelings of our naval Commanders may be gathered from Farragut's dispatches from before Mobile, on the outer forts of whose Bay he was fiercely pounding, while Sherman was traversing the State of Mississippi with the hope of lending him a helping hand. In the latter part of January, he had made a bold reconnoissance of Forts Morgan and Gaines, and, as a result of his observations, wrote to the Secretary of the Navy that he was satisfied that if he had had but a *single iron-clad*, he could have "destroyed the whole force in the Bay, and reduced the forts at his leisure." In the latter part of February, he shelled Fort Powell. Two or three months later, he wrote: "I deeply regret that the Department has not been able to give us *one* of the many iron-clads that are off Charleston and on the Mississippi. I have always looked for the latter, but it appears that it takes *us twice as long to build an iron-clad* as any one else. It looks as if the contractors and the fates were against us. While the rebels are bending their whole energies to the war, our people are expecting the war to close by default, and if they do not awake to a sense of their danger soon, it will be so." This was very plain talk, by one who stood at the head of the navy, to the Secretary, and shows how differently things would have been managed if he had been allowed to control matters.

Between the victory of Chattanooga and the next May, when Grant would be ready to begin his great simultaneous movement of the two grand armies of the republic, there was considerable activity in military affairs in various parts of the country. In January, quite a fight occurred at Strawberry Plains, Tennessee, and the rebels obtained some successes in Western Virginia. The President's proclamation, on the 1st of February, ordering a draft for five hundred thousand men to be made on the 10th day of March, showed what mighty preparations were in prospect.

Butler, having heard that Richmond was weakly garrisoned, started an expedition to liberate the prisoners there, but it turned out a miserable failure.

One of the most important expeditions—or, at least, most talked about—was one under General Seymour, that left Port Royal, the fore part of the month, for Jacksonville,

Florida. It was composed of twenty steamers, eight schooners, and about five thousand troops. It left Hilton Head on the morning of the 6th, and occupied Jacksonville the next day. Gillmore, the Commander of the Department, said the object of the expedition was: First, to procure an outlet for cotton, lumber, timber, &c. Second, to cut off one of the enemy's sources of supplies. Third, to obtain recruits for any colored regiments. And last, "to inaugurate measures for the speedy restoration of Florida to her allegiance, in accordance with instructions received *from the President, by the hands of Major John Hay, Assistant Adjutant-General.*" The three first reasons might as well have been omitted, as the last was the true one. Seymour, in accordance with his instructions, pushed a force on to Baldwin, twenty miles from Jacksonville, while another portion was sent forward to Sanderson. These preliminary steps being taken, Gillmore returned to Jacksonville, leaving Seymour in command in the field. The latter, on his own responsibility, now determined to advance inland a hundred miles, without supplies, in order to destroy the railroad, near the Savannah River. On the 18th, the army left its camp at Jacksonville, in light marching order, with ten days' rations, and made sixteen miles, over bad roads, that day. The next day, it marched seventeen miles, and encamped at a place called Barber's. In the morning, the march was resumed, the objective point being Lake City, nearly forty miles distant; but the columns had proceeded only sixteen or eighteen miles, when the enemy's skirmishers were met. Pushing these back four miles, the army came upon the rebels in force. The columns were at once deployed, and Hamilton's battery ordered forward to within a hundred and fifty yards of the hostile line. This close proximity, of course, brought the gunners completely under the fire of the sharpshooters. It went in with four pieces, fifty horses, eighty-two men and four officers. In twenty minutes, half of the guns, half of the officers, more than half of the men, and all but ten of the horses, were lost. The different regiments, as they came into position, were met by a murderous fire. One broke, another got out of place, and yet the conflict raged with terrible ferocity. Seymour was everywhere present, apparently reckless of death, striving to win the battle thus suddenly, unexpectedly thrown upon him; but his efforts were all in vain. He succeeded only in holding the men to a useless slaughter. From two o'clock till dark, the contest was close and deadly, when, as if by mutual consent, it ceased, and Seymour, leaving most of his wounded in the hands of the enemy, withdrew, and the troops, foot-sore and weary, marched all night to Barber's—having marched over thirty miles, and fought for four hours, since the previous morning. The next morning (Sunday), the shattered, dispirited army continued its retreat, and did not rest till it reached its old camps at Jacksonville. Over one-fifth of the army of five thousand men, and five pieces of artillery, were lost in this disastrous fight—called the battle of Olustee, because it occurred a few miles from this railroad station. The whole affair caused a great deal of indignation, and, as in the case of all foolish, unsuccessful expeditions, every one engaged in it was blamed by turns. Now the President and Hay—whom he had made Major on purpose to accompany the expedition—were blamed; now Seymour, for being ambuscaded, and now Gillmore, for allowing it to be so miserably conducted. So, too, the Seventh New Hampshire, and a colored regiment, were accused of losing the battle by their poltroonry. Of course, an investigation was called for, while the newspapers discussed it freely, without waiting for its developments. Gillmore asserted that Seymour moved inland in direct violation of his orders, and, after he started, required him, his superior, to make a naval demonstration in his behalf. Seymour has not seen fit to tell how much the presence of Major Hay had to do with this departure from the course marked out for him by Gillmore. We suspect it would be hard to fix the blame on any one man. It was one of those shrewd little plans got up between those at Washington and some civilians and officers—the success of which was intended to astonish the country, and show that all the wisdom did not rest in military quarters. All that need be said of it is, it was a foolish expedition from the start—badly carried out, and a total, disgraceful failure.

The rebel General, Patton Anderson, soon after the battle, did an act which should be mentioned to his honor. He made out and sent in a complete list of all our prisoners in his hands, both white and colored, together with a description of the character of the injuries of each of the wounded. This conduct was the more noticeable, being in such striking contrast with the brutality shown to the blacks at Fort Wagner and other places.

In the latter part of the month, Kilpatrick started on his great raid for the relief of our prisoners in Richmond, which were reported to be in a most suffering condition. Knowing that the rebel Capital was weakly garrisoned, he thought that he might, by a sudden dash, enter it and release them before a sufficient force could be brought up to arrest his progress. His plan was submitted to the President and Secretary of War, and after due deliberation accepted, and, on the last day of February, this daring leader, with four thousand chosen men, left his camp at Stevensburg, and marched for Ely's Ford, on the Rapidan. By the aid of a daring scout named Hogan, he succeeded in capturing the entire picket stationed there, without giving the alarm. He then pushed rapidly forward, and at daylight reached Spottsylvania Court House. Elated with his successful start, he now moved rapidly towards the Beaver Dam Station, on the Virginia Central railroad, which he reached at four o'clock, and where he went into camp for a few hours. Colonels Dahlgren and Cook, with five hundred men, had been sent across the James River, to move down its south bank and release the prisoners at Belle Isle, and then with them join Kilpatrick in the city, who was to enter it by the Brook turnpike. The latter carried the first line of rebel works, within two miles of the Capital, and opened on it with his artillery, the sound of which was to be the signal for Dahlgren to advance. The latter, however, misled by a negro guide, did not appear, and Kilpatrick, disappointed in not having his co-operation, and finding the rebel defenses stronger than he had anticipated, now spent some hours in reconnoitering to see if he could not find a weak place where he could dash in. In the meantime, the city was thrown into the wildest consternation. The bells were rung, and couriers sent off to hurry up the troops on the Chickahominy. Finding the obstacles in front of him too great to be surmounted, and the hostile forces concentrating fast, he was compelled reluctantly to abandon his bold design, and see to the safety of his command. Falling back, he swept around Richmond to the Chickahominy, which he crossed, at Meadow Bridge, and went into camp in the midst of a driving storm of sleet, and hail, and snow. Here he was attacked by a heavy force, but succeeded, after a sharp fight, in repulsing it, and moving off to Old Church, again went into camp, to wait the arrival of his scattered detachments. During the day, they all came in except Dahlgren's command. At length, hearing that the latter was over the Pamunkey, and making his way towards Gloucester Point, he moved leisurely down the Peninsula, and arrived safely at Yorktown. Dahlgren, becoming separated in the darkness from his main body, fought his way, with a hundred men, to within three miles of King and Queen Court-House, where he fell into an ambuscade and was shot down, and all but seventeen of his party killed or taken prisoners. The body of this gallant young officer was shamefully maltreated, and buried in the middle of the road by the rebels, to show their savage hate. They asserted, in extenuation of their conduct, that a paper was found in his pocket, directing that Richmond when captured should be laid in ashes and given over to plunder. This raid had a special, noble object in view, which would sanction the taking of heavy risks.

The sudden appearance of the rebels, the latter part of this same month, in the western part of Kentucky, took the country by surprise.

On the 24th of March, Forrest, in command of the rebel forces, attacked Union City, which was surrendered by Colonel Hawkins, the Commander, in a manner that called forth the bitterest condemnation. The next day, the combined rebel force, numbering in all six thousand men, attacked Paducah, which post was held by Colonel S. G. Hicks, with six hundred and fifty-five men. On the approach of the enemy, Colonel Hicks retired into Fort Anderson with his little band, resolved to hold it to the last extremity, while some gunboats in the river, commanded by Captain Shirk, moved up to his assistance. Forrest advanced to the attack, but failed to make any impression on the fort. He then sent a flag of truce to Colonel Hicks, demanding the surrender of the place, saying in conclusion, "If you surrender, you shall be treated as prisoners of war, but if I have to storm your works, you may expect no quarter." Hicks very quietly replied, that he had been placed there by his Government to defend the post, and should do it. Forrest, however, made a base use of the flag of truce, and advanced his troops, while the negotiations were going on, to advantageous positions. His sharpshooters also mingled with the women and children that had been sent out of town to avoid danger, and picked off the officers of the gunboats, knowing that they could not be fired on without killing the women and children. They also placed women in front of their lines as they moved towards the fort—a piece of dastardly cowardice that can hardly be believed of any American.

Forrest made three desperate assaults on the place during the day, but each time was met with such a destructive fire that he was repulsed with a loss of three hundred killed and about a thousand wounded, while on our side only sixty were killed or wounded. Finding that Colonel Hicks could be neither frightened nor forced into a surrender, he withdrew, and on the 12th of next month—the anniversary of the attack on Fort Sumter—drove in the pickets of the garrison of Fort Pillow. This fort was situated on a high bluff on the banks of the Mississippi, and was garrisoned with five hundred and fifty-seven men—two hundred and sixty-two of whom were colored troops.

MASSACRE AT FORT PILLOW.

The attack was made at sunrise. Major Booth, of the colored troops, the senior in command, was killed about nine o'clock, and Major Bradford succeeded him. Forrest pressed his attack vigorously, up to three o'clock, but without any success. The gunboat New Era, Captain Marshall, threw its shells with great effect into the rebel ranks, causing them to flee from one ravine into another, as she shifted from one position to another in answer to the signals from the fort. Forrest, finding that he could not carry the place by assault, resorted to a flag of truce, under cover of which, with true Mexican duplicity, he determined to gain a position that would enable him, with a single dash, to get into the fort. He now demanded a surrender of the place, and Major Bradford asked an hour in which to consult with his officers. Forrest replied that he would give him but twenty minutes, and in the meantime moved his men along a ravine to the position he desired. Bradford rejecting the summons to surrender, the rebels made a sudden rush, and, with the cry, "No quarter!" cleared the ramparts with a bound. There was no fighting—overwhelmed by superior numbers, the troops, black and white, threw down their arms, and precipitated themselves down the steep bluff near the fort—some hiding themselves under the brush that lined the river shore—some taking refuge in the water itself, and lying with their heads just far enough out to allow them to breathe. Then commenced a scene of cruelty and murder that finds its parallel in our land only in Forts Mimms and Raisin. All of the savage was there—the thirst for blood, remorseless hate and barbarity, and fiendish yells—all but the scalping-knife. Neither sex, nor age, nor color, was spared—everything went down before that bloody onslaught. Even children were hacked to death or coolly shot down, while their tearful, despairing faces were turned pleadingly on their murderers. The sick were not spared by these fiends, who seemed determined to enact a scene that should shock the civilized world. The matter was one that demanded some official action, and the Joint Committee on the Conduct and Expenditures of the War appointed Messrs. Wade and Gooch a sub-committee to proceed to the spot, and investigate it. That we may not seem to exaggerate the conduct of the rebels, we quote a portion of the report of this Committee:

"Immediately after the second flag of truce retired, the rebels made a rush from the positions they had so treacherously gained, and obtained possession of the fort, raising the cry of 'No quarter!' But little opportunity was allowed for resistance. Our troops, black and white, threw down their arms, and sought to escape by running down the steep bluff near the fort, and secreting themselves behind trees and logs, in the bushes, and under the brush—some even jumping into the river, leaving only their heads above the water, as they crouched down under the bank.

"Then followed a scene of cruelty and murder without a parallel in civilized warfare, which needed but the tomahawk and scalping-knife to exceed the worst atrocities ever committed by savages. The rebels commenced an indiscriminate slaughter, sparing neither age nor sex, white nor black, soldier or civilian. The officers and men seemed to vie with each other in the devilish work; men, women, and even children, wherever found, were deliberately shot down, beaten, and hacked with sabres; some of the children, not more than ten years old, were forced to stand up and face their murderers, while being shot; the sick and the wounded were butchered without mercy—the rebels even entering the hospital-building, and dragging them out to be shot, or killing them as they lay there unable to offer the least resistance. All over the hill-side, the work of murder was going on; numbers of our men were collected together in lines or groups, and deliberately shot; some were shot while in the river, while others on the bank were shot, and their bodies kicked into the water, many of them still living but unable to make any exertions to save themselves from drowning. Some of the rebels stood on the top of the hill, or a short distance down its side, and called to our soldiers to come up to them, and as they approached, shot them down in cold blood; if their guns or pistols missed fire, forcing them to stand there until they were again prepared to fire. All around were heard cries of 'No quarter!' 'No quarter!' 'Kill the damned niggers; shoot them down!' All who asked for mercy, were answered by the most cruel taunts and sneers. Some were spared for a time, only to be murdered under circumstances of greater cruelty. No cruelty which the most fiendish malignity could devise, was omitted by these murderers. One white soldier, who was wounded in one leg so as to be unable to walk, was made to stand up while his tormentors shot him; others who were wounded and unable to stand, were held up and again shot. One negro, who had been ordered by a rebel officer to hold his horse, was killed by him when he remounted; another, a mere child, whom an officer had taken up behind him on his horse, was seen by Chalmers, who at once ordered the officer to put him down and shoot him, which was done. The huts and tents in which many of the wounded had sought shelter, were set on fire, both that night and the next morning, while the wounded were still in them—those only escaping who were able to get themselves out, or who could prevail on others less injured than themselves to help them out; and even some of those thus seeking to escape the flames, were met by those ruffians and brutally shot down, or had their brains beaten out. One man was deliberately fastened down to the floor of a tent, face upward, by means of nails driven through his clothing and into the boards under him, so that he could not possibly escape, and then the tent set on fire; another was nailed to the side of a building outside of the fort, and then the building set on fire and burned. The charred remains of five or six bodies were afterward found, all but one so much disfigured and consumed by the flames that they could not be identified, and the identification of that one is not absolutely certain, although there can hardly be a doubt that it was the body of Lieutenant Akerstrom, Quartermaster of the Thirteenth Tennessee cavalry, and a native Tennesseean; several witnesses who saw the remains, and who were personally acquainted with him while living, have testified that it is their firm belief that it was his body that was thus treated.

"These deeds of murder and cruelty ceased when night came on, only to be renewed the next morning, when the demons carefully sought, among the dead lying about in all directions, for any of the wounded yet alive, and those they found were deliberately shot. Scores of the dead and wounded were found there the day after the massacre, by the men from some of our gunboats, who were permitted to go on shore and collect the wounded and bury the dead. The rebels themselves had made a pretense of burying a great many of their victims, but they had merely thrown them, without the least regard to care or decency, into the trenches and ditches about the fort, or the little hollows and ravines on the hill-side, covering them but partially with earth. Portions of heads and faces, hands and feet, were found protruding through the earth in every direction. The testimony also establishes the fact that the rebels buried some of the living with the dead, a few of whom succeeded afterward in digging themselves out, or were dug out by others—one of whom your Committee found in Mound City hospital, and there examined. And even when your Committee visited the spot, two weeks afterward, although parties of men had been sent on shore, from time to time, to bury the bodies unburied, and rebury the others, and were even then engaged in the same work, we found the evidences of this murder and cruelty still most painfully apparent; we saw bodies still unburied (at some distance from the fort) of some sick men who had been met fleeing from the hospital, and beaten down and brutally murdered, and their bodies left where they had fallen. We could still see the faces, hands and feet of men, white and black, protruding out of the ground, whose graves had not been reached by those engaged in reinterring the victims of the massacre; and, although a great deal of rain had fallen within the preceding two weeks, the ground, more especially on the side and at the foot of the bluff where the most of the murders had been committed, was still discolored by the blood of our brave but unfortunate men, and the logs and trees showed but too plainly the evidences of the atrocities perpetrated there.

"Many other instances of equally atrocious cruelty might be enumerated, but your Committee feel compelled to refrain from giving here more of the heart-sickening details, and refer to the statements contained in the voluminous testimony herewith submitted. Those statements were obtained by them from eye-witnesses and sufferers; many of them, as they were examined by your Committee, were lying upon beds of pain and suffering, some so feeble that their lips could with difficulty frame the words by which they endeavored to convey some idea of the cruelties which had been inflicted on them, and which they had seen inflicted on others.

"How many of our troops thus fell victims to the malignity and barbarity of Forrest and his followers, cannot yet be definitely ascertained. Two officers belonging to the garrison, were absent at the time of the capture and massacre. Of the remaining officers, but two are known to be living, and they are wounded, and now in the hospital at Mound City. One of them, Captain Potter, may even now be dead, as the surgeons, when your Committee were there, expressed no hope of his recovery. Of the men, from three hundred to four hundred are known to have been killed at Fort Pillow—of whom at least three hundred were murdered in cold blood, after the post was in possession of the rebels, and our men had thrown down their arms and ceased to offer resistance. Of the survivors, except the wounded in the hospital at Mound City, and the few who succeeded in making their escape unhurt, nothing definite is known; and it is to be feared that many have been murdered after being taken away from the fort.

"In reference to the fate of Major Bradford, who was in command of the fort when it was captured, and who had up to that time received no injury, there seems to be no doubt. The general understanding everywhere seemed to be, that he had been brutally murdered the day after he was taken prisoner.

"There is some discrepancy in the testimony, but your Committee do not see how the one who professed to have been an eye-witness of his death could have been mistaken. There may be some uncertainty in regard to his fate.

"When your Committee arrived at Memphis, Tennessee they found and examined a man (Mr. McLagan) who had been conscripted by some of Forrest's forces, but who, with other conscripts, had succeeded in making his escape. He testifies that while two companies of rebel troops, with Major Bradford and many other prisoners, were on their march from Brownsville to Jackson, Tennessee, Major Bradford was taken by five rebels—one an officer—led about fifty yards from the line of march, and deliberately murdered, in view of all there assembled. He fell—killed instantly by three musket-balls, even while asking that his life might be spared, as he had fought them manfully, and was deserving of a better fate. The motive for the murder of Major Bradford, seems to have been the simple fact that, although a native of the South, he remained loyal to his Government. The testimony herewith submitted, contains many statements made by the rebels, that they did not intend to treat 'home-made Yankees,' as they termed loyal Southerners, any better than negro troops."

The testimony taken was very voluminous—covering the whole ground; and, that there might be no charge of unfairness, the name and rank of each witness were given, together with all the questions put to him. A severe cross-examination would doubtless have caused many of the statements to be modified, and have impeached the credibility of some of the witnesses. As an example of the kind of testimony bearing hardest against the perpetrators of this enormous crime, we give a single statement made by a private:

"In about five minutes after the disappearance of the flag of truce, a general assault was made upon our works from every direction. They were kept at bay for some time, when the negroes gave way upon the left, and ran down the bluff, leaving an opening through which the rebels entered, and immediately commenced an indiscriminate slaughter of both white and black. We all threw down our arms, and gave tokens of surrender, asking for quarter. (I was wounded in the right shoulder and muscle of the back, and knocked down, before I threw down my gun.) But no quarter was given. Voices were heard upon all sides, crying: 'Give them no quarter; kill them; kill them; it is General Forrest's orders.' I saw four white men and at least twenty-five negroes shot while begging for mercy; and I saw one negro dragged from a hollow log within ten feet of where I lay, and as one rebel held him by the foot another shot him. These were all soldiers. There were also two negro women and three little children standing within twenty-five steps from me, when a rebel stepped up to them and said: 'Yes, God damn you, you thought you were free, did you?' and shot them all. They all fell but one child, when he knocked it in the head with the breach of his gun. They then disappeared in the direction of the landing, following up the fugitives, firing at them wherever seen. They came back in about three-quarters of an hour, shooting, and robbing the dead of their money and clothes. I saw a man with a canteen upon him, and a pistol in his hand. I ventured to ask him for a drink of water. He turned around, saying: 'Yes, God damn you, I will give you a drink of water,' and shot at my head three different times, covering my face up with dust, and then turned from me, no doubt thinking he had killed me, remarking: 'God damn you, it's too late to pray now;' then went on with his pilfering. I lay there until dark, feigning death, when a rebel officer came along, drawing his sabre, and ordered me to get up, threatening to run his sabre into me if I did not, saying I had to march ten miles that night. I succeeded in getting up, and got among a small squad he had already gathered up, but stole away from them during the night, and got among the dead, feigning death, for fear of being murdered. The next morning, the gunboat came up and commenced shelling them out, when I crawled out from among the dead, and with a piece of paper motioned to the boat; she came up, and I crawled on board.

WILLIAM F. his † mark MAYS."

It is hard to believe that native-born American citizens—men brought up in the light of the civilization of the Nineteenth Century, and educated under Christian influences, could be guilty of such deeds. Acts of violence have been committed on both sides, during this sanguinary struggle, which are undreamed of by the public. It always has been, and always will be so, in war; but such deeds as these, are not to be classed amid its ordinary cruelties, and should never find a place among the records of civilization. Their proper place is in the war song of the Indian, as he dances around the fire in which his bleeding captives are writhing.

Another event of considerable importance, occurred on the Eastern coast, at Plymouth, North Carolina, during the month. A land force of rebels made a furious attack, on the 18th, upon the garrison commanded by General Wessels, but were repulsed. The next day, the iron-clad rebel ram—Albermarle—came down the Roanoke River, and attacked the Southfield and Miami. These two boats were fastened together at the time, and were driven straight on the hostile steamer, as she came heavily down. The latter, reckless of the heavy rifled shot, that bounded like peas from her mailed sides, moved fearlessly on the two boats, striking the Southfield—sinking her immediately, and seriously damaging the Miami. Captain Flusser was killed in the engagement. It was feared that the ram would soon have possession of the whole Sound, and that Roanoke Island would be attacked. Plymouth had to be evacuated, and the public was loud in its denunciations of the Secretary of the Navy. A resolution of inquiry was passed by Congress, requesting him to give an explanation of the matter.

CHAPTER XXIII.

SANITARY FAIRS—BANKS IN NEW ORLEANS—INAUGURATION OF THE FREE STATE GOVERNMENT—THE RED RIVER COTTON EXPEDITION—PORTER'S ASCENT OF THE RED RIVER—CAPTURE OF BATTERIES BY GENERAL SMITH—MARCH OF BANKS ACROSS THE COUNTRY TO ALEXANDRIA—ADVANCE INTO THE INTERIOR—DEFEAT OF BANKS—RETREAT OF STEELE—RETURN OF THE GUNBOATS TO ALEXANDRIA—UNABLE TO GET BELOW THE FALLS—GRAND ENGINEERING SUCCESS OF COLONEL BAILEY—PASSAGE OF THE FALLS BY THE FLEET—AN EXCITING SPECTACLE—PROMOTION OF BAILEY—DESTRUCTION OF THE GUNBOATS SIGNAL, COVINGTON, AND TRANSPORT WARNER—RETURN OF THE EXPEDITION—CANBY SUPERSEDES BANKS IN THE FIELD—THE LATTER RETURNS TO NEW ORLEANS—VIEW OF THE EXPEDITION.

THOUGH having no direct bearing on the war, the great Fairs throughout the country the first few months of this year, deserve a special mention. The raising of funds on such a gigantic scale for the relief of our wounded and sick soldiers, had never before been witnessed. Independent of the amount of good done, and the vast number of soldiers thus saved to the army, it created a bond between the people and the soldiers that rendered it impossible for them ever to feel that their interests were separate.

Before the great decisive movements of the Spring commenced, the country was destined to suffer one more mortification from the failure of an ill-starred expedition.

General Banks in New Orleans after adjusting the labor system and seeing to the elections, on the 4th of March inaugurated the Free State government with the most imposing ceremonies. A multitude, estimated at fifty thousand in number, assembled in Lafayette Square, where a platform had been erected, and the newly elected Governor Hahn was installed into office amid the firing of cannon, the playing of patriotic airs, and the huzzas of the multitude.

The political machinery having been put in working order, Banks could turn his attention to affairs in the field, and in this month a combined naval and land expedition was fitted out destined to become famous as the "Red River Cotton Expedition."

Porter, with a large fleet of gunboats and transports carrying a portion of Sherman's army under A. J. Smith, left Vicksburg early in March, and proceeded towards Alexandria, where the main army, under Banks, was to meet him, after having marched across the country. The objective point in the expedition was Shreveport, in Caddo Parish, on the Red River, some six hundred and seventy miles by water from New Orleans, and a great depot for commissary stores of the rebel army. On the passage up the river, Fort DeRussey, a formidable work, was captured by a rapid land march of Smith, together with ten guns and three hundred prisoners. Alexandria surrendered to Porter without a battle, and here, on the 17th, the land force joined him, having marched a hundred and seventy miles in five days. The army by land, and the gunboats by water, now moved forward toward Shreveport, some three hundred miles distant. It was a long and weary march for the troops, and almost equally arduous work for the gunboats to make their way up the shallow, tortuous stream. Steele, commanding in Arkansas, was to co-operate with this force, moving on Shreveport from Little Rock—having these two objects in view—to keep Price, in Arkansas from joining the rebel force under Kirby Smith in Louisiana, and to take Shreveport in rear while Banks advanced against it in front. At Mansfield, forty-five miles from it, the rebels made a stand, where our cavalry came up with them on the 8th of April. The army was scattered over the country far back in the rear, which Kirby Smith seemed fully aware of. At first, on the 7th, the cavalry, commanded by Colonel Robinson, drove the enemy before it, and pursued him some fourteen miles, when the column came upon a body of infantry which, after a sharp contest, was also forced back. Colonel Landrum's brigade of infantry, and Colonel Lucas' of cavalry, coming up that night, the whole advanced in the morning, but on arriving near Sabine Cross-Roads, they found themselves suddenly confronted by fifteen or twenty thousand men. In the meantime General Ransom with his troops arrived, accompanied by General Banks. The latter immediately dispatched a courier to Franklin, in the rear, to hasten up with his Corps, but Kirby Smith saw his advantage, and pressed it vigorously. The cavalry in front were turned back in terrible rout, and the troops though struggling bravely to bear up against the disorder, were also at length overborne and their artillery captured—their ranks being broken by the fleeing wagon train which somehow had got in advance. But at this critical moment, when every thing seemed lost, Franklin arrived with his Corps, and waving his hat above his head fell furiously upon the exulting, shouting rebels. Two horses were successively shot under him, but leaping to the saddle of a third, he still led on his men. By his gallantry he succeeded in checking the victorious progress of the rebels for a time, but he also was at last borne back in the refluent tide. Fortunately, the Nineteenth Army Corps under General Emory, had been advised of the rout, and stood drawn up in line of battle as the fleeing army came in sight. Allowing the shattered, broken columns to pass to the rear, it closed sternly up and bravely breasted the storm till darkness put an end to the conflict.

In the meantime Smith, with the Sixteenth and Seventeenth Army Corps, had reached Pleasant Hill, and drawn up his forces behind a low ridge. The next day the rebels advanced, confident of success, and Emory, whose line of battle had been formed in front of Smith, and masked him, after dealing the enemy a heavy blow, fell back, according to pre-arrangement, when the confident, shouting foe dashed forward in pursuit. Smith's troops lay flat on the ground until the first rebel line was well up the slope, when seven thousand muskets suddenly blazed in its front, and the artillery swept the crowding columns with terrible slaughter. The rebels, stunned at the suddenness and awfulness of the blow, stopped and staggered back, and before they could recover their senses, Smith gave the order to charge, when his brave troops swept the field with a shout.

But nothing now could change the defeat into a victory, and next morning the retreat was continued. Banks sent word to Porter, acquainting him with his disaster, and directed him to fall back to Grand Ecore, whither he was retreating. From this point the retreat was continued to Alexandria without serious molestation, except at Monet's Bluff, where the rebels made an attack on him, but were repulsed with heavy loss. Here he halted to save the gunboats, which could not get over the falls above the place, on account of low water.

In the meantime Steele had advanced from Little Rock, but when near Camden his wagon train was cut off and destroyed. Marmaduke with a heavy force now confronted him, and Banks having retreated, the whole rebel force was free to operate against him, and he was compelled to fall back. At Saline Falls, however, Price pressed him so hard that he was forced to turn and give battle, and fell with such fury on his pursuers, that they let him alone during the rest of his retreat, and he reached Little Rock again in safety.

In the meantime the rebels were swarming along the shores of the Red River, both above and below Alexandria. Above, Porter was dreadfully harassed from the shores, and things began to wear a gloomy aspect. There was no appearance of a rise in the river, and without one, Porter's entire fleet must be destroyed, to prevent its falling into the hands of the enemy—for forage was getting short, and the protecting army would soon have to move. With its departure all attempts to save the boats would be abandoned. In this painful dilemma Lieutenant-Colonel Bailey, acting engineer of the Nineteenth Army Corps, proposed to build a series of dams across the rocks at the lower falls, and raise the water sufficiently to let the boats pass over the upper ones. His plan was ridiculed by the best engineers, but Bailey had tried it before, in floating logs down the western rivers, and was so sanguine of success, promising to complete the work in ten days, that Banks was requested to let him attempt it. Three thousand men, and two or three hundred wagons were put at his disposal, and the work commenced. Those quiet shores at once became a human hive, and the sound of the axe, the crash of falling trees and shouts of men, made the forests echo. The army and fleet looked on in astonishment at this new system of engineering adopted by this bold western man. On the left bank of the river, a dam, made of fallen trees, was run out some three hundred feet, and then four coal barges filled with brick were sunk at the end. From the other shore, cribs filled with stone to meet the barges, were built. The work was successfully accomplished, and the water rapidly rose. In one day more it would have been high enough to let the boats above the upper falls pass over; when, unfortunately, on the 9th of May, the pressure became so great that two of the coal barges were forced downward from their position, and swung round at right angles to the dam. The water immediately began to pour through like a cataract. Porter saw with a sinking heart the catastrophe, for he feared the men would have no heart to rebuild the dam. Determined if possible to save some of his vessels, he jumped upon a horse and galloping up stream, ordered the Lexington to try to pass the falls. She succeeded, and then headed straight for the fearful shute in the dam. Tens of thousands lined the shores, watching with breathless interest the perilous movement. Not a sound but the low steady rush of the torrent broke the stillness as she neared the boiling mælstrom. Crowding on all steam, her gallant Commander stood and calmly watched the approaching crisis. The vessel, impelled by a full head of steam, and the swiftly descending, sloping hill of water, rushed like a mad thing toward what seemed certain destruction. Leaping into the boiling cauldron, she settled heavily in the surge, and, for a moment, seemed going to the bottom. Rolling heavily from side to side, she at length caught on a rock, and hung for an instant suspended in the torrent, then, rising slowly, swept off into deep water, and rounded quietly to. The watching, excited multitude that had not uttered a word while the fate of the vessel was held in a fearful crisis, now rent the heavens with deafening shouts. From shore to shore the wild cheers echoed, and again and again were taken up and sent in thunder toward the sky. The Neosho now tried it, but the pilot becoming frightened as the vessel approached the abyss, stopped her engine. Porter saw the fatal mistake, and watched to see her disappear in the tumultuous waters. Her hull went out of sight, and she seemed lost, but slowly lifting herself again, she heaved forward and passed through, though with a hole in her bottom. The partial success of the experiment encouraged the men to rebuild the dam; though they had been working for eight days and nights up to their necks in water, they cheerfully entered on the herculean task. Bailey now left a gap of fifty feet in the dam, to avoid the tremendous pressure of the water, and built wing dams on the falls above, so as to make a deep channel for the current. In three days the work was accomplished, and on the 11th and 12th six gunboats and two tugs were got over the upper falls. They then one after another, with their hatches battened down, took the shute of the dam, cheered loudly by the whole army as they successively passed safely through. It was a great engineering success—the entire fleet being saved—thanks to the skill of an engineer who dared to attempt an undertaking that all had ridiculed. Porter could hardly moderate his delight at this unexpected deliverance of his fleet, and heaped encomiums on Bailey, whom the Government very properly rewarded with the star of a Brigadier-General.

Porter in his report said: "Words are inadequate to express the admiration I feel for the abilities of Lieutenant-Colonel Bailey. This is, without doubt, the best engineering feat ever performed. Under the best circumstances a private company would not have completed this work under one year, and, to an ordinary mind, the whole thing would have appeared an impossibility. Leaving out his abilities as an engineer, and the credit he has conferred upon the country, he has saved to the Union a valuable fleet worth nearly two millions of dollars. More, he has deprived the enemy of a triumph which would have emboldened them to carry on this war a year or two longer; for the intended departure of the army was a fixed fact, and there was nothing left for me to do, in case that event occurred, but to destroy every part of the vessels, so that the rebels could make nothing of them. The highest honors the Government can bestow on Colonel Bailey can never repay him for the service he has rendered the country."

The fleet, however, did not get off entirely scatheless. The gunboats Signal and Covington, having been sent down the river from Alexandria to convoy the Warner, a boat loaded with cotton, unexpectedly came upon a series of rebel batteries about thirty miles from the place. These batteries were so concealed, that their existence was not dreamed of until they opened on the boat loaded with cotton—piercing her boilers almost instantly, and sending her, a helpless wreck, against the opposite bank. The rebel troops fired at the same time with musketry, killing and wounding nearly two hundred soldiers that were aboard of her. Others were killed in trying to escape to the shore. The Signal and Covington at once rounded to and pushed back to help the transport, but soon found that they had enough to do to take care of themselves. Their steam pipes were soon cut, and their boilers perforated with shot, yet they gallantly maintained the unequal contest for five hours. Lieutenant George P. Lord, commanding the Covington, fired his last charge of ammunition—then spiked his guns, set fire to his vessel, and with what was left of his crew, escaped to the shore. Soon the flaming boat blew up with a loud explosion. Lieutenant Edward Morgan, of the Signal, maintained the contest for half an hour longer, but finding that he was only exposing his men to useless slaughter, abandoned it. His decks being strewn with the wounded who had gallantly stood by him to the last, he could not consent to set fire to his vessel, and so he gave permission for all to escape as they best could. But few, however, got off, for in attempting to climb the opposite bank they became a fair mark for the sharp-shooters, and were dropped, one after another, into the river.

When Banks heard of this disaster, he sent out a body of cavalry and dispersed the rebels.

Both fleet and army now came back to the Mississippi, and Canby was sent to take the place of Banks in the field, while the latter returned to New Orleans to confine himself to the civil duties of his department. This ended his military career of which his friends had expected so much.

The expedition, whoever planned it, was a foolish one, while Banks, in carrying it out, showed a great lack of military sagacity. With the enemy in his immediate front, he was caught with his army widely scattered apart, and his trains anywhere but where they should have been. Beaten in detail, he was driven back in disgrace, and the whole expedition turned out a mortifying failure, and came very near being a great catastrophe. Its chief object seemed to have been to gather cotton, of which large quantities were known to be in this section. It was a bad speculation, however, on the part of the Government, and most disastrous to the military reputation of the Commander. If Franklin, whom the Secretary of War had sent to Banks in a fit of spleen, had been at the head of it, a different result would have been reached.

It is proper to state that though this expedition was started almost simultaneously with the movement of the two great armies under Sherman and Grant, it had no connection whatever with it. It was organized previous to the assumption of supreme command by Grant, or it never would have been organized at all. It had been sanctioned by those unfortunate strategists, Halleck and Stanton, and hence had to proceed. Nothing was left for Grant to do but to hurry it forward as fast as possible, and have it out of his way before his great movements commenced. Hence, as far back as the 15th of March, he notified Banks of the importance of capturing Shreveport at the earliest possible day, and that if he should "find that the taking of it would occupy from ten to fifteen days more time, than General Sherman had given to his troops to be absent from their command—he would send them back at the time specified by General Sherman, even if it led to the abandonment of the main object of the Red River expedition, for this force was necessary to movements east of the Mississippi; that should his expedition prove successful, he would hold Shreveport and the Red River with such force as he might deem necessary, and return the balance of his troops to the neighborhood of New Orleans, commencing no move for the further acquisition of territory unless it was to make that then held by him more easily held; that it might be a part of the spring campaign to move against Mobile; that it certainly would be if troops enough could be obtained to make it without embarrassing other movements; that New Orleans would be the point of departure for such an expedition; also that he had directed General Steele to make a real move from Arkansas as suggested by him, (General Banks,) instead of a demonstration, as Steele thought advisable."

Grant told him, moreover, to move as quickly as possible—abandon Texas altogether, and, leaving only a portion of his army to guard the Mississippi, to prepare to co-operate with Farragut against Mobile. This would keep a part of the Southern army away from Richmond, while the farther he went toward Shreveport, the less use he was to Grant. Hence, as we have said, the only interest the General-in Chief took in the expedition, was to have it over with as speedily as possible.

But all these battles and expeditions in the East and West, were isolated affairs, having no bearing on the mighty movement about to be made. They caused some noise and much angry feeling and vituperation, but the burdened trains and crowded boats, steadily moving without noise and observation southward, were the really great events of those four months. These separate successes or disasters were the mere by-play to the great drama about to open—the dim and far-off flashes along the edge of the storm-cloud, which was soon to darken all the heavens, and shake the earth with its thunder.

CHAPTER XXIV.

GRANT'S DELAY IN FRONT OF WASHINGTON—THE PRESIDENT'S DETERMINATION NOT TO INTERFERE ANY MORE WITH THE ARMY OF THE POTOMAC—THE TWO ARMIES MOVE—THE ATLANTA CAMPAIGN—ITS DIFFICULTIES—COMPOSITION AND STRENGTH OF SHERMAN'S ARMY—DALTON FLANKED—BATTLE OF RESACA—A FIERCE STRUGGLE—FIGHT AT DALLAS—ALLATOONA FLANKED—BATTLE OF KENESAW MOUNTAIN—DEATH OF MAJOR-GENERAL POLK—SHERMAN DIRECTS THE SHOT THAT KILLS HIM—SHERMAN'S FIRST DEFEAT—KENESAW FLANKED—THE CHATTAHOCHEE REACHED AND CROSSED—ATLANTA IN SIGHT.

THE long delay of Grant in front of Washington awakened much surprise, but he had resolved not to move till he was ready. No order to move at a certain day, like that of President Lincoln formerly to the Army of the Potomac, without consulting the General-in-Chief, was given. The public might grumble and grow impatient, but he had learned from experience the folly of such a course, and determined to let Grant take his own time, if he did not move till mid-summer. The lesson he had learned, had been a costly one to the country, and to our brave soldiers, but it was learned at last—that the General-in-Chief should be left to carry out his own plans without interference from politicians or the Secretary of War. This settled determination of his, neither to meddle with military movements himself, nor let others do it, filled every one with hope, and was a good augury of the future. The public settled down patiently into the conviction that Grant was to be left untrammeled, and the Secretary of War to be confined to his legitimate duties, for which he was eminently qualified.

At length the first of May, the appointed time, came, and

the two mighty armies arose from their long apparent torpor, and the knell of the Confederacy from that hour began to toll. Their movement was simultaneous, and the campaigns practically parallel; yet their starting points were a thousand miles apart, with the lofty Alleghanies between. In some respects they were widely different. Grant had but little over half as far to go as Sherman, with no flank to guard but his right, and that easily made secure by an army of occupation in the defiles of the Shenandoah Valley. Neither was he confined to a single base like Sherman, but could change it at his pleasure, as he afterward did. The latter could reach his objective point only by a single line of railway, stretching for nearly two hundred miles through a comparative wilderness, with Forrest's daring cavalry threatening both flanks and his long line of communications, which, if once permanently cut, would secure the destruction of his army. They were different in another respect; Grant could at any time fling his army, by water, in front of Richmond, when the difficulties of his task would be only just commenced, while Sherman, if he should once get in front of Atlanta, would have achieved the most difficult part of his campaign.

The eyes of the whole country were fixed on the two armies, but Grant held more fully the attention of the East, and Sherman that of the West. The South saw the coming storm and braced itself to meet it.

Sherman, at the outset, had asked for one hundred thousand men, and two hundred and fifty pieces of artillery. The disgraceful failure of the Red River expedition, interfered somewhat with this arrangement, but the War Department, by great effort, succeeded in giving him all but twelve hundred of the required number of men. His force was divided as follows:—the Army of the Cumberland, Major-General Thomas, sixty thousand, seven hundred and seventy-three men, and one hundred and thirty guns; Army of the Tennessee, McPherson, twenty-four thousand, four hundred and sixty-five men, and ninety-six guns; Army of the Ohio, Schofield, thirteen thousand five hundred and fifty-nine men, and twenty-eight guns. Kilpatrick commanded the cavalry of the Army of the Cumberland. The Confederate Army opposed to him was sixty thousand strong, including ten thousand cavalry; the latter superior to that of Sherman. Hardee, Hood and Polk commanded the three Corps, composing this army.

Sherman had a most difficult task before him. If he succeeded, he would solve a new problem in war—or rather introduce a new principle into military science, viz.:—that an army of a hundred thousand men could be marched three hundred miles from its actual base, (which was Nashville,) and yet this long line of communication be kept open. Such a thing had been considered an impossibility; and when the news of his advance reached Europe, there was no discussion among military men respecting his probable success; it was settled that he was going to certain defeat. The South also had no doubt on the subject.

The public will never appreciate the skill which Sherman showed in arranging his forces, securing his transportation, and guarding his communications—a skill that astonished and baffled his foes, and yet retained his army almost intact. By all ordinary rules, in order to guard his transportation and secure his communications as he advanced, he would have had to deplete his army and string it along his rear, till but a handful would be left by the time he reached Atlanta, if he got there at all. One of his devices to protect his line was an admirable and successful one. By a glance at the map, it will be seen that the railroad in its course to Atlanta frequently crosses streams. The bridges over these had to be protected at all hazards. The destruction of the railroad between them was comparatively of small account as it could be repaired in a few hours. To protect the bridges, and at the same time, not materially lessen his force, he had small bomb-proof block houses, or fortifications, built near them, as he advanced, large enough to hold a few hundred men, and provisioned for a long time. These the enemy could not beat down with their cannon, nor carry by assault, nor could they starve out the garrisons. In the meantime, a few pieces of artillery completely commanded the approaches to the bridges, so that no force could advance to destroy them. He also accumulated at different points, as he advanced, vast stores of imperishable provisions, so that in case of accident, he could subsist his army until communications could be restored. Although it was necessary to the success of his campaign that the railroads should be kept exclusively for military purposes, the fact that they were, caused incalculable suffering to the people of East Tennessee.

Having thus anticipated almost every contingency that could arise, he, early in May, put his magnificent columns in motion. Johnston lay in and about Dalton, which was so strongly fortified that an attack in front would have been madness, and Sherman here began that series of movements which won for him the sobriquet of the "great flanker." Resaca lay eighteen miles south of Dalton, directly on the railroad, and he determined, if possible, to reach this by a circuitous route, and seize it, thus compelling Johnston to retreat or accept a battle, unprotected by his fortifications. McPherson's army was at once started westward on a circuit of some thirty or forty miles, through Snake Creek Gap to this point, while Thomas moved directly up in front of Dalton, as if about to force a passage there. But Dalton was covered by Rocky-Face Ridge, cleft in two by Buzzard-Roost Gap, through which ran the railroad. This narrow defile was filled with abattis, artificially flooded by a neighboring creek, and swept from end to end by artillery posted on every commanding spur, and on a height at the farther extremity. Against this Thomas made first a feint, and then a vigorous attack, in which Veatch's division of Howard's Corps actually carried the rocky ridge, but could not, from the obstacles opposed to it, reach the gorge—while Geary's division of Hooker's Corps made a gallant, desperate push for the summit. Added to the natural obstacles and fire of the enemy, huge rocks were sent down, crashing through the trees and advancing lines with resistless fury. No decisive advantage was gained by our forces, but the enemy was kept so well occupied that McPherson was left to make his difficult march undisturbed, till he got within a mile of Resaca If, by a sudden bold push, he could have taken this place, Johnston's army would, doubtless, have been annihilated. But, on reconnoitering, he found it too strong to be carried by assault, for the wily Johnston had provided against this possible contingency, by hurrying off troops thither. McPherson therefore fell back on Snake Creek Gap, ready to strike the rebel flank when the army should retreat. Hooker's Corps was immediately sent over to McPherson's aid, followed by all of Schofield's army, until Howard's Corps alone remained in front of Dalton. Johnston, seeing the trap that was set for him, immediately evacuated his stronghold and fell back rapidly to Resaca, when Howard entered Dalton and kept on directly in the enemy's track.

Thus was the first eighteen miles won. Sherman lost about a thousand men in these first movements.

BATTLE OF RESACA.

Reaching Resaca, Sherman found his adversary strongly posted, and he at once initiated another flank movement. The Oostenaula stream, which is here crossed by a railroad bridge, he pontooned, and then hurried off Sweeney's division, with orders to move around, and threaten Calhoun, still farther down on the railroad, while Garrard's division of cavalry was sent to destroy the railroad beyond. There was some heavy fighting here during the first day. Judah's division of Schofield's Corps charged bravely on the enemy, but was repulsed. Cox, getting out of ammunition, ordered a charge of the enemy's breastworks in his immediate front, and carried them with a cheer. Palmer's Corps also pressed the enemy vigorously, who, after vainly endeavoring to break our centre, massed his forces against our left, and came down in one of those impetuous overwhelming assaults, for which the rebels were distinguished. Stanley caught the blow on his flank, and, for awhile, bore up firmly against it. At last, however, he gave way, and the broken confused ranks began to retire in disorder, when there suddenly arose a cheer, heard above the roar of artillery. Robinson's brigade was coming to the rescue on a run. With one terrible blow, it stopped the shouting, exultant enemy, and sent him bleeding, discomfited back to his breastworks. Darkness, at length, closed the combat, and night came down on the valley and ridges, strewed with the dead and wounded. Though no material advantage was gained, the enemy had failed to break our extended, incomplete line at any point.

Quiet reigned over the two armies that night, except that the incessant blows of the axe, and the falling of trees showed that Johnston was busy in piling obstructions in his front. Sunday morning, the 15th, dawned mild and peaceful, but by the time the sun was an hour high, the scattering fire of the skirmishers told that the day was to be one of blood, not of rest. By noon Sherman had his army well up, extending for miles in a sort of semi-circle—McPherson on the right, Thomas in the centre, and Schofield on the left, with Howard extending beyond. The rebel army—Hood on the right, Hardee in the centre, and Polk on the left, was drawn up behind breastworks, calmly awaiting the coming shock. At a given signal, the whole army moved forward, and the battle began. Into our uncovered ranks the enemy hurled shot and shell with desolating effect, until the dead lay everywhere, but not a brigade wavered. Inch by inch the gallant regiments worked their way on, pressing heavier and heavier, every moment, the astonished enemy—determined, at whatever sacrifice, to carry the strong position that confronted them.

Hooker threw forward Butterfield's division against the enemy's strongest position, supported by Williams' and Geary's divisions, and the battle opened vigorously on both sides. Hooker fought for three or four hours and made steady headway, carrying line after line of rifle-pits, until Butterfield's division encountered a lunette of formidable size. Several attempts were made to carry this and capture its guns, which were pouring a destructive fire into our lines, but they did not succeed. The troops fought with great desperation, but as often as they advanced upon the lunette, the terrific volleys of musketry from the enemy in the fortifications hurled them back in confusion. At last Butterfield charged forward and took a position under the protecting works of the fort, and so close to the guns within, that they could be touched by the men's hands. "In the effort to gain this exposed position, the contest was a bloody one, Geary's division supporting Butterfield. Ward's brigade, which were participating in their first battle, fought with marked determination, and contributed much to secure the position."

"After vain efforts to capture the lunette, from which the enemy poured into our ranks grape, canister and shrapnel, Hooker's forces gave up the unequal contest, and during the balance of the day lay under the breastworks protected from the enemy's fire, and picking off every rebel who showed himself above the ramparts. Night found him in this position, and he at once matured plans for capturing the works by strategy, under cover of darkness. The pioneers were brought up; the ends were dug out of the works, and the guns drawn out by the aid of ropes, under a destructive fire from the occupants of the lunette, who were driven out or captured, as our troops swarmed in through the opening in overwhelming numbers."

This Corps lost very heavily. At ten o'clock at night, Hooker began to throw up breast-works to protect himself, and in the meantime advanced his skirmish line. This in the darkness moved upon the enemy, and a night battle commenced, lighting up the gloom with flame, and sending its heavy thunder all along our expectant line. At two o'clock in the morning, the rebels gave way, and the low moans of the dying, and cries for water succeeded to the uproar that made the night hideous. In this battle the gallant Kilpatrick was wounded, and had to leave the army till his recovery.

Monday morning dawned bright and clear, but as the sun climbed the heavens it revealed the whole valley filled with smoke and fog, that lay like a great pall over the spring brightness and beauty. It was soon discovered that the rebels, not wanting to risk another battle, had evacuated their works, and were in full retreat. Our line immediately advanced, and the cavalry pressed fiercely on the enemy's rear. The latter succeeded in getting off his artillery, but was compelled to burn his wagon trains to prevent them from falling into our hands.

An officer visited the spot where the desperate hand-to-hand fight had occurred, for the lunette, and says, "this was thickly strewed with the dead and wounded. Inside and around the work, rebel and Union officers and men lay piled together; some transfixed with bayonet wounds, their faces wearing that fierce contorted look which marks those who have suffered agony. Others, who were shot dead, lay with their calm faces and glassy eyes turned to heaven. One might think they were but sleeping. Others had their skulls crushed in by the end of a musket, while the owner of the musket lay stiff beside them with the death-grip tightened on the piece. Clinging to one of the guns with his hand on the spoke and his body bent as if drawing it, lay a youth with the top of his head shot off. Another with his body cut in two still clung to the ropes." *

Crossing the Oostenaula, Johnston partially destroyed the bridge, so that the pursuit was delayed. McPherson endeavored to throw over pontoons, and get in his rear, but was unable to do so under the heavy fire to which he was exposed, and the former got off with his army. Our loss in these two days had been heavy—about five thousand in all. That of the enemy was not probably so great, for he fought behind breastworks—but we took nearly a thousand prisoners, and eight guns, and a large quantity of stores.

The whole army at once pressed rapidly in pursuit—a portion going by circuitous roads—struggling through the rough country as it best could—fording the shallow streams—pontooning the deep ones, and hovering like a storm-cloud on the fleeing enemy. The movements were complicated and often wide apart, yet Sherman's grasping mind embraced them all, so that the entire army moved like a single piece of mechanism.

On the 17th, Newton's division had a snarp artillery fight at Adairville, near Calhoun, but Johnston never halted in his flight; and on the 18th, after some heavy skirmishing, Clinton fell into our hands. Here Sherman gave his gallant weary troops a few days rest, while he hurried forward his supplies and re-established telegraphic and railroad communication with Chattanooga.

* Captain Conyngham.

It was beautiful spring weather, and the country around being fine, a perfect carnival reigned in the camps that were scattered for miles in every direction. Racing and hunting parties were got up, and mirth and gaiety took the place of battles and marches. But the vast extent of country occupied by the army, and its wooded character, gave opportunity to the base and villainous soldiers that belong to every army to carry out a system of pillage and house burning that filled the inhabitants with terror, and spread suffering on every side. Cold-blooded murders were not wanting to complete the dark list of crimes committed by them.

Leaving a garrison here, and also one at Rome, which had been captured with all its warehouses, foundries, workshops, and fifteen hundred bales of cotton, without a fight, Sherman on the 23rd, again put his army in motion toward Dallas—that lay west of the railroad, south of Allatoona—a place strong by nature, and covered with fortifications. If this point could be reached before Johnston abandoned Allatoona, he would be cut off from Atlanta. This he must prevent at all hazards, and the rugged character of the country gave him every facility for making obstinate defense all along our line of march. Day after day more or less fighting occurred, but still swinging steadily off to the right, Sherman continued to push his victorious columns forward till he approached Dallas. The junction of the Acworth, Marietta and Dallas railroad, he was very anxious to secure, and Hooker was ordered to hasten forward and seize it. Near New Hope Church, the latter came upon the enemy in strong force, and attacked him fiercely. The Corps fought with its accustomed gallantry, and Geary's division especially distinguished itself. The rebels also fought desperately, disputing bravely every inch of ground, yet Hooker drove them steadily toward the junction. But night came on before he reached it, and a drenching, pelting rain storm set in, which arrested the fight; and the tired Corps sunk to rest on the flooded field.

For three days now, there was constant skirmishing, and some heavy fighting between portions of the army, while Sherman was developing his line, preparatory to a general onward movement. On the 28th, Johnston, taking advantage of the somewhat disintegrated state of our army, fell furiously on McPherson, while closing in on the army of Thomas. Hardee's and Polk's Corps made the assault, which was sudden and terrible. Our men were behind rifle pits extending for two miles, waiting, as the skirmishers fell back, to receive the shock. Logan, hat in hand, rode along his division, encouraging the men, who replied with shouts. Soon after, McPherson with his staff, rode along the whole line, received with deafening cheers as he passed. The assaulting columns came down with shouts and yells, that rose over the crash of their volleys; but our troops reserved their fire until the enemy were within a few yards, when a volley from the first rank leaped forth like a sheet of lightning, cutting with its fiery blade the rebel line of battle. A second one from the rear rank instantaneously followed, and the rash, brave foe fell like grass before the swinging scythe. Rolled back before this withering fire, they rallied again and again, and came on with the same defiant shouts, charging up almost to the muzzles of the guns. But it was like the waves beating the rocks. The Army of the Tennessee never wavered, but steady and stern, stood and reaped that harvest of death, till night fell, when the baffled foe gave it up, and retired, leaving the ground covered with dead. His loss in this desperate assault was fully three thousand, while McPherson's was not over a third as great.

Sherman now paused a few days to mislead the enemy, and on the 1st of June sent McPherson around to the left on another flank movement. Johnston was confounded at these continual flank movements—now around his right, and then around his left, ever threatening his communications with Atlanta. As before, so now he was compelled to abandon his stronghold which he had fortified with so much care, and fell back to Kenesaw Mountain, if possible a still stronger position than any he had thus far abandoned. Making Allatoona Pass a secondary base, and leaving a garrison there to hold it, and repairing the railroad behind him, Sherman prepared to advance again.

On the 9th of June "Forward" sounded from our bugles, and the conquering army took up its march for Kenesaw Mountain.

BATTLE OF KENESAW MOUNTAIN.

It drew up in front of this formidable height, whose crest, four hundred feet high, was seen to be lined with artillery. On the right arose other mountains, and, farther back, Lost Mountain—all dark with batteries, while every spur was alive with men, "felling trees, digging pits, and preparing for the grand struggle impending." Says Sherman, "the scene was enchanting, too beautiful to be disturbed by the rude clamors of war, but the Chattahoochee lay beyond, and I had to reach it." "By the 11th of June our lines were well up, and we made dispositions to break the line between Kenesaw and Pine Mountains. General Hooker was on its right and front, General Howard on its left and front, and General Palmer between it and the railroad." On the 14th, during a sharp cannonade, General Polk was killed, and the next morning Pine Mountain was discovered to be abandoned.

The death of Polk, as related by Captain Conyngham, reminds one of the death of Moreau, at Leipsic. Bonaparte, seeing a group of officers on a distant elevation, ordered a captain of artillery to throw a shot into it, saying, perhaps some little Generals are there. The latter did so, and the cannon ball smote Moreau.

Sherman, riding up to a battery, took a careful survey of Pine Mountain with his glass. Then turning to Captain Simonson, he said, "Can you send a shell right on the top of that knob? I notice a battery there, and several general officers near it." "I'll try, General," was the reply. He fired. "A little too high, try again, with a shorter fuse," said Sherman. The second shell flew through the air, and entering the distant group, crashed through the side of Polk, tearing his body into fragments.

Thomas and Schofield now advanced, and found the enemy again strongly intrenched along the line of rugged hills that connect Kenesaw and Lost Mountains. On the 17th, the enemy abandoned Lost Mountain, and took position on Kenesaw; his right wing thrown back, so as to cover Marietta, and his left covering the railroad in the rear, thus contracting his lines, and leaving no weak spot open to an attack. From his high position he could look down on every movement of our troops, while his cannon thundered away upon our long line. To make matters worse, a heavy rain storm had set in, and day and night, week after week, it poured down on the exposed army, turning the narrow country roads into gulleys, and every open space into a marsh, and thus preventing any general movement. The troops suffered greatly, yet kept steadily at work. "General McPherson watching the enemy on Kenesaw, and working his left forward; General Thomas, swinging, as it were on a grand left wheel, his left on Kenesaw, connected with General McPherson, while General Schofield was all the while working to the south and east along the old Sandtown road."

Thus matters went on, amid the pelting rain, when on the 22nd, Hood made a sudden attack on Hooker's Corps. Driving in the advanced detachments, he fell furiously on

Williams' division. The onset was fierce, but failed—the enemy losing seven or eight hundred men. Sherman now determined to assault in turn; and, on the 27th, the army advanced against the stronghold. The long rain storm had cleared away, the roads were good—and a warm summer sun was shining, as the columns moved off on the desperate undertaking. The grand assault was made by the two armies of Thomas and McPherson, at two different points. Gulleys, rocks, trees, and underbrush, lay on the line of march, before the mountain, swarming now with men like bees, could be reached. Heralded by the crash of artillery, the columns moved steadily forward, and the battle soon raged furiously. Kenesaw seemed a volcano there in the summer air, while a surge of fire kept rolling steadily up its base. Troops never behaved more gallantly, and the officers held them to their deadly work with unparalleled devotion. Generals McCook and Harker fell at the head of their brigades, cheering on the men, and many other officers went down before the awful fire that swept, without cessation, the rugged slopes of the mountain. But it was vain valor, for the position was too strong to be carried by direct assault. Some brave regiments mounted half way up the slope, but only to be hurled back broken and bleeding; and at length the bugles rung out the order to cease firing, and the battle was over. Sherman had met his first defeat. His loss was severe, reaching full three thousand, among whom were many valuable officers.

If Sherman made any mistake in this remarkable campaign, it was in ordering this assault. His own reasons for making it are not satisfactory. He says, "all looked to outflank. An army to be efficient must not settle down to one single mode of offense," &c. An army must "settle down" just to that "mode of offense" which will bring victory with the least loss of life. He thought also that the "moral effect" of a successful assault would be good. But it is equally true that the "moral effect" of an *unsuccessful* one is bad, and the chances here were nine to one against him. Besides, he after all, had to fall back again to his old flanking system, the only wise course when it can be taken against such a strong position as Kenesaw mountain was.

Gathering up his bleeding army, and, burying his dead, under a flag of truce, he sent McPherson forward to the Chattahoochee, far in the rear of Kenesaw Mountain. As soon as Johnston was aware of this movement, he evacuated his strong position, and Sherman rode into Marietta. The result showed that this would have been the proper course at first, and that he could have had the strong position without the loss of a man.

Sherman now pressed forward, in hope of catching Johnston in the confusion of crossing the Chattahoochee. But the latter had provided against such a contingency, and covered his movements so well that no considerable advantage could be gained over him, though more or less fighting occurred all the way to its banks. On the 4th and 5th of July, the rebel army crossed the river in safety. On the 7th, Schofield effected a lodgment on the farther bank, and laid a good pontoon and trestle bridge. Sherman handled his troops with such skill, that by the ninth, he had secured three good points for crossing over his army above the enemy's *tete-du-pont*, when the latter reluctantly abandoned his last line of defense, and fell back to Atlanta.

In the meantime Rousseau, with two thousand cavalry, was sent around Atlanta, to destroy the railroad at Opelika, Ala., south, and cut off Johnston's supplies. This force was gone twelve days, and succeeded in accomplishing its object, and returned, with the loss of only thirty men.

The control of the Chattahoochee, Sherman said, "was one if not the chief object of the campaign," but Atlanta lay only eight miles distant, and he determined to capture it. But after the heavy marching and fighting of the past few weeks, the army needed rest before entering on such a desperate undertaking, and it pitched its camps along the stream, and gave itself up to several days' repose. From a neighboring hill the steeples of Atlanta, and the smoke of its foundries could be seen. Around it stretched a beautiful country, dotted with plantations, while in every direction, the smoke of locomotives, as they sped along the plains, revealed the various lines of railroad that centered in the place.

CHAPTER XXV.

ATLANTA REACHED—HOOD'S FIRST ATTACK—HIS ASSAULT ON MC PHERSON—DEATH OF THE LATTER—HOWARD PLACED OVER THE ARMY OF THE TENNESSEE—STONEMAN AND MC COOK'S RAID—HOOKER RESIGNS—FIERCE ATTACK ON HOWARD—SHELLING OF ATLANTA—AN UNSUCCESSFUL ASSAULT—WHEELER SENT TO CUT SHERMAN'S COMMUNICATIONS—KILPATRICK DISPATCHED TO CUT HOOD'S—SHERMAN RESOLVED TO PLANT HIS ARMY ON THE MACON ROAD—BATTLE OF JONESBORO'—ATLANTA CUT OFF—HOOD EVACUATES IT—SLOCUM TAKES POSSESSION—THE REBEL ARMY PURSUED TO LOVEJOY'S STATION—REST TO THE ARMY—SUMMING UP OF THE CAMPAIGN—SHERMAN ORDERS ALL THE INHABITANTS TO LEAVE—HIS CORRESPONDENCE WITH HOOD AND THE MAYOR, ON THE SUBJECT.

ON the 17th of July, the whole army moved forward, fighting as it advanced, and, at length, Atlanta greeted the eyes of the weary, suffering, yet enthusiastic troops.

Johnston, at this time, was removed from command, and Hood put in his place. A new mode of conducting the campaign was now to be inaugurated. The Fabian policy was dropped at once, and the impetuous Hood, the moment he obtained the control of the army, broke into a furious offensive. On the 20th, Sherman was in the act of forming his new lines, about five miles from Atlanta, with no enemy in force apparently near, when suddenly, nearly the whole of Hood's army came pouring forward with shouts and yells, that rolled like thunder over the field. Newton's division of Howard's Corps, and Johnson's of Palmer's, received the first shock. They had just before thrown up a breastwork of rails, behind which they poured in a galling fire. Hooker's Corps, however, was entirely uncovered, yet stood like a flaming citadel in the open fields. Where this onset was made, a gap in the lines existed, which Hood hoped to penetrate. Had he succeeded, disastrous consequences would, doubtless, have followed. But though the assault was sudden as a thunder-clap, and found our troops partially unprepared, it failed to break through our lines. The rebels threw themselves forward on our batteries with a recklessness that was frightful to behold. Their ranks melted away before the fire like the sand bank when caved by the torrent, yet the living never faltered. Over their own piled-up dead, they still crowded the gates of death with a self-devotion never surpassed. The sacrifice was great, but it did not avail, and the bleeding, shattered host fell back to its intrenchments, having lost in this short, fierce engagement, according to the estimate of Thomas, five thousand men. Our loss was about half that number.

Two days after, Hood abandoned his extensive line of defenses, falling back to his interior position of redoubts, in front of which were almost impenetrable *chevaux-de-frise*, with water between them.

While Thomas was thus pushing forward in front, McPherson, from Decatur to the eastward, was moving down the railroad toward the city.

Hood, two days after this terrible repulse, made another desperate attempt to break through the net that was steadily closing round him. Leaving just enough troops in the intrenchments to hold them, he massed his entire army against McPherson on the left, who had not yet got into position. The onset, if possible, was more terrific than that of two days before, and, at one time, came very near overwhelming the Army of the Tennessee. Blair caught the first blow, and then the shouting, yelling, frantic mass poured down on the whole line with a fury that, at first, seemed irresistible. In the meantime, a heavy force got in the rear and captured some twelve guns. The enraged gunners rushed back for their pieces, and a bloody, hand to hand fight took place over them. In front, the rebels, with their usual daring, dashed unflinchingly through the fire that wasted them, up to the very breastworks, and planted their colors alongside of our own, and fought like tigers around them. "*For a half an hour, the two armies fought face to face each side of the same line of intrenchments, with the battle colors of the respective parties flying from the same works.*" The struggle was so close and deadly that orders were of little avail—it was a contest of the old Greeks and Romans, when everything, for a time, rested solely on the valor of the soldiers. Sherman, with Schofield and Howard, stood on an elevation that commanded a view of the battle field. Planting two batteries on two hills—one on each side of him—which poured a converging fire into the enemy, he sent word to Logan, in the centre, to mass his troops and charge. "You must retake those guns," was the stern order. No sooner did the gallant Logan receive it, than he swiftly massed his troops, and riding alternately at the heads of the columns, shouted them on. Wood's division led the charge, and a loud cheer rolled down the line, as it advanced. The enemy supposing we were thoroughly beaten, were astonished at the sight, but moved boldly out to meet the onset—the artillery, on both sides, playing over the heads of the troops. Soon, however, it ceased as the approaching lines came close together. A crushing fire, a cheer, and then we were upon and over them, scattering them in flight, and retaking part of the guns.

The struggle was a short one, but while it lasted, death reaped the field with rapid strokes. Six tremendous assaults were made on the Fifteenth, Sixteenth and Seventeenth Corps, but when darkness closed over the field, victory was ours. The dead lay everywhere—sometimes in ranks, as though whole companies had been swept away by a single volley. Logan reported the enemy's dead at over three thousand, and the whole rebel loss was estimated at twelve thousand, including seventeen hundred prisoners. We captured, also, eighteen stand of colors, and five thousand small arms. Our loss was only a little over seventeen hundred. The enemy, however, succeeded in carrying off eight pieces of artillery. Our greatest loss, however, was the death of General McPherson, who fell while crossing a piece of woods, attended only by an orderly. He came unexpectedly upon a detachment of rebels, who fired upon him as he attempted to escape.

A comparatively young man, he was one of the ablest officers in the army. Long before he was known to the public, Grant leaned on him, and the enemy, who knew his worth, feared him. Noble and pure-minded, he was beloved by all. Able in council, his opinions carried great weight, while in "the high places of the field," he moved, a tower of strength. As Napoleon, when it was told him that the noble, true-hearted Duroc had fallen, so the iron-hearted Sherman, when the tidings reached him that McPherson was dead, burst into tears.

The next day, Garrard returned from a cavalry raid to Covington, forty-two miles east of Atlanta, in which railroads, bridges, cotton, stores, &c., were destroyed, he having lost but two men in the expedition.

Sherman was now able to move his lines so as to lay regular siege to Atlanta, but to cut off its supplies, it was neccessary that the Macon road should be broken up. To accomplish this, Stoneman was dispatched with a cavalry force of five thousand, while McCook, with four thousand infantry was to meet him on the railroad near Lovejoy's, and co-operate with his movement. The former got in front of Macon, but on his return, he was surrounded by Iverson, and captured, with a thousand of his men. McCook performed his part of the task assigned him, but getting hemmed in by a large force of infantry and cavalry, had to cut his way out, which he did in the most gallant style. On the whole, the expedition was a sad failure. Sherman, in the meantime, kept extending his lines and tightening his coils around the doomed place. Like a scorpion girt with fire, Hood turned and turned to find some way of escape, and on the 28th, at noon, again flung his army in a desperate assault on our lines. Again the Army of the Tennessee received the rebel assault, but, this time, under the leadership of Howard. Sherman had put him in McPherson's place, which so offended Hooker, who felt his claims were overlooked, that he resigned his position and came home. Howard had assumed direct command only the day before the battle.

Says Sherman, "The enemy had come out of Atlanta by the Bell's Ferry road, and formed his masses in the open fields, behind a swell of ground, and after the artillery firing, advanced in parallel lines, directly against the Fifteenth Corps, expecting to catch that flank in air. His advance was magnificent, but founded on an error that cost him sadly; for our men coolly and deliberately cut down his men, and, in spite of the efforts of the rebel officers, his ranks broke and fled. But they were rallied again and again, as often as six times, at some points, and a few of the rebel officers and men reached our lines of rail-piles, but only to be killed or hauled over as prisoners." These assaults continued from noon until four in the afternoon, when the enemy disappeared, leaving his dead and wounded in our hands. The splendid and daring manner in which the rebel troops, right on the top of repeated defeats, were brought to the assault, speaks volumes for their bravery. After being driven for nearly two hundred miles, and then, when turning and breaking into a furious offensive, remorselessly slaughtered, it showed the highest order of bravery, and marvellous endurance, to move with confident bearing, as they did, against overwhelming numbers, protected by breastworks. The enemy's loss, in this last attack, was estimated at six thousand, while our own was under six hundred—a great disparity, if true. Five stand of colors were taken, and two thousand muskets.

Hood now let Sherman advance his lines without interruption. He was dashing his army to pieces against the adamantine wall closing around him; and he saw that some other course must be adopted, or his fate was sealed.

Sherman now began to shell the place, and, at one point, made an assault, in which he lost some four hundred men. But, on a careful examination of the enemy's works, he saw that the place could not be carried by storm without a loss that would leave him without an army, and he cast about for other means of reducing it. If he could once plant his army on the Macon road, he knew that Hood would have to leave, for this, now, was his only line of supplies. He at once resolved to do this, and the 18th day of August being chosen for the movement, the wagons were loaded with fifteen days' provisions.

But Hood, in the meantime, had formed a similar plot against Sherman. Finding himself unable to break through his lines and defeat his army, he determined to cut his communications, and starve him into a retreat. Wheeler, with all his cavalry, was sent off toward Chattanooga, to operate on the single line of railroad by which Sherman's army was fed. When this was told the latter, instead of being alarmed, he said, "I could not have asked anything better, for I have provided well for such a contingency." He knew that Wheeler would fail, while it relieved him from the annoyances of cavalry. He, therefore, resolved to cut the West Point railroad at Fairburn, and the Macon road at Jonesboro', by cavalry alone, and Kilpatrick, who had returned to duty, was dispatched with four thousand men and eight pieces of artillery to carry out his plan. Although this bold rider made a complete circuit of Atlanta, yet the expedition was only partially successful. Breaking the roads was comparatively a small matter; they must be held permanently, and so Sherman returned to his original plan. The surplus wagons were sent back to his intrenched bridge on the Chattahoochee river, whither the Twentieth Corps was also dispatched, and the various movements at once commenced for carrying it out. The separate columns moved like clockwork, and reaching without delay the points aimed at, showed the highest stragetic skill on the part of Sherman.

To a common observer, only a vast army could be seen marching by various roads over the country; but, in Sherman's plan, they were like the several wheels of a mighty machine, whose steady revolutions lift the ponderous hammer, which by its descending blows grinds every-thing beneath it to powder.

The West Point railroad was reached and torn up, and then the army moved eastward to Jonesboro'. On the 31st, Howard, who was on the right, arrived, while Thomas, in the centre, was at Couch's, and Schofield commanding the left, at Rough and Ready. A glance at the map, will show in what a desperate position Hood was now placed. He was completely cut off south and east, by railroad, and he must demolish this living wall, closing around him, or leave Atlanta at once. He attempted to effect the former, and S. D. Lee and Hardee, with their Corps, fell on Thomas with desperate resolution, and a fierce battle followed. The rebels fought with their accustomed gallantry, and, for a while, pressed Thomas' veterans sorely, but they were finally repulsed with a loss of some four thousand men. Davis' Corps now came up, and, at four o'clock on the 1st of September, moved majestically on the rebel position, sweeping it like an inundation, and capturing an entire brigade, with its General and eight guns.

Five thousand more were here put *hors-du-combat*, while our loss, in both engagements, was but little over two thousand. Hood's army was fast melting away, and the shattered remnant must now flee or be captured. He saw plainly that all was lost, and that night, hastily evacuated Atlanta, blowing up magazines and stores, and destroying seven locomotives and eighty-one cars.

The torch was applied, also, to a thousand bales of cotton, which made the midnight heavens lurid with flame. Lighted on his gloomy march by this sea of fire, Hood moved swiftly forward over the country toward Macon. The inhabitants of Atlanta, filled with consternation, streamed after him in every vehicle they could lay their hands on, making a scene of terror and confusion that baffles description. Slocum, of the Twentieth Corps, seven miles north, on the Chatahoochee, heard the explosions, caused by the blowing up of the cars, and saw the ruddy heavens, and suspecting the cause, sent out, at day-break, a strong column to reconnoitre. Atlanta was found deserted, and he marched in and took possession of it.

At daylight, next morning, the army started in pursuit of Hood, and kept up the chase, for thirty miles, to Lovejoy's, where he was found strongly fortified. Here it was arrested and moved back to Atlanta, for the campaign was over, and the tentless, almost shoeless, ragged soldiers needed rest. Sherman wrote, "Atlanta is ours, and fairly won," and so it was—won by genius, skill, and downright hard fighting. He had given the lie to all prognostications, and stamped himself the foremost General of the age.

This extraordinary campaign cannot be summed up better than in these words of Colonel Bowman. "When we reflect upon the enormous distance traversed—upon its rugged and defensible character; it being nothing less than a penetration of the entire series of parallel Alleghany ranges—upon the strong army and able General of the enemy, contesting our advance, inch by inch, over ground entirely known to them and unkown to us, after years of preparation in roads and fortified places—upon the fact that Sherman was obliged to rebuild bridges and railroads, as he advanced, and protect his line of supplies, all the way from Nashville to Atlanta, three hundred miles long—upon the dazzling series of victories unbroken, save at Kenesaw, which crowned our banners—upon the miraculous handling of troops, as if by mechanism, over the most wretched of roads, in the most impracticable of countries—upon the skillful and extraordinary system of supplies, of food, forage and ammunition—upon the tremendous disparity of loss inflicted on the enemy, although he fought a defensive campaign—upon the wonderful, tactical genius of the great Commander, whether on the march or in battle—this campaign must stand unsurpassed in the annals of history." Even the momentous events transpiring East, could not overshadow this great campaign, not only great in its actual character, but also in its results. The centre of Southern railroads was reached, the Confederacy again bisected, and Sherman's hand was feeling its great arteries.

He now placed his camp in order and showed that he had come to stay. He commenced putting Atlanta in a state of defense, and ordered all non-combatants to be removed to Hood's lines, with their servants and effects. He asked the latter for his co-operation in effecting this. Hood acceded to his proposition, but bitterly denounced the measure as "*unprecedented, studied and ungenerous cruelty.*"

This was a charge so wholly contrary to Sherman's character, and so repugnant to his feelings, that he replied to it. He had before shown that he wielded a trenchant pen, as well as sword. His letter to the Massachusetts agent, who asked to enter his lines to get blacks to fill up the quota of the State, under the President's call for troops, struck a hard blow at that miserable, pseudo patriotism, that wished to keep the able-bodied whites from the war, and place its tremendous responsibilities on mercenary foreigners, or the poor, liberated blacks. His answer to Hood showed the same capacity to strike hard blows. He says:—

"GENERAL,—I have the honor to acknowledge the receipt of your letter, of this date, at the hands of Messrs. Ball and Crew, consenting to the arrangements I had proposed to facilitate the removal south, of the people of Atlanta, who prefer to go in that direction. I inclose you a copy of my orders, which will, I am satisfied, accomplish my purpose perfectly. You style the measures proposed 'unprecedented,' and appeal to the dark history of war for a parallel, as an act of 'studied and ungenerous cruelty.' It is not unprecedented, for General Johnston himself very wisely and properly removed the families all the way from Dalton down, and I see no reason why Atlanta should be excepted. Nor is it necessary to appeal to the dark history of war, when recent and modern examples are so handy. You, yourself, burned dwelling-houses along your parapet, and I have seen to-day fifty houses that you have rendered uninhabitable because they stood in the way of your forts and men. You defended Atlanta on a line so close to the town that every cannon-shot, and many musket-shots, from our line of investments, that overshot their mark, went into the habitations of women and children. General Hardee did the same at Jonesboro', and General Johnston did the same last Summer at Jackson, Mississippi. I have not accused you of heartless cruelty, but merely instance these cases, of very recent occurrence, and could go on and enumerate hundreds of others, and challenge any fair man to judge which of us has the heart of pity for the families of a 'brave people.' I say it is a kindness to these families of Atlanta, to remove them now at once from scenes that women and children should not be exposed to; and the brave people should scorn to commit their wives and children to the rude barbarians who thus, as you say, violate the laws of war, as illustrated in the pages of its dark history. In the name of common sense, I ask you not to appeal to a just God in such a sacrilegious manner—you, who, in the midst of peace and prosperity, have plunged a nation into civil war, 'dark and cruel war;' who dared and badgered us to battle; insulted our flag; seized our arsenals and forts, that were left in the honorable custody of a peaceful ordnance sergeant; seized and made prisoners of war the very garrisons sent to protect your people against negroes and Indians, long before any overt act was committed by the (to you) hateful Lincoln-Government; tried to force Kentucky and Missouri into the rebellion in spite of themselves; falsified the vote of Louisiana; turned loose your privateers to plunder unarmed ships; expelled Union families by the thousand; burned their houses, and declared, by Act of your Congress, the confiscation of all debts due Northern men for goods had and received. Talk thus to the marines, but not to me, who have seen these things, and who will this day make as much sacrifice for the peace and honor of the South, as the best-born Southerner among you. If we must be enemies, let us be men, and fight it out as we propose to-day, and not deal in such hypocritical appeals to God and humanity. God will judge us in due time; and He will pronounce whether it be more humane to fight with a town full of women and the families of a "brave people" at our back, or to remove them, in time, to places of safety among their own friends and people.

I am, very respectfully, your obedient servant,
(Signed,) W. T. SHERMAN, Major-General Commanding."

This policy, at the first blush, did seem cruel, and the fact that the enemy committed acts of barbarity, was no justification for Sherman's committing similar acts. It is, therefore, but right that he should be heard in his own defense. So heavily did this order fall on the innocent women and children, that the Mayor begged him, in the name of mercy, to revoke it. Among other things, he says:—

"Many poor women are in an advanced state of pregnancy; others, having young children, whose husbands, for the greater part, are either in the army, prisoners, or dead. Some say, 'I have such a one sick at my house; who will wait on them when I am gone?' Others say: 'What are we to do? we have no houses to go to, and no means to buy, build, or rent any; no parents, relatives, or friends to go to.' Another says: 'I will try and take this or that article of property; but such and such things I must leave behind, though I need them much.' We reply to them: 'General Sherman will carry your property to Rough and Ready, and then General Hood will take it thence on;' and they will reply to that: 'But I want to leave the railroad at such a place, and cannot get conveyance from thence on.'

"We only refer to a few facts to illustrate, in part, how this measure will operate in practice. As you advanced, the people north of us fell back, and before your arrival here a large portion of the people here had retired South; so that the country south of this is already crowded, and without sufficient houses to accommodate the people, and we are informed that many are now staying in churches and other outbuildings. This being so, how is it possible for the people still here (mostly women and children) to find shelter, and how can they live through the Winter in the woods—no shelter or subsistence—in the midst of strangers who know them not, and without the power to assist them much if they were willing to do so.

"This is but a feeble picture of the consequences of this measure. You know, the woe, the horror and the suffering cannot be described by words. Imagination can only conceive of it, and we ask you to take these things into consideration. We know your mind and time are continually occupied with the duties of your command, which almost deters us from asking your attention to the matter, but thought it might be that you had not considered the subject in all of its awful consequences, and that, on reflection, you, we hope, would not make this people an exception to all mankind; for we know of no such instance ever having occurred—surely not in the United States. And what has this helpless people done, that they should be driven from their homes, to wander as strangers, outcasts and exiles, and to subsist on charity?"

Sherman felt the truth of all this, and saw that his course might be deemed harsh in the sight of the world, so, to clear himself from an unjust charge, and place the reason of his conduct on record for the future historian, he wrote the following letter:—

"ATLANTA, Ga., Sept. 12, 1864.

JAMES M. CALHOUN, Mayor, E. E. RAWSON, and S. C. WELLS, representing the City Council of Atlanta:

GENTLEMEN:—I have your letter of the 11th, in the nature of a petition, to revoke my orders removing all the inhabitants from Atlanta. I have read it carefully, and give full credit to your statements of the distress that will be occasioned by it, and yet shall not revoke my order, simply because my orders are not designed to meet the humanities of the case, but to prepare for the future struggles, in which millions, yea hundreds of millions, of good people outside of Atlanta have a deep interest. We must have *Peace*, not only at Atlanta, but in all America. To secure this, we must stop the war

H. W. Smith, N.Y.

W. T. Sherman

that now desolates our once happy and favored country. To stop war, we must defeat the rebel armies that are arrayed against the laws and Constitution, which all must respect and obey. To defeat these armies we must prepare the way to reach them in their recesses, provided with the arms and instruments which enable us to accomplish our purpose.

Now, I know the vindictive nature of our enemy, and that we may have many years of military operations from this quarter, and, therefore, deem it wise and prudent to prepare in time. The use of Atlanta for warlike purposes is inconsistent with its character as a home for families. There will be no manufactures, commerce, or agriculture here for the maintenance of families, and, sooner or later, want will compel the inhabitants to go. Why not go *now*, when all the arrangements are completed for the transfer, instead of waiting till the plunging shot of contending armies will renew the scene of the past month? Of course, I do not apprehend any such thing at this moment, but you do not suppose that this army will be here till the war is over. I cannot discuss this subject with you fairly, because I cannot impart to you what I propose to do; but I assert that my military plans make it necessary for the inhabitants to go away, and I can only renew my offer of services to make their exodus in any direction as easy and comfortable as possible. You cannot qualify war in harsher terms than I will.

War is cruelty, and you cannot refine it; and those who brought war on our country, deserve all the curses and maledictions a people can pour out. I know I had no hand in making this war, and I know I will make more sacrifices to-day than any of you, to secure peace. But you cannot have peace and a division of our country. If the United States submits to a division now, it will not stop, but will go on till we reap the fate of Mexico, which is eternal war. The United States does and must assert its authority wherever it has power; if it relaxes one bit to pressure, it is gone, and I know that such is not the national feeling. This feeling assumes various shapes, but always comes back to that of *Union*. Once admit the Union, once more acknowledge the authority of the National Government, and instead of devoting your houses and streets and roads to the dread uses of war, I and this army, become at once your protectors and supporters, shielding you from danger, let it come from what quarter it may. I know that a few individuals cannot resist a torrent of error and passion, such as has swept the South into rebellion; but you can point out, so that we may know those who desire a Government, and those who insist on war and its desolation.

You might as well appeal against the thunder-storm, as against these terrible hardships of war. They are inevitable; and the only way the people of Atlanta can hope once more to live in peace and quiet at home, is to stop this war, which can alone be done by admitting that it began in error, and is perpetuated in pride. We don't want your negroes or your horses, or your houses or your land, or anything you have; but we do want, and will have a just obedience to the Laws of the United States. That we will have, and if it involves the destruction of your improvements, we cannot help it. You have heretofore read public sentiment in your newspapers, that live by falsehood and excitement, and the quicker you seek for truth in other quarters, the better for you.

I repeat, then, that, by the orginal compact of government, the United States had certain rights in Georgia, which have never been relinquished, and never will be; that the South began war by seizing forts, arsenals, mints,

52

custom-houses, &c., &c., long before Mr. LINCOLN was installed, and before the South had one jot or tittle of provocation. I, myself, have seen in Missouri, Kentucky, Tennessee and Mississippi, hundreds and thousands of women and children fleeing from your armies and desperadoes, hungry and with bleeding feet. In Memphis, Vicksburg and Mississippi, we fed thousands upon thousands of the families of rebel soldiers left on our hands, and whom we could not see starve. Now that war comes home to you, you feel very different; you deprecate its horrors, but did not feel them when you sent carloads of soldiers and ammunition, and moulded shell and shot, to carry war into Kentucky and Tennessee, and desolate the homes of hundreds and thousands of good people, who only asked to live in peace, at their old homes, and under the Government of their inheritance. But these comparisons are idle. I want peace, and believe it can only be reached through Union and war, and I will ever conduct war purely with a view to perfect and early success.

But, my dear Sirs, when that peace does come, you may call on me for anything. Then will I share with you the last cracker, and watch with you to shield your homes and familes against danger from every quarter. Now, you must go, and take with you the old and feeble; feed and nurse them, and build for them, in more quiet places, proper habitations to shield them against the weather, until the mad passions of men cool down, and allow the Union and peace once more to settle on your old homes at Atlanta.

Yours, in haste,

W. T. SHERMAN, Major-General."

It is a noble defense.

But, while these momentous events were passing in the West, others, calculated to move the nation to the centre, and which arrested and held the attention of the civilized world, were transpiring in the East. Amid the mighty movements, gigantic battles, and fearful slaughter, that shook and crimsoned the earth between Washington and Richmond, the news of the fall of Atlanta came like a faint and far-off echo.

CHAPTER XXVI.

NECESSITY OF UNITY OF ACTION—SIGEL IN THE SHENANDOAH VALLEY—GRANT'S INSTRUCTIONS TO BUTLER—FOLLY OF PLACING THE LATTER IN THE IMPORTANT POSITION HE HELD—NUMBER OF THE TROOPS CO-OPERATING DIRECTLY WITH GRANT—OUR ENTIRE MILITARY FORCE—GRANT'S PLAN OF CAMPAIGN—ADVANCE OF THE ARMY OF THE POTOMAC—CROSSING THE RAPIDAN—COMMENCEMENT OF THE "BATTLES OF THE WILDERNESS"—FIRST DAY—SECOND DAY—THIRD DAY—RETREAT OF THE ENEMY—ADVANCE OF OUR ARMY—FIGHT OF WARREN'S CORPS—DEATH OF SEDGWICK—GRAND ASSAULT ON THE ENEMY'S WORKS—HANCOCK'S BRILLIANT NIGHT ATTACK—FEARFUL APPEARANCE OF THE BATTLE-FIELD—A WEEK'S COMPARATIVE REST—CHANGE OF BASE, AND BRINGING UP OF REINFORCEMENTS—THE DEAD OF THE WILDERNESS.

THE simultaneous movement of the combined forces of the Republic, East and West, was a sublime spectacle. The tread of more than a half a million of men, suddenly shook the earth, as, with faces turned southward, they moved on the tottering Confederacy. All of Grant's energies, for months, had been directed to secure this unity of action, this consolidation of Northern strength. With forces far outnumbering those of the South, backed by an overwhelming navy, we yet had made but little progress toward putting down the rebellion. First a blow would be struck East, and then one West, with sufficient intervals between them, to allow the rebel leaders, with their shorter interior lines, to transfer troops from one section to another, so as always to present a force at the menaced point, nearly, if not quite equal to the one we had there.

The armies, under Halleck's and Stanton's administration, had, to use Grant's homely but expressive phrase, worked "*like a balky team.*" His great object, therefore, was to reverse all this, and when he had attained his object, he was ready to move; and the roll of the drum, and the pealing bugle awoke the Army of the Potomac from its long slumbers, and, for the fourth time, it turned its face toward Richmond.

As before stated, Grant had only his right flank to protect, and thus keep Lee from threatening Maryland and Washington, by way of the Shenandoah Valley. To secure this, he says:—

"General Sigel was, therefore, directed to organize all his available force into two expeditions, to move from Beverly and Charlestown, under command of Generals Ord and Crook, against the East Tennessee and Virginia railroad. Subsequently, General Ord having been relieved at his own request, General Sigel was instructed, at his own suggestion, to give up the expedition by Beverly, and to form two columns, one under General Crook, on the Kanawha, numbering about ten thousand men, and one on the Shenandoah, numbering about seven thousand men. The one on the Shenandoah to assemble between Cumberland and the Shenandoah, and the infantry and artillery advanced to Cedar Creek with such cavalry as could be made available at the moment, to threaten the enemy in the Shenandoah Valley, and advance as far as possible; while General Crook would take possession of Lewisburg with part of his force, and move down the Tennessee railroad, doing as much damage as he could, destroying the New River bridge, and the salt works at Saltville, Virginia."

A still more important co-operating force was under Butler, who commanded at Fortress Monroe. In this department, including North Carolina, were a little over fifty-nine thousand troops. On Butler's proper co-operation, Grant mainly depended for success; and it was one of those stupendous follies the Administration seemed determined to commit to the last, to let this man, without military education, or experience in the field, hold so vital a command. The following were Grant's instructions to him:—

"FORTRESS MONROE, Va., April 2, 1864.

GENERAL:—In the spring campaign, which it is desirable shall commence at as early a day as practicable, it is proposed to have a co-operative action of all the armies in the field, as far as this object can be accomplished.

It will not be possible to unite our armies into two or three large ones, to act as so many units, owing to the absolute necessity of holding on to the territory already taken from the enemy. But, generally speaking, concentration can be practically effected by armies moving to the interior of the enemy's country, from the territory they have to guard. By such movement, they interpose themselves between the enemy and the country to be guarded, thereby reducing the number necessary to guard important points, or, at least, occupy the attention of a part of the enemy's force if no greater object is gained. Lee's army and Richmond being the greater objects toward which our attention must be directed, in the next campaign, it is desirable to unite all the force we can against them. The necessity of covering Washington with the Army of the Potomac, and of covering your department with your army, makes it impossible to unite these forces at the beginning of any move. I propose, therefore, that what comes nearest us of anything that seems practicable:—The Army of the Potomac will act from its present base, Lee's army being the objective point. You will collect all the forces from your command, that can be spared from garrison duty—I should say not less than twenty thousand effective men—to operate on the south side of James River, Richmond being your objective point. To the force you already have, will be added about ten thousand men from South Carolina, under Major-General Gillmore, who will command them in person. Major-General W. F. Smith is ordered to report to you, to command the troops sent into the field from your own department.

General Gillmore will be ordered to report to you at Fortress Monroe, with all the troops on transports, by the 18th instant, or as soon thereafter as practicable. Should you not receive notice by that time to move, you will make such disposition of them and your other forces, as you may deem best calculated to deceive the enemy as to the real move to be made.

When you are notified to move, take City Point with as much force as possible. Fortify, or rather intrench, at once, and concentrate all your troops for the field there as rapidly as you can. From City Point directions cannot be given, at this time, for your further movements.

The fact that has already been stated—that is, that Richmond is to be your objective point, and that there is to be co-operation between your force and the Army of Potomac—must be your guide. This indicates the necessity of your holding close to the south bank of the James River, as you advance. Then, should the enemy be forced into his intrenchments, in Richmond, the Army of the Potomac would follow, and by means of transports the two armies would become a unit.

All the minor details of your advance are left entirely to your direction. If, however, you think it practicable to use your cavalry south of you, as to cut the railroad about Hick's Ford, about the time of the general advance, it would be of immense advantage.

You will please forward for my information, at the earliest practicable day, all orders, details, and instructions, you may give for the execution of this order.

U. S. GRANT, Lieutenant-General.

Major-General B. F. BUTLER."

These instructions he subsequently reiterated, and informed him farther, that he expected him to move from Fortress Monroe the same day that Meade advanced from Culpepper, and also stated the plan which he proposed to follow.

The Army of the Potomac proper, numbered, at this time, a little over one hundred and twenty thousand men. The Ninth Corps, under Burnside, held in reserve, and numbering a little over twenty thousand men, was stationed on the road near Bull Run. His orders were, not to move until he heard that the Army of the Potomac had crossed the Rapidan, and then to move promptly.

Thus, it will be seen, that Grant had directly co-operating with him, in various directions, over two hundred thousand troops. Although our military force, at this time, was nine hundred and seventy thousand and seven hundred men, only a little over six hundred and sixty-two thousand were available for duty; hence, a third of our actual force was operating against Richmond. More or less remotely and directly, more than two hundred thousand bayonets were pointing toward the rebel Capital.

The general plan of operations, adopted by Grant, in the important campaign on which he was entering, he states to be as follows:—

"My first object, being to break the military power of the rebellion, and capture the enemy's important strongholds, made me desirous that General Butler should succeed in his movement against Richmond, as that would tend more than anything else, unless it were the capture of Lee's army, to accomplish this desired result in the East. If he failed, it was my determination, by hard fighting, either to compel Lee to retreat, or to so cripple him that he could not detach a large force to go North, and still retain enough for the defense of Richmond. It was well understood, by both Generals Butler and Meade, before starting on the campaign, that it was my intention to put both their armies south of James River, in case of failure to destroy Lee without it."

This shows how important was the position held by Butler, and how absurd it was to place him in it. The General in the Army of the Potomac, second only to Grant, should have commanded there—one who would not have been "corked up" at the very outset.

The quotation above, however, does not give a clear view of Grant's entire plan. The success of Butler's operations against Richmond were, at the best, problematical, and his own plans had to be formed on their possible failure.

It appears, in other parts of Grant's report, that his first object was to turn Lee's left flank at Mine Run—where the latter held a strong position—and compel him to a decisive, pitched battle. If he accomplished this, he believed that, with his superior force, he could destroy him, or so utterly shatter him, that he could present but feeble resistance anywhere between that point and the rebel Capital. If Butler could capture Petersburg, destroy the South Side railroad, and work around Richmond till his left rested on the James above the city, Grant could form a junction with him there, which would leave the Capital completely invested. The course he was actually compelled to pursue, was the last one he desired. Butler not only failed in performing what was expected of him, but he, himself, also failed to get a decisive battle out of Lee, and was beaten back in every attack, from the Wilderness to the James.

On the night of the 3rd of May, all was in commotion in the Army of the Potomac, and the next morning, it moved in splendid array across the Rapidan. It was divided into three Corps—the Second, commanded by Hancock, the Fifth, by Warren, and the Sixth, by Sedgwick. Two Corps crossed at Germania Ford, and the other at the United States Ford. Sheridan, commanding the cavalry, led the advance, and protected the immense trains, composed of over four thousand wagons, which were to be carried through that broken, wooded country.

This day, the army marched about twelve miles. Grant expected that his passage of the Rapidan would be stubbornly contested; but Lee seemed to think that his chances of success, with his inferior force, would be better, to attack the army while on the march, and separated in the forest—for the course, it was compelled to take, led across a wild and desolate tract of country, overgrown with stunted pines, and as unfit for a battle-field as could be imagined. This "Wilderness," as it was called, extended from Chancellorsville up to Mine Run, where Lee lay intrenched. Besides, by the road that Grant was compelled to take, Lee could come down on him on the Orange and Chancellorsville turnpike and the Orange and Chancellorsville plank road, and strike him at right angles, while on the march. This, as soon as Grant's plan was fully developed, he did, compelling the latter to halt, and form line of battle in the woods, so as to cover the fords over which the trains were passing. This was the last thing Grant desired. He knew the country imperfectly, and could in no way overlook it, while every highway and byway was familiar to Lee and his corps-commanders.

On Thursday morning, Warren reached the Old Wilderness Tavern, ten miles south of the ford, and situated on the Germania and Chancellorsville plank road—Sedgwick being on his right with his line extending back to the river. Hancock, who had crossed five or six miles farther down the river, was directed to move forward to Shady Grove Church from Chancellorsville, but Grant, finding that a battle was to be thrown upon him on this unfortunate spot, countermanded the order, and Hancock was directed to swing round and hasten forward, by a cross-road, with all possible dispatch and close up with Warren, and form the left wing. Lee, aware of the gap here, made a desperate effort to get into it, and thus divide the armies. Previous to this, however, a part of Griffin's division had been pushed forward to ascertain the designs of the enemy, in doing which a severe fight occurred, and the force was compelled to fall back with a loss of several hundred men.

About three o'clock, Lee attempted to get between Hancock and Warren; Grant penetrating his design—and Mott's division, the advance of Hancock's Corps, just then coming up—he ordered this, with Getty's, on Warren's left, to charge the enemy, so as to hold him back until the rest of Hancock's Corps could arrive. They, at once, plunged into the woods, which were so dense that artillery was almost entirely useless, and the real

BATTLE OF THE WILDERNESS

commenced. The woods were soon ablaze with the fire of the musketry, but every effort of the enemy to advance at this point, was baffled, and he was held sternly back until Hancock's Corps arrived and closed up the line on the left. The battle was a singular one. Says an eye-witness:—

"The fighting—who shall describe it? Not a thousand men can be seen at once, yet for miles, in the front, thousands are engaged. The volleyed thunders of the combat roll among the glens and ravines, hoarser and higher than the voices of an Eastern jungle. The woods are alive with cries and explosions, and the shrill, anvil clatter of musketry. One cannon, pitched afar, times the wild tumult like a tolling bell. The smoke is a shroud about our heroes; there is not wind enough to lift it into a canopy.

"And now, out of the concealed and awful scenery, where the fight goes on, there come the ruins it has wrought, in shapes, borne in blankets and on litters—maimed, tortured, writhing; with eyes dull with the stupor of coming death; or bright with delirious fire. Listen to the hell, raging beyond and below; behold this silent, piteous procession, that emerges ceaselessly, and passes on. Into and out of the ordeal of fire; from the pride of the ranks to the suffering of the hospital, these forms have been, and come, and are of no more avail."

Darkness, at length, put an end to the contest. Grant saw, at a glance, the peril he was in, and that Lee needed but slight success at this point to compel him to re-cross the river, as Burnside and Hooker had done before him, and he, therefore, brought over a part of Sedgwick's Corps, to which he added some of Warren's force to strengthen Hancock. Burnside's Corps, too, which had strained forward all night, was up in the morning. Grant had notified him at four o'clock, the afternoon before, that he was over the Rapidan, and directed him to hasten forward. So swiftly did he march that, says Grant:—

"By six o'clock of the morning of the 6th, he was leading his Corps into action near the Wilderness Tavern, some of his troops having marched a distance of thirty miles, crossing both the Rappahannock and Rapidan Rivers. Considering that a large proportion, probably two-thirds of his command, was composed of new troops. unaccustomed to marches, and carrying the accoutrements of a soldier, this was a remarkable march."

SECOND DAY'S BATTLE.

Grant, however, did not wait his arrival. He had given his orders the night before, for a general advance of the whole line, at five o'clock in the morning. The army, at this time, stretched for about seven miles through the Wilderness, and as no general survey of it could be had, much had to be left to the separate Commanders. At five o'clock, Sedgwick attacked on the right, moving with his accustomed gallantry on Ewell—on the left, Hancock burst like a torrent on the enemy, and drove him back in confusion, and, for hours, the battle roared like a tornado for seven miles through the pine forest. Grant stood under a tree and listened to the crashing volleys that receded away in the distance, while aids were constantly coming and going with reports and orders.

Still, the line of that terrific fire seemed to advance nowhere, except on the left. Hancock steadily pushed the enemy before him for a mile and a half, taking a rebel rifle-pit and five stand of colors. Wadsworth, connecting with his right, put forth desperate efforts. Apparently forgetful that he had a life to lose, he again and again led the charge in person. Two horses were shot under him, and, at length, a shot pierced his own head and he fell. His body was seized by the enemy, and he died in their hands.

But, at length, Hancock's victorious career was stopped. The rebels rallying fiercely, fell on his exhausted battalions, whose ammunition was now getting low, and bore them steadily back, until, at eleven o'clock, he occupied the ground which he held in the morning. His extreme left, for the moment, was turned, but the mischief was quickly repaired, and a lull at this point came in the contest. But, at four o'clock, Longstreet coming up, having made a forced march of twenty-five miles, Lee resolved to make one more desperate effort to turn our left and double it up on the army.

The enemy came on in four lines, and fell with such desperation on Hancock that he succeeded in breaking his firm formation, and, for a moment, the battle seemed lost. When the startling news was borne to Grant, he replied, "I don't believe it." But Gibbon's division was promptly formed in rear of the break, and the headlong torrent that was pouring through was stopped. For three-quarters of an hour, the battle raged here with terrible ferocity. Longstreet was determined to complete what he had so auspiciously begun, and hurled his columns forward with a desperation and gallantry, that could not be surpassed. Hancock, however, knowing that the battle lost here was lost everywhere, disputed every inch of ground with a stubbornness that neither valor nor numbers could overcome.

The use of so little artillery, made this one of the most remarkable battles on record—over two hundred thousand men fought in a vast jungle.

"There in the depths of those ravines, under the shadows of those trees, entangled in that brush-wood, is no pomp of war, no fluttering of banners in an unhindered breeze, no solid tramp of marching battalions, no splendid strategy of the fields Napoleon loved to fight on. There a Saturnalia, gloomy, hideous, desperate, rages confined. That metallic, hollow rack of musketry, is like the clanking of great chains about the damned; that sullen yell of the enemy, a fiendish protest and defiance. How the hours lag; how each minute is freighted with a burden that the days would have groaned to bear in other times! Still, the sad, shuddering procession, emerging out of the smoke and tumult and passing on. Still the appealing eyes, and clenched hands, and quivering limbs of human creatures, worse than helpless, whose fighting is over. The paths are full of them, the roads are thick with them, the forest seems to take up the slow movement, and move with them like giants hovering over the funeral of Lilliputians. Piled in ambulances, they move on further yet, while the torturer of battle plies on below, making more victims. Here and there, beside some path, you shall see a heaped blanket, labeled by some thoughtful bearer with the name of the corpse beneath it bore in life; here and there, you shall come across a group of men bending over one wounded, past help, and dying an agonized death. And often—too often—the shameful spectacle of one bearing a weapon, unhurt, pallid and fear-stricken, flits through an opening toward the rear, and is gone. You shall meet with soldiers, in groups of one, or two, or three, hidden in some thicket, or coolly making coffee by the road-side. And hearing the roar of the battle below, and seeing the bloody trail of the battle behind, it shall be a glad thing to see these men hunted by officers back, with curses, to the ranks, to share the dangers of their nobler comrades.

"About this battle there is a horrible fascination. It is like a maelstrom. You feel it sucking you in, and you go nearer to see men fall like those you have seen fallen. Down through the break, underneath the edges of the smoke, where the bullets are thick, and the trunks of trees, like the ranks of men, sway and fall with the smiting of shells, you have a little view of the courage and the carnage of this fight. There are the enemy, retreated to the breastworks—a ragged pile of fallen trees and heaped up earth—hiding their heads, spitting lead and flame. Here is the Sixth Corps—what you can see of it—plunging on, firing continually, tumbling over branches and limbs, sinking waist-deep in swamps, fighting with its might, and bleeding at every pore."

The covering of the trees, and the absence of cannon, made it a very close contest—the lines often almost meeting in the fierce encounter. For seven miles, the forest was alive with the confused sounds of this awful struggle, out of which arose fierce jets of smoke, that settled in a vast and sulphurous cloud above the green tree-tops. The dead and wounded lay thick as autumn leaves along the low ridges and slopes, and in front of the hastily thrown up intrenchments, and when night put an end to the contest, the "Wilderness" was dreary and desolate indeed. After dark, the enemy made an attack on our left, in which Seymour and Shaler were taken prisoners, with a large number of troops.

The battle, on this day, was the decisive one, and at its close, it was evident that Lee had put forth his greatest effort, and just at the moment too when Grant was in a position to be beaten, if ever he could be. Still the latter was not certain that the attack would not be renewed in the morning, and he, therefore, during the evening, selected a new and stronger position, and contracted his lines. But Saturday brought no renewal of the attack, and the day was spent in reconnoissances and skirmishes along the whole line. The result of the day's operations, was a conviction, on the part of Grant, that the enemy was preparing to retreat, and he, therefore, determined, weary as his army was, to throw it forward by a rapid, night march towards Spottsylvania. If he reached this place first, Lee would be cut off from Richmond, and compelled to give him battle in the open field. Accordingly, at ten o'clock, our advance started off through the gloom.

The moon had been down for an hour, and the army passed like a mighty shadow over the sterile country. "The fires burned brightly, and at a distance, upon the wooded hillsides, looked like the lights of a city. Standing upon an eminence, at the junction of the Germania, Chancellorsville, and Orange Court-House roads, along which the tramp of soldiers, and the rumble of wagon-trains, made a smothered din, one could almost imagine himself peering down through the darkness on the streets of a metropolis, in peace. Back in the forest, from the hospitals, from the trees, from the roadside, the wounded were being gathered in ambulances for the long, night journey. That part of the army, not on the move, was slumbering by its fires, waiting for the signal."

Lee, however, was soon made aware of the movement, and dispatched Longstreet, an hour later, to the same point. The two exhausted columns marched by parallel roads, but Longstreet had the shortest distance to go in the race, and reached Spottsylvania first.

BATTLE OF SUNDAY, MAY 8TH.

Warren's Corps was in the advance, in the march for this vital point, and Bartlett's brigade, of Griffin's division, was ordered to attack the place at once, on the supposition that only cavalry held it. But, to his astonishment, this Commander run into Longstreet's whole Corps, and was shivered to fragments—one regiment, the First Michigan, losing three-fourths of its number in fifteen minutes. Robinson's division, on the left, finding itself confronted by an overwhelming force, also gave way in disorder.

At that critical moment, Warren, with his Staff, arrived on the field, and fired at the sight of the disordered ranks, spurred forward and seizing a division flag, rallied the troops by his gallant bearing, and held them firmly to the shock, until the other portions of his Corps could arrive. From eight till twelve—for four hours—he maintained the unequal struggle, and, at length, gained an open space which led up to the rebel line of battle, that stretched through a piece of woods.

Two fresh divisions coming up—Crawford's and Getty's—an attack was made on the enemy's position just at evening, and after an hour and a half of severe fighting, the first line of breastworks was carried, though with heavy loss to us. The next morning Grant saw his line advanced to within less than three miles of Spottsylvania Court-House, and well intrenched.

MONDAY.

This was a sad day, for it took from the army one of its ablest Commanders. Sedgwick having gone out in advance to superintend the placing of some batteries, noticed that one of the gunners dodged, as the sharp whistle of a bullet sounded near. Amused at the man's nervousness, he said, pleasantly, "Pooh, man, you can't hit an elephant at that distance"—referring to the nearest enemy in sight—when the bullet, of a sharp-shooter ensconced in one of the neighboring trees, entered his eye, and passed directly into his brain. The blood gushed from his nostrils, and with a serene smile on his face, he fell into the arms of his Assistant Adjutant-General. A noble man, a strong leader, a great General, and one of the firmest props of Grant, he fell where he always preferred to fall, on the field of battle, with his face to the foe.

Monday was a day of comparative quietude, though there was constant skirmishing. Hancock had crossed the Po and thrown up intrenchments, working all night by the light of lanterns, hung in the blossoming cherry trees. Heavy cannonading occured at intervals, along the line, and an attack of the enemy was expected, but was not made in any force or determination.

Both armies were fearfully exhausted. For the last three days, the line of battle had been constantly formed, and, for forty-eight hours, many of the troops had been without rest or regular rations.

Soldiers had never shown greater endurance on any battle-field, and the "three days' battle in the Wilderness" will remain to all time, as an evidence of the superiority of American troops—when once inured by long service--to any others in the world.

On this day, Sheridan, with the cavalry force, started on a raid to sever Lee's communications with Richmond. The very next day he sent a dispatch to the Secretary of War, stating that he had "turned the enemy's right, and got into their rear; had destroyed from eight to ten miles of railroad, two locomotives, and three trains, and a very large quantity of supplies; and that since he had got into their rear, there was great excitement among the inhabitants and with the army. The enemy's cavalry had tried to annoy his rear and flank, but had been run off, and he had recaptured five hundred of our men—two of them colonels."

From this point he moved on, spreading destruction in his path, until he reached the suburbs of Richmond, and actually entered the first line of works. But finding it impossible to proceed farther, he wheeled about and crossed the Chickahominy at Meadow Bridge, having suffered but slight loss in his daring ride. But, like every movement of the kind, since the war commenced, it was of no practical importance, for it had no effect whatever on Lee's movements.

On Tuesday, the 10th, Grant having finished his reconnoissances, and got his army into position, determined to assault the enemy's works. It was ordered to take place at five o'clock in the afternoon, and all day long the artillery beat in a steady, awful storm on the rebel position—in some places setting fire to the forest, that smoked and flamed above the dead and wounded. More or less fighting occurred all along the lines, and at about four o'clock, the enemy came out and attacked Barlow's division, which occupied a flanking and somewhat isolated position over the stream, and compelled it to re-cross and join the Second Corps. This delayed the proposed attack for an hour and a half, so that it was sundown before the columns began to advance.

During this interval, however, the cannonading was terrific, and shot and shell fell in a ceaseless shower on the rebel works. At half past six, Grant and Meade, with their staffs, took positions on an eminence that overlooked, to some extent, the field of operations, and the signal—twelve cannon shots—sounded the advance. With cheers that rose over the crash of cannon, the assaulting columns at once leaped forward and pressed over the broken field. Through patches of wood—over ridges, across swampy holes and ravines—swept at every step by a destructive fire—the dark lines steadily advanced, although the brave battalions crumbled away like frost-work before the enfilading fire that ploughed through the ranks. It was a vain effort, however, and it was soon evident that the troops were held to a useless slaughter—those strong works could not be carried. The only success, of importance, was achieved by the Sixth Corps, that, since the death of Sedgwick, had been commanded by General Wright.

"About three hundred yards in front, the enemy occupied a work very strongly constructed, as high as a man's head, and loop-holed at the top. The party organized to attack this work, was disposed by General Russell and led by Colonel Upton. It consisted of a portion of the First division, the Vermont brigade of the Second division, and some picked troops of General Neill's command, who were massed, on the eve of the attack, to the left and front of three batteries—Cowan's, McCartney's and Rhodes'. Some companies of the Forty-ninth New York regiment had occupied, during the afternoon, a work in advance of the general line, and just to the left of the line of march of the column of attack. As the column pressed forward, these companies moved by the left flank, engaging a battery of the enemy on the right of his work.

"The batteries of McCartney, Cowan and Rhodes opened on the work, over the heads of the attacking column, which moved steadily on in the face of a terrific blaze of musketry, with arms a-port, and without firing a shot, up to the very face of the enemy's position. It poured—a flood of savage faces and plunging bayonets—over the crest of the work and into the midst of the enemy, capturing, in an instant, nine hundred and fifty of the very men who had stampeded the brigades of Shaler and Seymour, on Friday night, in the Wilderness, and sending a scattering volley after a host of flying rebels. Twelve guns, also, came into our possession."

Shouts of laughter greeted these prisoners, as they were run back into our lines at full speed, before the bayonets of their captors. Darkness, at length, closed the conflict, and our bleeding lines retired from the hopeless struggle. Our losses this day were fearful, and the moon that night, looked down on hetacombs of brave men, piled everywhere around the rebel works and over the fields.

The next day was spent in skirmishing and manœuvering. In the afternoon, a heavy storm set in, followed by a dark and foggy night. Hancock took advantage of the darkness and rain to change his position, and, unobserved by the enemy, planted himself on his right flank. Between four and five o'clock in the morning, in the midst of a pouring rain, the troops moved silently forward against a salient or angle of the enemy's works, held by Johnston, which here were exceedingly strong, with a wide ditch in front. Barlow's division had the advance, Miles' brigade leading. The assaulting columns moved swiftly, and in dead silence, forward, and without a cheer or a shot, swept in one dark flood over the ramparts, capturing almost the entire division of Johnston.

Hancock now turned the captured artillery on the enemy, and drove them back for nearly a mile. But here they rallied, and a long and bloody fight followed. The other Corps were brought up, and a desperate effort was made to turn this brilliant success into a complete victory; and all through the forenoon, in the midst of the pelting rain, the fearful conflict continued to rage. At noon the storm broke, and the sun came out, but, alas! not to light us to victory. The first advantage was the last, of any importance, that was gained, and after hours of heavy fighting, it was evident that the enemy's position could not be carried. The rebels, fighting with a desperation never surpassed, made five successive charges to re-take the works that had been carried by Hancock. The two armies were rapidly concentrated around this single spot—the one to retake, and the other to hold the captured works—hence, the struggle and the slaughter here were awful.

"Column after column of the enemy penetrated to the very face of the breastwork, to be hewn down and sent back like a broken wave. Column after column still came on, dealing death and meeting it, and making way for other columns and others still; and all the day long, against this rush of a foe, that seemed disdainful of life, the angle was held by our troops, fighting, falling, but unyielding, to the close. Our artillery made havoc on that day; from dawn to dusk, the roar of the guns was ceaseless; a tempest of shell shrieked through the forest, and plowed the field.

"When the night came, the angle of those works, where the battle had been hottest and from which the enemy had been finally driven, had a spectacle for whoever cared to look, that would never have enticed his gaze again. Men in hundreds, killed and wounded together, were piled in hideous heaps—some bodies that had lain for hours under the concentric fire of the battle, being perforated with wounds. The writhing of the wounded beneath the dead, moved these masses at times; at times, a lifted arm or a quivering limb, told of an agony not yet quenched by the Lethe of death around."

Says another correspondent:—"The angle of the works at which Hancock entered, and for the possession of which the savage fight of the day was made, is a perfect Golgotha. In this angle of death the dead and wounded rebels lie, this morning, literally in piles—men in the agonies of death groaning beneath the dead bodies of their comrades. On an area of a few acres, in the rear of their position, lie not less than a thousand rebel corpses, many literally torn to shreds by hundreds of balls, and several with bayonet thrusts through and through their bodies, pierced on the very margins of the parapet, which they were determined to retake or perish in the attempt. The one exclamation of every man who looks on the spectacle is, 'God forbid that I should ever gaze upon such a sight again.'"

Hancock's achievement was a brilliant one, and, for a time, promised success, but as it turned out, it was a useless waste of life.

Grant's losses, since he crossed the Rapidan, had been fearful—a whole army had disappeared—and it was necessary that these should be repaired, and now for six days the army had comparative rest, while reinforcements were hurried up from Washington. The manner in which the troops came pouring in showed the forecast of Grant. He had anticipated no easy victory—he knew Lee and his gallant veterans, and hence prepared for the frightful loss of life which had now taken place. These gathering hosts showed too the almost exhaustless resources of the North, and that they were at last being employed by a man who knew how to use them.

Grant a few days before, had telegraphed to the Secretary of War, "I propose to fight it out on this line, if it takes all Summer," and it was evident that he meant to. This was said in no spirit of obstinacy, as it was generally supposed—it was a mere re-affirmation of judgment on the plan he had adopted, notwithstanding the frightful sacrifices of life the carrying it out had demanded.

The base of supplies, in the meantime, had been changed to Fredericksburg. Manœuvering of the forces, skirmishing and heavy artillery firing, kept the troops on the alert, but Grant had resolved not to dash his army to pieces again on the strong works before him.

The ceaseless energy with which he had pushed the enemy, had not left him sufficient time to bury his dead properly, and the "Wilderness" presented a shocking spectacle, with its uncovered, or but partially interred bodies, scattered amid the shattered trees of the forest and wreck of the fight.

During these seventeen fearful days, Sherman's army had been sending up its victorious shouts amid the mountains of Georgia, as it hewed its way toward Atlanta, and Butler causing consternation among the inhabitants of Richmond, as the sound of his cannon broke over the rebel Capital.

CHAPTER XXVII.

BUTLER'S ADVANCE TO CITY POINT—BUTLER'S CAMPAIGN—BERMUDA HUNDRED—POSITION OF THE ARMY—KAUTZ'S CAVALRY EXPEDITION—TORPEDOES—RICHMOND AND PETERSBURG RAILROAD SEVERED—BUTLER'S DISPATCH—OPERATIONS AGAINST DRURY'S BLUFF—DILATORINESS OF BUTLER—REFUSES TO INTRENCH HIMSELF ON THE RAILROAD—MORNING ATTACK OF THE ENEMY—CAPTURE OF HECKMAN AND HIS BRIGADE—GILLMORE AND BUTLER ON THE SITUATION OF THE ARMY—RETREAT TO BERMUDA HUNDRED—TOTAL FAILURE OF THE PENINSULA MOVEMENT—GRANT'S OPINION OF BUTLER'S CONDUCT—BUTLER'S TREATMENT OF WAR CORRESPONDENTS—BRUTAL TREATMENT OF A CHAPLAIN—NAVAL OPERATIONS ALONG THE COAST—IN FLORIDA—LOSS OF THE COLUMBINE—INVESTMENT OF NEWBERN—REBEL IRON-CLADS—GALLANT FIGHT OF SMITH WITH THE ALBEMARLE IN ALBEMARLE SOUND—CONDUCT OF THE SASSACUS—STEELE IN ARKANSAS.

IN accordance with Grant's orders, General Butler, on the 4th of May, moved his army from Fortress Monroe, to co-operate, by an advance on Richmond, with the former, and keep reinforcements back from Lee. While Grant was entering on the terrific "Battles of the Wilderness," and its dreary solitudes were echoing to the roar of his guns, Butler with his army on transports, guarded by iron-clads, was steaming up the James River, toward City Point, that lay about fifteen miles below the rebel Capital. A landing was made at this place without opposition, and soon the army was planted securely on the narrow strip of land, known as Bermuda Hundred.

The river here takes a sharp bend, so that the army rested both its right and left flank on it, though, by the stream, they were many miles apart. A line of intrenchments was also stretched across the neck, while either extremity was protected by gun-boats. A more secure position could not have been selected. The difficulty was that while an army here could repel a large force, a small one, on the other hand, could coop it up so as to render it inoperative. It was like a cavern, the mouth of which could be defended by a few men within, against great odds without; and, on the other hand, a few men could prevent any egress from it.

Simultaneous with the advance of the army, a cavalry expedition, under General Kautz, was sent off to strike the Richmond and Weldon railroad, at a point some eighty miles distant, and destroy a bridge three thousand feet long, and then act as circumstances might dictate.

A strong fleet of gun-boats and iron-clads, under Admiral Lee, co-operated with the army. It was known that torpedoes had been sunk in the river, and hence they were dragged for in advance. But, notwithstanding the utmost precaution was taken, about noon, on the 6th, one that had escaped discovery, exploded under the Commodore Jones, near Four Mile Creek, utterly destroying the vessel, and killing and wounding half of the crew. A party of marines and sailors immediately landed at the point and discovered three galvanic batteries sunk in the ground. Two men also were captured in a battery near.

One of these being interrogated respecting the locality of the torpedoes, at first professed entire ignorance, but being placed in the advance boat of those dragging for them, and told that he would be blown up with the rest, he became more communicative, and stated where those he knew of were placed. He said, moreover, that the one which exploded under the Commodore Jones contained two thousand pounds of powder—that the large ones were exploded by galvanic batteries, but the smaller ones, either by contact or a line from shore. Those that were sunk, were put down by Hunter Davidson, formerly of the United States Navy, who commanded a boat named the Torpedo, which was built for this especial service.

The next day, the 7th, the tug gun-boat Shawsheen, while looking for one of these submarine terrors, near Turkey Bend, came under the fire of a rebel battery, and was destroyed, and most of the officers and crew captured.

First Assistant-Engineer Young sent to the department a sketch of these galvanic batteries, by which the torpedoes were exploded, which is curious, as a part of our naval history during a war, that brought into service so many new missiles of destruction.

He says:—"The galvanic batteries were formed of nine zinc cups, each one battery, or a set of cups being placed on shelves directly over the other. In each zinc cup was placed a porous clay cup. In the zinc cup, and outside the porous cup, was placed the sulphuric acid and water, and inside the porous cup was placed the nitric acid. The zinc of one cup was connected to the cast-iron of the other, by a clamp and thumb screw. The negative wires led directly to the torpedoes, (one to each.) The positive wires ran along near a foot-path, parallel with the river, for about two hundred feet, and terminated at a sub-battery. In this sub-battery, were two large wooden plugs, with a hole about one-half inch in diameter in each; these holes being filled with mercury; the positive wires connecting from the torpedoes to the bottom of these plugs; the positive wires, from the charged batteries, being inserted in the mercury at the top of its respective plug, to form the connections and explode the torpedoes. The wires from the river bank to the torpedoes were supported by a three inch rope, being stopped to rope about every four feet. At a distance of every fifteen feet of the rope, were some five or six feet of three-quarter link chain to assist in keeping it on the bottom. The wires were covered with gutta percha, about one-quarter inch thick. The battery used is generally known as the Bunsen battery."

With such infernal mechanism lining the banks of a narrow river, and connecting with vast masses of gun-powder, lying concealed on the bottom, and all under the control of hidden operators on shore, the navigation of the stream was made most perilous. We had not a Commander afloat who would not rather at any time engage a hostile fleet, of vastly superior force, than carry his vessels, without an enemy in sight, up such a river. There is something infinitely more appalling in sailing over such hidden engines of destruction, than there is meeting any danger face to face.

About the time the rebel batteries opened on our fleet—destroying the Shawsheen—a fight commenced on land. Butler moving out his army toward the Richmond and Petersburg railroad, the rebels attacked him. The day was excessively warm, but, about eleven o'clock, the enemy opened with artillery, and a sharp cannonade was kept up along the lines.

While the left and centre were thus engaged, a brigade, on the right, under Colonel Barton, pressed forward, and striking the railroad, succeeded in tearing up the track for some distance, and setting a bridge on fire. But being heavily pressed in turn, it was compelled to retire.

The action continued with more or less severity till four o'clock in the afternoon, when the order was given for the army to fall back to the lines held in the morning.

On the 9th, Butler again moved forward to break up more effectually this important railroad. With General Smith's Corps, on the left, and Gillmore, with the Tenth Corps, on the right, the columns began their march at daylight, and passed cautiously through the thick woods in front, without meeting the enemy. About nine o'clock, Smith struck the railroad at Port Walthall Junction, and Gillmore at Chester Station, and the work of destruction commenced. But little resistance was made by the enemy, and it was evident that he had been taken wholly by surprise.

Butler now determined to advance on Petersburg, and the army, the same afternoon, moved forward. The place was held by Beauregard with a large force, who had been ordered up from the south to take charge of affairs around Richmond.

Butler, elated with his easy success, and fully believing that he could hold possession of the railroad communication between Richmond and Petersburg, sent the following telegram to Washington, summing up his achievements, and announcing the separation of Beauregard's forces from those of Lee:—

"MAY 9, 1864.

Our operations may be summed up in a few words. With one thousand and seven hundred cavalry we have advanced up the Peninsula, forced the Chickahominy, and have safely brought them to our present position. These were colored cavalry, and are now holding our advanced pickets toward Richmond.

General Kautz, with three thousand cavalry, from Suffolk, on the same day with our movement up James River, forced the Blackwater, burned the railroad bridge at Stony Creek, below Petersburg, cutting in two Beauregard's force at that point.

We have landed here, intrenched ourselves, destroyed many miles of railroad, and got a position which, with proper supplies, we can hold out against the whole of Lee's army. I have ordered up the supplies.

Beauregard, with a large portion of his force, was left south by the cutting of the railroads by Kautz. That portion which reached Petersburg under Hill, I have whipped to-day, killing and wounding many, and taking many prisoners, after a severe and well-contested fight.

General Grant will not be troubled with any further reinforcements to Lee from Beauregard's force.

BENJAMIN F. BUTLER, Major-General."

More or less fighting occurred between the hostile forces, without bringing on a decisive battle, and Butler, at length, determined to advance against Fort Darling, located on

Drury's Bluff. The batteries here were the main obstacle that prevented our gun-boats from moving as near to Richmond as the depth of water would allow, and if they were once silenced, it was believed that the advance of the fleet would compel the evacuation of the rebel Capital.

Butler having reached Kingsland Creek, formed line of battle on the south-east side, in view of James River. The fleet, in the meantime, moved to the vicinity of the fort to co-operate with the land forces.

The news of Hancock's brilliant success at Spottsylvania, reached the army on this day, causing immense cheering all along the front.

For five days there had been more or less fighting, and much of the time in a pouring rain, but no decisive advantage had been gained by either side. Butler succeeded in taking some of the outer works of Fort Darling; and from the daily bulletins, published by war correspondents, the public expected the speedy capture of this stronghold. Foiled here, Butler attempted to get toward Petersburg—the fall of which had been prematurely announced—but meeting with strong opposition, he, on Monday, changed front, and moved toward Richmond. His line, at this time, was three miles long, extending from the James River to the Richmond and Petersburg railroad. He had been molested so little in the occupancy of this road, that he seemed to think the enemy had abandoned all hope of re-occupying it, and hence neglected to take those precautions which a skillful Commander would have adopted.

Gillmore, one of the ablest engineers of the age, and of much experience in the field, advised him to throw up intrenchments so as to be able to hold this important position against any attack of the enemy. But Butler, in a pompous manner, replied, that he was acting on the *offensive*, and not *defensive*, and refused to follow his advice.

Gillmore, clearly, did not believe that the rebels had abandoned all hope of re-taking this important railroad, and the event proved the correctness of his opinion. The movement to City Point had evidently been a surprise, and had Butler advanced at once, before the enemy recovered from it, Petersburg, if not Richmond, could have been easily captured.

But the five days, or more, that he had been campaigning in the open country, had been improved by Beauregard in hurrying up troops, which, the moment they were well in hand, he meant to hurl with resistless fury on our army. Monday morning, the 16th, was selected for the assault, and a better time could not have been chosen. The night had been exceedingly dark, and toward morning a dense fog wrapped everything in impenetrable gloom. Shrouded in this, the enemy came noiselessly down on our unsuspecting line, striking it first on the right flank. Heckman's brigade was posted here, on which the onset came with the suddenness of a thunder-clap.

The fog lay so thick over the fields, that a person, a few rods distant, was invisible; hence the proximity of the enemy was unknown till his unearthly yells rose out of the mist, right in the face of the brigade. Heckman, than whom a braver man never lived, dashed through the gloom, shouting to his men to stand firm, and succeeded, by great effort, in rallying a portion of his brigade, whose loud cheers soon answered the defiant yells of their assailants. So dense was the fog, that the troops were brought breast to breast, before they could see each other, and the fight became a hand-to-hand contest. Wholly unable to see the ground occupied by the enemy, Heckman could not tell what disposition to make of his regiments—in fact, was totally ignorant of the strength of the force opposed to him.

Under such circumstances, the contest could not be otherwise than a short one. The rebels knew the exact position of the brigade, and swiftly overlapping it, took it in rear, and captured nearly the whole, and with it its leader, the gallant Heckman. Two regiments of Gillmore's Corps had been detached from it, and, under Weitzel, lay in rear of the brigade as a reserve. These, aroused by the firing and yells, that rent the fog in advance, sprung to their arms, and were led, by Colonel Drake, swiftly forward toward the spot where the conflict was raging. Charging fiercely on the exultant foe, they bore him back, and rescued some three or four hundred of our prisoners. The rebels rallying, charged back, but could not move those noble regiments from their places.

The battle raged furiously here, for a long time, for both sides brought up reinforcements to this vital point. The contest, however, was not confined to the right flank, but drifted steadily down the line for two miles and a half.

"The rebel plan of massing brigade after brigade, in line of battle, and hurling them in rotation against us, was here tried with very bad results. General Smith, with that forethought which is characteristic of him, anticipating some such move on the part of the enemy, had ordered a large quantity of telegraph wire to be intertwisted among the trees and undergrowth which lay in front of our position. Wister and Burnham received the order and obeyed it. Heckman failed, unfortunately, to get it. When, therefore, the rebels charged upon our intrenchments, in the dull light, hundreds of them were tripped down, and unable to tell the cause. As they lay upon the ground, our musketry-fire kept many of them from ever rising more. As with the first line, so with the second. They met the same fate. The third line fared no better, and this simple agency of a telegraphic wire, interlaced among the trees, played more havoc in the rebel ranks than anything else. The dead lay like autumn leaves before the front of Wistar and Burnham."

About eight o'clock, there was a lull, and Butler, now thoroughly alarmed, ordered a retreat. For the first time in his life, he had experienced a real rebel charge, and his confidence in his own powers seemed suddenly to vanish. Notwithstanding the disaster that had overtaken the army, Gillmore was not disposed to abandon so readily this position on the railroad, the holding of which was so necessary to ultimate success; and when he received the order to fall back, sent an urgent remonstrance to Butler to withdraw it, saying that he believed he could hold his position. Receiving, in reply, a peremptory order to retreat, he reluctantly obeyed, and the army fell back to its intrenched position at Bermuda Hundred.

Thus, in a single morning, the whole value of the Peninsula movement was lost, and might as well have not been undertaken at all, for the rebels not only had possession of the railroad again, by which they could forward troops and supplies to Lee, but had cooped up Butler in his strong position, so that he was as powerless to make any aggressive movement, as though locked up in an iron cage. There never was a movement begun with such a promise of success, that ended so disgracefully.

Grant saw a most important part of his great plan thus suddenly broken up, thereby increasing four-fold the magnitude of the work before him. The chagrin and feeling with which he received the news, may be gathered from the manner in which he alludes to the subject in his official report. He says:—

"On the 16th, the enemy attacked General Butler in his position in front of Drury's Bluff. He was forced back, or drew back, into his intrenchments between the forks of the James and Appomattox Rivers—the enemy intrenching strongly in his front, thus covering his railroads, the city, and all that was valuable to him. His army, therefore, though in a position of great security, was as completely shut off from further operations, directly against Richmond, as if it had been in a bottle strongly corked. It required but a comparatively small force of the enemy to hold it there."

A little farther on, referring to the same lamentable affair, he says:—

"The army sent to operate against Richmond, having hermetically sealed itself up at Bermuda Hundred, the enemy was enabled to bring the most, if not all, the reinforcements brought from the south by Beauregard, against the Army of the Potomac. In addition to this reinforcement, a very considerable one—probably not less than fifteen thousand men—was obtained by calling in the scattered troops, under Breckenridge, from the western parts of Virginia."

The public was not aware, at first, of the extent of the misfortune, and rested comparatively satisfied with the announcement that Butler's "position was impregnable." It was as much as the position of a war correspondent was worth, in the Army of the James, to breathe one word in disparagement of Butler's skill, or express a doubt of the wisdom of his movements.

This had a striking illustration in the case of a chaplain in Gillmore's Corps. In a private letter to the editor of *The Evening Post*, he stated some very unwholesome truths, respecting this unfortunate battle. This was published anonymously, but Butler having discovered its author, under a trumped-up charge of his being absent without leave, got the unsuspecting clergyman within his department, and, unable to make him consent to unsay the truth, and state a falsehood, threw him into confinement among rebels and negroes, where he kept him for more than a month, subjected to exposures that well nigh destroyed his life. Refusing to grant him a trial, in direct violation of his duty; refusing, also, to allow him to hold religious service with his fellow-prisoners, he continued his unmanly persecutions until powerful friends of his victim, from without, took up the case, when he was compelled to release his despotic grasp, and let the injured man go free to paint his persecutor in his true colors.

Kautz's cavalry raid, which started two or three days before this disastrous battle, accomplished its work successfully. The damages inflicted upon the enemy have been described as follows:

"Going direct to Walthall Junction, the depot of the Richmond and Petersburg railroad was destroyed, together with its contents. Moving on to Chester Station, a similar scene was enacted.

"Marching on to the Richmond and Danville road, the depot at the coal mines, with a large number of cars, was demolished. The same occurred at Tomahawk Station. At Powhatan, a locomotive and train were destroyed, together with the railroad buildings. When the Third New-York and Eleventh Pennsylvania cavalry approached Chola, on the line of the Lone road, their further progress was contested by a rebel infantry regiment stationed there. After a brisk fight, our men drove the rebels. In the short engagement, but few were killed or wounded, on our side.

"The rebels having retired, the command pushed on, after destroying considerable of the property, a train of cars, and a locomotive included. The expedition then struck for the South-side road. Here, at Black's and White's, another train was destroyed, with a large amount of commissary stores. At Wellsville and Wilson's Station, railroad property was demolished.

"At Lawrenceville, the Court-House of Brunswick County, a large amount of corn, tobacco and flour, belonging to the Confederate Government, and which had been taken from farmers, for taxes, was burned.

"On the Nottaway River, near Jarrett's Station, a pontoon bridge was destroyed. The part of the Petersburg and Weldon railroad, which was tapped by the former raid, had been repaired, but this time the raiders broke it more effectually. At all the stations, where the expedition halted to destroy depots, the railroad track was torn up for several miles on each side. Bridges were leveled, not only on the railroads, but on several turnpikes.

"There were large quantities of commissary stores all along the line of the road, which were rendered thoroughly useless for the Confederates. The work done by this expedition was most effectual; four railroads being rendered useless to the rebels, to say nothing of what else was done, which will cripple them very materially.

"Our men penetrated within four miles of Richmond, and three of Petersburg. Encounters with the enemy occurred on several occasions, but they always were compelled to retire."

With small loss, the force again reached City Point, on the evening of the 18th.

Butler now being "corked up," but little interest was felt by Grant, in his action, for he knew that nothing more could be done in that direction until he should arrive with the Army of the Potomac. There was plainly, now, but one way to form a junction with Butler, and that was to march to the spot where he lay helpless. The Army of the James being "hermetically sealed," it must remain useless to him until, by his presence, he could unseal it.

The rebels, emboldened by their success, endeavored to get possession of the James River, below Butler, and cut off his supplies; they accordingly attacked both Fort Powhatan and Wilson's Wharf, but were repelled by the monitors under Admiral Lee.

But, while the month of May will be forever marked in our calendar for the mighty military movements it witnessed, East and West, its record would not be complete without giving the naval operations along our coast.

When Grant set in motion our great armies, it was understood that the navy should, at the same time, threaten the rebel ports, not yet in our possession, and thus keep from Lee reinforcements that otherwise would reach him. With all our borders at peace, the entire military force of the North was available, and could be sent in any desired direction. At the South, this state of things was reversed, and with fewer men to bring into the field, she had to keep back many, even of these, to protect the few ports that still remained to her.

At Mobile, Farragut lay waiting for one or two iron-clads to boldly force his way into the bay, while expeditions up the rivers of Florida kept detachments of troops there, which Lee would soon be in sore need of. In one of these up the St. John's, we lost the steam tug, Columbine, which fell into the hands of the enemy. Our batteries and iron-clads were also pounding away on the defenses of Charleston harbor—holding strong garrisons there to defend the place.

Thinking that we had drawn away our forces from Newbern, to fill up our armies, the rebels organized an expedition against it, and in the fore part of the month, news was received that it was closely besieged by the enemy, and fears were entertained that it might fall into his hands, but he was driven back in disgrace.

Although nothing but disaster had overtaken the Southern navy from the outset, two formidable rams, on the eastern coast, this Spring, caused a good deal of alarm to our shipping. One, at Wilmington, was reported to be a powerful vessel, and a strong force was kept watching her. The Albemarle, that had wrought such mischief to the Miami and Southfield, in Albemarle Sound, was decoyed out of the Roanoke River, by Melancthon Smith, senior officer in the Sound, and attacked by eight steamers. The gun-boat Bombshell, which accompanied it, was captured, and the ram was compelled to retire from the conflict, apparently, somewhat damaged. The Sassacus behaved nobly in the combat. Laying herself alongside her formidable antagonist, she poured in her heavy shot at close quarters. After the capture of the Bombshell—she being some distance off, and the ram lying broadside too—Roe, the Commander, "ordered full steam on and open throttle, and laid the ship fair for the broadside of the ram, to run her down. The Sassacus struck her fairly just abaft her starboard beam, in the position, in the rear of the house or casemate, with a speed of nine or ten knots, making twenty-two revolutions with thirty pounds of steam. As I struck, (he says,) she sent a one hundred-pounder rifle-shot, through and through, from starboard bow to port-side, at the berth-deck. The collision was pretty heavy, and the ram careened a good deal,—so much so that the water washed over her deck, forward and aft the casemate. At one time, I thought she was going down; I kept the engine pushing, as I hoped, deeper and deeper into her, and also hoping it might be possible for some one of the boats to get up on the opposite side of me, and, perhaps, enable us to sink her, or, at least, to get well on to her on all sides. I retained this position full ten minutes, throwing grenades down her deck hatch, and trying in vain to get powder into her smoke-stack, and receiving volleys of musketry, when the stern of the ram began to go round, and her broadside port bearing on our starboard bow, when the ram fired, and sent a one hundred-pounder, Brook's rifle-shot, through the starboard side, on the berth-deck, passing through the empty bunkers into the starboard boiler, clear through it, fore and aft, and finally lodging in the ward-room. In a moment, the steam filled every portion of the ship, from the hurricane-deck to the fire-rooms, killing and stifling some, and rendering all movements, for a time, impossible."

Just before receiving this shot, he sent a one hundred-pounder, solid shot, against the monster, which broke into fragments against his mailed sides, one of the pieces actually bounding back upon his own deck. The flag-ship, Mattabesett, and the Wyalusing, engaged the ram with equal gallantry, laying their vessels alongside of it, with a boldness never surpassed in any naval combat. They rained their heaviest shot and shell on the huge structure, at close quarters, cutting away the flag; but failing to reach any vital part.

In Arkansas, Steele pushed Price at every point and forced him into disastrous retreat.

CHAPTER XXVIII.

SURVEY OF GRANT'S POSITION—SIGEL'S FAILURE IN THE SHENANDOAH VALLEY—SPOTTSYLVANIA FLANKED—THE RACE FOR THE NORTH ANNA RIVER—HANCOCK'S AND WARREN'S CORPS—FIGHT OF THE LATTER AT JERICHO FORD—GALLANTRY OF GRIFFIN—ASSAULT OF A REDAN BY HANCOCK—GALLANT CHARGE—THE ENEMY FALLS BACK TO THE SOUTH ANNA—STRENGTH OF HIS POSITION—TRANSFER OF BASE TO PORT ROYAL—GRANT AGAIN FLANKS THE ENEMY AND CROSSES THE PAMUNKEY AT HANOVERTOWN—MOVEMENT TO COLD HARBOR—BATTLE OF COLD HARBOR—GRANT RESOLVES TO TRANSFER THE ARMY TO THE JAMES RIVER—A DELICATE OPERATION—GILLMORE'S FAILURE TO TAKE PETERSBURG—LEE DECEIVED—THE JAMES SAFELY CROSSED—ATTACK ON PETERSBURG BY SMITH—OUTER WORKS CARRIED—VARIOUS ASSAULTS—BUTLER AGAIN CUTS THE RICHMOND AND PETERSBURG RAILROAD, AND AGAIN DRIVEN BACK—LAST GRAND ASSAULT—THE POSITION OF AFFAIRS—REVIEW OF THE CAMPAIGN—GRANT'S SAGACITY AND JUDGMENT VINDICATED.

DURING the time that Grant lay before Spottsylvania, waiting for reinforcements to come up, and recruiting his overtasked army, he had ample time to survey his position. As, he said, "during three long years the Armies of the Potomac and Northern Virginia had been confronting each other," and "in that time they had fought more desperate battles than it probably ever before fell to the lot of two armies to fight, without materially changing the vantage-ground of either." It was not a pleasant reflection to think of these terrible struggles and fearful losses—all made without giving him any "*vantage ground.*"

To make matters worse, Butler had totally failed in his co-operative movement, so that, practically, he must be left out of any plan Grant might adopt to reach Richmond. Sigel also had miserably failed in the Shenandoah Valley, and the prospect was that he must look to himself, and his gallant army alone, for success. The part this officer performed in the grand campaign cannot be better given than in the following few sentences of Grant:—

"The movement of the Kanawha and Shenandoah Valleys under General Sigel, commenced on the first of May. General Crook, who had the immediate command of the Kanawha expedition, divided his forces into two columns, giving one, composed of cavalry, to General Averill. They crossed the mountains by separate routes. Averill struck the Tennessee and Virginia railroad, near Wytheville, on the 10th, and proceeding to New River and Christiansburg, destroyed the road, several important bridges and depots, including New River bridge, forming a junction with Crook at Union, on the 15th. General Sigel moved up the Shenandoah Valley, met the enemy at New Market, on the 15th, and after a severe engagement, was defeated with heavy loss, and retired behind Cedar Creek. Not regarding the operations of General Sigel as satisfactory, I asked his removal from command, and Major-General Hunter was appointed to supersede him."

Grant having, at length, established his base of supplies, and received his reinforcements, gave orders for the army to move on the 18th. Still determined, if possible, to get a field-fight out of Lee, he planned a flank movement around the right of the rebel army to the North Anna River. If he succeeded in reaching this point first, it would place him in Lee's rear, cut off his communications, and compel him to evacuate the strong works at Spottsylvania.

The movement was postponed, however, on account of an unexpected attack of Ewell, who came out of his intrenchments and assailed our right, so that it did not commence till the night of the 21st.

To mask it more effectually, Hancock and Wright were

previously ordered to attack the rebel left, as though it were Grant's intention to turn that flank. After losing several hundred men in this feint, the former was shifted over, by night, to our extreme right, and at once commenced his march for the North Anna. Torbert's cavalry, in the meantime, moved off ten miles east of Spottsylvania, on the Fredericksburg railroad, to clear the country for the march. Hancock at first struck off with his Corps east to Massaponax Church, then wheeled south, and moving rapidly forward all night, and all next day, reached Bowling Green at evening—the head of his column being seventeen miles from Spottsylvania.

Lee, however, having in some way obtained information of this movement, and penetrating Grant's design, at once proceeded to checkmate it. At midnight, the reveillè was beat in the rebel camp, and, by one o'clock, Longstreet's Corps was pushing on through the darkness toward the North Anna. In the presence of such an enemy as Lee, Hancock's movement was a perilous one, for it exposed him to a flank attack while on the march.

To guard against this, he took a somewhat circuitous route, which, of course, gave Longstreet all the advantage in the race, as he, moving directly to the rear, had a much shorter line to traverse.

Warren broke off from the main army a few hours after Hancock started—taking, for a while, the same road. With a promptness, that could hardly have been surpassed had there been a mutual understanding, Ewell's Corps at once moved off in the same direction. Saturday afternoon, Burnside followed the other two Corps, leaving Wright—in command of Sedgwick's old Corps—alone in front of Spottsylvania.

Hill, with his Corps still remaining behind in the intrenchments, at once came out and attacked him, evidently for the purpose of ascertaining the actual force left behind. Breaking through our skirmish line he was received with such a terrible artillery fire that he dared not push his attack, and fell back to the cover of the works.

That night Wright followed the rest of the army, when Hill also moved off, and Spottsylvania, in front of which such rivers of blood had flowed, was left silent and deserted.

The country, over which these two mighty armies now marched, seeking a new battle-field, had thus far escaped the ravages of war, and sprouting wheat and clover fields, and quiet farm-houses, greeted the eyes of the weary soldiers as they toiled forward toward the North Anna. From the outset, it was plain that, unless the movement could be kept secret for several hours at least, we could not reach the desired point, before the enemy. As he started almost simultaneously with us, there could be but one result to the race, and when, on Monday, the heads of our columns approached the North Anna, the enemy was found to be there in position.

This river was sixty-five miles from the Rapidan, and but twenty-five from Richmond, but though distance had been overcome, the obstacles that intervened between Grant and the rebel Capital, remained great as ever. Hancock struck the stream near where the Fredericksburg and Richmond railroad crosses it—Warren, who had the right, four miles farther up, at Jericho. Griffin's division of the latter Corps, in advance, at once plunged into the stream, and waist-deep, floundered over the rocky bed to the farther bank. The enemy apparently not expecting that any part of our force would cross so high up, had no troops to oppose the passage here. The rest of the Corps rapidly followed, and Griffin moving swiftly over an open space, a third of a mile wide, took position in a piece of woods, and soon encountered a heavy skirmish line of the enemy.

The rebel leaders, made aware of Warren's movement, hurried up reinforcements to this point, and, at five o'clock, fell furiously on Griffin—coming on in two lines of battle, and suddenly opening with three batteries on his uncovered ranks. But Griffin, with his accustomed gallantry and firmness, held his position, and gave the on-sweeping battalions such a murderous fire, that the attack in front was soon abandoned, and the rebel Commander detached a brigade to make a detour and fall on his right flank. Cuyler, who commanded here, had not yet got into position, and his brigade gave way before the sudden onset.

This was a critical moment for Griffin, but with that promptness which has always distinguished him, he quickly ordered up three regiments of Bartlett's brigade, and restored the line. The Eighty-third Pennsylvania regiment, commanded by Lieutenant-Colonel McCoy, ran into the rebel brigade while on the march. With great presence of mind, he quickly moved his forward companies into line, and poured in a sudden volley, while one of his men seized the rebel leader by the collar, and pulled him into our lines a prisoner. Caught in flank and rear, by the fire of the regiment, the rebel brigade broke and fled.

The brilliancy and success of this engagement called forth a congratulatory order from Meade. A failure here, at the outset, would have complicated matters much, and for a few moments, it seemed inevitable.

While, on the right, this conflict was passing on the south bank of the stream, Hancock, on the left, was engaged in a desperate fight on the north side. Here, on either bank, the rebels had, long before, erected strong works, which now swept the shores with a destructive fire. Hancock saw, at once, that there must be no delay; that the redan on the side nearest him, must be taken at all hazards, by assault. This perilous task was assigned to Birney's gallant division.

"On the left, was the brigade of Colonel Egan; on his right, Pierce's brigade, and General Mott's brigade on the right of Pierce. The Fourth brigade (the Excelsior, commanded by Colonel Blaisdell, of the Eleventh Massachusetts) came up partly in the rear, its left to the right of the redan. To cover the assault, three sections of artillery were put in position, and replied to the artillery fire of the enemy. On the left of Birney's division, was Barlow's division, the left of which connected with the right of Gibbon's division, while Tyler's heavy artillery division was held in reserve.

"An hour before sundown, on Monday, the assault was begun and most brilliantly executed, by Birney's command, which swept across the open space at double quick, under a storm of artillery and volleys of musketry. Two regiments of the Excelsior brigade, (the Seventy-first and Seventy-second New-York,) first reached the redan, the garrison of which ran precipitately, as the menacing line of fixed bayonets came sweeping along. Making a foothold in the parapet with their muskets, the brave fellows clambered up and simultaneously planted their colors on the rebel stronghold.

"Thirty rebels, unable to get away in time, were captured in the ditch. The total loss in this brilliant exploit, the very rapidity and daring of which astonished and paralyzed the rebels, did not exceed a hundred men, and secured us the possession of the bridge, across which a portion of Hancock's Corps immediately crossed, and held the bridge-head during the night."

Wright's Corps, crossing at Jericho's Ford, took position in rear of Warren. The enemy being swept from the line of the stream, Burnside's Corps, on the 25th, crossed over between Hancock and Warren. The Army of the Potomac now lay south of the North Anna, with the exception of Hancock's Corps, which was unable to cross, as the rebels had burnt the bridge, when they found they could no longer hold it.

Grant now changed his base to Port Royal, on the Rappahannock, and a long, sad train, containing our wounded, was soon winding its way to that point. In the meantime, he pushed on his advance columns three miles toward the South Anna, which was found to be the real rebel line of defense—having evidently been selected, long ago, and strongly fortified.

For the last few days, the heat had been overpowering, and the troops were much exhausted; still there seemed no end to their labors. Wherever they moved, strong defenses sprung up in their faces, behind which the enemy mocked at their efforts to force him into a decisive engagement.

Lee lay here with his centre advanced, and his flanks thrown back, and strongly protected, hoping that Grant would dash his army against the intrenchments, as he did at Spottsylvania. But the latter, after a thorough reconnoissance of the position, was satisfied, he said, that it was stronger than any the enemy had hitherto taken up, and so, on the night of the 26th, he withdrew his army to the north bank of the North Anna, and again moved around Lee's right flank, crossing the Pamunkey at Hanovertown. Sheridan, with Merritt's and Torbert's divisions of cavalry, cleared the advance for the Sixth Corps, which this time took the lead—Hancock bringing up the rear.

Some sharp fighting occurred before the Corps effected a lodgment on the opposite bank; and on the 28th, Sheridan had a severe cavalry engagement with Fitz-hugh Lee—driving him from the field. The whole army now rapidly crossed and advanced toward the Chickahominy. Grant, therefore, transferred his base from the Rappahannock to the White House, which had become a historic place to the Army of the Potomac.

In the meantime finding, as he said, Butler "hermetically sealed," at Bermuda Hundred, and that the position could be held with a less force than the one under him, he ordered W. F. Smith to join him with the Eighteenth Corps, by way of the White House. The troops were placed on transports, which, passing down the James, advanced up the York River to the White House, from which point, it was scarcely fifteen miles to the Army of the Potomac.

On Monday, the 30th, Grant pushed energetic reconnoissances, which showed the enemy to be in full force, in front; when Warren, on the left, made an effort to get possession of the Mechanicsville pike, but failed. Grant now determined to seize Cold Harbor, for the purpose of forcing the Chickahominy at that point, by carrying, if possible, the enemy's works between him and it.

On Tuesday night, Warren's Corps, holding the extreme right, was transferred to the left, where, the next day, it was joined by the Eighteenth Corps from the White House. The rest of the army came up this day, and a sharp conflict ensued for the position of Cold Harbor. We finally carried it, though with a loss of two thousand men. It was an important point to hold, for nearly all the roads leading out of Richmond converge here, as well as those coming from the White House. Hence, Lee made a great mistake in not securing it in advance, and holding it all hazards.

Grant now determined to give battle the next day; and Hancock's Corps which, after the withdrawal of Warren's, held the extreme right, was brought over to the extreme left, during the night. He had to fight his way into position, so that he was not ready to advance until afternoon. The attack was ordered to commence at five o'clock, but just before the hour arrived, the heavens grew black as night, and a heavy thunder cloud rapidly pushed its way across the sky. Its dark bosom was incessantly riven by lightning, and the thunder boomed louder than artillery, above the waiting armies. The wind swept by in fierce gusts, bending the trees like wands, in its path, and everything betokened a wild and stormy evening. Soon the burdened clouds opened, and the rain came down in a perfect deluge, turning the fields into standing pools, and swelling the Chickahominy into a turbid flood.

The order for the attack had, therefore, to be countermanded, and the drenched army went into bivouac for the night. A new order was issued, fixing the attack at half-past four in the morning.

BATTLE OF COLD HARBOR.

Hancock's Corps was on the extreme left, Wright's next, the Eighteenth, under Smith, next, then came Warren, and last, Burnside, holding the extreme right. The rebel army was drawn up in front of the Chickahominy, two lines deep, with a heavy skirmish line well advanced. It was irregular, in order to conform to the ridges, woods and swamps, over or across which it extended. Between the two armies, lay a low, swampy region, made worse by the thunder storm of the night before—and this was to be the battle-field.

The morning was dark and gloomy, and a gentle rain was falling, as the firm-set lines moved out from behind their breastworks, and began to advance over the field. The skirmish line pushing rapidly forward, soon encountered that of the enemy, and their sharp, irregular volleys awoke the morning echoes. The next minute the artillery opened, and from right to left, for miles along the Chickahominy, the deep reverberations rolled like heaven's own thunder of the night before.

The advance of that mighty host, as the long lines of glittering steel rose and fell along the uneven ground, was a magnificent spectacle. Hancock, on the left, first came up to the enemy's works. Barlow, with four brigades, formed his extreme left; and this gallant Commander carried his troops for half a mile, through woods and over open spaces, under a heavy fire, square up to the rebel works.

These were the immortal brigades that made the gallant dash into the works at Spottsylvania, and here, enacting over again their heroic deeds, they sprung with a shout over the enemy's parapets, capturing the guns, colors, and several hundred prisoners. This was the key to the rebel position, and could this gallant charge have been properly supported, Lee's army, in all probability, would have been driven over the Chickahominy. The latter was aware of this, and had guarded well against such a catastrophe, for Barlow had not yet turned the captured guns upon him, when a heavy force, under Hill, was seen advancing to retrieve the disaster.

These bold brigades saw the approach of these overwhelming numbers without fear, but the position they had gained was so far in advance, that it was exposed to a deadly, enfilading fire from the rebel artillery, that now ploughed through them with awful havoc. Two of their leaders, Brooks and Byrnes, fell mortally wounded; other officers were fast disappearing; and shattered, rent, and bleeding, they, at length, fell back, bringing with them a part of their prisoners, but not the captured guns.

The whole of Hancock's Corps advanced simultaneously with Barlow's division, and came like it, upon the rebel works, and made desperate efforts to carry them. Deafening yells, rising from behind the hostile intrenchments, answered with shouts all along our lines—incessant explosions of artillery, and crashing volleys of musketry—the long, low sulphurous cloud hanging in the damp air above the combatants—the never-ceasing stream of the wounded, borne back to the rear, made that summer morning one of gloom and terror to the beholder.

The Sixth Corps, under a desolating fire, swept the first line of rifle-pits, in its front, and with five batteries played furiously on the rebel position, but could make no serious impression on the main works. Warren and Burnside, on the right, suffered less than the rest of the army, especially the latter, who did little more than keep up a heavy artillery fire. The brunt of the battle was borne by Hancock's Corps, which, also, gained most of the advantage that was even temporarily secured.

The Army of the Potomac had again flung itself against the rebel works in vain, and rent and bleeding, fell back, though not to its original position. A lull came in the battle, and the anxious question asked by all was, "Will the assault be renewed?" Grant and Meade stood on a naked eminence in consultation; the latter, nervous and emphatic in his manner; the former, cool and imperturbable as ever, looking gravely, sternly on the embattled hosts and the ensanguined field.

Intervening woods hid much of the country, and, apparently, wishing to ascertain for himself the true condition of things, he called for his horse, and, mounting it, rode down to Hancock's head-quarters, and after consulting with him, went over to Wright's. All this time, occasional firing was heard along the lines, for they were still in close proximity, especially on the left—Barlow being on one side of a ridge, and the enemy on the other, not more than fifty yards apart.

The war correspondent of the *Times*, in speaking of the position of the lines, and their nearness to each other, at some points, relates the following singular incident, which we give in his own words.

"One portion of our line retained all day a position within

fifteen yards of the rebel works. This heroic band was the brigade of Colonel McKean, a brigade of Gibbon's division of Hancock's Corps, and numbering about eight hundred men. The conduct of these eight hundred, is as splendid a stroke of heroism as ever lit up the story of 'the glory we call Greece and the grandeur we call Rome.' Through the live-long day, these men held their line, within fifteen yards of the enemy, and all his forces could not dislodge them. Repeatedly, during the day, the rebels formed double columns of attack to come over the work and assail them, and the officers could be heard encouraging their troops, saying to them 'There are only four or five hundred of them—come on.' But the moment the rebels showed themselves above their parapet, a line of fire flashed out from behind the earthern mound, where those eight hundred heroes stood in a new Thermopylæ, and many a rebel threw up his arms and fell prone, under their swift avenging bullets.

"The sequel of this bit of history is as curious as the deed itself—for while the rebels dared not venture out to assail McKean's men, neither could he, nor his command, recede from the perilous position. He could not get back to us—we could not go forward to him. In this dilemma, the ingenious device was hit upon of running a 'sap,' or zig-zag trench, up from our line to his. In this way, a working party were able tc dig up to where they lay, begrimed with powder and worn down with fatigue, and a few hours ago they were brought safely away—'all that was left of them, left of six hundred!' But McKean, their gallant leader, he came not away alive. Since eleven in the morning, he had lain behind the bulwark his valor defended—a corpse. While preparing to resist a rebel assault, he fell, pierced by the bullet of a sharp-shooter, and, after living for an hour or two, in an agonizing death-in-life, begging his staff-officers to put an end to his misery, his heroic soul forsook the turmoil of this weary, warring world."

The two armies remained in this relative position, all day, neither making any decided demonstration. But, just after dark, the rebels came down on Hancock's Corps in one of their tremendous charges. Our brave troops, however, had moved too often on formidable works, without flinching, to be driven from behind their own intrenchments, by any force; and as the dark mass became well defined in the grey gloom, they poured in volley after volley of musketry, with a coolness and precision, that made the hostile lines melt away as though swallowed up by the night, while the deadly batteries tore huge gaps through the dim formations.

The assault, however, was a most gallant one, and the great openings made in the ranks were closed up with steadiness and a noble devotion; and they pressed forward until they reached the breastworks, and poured their fire over the very parapets—some even getting upon them, but only to fall dead before the terrible fire that met them. Their shouts of defiance rung over the din of battle, and the order "*Forward*, FORWARD," rose steady and strong through the darkness, but all their efforts to carry the intrenchments were vain. Our troops had been compelled again and again to attack the enemy behind their breastworks, and been repulsed, and now they had their revenge, and hurled the assailants back with terrible slaughter.

This ended the battle of Cold Harbor, or, as it has been sometimes called, of Chickahominy. Grant had failed here as at Spottsylvania, and it was plain that he could not force the Chickahominy. It then became a serious question what the next move on this mighty chess-board would be.

The aspect of affairs here had materially changed since McClellan, two years before, attempted to move on Richmond from the same point. *He* found no trouble in crossing the Chickahominy; indeed, had but little difficulty in advancing two miles beyond it. But that campaign taught the rebels wisdom; and now strong works dotted the country in every direction, and for five miles out of Richmond, every available point was fortified.

It was very plain, therefore, that Richmond could not be taken in this direction, and but one of two courses remained for Grant to pursue—either to retrace his steps far enough to turn Lee's *left* flank, and so come down on Richmond from the north, or continue on as far as the James River, and join Butler.

The former course would cover Washington and save the Government from its former fears for its safety; but, in this case, the Fredericksburg railroad would be the line of communication, over which his supplies must pass, while the length of it would require an army to protect it.

Grant, therefore, resolved to keep on to the James. He, however, remained for more than a week in front of the rebel position, gradually working his way, with the spade, toward it, as though he intended another assault; but in the following paragraph he gives the true reason of his delay:—

"I therefore determined to continue to hold substantially the ground we then occupied, taking advantage of any favorable circumstances that might present themselves, until the cavalry could be sent to Charlottesville and Gordonsville, to effectually break up the railroad connection between Richmond and the Shenandoah Valley and Lynchburg; and when the cavalry got well off, to move the army to the south side of the James River, by the enemy's right flank, where I felt I could cut off all his sources of supply, except by the canal."

To withdraw such a vast army from the immediate front of the enemy, was a dangerous undertaking; for it was hardly to be expected that it could be done unobserved by him, and he would not fail in case of discovery to attack both in flank and rear.

Hitherto all of Grant's movements had been by his left flank, and made in the same way; at night, the Corps holding the extreme right would throw out a strong picket line in front, to cover its movements, and then fall back, and marching in rear of the army, take position on the extreme left. The next Corps would follow in the same manner, until, by this simple process, the army was advanced the entire length of its line, some eight or ten miles. But Grant was now not to advance his lines so as to lap the enemy's flank and threaten his rear, but, if possible, to swing loose entirely from him, and make a rapid march of fifty miles, with all his trains and artillery. To secure himself in case of attack, while doing this, he gradually concentrated his lines until, in front, they were scarcely more than four miles long. This, consequently, forced the several Corps back, until the army assumed the form of a square, in its main outline; all along the sides of which, and beyond, strong earth-works were thrown up to protect the flanks.

Having completed all his preparations, and Sheridan, with his cavalry, being off, he, on the night of the 12th, silently withdrew from the enemy's front. Wilson's cavalry and the Fifth Corps crossed the Chickahominy, at Long Bridge, and proceeded to the White Oak Swamp, to cover the crossing of the rest of the troops. The Eighteenth Corps, in the meantime, marched back to the White House and again embarked in the transports for Bermuda Hundred.

With such secrecy and dispatch did the Army of the Potomac move away, that its departure was not known by Lee till next morning, when it was miles away. It marched below the White Oak Swamp instead of through it as it did under McClellan and by different roads stretched forward toward the James River. Meade, to whom was intrusted the management of the army, in this delicate movement, evinced the highest skill, and everything went on with the precision and regularity of machinery. There was some skirmishing on the way, but none serious enough to check the onward movement; and the grand army swept steadily and swiftly forward and crossed the James River without molestation. This probably would hardly have happened, if Lee had been aware of Grant's plan; but supposing his design was to advance on Richmond by the way of Malvern Hill, he disposed his forces to meet this imaginary movement.

Two days before Grant broke up his camps at Cold Harbor, a demonstration was made against Petersburg by Kautz's cavalry, and an infantry force under Gillmore. The cavalry penetrated beyond the outer works, but not being supported by the infantry, was compelled to retire. Gillmore thought the works too strong to be carried by assault, and, hence, did not make the attempt, for which he was much blamed.

Grant having deceived Lee, as to his intentions, determined to capture Petersburg before the latter could throw reinforcements into it; and hence, before the army was over the river, planned an assault upon it. As the failure of this well-laid plan, on the success of which everything, for the time, depended, has been the cause of much dispute, we let General Grant give his own account of it. He says:—

"After the crossing had commenced, I proceeded by a steamer to Bermuda Hundred, to give the necessary orders for the immediate capture of Petersburg.

"The instructions to General Butler were verbal, and were for him to send General Smith immediately, that night, with all the troops he could give him without sacrificing the position he then held. I told him that I would return at once to the Army of the Potomac, hasten its crossing, and throw it forward to Petersburg, by divisons, as rapidly as it could be done; that we could reinforce our armies more rapidly there than the enemy could bring troops against us. General Smith got off as directed, and confronted the enemy's pickets near Petersburg, before daylight next morning, but, for some reason, that I have never been able to satisfactorily understand, did not get ready to assault his main lines until near sundown. Then, with a part of his command only, he made the assault, and carried the lines northeast of Petersburg, from the Appomattox River, for a distance of two and a half miles, capturing fifteen pieces of artillery, and three hundred prisoners. This was about seven o'clock, p. m. Between the lines thus captured and Petersburg, there were no other works, and there was no evidence that the enemy had reinforced Petersburg with a single brigade from any source. The night was clear—the moon shining brightly—and favorable to further operations. General Hancock, with two divisions of the Second Corps, reached General Smith just after dark, and offered the service of these troops as he (Smith) might wish, waiving rank to the named Commander, who he naturally supposed knew best the position of affairs, and what to do with the troops. But, instead of taking these troops, and pushing at once into Petersburg, he requested General Hancock to relieve a part of his line in the captured works, which was done before midnight.

"By the time I arrived the next morning, the enemy was in force. An attack was ordered to be made at six o'clock that evening, by the troops under Smith, and the Second and Ninth Corps. It required until that time for the Ninth Corps to get up and into position. The attack was made as ordered, and the fighting continued, with but little intermission, until six o'clock the next morning, and resulted in our carrying the advance and some of the main works of the enemy to the right (our left) of those previously captured by General Smith, several pieces of artillery, and over four hundred prisoners."

It seems that this sudden victory was gained by the skirmish line alone, which, at a single bound, captured thirteen redoubts, sixteen guns and several colors, with three or four hundred prisoners. The colored troops took three of the redoubts, and six of the guns.

As soon as Lee was made aware of the danger threatening Petersburg, he had the garrison reinforced with the troops nearest it; in doing which, he weakened the force on the railroad in front of Butler. The latter informed of this, immediately sent out a few thousand men, under Terry, who succeeded in reaching the road, and tore up the track for three or four miles, but was in turn driven back by Longstreet's Corps.

For not holding this important road, gained thus a second time, Butler again receives the lash of the Lieutenant-General. He says:—

"As soon as I was apprised of the advantage thus gained, to retain it I ordered two divisions of the Sixth Corps, General Wright commanding, that were embarking at Wilcox's Landing, under orders for City Point, to report to General Butler, at Bermuda Hundred, of which General Butler was notified, and the importance of holding a position in advance of his present line, urged upon him.

"About two o'clock in the afternoon, General Butler was forced back to the line the enemy had withdrawn from in the morning. General Wright, with his two divisions, joined General Butler on the forenoon of the 17th; the latter still holding, with a strong picket line, the enemy's works. But instead of putting these divisions into the enemy's works to hold them, he permitted them to halt and rest some distance in the rear of his own line. Between four and five o'clock in the afternoon, the enemy attacked and drove in his pickets, and re-occupied his old line.

"On the night of the 20th, and morning of the 21st, a lodgment was effected by General Butler, with one brigade of infantry, on the north bank of the James, at Deep Bottom, and connected the pontoon bridge with Bermuda Hundred."

On Thursday, the assault was made on the rebel lines, and no permanent success gained. The next morning, Friday, at daylight, Burnside, with Miles' division of the Second Corps, made an attack on the right of the enemy's line, capturing three redoubts, and five hundred and fifty prisoners. The Second Corps was then thrown forward, and struggled nobly to gain the works, but failed.

On the right, Neill's division of the Sixth Corps, and Martindale's of the Eighteenth, pushed the enemy handsomely, for some distance, but gained no material advantage. We had lost, probably, six thousand men during these two days, which showed that the fighting had been very severe.

This was the condition of things when Grant arrived at the scene of action. The result thus far, of his grand *coup-de-main*, was most deplorable. Two lines, however, of the enemy's works had been captured, and so, on Saturday, he resolved to carry the third and last, by general assault. Three times during the day did the gallant battalions move steadily up in the face of a deadly fire, and were swept down by thousands, but each time failed to gain the coveted position.

Grant succeeded in occupying and holding a ridge that completely commanded Petersburg, into which he could hurl his shells, but the "Cockade City," as it was called, was of no consequence whatever, so long as the rebels held the heights beyond. The city lay in a hollow, with two ridges on either side, frowning with hostile batteries, and dark with earth works. Hence, the place was commanded by both parties, and, therefore, could be occupied by neither till the strong works on one or the other side were carried.

It was now very plain that the campaign had ended for the present, and a second one, of siege operations chiefly, was to commence.

It must be confessed that the sum total of this frightful campaign, of a month and a half, was anything but satisfactory. As Grant said, no material advantage had been gained. Nearly a hundred thousand men had disappeared in its progress, and now, at the end of the long marches and bloody battles, he found himself twice as far from Richmond as he was when on the Chickahominy. The distance, however, was a small matter—the obstacles that intervened between him and the coveted prize were well-nigh insurmountable. Assault after assault, the determined character of which was attested by the ghastly piles of dead, had been made in vain, and that, too, while the works were incomplete and, comparatively, weakly garrisoned. But Lee's army was now well up, and, as at Spottsylvania and Cold Harbor, lay behind the strong works.

The prospect, at this time, was enough to discourage any heart less resolute than Grant's. He had failed, at the outset, in the effort to get a decisive battle out of Lee. That of the Wilderness was only a drawn one. He had been repulsed at Spottsylvania with terrible loss. The same calamity had overtaken him at Cold Harbor. Sigel had failed in the Shenandoah Valley. Butler had twice lamentably failed in front of Bermuda Hundred. Smith and Gillmore had both failed; and to crown the climax, his last grand assault had failed, and the anxious inquiry arose, "What is next to be done?" Besides all this, those who had, at the outset, condemned the campaign across the country, now pointed to the result as the fulfillment of their prophecies.

Some of the English papers called him the great butcher, and the rebel press tauntingly asked why he did not take his army by transports to the James, instead of dragging it through rivers of blood across the country. It was said, and truly, that he could have put his army where it now was, without the loss of a man, had he adopted McClellan's course. It was said, moreover, and with equal truth, that he had lost two to one of the enemy in this long and bloody march, and, sadder than all and incapable of contradiction, he had not won a single decisive battle, but on the contrary, from the Wilderness to Petersburg, had been repulsed in every attack.

This seemed a gloomy summing up of the campaign, and, at first sight, conclusive that it was wrong throughout. There could be, apparently, no dispute that he erred egregiously in not following McClellan's plan of operations against the rebel Capital. Yet, after events showed that such a conclusion was entirely false, and fully vindicated the wonderful sagacity and sound judgment of the Lieutenant-General. He was not responsible for the condition in which two years of mismanagement had placed things. When McClellan undertook the Peninsula campaign, Richmond, from Hanover to Petersburg, was poorly fortified, so that when threatened on this long line, the Confederate Government was compelled to call in all its troops for the defense of its Capital. Hence, McClellan's declaration that Washington was best defended at Richmond, was true.

But matters were now reversed—the rebels, admonished of their danger in this direction, had, for the last two years, been erecting elaborate defenses, and guarding every point, so that there could be no strategy that did not involve hard fighting and terrible losses. Besides, the strength of the works around Richmond enabled a comparatively small force to hold the place, so that a portion of the army could operate against Washington, or threaten Maryland and Pennsylvania by way of the Shenandoah Valley. This was actually done, and, as we said, after events abundantly vindicated the wisdom of Grant's course.

Granting that we lost nearly one hundred thousand men, from May to July, and Lee but fifty thousand, yet Grant received reinforcements to the full amount of his losses, and sat down before Petersburg with an army as large, in fact larger than the one with which he crossed the Rapidan, so that he was as strong as though, at the outset, he had transferred his army by water to Petersburg. Notwithstanding this, Lee was able to hold his works and yet dispatch twenty thousand men, under Early, to ravage the Shenandoah Valley, thunder at the very gates of the Capital, and sever its great line of communication with the North—in short, spread such ruin and consternation that, though the Nineteenth Corps opportunely arrived from New Orleans, Grant was compelled to detach one of his own veteran Corps to the defense of Washington.

Now, if the fifty thousand men strewing the fields and crowding the hospitals, along the track of Lee's army, from the Wilderness to Petersburg, had been alive, to have swelled that twenty thousand, under Early, to seventy thousand men, what force would Grant have been compelled to send back to the National Capital? In other words, if twenty thousand rebels required the presence there of two Corps, how many Corps would seventy thousand men have required? The answer is very obvious. The whole army would have been recalled—the siege of Richmond raised, and the campaign have proved a failure.

Hence the course which Grant took was the only one that could bring success. True, it required frightful slaughter, but it was a saving of life in the end. Lee could not replenish his army as fast as we could ours.

Grant's perseverance in the course he marked out, was not, as many supposed, the result of obstinacy, but of sound judgment, which subsequent events fully confirmed. He had reduced Lee so that he could not dispatch sufficient troops up the Shenandoah Valley to make him loose his death-grip on Richmond, and had effected it in the only way possible.

CHAPTER XXIX.

DIFFICULTIES OF GRANT'S POSITION—HIS PLAN TO SEVER THE COMMUNICATIONS OF RICHMOND—SHERIDAN'S EXPEDITION—HUNTER'S—AVERILL'S AND CROOK'S—THE ENEMY DEFEATED AT STAUNTON—HUNTER AT LYNCHBURG—HIS DISASTROUS RETREAT—THE ENEMY IN POSSESSION OF THE SHENANDOAH VALLEY—WILSON'S EXPEDITION—DEFEAT OF THE SECOND AND SIXTH CORPS NEAR THE WELDON RAILROAD—A GLOOMY PROSPECT—OPERATIONS ALONG THE ATLANTIC COAST—CAPTURE OF THE WATER WITCH—FEDERAL OFFICERS PLACED UNDER FIRE AT CHARLESTON—MR. LINCOLN RENOMINATED FOR PRESIDENT—OPENING OF THE POLITICAL CAMPAIGN.

THE problem now left for Grant to solve, was one of the most difficult ever presented to a Commander. As before remarked, every part of his great plan had failed, except the killing of a certain number of the enemy. Getting his army on the James was not accomplishing anything of moment, because it could have been placed there at any time by transports. Richmond was neither invested, nor even approached—at least, it was no nearer than Butler's Army of the James, as it was called, had been to it for a long time. To dig his way from five to twelve miles to the rebel Capital, was a process too long to be attempted until every other measure had failed.

In carrying out his siege operations, therefore, it was plain that the first step to be taken was to sever the communications which united Richmond with the other parts of the Confederacy.

The Peninsula was in our possession, but this only shut the rebel Capital off from the sea. There were four channels of communication, with the interior, which Grant did not control. First, the railroad to Fredericksburg, connected with which was the railroad to Gordonsville, running south to the James River. Second, the James River canal, running along the James River, which, though but little spoken of by the Northern press, was the great channel for the transportation of provisions of all kinds to Richmond. Third, the railroad running south-west to Danville. Fourth, the Weldon railroad running directly south.

So long as any one of these channels of communication was left open, Richmond could not be regarded as invested; hence it was necessary that they all should be severed. This was the herculean task which Grant had assigned himself. To have captured Petersburg, and thus hold the Weldon road, and be in striking distance of the South-side road connecting with the Danville road, would have simplified it much. But the failure to do this, complicated matters greatly, and increased the magnitude of the work before him.

If he had succeeded, as he anticipated, in getting possession of the communications south of Richmond, and holding them by his army, the failure to destroy the other lines would not have been so disastrous—but he failed in every direction. Sheridan, whom he had sent off, before he left Cold Harbor, failed to accomplish the object of his expedition; while Hunter, in the moment of victory, and just as he seemed about to seize Lynchburg, had to flee over the mountains. Hence, new expeditions had to be started, and other efforts made to carry out the great plan.

As before remarked, Sheridan started off a few days previous to the evacution of Cold Harbor, to break up the Virginia Central railroad—the first of the channels of communication above mentioned—and, if possible, co-operate with Hunter, in the neighborhood of Lynchburg. He crossed the Pamunkey on the 7th and meeting with no resistance, moved rapidly forward, and on the 10th crossed the North Anna, and encamped at Buck Child's, about three miles from the Trevillian Station.

His intention was, he says, "To break the railroad at this station, march through Mechanicsville, cut the Gordonsville and Charlottesville railroad, near Lyndsay's House, and then to march on Charlottesville; but, on our arrival at Buck Child's, I found the enemy's cavalry in my immediate front.

"On the morning of the 11th, General Torbert, with his division, and Colonel Gregg, of General Gregg's division, attacked the enemy. After an obstinate contest they drove him from successive lines of breastworks, through an almost impassable forest, back on Trevillian Station.

"In the meantime, General Curtis was ordered, with his brigade, to proceed by a country road so as to reach the station in the rear of the enemy's cavalry. On his arrival at this point, the enemy broke into a complete rout, leaving his dead, and nearly all his wounded, in our hands; also, twenty officers, five hundred men, and three hundred horses."

That night he encamped at Trevillian Station, and on the morning of the 12th, commenced destroying the railroad up to Louisa Court-House. He was occupied in this work until three o'clock in the afternoon. But the enemy, in the meantime, had not been idle, and Sheridan suddenly found himself confronted by a large force, protected by rifle-pits. He at once advanced to give battle, but a careful reconnoissance showed that the enemy's works were too strong to be carried by assault. On the right, however, the bugles sounded the charge, and a portion of his troops entered the works but were quickly driven out.

Night, at length, closed the contest. The next day trains of cars, bearing rebel reinforcements, came down to prevent the capture of Gordonsville, and Sheridan was compelled, reluctantly, to wheel about and fall back toward the White House. Wade Hampton followed him, though at a respectful distance.

At the Pamunkey, the rebel leader made a detour and attacked Sheridan's trains at the White House, but Abercrombie, commanding there, maintained his ground until Sheridan came up, when the enemy was driven off. Resting his command here a short time, he started with all his trains and guns, for the James River, to join Grant.

Hampton followed, and attacked him on the Chickahominy, but without obtaining any advantage. On the 24th, near Charles City Court-House, he again attacked him, and made a desperate effort to capture his trains. A sharp contest followed, and the rear-guard was badly cut up; but Grant sending a brigade of infantry to Sheridan's relief, he was able to get off with all his guns and trains, though he lost some five hundred men. The next day he crossed the James, under cover of the gun-boats, and joined the main army.

The success of the expedition was very much magnified at the time, for, notwithstanding Sheridan beat the enemy in every encounter, it was a total failure as a part of Grant's great plan. Gordonsville was not reached, and the few miles of railroad destroyed were easily repaired, so that this line of communication remained to Lee. Butler's movement against the Richmond and Petersburg road, as we have seen, had failed, and Kautz's raid, on the Danville road, inflicted no permanent injury. Transient success, but ultimate failure, characterized, also, Hunter's expedition. When he was ordered to supersede Sigel, he hastened to Cedar Creek, where the demoralized army lay, and found two thousand of the troops without shoes, and one thousand without arms, they having thrown them away in their flight.

Re-organizing the command and receiving reinforcements,

he moved forward upon Staunton, and the day before Sheridan started on his raid with the intention of co-operating with him, had a severe battle with the rebels, under General Jones, and defeated him utterly, capturing fifteen hundred prisoners, and several guns. The next day, he was joined by Averill, who had been raiding in South-western Virginia, on the line of the Lynchburg and East Tennessee railroad. This Commander started simultaneously with Sheridan; one object of his expedition being to make a diversion in favor of General Crook, who was operating on the Virginia and East Tennessee road, and who succeeded in breaking it up and destroying a vast amount of stores.

Averill moving rapidly, from point to point, destroyed stores and trains, and spread terror and consternation on every side. He, at length, met Morgan with a force estimated at five thousand men, at Cave Mountain Gap, five miles from Wytheville.

The rebels were strongly intrenched, and it was evident that their position could not be forced.

"Scarcely had the rebels, thus impregnably ensconced, been revealed in front, ere two heavy lines of skirmishers, strongly supported, were discovered rapidly advancing, and in splendid style, over a clearing, and upon our right flank. The two discoveries were almost simultaneous. General Averill at once took in the perilous situation; to retreat was ruin, to advance certain destruction, to surrender was never thought of. Nothing was to be done but to hold his ground, make desperate, stubborn resistance, and during it to await the cover of the night.

"The gallant Colonel Schoonmaker, commanding the Second brigade, was, with the Fourteenth Pennsylvania and First Virginia, (mounted,) hurriedly thrown out across to the right of the road on a rise, there to meet the approaching columns, which they nobly did, receiving the fire of the enemy—presenting a front of twice their own—at close range, and returning it so rapidly, and with such deadly effect, that repeated attempts to charge upon them failed. Colonel Schoonmaker made no attempt to advance, but held his position under a constant fire for one hour, when, upon a threatened flank movement on his right, by the rebel cavalry, General Averill ordered him to fall back across the road, and on the right of the second column, which had been formed there, consisting of the Thirty-fourth Ohio and Second and Third Virginia, all dismounted, under the command of Brigadier-General Duffie. He had suffered considerably, and was compelled to leave his dead and badly wounded on the line where they had fallen. The movement was made leisurely, and in excellent order. It was greeted with exultant shouts by the rebels, who pressed rapidly forward as far as the abandoned line, but the now united columns, presenting a solid and unflinching front, delivered with rapidity and withering precision a fire which prevented further advance, and temporarily staggered into confusion the opposing ranks.

"From the outset of the fight, both columns, while holding in check the vastly superior force in front, were subjected, at easy musketry range, to the cross-fire of the infantry and artillery at the Gap. The terrible position of General Averill's command, no description can convey the correct idea of. They were on a cleared section with a force double their own to the left, and another double their own to the front, with no cover of hills or woods to fall back to, and with but the one thing to do—to maintain their position under the heavy and continuous fire of shot and shell. The gallantry of General Averill and his Staff shone conspicuously during the terrific ordeal, as did that of every officer and man in his command. Not one was seen to falter. The Second Virginia, on the left of the second column, and in close range of the Gap, constantly under murderous fire, extorted the admiration of the enemy, and won that of its own command by its splendid conduct. It was firm as a rock; every movement was executed with the ease and precision of a dress-parade, and the moral effect of its splendid bearing infused the strength of another regiment. On the field, as in general orders, it received from General Averill the warmest praise.

"General Averill was constantly at the front of the first column, and on its falling back, at the front of the command, encouraging and stimulating it to the noble heroism displayed by his own fearless exposure and dauntless courage. About midway of the fight, he was struck in the middle of the forehead by a musket ball, which, glancing, passed off over the left eye, inflicting a deep wound; with the blood flowing profusely, his face undistinguishable from gore, he continued in his saddle until, by weakness, he was compelled to retire to the rear. Here the blood was staunched, the wound dressed, and, after a few moments' rest, he was again in the saddle and at the front, there remaining until the close of the fight."

When night closed the contest, Averill withdrew, leaving his dead and wounded in the hands of the enemy.

"When Walker Mountain was reached, it was found that there was but a bridle-path over it, and the wearied men dismounting, dragged themselves and their jaded horses up the steep ascent. The advance reached the top at midnight, and here the guide irrecoverably lost his way. To continue in the pitchy darkness was impossible. The order was given to halt, and the worn-out men and horses, stretched in single file from base to summit, on the precipitous, rocky mountain's side, lay down to rest.

"Singularly enough, yet confirmatory of the terrible punishment the enemy had received, they were not disturbed, and at daylight were on the march again. The mountain was passed, and a forced march made, during the day, of thirty-two miles, to Dublin. Here was a sad disappointment, for, though the good work of destruction which General Crook had done, was seen, yet he was not met. Remaining over night, an early march was made of seven miles to New River; it was greatly swollen, but was crossed with the loss of two men, four horses, and destruction of all the ammunition, and ten miles further on, the Virginia and Tennessee railroad was struck at Christiansburg. Some scattering rebel forces were found here, but were charged on and driven through and beyond the town, giving no after trouble.

"The depot here, stored with large amounts of flour, bacon and forage, was burned, the telegraph office instrument and wires destroyed, the railroad torn up and the rails rendered useless, and the bridge, two miles below, burned. Two field-pieces were captured in the village. The command occupied the town over night, moving nineteen miles to Gap Mountain the next morning, where fifteen hundred rebels, under Colonel (or General) W. E. Jackson, were found strongly posted in a gap, and strengthened by two pieces of artillery.

"General Averill's command was now entirely without ammunition. What little was left, after the battle at Cave Mountain, had been destroyed while crossing New River. A fight, therefore, was hopeless. So, by a strategic and hasty movement, he turned the enemy's left flank, seeking a bridle-path over the mountain, and thence to Sinking Creek Valley, twelve miles distant; Jackson making no pursuit. On the next day, the 14th, he pushed on twenty-nine miles toward Union, and, within five miles thereof, fell in with the rear-guard of General Crook's command. It was a gladdening sight and hailed vociferously."

The two commands now joined Hunter. The latter, after

the battle near Staunton, occupied the town. Destroying here a vast amount of property, he advanced with his force, now about seventeen thousand strong, to Lexington, which was held by McCausland. The latter finding himself threatened in flank and rear, evacuated the place, and Hunter marched in and sat down, to wait the arrival of Sheridan from Gordonsville, which point, we have seen, he was unable to reach.

Receiving no tidings from him, he moved forward toward Lynchburg, the grand end of his expedition. If he could reach and hold this place, one very important part of Grant's plan would be carried out, and the supplies for Richmond sadly interfered with.

On his arrival before the town, he found it too strong to be carried by assault; but on the 18th, the very day the Army of the Potomac was moving against Petersburg, he made an attempt to capture it, but was repulsed. Sheridan having failed to destroy the Virginia Central road, Lee was able to transport troops rapidly from Richmond and its vicinity to the point of danger, and hurried off Ewell's Corps, with a part of Hill's and Breckenridge's command.

Hunter, at this time, was fifteen days' march from his base of supplies, and hence depended, for subsistence, on the country. Advised of the approach of this formidable force, he, on the 19th, commenced to retreat down the Valley. He had not proceeded far, however, when he found himself so closely pressed by the enemy that escape, in this direction, was hopeless. He, therefore, hastily abandoned a great part of his trains and guns, and struck across the mountains to Kanawha Valley, from whence he designed to return by the way of the Ohio River.

Thus, of course, Grant lost the use of these troops for several weeks. Hunter not only failed to accomplish the object of his expedition, but being compelled to flee over the mountains, he left the Shenandoah Valley as defenseless as though his entire army had been captured.

The enemy, now between twenty and thirty thousand strong, marched down it, unopposed, sending consternation into Washington. The failure of Hunter was another sad blow to Grant, whom fate seemed determined to try to the uttermost. Though disappointed, he did not blame him as he did Butler, yet says:—

"Had General Hunter moved by way of Charlottesville, instead of Lexington, as his instructions contemplated, he would have been in a position to have covered the Shenandoah Valley against the enemy, should the force he met have seemed to endanger it. If it did not, he would have been within easy distance of the James River canal, on the main line of communication between Lynchburg and the force sent for its defense. I have never taken exception to the operations of General Hunter, and I am not now disposed to find fault with him, for I have no doubt he acted within what he conceived to be the spirit of his instructions and the interests of the service. The prompitude of his movements and his gallantry should entitle him to the commendation of his country."

The effort, by Sheridan and Hunter, to destroy, permanently, the enemy's communications, north and west, having failed, it was hoped that success would crown Grant's measures to sever those farther south. While the latter was fleeing over the mountains to the Kanawha Valley, a strong cavalry expedition was sent out against the Weldon and Danville railroad—the success and result of which, Grant sums up in a few words. He says:—

"On the 22nd, General Wilson, with his own division of cavalry of the Army of the Potomac, and General Kautz's division of cavalry of the Army of the James, moved against the enemy's railroads south of Richmond. Striking the

Weldon railroad, at Ream's Station, destroying the depot and several miles of the road and the South-side road—about fifteen miles from Petersburg, to near Nottoway Station, where he met and defeated a force of the enemy's cavalry; he reached Burksville Station, on the afternoon of the 23d, and from there destroyed the Danville railroad to Roanoke bridge, a distance of twenty-five miles, where he found the enemy in force, and in a position from which he could not dislodge him. He then commenced his return march, and on the 28th met the enemy's cavalry in force at the Weldon railroad crossing of Stony Creek, where he had a severe but not decisive engagement. Thence he made a detour from his left, with a view of reaching Ream's Station, (supposing it to be in our possession.) At this place he was met by the enemy's cavalry supported by infantry, and forced to retire with the loss of his artillery and trains. In this last encounter, General Kautz, with a part of his command, became separated, and made his way into our lines. General Wilson, with the remainder of his force, succeeded in crossing the Nottoway River, and coming in safely on our left and rear. The damage to the enemy, in this expedition, more than compensated for the losses sustained by us. It severed all connection by railroad, with Richmond, for several weeks."

It is possible that the damage sustained by the enemy would "compensate" for our loss, though we apprehend that, on a careful estimate, the balance remaining in our favor would be hardly worth mentioning. The evil done was soon remedied, and Grant learned what Sherman found out at Atlanta, that the breaking up of railroads, by cavalry, inflicted only temporary inconvenience. They must be *held* to be of permanent service.

A more serious movement was made at this time against the Weldon railroad, by the Second Corps and Griffin's division of the Fifth, with this latter Corps itself in reserve. The Second Corps moved to the left, on Monday night, and the next day, the 22nd, marched rapidly southward until it came upon the enemy at the Jerusalem plank road. An engagement followed, when the Corps fell back into position for the night. The Sixth Corps now came up and formed on its left, when a consultation was held between the Commanders, and it was resolved to attack the enemy at day-break next morning. There being some misunderstanding with regard to orders, the two Corps did not move forward in unison, but independent of each other.

Barlow, with his immortal brigades, dashed into the woods, in his front, and pressing on, soon opened a gap between his left and the right of the Sixth Corps. Having advanced far enough, he was about to intrench himself when he was startled by a heavy firing on his flank and rear. Hill moving up his Corps to check our advance perceived the fatal gap in our lines, and quick as thought, dashed into it—a whole division driving like a storm through it. Struck in flank, Barlow's division was rolled up like a piece of paper, and several hundred men taken prisoners. Mott's flank being now uncovered, he, also, was compelled to fall back with heavy loss. Gibbon's turn came next, and his whole line of intrenchments was carried, and the army seemed about to break in utter rout.

But Miles' reserve division coming up opportunely, Gibbon rallied his division on it, and the enemy being apparently exhausted by his own efforts, the two Corps were enabled to form a new line of battle. The order for the whole line to advance was then given, when the enemy slowly retreated. The army proceeded, however, but a short distance, when it halted and passed the night in intrenching, while the rebels intrenched on the other side of the railroad.

Our loss in this engagement was probably two thousand,

while four guns and several stand of colors were left in the enemy's hands.

On Thursday, Wright, having ascertained that the enemy was weak on the extreme left, sent three Vermont regiments to occupy the railroad there. Before they reached their destination, however, they were furiously attacked and driven in confusion back to the main body, losing many prisoners. Flushed with success, the rebels now came down with loud yells on our whole line, and compelled it to withdraw to the cover of breastworks.

For the balance of the month, nothing more was done at this point, and the two armies seemed once more at a deadlock.

Grant had now felt his way all around Richmond, but could find no entrance to the rebel Capital. Every expedition to sever its communications had succeeded in inflicting only temporary damage, and, to an ordinary observer, nothing more could be done. Not a gleam of success lightened the dismal prospect; and added to all, came the news that the enemy was thundering down the Shenandoah Valley. Nothing, however, could shake the iron resolution of Grant, and he cast about for some new mode of reaching the enemy, while his artillery kept pounding away on the rebel intrenchments.

While the month of June was thus closing without witnessing any material success to the Army of the Potomac, Sherman had met his first repulse at Kenesaw and was burying his dead in the mountains of Georgia. In other parts of the West, the enemy was active, and the country was infested with guerilla parties. Marmaduke was operating along the Mississippi, and Shelby on the Arkansas.

The defeat of Sturgis in Mississippi, with the loss of twelve guns—the surrender of Hobson at Cynthiana, with fifteen hundred men, and the raid of Morgan through Kentucky, had no effect on Sherman's grand movement. The defeat of the latter at Mount Sterling, by Burbridge, reflected great credit on the latter.

Nothing, of especial interest, occurred along the Atlantic coast, during the month, except the capture of the Water Witch, by the rebels, and the placing of Federal officers under our own fire at Charleston.

The Water Witch, attached to the Fernandina, in Ossabaw Sound, was captured early on the morning of the 3rd of June. The night had been dark and squally, so that an object could not be seen twice the ship's length, except by the flashes of lightning. About two o'clock in the morning, the officer of the deck saw, by the uncertain light, a boat ahead, filled with men, and hailed it. The reply was, "Who the h–ll are you hailing?" followed by a volley of musketry. He immediately sprung his rattle, when from six other launches, which now swept out of the gloom, arose loud yells of defiance. The next moment, wrathful visages were seen, by the vivid flashes of lightning, peering over the railing, as the enemy climbed swiftly on board. Pendegrast, the Commander, was by this time on deck, and to his inquiry, "What is the matter," received the reply, "Rebels, rebels," from the rebels themselves. Instantly shouting, "Call all hands to repel boarders," "slip the chain and start the engine," he sprang to his state-room for his arms. When he reached the deck again, a motley crowd was struggling upon it, cursing and firing—the flashes of fire-arms and flashes of lightning mixing strangely in the turbulent scene.

Making his way to the hurricane-deck, he was struck by a cutlass and fell, for a moment, insensible. Recovering himself, he leaped upon the hurricane-deck, and rang the bell for the engineer to go ahead, hoping to swamp the boats alongside; but the engine made only a single revolution, and then stopped.

In the darkness and suddenness of the attack, no time was given to organize any resistance, and it was a short hand-to-hand fight. Most of the crew seemed paralyzed with fear, and made but feeble defense, and the rebels soon had entire possession of the vessel.

That a vessel, occupying the position she did, should be taken by surprise, argued, in the eyes of the Department, great criminality on the part of the Commander, and he had to bear the weight of its indignation.

The rebel Commander, in Charleston, indignant at our bombardment of the place, thought he would put a stop to it by placing fifty of our officers, some of them Major-Generals, in confinement, at a point reached by our fire. The following correspondence explains this diabolical act:—

"HEAD-QUARTERS, DEPARTMENT OF SOUTH CAROLINA, GEORGIA AND FLORIDA.
CHARLESTON, June 13, 1864.

GENERAL:—Five Generals and forty-five Field Officers, of the United States Army, all of them prisoners of war, have been sent to the city for safe keeping. They have been turned over to Brigadier-General Ripley, commanding the First Military District of this department, who will see that they are provided with commodious quarters in a part of the city occupied by non-combatants, the majority of whom are women and children.

It is proper, however, that I should inform you that it is a part of the city which has been for many months exposed, day and night, to the fire of your guns.

Very respectfully, your obedient servant,

(Signed,) SAMUEL JONES, Major-General Commanding.

Major-General J. G. FOSTER, Commanding United States Forces on coast of S. C., C. S."

"HEAD-QUARTERS, DEPARTMENT OF THE SOUTH.
HILTON HEAD, S. C., June 16, 1864.

Major-General SAMUEL JONES, Commanding Confederate Forces, Department of South Carolina, Georgia and Florida:—

GENERAL:—I have to acknowledge the receipt, this day, of your communication, of the 13th instant, informing me that five Generals and forty-five Field Officers, of the United States Army, prisoners of war, have been sent to Charleston for safe keeping; that they have been turned over to Brigadier-

General Ripley, with instructions to see that they are provided with quarters in a part of the city occupied by non-combatants, the majority of which latter, you state, are women and children. You add that you deem it proper to inform me that it is a part of the city which has been, for many months, exposed to the fire of our guns.

Many months since, Major-General Q. A. Gillmore, United States Army, notified General Beauregard, then commanding at Charleston, that the city would be bombarded. This notice was given that non-combatants might be removed, and thus women and children spared from harm. General Beauregard, in a communication to General Gillmore, dated August 22, 1863, informed him that the non-combatant population of Charleston would be removed with all possible celerity. That women and children have been since retained by you, in a part of the city which has been for many months exposed to fire, is a matter decided by your own sense of humanity.

I must, however, protest against your action, in thus placing defenseless prisoners of war in a position exposed to constant bombardment. It is an indefensible act of cruelty, and can be designed only to prevent a continuance of our fire upon Charleston. That city is a depot for military supplies. It contains not merely arsenals, but also foundries and factories for the manufacture of munitions of war. In its ship-yards, several armed iron-clads have already been completed, while others are still upon the stocks in course of construction. Its wharves and the banks of the rivers, on both sides of the city, are lined with batteries. To destroy these means of continuing the war is, therefore, our object and duty. You seek to defeat this effort, not by means known to honorable warfare, but by placing unarmed and defenseless prisoners under fire.

I have forwarded your communication to the President, with the request that he will place in my custody an equal number of prisoners, of the like grades, to be kept by me in positions exposed to the fire of your guns, so long as you continue the course stated in your communication.

Very respectfully, your obedient servant,

(Signed,) J. G. FOSTER, Major-General Commanding."

Foster's request was complied with, and the rebels were soon glad to abandon this barbarous mode of carrying on war, and to propose an exchange of prisoners.

Outside of military operations, nothing caused so much excitement, this month, as the re-nomination of Mr. Lincoln by the Republican party, as the candidate for the Presidency, in the election to come off in the ensuing Fall.

The two great political parties were organizing for a political campaign which was to be almost as bitter and deadly as that which was carried on in the field.

CHAPTER XXX.

BUILDING AND FITTING OUT OF THE ALABAMA IN AN ENGLISH PORT—COMPLAINT BY OUR GOVERNMENT—THE TWO YEARS' CRUISE—RETURNS TO CHERBOURG, FRANCE—BLOCKADED BY WINSLOW—SEMMES CHALLENGES WINSLOW—MORNING OF THE COMBAT—SPECTATORS COMING DOWN FROM PARIS TO WITNESS IT—THE ALABAMA STEAMS OUT OF THE HARBOR—THE COMBAT—LUDICROUS BY-PLAY ON THE KEARSARGE—SUPERIOR FIRING OF THE FEDERAL SHIP—SURRENDER OF THE ALABAMA IN A SINKING STATE—PICKING UP OF THE CREW AND CAPTAIN BY THE ENGLISH YACHT DEERHOUND—THE DEERHOUND SAILS OFF WITH THE PRISONERS TO SOUTHAMPTON—SEMMES' REPORT OF THE FIGHT—HIS SLANDERS AND FALSEHOODS—THE TWO VESSELS COMPARED—DEFENSE OF THE COMMANDER OF THE ENGLISH YACHT—EXCITEMENT IN EUROPE OVER THE ENGAGEMENT—WINSLOW AND THE SECRETARY OF THE NAVY.

THE KEARSARGE AND ALABAMA.

BUT while the month of June was pregnant with such great events in our own borders, there occurred a sea-fight on the other side of the Atlantic, that will ever occupy a prominent place in our naval history. On Sunday, the 19th of June, the same Sabbath that followed the last grand assault on Petersburg, and while we were gathering up our wounded, and burying our dead, that fell in front of the rebel works, and while Sherman was lying at the base of Kenesaw Mountain, preparing to storm its impregnable defenses, the Kearsarge and Alabama were engaged in mortal combat, off the quiet port of Cherbourg, in France. The Alabama, with other vessels, had been built by private enterprise, in England, ostensibly for neutral powers, or commercial purposes, but, after clearing the English coast, took in their armaments and crews, and hoisting the Confederate flag, preyed upon our commerce.

The Alabama was a powerful steamer, a swift sailer, and carrying guns of the heaviest kind. She had been a bold, successful cruiser for two years, though she had carefully avoided a contest with our war vessels, except in the single instance, when she attacked and sunk the Hatteras, which was no match for her, off Galveston harbor. Standing fearlessly along the track of our commerce, on the Atlantic, she had made the ocean lurid with the flames of burning merchantmen. Our fastest vessels had been sent in search of her, and the Vanderbilt had steamed half-way round the globe in the vain effort to capture her.

Down the coast of the Eastern Continent, around the Cape of Good Hope, into the Indian Ocean, she had proudly flaunted her hated flag, and destroyed our merchantmen. She with others, had well-nigh driven our ships from the ocean, so that our commerce was carried on almost entirely in foreign bottoms.

Her launch from an English dock-yard, had caused the most serious complaints to be made, by our Government, against Great Britain; such conduct being denounced as a breach of neutrality. The discussion of the question is not ended yet, and though the steamer lies at the bottom of the sea, she may, in the end, be the cause of the gravest difficulties between the two nations.

Unable to carry her prizes into any port, she plundered them of what she needed, sparing some, on the captains' giving bonds to pay a certain sum of money after the establishment of Southern independence, and burning the rest on the high seas. She had been the terror of our commerce, as far as the Indian Ocean, from which she had just returned and entered the port of Cherbourg for repairs. Captain Winslow, commanding the Kearsarge, had long been in search of her, and the moment he heard of her arrival, set sail, and lay off the mouth of the harbor, for the purpose of following her to sea when she again left port, and forcing her to a combat.

On the 14th, Semmes sent Captain Winslow the following challenge:—

"CONFEDERATE STATES' STEAMER ALABAMA,
CHERBOURG, June 14, 1864.

SIR—I hear that you were informed by the United States Consul that the Kearsarge was to come to this port solely for the prisoners landed by me, and that she was to depart in twenty-four hours. I desire you to say to the United States Consul that my intention is to fight the Kearsarge as soon as I can make the necessary arrangements. I hope these will not detain me more than till to-morrow evening, or after to-morrow morning, at the farthest. I beg she will not depart before I am ready to go out.

I have the honor to be, very respectfully, your obedient Servant,

R. SEMMES, Captain.

He very much mistook the Commander of the Kearsarge, if he supposed it was necessary to send a challenge to get a fight out of him. He had come to Cherbourg for no other purpose, and intended, by no means, to leave till he could follow the bold corsair out on the deep, and there sink him, or be sunk himself.

The Sabbath morning, of the 19th of June, broke in all the loveliness of early Summer over the rippling sea. A gentle breeze drifted lazily in from the ocean, and the sun, half shorn of his brightness, looked down through a hazy atmosphere, on the town and port, and revealed the Kearsarge gently swaying to the easy swell, as she lay three miles off the entrance, watching the movements of her antagonist. News of the expected fight had spread to Paris, and, in the morning, an excursion train came down from the French Capital loaded with passengers, eager to witness the combat. The boatmen of the port swarmed like hackmen around the terminus of the railway, offering the services of their boats to those who wished "to see a genuine naval battle, that was to come off during the day." A photographer, with all his apparatus and materials, perched himself on a church tower, to take an impression of the contest. Spectators swarmed upon every spot, commanding a view of the harbor and sea beyond, while boats flew about in every direction as on a great holiday.

The bells of the churches of Cherbourg had not yet done pealing, when the rebel steamer cast off her fastenings and began to steam slowly out of port. Semmes had taken the precaution to send ashore sixty chronometers that he had taken from his prizes, his money, and bills of ransomed vessels; thus showing that he was fully aware of the desperate character of the conflict that awaited him. As the steamer slowly drifted past the end of the mole, crowded with human beings, a great shout rent the air, and "God speed you," rolled over the waters. The next moment the drums were heard beating to quarters.

The iron-plated frigate, Couronne, accompanied her to the limit of the French waters, while the English yacht, Deerhound, followed in her wake out to sea. This was about half-past ten, and Winslow, as soon as he descried his adversary approaching, turned his ship's head seaward, to avoid the question of jurisdiction, and to draw the Alabama so far off that, in case of being disabled, she could not get back into port, and thus escape capture. The Alabama followed after, till the former was about seven miles from shore, when Winslow turned short about, and steered straight for the privateer, intending to run her down. The latter immediately sheered off and slowed her engines, presenting her starboard battery to her enemy. While the Kearsarge was still a mile off, there suddenly came sharp puffs of smoke from the side of the Alabama, followed by the heavy, dull reports of the guns that rolled heavily away over the shuddering waters.

The ponderous shell and shot flew over the Kearsarge and cut up her rigging, but did no serious damage. Winslow made no reply, but ordered the engineer to put on more speed, and the gallant steamer rolled the foam away from her bows as she dashed silently forward to a close death-grapple with her antagonist. In two minutes came another broadside—and then another; yet not a gun of the Kearsarge replied. Coming head on to the rebel steamer as she lay with her broadside to, she was in great danger of being raked, and so when about a half a mile distant, Winslow sheered in order to bring his own broadside to bear—and the battle commenced.

The firing now was rapid and incessant, and the two guns of the Kearsarge, carrying eleven-inch shell, sent their ponderous missiles with terrible accuracy into the hull of the Alabama. Winslow, fearing that his antagonist might after a while make again for the shore, ordered a full head of steam on, with directions to run under the stern of the Alabama and rake her. Semmes, however, discovered his design and sheered off so as to keep his broadside bearing on his antagonist. Hence the two vessels kept moving in independent circles round a common, yet ever changing centre. Sailing at the rate of nearly eight miles an hour, they thus swung steadily around each other, wrapped in the smoke of their own guns—the Alabama getting deadly blows from the calm and accurate firing of the Kearsarge, while the latter received no material injury for nearly twenty minutes. At length a sixty-eight pound Blakely shell passed through the starboard bulwarks, below the main rigging, and exploded on the quarter-deck, wounding three of the crew of the pivot gun, and among them a seaman named William Gowin, who, though suffering acutely, wore a smile on his face as he was brought to the surgeon. "It is all right," said he; "I am satisfied, for we are whipping the Alabama;" adding "I willingly will lose my leg or life, if necessary."

In the meantime the fight went on, and as the heavy broadsides shook the deck, he would comfort his two wounded comrades by telling them that "victory was certain;" and as ever and anon the cheers of the guns' crews on deck were borne to his ears, as they saw a shot planted in a vital part of the Alabama, he would wave his hand over his head, and with a smile lighting his pallid features, give a faint, answering cheer. His heroic spirit kept in this buoyant state till long after the victory, and he passed away, reiterating again and again as the sands of life ran low, "I am willing to die, for we have won a glorious victory."

Winslow fought his ship as coolly as though engaged in a simple manœuvre, telling the officers not to let the men fire too rapidly, but take deliberate aim. "Point," said he, "the heavy guns below rather than above the water line, and sweep the decks with the lighter ones."

In addition to her regular and effective armament, the Kearsarge had a twelve-pounder boat-howitzer, which was totally useless in the fight. This was put in charge of two old quartermasters, "the two Dromios" of the ship, with orders not to fire until directed to do so. But those rollicking old salts had no idea of remaining idle while their messmates were stripped to such deadly work, and having, as they said, all the fun. So without waiting for orders, when the heavy guns began to thunder over the sea, they loaded and fired their solitary howitzer as though the fate of the combat depended on their activity. Though perfectly aware of the harmlessness of their shots, they peppered away with all the gravity of men in dead-earnest, pausing between each discharge to curse and swear at each other in the most approved man-of-war style. Standing thus apart and firing their pop-gun in any direction with the most perfect gravity, and then pausing to abuse each other roundly, while the enemy's heavy shells were screaming and bursting above and around them, they made such an exceedingly ludicrous by-play, that the crew burst into peals of laughter. The officers, seeing in what excellent humor for cool fighting this farce kept the men, and amused at the mock earnestness and droll abusive language of these old weather-beaten favorites of the ship, did not interfere with them, and they kept on firing till they had exhausted the entire box of ammunition.

In the meantime the vessels, moving steadily in their respective circles, kept pouring in their heavy broadsides; the Alabama firing twice to the Kearsarge once; yet, so bad was her gunnery that out of over three hundred shots only twenty hit her antagonist, and only some fourteen of these pierced her hull—not killing a single man, and wounding but three. On the other hand, the slow and accurate firing of the Kearsarge told with terrible effect on the enemy. One shot alone killed and wounded eighteen men. Her two hundred pound shells, pierced the rebel ship at the water line, and bursting within, opened huge gaps, through which the water poured in torrents. The rudder of the latter was soon rendered useless, and by the time the vessels had made seven complete circles, report was made to Captain Semmes that his ship was sinking. He immediately hoisted sail, and ordered all steam on, hoping to be able to reach the French coast; but, finding the steamer fast settling in the water, he hauled down his colors and dispatched a boat to the Kearsarge to state that he had surrendered. In the meantime, he lowered the boats that had not been shot away, to receive the sick and wounded; but before all could be got off, the stern of the steamer sunk deep in the sea, lifting her bow into the air as though making a last effort to escape destruction,—ner mainmast breaking short off in the struggle—and then with one heavy lurch she went to the bottom. The parted waves closed with a loud splash above her form, as with all her guns, and some of her brave defenders she disappeared from sight forever. Thus perished this terror of the seas, after a fight of only an hour and two minutes. Amid the foam that tossed above the spot where she went down, appeared a mass of human heads struggling for life, and among the strong swimmers was Captain Semmes himself. The Yacht Deerhound having now approached within hailing distance of the Kearsarge, Winslow begged the Commander to go to the assistance of the drowning men, as he had but two boats. The latter did so, picking up Semmes and many of the crew, and carried them, together with the officer who had surrendered the ship, to Southampton.

Semmes in his report, by implication, charges Capt. Winslow with inhumanity. He not only declares that he fired on him after he struck his flag, but says: "There was no appearance of any boat coming to me from the enemy after my ship went down. Ultimately, the steam yacht Deerhound, owned by a gentleman of Lancashire, England, Mr. John Lancaster, who was himself on board, steamed up in the midst of my drowning men and rescued a number of both officers and men from the water. About this time the Kearsarge sent one, and then tardily another."

Now Mr. Lancaster, who was evidently hand and glove with the rebel Commander, contradicts this statement. His log book says, "At half past twelve, we observed the Alabama to be disabled, and in a sinking state. We immediately made toward her, and in passing the Kearsarge were *requested to assist in saving the Alabama's crew.*" And again, in a published letter, he says, "when we passed the Kearsarge, the captain cried out, 'For God's sake do what you can to save them.'" It was unquestionably very mortifying to Semmes to lose his ship; but that is no reason why he should endeavor to slander a gallant opponent. Again he says, "the enemy was heavier than myself, both in ship, and battery, and crew; but I did not know till the action was over that she was also iron-clad." This assertion is not borne out by the following figures:

	Alabama.	*Kearsarge.*
Length over all,	220 feet,	214 1-4
Length on water line,	210 "	198 1-2
Beam,	32 "	33
Depth,	17 "	16
Horse power—two engines,	300 each,	400 h. p.
Tonnage,	1,150	1,031

Thus much as to the size and tonnage of the two ships.

The armament of the Alabama was one seven-inch rifle-gun; one eight-inch smooth bore sixty-eight pounder; six thirty-two pounders.

That of the Kearsarge was two eleven-inch smooth bores; one thirty pounder rifle; four thirty-two pounders.

It will be seen by these figures, that the Alabama was the larger ship, and had one more gun than the Kearsarge, although the weight of the latter's broadside was the greater. The simple truth is, two more equally matched ships could not well be found. The "iron plating," which Captain Semmes makes so much of was simply some spare chain cable hung over the sides of the vessel midships, and boxed over with planking. This had been done a year before, and was well known in every port where she had since touched. Semmes was also aware of it, for he spoke about it some days previous to the fight, saying, "that the chains were only attached together with rope-yarn, and would drop into the water when struck with the first shot." If

Capt. Semmes wishes his character as a fighter to be judged by his reputation as a man of veracity, we fear his capture and firing of helpless merchantmen will furnish his greatest laurels.

In speaking of the conduct of the Deerhound, Captain Winslow says: "I could not believe that the commander of that vessel could be guilty of so disgraceful an act as taking our prisoners off, and, therefore, took no means to prevent it." The act of Mr. Lancaster was so generally condemned on both sides of the water, that this gentleman deemed it incumbent on him to make a public defense.

He says, "I had the earnest request of Captain Winslow to rescue as many of the men as were in the water, as I could lay hold of, but that request was not *coupled with any stipulation to the effect that I should deliver up the rescued men to him as his prisoners.* If it had been, I should have declined the task, because I should have deemed it dishonorable—that is, inconsistent with my notions of honor—to lend my yacht and crew for the purpose of rescuing those brave men from drowning, only to hand them over to their enemies for imprisonment, ill-treatment, and, perhaps, execution."

Now, there are several things to be noticed in this curious portion of his defense. First, a falsehood in the expression of fear that they might be delivered over "to execution." The war had been going on for over two years, and our Government had, at the very outset, in the first capture of a privateer, decided that the crews of such vessels should be treated as prisoners of war. In the second place, we are called upon to admire this gentleman's peculiar "notions of honor," which would have prevented him from "rescuing those brave men" from death, to hand them over as "prisoners," to a nation, distinguished for its humane treatment of the captured.

One would think that a proper sense of "honor" would prompt a man to give the poor fellows, at least, the choice of being rescued, or of drowning. We are quite sure the spent swimmers did not take his view of the case, as they cried for help, and struck out toward the boats. His logic, however, is more peculiar than his "notions of honor," or his veracity. He says that Captain Winslow accompanied his request to help save the sinking crew, "*with no stipulation* to the effect that I should deliver up the rescued men to him as prisoners." That is to say, because Captain Winslow did not wait to draw up a contract that he should deliver into his hands men that had already given themselves up as prisoners of war, there was no obligation resting on him to do so. To see the full beauty of this logic, let us suppose it had been property, not prisoners of war, floating on the sea; and Captain Winslow had requested the Commander of the yacht to assist him in saving it. By Mr. Lancaster's code of morals, after he had loaded his vessel down with a choice assortment, he would have steered away for Southampton with his spoils, and when called to account for them, have replied that Captain Winslow made "no stipulation with me to deliver up his goods." His high notions of honor would have compelled him to keep them—in other words, turn thief because "no stipulation" was made that he should not be one.

After clearing himself, as he supposes, from all blame, by this extraordinary defense, he says, that "the hero's (Captain Winslow's) forbearance," for not bringing him to, with a shot, when making off with the prisoners, may be "imagined in the reflection that such a performance as that of Captain Wilkes, who dragged two 'enemies,' or 'rebels,' from an English ship, would not bear repetition." Our fear, on the contrary, is, that such conduct, on the part of a member of "The Royal Yacht Squadron," will not "bear repetition."

This novel engagement, in which such heavy metal was thrown, caused much excitement in Europe. That the Kearsarge, without ever coming nearer than a quarter of a mile of her antagonist—a vessel of war heavier, even, than herself—should sink her in one hour, was a warning to the English Admiralty which, it was urged, they had better not disregard. There was not an eleven-inch gun in the English navy, yet the Kearsarge had two of these, throwing metal of two hundred pounds weight. Said one writer in the English press:—

"When the Kearsarge was recently at Cork, the Commander of her Majesty's ship, Hawke, was instructed by the Admiralty to report as to the construction and fitting up of the American cruiser, and more particularly as to her armament. He replied that the Kearsarge had no more effective guns than the ordinary sixty-eight pounder of the British navy. The Kearsarge is fitted up with a special contrivance for raising and lowering her great guns, so that they may be mounted on deck, or kept snugly below, as occasion requires.

"It is a curious speculation whether, when the Commander of the Hawke visited the vessel, a smart 'Yankee trick' was played upon him by this contrivance, or whether he made an actual blunder as to the armament."

Captain Winslow paroled his prisoners, which brought on him the condemnation of the Navy Department. In one letter to him, Mr. Welles says that it is reported, in the English papers, that he "has paroled the foreign pirates captured in the Alabama," and adds, "I trust you have not committed this error of judgment." In another, he says, "in paroling the prisoners, however, you have committed a grave error."

This is a fair specimen of the wise blunders constantly committed by our Navy Department; the head of which changes with every Administration, and who receives his appointment without reference to his knowledge of naval matters, but solely on political grounds. A serious war with one of the great maritime nations of Europe, will work a change, we apprehend, in this respect, and give us, at least, something in the Navy to correspond with Lieutenant-General in the Army.

The following reply of Captain Winslow, exhibits the vast difference between theoretical and practical knowledge:—

"I beg the Department will consider the circumstances in which this vessel was placed at the termination of the action with the Alabama. The berth-deck, contracted as it is, with insufficient storage for our own men, was covered with bedding of the wounded, the quarter-deck was similarly crowded, and the forward part of the ship, on the spar-deck, was filled with prisoners under guard.

"The ship was damaged both in rigging and hull. A shot had entered the stern-post, raising the transom-frame, and binding the rudder so hard as to require four men at the helm. It was, therefore, important that an examination should be made of the damages sustained. On our arrival at Cherbourg, I received information from our Consul at London, that the Florida was in the Channel, on the French coast, and, at the same time, information came that the Yeddo was out, and the Rappahannock was expected to follow; and, in addition to this, that the St. Louis had sailed for Madeira.

"The Kearsarge had been acting alone and independently for the last nine months, and I was not aware that any of our cruisers had been ordered in the Channel. It became, therefore, in my mind, of the utmost importance that the Kearsarge should at once be put in a state to meet these vessels, and protect our commerce. This could not be done with prisoners on board equaling the half of our crew, and the room occupied by the wounded taken to the exclusion of our own men; to have kept them would have required a quarter-watch as guards, and the ship would have been wholly ineffective, as a man-of-war, to meet this emergency which threatened.

"Under these circumstances, and without an American vessel in port by which any arrangement could be made for transhipping the prisoners outside, I felt it my duty to parole them."

CHAPTER XXXI.

MR. CHASE'S RESIGNATION—WANT OF A FINANCIAL SYSTEM—LOW STATE OF PUBLIC CREDIT WHEN HE ENTERED ON THE DUTIES OF HIS OFFICE—ESTIMATE OF EXPENDITURES FOR 1862—ISSUES OF FIVE-TWENTY BONDS AND TREASURY NOTES—FIRST LOAN MADE IN NEW YORK—LOAN TAKEN BY THE BANKS OF PHILADELPHIA, NEW YORK AND BOSTON—SALE OF BONDS, &C.—CUSTOMS TO BE PAID IN GOLD—SUSPENSION OF THE BANKS—STATEMENT OF REVENUE AND EXPENDITURES—PUBLIC DEBT AT THE CLOSE OF THE YEAR—OPENING OF THE YEAR 1863—AN EXCISE LAW RESOLVED UPON—RAISING OF MONEY IN THE MEANTIME—ISSUE OF PAPER MONEY—NATIONAL BANKING LAW—ITS EFFECT IN NEW YORK—GOLD BILL—STATEMENT OF REVENUE AND EXPENDITURE FOR THE YEAR—PUBLIC DEBT—MR. FESSENDEN SUCCEEDS MR. CHASE—CONDITION OF THE TREASURY AND MEANS AT ITS DISPOSAL—PUBLIC DEBT WHEN HE RESIGNED IN MARCH, 1865.

OUTLINE OF OUR FINANCIAL HISTORY DURING THE WAR.

THE first day of the month of July, 1864, was signalized by an event in the political field, that caused almost as much sensation as the news of the proposed invasion of the rebels. This was the announcement of the resignation of Mr. Chase, as Secretary of the Treasury

In a war of the magnitude of the one in which we were engaged, the question of finance was really the vital one; for all knew that money would give out before men would. Mr. Chase had never perfected and carried out any financial system whatever; his system had been one of expedients, based on the assumption that the war was always just on the eve of closing, and that it was only necessary to raise money on the public credit to meet a present emergency. In short, the Government appeared, in the eyes of the world, very much like a shaky railroad company, willing to mortgage its present property and future prospects, to get over present difficulties; or that of a heavy operator, who is willing to make any sacrifices, if he can only be tided over a dangerous crisis.

Still, in the new and unexpected condition of things, in which the Secretary of the Treasury found himself—the sudden and frightful call on the Government for money, and in our want of credit in the foreign market, it was hard to see what other course could be pursued. Fabulous sums were needed to carry on the gigantic war into which we had been forced, and there seemed no way to raise them except by the system of expedients which was adopted. The resignation of the Secretary of the Treasury, therefore, in the very crisis of our affairs, created a profound sensation, and various causes were assigned for it—some asserting that despair of meeting the enormous demands of the Government, was the motive—others, that personal disagreement with the President, in the matter of appointments; others, still, that he was a candidate for the Presidency, and could not support his successful rival; and still, others, that it was in consequence of the repeal of the "Gold Bill," as it was called.

Although the present work was designed to be only a history of the more important military events of the war, yet a brief account of the financial measures, by which it was carried on, seems necessary to its completeness.

As the financial policy was not changed, on the resignation of Mr. Chase, and Mr. Fessenden, who succeeded him, simply completed what was already begun, a history of our finances, under the former, is the history of them during the war.

Some faint idea of the difficulties that beset Mr. Chase's path, at the outset, may be gathered from the fact, that in the December previous to his inauguration into office, Howell Cobb, Mr. Buchanan's Secretary of the Treasury, put into the market five million dollars of treasury notes, payable in one year, and received bids for only a half a million, at twelve per cent.

If such was the credit of the Government, and such the difficulty in raising a small sum of money when war was threatened, one can imagine the prospect before the new Secretary, when war, the end of which no one could see, had actually commenced, and when, according to his own estimate, not five millions of dollars, but three hundred and nineteen millions, would be needed the first year to meet the wants of the Government.

Congress, which adjourned the first week in August, 1861, passed an act authorizing him to borrow two hundred and fifty million dollars by the issue of bonds not to be redeemed for twenty years, and bearing a no greater interest than seven per cent.; also to issue fifty million dollars in seven and three-tenths per cent. treasury notes, payable in three years, and of United States notes without interest, and payable on demand. A direct tax of twenty million dollars was also ordered to be levied—while the customs were increaed Of this, one hundred and eighty million dollars were appropriated to the Army, thirty millions to the Navy, and three millions to purchase and hire vessels.

It was an easy matter to authorize the Secretary to borrow money by the issue of interest-bearing bonds, and treasury demand notes, but it was another thing to find lenders. If it had been a foreign war in which we were engaged, we could have borrowed an unlimited amount of money abroad; but, in a war, which, in the eyes of other nations would end in the total disruption of the Government, not a dollar could be obtained. It must be raised at home or not at all, and obviously, to obtain the enormous sums that would be needed, the only course to be pursued was the one adopted by the Emperor of France,—viz.: make it a people's loan, by distributing it in small sums over the entire country. This could be done only through agencies established at every important point, to receive subscriptions. But it would take some time to get the machinery in complete working order and prepare the Seven and three-tenths treasury notes. In the meantime money was needed, and the Secretary therefore resorted to a temporary loan of five million dollars for sixty days, giving the Twenty-years' bonds as collateral security. This was taken up in a few hours in New York. He then visited the three great commercial cities on our Northern sea-board—Philadelphia, New York and Boston—and after a frank interview with the heavy capitalists, succeeded in getting the Banks to take fifty million dollars of the Seven-thirties at par; of which New York alone took more than two-thirds. It was left optional with the Banks to take two more issues to the same amount.

The various agencies established were very successful, so that thirty-eight millions of the fifty millions of dollars were taken up. The Banks then took the second issue of fifty million dollars, bearing date October 1st, 1861. In the meantime the demand notes, as they were called, were put in circulation, and a vast amount of State loans thrown upon the market, which so diverted the investment by the people in the treasury notes that the Banks refused to take the third issue of fifty million dollars, preferring the Twenty-years' six per cent. stock at a discount, that made it equivalent to a seven per cent. stock at par.

On the 1st of January, 1862, only a little over fifty million dollars of the treasury notes had been subscribed for, outside of the Banks, while twenty-four million dollars of demand notes had been issued, and fifty millions of Twenty-years' stock—though this sum had not been realized. Two years' six per cent. notes to the amount of fourteen million, nineteen thousand, three hundred and forty dollars and sixty-six cents had also been issued, and nearly thirteen million dollars had been borrowed on sixty days six per cent. notes—making in all one hundred and ninety-seven million, two hundred and forty-two thousand, five hundred and eighty-eight dollars and fourteen cents.

The tax of twenty million dollars gave us no revenue. It was apportioned to the several States, but of course was collectable only in the loyal ones; and in most cases as the amount they had already furnished in equipping the national troops equaled the amount of the tax, they were given credit for it, so that the only effect of the tax was to pay a debt which might have been deferred. In the firm belief that the war would be a short one, the Government had expended its wealth with an extravagance never before witnessed in any nation, and which, if persisted in for any length of time, whatever other national resources we might possess, threatened to end the war by national bankruptcy.

In the beginning of the year 1862, fifty million dollars of paper money had been set afloat, redeemable in coin, and receivable for customs. Government stocks were at a discount, and in the general panic and upheaving, the Banks, utterly indifferent to the laws under which they had been organized, suspended specie payment, and yet went on doing business as before. The increase of the army, and the lavish expenditures had raised the expenses of the Government to about two million dollars per day; and yet the first step had not yet been struck toward putting down the rebellion. The Army of the Potomac lay in front of Washington—the Mississippi was closed nearly up to the Ohio, and the lines of the enemy, with scarcely a break, extended along the southern border of the Northern States from Missouri to the Atlantic.

The financial prospect under these circumstances was appalling, and the question, "Where is all the money needed, to come from?" was one which might well stagger any Secretary of the Treasury. Congress might authorize loans, but who would take them, unless they could see some certain method adopted by which the interest would be paid. Direct taxation to the amount needed was not to be thought of, for the Constitution required that a direct tax should be laid according to population, which, as between the Eastern and Western States would be grossly unjust. It was very plain to men familiar with the financial history of Governments, that we must fall back on some system of *internal* taxation. But the excise laws of England were odious to our people, and regarded as fit only for an oppressive Government, and hence the party in power feared to enact them, lest it should be overthrown in the next election. Besides, the perfection of a system of internal revenue required time, while the Government was in pressing need of money, for it was heavily in arrears, both to the army and to contractors.

Still hugging the miserable delusion that the war would be over in a few months, Congress cast about for some way to raise enough for immediate wants, thinking that if these were once met, the danger would be over, and then the Government could gather up the raveled ends of its financial schemes, and once more bring order out of chaos.

The only method of immediate relief, therefore, seemed to be the issue of paper money—the last desperate resort of Governments on the verge of bankruptcy. So in the last of February the Secretary was authorized to issue one hundred and fifty millions of dollars in notes, in such denominations as he chose, down to five dollars. But knowing that paper money depreciated just in proportion to the amount issued, Congress saw that the public loan would not be taken if the interest was payable in paper, for a seven per cent. stock might actually turn out by this depreciation to be worth no more than an ordinary two or three per cent. stock, and it therefore enacted that the interest on the public debt should be paid in coin. This, of course furnished a strong inducement to invest in public securities, for the more paper depreciated the higher coin would go, and hence the higher the rate of interest would be. But the next question was, "Where shall the Government get this coin?" To go into the market and buy it, would stimulate speculation so that it could be obtained only at ruinous rates. It was therefore decreed that all customs should be paid in coin. This was in effect enacting over again the old protective tariff; for importers being compelled to go into market and buy their gold, its rise would be inevitable. Practically, therefore, the duties would be increased indefinitely, causing a corresponding rise in the price of goods. This of course would stimulate home manufacture. As from the embargo of 1812, and the protective tariff afterward, New England was made a manufacturing country, so now, by this practically high tariff all her machinery was set in full motion.

Another ingenious device was adopted for obtaining money for present use. The war had locked up a vast amount of wealth ordinarily invested in trade. But the holders, like every body else, believed the war was to be a short one, and therefore preferred that their capital should lie idle for a while, so that with peace it could be employed again in the more remunerative way of trade and commerce, than by being invested in Government securities at a fixed rate of interest. To get hold of this, the Secretary of the Treasury was authorized to receive twenty-five million dollars on deposit to be paid on ten days' notice, and to bear interest at the rate of five per cent. per annum, payable in gold. The bait took, and the whole amount was so quickly taken, that Congress authorized the reception of one hundred million dollars, interest payable in paper. Fruitful in all kinds of shifts, it also authorized the Secretary to issue certificates of indebtedness to the public creditors, bearing interest of six per cent.—at first payable in gold, but afterward in paper.

The Department had had for use during the year, two hundred and thirty-five million dollars—all but ten millions granted by the tariff law—being in seven and three-tenths three years' bonds, legal tender, and certificates of deposit. It had besides, one year six per cent. certificates to issue to any amount it chose.

The debt at the close of the fiscal year, as ascertained, was five hundred and fourteen million, two hundred and eleven thousand, three hundred and seventy-one dollars, while gold was at ten per cent. premium. There should be added to this, however, probably over a million dollars of arrears not yet audited. On this debt, twenty-two million dollars of interest in gold was to be paid. It had now become very evident that the war was not to be terminated speedily, and hence that these various expedients to raise money for present emergencies would not answer. No matter how unpopular a system of internal taxation might be for the party in power, it must be resorted to or the war be abandoned for want of means to carry it on. Congress therefore resolved to pass an excise law that should tax the entire industry of the country, and levy a tax on all incomes over six hundred dollars. We had taunted England with her oppressive taxation, saying that the poor man was taxed even for the light of heaven, and after his eyes had closed on that light forever, the very nails in his coffin were taxed, little dreaming that our boasted Republic would so soon follow her example.

But there was no help for it. Under this law stamp-duties were to be paid on all transactions and legal demands, and a three per cent. tax on all manufactures.

Such a law was something entirely new to our legislators, and it required time to perfect it—besides, the income tax was not to be collected till June of 1863. In the meantime, money must be had, for the Secretary had estimated that the expenditures, for the fiscal year of 1863, would be six hundred and ninety-three million, three hundred and forty-six thousand, three hundred and twenty-one dollars, independent of the public debt of ninety-five million, two hundred and twelve thousand, four hundred and fifty-six dollars.

This, however, was an under-estimate, for the military necessity, which soon after required the calling out of six hundred thousand men, swelled these expenditures so that Congress, instead of making an appropriation to meet the Secretary's estimate of nearly seven hundred million dollars, made one of eight hundred and eighty-two million, two hundred and thirty-eight thousand, and eight hundred dollars. To raise this amount, it authorized the issue of five hundred million dollars of six per cent. stock, redeemable in five to twenty years, and also an issue of notes for one hundred million dollars, which could be exchanged at par for the stock, making in all seven hundred million dollars. To make up the balance, the Secretary was empowered to issue fractional notes, under a dollar, to any amount.

This, apparently, reckless issue of Government paper, created general distrust, and gold, which only reached, the year before at any one time, one hundred and thirty-six and one-half per cent., touched, this year, one hundred and seventy-two and one-half per cent. To keep up the public credit, it was ordered that the Five-twenty bonds should not be sold at less than market value, while the holders of Government notes were allowed to exchange them for the bonds at par.

When Congress again met, the debt was stated to amount to fourteen hundred million dollars, without computing the enormous arrears that could only be guessed at, and which somehow must be met. In the beginning of the actual year the Secretary was authorized to issue one hundred million dollars of paper money, in order to meet the present obligations of the Government. He now asked Congress to amend the law respecting the sale of the Five-twenty bonds, fixing July as the limit, beyond which Government notes could not be converted into them at par. A law was also passed authorizing five hundred million dollars six per cent. stock to be issued, redeemable within forty years, but not till after ten—also, the issue of four hundred million dollars of notes, as low as ten dollars, to be legal tenders, bearing six per cent. interest in paper, and redeemable in three years. To these were added one hundred and fifty million dollars more, into which the smaller interest-bearing notes could be converted.

The unbounded license given to the Secretary to issue fractional paper currency was now taken away, and the amount fixed at fifty million dollars.

This enormous issue of paper bewildered the public, and it seemed as though nothing short of a miracle could save the nation from hopeless bankruptcy. Abroad, there was not the slightest doubt that we were rushing headlong into financial ruin.

Another law was passed which caused great excitement, completely revolutionizing the whole banking system of the country. This was the National Banking Law, authorizing Banks, in all the States, secured in Government stocks, to circulate notes redeemable in Government paper. This circulation was limited to three hundred millions of dollars, based on the same amount of Government securities. But there were already more Banks in the country than the wants of the community required, and it was plain that these must be converted into National Banks, or be killed, or the system would fail of success. The change could be easily made, for it was only necessary to change the securities which they held into Government securities.

But many of the States preferred their own banking system, especially the great State of New York, which compelled its Banks, in the main, to be secured by the State stocks. It had so perfected its banking system, that should every Bank in the State fail, its notes would be redeemed dollar for dollar. Besides, by making its own stock the basis of banking, it enhanced the value of it, so that whenever it wished to make a loan, the Banks not only took all the stock with avidity, but the competition was so great to secure it, that it was always at a large premium—its six per cent. stock, having a long time to run, going, in some instances, as high as seventeen per cent. above par. Thus its banking system not only made loans easy, but caused them to be taken at a premium that materially lessened the interest. To change it, therefore, was to depreciate at once the value of its own securities. This depreciation would, also, cause a great loss to the Banks, for the stocks held by them could not bring, in the market, the prices they had paid for them. Hence, in every way the law was distasteful to the State.

To force the State Banks to change into National Banks, Congress passed a law taxing their notes ten per cent. As it had long ago been decided that Government securities were not taxable, the States could not retaliate by taxing the National Banks—at least, it was very questionable whether any State legislation could offset this discrimination against the State Banks, and so the latter gradually converted themselves into National Banks. This, of course, required the absorption of a large amount of Government securities.

But, independent of its being a present benefit, this system, if let alone by new administrations, will be a lasting one, by giving us a uniform currency throughout the country; a desideratum acknowledged by every business man.

Under the agencies and commissions authorized by the Treasury Department, the sale of the Five-twenties went briskly on, and the Secretary extended the limit in order to dispose of the whole. The deposits on five per cent. certificates filled up the limit of one hundred millions of dollars, so that for the last three months of the fiscal year, ending with June, the Treasury was well supplied.

Gold fell nearly a half, goods went down, and in the very midst of our troubles, everything seemed about to revive. At its close the debt was one thousand and ninety-eight million, seven hundred and ninety-three thousand, one hundred and eighty-one dollars, without reckoning in the arrears, amounting probably to two hundred millions more. The interest on the funded debt was forty-two million, two hundred and seventy-eight thousand and two dollars, and seventy-three cents. Unfunded, one hundred and eighty millions of dollars.

At the beginning of the fiscal year of 1864, there were over four hundred and eleven million dollars of outstanding legal tender money. The constant forcing of paper issues on the market depreciated necessarily its value, and again raised the price of gold. Still the financial resources of the country had been developed in a manner that astonished the most hopeful, showing an amount of available wealth never dreamed of before. Our unparalleled prosperity for so many years had induced an extravagant, expensive mode of living, so that the extraction of these vast sums from the people produced comparatively little suffering—it demanded only the practice of a wholesome economy.

The total revenue from all sources this fiscal year was one hundred and eleven million, three hundred and ninety-nine thousand, seven hundred and sixty-six dollars. Added to this, we borrowed seven hundred and seventy-six million, six hundred and eighty-two thousand, three hundred and sixty-one dollars; making in all eight hundred and eighty-eight million, eighty-two thousand, one hundred and twenty-eight dollars with which to meet an expenditure of eight hundred and ninety-five million, seven hundred and ninety-six thousand, six hundred and thirty dollars. It was impossible to estimate very closely the expenditures of the year 1864, for the constant depreciation of paper brought up the price of every thing the Government would have to buy. It was plain that the taxes would not meet it, and therefore the Government must go on borrowing. The Secretary stopped in January the sale of the Five-twenty bonds. Having previously issued fifteen million dollars more of legal tender notes, he now, with the stoppage of the sale of these bonds issued one hundred and fifty million dollars more of these notes, bearing interest.

In the meantime, the amount of customs largely exceeded the estimate, so that after paying the interest on the public debt a surplus of gold was left, which by law was to be applied to the purchase of one per cent. of the public debt as a sinking fund.

This whole surplus was eventually sold in the market, and the premium obtained credited to the Government. It seemed a very discreditable thing for the Government to go into the market to speculate on its own depreciated paper, but the object was to bring down the price of gold, which speculators were forcing up to a ruinous rate. But the most remarkable effort to bring down the price of gold this year, remarkable from the enormous *advance* it produced, was what was called the "Gold Bill." Congress having passed a resolution increasing the duties on imported goods fifty per cent., for sixty days, to take effect on the 28th of April, large entries of goods were made, which increased the demand for gold, and hence caused it to advance in price. To stop its farther advance, the "Gold Bill" was concocted, which forbade any one to sell exchange for specie at more than ten days time, and no where except over the counter of the individual banker. This law was odious not only as infringing on personal rights, but it crippled bankers, by making them afraid to act as their business relations required. It besides, exposed them to informers, who were ready to make complaints on any pretense, as half the fine would go to them. Moreover, the short term fixed by the law for which a contract for exchange might run, interfered sadly with the ordinary shipping business done in New York for the West. Fifteen or sixteen days were required to complete arrangements between even Chicago and New York, hence foreign exchanges were at a dead stand-still. If, for instance, certified checks could not be used, it was difficult to see how ordinary business could be carried on. It is true that the Solicitor of the Treasury finally gave it as his opinion that the Act did not require the "formal delivery of the notes in currency by the buyer to the seller," for the amount of gold or bullion purchased on the day in which the contract was made, but that a bona-fide check for the amount in United States notes or currency was valid payment, and also, that although the law "prohibits contracts for the purchase or sale and delivery of foreign exchange, except on conditions of immediate payment in full of the agreed price thereof on the day of delivery in United States notes, or national currency," yet, "that a payment for exchange in gold coin of the United States was a legal and valid payment;" thus relieving bankers from their greatest fears. Still gold went steadily up, till at the close of the fiscal year it stood at *two hundred and ninety.* On the last day of the fiscal year this absurd bill was repealed, and the same day Mr. Chase resigned and Mr. Fessenden took his place.

The total receipts of this year, from receipts of customs, loans, taxes and every source, were two hundred and sixty million, six hundred and thirty-two thousand, seven hundred and fifty-seven dollars, while the expenses, and interest on this debt, amounted to eight hundred and sixty-five million, two hundred and thirty-four thousand and eighty-seven dollars. The revenue, therefore, fell short six hundred and four million, six hundred and one thousand, three hundred and seventy dollars of meeting the expenditures. This enormous balance was borrowed as we have seen, on bonds of various kinds, notes, certificates of indebtedness, fractional currency, &c., the whole amount so borrowed being seven hundred and thirty million, six hundred and forty two thousand, four hundred and ten dollars and ninety-seven cents; of which, one hundred and twelve million, five hundred and twenty-seven thousand, five hundred and twenty-six dollars and five cents were expended in repayment of the public debt, leaving over six hundred and eighteen millions to be applied to the expenditures. The receipts from customs this year, reached the large sum of one hundred and two million, three hundred and sixteen thousand, one hundred and fifty-three dollars, while the interest to be paid in coin was only fifty-three million, six hundred and eighty-five thousand, four hundred and twenty-one dollars, leaving over forty-eight and a half millions in gold in the public treasury, which, as we previously stated, was sold, and a premium of over nineteen million dollars obtained, and put down as miscellaneous receipts.

When, in 1864 Mr. Fessenden came into office, he found as we have seen, the Government paper worth only thirty-five cents on the dollar, with customs falling off. But the tax law had been revised and now promised to furnish a larger amount of money than before, while a five per cent. extra income tax was levied on the incomes of the year before, which of course would increase the amount of revenues. There were nearly nineteen million dollars in the Treasury, when he accepted the office of Secretary, while under laws previously passed, he had a right to borrow, first, thirty-two million, four hundred and fifty-nine thousand, seven hundred dollars—that portion of the seventy-five million dollars advertised before the close of the former fiscal year, and which had not been awarded to bidders—and also one hundred and twenty-seven million, six hundred and three thousand, five hundred and twenty dollars, the amount which had not been subscribed for, and paid under the Act of March 3d, 1864, besides four hundred million dollars under an Act passed the last day of the fiscal year. A little over sixty-two million dollars of treasury notes had been redeemed and canceled, which he had authority to replace, so that altogether the available resources in the hands of the new Secretary amounted to six hundred and forty-one million, one hundred and twenty-seven thousand, two hundred and thirteen dollars and seventy-one cents. Of course he could not do otherwise than follow on in the track of his predecessor.

Our bonds now began to sell abroad, which obviated very much the issue of legal tender notes.

Mr. Fessenden continued in office until March, 1865, when the war was drawing to a close, at which time the public debt was twenty-four hundred and twenty-three million, four hundred and thirty-seven thousand and one dollars.

It had increased at the rate of two and a half million dollars a day since he took charge of the Treasury Department.

From what revenues we are to establish a sinking fund to pay off this enormous debt, it does not yet appear. Of course when the tax for paying the interest, now levied on the North, shall be distributed in proper proportion over the South, the burden will be lightened; but this generation, we fear, will look in vain for any material diminution of the debt. Still, returning prosperity may develop resources of which we are now ignorant.

CHAPTER XXXII.

ALARM PRODUCED BY EARLY'S INVASION—SIGEL'S RETREAT—WEBER ABANDONS HARPER'S FERRY—THE PIRATE FLORIDA ON OUR COAST—THE REBELS CROSS THE POTOMAC AND OCCUPY HAGERSTOWN—HEGIRA OF THE PEOPLE—MILITIA CALLED OUT—GENERAL WALLACE GIVES BATTLE AT MONOCACY—RETREATS—ALARM IN BALTIMORE—RAILROAD CUT BETWEEN BALTIMORE AND PHILADELPHIA—GENERAL FRANKLIN TAKEN PRISONER—GOVERNOR BRADFORD'S HOUSE BURNED—THE MAIN ARMY MOVES ON WASHINGTON—SKIRMISHING IN FRONT OF FORT STEVENS—ARRIVAL OF THE NINETEENTH AND SIXTH CORPS—THE REBELS RETREAT—PURSUIT BY WRIGHT—ESCAPE OF THE INVADERS—AVERILL AND CROOK AND DUFFIE ENGAGE A PORTION OF THE ENEMY—COMPELLED TO RETREAT ACROSS THE POTOMAC—THE REBEL MCCAUSLAND ADVANCES TO CHAMBERSBURG AND BURNS IT—ATTACKED IN HIS RETREAT AND HIS FORCES SCATTERED AMONG THE MOUNTAINS—EARLY PREPARES TO REMAIN IN THE SHENANDOAH VALLEY—GRANT VISITS HUNTER—HIS LETTER OF INSTRUCTIONS—SHERIDAN PUT IN HIS PLACE—POLITICAL EVENTS—FIVE HUNDRED THOUSAND TROOPS CALLED FOR—PEACE NEGOTIATIONS—JACQUES AND KIRK—GREELY, JEWETT, SANDERS AND OTHERS—"TO WHOM IT MAY CONCERN"—ABSURDITY OF THE PEACE NEGOTIATIONS.

ALTHOUGH the months of May and June, both West and East, had been crowded with events of a magnitude and national interest, hitherto unknown in our history, yet the month of July saw Washington in a state of excitement scarcely equaled since the disastrous battle of Bull Run in July, 1861; while in Maryland and Pennsylvania, the alarm and consternation of the year before, on the invasion of Lee, were repeated over again.

The disappearance of Hunter from the Valley of the Shenandoah, as before remarked, was the signal for a new invasion of Maryland. On the 2nd, it was announced that the enemy was approaching Martinsburg, on his way to the Potomac. On the 3rd, Sigel, in command there, retreated across the river, at Shepardstown, with his immense trains, and Weber, in command of Harper's Ferry, also crossed over and occupied Maryland Heights. Frederick City was thrown into consternation, the public stores were removed, and the streets thronged with people bearing their goods with them, fleeing to a place of safety. On the 6th, Hagerstown was occupied by the enemy, who was found not to be on a mere raid, for his force was altogether too large for such a purpose. The roads were now thronged with refugees, some with vehicles of every kind pressed into service, to carry their little possessions toward Baltimore; others, on foot, driving their cattle before them—all filled with terror, and circulating the most extravagant reports of the number and blood-thirstiness of the enemy. The region around Hagerstown became depopulated, and a universal hegira of the inhabitants seemed about to take place.

There were no troops, or scarcely none, to oppose this sudden invasion. The enormous losses of Grant had caused him to call forward the troops in the neighborhood of Washington and Baltimore, even in the garrisons over the Potomac; and Early, for the time being, had a clear field. On the 6th, he moved a strong column toward Frederick City. General Wallace, with Rickett's division, and such troops as he could gather, most of them new and undisciplined, moved out from Baltimore to arrest his progress, and met him in force, on the Monocacy, near where the railroad bridge crosses it, and gave him battle. After a severe loss, Wallace was compelled to retreat.

In the meantime, the President had called on New York, Massachusetts, and Pennsylvania, for their quotas of militia, and the scenes of the Summer previous were enacted over again. Railroads and steamboats groaned under the weight of troops hurrying on toward Washington, and it was feared by many that the consternation there would compel the President to demand the presence of Grant's army around the National Capital, and the war once more be transferred to the neighborhood of the Potomac.

The Mayor of Baltimore called on the citizens to man the fortifications, as the enemy was marching on the city. "Come as leagues, or come in military companies, only come in crowds, and come quickly," he said, and the drum and fife rang through the streets, to call out volunteers to meet the pressing danger. Fortunately, immediately after the failure of the Red River expedition, Grant had ordered home the Nineteenth Army Corps, which now began to arrive at Hampton Roads, and was immediately hurried on to Washington. Hunter, the Commander of the Shenandoah Department, with his army, being unavailable at present, Grant also dispatched the Sixth Army Corps, under Wright, to assist in repelling the invasion, and two divisions followed fast on the heels of the Nineteenth Corps.

Early having swept Wallace from his path, moved rapidly down on Washington, by the Washington and Frederick turnpike. In the meantime, a body of rebel cavalry, under Gillmore, pushed on toward Baltimore, and striking the railroad between that city and Philadelphia, captured a train, and setting it on fire, run it upon Gunpowder bridge, destroying for a time, direct communication between Washington and the North. Major-General Franklin, just from New Orleans, was on board, and being pointed out by a rebel sympathizer, was taken prisoner. He, however, afterward managed to escape while his guard were asleep. A rebel squad boldly pushed to the suburbs of Baltimore, and burned the house of Governor Bradford, in retaliation, they said, for the burning, by our forces, of the dwelling of Governor Letcher, of Virginia. Other detachments wandered hither and thither unmolested, collecting forage and supplies for the army, and levying contributions on the inhabitants. The main army, however, which had grown, by popular rumor, from four or five thousand to forty thousand, pressed rapidly toward Washington, hoping to take it by surprise before the weakened garrisons could be reinforced. Five miles from the city and two miles from the fortifications, it drove in, on Sunday night, our pickets, and, next morning, the skirmishers were in rifle-shot of Fort Stevens, three miles from Georgetown. Firing continued here all the forenoon, and, by two o'clock, the sharp-shooters, under cover of the houses, had advanced to within thirty or forty rods of the fort. During the afternoon, the main column arrived and showed a strong line in front of it. From appearances, it was conjectured that a general assault would take place next morning. The skirmishing had been heavy the latter part of the day, our loss reaching nearly three hundred. The Sixth happily arrived just in time to save the fort. The rebels, doubtless, learned of the sudden reinforcement of the garrison, by this veteran Corps, and that night retreated—their chief conquest being some papers taken from the residence of Francis P. Blair in the vicinity.

Grant understanding the exact condition of things, telegraphed to Washington to have General Wright placed in command of all the troops in the field, operating against the enemy, and directed him to move at once outside of his trenches, and "push Early to the last moment."

With the retreat of the rebel army, the cavalry that had threatened Baltimore, and carried consternation even to Annapolis, began to fall back to the main body.

Although Wright pushed on after Early, the latter was able to cross the Potomac, near Poolesville, with his immense plunder—vast herds of cattle being not the least conspicuous figure in the moving caravan.

In the midst of these exciting events, came the startling news that the rebel privateer Florida was on our coast, and had captured five vessels. War vessels were immediately sent in pursuit of this daring cruiser, which seemed to vie in the boldness of his movements with the presumptuous invaders that were pressing up to the very gates of the Capital.

General Wright, in pursuing Early, whose force it was pretty well understood was about twenty thousand men, crossed the Potomac at Edward's Ferry and advanced toward Leesburg, where Rickett's division, which had parted from the corps, to aid Wallace, joined it. Four days after, a portion of Crook's cavalry, under Duffie, captured a part of the rebel trains near Snicker's Gap. Crook, with the main body, coming up, was repulsed, and the following day Duffie was roughly handled by Breckenridge, at Island Ford, on the Shenandoah, losing three hundred men. As the enemy moved on toward Winchester, Averill near this place had an engagement with a rebel division, defeating it with heavy loss and capturing four guns. Crook and Averill now joined their forces, and Early, finding himself closely pressed by this large body of cavalry, rapidly concentrated a large force, which on the 24th fell with such fury on the Union cavalry, that it was compelled with severe loss to retreat, and recrossed the Potomac, leaving the southern shore in possession of the rebels, from Williamsport to Shepardstown. The latter occupied Martinsburg, and again commenced to tear up the Baltimore and Ohio railroad track, which had suffered so severely in every advance of the rebels to the Potomac.

Hunter had now got back with his shattered army, and once more confronted his old enemy that chased him over the mountains from Lynchburg. On the 30th McCausland with a body of cavalry recrossed the Potomac, and, moving rapidly upon Chambersburg, demanded a ransom of half a million of dollars from the inhabitants, which they refusing to pay, he fired the town, destroying a vast amount of property. Retreating toward Cumberland, the force was met and defeated by General Kelley, and scattered among the mountains of Western Virginia. The rebels now held the Shenandoah Valley, and evidently meant to hold it till the crops were harvested, for Early had made a requisition on the inhabitants for a large amount of grain.

Communications between Hunter, whose forces were concentrated on the Monocacy, and Grant at City Point, were very uncertain, and movements would often take place in the interim materially changing the aspect of affairs, so that orders given to day, might by the time they reached Hunter be such as Grant would not give. He, therefore, left City Point on the 4th to visit him, and see for himself what was best to be done. On reaching Hunter's head-quarters, and consulting with him, he gave him the following instructions:—

"MONOCACY BRIDGE, Md., August 5, 1864—8 P. M.

GENERAL:—Concentrate all your available force without delay in the vicinity of Harper's Ferry, leaving only such railroad guards and garrisons for public property as may be necessary. Use, in this concentrating, the railroads, if by doing so time can be saved. From Harper's Ferry, if it is found that the enemy has moved north of the Potomac in large force, push north, following him and attacking him wherever found; follow him if driven south of the Potomac, as long as it is safe to do so. If it is ascertained that the enemy has but a small force north of the Potomac, then push south with the main force, detaching under a competent commander a sufficient force to look after the raiders, and drive them to their homes. In detaching such a force, the brigade of cavalry now *en route* from Washington *via* Rockville may be taken into account.

There are now on their way to join you three other brigades of the best cavalry, numbering at least five thousand men and horses. These will be instructed, in the absence of further orders, to join you on the south side of the Potomac. One brigade will probably start to-morrow. In pushing up the Shenandoah Valley, where it is expected you will have to go first or last, it is desirable that nothing should be left to invite the enemy to return. Take all provisions, forage, and stock wanted for the use of your command: such as cannot be consumed destroy. It is not desirable that the buildings should be destroyed—they should rather be protected—but the people should be informed that so long as an army can subsist among them, recurrences of these raids must be expected, and we are determined to stop them at all hazards.

Bear in mind the object is to drive the enemy south, and to do this you want to keep him always in sight. Be guided in your course by the course he takes.

Make your own arrangements for supplies of all kinds, giving regular vouchers for such as may be taken from loyal citizens in the country through which you march.

U. S. GRANT, Lieutenant-General.

Major General D. HUNTER."

The troops were immediately put in motion, and the advance reached Halltown that night. Grant, however, had no intention of leaving Hunter in command of the Department. He felt that he needed a different kind of a man—one who would require no instructions, and no watching; and, though he speaks in as delicate a manner as possible of Hunter's removal, saying, that in "his conversation with him the latter expressed his willingness to be relieved from command," yet that conversation was evidently of a character to leave no room for choice, for two days before Grant left City Point, he sent on Sheridan to report to Halleck, for the sole purpose of taking Hunter's place. Carrying out this purpose, he immediately telegraphed to Washington to have Sheridan come on by the morning train, to assume command of all the forces designed to operate against Early. He arrived on the morning of the 8th, and had a consultation with the Lieutenant-General in relation to military matters in that section, after which the latter returned to City Point.

On the 11th, the Middle Department, the Departments of West Virginia, Washington, and Susquehanna were constituted into the "Middle Military Division," and Major General Sheridan was assigned to temporary command of the same, and the Shenandoah Valley, the scene of so many disasters was to enter on a new history.

The army around Petersburg this month, parched with heat, and suffering for want of water, lay comparatively quiet.

The month closed, however, with another desperate attempt to carry Petersburg by assault. A part of Butler's army had been thrown across the James River, on the north side, so that Grant's lines extended at this time over twenty miles. A strong fort crowned an eminence in front of Burnside's Corps, (the Ninth,) which it was thought, if once carried, would let the assaulting columns into the very heart of the enemy's works. It was, therefore, determined to undermine this and blow it up, and in the terror and confusion of the explosion, to charge through, and take the rebel works in flank and rear.

The mine that was to lift it, like an earthquake, from its firm foundations, was commenced at the distance of five hundred feet, in the sides of a ravine. It was said that the plan originated with Lieutenant-Colonel Pleasants, of the Forty-eighth Pennsylvania regiment, which was composed chiefly of miners.

A gallery like one leading to a coal mine, was constructed about four and a half feet high, and four feet wide, ending at a point directly under the fort, and twenty feet below it. When, as ascertained by actual scientific measurement, this subterranean arch-way got directly beneath the fort, two wings were sent out, to the right and left, extending under the entire structure. It was a work of great labor, but, in the latter part of the month, was finished, and eight tons of powder placed in the subterranean gallery to which was attached a fuse that led outside.

The plan was to have assaulting columns, which in the confusion of the explosion and under cover of a horrible fire of nearly a hundred pieces of artillery, would open simultaneous with the explosion, rush in and occupy a crest beyond, that completely commanded the enemy's defenses.

The 30th was fixed for the explosion of the mine. To give however a greater chance of success, Grant determined to make a strong demonstration against the enemy, on the north side of the James, as though he contemplated an advance on Richmond in that direction, and thus draw off the rebel force from the real point of attack. In carrying out this plan, Grant says, "that on the night of the 26th of July, the Second Corps, and two divisions of the Cavalry Corps, and Kautz's cavalry, were crossed to the north bank of the James River, and joined the force General Butler had there. On the 27th, the enemy was driven from his intrenched position, with the loss of four pieces of artillery. On the 28th, our lines were extended from Deep Bottom to New Market road, but in getting this position were attacked by the enemy in heavy force. The fighting lasted for several hours, resulting in considerable loss to both sides. The first object of this move having failed, by reason of the very large force thrown there by the enemy, I determined to take advantage of the diversion made, by assaulting Petersburg before he could get his force back there. One division of the Second Corps was withdrawn on the night of the 28th, and moved during the night to the rear of the Eighteenth Corps, to relieve that Corps in the line, that it might be foot-loose in the assault to be made. The other two divisions of the Second Corps and Sheridan's cavalry were crossed over on the night of the 29th, and moved in front of Petersburg."

The 30th being, as before stated, fixed upon for the explosion of the mine, a little after midnight, on the 29th, the Ninth Corps, which was to make the assault, was drawn up and closely massed in front of it, to rush in the moment it took place. Half-past three o'clock in the morning was the hour fixed upon for lighting the train, and as it approached, the troops were greatly excited. But three o'clock passed, and all remained quiet as before. The waiting troops looked on each other in mute inquiry, and the gunners standing beside their loaded pieces, wondered at the delay. The fuse had gone out in the gallery, and for an hour the mighty host watched and waited in vain. Daylight in the meantime had broadened in the East, revealing every object distinctly, and the rebel flag was seen waving listlessly above the unsuspecting garrison.

The fuse was now again lighted, and just as the sun burst in blazing splendor above the horizon, the explosion took place; but it being so deep underground, the heaving and trembling of the earth was felt before any sound was heard. The next moment, the fort rose into the air in fragments, and mingled with great clods of earth, guns, caissons and limbers, was seen a cloud of human forms tossing in the air. The mighty mass rose like the jet from some huge fountain, and when it reached its highest elevation, balanced a moment in space, and then fell back with a dull, heavy, thunder sound, in wreck to the earth.

A crater, a hundred feet long, and fifty feet wide, and twenty feet deep, appeared where the six-gun fort had been, over which hung a cloud of mingled dust and smoke like a great pall. The next moment, came the roar of a gun, and then another and another, till a hundred cannon along our line were playing upon the rebel batteries. The bugles rang out, the drums beat, and in dashed Ledlie's division—Marshall's brigade leading the advance. Though taken wholly by surprise, the rebels rallied with wonderful quickness, and in a short time, from right and left, their artillery was in full play on the storming party, that, with loud cheers, charged on a run over the intervening space. The Fourteenth New York heavy artillery first entered the gap, followed by Marshall's second brigade, which went pellmell into the smoking crater, from the bottom of which protruded half buried limbs and mangled bodies of men.

To the right and left, Hartranft's and Griffin's brigades

spread out, enveloping the flanking rifle-pits, and, for a moment, success seemed certain. But instead of pushing on, the troops began to dig out the wounded and the captured guns, and throw up breastworks to protect themselves from the enemy's shells. This gave the rebel gunners time to train their guns with fearful accuracy on the spot, and by the time the troops were re-formed and ready to push on, a fire awaited them, before which nothing human could stand. Still undaunted, the Corps in three divisions—Ledlie in the centre, Potter on the right, and Wilcox on the left—moved swiftly forward; Marshall again leading, followed close by the gallant Bartlett. They breasted the horrible fire until they reached the side of the coveted crest, when they halted. From every redoubt, salient, and earthwork, shot and shell and canister came in one ceaseless stream, and the shattered Corps, after swaying a moment in the vain effort to breast it, recoiled bleeding, to the crater they had just left. Ferrero's colored division was now sent in to do what white troops had failed to accomplish, but though they charged gallantly, it was madness to expect them to succeed where veteran soldiers, under such leaders as Griffin, Marshall, and Bartlett, failed. Recoiling, they only helped to swell the confusion, as they plunged headlong amid the ruins for shelter.

The enemy now concentrated his fire on this single spot, and swept the space in rear of it, so frightfully, that an orderly retreat over it was out of the question. Unable to advance, cooped up in the crater, over which swept an incessant storm of shot and shell, the position of the troops was most distressing. But little order could be maintained, and the men in squads began to flee back to our lines. About noon, a general retreat was ordered, but a portion preferred to remain in the fort, and left alone were soon after charged upon and captured. Among the prisoners was General Bartlett, with most of his Staff.

Our loss in this fruitless assault, was about four thousand, while that of the enemy was not over fourteen hundred, two hundred of whom were supposed to have perished in the blowing up of the fort. The next day was a gloomy Sabbath, and we sent in a flag of truce to obtain permission to bury our dead, but, through some informality, it was not granted until next day.

The Army of the Potomac seemed doomed to useless butcheries, and this one, like others that preceded it, caused intense excitement throughout the country. The blame fell now on this Commander, and now on that, but Burnside had to bear the brunt of it, and in the end was relieved from his command to await an investigation. This ended his military career. It is not so easy to fix the blame on one person.

The great error, however, seems to have been the neglect to have the storming force consist of picked regiments and brigades from the whole army.

Along the coast but little was done. Farragut was getting ready for his grand attack on Mobile, while our batteries kept playing on Charleston. An attempt was made by our land forces and iron-clads to get possession of James Island, but failed.

In the political world, the chief events were the adjournment of Congress, after perfecting the income-tax bill, and the organization of the two great parties for the coming political campaign. Perhaps the most important event outside of operations in the field, was the proclamation of the President, calling for five hundred thousand additional troops. This requisition for half a million of men, right on the top of Grant's campaign, looked as if the war had only just begun, and filled the timid with alarm.

This call for troops, which we give below, shows no timidity on the part of the President, but if possible, a more fixed determination than ever to put down, at all cost, the wicked rebellion.

"WASHINGTON, July 18, 1864.

By the President of the United States of America:

A PROCLAMATION.

WHEREAS, by the Act, approved July 4, 1864, entitled 'An Act further to regulate and provide for the enrolling and calling out the National forces, and for other purposes,' it is provided that the President of the United States may, at his discretion, at any time hereafter, call for any number of men as volunteers, for the respective terms of one, two, and three years, for military service, and 'that in case the quota, or any part thereof, of any town, township, ward of a city, precinct, or election district, or of a county, not so subdivided, shall not be filled within the space of fifty days after such call, then the President shall immediately order a draft, for one year, to fill such quota, or any part thereof, which may be unfilled.'

AND WHEREAS, the new enrollment heretofore ordered is so far completed as that the afore-mentioned Act of Congress may now be put in operation for recruiting and keeping up the strength of the armies in the field, for garrisons and such military operations as may be required for the purpose of suppressing the rebellion and restoring the authority of the United States Government in the insurgent States;

Now, therefore, I, ABRAHAM LINCOLN, President of the United States, do issue this, my call for five hundred thousand volunteers for the military service, provided, nevertheless, that all credits which may be established under section eight, of the aforesaid Act, on account of persons who have entered the naval service during the present rebellion, and by credits for men furnished to the military service in excess of calls heretofore made for volunteers, will be accepted under the call for one, two or three years, as they may elect, and will be entitled to the bounty provided by law for the period of service for which they enlist.

And I hereby proclaim, order and direct, that immediately after the fifth day of September, 1864, being fifty days from the date of this call, a draft for troops, to serve for one year, shall be held in every town, township, ward of a city, precinct, election district, or a county, not so subdivided, to fill the quota which shall be assigned to it under this scale, or any part thereof, which may be unfilled by volunteers on the said fifth day of September, 1864.

Done at the City of Washington, this 18th day of July, in the year of our Lord, 1864, and of the Independence of the United States, the eighty-ninth.

[L. S.] In testimony whereof I have hereunto set my hand and caused the seal of the United States to be affixed.

ABRAHAM LINCOLN.

By the President,

WILLIAM H. SEWARD, Secretary of State."

The promptness with which the country responded to the call, would have reflected the highest credit on its patriotism, but for the manner in which that response was made. Instead of the bone and sinew of the land stepping forward to sustain the Government in its last great effort, every man seemed desirous to shirk personal responsibility, and non-tax-payers, or men of small means, in the various towns, voted away fabulous sums for bounties to get recruits from any-where and every-where, and of all conditions, to fill up their quotas—often forcing on the Government the halt, the lame, and the blind, and at the best, mere mercenaries, who would enlist for the enormous bounties, but without any intention of risking their lives in battle.

Getting such men away, after they had enlisted, became a regular business, so that, of the five hundred thousand called for, not more than half ever reached the field, and probably not half of those, the front. At all events, one hundred and fifty thousand strong-bodied, patriotic, willing men, would have been worth more than the whole half-million proved to be. Nor was this the worst of it. The country got saddled with a debt, in the shape of bounties, that bore heavily on its industry. Had the war been prolonged another year, the North would, unquestionably, have broken down under this false and ruinous system.

The month, moreover, was distinguished for peace negotiations—ludicrous, except from the importance of the personages, on one side or the other, engaged in them. Colonel Jacques, of Illinois, a Methodist clergyman who had enlisted in the army, and a Mr. Kirke, by some extraordinary process, appointed themselves peace ambassadors to Richmond, and though clothed with no authority, were permitted to pass through our lines to the rebel Capital, where they actually had an interview with the rebel President and Members of his Cabinet, and talked over, with the gravity of two potentates, the momentous question of peace, and the duties of the two Governments.

What motive Davis could have had for seriously entering into such a discussion with these unauthorized, unknown and uninfluential men, unless that he wished to give utterance to views that might help the peace-party North, it is difficult to conjecture. That a fighting parson, ranking no higher than a colonel, and an obscure individual spoken lightly of among business men at home, should by any management, have got into this position, will remain one of the curious things of the war.

The other attempt was equally absurd, though dignified by the employment of a little more political machinery.

Early in July, Horace Greeley, of *The New York Tribune*, received a letter from W. Cornell Jewett—a political adventurer, who had acquired at home and abroad a certain doubtful notoriety—stating that some prominent rebels then residing in Canada, desired to have an interview with him at Niagara Falls, respecting terms of peace. It was flattering to Mr. Greeley, to be thus selected out among all the distinguished men of the country as the proper person to influence the President, and stand in the great gap that divided the North and South. Fully impressed with the responsibility thus laid upon him, he addressed a letter to the President, and vouchsafed to state conditions of peace, which he thought the President might safely adopt.

A few days after, the notorious rebel agent, George N. Saunders, informed Mr. Greeley that Clement C. Clay, of Alabama, Professor Holcomb, of Virginia, and himself were ready, the moment they could be assured of their personal safety, to proceed at once to Washington and enter on their momentous mission.

To this Mr. Greeley replied, that if they were "duly accredited from Richmond, as the bearer of propositions looking to the establishment of peace," &c., that he was "authorized by the President of the United States to tender them his safe-conduct on the journey proposed," and that he would accompany them "at the earliest time convenient" to them.

That accredited ambassadors for peace should fear to come to the head of a Christian Nation, in this enlightened age, without having a promise that their heads should not be cut off, was certainly very extraordinary, and not very complimentary to Mr. Lincoln's civilization.

To this offer, these gentleman replied that there had been some misapprehension, as they were not accredited from Richmond as the bearers of dispatches, but, being in the confidential employment of the Confederate Government, familiar with its wishes, views, &c., they had no doubt if the rebel President was aware of what they had done, that they would be at once accredited, &c. On the reception of this statement, Mr. Greeley telegraphed to Washington for further information, and received the following extraordinary document:—

"EXECUTIVE MANSION, July 18th, 1864.

To whom it may Concern:—

Any proposition which embraces the restoration of peace, the integrity of the whole Union, and the abandonment of Slavery, and comes by and with an authority that can control the armies now at war against the United States, will be received and considered by the Executive Government of the United States, and will be met by liberal terms, on substantial and collateral points, and the bearer or bearers thereof, shall have safe-conduct both ways.

Signed, ABRAHAM LINCOLN."

This was certainly a very safe circular, but not one that should have proceeded from the Executive Mansion, for it cannot be regarded as a serious act—it must have been either a political move to disarm the peace-party, or a somewhat grave joke, which would put an end to Mr. Greeley's importunity, and, at the same time, throw a shell into this self-constituted embassy. Viewed in this light, it was, perhaps, a good stroke of policy. Though correspondence and lengthy statements followed this *denouement*, the whole thing collapsed, and was heard of no more.

It was very plain to the President, and to every man of common sense, that if Jefferson Davis wanted peace on the only terms the North would accept it, he would not have to go around by way of Canada, to commence negotiations. The two Capitals were close to each other, and no such farce as this was needed to bring the conflicting powers face to face, if both were desirous of peace.

Personal notoriety and political effect were, doubtless, the motives that prompted these gentlemen to undertake this self-imposed task.

CHAPTER XXXIII.

FORTS MORGAN AND GAINES—DEFENSES OF MOBILE BAY—A LAND FORCE UNDER GENERAL GRANGER SENT TO CO-OPERATE WITH FARRAGUT—ARRIVAL OF THE TECUMSEH—FARRAGUT READY TO RUN THE REBEL BATTERIES—MORNING OF THE BATTLE—THE SHIPS LASHED TWO TOGETHER—THE BROOKLYN TO LEAD THE FLEET AGAINST FARRAGUT'S WISHES—THE FIRST GUN—THE BROOKLYN FEARING TORPEDOES—BACKS AND AWAITS THE FLEET—FARRAGUT LASHED IN THE MAIN-TOP, SEEING THE DELAY, TAKES THE LEAD JUST AS THE TECUMSEH GOES DOWN—HE SENDS A BOAT TO SAVE THE SURVIVORS—STEAMS AHEAD—ENTERS THE BAY—ATTACKED BY REBEL GUNBOATS—THE SELMA CAPTURED BY THE METACOMET—THE REBEL RAM TENNESSEE ATTACKS THE FLEET—THE COMBAT—SURRENDER OF THE RAM—THE TECUMSEH—A BRAVE ENSIGN—GALLANT DEEDS AND GALLANT MEN—SURRENDER OF FORTS POWELL AND GAINES—SIEGE AND BOMBARDMENT OF FORT MORGAN—ITS SURRENDER—DISGRACEFUL CONDUCT OF ITS COMMANDER AND OFFICERS—MOBILE NOT TAKEN—CAPTURE OF THE PRIVATEER GEORGIA.

FARRAGUT ENTERS MOBILE BAY.

THE beginning of August was made memorable by one of the most gallant naval achievements on record. Farragut, who had been lying for a long time, outside of Mobile harbor, the entrance to which was defended by two forts—Morgan and Gaines—determined, the moment that the iron-clads which he had asked for arrived, to force his way inside, when he knew they must surrender. The former fort, located on a long spur of land, commanded the two channels to the east, while the latter commanded the western one. Beyond these, toward the city, the channel was obstructed by piles driven deep into the mud. Several rebel steamers were also in the bay, and a formidable iron-clad ram, named the Tennessee. In July, a land force, under General Granger, was sent from New Orleans to assist Farragut in taking the forts. On the first of August, General Granger visited him on the Hartford, and after a consultation, it was decided that a combined movement of the fleet and army should be made on the 4th.

The Tecumseh had arrived at Pensacola on the 1st, and Captain Craven, the Commander, had informed the Admiral that he would be ready in four days for any service. He was delayed, however, in getting aboard coal, so that Farragut, to his mortification, could not keep his engagement with Granger. The latter, however, as he said, "was up to time," and landed his troops (some four or five thousand in number) on Dauphin Island, in rear of Fort Gaines. That evening, the Tecumseh came steaming up from Pensacola, and Farragut at once prepared to force the entrance to the harbor.

The morning of the 5th dawned warm and hazy—a light south-west breeze came drifting across the Gulf, raising a gentle swell, on which the fleet rocked lazily, and all was peaceful as though no preparations were afoot to change the quiet scene into one of tumult, terror and death. But just as the half-veiled sun was sending his dim beams aslant the sea, the drum on the flag-ship was heard beating to quarters, and soon every ship was cleared for action.

At a quarter before six, the whole fleet was moving steadily forward toward the entrance to the bay, where, every Commander knew, slumbered a volcano whose earthquake throes would make land and sea tremble. There were twelve wooden vessels in all, and four iron-clads. The latter already inside the bar, were ordered to take up a position between the wooden vessels and Fort Morgan, to keep down the fire of the water-battery and the parapet guns of the fort, as well as to engage the rebel ram, Tennessee, waiting to pounce down on the fleet.

The wooden vessels were lashed two abreast. The Brooklyn, Captain James Alden, led the fleet, with the Octorara, Lieutenant-Commander C. H. Greene, on the port side—next came the flag-ship Hartford, Captain Percival Drayton, with the Metacomet, Lieutenant-Commander J. E. Jouett; followed by the Richmond, Captain T. A. Jenkins, with the Port Royal, Lieutenant-Commander, B. Gherardi; Lackawanna, Captain J. B. Marchand, with the Seminole, Commander E. Donaldson; Monongahela, Commander J. H. Strong, with the Kennebec, Lieutenant-Commander W. P. McCann; Ossipee, Commander W. E. LeRoy, with the Itasca, Lieutenant-Commander George Brown; Oneida, Commander J. R. M. Mullany, with the Galena, Lieutenant-Commander C. H. Welles.

The Brooklyn, with her consort, took the lead, much against Farragut's wishes. He yielded, however, to this arrangement at the earnest request of the Commanders, who represented that the Brooklyn had four chase guns to the Hartford's one; and also an ingenious machine for picking up torpedoes with which they believed the channel to be lined. They stated, moreover, that in their judgment, the flag-ship, on whose movements and signals, everything depended, ought not to be so much exposed as she would be at the head of the fleet.

Although Farragut yielded to their united petitions, he demurred, saying that "exposure was one of the penalties of rank in the navy," and, moreover, that it made but little difference where the flag-ship was, as it would always be the main target of the enemy's fire.

The fleet steamed slowly on, and at a quarter to seven, the Tecumseh fired the first gun. Twenty minutes later, the fort opened her fire, to which the Brooklyn replied with her two one hundred-pounder Parrott rifles, on the bow—and the battle commenced. The rebel ram and iron-clads lying under the protection of the fort, added their fire to the guns of the latter, all playing, almost exclusively, on the wooden vessels. Farragut stood lashed in the main-top, so that he could overlook the fleet, and have a clear view of the whole field of action.

The Brooklyn, for a while, gallantly led the fleet, but as she entered the narrow channel, some suspicious looking buoys ahead, indicating torpedoes, caused her to stop, which of course, at once brought to a halt, the vessels that were crowding after. Farragut, from his high perch, saw with alarm this unexpected arrest of the onward movement right under the terrible fire that was raining on the advance vessels, and looking anxiously around, saw, with amazement, the turrets of the Tecumseh disappearing under the water, as she went down with her gallant crew. In an instant, his determination was taken, and regretting that he had not originally followed his own judgment and led the fleet, he steamed rapidly ahead, and his glorious signal flew where he wanted it, in advance. Ordering the Metacomet to send a boat to save any of the survivors of the ill-fated Tecumseh, who might be struggling in the water, he swept fearlessly onward.

Wrapped in the smoke of his own guns, he pressed on into the fire, followed by the ships, "their officers," he heroically says, "believing they were going to a noble death, with their Commander-in-Chief." Shot and shell crashed through the wooden sides of his vessel yet his flag still flew, and those astern ever and anon caught glimpses of his signal through the rifts of smoke, still beckoning them on. He too saw the buoys that had caused the Brooklyn to hesitate and back water, and knew that torpedoes were lining the bottom of the channel beneath him, but this was no time to hesitate.

He "determined," he says, "to take the chances of their explosion," and still kept on, his gallant crew expecting every moment to feel the vessel lift beneath them, yet working their guns as coolly as though standing on solid ground, and, meanwhile, pouring in such terrific broadsides that the rebel batteries fired wildly, or were silent. At ten minutes before eight, he was past the fort, when suddenly the rebel ram dashed out to run his vessel down, firing as it came on. Taking no notice of the monster, except to return the fire, he steamed ahead toward the rebel gun-boats, Morgan, Gaines and Selma, which poured a raking fire into him. The latter especially cut down his crew fearfully, and spread ruin and destruction over his deck.

Not being able to return the fire, he cast off the Metacomet, with orders to go after these boats. Seeing the vessel approaching, the latter retreated up the bay, firing as they fled. The Gaines soon took refuge under the guns of the fort, but was so injured that she had to be run ashore and burned—the Morgan hauled off and left the Selma to her fate, which soon after struck her flag.

The other vessels gallantly following in the wake of their noble Commander, one after another swept past the hostile batteries and passed up the bay, their crews loudly cheering, and were signaled by Farragut to come to anchor. But the officers had hardly commenced clearing their decks, and caring for the wounded, when the rebel ram was seen boldly standing out from under the guns of the fort, and bearing down, with the evident intention of engaging the whole fleet. If she had waited till dark this would not have been such an act of temerity, for with her perfect knowledge of the bay, and in the confusion that would have prevailed in the fleet in a nocturnal fight, she might have run down many vessels—at least, made sad havoc before her progress could have been arrested.

The moment it was reported to Farragut that the ram was standing toward the fleet, he signaled the vessels to run her down, and ordered up the anchor of his own ship, and directed the pilot, with a full head of steam on, to carry the Hartford straight against the iron-clad structure, hoping, by the concussion, though his own bows should be crushed in the shock, to stave in its mailed sides. The Monongahela, Commander Strong, first struck the ram, carrying away her iron prow and cut-water. The Lackawanna came next and struck with such force that her stern was cut and crushed for the distance of three feet above the water's edge, to five feet below. The only effect on the ram, however, of this tremendous blow, was to give her a heavy list. As the Hartford came down, the ram sheered so that it was a glancing blow.

Deadened in her headway, as she rasped along the iron-plating, the flag-ship fell along side, and at once poured in, at a distance of not more than eight or ten feet, her broadside of nine-inch solid balls, sent with a charge of thirteen pounds of powder. The heavy shot, hurled with this awful force, and in such close proximity, fell on the mailed sides of the ram with a power that seemed irresistible, and yet, apparently, had no more effect than if they had been mere India-rubber balls.

On the other hand, the shot and shell from the Tennessee pierced the Hartford as though her sides were mere pasteboard—one one-hundred-and-fifty-pound shell, fired with the muzzle of the monster gun almost touching the sides of the ship, exploded inside, killing and wounding several men—the fragments going through the spar and berth-decks, "even going through the launch and into the hold where were the wounded."

The Hartford now stood off, and though her bow was badly crushed, began to make a circuit, in order to come down again on the ram, when the Lackawanna, which was driving, with a full head of steam, straight on the monster, struck the flag-ship instead, a little forward of the mizzen-mast, and cut her down to within two feet of the water.

The monitors, in the meantime, poured in their fire—the Chickasaw got under the monster's stern, while the Manhattan sent a fifteen-inch shell through the iron plating.

"At this time," says Farragut, "she was sore beset—the Chickasaw was pounding away at her stern, the Ossipee was approaching her at full speed, and the Monongahela and Lackawanna, and this ship, were bearing down on her, determined on her destruction. Her smoke-stack had been shot away, her steering chains were gone, compelling a resort to her relieving tackles, and several of her port shutters were jammed. Indeed, from the time the Hartford struck her, until her surrender, she never fired a gun. As the Ossipee, Commander LeRoy, was about to strike her, she hoisted the white flag, and that vessel immediately stopped her engine, though not in time to avoid a glancing blow."

This ended the fight, and at ten minutes past ten Farragut again brought his shattered vessels to anchor, within four miles of Fort Morgan. Admiral Buchanan, the Commander of the ram, was wounded in the leg, which afterward had to be amputated; and some eight or ten of his crew were killed or wounded.

The killed and wounded on board the fleet, amounted to two hundred and twenty-two. Only fifty-two were killed, of which number twenty-five, early half, were killed on board the flag-ship—showing that the enemy's fire was concentrated on this vessel, and that she bore the brunt of the conflict.

The loss of the Tecumseh, with her gallant Commander

and crew, nearly all of whom went to the bottom with her, chastened somewhat the joy of this great victory. Craven was in the turret when the torpedo exploded beneath his ship. He saw the buoys that marked the line along which the torpedoes lay, and endeavored to carry the vessel between two, but just as it got in range, the explosion took place, almost lifting the iron-clad from the water, and blowing a great opening in the bottom, through which the water rushed in such a deluge that she went down before those below had time to get on deck.

Acting-Ensign Henry C. Nields had charge of the boat, sent by Farragut to rescue any survivors that might be struggling in the water, and right gallantly did this noble, young officer perform the perilous duty, with which he was intrusted. Sitting in the stern of the open boat, he gave his orders as coolly as his great Commander could have done, and the rowers bent steadily to their oars, while shot were striking and shells bursting momentarily, on every side of them.

A boat was never carried through a more terrible fire, and it rained an iron tempest on the spot where the ill-fated monitor had gone down; but the fearless ensign rowed calmly through it, picking up the few swimmers that were struggling in the water, and succeeded in rescuing ten within six hundred yards of the fort. Farragut, from the main-top, saw with pride how steadily he entered the horrible fire, and afterward asked that he might be promoted.

The only other vessel lost was the steamer Philippi, which followed the fleet in against orders, and being struck by a shot, was run ashore by her Commander and deserted, when the rebels burnt her.

There were many cases of individual heroism—indeed, all were heroes—there was no flinching any where, although every captain knew that the probabilities were against his being able to save his ship. Of his Flag-Lieutenant, J. Crittenden Watson, who stood on the poop during the entire action, attending to the signals, Farragut says, "He is a scion worthy the noble stock he sprung from."

"The last of my Staff," he says, "to whom I would call the attention of the Department, is not the least in importance. I mean Pilot Martin Freeman. He has been my great reliance in all difficulties, in his line of duty. During the action, he was in the maintop, piloting the ships into the bay. He was cool and brave throughout, never losing his self-possession. This man was captured early in the war, in a fine fishing smack, which he owned, and though he protested that he had no interest in the war, and only asked for the privilege of fishing for the fleet, yet his services were too valuable to the captors, as a pilot, not to be secured. He was appointed a first-class pilot, and has served us with zeal and fidelity, and has lost his vessel, which went to pieces on Ship Island. I commend him to the Department."

Indeed, every man on the flag-ship was worthy of his Commander. Drayton, the Flag-Captain, says:—

"Of the crew, I can hardly say too much. They were, most of them, persons who had never been in action, and yet I cannot hear of a case where any one attempted to leave his quarters, or showed anything but the sternest determination to fight it out. There might, perhaps, have been a little excuse, had such a disposition been exhibited, when it is considered that a great part of four guns' crews were, at different times, swept away almost entirely by as many shells. In every case however the killed and wounded were quietly removed; the injury at the guns made good, and in a few moments, except from the traces of blood, nothing could lead one to suppose that any thing out of the ordinary routine had happened."

Kimberly, the executive officer of the ship, said, "nothing could be more noble than the spirit displayed by our wounded and dying, who cheered and smiled, in their agony, seemingly contented at the sacrifice of their lives for the victory vouchsafed to their country. Such men are heroes."

No higher commendation could be passed on a ship's crew, and yet all the Commanders spoke in the same strain of their own crews.

In one case, a rifle-shell burst between two guns on the Hartford, killing and wounding fifteen men. They presented a terrific sight, as they lay scattered, mangled and bleeding on deck. One of them, Charles Melville, was taken down to the surgeon, but almost immediately appeared on deck again, and though scarcely able to stand, refused to go below, and bravely worked at his gun till the close of the action.

"Thomas Fitzpatrick, Captain of Number One gun, was struck several times in the face by splinters, and had his gun disabled by a shell. In a few minutes he had his gun in working order again, with new truck breeching, side-tackle, &c., his wounded below, the deck clear, and was fighting his gun as before, setting a splendid example to the remainder of the crew."

James R. Garrison, coal-heaver, had his great toe shot off, but dressing the wound himself, returned to his station, and remained there till struck in the breast, when he was carried below. Thomas O'Connel, though sick, and scarcely able to stand, took his station and kept it till his right hand was shot away. James E. Sterling, coal-heaver on board the Brooklyn, continued to pass shell after he was wounded, and until hit a second time and completely disabled. Alexander Mack, Captain of top, was wounded and sent below, but immediately returned and took charge of his gun, working it until he received two more wounds. Others left a sick-bed to fight, and each seemed to vie with the other to set an example of gallant daring.

The Hartford was struck twenty times, and fired nearly two hundred and fifty shot and shell. The Brooklyn picked out eleven hundred pounds of iron from her wood-work after the battle was over.

Farragut exhibited great foresight in the plan he adopted in passing the fort. By lashing two ships together, he saw if one got disabled, she would not drift about and disorder the line, for her consort could take her along—neither would any vessel be left helpless under the fire of the batteries.

The night after the battle Fort Powell was evacuated, the rebels blowing it up, but all the guns fell into our hands. The next afternoon, the Chickasaw went down and shelled Fort Gaines, and the following morning, Colonel Anderson, the Commander, sent a note to Farragut, stating that he knew he could not hold the fort, if the fleet opened upon it, and offered to surrender it—asking for terms. Farragut, after communicating with General Granger, on Dauphin Island, replied,

"First, The unconditional surrender of yourself and the garrison of Fort Gaines, with all of the public property within its limits.

"Second, The treatment which is in conformity with the custom of the most civilized nations toward prisoners of war.

"Third, Private property, with the exception of arms, will be respected."

These terms were accepted, and at a quarter to ten, the rebel flag came down and the Stars and Stripes went up, amid the prolonged and vociferous cheering of the fleet.

Fort Morgan, however, still held out, and Granger at once commenced his siege operations against it landward, and on Sunday evening, the 21st, announced to Farragut that he was ready to open with his batteries upon it. The latter immediately ordered the monitors and vessels to move up, and be ready next morning at daylight, to commence the bombardment, in conjunction with the land batteries, and at the same time, landed four nine-inch guns, and placed them in battery under the Commanding-Lieutenant, H. B. Tyson.

Everything being ready at daylight the signal was given, and from land and water, the bombardment commenced. As the sun rose in the East, his beams fell on a scene as terrific as that which they lighted up on the morning of the 8th, when Farragut steamed boldly into Mobile Bay. Gun answered gun, and shell crossed shell in their fiery tracks, mingling their explosions with the roar of cannon, and combining to make that summer morning one long to be remembered.

As Farragut said, "a more magnificent fire has rarely been kept up." All day long it rained a steady, horrible tempest of iron, on that solitary fort. As the beams of the *rising* sun fell on a tossing, sulphurous cloud—covering land and water—so now his departing rays cast a lurid light on the heaving masses of vapor, that shut out half the terrors of the scene.

Just as twilight began to creep over the deep, the citadel of the fort took fire, and Granger seeing the flames burst forth, ordered all the batteries to re-double their fire to prevent their extinguishment. The enemy finding that the fire had got under uncontrollable headway, flooded the magazine, and threw large quantities of powder into the wells to prevent an explosion.

A fierce bombardment was kept up all night, ribbing the darkness with ghastly seams of light, as shell after shell, with scarcely a moment's intermission, dropped inside the rebel works. At six in the morning, a dull, heavy explosion was heard in the fort, and half an hour afterward, a white flag was seen to emerge from it. General Page, the Commander, offered to surrender the fort, and asked the terms of capitulation. Unconditional surrender at two o'clock that day, was the reply, which the rebel General was forced to accept.

In his indignation and mortification, however, he determined to lessen as much as possible the value of the victory, for after the surrender, Farragut says, "It was discovered, on an examination of the interior, that most of the guns were spiked, and many of the gun-carriages wantonly injured, and arms, ammunition, provisions, &c., destroyed; and that there was every reason to believe that this had been done after the white flag had been raised. It was also discovered that General Page, and several of his officers, had no swords to deliver up, and further, that some of those which were surrendered, had been broken."

He contrasts this conduct with that of Colonel Anderson, of Fort Gaines, who "from the moment he raised the white flag, scrupulously kept every thing intact, and in that condition delivered it over; whilst General Page and his officers, with a childish spitefulness, destroyed the guns which they said they would defend to the last, but which they never defended at all, or threw away, or broke those weapons which they had not the manliness to use against their enemies; for Fort Morgan never fired a gun after the commencement of the bombardment, and the advanced pickets were repeatedly on the glacis."

There never was a more striking illustration of the ease with which a mean and dishonorable Commander may increase his disgrace, by the attempt to lessen it, than this. These few sarcastic words of Farragut, who knew how to admire a brave and honorable foe, will stick to General Page as long as the history of the country endures.

Though the outer defenses of Mobile were now all taken, the city was as far as ever from falling into our hands. The water was too shallow to allow the approach of our vessels to within shelling distance, and though Farragut used every device to reach the place, it soon became evident that it could be taken only by a land force.

In the latter part of this month, the Niagara captured off the coast of Europe, the Japan, or Georgia, a noted rebel privateer, though at the time of her seizure, she was sailing under English colors, and chartered to the Portuguese Government.

CHAPTER XXXIV.

GRANT'S CEASELESS ACTIVITY—BLOWING UP OF AN ORDNANCE BOAT—DUTCH GAP CANAL—WARREN'S FIGHT FOR THE WELDON RAILROAD—BATTLE AT REAM'S STATION—DEFEAT OF HANCOCK'S CORPS—MEADE'S DISPATCHES—SHERIDAN'S OPERATIONS IN THE SHENANDOAH VALLEY—PURSUIT OF EARLY—CAPTURE OF OUR TRAINS BY MOSBY—RETREAT OF SHERIDAN—HIS POSITION AT BOLIVAR HEIGHTS—A SECOND ADVANCE—TAKES POSITION AT BERRYSVILLE—UNSATISFACTORY CAMPAIGN—DISAPPOINTMENT OF THE COUNTRY—GRANT'S EXPLANATION OF THE WHOLE MATTER—THE PERMISSION TO "GO IN"—SHERIDAN MOVES IN EARNEST—BATTLES OF OPEQUAN CREEK AND FISHER'S HILL—TOTAL ROUT OF THE ENEMY—EARLY TAKES A NEW POSITION AT BROWN'S GAP—SHERIDAN FALLS BACK.

THE month of August, which gave such laurels to the navy under Farragut, at Mobile, and saw Sherman's gallant army virtually in possession of Atlanta, witnessed no triumphs of the Army of the Potomac. It brought instead what seemed to be the heritage of this sadly tried, but noble army—terrible fighting, heavy losses, but no success. Grant, though apparently at a dead-lock with the enemy in front of Petersburg, did not sit down in idleness. He kept the heavens, around Lee, constantly muttering thunder-notes of alarm, and almost every day the bolt threatened to fall in one direction or another. Indefatigable, untiring, and exhaustless in resources, no sooner did one thing or measure fail, than he tried another. He was the most unsleeping, merciless antagonist that an enemy ever had to deal with, and Lee soon discovered that he never could calculate on a moment's repose. At the very time when he thought his enemy exhausted, and would naturally seek rest, the greatest energy would be put forth.

The rebels, taught wisdom by the mine that destroyed one of their forts, began to countermine, and on the 5th, sprung a mine in front of the Eighteenth Corps, where they supposed we were running one of our own, but it produced no effect. One of our own ordnance boats, however, blew up five days after, at City Point, killing and wounding two hundred men.

Butler now commenced the famous Dutch Gap canal, which, like the one he dug around Vicksburg, was expected to work wonders. The James River, just below Fort Darling, makes an immense bend, inclosing a peninsula, called Farrar Island, the neck of which, where it joins the mainland, is only a half a mile across, while it is six miles around it by the stream. It was prosecuted under the constant fire of the enemy, but, like the Vicksburg canal, was useless labor.

At this time, Grant says, "reports from various sources led me to believe that the enemy had detached three divisions from Petersburg to reinforce Early in the Shenandoah Valley. I therefore sent the Second Corps, and Gregg's division of cavalry, of the Army of the Potomac, and a force of General Butler's army, on the night of the 13th of August, to threaten Richmond from the north side of the James, to prevent him from sending troops away, and, if possible, to draw back those sent. In this move we captured six pieces of artillery and several hundred prisoners, detained troops that were under marching orders, and ascertained that but one disvision, (Kershaw's,) of the three reputed detached, had gone.

"The enemy having withdrawn heavily from Petersburg to resist this movement, the Fifth Corps, General Warren commanding, was moved out on the 18th, and took possession of the Weldon railroad."

Here he was attacked furiously, the next day, by Hill,

with two divisions, and a portion of our army was overwhelmed; and for a time, a second disaster at this point, seemed inevitable. But the gallant Fifth Corps succeeded in rallying, and, by a desperate charge, retrieved its ground, driving the rebels in confusion, and capturing many prisoners. Night, at length, closed the conflict. Our loss, this day, was between three and four thousand—that of the enemy, in killed and wounded, probably about the same as ours, though he took many more prisoners than we.

A few days after, the rebels again attacked Warren's position, but this time they were handsomely repulsed, with heavy loss—Generals Saunders and Lamar being among the killed. Warren now pushed his lines toward Petersburg, while the Second Corps, which had in the meantime arrived. began to tear up the railroad in rear of him.

At Ream's Station, this gallant Corps of Hancock, on the 25th, suffered a severe repulse. The rebels, under Hill, at about half-past three in the afternoon, suddenly emerged from the woods, in front of Miles and Gibbon, and with fixed bayonets and loud cheers, swept swiftly over the intervening space. Four batteries at once concentrated their fire on the column, and shot and shell and canister tore through it with awful destruction. Yet, through it, and through the steady fire of musketry, that swept without cessation the close formations, they kept on till within twenty paces of our line, when, unable to breast the fiery sleet any longer, they recoiled. Undismayed, they not long after repeated the desperate charge, but with similar results. They then brought up their batteries, and played furiously on our lines for nearly a half an hour, when the firing suddenly ceased, and with loud yells, and without firing a shot, they again sprang forward—crossed the interval that separated them from our lines, reached the breastworks, mounted them with deafening shouts, and forced Miles back, capturing several guns.

A part of Gibbon's men, a half a mile distant, were hurried over, to check the disaster, when his own line was attacked in turn by the dismounted rebel cavalry, under Wade Hampton, and his works carried. The enemy now pressed his advantage on all sides. Our troops fought desperately—some regiments being almost annihilated—but could not arrest the onset; and as night came on, Hancock withdrew his Corps, and left Ream's Station in possession of the enemy. In this disastrous conflict, we lost thirty-five hundred men, seven colors, and five guns.

The loss, however, had not been all on one side, as is evident from the two dispatches sent from Meade to Grant. In the first he says that a safeguard left on the battle field until after daylight next morning reported that "at that time the enemy had all disappeared, leaving their dead on the field unburied. This shows how severely they were punished, and doubtless hearing of the arrival of reinforcements, they feared the results of to-day if they remained." In the second he says, "since sending my last dispatch, I have conversed with the safeguard referred to. He did not leave the field until after sunrise. At that time nearly all the enemy had left, moving toward Petersburg. He says they abandoned not only their dead, but wounded also. He conversed with an officer, who said that their losses were greater than ever before during the war. The safeguard says that he was over the field, and it was covered with the enemy's dead and wounded. He has seen a great many battle fields, but never such a sight. Nearly all the enemy's and all our wounded were brought off, but our dead were unburied. I have instructed General Gregg to make an effort to send a party to the field to bury our dead." There can be no doubt that the enemy in their desperate charges through the concentrated fire of our batteries, and into the very faces of such veterans as composed Hancock's Corps, must have suffered terribly. Still General Meade's dispatches bear the marks of an effort to put the best possible face on a very bad business. When the results of a desperate battle are made to depend on the statements of a single individual, who has been over the field, they should be received with many grains of allowance. One would infer from these dispatches that the battle field was so entirely ours that a single safeguard could roam over it unmolested, making such observations as he liked. But if this were the fact, it seems rather strange that the Chief of cavalry should be "instructed to make an effort to send a party to the field and bury our dead." The fact is the battle put the rebels in possession of the Weldon railroad at Ream's Station—which was only ten miles from Petersburg—up to Yellow Tavern, while Warren held some four miles of it further north.

This ended all active operations on the part of Grant for several weeks. In the meantime the country was expecting great things from Sheridan in the Shenandoah Valley. He had under him the Sixth, Eighth and part of the Nineteenth Corps of infantry, and the troops that composed the old Army of the Kanawha under Crook, and Torbett's and Averill's divisions of cavalry, with Kelley's command, and Lowell's brigade, to which in a few days was added the second cavalry division of Wilson, from the Army of the Potomac. To meet this force Early had about twenty thousand men, who, previous to Sheridan's assumption of command, seemed to be principally engaged in thrashing out grain.

On the 10th of August, Sheridan moved his forces up the Valley, when the enemy retired toward Strasburg. Occasional skirmishing, and once a partial engagement took place, but without any decisive result except to delay our progress, and inflict on us more or less loss. At Newtown, Early made another stand in order to cover the passage of his trains, and repulsed a charge of our cavalry. Still falling back, he evacuated Winchester, and on the 13th encamped at Cedar Creek, three miles north of Strasburg. Two days after, he withdrew his skirmishers from the place and took position on Fisher's Hill, which completely commanded the town. Sheridan in pushing on, had passed several gaps in the Blue Ridge, which he had not sufficient force to guard. Through one of these,—Snicker's Gap—Mosby suddenly rushed, pouncing on the supply train at Berrysville, seized and burned seventy-five wagons, captured two hundred prisoners, two hundred beef cattle, and nearly six hundred horses and mules, besides a large quantity of stores.

This of course, compelled Sheridan to retreat in turn. In doing this, he with his flanking cavalry destroyed every thing that could feed the enemy, except the live stock which he drove before him as he fell back toward the Potomac. Houses of suspected persons were burned, in retaliation of Mosby's murderous conduct, by some cavalry-men who in turn were attacked by the rebels and deliberately murdered. Again retaliation was resorted to by Sheridan, and the heavens were darkened by the smoking, burning buildings.

Falling back through Winchester, which had been so often successively occupied by rebel and Union troops, Sheridan took position near Charlestown where he was attacked by Early, who inflicted severe punishment on Wilson's cavalry. The Sixth Corps bore the brunt of the conflict, which lasted from two hours before noon till dark. The Corps then fell back to Bolivar Heights, where Sheridan posted his army, with his right on the Potomac, and his left on the Shenandoah, near Harper's Ferry, his head-quarters being at Halltown.

MAJ. GEN. QUINCY A. GILLMORE.
MAJ. GEN. W. B. FRANKLIN.
MAJ. GEN. W. S. HANCOCK.
MAJ. GEN. G. H. THOMAS.
MAJ. GEN. A. H. TERRY.
MAJ. GEN. JOHN A. LOGAN.
MAJ. GEN. P. H. SHERIDAN.
MAJ. GEN. GEO. STONEMAN.
MAJ. GEN. J. KILPATRICK.
MAJ. GEN. H. W. SLOCUM.
UNION GENERALS.
Engd by H.B. Hall.

The two armies lay confronting each other here for several days, when Early once more fell back up the Valley. As soon as Sheridan was informed of this he again started in pursuit. On the morning of the 28th he advanced in line of battle toward Charlestown, the cavalry leading the advance. Passing through this place, the army moved forward to its old battle ground of the week before, and halted. The next morning Merritt made a vigorous attack on the rebel cavalry, driving it through the town of Smithfield, and beyond Opequan Creek, where he was brought to a halt by the rebel infantry. Some skirmishing followed, when Sheridan fell back upon Charlestown. But on the 3d of September he again put his army in motion, and near Berrysville was attacked by the rebels, whom he repulsed. He then commenced throwing up breastworks, and, having secured his position, remained quietly in it for two weeks, doing nothing except to make reconnoissances with his cavalry.

After nearly a month's operations, to leave off where he begun, was a sorry summing up of the campaign for Sheridan, and a sad disappointment to the country, which had expected so much from the well-known enterprise and daring of the man. It seemed very evident, either that Sheridan was incompetent to fill the place he occupied, or that Grant refused to give him the men he needed to carry out his orders. This indecision and apparent fear of risking a battle were wholly unaccountable to the public, and much to the chagrin of those who were tired of seeing Early roaming up and down the Shenandoah Valley at his leisure. It turns out, however, that Grant, not Sheridan was in fault for this state of things, and the former in his report gives the reasons that governed him. He says:

"His operations during the month of August and the fore part of September were both of an offensive and defensive character, resulting in many severe skirmishes, principally by the cavalry, in which we were generally successful; but no general engagement took place. The two armies lay in such a position—the enemy on the west bank of the Opequan Creek, covering Winchester, and our forces in front of Berrysville—that either could bring on a battle at any time. Defeat to us would lay open to the enemy the States of Maryland and Pennsylvania for long distances, before another army could be interposed to check him. Under these circumstances, I hesitated about allowing the initiative to be taken. Finally the use of the Baltimore and Ohio railroad and the Chesapeake and Ohio canal, which were both obstructed by the enemy, became so indispensably necessary to us, and the importance of relieving Pennsylvania and Maryland from continuously-threatened invasion so great, that I determined the risk should be taken. But fearing to telegraph the order for an attack without knowing more than I did of General Sheridan's feelings as to what would be the probable result, I left City Point on the 15th of September to visit him at his head-quarters, to decide, after conference with him, what should be done. I met him at Charlestown, and he pointed out so distinctly how each army lay; what he could do the moment he was authorized, and expressed such confidence of success, that I saw there were but two words of instructions necessary—Go in!"

This permission was all that Sheridan wanted. The Fabian policy under which he had been compelled to act irritated him, and he constantly felt like a caged lion. Now he was a free man once more, and it needed no spirit of prophecy in one who knew him, to foretell that bloody work was at hand.

Grant after hearing Sheridan's plans and approving them, asked if he could get ready to move by the following Tuesday. "Yes," replied the latter, "by Monday;" and before daylight that morning the army was in motion. By three o'clock in the afternoon it was drawn up in line of battle in front of the rebel position, at Opequan Creek, and as soon as the cavalry, under Torbert, arrived at the desired point on the extreme rebel right, Sheridan ordered a general advance. The artillery opened along the whole line—the columns moved steadily forward, and Early soon discovered that Sheridan was at last in earnest. His position, however, was a strong one, and he stubbornly held it until Averill's and Merritt's bugles were heard on his right, as the firm-set squadrons bore fiercely down. Rolled up before the impetuous charge, the rebel line at length crumbled into fragments, and the whole army broke in utter confusion, and streamed on toward Winchester and through it, halting only when it reached Fisher's Hill thirty miles beyond.

Early left his wounded and dead in our hands, and nearly three thousand prisoners, together with five pieces of artillery, and nine battle flags. Several rebel Generals were killed, while on our side, we had to lament the death of the gallant Russell, commanding a division of the Sixth Corps. The dispatch announcing this glorious victory, closed thus: "We have just sent them whirling through Winchester, and we are after them to-morrow. This army behaved splendidly. I am sending forward all the medical supplies, subsistence stores, and ambulances."

Following up Early vigorously, Sheridan, on the 21st, found himself in front of his strong position, at Fisher's Hill. Skillfully disposing his forces, he closed so suddenly, and with such fury on the enemy, that they broke, and fled in disorder toward Woodstock. Eleven hundred prisoners and sixteen pieces of artillery fell into our hands here, while the road, for miles, was strewed with abandoned wagons, knapsacks, muskets, and everything that impeded the headlong flight. Sheridan pushed on to Woodstock, where he halted to get his supplies up.

Averill, however, kept up the pursuit to Mount Jackson, twenty-five miles south of Strasburg. Here Early rallied his disordered battalions, and once more turned at bay. But, on Sheridan's arrival, he again retreated, though stubbornly contesting every inch of ground, and, at last, made a determined stand in Brown's Gap, on the Blue Ridge, eight miles south-east of Port Republic. Sheridan pursued as far as this place and halted. In the meantime, Torbert, with his cavalry, moved on Staunton and Waynesboro', destroying bridges, Government property, and everything that could be of benefit to the enemy.

Early's position, at Brown's Gap, was too strong to be carried by assault, while it seriously threatened Sheridan's flank, should he attempt to march on Lynchburg—the goal of all the expeditions up the Shenandoah Valley. It was hard to abandon this coveted prize; but he saw that, unless Early could be driven from Brown's Gap, it would be madness to advance farther. Besides, his supplies in the rear were in danger of being cut off by Mosby, and he, therefore, resolved to fall back.

In killed, wounded, prisoners, and missing, Early must have lost, in those two battles and the retreat, nearly half of his army.

While Sheridan was thus sweeping the enemy from his path in the Valley of the Shenandoah, Grant, who, under the most adverse circumstances, still always found some means of assailing the enemy, made a sudden movement north of the James—the object and result of which he thus sums up:—

"By the 12th of September, a branch railroad was completed from the City Point and Petersburg railroad to the

Weldon railroad, enabling us to supply, without difficulty, in all weather, the army in front of Petersburg.

"The extension of our lines across the Weldon railroad, compelled the enemy to so extend his that it seemed he could have but few troops north of the James for the defense of Richmond. On the night of the 28th, the Tenth Corps, Major-General Birney, and the Eighteenth Corps, Major-General Ord commanding, of General Butler's army, were crossed to the north side of the James, and advanced on the morning of the 29th, carrying the very strong fortifications and intrenchments below Chapin's Farm, known as Fort Harrison, capturing fifteen pieces of artillery, and the New Market road and intrenchments. This success was followed up by a gallant assault upon Fort Gillmore, immediately in front of the Chapin Farm fortifications, in which we were repulsed with heavy loss. Kautz's cavalry was pushed forward on the road to the right of this, supported by infantry, and reached the enemy's inner line, but was unable to get further. The position captured from the enemy, was so threatening to Richmond that I determined to hold it. The enemy made several desperate attempts to dislodge us, all of which were unsuccessful, and for which he paid dearly. On the morning of the 30th, General Meade sent out a reconnoissance, with a view to attacking the enemy's line, if it was found sufficiently weakened by withdrawal of troops to the north side. In this reconnoissance we captured and held the enemy's works, near Poplar Spring Church. In the afternoon, troops moving to get to the left of the point gained, were attacked by the enemy in heavy force, and compelled to fall back until supported by the forces holding the captured works. Our cavalry under Gregg was also attacked, but repulsed the enemy with great loss."

The enemy made a raid during this month, (on the 19th,) which, from its daring and success, caused some mortification and excitement. Two thousand cattle, which had been brought on for the use of the Army of the Potomac, were feeding near Coggin's Point, on the James River, guarded by two regiments of cavalry, on which Wade Hampton, with W. F. H. Lee's cavalry division and two other brigades, suddenly pounced and carried off the whole, together with several prisoners.

Starting from Ream's Station, this force had passed around our extreme left, and got in the rear of the army, and yet with such secrecy and celerity did it move, that though hotly pursued, it succeeded in reaching the rebel lines again with all its booty.

CHAPTER XXXV.

RAVAGING OF THE SHENANDOAH VALLEY—SHERIDAN'S DISPATCH—HIS NEW POSITION—LEAVES THE ARMY FOR WASHINGTON—EARLY RESOLVES TO MAKE A NIGHT ATTACK—SECRECY OF HIS MARCH—ROUT OF THE ARMY OF WESTERN VIRGINIA AND OF THE NINETEENTH CORPS—RETREAT OF THE WHOLE ARMY—SHERIDAN AT WINCHESTER—HIS APPROACH TO THE FIELD—HIS SUDDEN ARRIVAL AND STIRRING APPEALS—FORMS A NEW LINE OF BATTLE—REPULSE OF THE ENEMY—ADVANCE OF HIS LINE—THE ENEMY'S POSITION CARRIED—COMPLETE OVERTHROW OF THE REBEL ARMY—THE PURSUIT—A SUPPERLESS ARMY—ENTHUSIASM OF OFFICERS AND MEN—THE GENERALSHIP AND PERSONAL POWER OF SHERIDAN—THE REBELS ABANDON THE VALLEY—HATCHER'S RUN—GRANT FAILS TO TURN THE REBEL RIGHT—BUTLER'S DEMONSTRATION NORTH OF THE JAMES—DESTRUCTION OF THE RAM ALBEMARLE BY LIEUTENANT CUSHING—THE REBELS IN CANADA—RAID ON ST. ALBANS, VERMONT.

SHERIDAN when he fell back from the pursuit of Early took position on the north side of Cedar Creek, near Strasburg. But in his advance and retreat he had ravaged the country with a ruthlessness that reminds one of the old, barbaric wars. How much of this destruction of private property is chargeable to the Secretary of War, from whom he received his orders, and how much to himself, we are unable to say, but it is a lasting disgrace to its authors whoever they were. The following is his own account of what he did, and the reasons which actuated him:

"WOODSTOCK, VIRGINIA, October 7, 1864—9 P. M.

Lieutenant-General U. S. GRANT:

I have the honor to report my command at this point to-night. I commenced moving back from Port Republic, Mount Crawford, Bridgewater, and Harrisonburg yesterday morning. The grain and forage in advance of these points had previously been destroyed. In moving back to this point the whole country from the Blue Ridge to the North Mountain has been made entirely untenable for a rebel army. I have destroyed over two thousand barns filled with wheat, and hay, and farming implements, over seventy mills filled with flour and wheat; have driven in front of the army over four thousand head of stock, and have killed and issued to the troops not less than three thousand sheep. This destruction embraces the Luray Valley and Little Fort Valley, as well as the main Valley. A large number of horses have been obtained, a proper estimate of which I cannot now make. Lieutenant John R. Meigs, my engineer officer, was murdered beyond Harrisonburg, near Dayton. For this atrocious act all the houses within an area of five miles were burned. Since I came into the Valley from Harper's Ferry, every train, every small party, and every straggler has been bushwhacked by the people, many of whom have protection-passes from commanders who have been hitherto in that Valley. The people here are getting sick of the war. Heretofore they have had no reason to complain, because they have been living in great abundance. I have not been followed by the enemy to this point, with the exception of a small force of the rebel cavalry that showed themselves some distance behind my rear-guard to-day. A party of one hundred of the Eighth Ohio cavalry, which I had stationed at the bridge over the North Shenandoah, near Mount Jackson, was attacked by McNeil with seventeen men, while they were asleep, and the whole party dispersed or captured. I think they will all turn up. I learn that fifty-six of them had reached Winchester. McNeil was mortally wounded, and fell into our hands. This was fortunate, as he was the most daring and dangerous of all the bushwhackers in this section of the country.

(Signed) P. H. SHERIDAN, Major General."

This is a sad record for one to make of himself, in this age of civilized warfare. The burning by wholesale, of barns and mills, because the hay and grain in them might be seized by the rebels, would by the same logic justify an invading army at all times for "razing every house, and burning every blade of grass" on the line of its march. "War," Sherman said, "is necessarily cruel;" but to mitigate its severity as much as possible, it has been established as a rule of civilized warfare, that private property shall be respected, except when it is needed for the sustenance of the army, or where the owners are convicted of open hostility. For a General to justify such wholesale destruction of property, and thereby inflict suffering and want on women and children, on the ground that the enemy would rob them if he did not, is not only a violation of the rules of civilized warfare, but very miserable logic.

This mode of reasoning was far better carried out by the ancient barbarians, who killed the children of their enemies, lest they should grow up to be warriors, and the mothers, lest they should give birth to heroes. The ravages of war have their limit without reference to consequences, and civilized nations have fixed that limit. "To make a solitude and call it peace," was in the old dark, rude times the motto, but it does not belong to this age. The massacre of all the young men just entering the age that would render them subject to military duty, would injure an enemy far more than the burning of barns, and mills, and houses, but we suspect that but few would justify it. Because some wretch murdered a man, to burn all the houses—many of them containing helpless widows, "within an area of five miles" is a wilder sort of justice than any man of sound judgment, or an educated conscience will approve. That punishment was deserved and severity needed in many cases, no one will doubt, but if they could not be meted out with some discrimination, they had better have been let alone. England did nothing half so bad as this in our Revolution.

During his retreat, Sheridan was attacked on the 9th of October, by the rebel General Rosser with a large body of cavalry, but defeated him, taking three hundred and fifty prisoners, and eleven pieces of artillery—keeping him, as the former said, "on the jump" for twenty-six miles.

Sheridan, now thinking that the enemy was too severely punished to molest him for the present, left the army for a short visit to Washington.

BATTLE OF CEDAR CREEK, OR MIDDLETOWN.

The army at this time was posted on three moderate hills, extending for three miles across the country, each one a little back of the other.

The first and foremost one, some four or five miles north

of Fisher's Hill, was held by the army of West Virginia under Crook; the second, half a mile to the rear of this, by the Nineteenth Corps, under Emory, the turnpike running between them. The third and last, still farther back was occupied by the Sixth Corps, with Torbert's superb cavalry covering its right flank. Early, who had been reinforced by twelve thousand men, heard that Sheridan was in Washington, and at once resolved to attack the army before his return. On the night of the 18th, he crossed the mountains which separate the branches of the Shenandoah, and forded the north fork, marching in five columns. There was a dense fog at the time, wrapping everything in impenetrable darkness; but Early knew the ground thoroughly, and with trusty guides was in no danger of being misled. He ordered all the men to leave their canteens behind, lest their clanking against the shanks of the bayonets should be heard by our pickets and give the alarm. His march was to be noiseless, and he directed that all the orders should be given in a low tone, for although the movement was to be made with an army of between twenty and thirty thousand men, it must be with the utmost secrecy. Discovery would be fatal.

The whole enterprise was hazardous beyond expression. He, however, moved off toward our left, unperceived, though about two o'clock in the morning, some of the pickets on duty reported that they heard a heavy, muffled tramp and rustling through the underbrush, as though a multitude was marching along the front. This information caused some precautions to be taken, but no reconnoissance was sent out. The truth is, a serious attack by Early was not dreamed of, and the main army slumbered on wholly unsuspicious of danger.

All this time, the steady columns were sweeping on through the gloom, now pushing through the dripping trees, and now fording a stream—skirting our position for miles—till at length, an hour before day-break, the rebel troops, shivering with cold, stood within six hundred yards of our camps.

Crook had ordered a reconnoissance to be made on this morning, and the force was preparing to march, when there suddenly burst through the fog, a deafening yell from ten thousand throats, and then came the blaze and crash of musketry. The surprise was complete and the panic frightful. The roll of drums, bugle calls, and shouts of officers, arose on every side, and the troops rushed frantically to arms, but before any line of battle could be formed, the shouting, clamorous rebels were upon them. Without a moment's check or hindrance, they swept like a billow, up and over the hill, and over the breastworks. A brief struggle of five minutes at the latter, and then the Army of Western Virginia became a herd of fugitives, fleeing in wild disorder back toward the second hill, a half a mile in the rear, where lay the Nineteenth Corps.

A few regiments wheeled and tried to make a stand, but were borne swiftly back before the impetuous flood. The Nineteenth Corps, having a little time to prepare for the shock, attempted to arrest the progress of the enemy, but the latter sweeping down the road, got in its rear, and it soon broke and fled toward the hill, on which the Sixth Corps lay. The batteries which had been captured, were now turned upon us, and enfiladed our entire line. Wright at once formed a new line of battle, and attempted to check the frightful rush of the fugitives.

The force of the onset seemed now very much spent, for the rebels began to advance with more caution, and bring forward their artillery. Besides, the rich plunder of two camps was too tempting a prize for the half-starved troops of Early, and they left their ranks in crowds, and began to pillage.

Had Wright known this, it is possible that he might have made a successful stand where he was, but the rebels having possession of the turnpike that led toward Winchester, he feared that his communications would be severed, and therefore fell back toward Middletown. He had repulsed, in the meantime, a tremendous charge of the enemy, which gave him breathing space, and enabled him to cover the immense crowd of fugitives that darkened all the fields and the highway in the rear. Amid the roar of artillery, incessant volleys of musketry, and shouts and yells of the pursuers, were heard the cries and screams of teamsters as they endeavored to get off with the heavy trains.

The rebels still assailing our left flank, kept up a murderous fire, shaking it terribly, so that Merritt and Custer, with two divisions of cavalry, were sent over to check them, when a severe contest followed in the wooded fields, near Middletown. Strengthened by our captured artillery, they brought their overwhelming batteries to bear on our exhausted columns, and so shattered the hard-pressed left, that only a short stand could be made at Middletown, and the army passed through it toward Newtown, five miles in the rear. On the heights around the former place, Early planted his batteries, which poured in a terrible fire on the uncovered army, as it slowly fell back along the highway, and across the fields.

Sheridan, on his way back to the army, had slept at Winchester, twenty miles distant, the night before. In the morning, little dreaming of the terror reigning in his camp in front, he sat down to his breakfast, and after it was finished, he mounted his horse and with his escort rode leisurely forward. His noble army had then been struggling on the brink of destruction, for four long hours. As it fell back, and he rode forward, and the enemy began to open with his numerous artillery, the deep vibrations that made the earth tremble, caused him to look up in surprise. Still, he felt no uneasiness, for he was confident that if Early had attacked his strong position at Cedar Creek, he would be terribly beaten.

But as the thunder of the guns grew louder and more continuous, and was evidently rolling back toward him, his practised ear told him too well that a heavy battle was raging in front, and that his army was retreating. Startled from his composure, as the terrible truth flashed over him, he dashed the spurs into his horse, and was soon far ahead of his escort, tearing madly along the road. Soon he met camp-followers and fugitives from the field, who declared that all was lost.

What! his noble army, that only a few weeks before he had led twice to victory, broken, shattered, gone! In a moment, the lion in his nature was roused, and instead of being overwhelmed at the disaster, he rose above it—it shall not be so, he mentally exclaimed. As the cloud of fugitives deepened, he shouted—as he drove on and swung his cap over his head—" Face the other way, boys, face the other way; we are going back to our camps; we are going to lick them out of their boots."

The frightened stragglers paused and shouted, as they saw their gallant Chieftain fly past, and even the wounded, lying along the road-side, cheered him. With his face blazing with excitement, and his horse covered with foam, he suddenly appeared in front of his astonished army, and at once ordered the retreat to stop. The enemy had paused in his pursuit, so that our army was, at this time, out of the range of his guns, which enabled Sheridan to take measures to arrest the fugitives and bring them back, and in a short time he had a new line of battle formed.

Then, for two hours, he rode backward and forward along the front, now looking over the ground, and now encouraging the men. "Boys," said he, "if I had been here, this never should have happened. I tell you it never should have happened. And now we are going back to our camps. We are going to get a twist on them. We are going to lick them out of their boots."

Shouts and cheers followed him, and though they had eaten nothing since the night before, and been fighting for five hours, the excited soldiers felt a new strength infused into them by the confident bearing and language of their heroic Commander.

At length the rebel army was seen advancing across the autumnal fields, moving straight on the position held by the Nineteenth Corps. Sheridan sent word to Emory to stop them at all hazards. He did so, after a severe but short contest, in which General Bidwell was killed, and Grover wounded.

Emory immediately dispatched an aid to Sheridan with the news that the enemy was repulsed. "That's good, that's good," laughed Sheridan. "Thank God for that. Now, then, tell General Emory if they attack him again to go after them, and follow them up, and to sock it into them, and to give them the devil." And, with almost every word, bringing his right hand down into the palm of his left with a sharp blow, he added, "We'll get the tightest twist on them yet you ever saw—we'll have all those camps and cannon back again."

Whether aware of Sheridan's arrival, or astounded at the new and formidable line of battle that appeared before him, while a large part of his own army was rioting amid the the camps, at all events, Early at once abandoned the offensive and fell back, and began to throw up breastworks—evidently designing to hold the position till next day, which by all ordinary rules, should be the earliest moment that our hungry, exhausted, and discomfited army could be ready to make any movement. But Sheridan had no intention of waiting till his army was thoroughly re-organized and recruited. Right then and there, he was determined to wipe out the stigma of this disgraceful defeat, and make the same dispatch that carried the news of the overthrow of his army, carry also the thrilling tidings of its glorious victory.

At half past three, the orders were given for a general advance—the drums rolled along the line, the bugles pealed out, and, heralded by the deep-mouthed cannon, the steady battalions moved forward. It was a magnificent sight—the solid advance of that, but just now, fugitive host. Emerging from the woods that had concealed it, the army swung boldly out into the open field, and moved swiftly forward toward the enemy's position. In an instant, the rebel batteries opened, followed by a tremendous volley of musketry. The steady lines were rent before it, and fell suddenly back.

The sight roused Sheridan almost to frenzy, and galloping amid the broken ranks, he, by his thrilling appeals, and almost superhuman efforts, restored order, and although his few remaining cannon could make but a feeble response to the overwhelming batteries of the enemy, he ordered the advance to be resumed.

"The next moment, came a prolonged roar of musketry, mingled with the long-drawn yell of our charge—then the artillery ceased—the musketry died into spattering bursts, and over all the yell triumphant. Every thing on the first line, the stone walls, the advanced crest, the tangled wood, and the half-finished breastworks, had been carried." But the rebels, from a new position, opened with their artillery, and shot and shell crashed through our ranks. Sheridan, heedless of the storm, dashed along the front—giving all his orders to division and corps commanders in person; for in this fearful crisis, he would trust no subordinates. His eyes flashed fire, and his countenance wore a confident expression, while his short, emphatic appeals rung like a bugle-call to his excited troops, who responded with a shout, as through the thickets, over the stone-walls and ridges, they went with a thrilling cheer. The astonished enemy turned and fled in confusion over the fields.

As they streamed down into the Middletown meadows, Sheridan saw that the time for the cavalry had come, and ordered a charge. The bugles pealed forth their stirring notes, and the dashing squadrons of Custer and Merritt came down like a clattering tempest on the right and left, doubling up the rebel flanks, and cleaving a terrible path through the broken ranks. Back to, and through our camps, which they had swept like a whirlwind in the morning, the panic-stricken rebels went, pellmell, leaving all the artillery they had captured, and much of their own, and strewing the way with muskets, clothing, knapsacks, and every thing that could impede their flight. The infantry were too tired to continue the pursuit, but the cavalry kept it up, driving them through Strasburg to Fisher's Hill, and beyond, to Woodstock, sixteen miles distant.

The wearied troops stacked their arms in their pillaged camps, "and slept that night as they had fought that day, without food;" yet ever and anon, as reports would come in from the pursuing cavalry, announcing the capture of guns and prisoners, loud cheers would be sent up. Notwithstanding the dead and wounded lay every where, and the field presented a ghastly spectacle, nothing could check the wild excitement and enthusiasm of officers and men at their great, unexpected victory.

This, in some respects, was one of the most remarkable battles in history. Other lost fields have been won, but rarely by the presence of a single man. Marengo was lost to Napoleon, but won again by the arrival of the gallant Desaix, with his fresh column. Shiloh was lost to Grant, but won again by the opportune arrival of Buell, with his trained battalions; but here a lost battle was won by the arrival of Sheridan alone. By the power of his single presence as he dashed along the shattered lines, and the magic of his voice, as, now gay and confident, and now stern and terrible, he strengthened the discouraged, or awed the timid, and recalled the fugitives, he was able to reorganize the broken ranks almost under the guns of the enemy. He not only dissipated despair, and restored confidence, but breathed into the army enthusiasm, and daring, and positive strength, so that after hours of defeat and terrible losses in men and artillery, it not merely made a successful stand, but broke into a furious offensive, and charging the victorious enemy behind his intrenchments, drove him in utter rout from the field. This single battle, if he had fought no other, would stamp Sheridan as a great Commander.

It could be truly said of him as Carlyle said of Cromwell: "He was a strong man in the high places of the field, and hope shone in him like a pillar of fire, when it had gone out in all other men."

Our loss in this battle amounted to over six thousand men, while that of the enemy was not probably much over a third as great—thus showing under what immense disadvantage Sheridan snatched victory from the very jaws of defeat. After this there was some skirmishing and cavalry engagements in the Valley of the Shenandoah, but it was finally abandoned by the enemy, and in six weeks the Sixth Corps returned to the army before Richmond.

Soon after this great victory, Grant made another attempt to get nearer Richmond, by operating heavily on the enemy's right flank as he had done before. The movement was kept a profound secret, and several days were spent in preparation for it. The sick, together with the baggage and commissary stores, were sent to City Point, where the gun-boats could protect them, and three days' rations and forage were issued to the cavalry, and four days' rations to the infantry. The long line of intrenchments were almost denuded of men, and it looked as though the army did not intend to return. The point of attack was Hatcher's Run—the termination of the enemy's works on his right—and to render it more successful, Butler at the same time was to make a demonstration on the north side of the James, in order to draw off the rebel force in that direction. But, like all the other movements hitherto made around Richmond and Petersburg, this also proved a sad failure. We will not give a detailed account of the causes that prevented success. The whole movement, and its results are thus summed up by General Grant.

"On the 27th the Army of the Potomac, leaving only sufficient to hold its fortified line, moved by the enemy's right flank. The Second Corps, followed by two divisions of the Fifth Corps, with the cavalry in advance and covering our left flank, forced a passage of Hatcher's Run, and moved up the south side of it toward the South-side railroad, until the Second Corps and part of the cavalry reached the Boydton plank road, where it crosses Hatcher's Run. At this point we were six miles distant from the South-side railroad, which I had hoped by this movement to reach and hold. But finding that we had not reached the end of the enemy's fortifications, and no place presenting itself for a successful assault by which he might be doubled up and shortened, I determined to withdraw to within our fortified line. Orders were given accordingly. Immediately upon receiving a report that General Warren had connected with General Hancock, I returned to my head-quarters. Soon after I left, the enemy moved out across Hatcher's Run, in the gap between Generals Hancock and Warren, which was not closed as reported, and made a desperate attack on General Hancock's right and rear. General Hancock immediately faced his corps to meet it, and after a bloody combat, drove the enemy within his works, and withdrew that night to his old position.

"In support of this movement General Butler made a demonstration on the north side of the James, and attacked the enemy on the Williamsburg road, and also on the York River railroad. In the former he was unsuccessful; in the latter he succeeded in carrying a work which was afterward abandoned, and his forces withdrawn to their former positions.

"From this time forward the operations in front of Petersburg and Richmond until the spring campaign of 1865, were confined to the defense and extension of our lines, and to offensive movements for crippling the enemy's lines of communication, and to prevent his detaching any considerable force to send south."

The night before this grand movement took place, a most daring expedition was successfully carried out by a young lieutenant in the navy, on the Roanoke River. The Ram Albemarle, since its fight with our fleet, had lain at Plymouth, carefully guarded and protected. The Navy Department, wishing to get rid of this monster, had sent, the Summer previous, Lieutenant W. B. Cushing to New York with full powers to make all necessary preparations for the perilous undertaking of effecting her destruction. Having at length constructed a torpedo boat, he returned with it to the Sound, and on the night of the 27th of October proceeded with it, in his steam launch up the river. Thirteen officers and men composed the entire crew, all of whom felt that the chance of their return was more than doubtful. It was eight miles from the mouth of the river to where the ram lay, while the stream, which would not average over two hundred yards in width, was lined the whole way with pickets. About a mile below the ram, lay the wreck of the Southfield, which the former had destroyed, surrounded by schooners. The night was dark, and so cautiously did Cushing move that he was undiscovered by the pickets on shore, and passed within twenty yards of the Southfield, unnoticed by those on guard there. Having now got close to the ram, which by a light on shore could be seen, made fast to the wharf, he ordered on a full head of steam and pressed forward. As he steamed past the vessel he saw she was surrounded by a pen of logs thirty feet wide, placed there to prevent any such attack as the one he was now making. Performing a complete circle so as to come squarely down, he sent the launch's bows full against the pen of logs. The rebels had however discovered his approach, and opened on him with a terrible fire. Many were struck. "The bullets," says Cushing, "struck my clothing three times, and the air seemed full of them. In a moment we had struck the logs, just abreast of the quarter port, breasting them in some feet, and our bows resting on them. The torpedo boom was then lowered, and by a vigorous pull I succeeded in driving the torpedo under the overhang and exploded it, at the same time that the Albemarle's gun was fired. A shot seemed to go crashing through my boat and a dense mass of water rushed in from the torpedo, filling the launch and completely disabling her." He was now within fifteen feet of the ram, from the deck of which an incessant stream of fire fell into his gallant little band. Seeing his hopeless condition, the enemy hailed him and ordered him to surrender. The young hero sent back his stern refusal, and took unflinchingly the desolating fire.

Seeing, by the light of their own fire, that he was fast going to the bottom, they again hailed him, demanding his surrender. Again he refused, and coolly taking off his coat and shoes, he told the men to save themselves as they best could, and sprang into the river, and struck out for the middle of the stream. He then swam with the current, and when a half a mile below the ram, came upon Acting-Master's-mate Woodman, very much exhausted, and nobly tried to get him ashore but was unable to do so, and had to see him sink by his side, when he again turned for the shore. He had barely strength to reach it, but not enough to crawl up the bank, and so lay until near daylight, when he crept into a swamp close to the fort.

After he had rested awhile, he arose and traveled for several hours through the swamp, until he came to its termination, when he plunged into another, and, at length, reached a creek, in which he found a skiff belonging to the picket of the enemy. Capturing this, he pulled out into the stream, and by eleven o'clock, was once more safe among his friends. A more daring, gallant deed is scarcely to be found in the records of our glorious navy.

Secretary Welles sent him a complimentary letter, and the country rung with his praises. He had done his work well, for this much-dreaded ram, blown up by the torpedo, sunk at her moorings. Only one, besides himself, escaped, of all this gallant crew—the rest being killed, captured, or drowned.

During this month, also, an event occured on our Northern frontier, which caused the most intense excitement throughout the country. The Canadian Provinces from the commencement of the war, had been the resort of rebel refugees, who were constantly organizing plots against the Federal Government. One was set on foot the year before, to release twenty-five hundred rebel prisoners on Johnson's

Island, in Lake Erie, who, with rebels in Canada, were to burn Buffalo and other Lake cities, but it was discovered in time, and hence abandoned. So also in September, of this year, John Y. Beall, a rebel officer, captured and destroyed two steamboats on the lakes.

On the 19th of this month, forty armed men, headed by one Young, suddenly rode into the village of St. Albans, Vermont, fifteen miles from the Canadian frontier, and robbing the Bank of two hundred thousand dollars, escaped in safety. They fired upon the panic-stricken inhabitants, mortally wounding one.

They were afterward seized and tried in Canada, but were all finally discharged. The Bank recovered a part of its money, but no concessions were made to our Government for this violation of its territory, which caused it to adopt measures that interrupted, for a time, the usual communications between the Provinces and the States.

CHAPTER XXXVI.

OPERATIONS WEST DURING THE AUTUMN—IN ARKANSAS, KANSAS, AND MISSOURI—PRICE, STEELE, AND ROSECRANS—CAPTURE OF ATHENS BY FORREST—HIS FARTHER OPERATIONS—GENERAL BURBRIDGE SENT TO DESTROY THE SALT-WORKS AT SALTVILLE, VIRGINIA—SHERMAN AT ATLANTA—DAVIS IN GEORGIA—HOOD AGAIN TAKES THE FIELD—FALLS ON SHERMAN'S COMMUNICATIONS—GALLANT DEFENSE BY CORSE, OF ALLATOONA—PURSUIT OF HOOD—THOMAS AT NASHVILLE—SHERMAN PREPARES FOR HIS GEORGIA CAMPAIGN—ROME BURNED—DESTRUCTION OF PROPERTY—BURNING OF ATLANTA.

ALTHOUGH during the Spring, Summer, and Autumn of 1864, the two great campaigns of Sherman and Grant occupied almost the undivided attention of the country, still, as we have seen, in Missouri, Arkansas, Kentucky, Tennessee, and the Carolinas, hostilities were kept up, though they apparently had no direct bearing on the final result.

Those minor events of the East we have already traced till nearly the close of Autumn. The military operations outside of Sherman's army, during the months of September and October, West, are thus summed up by Grant:—

"About the last of August, it being reported that the rebel General Price, with a force of about ten thousand men, had reached Jacksonport, on his way to invade Missouri, General A. J. Smith's command, then *en route* from Memphis to join Sherman, was ordered to Missouri. A cavalry force was also, at the same time, sent from Memphis, under command of Colonel Winslow. This made General Rosecrans' forces superior to those of Price, and no doubt was entertained he would be able to check Price and drive him back, while the forces of General Steele, in Arkansas, would cut off his retreat. On the 26th day of September, Price attacked Pilot Knob and forced the garrison to retreat, and thence moved north to the Missouri River, and continued up that river toward Kansas. General Curtis, commanding the Department of Kansas, immediately collected such forces as he could to repel the invasion of Kansas, while General Rosecrans' cavalry was operating in his rear.

"The enemy was brought to battle on the Big Blue and defeated, with the loss of nearly all his artillery and trains, and a large number of prisoners. He made a precipitate retreat to Northern Arkansas. The impunity with which Price was enabled to roam over the State of Missouri, for a long time, and the incalculable mischief done by him, shows to how little purpose a superior force may be used. There is no reason why General Rosecrans should not have concentrated his forces, and beaten and driven Price before the latter reached Pilot Knob.

"September 20th, the enemy's cavalry, under Forrest, crossed the Tennessee, near Waterloo, Alabama, and on the 23rd attacked the garrison at Athens, consisting of six hundred men, which capitulated on the 24th. Soon after the surrender, two regiments of reinforcements arrived, and after a severe fight were compelled to surrender. Forrest destroyed the railroad westward, captured the garrison at Sulphur Branch trestle, skirmished with the garrison at Pulaski on the 27th, and on the same day cut the Nashville and Chattanooga railroad, near Tullahoma and Dechard. On the morning of the 30th, one column of Forrest's command, under Buford, appeared before Huntsville and summoned the surrender of the garrison. Receiving an answer in the negative, he remained in the vicinity of the place until next morning, when he again summoned its surrender and received the same reply as on the night before. He withdrew in the direction of Athens, which place had been regarrisoned, and attacked it on the afternoon of the 1st of October, but without success. On the morning of the 2nd, he renewed his attack, but was handsomely repulsed.

"Another column under Forrest, appeared before Columbia, on the morning of the 1st, but did not make an attack. On the morning of the 3rd, he moved toward Mount Pleasant. While these operations were going on, every exertion was made by General Thomas to destroy the forces under Forrest, before he could recross the Tennessee, but he was unable to prevent his escape to Corinth, Mississippi.

"In September, an expedition, under General Burbridge, was sent to destroy the salt-works at Saltville, Virginia. He met the enemy on the 2nd of October, about three miles and a half from Saltville, and drove him into his strongly intrenched position around the salt-works, from which he was unable to dislodge him. During the night he withdrew his command and returned to Kentucky."

The interest, however, in these various expeditions and movements was more local than general. East, as has been stated, with the failure at Hatcher's Run, in October, closed, for the Autumn, all movements of importance with the Army of the Potomac. It was evidently at a dead-lock with the enemy.

It was not so, however, with the other great army encamped at Atlanta. The fall of this place which threatened to bisect again the Southern Confederacy, caused the most intense feeling South, and Davis hastened from his Capital to Georgia to still the clamors of the disaffected, and raise the courage of the desponding. He made violent speeches, in which he seemed to lose both his reason and temper, using language that can hardly be accounted for, except on the ground of temporary insanity, arising from some cause or other. Still with his aid, Hood was reinforced with forty thousand militia, and by the last of September, declared himself ready to move. Unable to cope with Sherman in the open field, he resolved to throw himself on his long line of communications, and compel him to fall back to Chattanooga.

Moving rapidly, he broke up the railroad in various places. Beyond Allatoona, nearly to Dallas, he had it pretty much all his own way, so that during the entire month of October, Sherman was cut off from Chattanooga. The foresight of the latter, in making Allatoona a secondary base, was now apparent. If it could be taken, his army would be in a perilous position. This Hood knew, and dispatched a whole rebel division, under French, to capture it. Sherman, aware of his designs, sent a signal from the distant Kenesaw Mountains to General Corse, who was in command of Rome, to take his brigade, and move with the utmost speed to Allatoona, and hold it against all opposition, until he himself could arrive with help.

Pushing forward by railroad, this gallant officer reached the place with about two thousand men before French did, and at once made his dispositions to defend it to the last. As soon as the rebel General, with his overwhelming force, arrived, he sent the following message to Corse:—

"AROUND ALLATOONA, October 5, 1864.

Commanding Officer U. S. Forces, Allatoona:

SIR,—I have placed the forces under my command in such positions, that you are surrounded, and to avoid a needless effusion of blood, I call on you to surrender your forces at once, and unconditionally. Five minutes will be allowed you to decide. Should you accede to this, you will be treated in the most honorable manner as prisoners of war.

I have the honor to be, very respectfully yours,

S. G. FRENCH,

Major-General Commanding Forces C. S."

To this peremptory order, backed by an entire division, the gallant Corse replied in the following droll, yet curt language:—

"HEAD-QUARTERS FOURTH DIVISION, FIFTEENTH ARMY CORPS, ALLATOONA, GA., 8.30 A. M., October 5, 1864.

Major-General S. G. French, C. S. Army, etc.:

Your communication demanding surrender of my command, I acknowledge the receipt of, and respectfully reply that we are prepared for the "needless effusion of blood," whenever it is agreeable to you.

I am, very respectfully, your obedient servant,

JOHN M. CORSE,

Brigadier-General Commanding Forces U. S."

Corse had but little time to arrange his defense, as he reached the place that very morning, a little after midnight. Sherman, in his dispatch, says of Corse, in the desperate engagement that followed—"his description of the defense is so graphic that it leaves nothing for me to add." We agree with him, and therefore let him tell his own story.

"I had hardly issued the incipient orders, when the storm broke in all its fury on the Thirty-ninth Iowa and Seventh Illinois. Young's brigade of Texans, one thousand nine hundred strong, had gained the west end of the ridge, and moved with great impetuosity along its crest, till they struck Rowett's command, where they received a severe check; but undaunted, they came again and again. Rowett, reinforced by the Ninety-third Illinois, and aided by the gallant Redfield, encouraged me to hope we were safe here, when I observed a brigade of the enemy, under General Sears, moving from the north, its left extending across the railroad. I rushed to the two companies of the Ninety-third Illinois, which were on the brink of the cut running north from the redoubt and parallel with the railroad—they having been reinforced by the retreating pickets—and urged them to hold on to the spur; but it was of no avail. The enemy's line of battle swept us like so much chaff, and struck the Thirty-ninth Iowa in flank, threatening to engulf our little band without further ado. Fortunately for us, Colonel Tourtellotte's fire caught Sears in flank, and broke him so badly as to enable me to get a staff-officer over the cut, with orders to bring the Fiftieth Illinois over to reinforce Rowett, who had lost very heavily. However, before the regiment sent for could arrive, Sears and Young both rallied, and made their assaults in front and on the flank with so much vigor and in such force, as to break Rowett's line, and had not the Thirty-ninth Iowa fought with the desperation it did, I never would have been able to get a man back into the redoubt. As it was, their hand-to-hand conflict and stubborn stand broke the enemy to that extent, he must stop and re-form, before undertaking the assault on the fort. Under cover of the blow they gave the enemy, the Seventh and Ninety-third Illinois, and what remained of the Thirty-ninth Iowa, fell back into the fort.

The fighting up to this time (about eleven A. M.) was of a most extraordinary character. Attacked from the north, from the west, and from the south, these three regiments, Thirty-ninth Iowa, Seventh and Ninety-third Illinois, held Young's and a portion of Sears's and Cockeral's brigades at bay for nearly two hours and a half. The gallant Colonel Redfield, of the Thirty-ninth Iowa, fell shot in four places, and the extraordinary valor of the men and officers of this regiment, and of the Seventh Illinois, saved to us Allatoona. So completely disorganized was the enemy, that no regular assault could be made on the fort, till I had the trenches all filled, and the parapets lined with men.

The Twelfth Illinois, and Fiftieth Illinois arriving from the east hill, enabled us to occupy every foot of trench and keep up a line of fire that, as long as our ammunition lasted, would render our little fort impregnable."

But the ammunition gave out, and a brave fellow, whose name he forgot, crossed over to another fort under the enemy's fire, and brought back an armful and the fight went on.

Sherman, anxious about Allatoona, hastened forward, and about ten o'clock reached the top of the Kenesaw, eighteen miles distant. He says, "I could see the smoke of battle, and hear the faint sound of artillery." He immediately pushed forward a brigade, and flew his signal telling Corse that help was coming. But this heroic Commander had too much on his hands to be looking out for signals. He knew, without them, that Sherman was hurrying forward troops to his relief as fast as they could march.

The fight was kept up, and the smoke of battle wrapped the combatants, while far away on the serene heights of Kenesaw stood Sherman flying his signals and watching through his glass to see if they were answered. For a long time they waved unheeded, but at last an answer came, and he knew then that while Corse lived, the rebel force would never have Allatoona. At three o'clock in the afternoon, the rebel General gave it up—for, repulsed in every attack, he saw he was only increasing his piles of dead, and ordered his bugles to sound retreat.

Sherman, hurrying forward his army, passed through Allatoona to Kingston, which he reached on the 6th, and at once reinforced Resaca—before which Hood had appeared and demanded its surrender—and pushed forward toward the same point with the main army. The succeeding movements, until the pursuit was abandoned, and Hood left to move north, while he prepared his Georgia campaign, are best described in his own language. He says:

"Arriving at Resaca on the evening of the fourteenth, I determined to strike Hood in flank, or force him to battle, and directed the Army of the Tennessee, General Howard, to move to Snake Creek Gap, which was held by the enemy, whilst General Stanley, with the Fourth and Fourteenth Corps, moved by Tilton across the mountains to the rear of Snake Creek Gap, in the neighborhood of Villanow.

"The Army of the Tennessee found the enemy occupying our old lines in the Snake Creek Gap, and on the 15th skirmished for the purpose of holding him there until Stanley could get to his rear. But the enemy gave way about noon, and was followed through the Gap, escaping before General Stanley had reached the further end of the Pass. The next day, the sixteenth, the armies moved directly toward Lafayette, with a view to cut off Hood's retreat. We found him intrenched in Ship's Gap, but the leading division (Wood's) of the Fifteenth Corps rapidly carried the advanced posts held by two companies of a South Carolina regiment, making them prisoners. The remaining eight companies escaped to the main body near Lafayette. The next morning we passed over into the Valley of the Chattooga, the Army of the Tennessee moving in pursuit by Lafayette and Alpine, toward Blue Pond; the Army of the Cumberland by Summerville and Mellville Post-Office to Gaylesville; and the Army of the Ohio and Garrard's cavalry from Villanow, Dirttown Valley, and Goover's Gap to Gaylesville. Hood, however, was little encumbered with trains, and marched with great rapidity, and had succeeded in getting into the narrow gorge formed by the Lookout Range abutting against the Coosa River, in the neighborhood of Gadsden. He evidently wanted to avoid a fight.

"On the nineteenth, all the armies were grouped about Gaylesville, in the rich Valley of the Chattooga, abounding in corn and meat, and I determined to pause in my pursuit of the enemy, to watch his movements and live on the country. I hoped that Hood would turn toward Guntersville and Bridgeport. The Army of the Tennessee was posted near Little River, with instructions to feel forward in support of the cavalry, which was ordered to watch Hood in the neighborhood of Will's Valley, and to give me the earliest notice possible of his turning northward. The Army of the Ohio was posted at Cedar Bluff, with orders to lay a pontoon across the Coosa, and to feel forward to centre, and down in the direction of Blue Mountain. The Army of the Cumberland was held in reserve at Gaylesville; and all the troops were instructed to draw heavily for supplies from the surrounding country. In the meantime communications were opened to Rome, and a heavy force set to work in repairing the damages done to our railroads. Atlanta was abundantly supplied with provisions, but forage was scarce; and General Slocum was instructed to send strong foraging parties out in the direction of South River, and collect all the corn and fodder possible, and to put his own trains in good condition for further service.

"Hood's movements and strategy had demonstrated that he had an army capable of endangering at all times my communications, but unable to meet me in open fight. To follow him would simply amount to being decoyed away from Georgia, with little prospect of overtaking and overwhelming him. To remain on the defensive, would have been bad policy for an army of so great value as the one I then commanded; and I was forced to adopt a course more fruitful in results than the naked one of following him to the Southwest. I had previously submitted to the Commander-in-Chief a general plan, which amounted substantially to the destruction of Atlanta and the railroad back to Chattanooga, and sallying forth from Atlanta through the heart of Georgia, to capture one or more of the great Atlantic seaports. This I renewed from Gaylesville, modified somewhat by the change of events.

"On the twenty-sixth of October, satisfied that Hood had

moved westward from Gadsden across Sand Mountain, I detached the Fourth Corps, Major-General Stanley, and ordered him to proceed to Chattanooga and report to Major-General Thomas at Nashville."

Thomas had been sent on from Atlanta to take charge of all the troops in the State, and those *en route* to reinforce the army, and Sherman says:—

"Subsequently, on the 30th of October, I also detached the Twenty-third Corps, Major-General Schofield, with the same destination; and delegated to Major-General Thomas full power over all the troops subject to my command, except the four Corps with which I designed to move into Georgia. This gave him the two divisions under A. J. Smith, then in Missouri, but *en route* for Tennessee, the two Corps named, and all the garrisons in Tennessee, as also all the cavalry of my Military Division, except one division under Brigadier-General Kilpatrick, which was ordered to rendezvous at Marietta."

General Wilson had been sent from the Army of the Potomac to take charge of his cavalry, and he ordered him also to report to Nashville with all the dismounted detachments, and collect, equip, and organize all the cavalry in Tennessee and Kentucky and report to Thomas.

"These forces I judged would enable General Thomas to defend the railroad from Chattanooga back, including Nashville and Decatur, and give him an army with which he could successfully cope with Hood, should the latter cross the Tennessee northward.

"By the 1st of November, Hood's army had moved from Gadsden, and made its appearance in the neighborhood of Decatur, where a feint was made; he then passed on to Tuscumbia, and laid a pontoon-bridge opposite Florence. I then began my preparations for the march through Georgia, having received the sanction of the Commander-inChief for carrying into effect my plan, the details of which were explained to all my corps commanders and heads of staff departments, with strict injunctions of secrecy. I had also communicated full details to General Thomas, and had informed him, I would not leave the neighborhood of Kingston until he felt perfectly confident that he was entirely prepared to cope with Hood, should he carry into effect his threatened invasion of Tennessee and Kentucky. I estimated Hood's force at thirty-five thousand infantry, and ten thousand cavalry."

Sherman then moved his army by easy marches back to the neighborhood of Smyrna camping ground, sent all surplus artillery and baggage to Chattanooga, put Kilpatrick's cavalry force in the best possible condition, ordered Corse, at Rome, to burn every thing there that could be of service to the enemy, and, at the same time, destroyed all the railroads in and around Atlanta, and finally ordered all the garrisons north of Kingston to fall back to Chattanooga, taking with them the public property and railroad stock, and the rails from Resaca, saving the latter for future use. He thus rapidly and effectually cut himself clear from the outer world, and stripped himself for the race.

Rome was first burned; and a thousand bales of cotton, two flour mills, two tanneries, a foundery, machine shops, store-houses, and bridges, were set on fire, making a fearful conflagration. The soldiers seeing the work of destruction commenced, applied the torch to the private dwellings, and soon the flames leaped and roared through the murky atmosphere, lighting up the nightly heavens with a lurid glare, and flooding field and mountain in flame.

A few days after, Atlanta shared the same fate. The Michigan engineers were detailed to effect its destruction. A foundery, worth a half a million of dollars, was first in a blaze, then an oil refinery, followed by a freight ware-house, in which were stored several bales of cotton. The depot, turning-tables, freight sheds, and stores around, were soon a fiery mass. The heart was burning out of beautiful Atlanta.

"The few people that had remained in the city, fled, scared by the conflagration and the dread of violence.

"The Atlanta Hotel, Washington Hall, and all the square around the railroad depot, were soon in one sheet of flame. Drug stores, dry goods' stores, hotels, negro marts, theatres, and grog-shops, were all now feeding the fiery element. Worn-out wagons and camp equipage were piled up in the depot, and added to the fury of the flames.

"A stone ware-house was blown up by a mine. Quarter-masters ran away, leaving large stores behind. The men plunged into the houses, broke windows and doors with their muskets, dragging out armfuls of clothes, tobacco, and whiskey which was more welcome than all the rest. The men dressed themselves in new clothes, and then flung the rest into the fire.

"The streets were now in one fierce sheet of flame; houses were falling on all sides, and fiery flakes of cinders were whirled about. Occasionally shells exploded, and excited men rushed through the choking atmosphere, and hurried away from the city of ruins.

"At a distance the city seemed overshadowed by a cloud of black smoke, through which, now and then, darted a gushing flame of fire, or projectiles hurled from the burning ruin.

"The sun looked, through the hazy cloud, like a blood-red ball of fire; and the air, for miles around, felt oppressive and intolerable. The Tyre of the South was laid in ashes, and the 'Gate City' was a thing of the past."*

On the 12th of November, Sherman stood detached from

* Captain Conyngham.

all its communications ready to move. His army "was composed of four Corps: the Fifteenth and Seventeenth, constituting the right wing, under Major-General O. O. Howard; the Fourteenth and Twentieth Corps, constituting the left wing, under Major-General H. W. Slocum, making an aggregate strength of sixty thousand infantry, with one cavalry division of five thousand and five hundred men, under Brigadier-General Judson Kilpatrick, and the artillery reduced to the minimum, one gun per one thousand men.

"The whole force was moved rapidly, and grouped about Atlanta on the 14th of November."

CHAPTER XXXVII.

SHERMAN PREPARES TO MARCH—ORDERS RESPECTING FORAGING PARTIES—DIVISION OF THE ARMY—SLOCUM'S WING—HOWARD'S WING—KILPATRICK'S CAVALRY—MARCH OF THE FORMER—PILLAGE OF MADISON—SLOCUM ENTERS MILLEDGEVILLE—MARCH OF THE RIGHT WING—THE ENEMY AT LOVEJOY'S—KILPATRICK'S CAVALRY—MACON LEFT IN THE REAR—SHERMAN ENTERS MILLEDGEVILLE AND OCCUPIES THE GOVERNOR'S HOUSE—THE SOLDIERS ORGANIZE A LEGISLATURE—REBELS REPULSED AT GRISWOLDVILLE—KILPATRICK DRIVES WHEELER BEFORE HIM AND THREATENS AUGUSTA—THE ARMY AT MILLEN—MARCH TO SAVANNAH—CAPTURE OF FORT MC ALLISTER BY HAZEN—SAVANNAH INVESTED—HARDEE SUMMONED TO SURRENDER—SHERMAN STARTS FOR PORT ROYAL—THE CITY EVACUATED—SHERMAN'S DISPATCH TO THE PRESIDENT—REVIEW OF THE CAMPAIGN.

IN preparing for his march across the State of Georgia, Sherman gave stringent rules for the conduct of his troops. Of necessity, they must live off the country. He therefore, issued the following order:—

"The army will forage liberally on the country during the march. To this end, each brigade Commander will organize a good and efficient foraging party, under command of one or more discreet officers. To regular foraging parties must be intrusted the gathering of provisions and forage at any distance from the roads traveled.

"As for horses, mules, wagons, &c., the cavalry and artillery may appropriate freely and without limit. Foraging parties may also take mules or horses to replace the jaded animals of their trains, or to serve as pack-mules for the regiments or brigades."

This order shows that Sherman possessed the right spirit, and desired that his army should not behave like banditti.

Every brigade and regiment had its organized foraging party, which was to forage under established rules, and be under the command of one or more discreet officers. It was also ordered,—

"Soldiers shall not enter the dwellings of the inhabitants or commit any trespass; but, during the halt or camp, they may be permitted to gather turnips, potatoes and other vegetables, and drive in stock in front of their camps."

Officers were also directed "to leave with each family a reasonable portion for their maintenance."

These were humane regulations, and shed as much lustre on Sherman's character, as his great victories. But who, familiar with the history of invading armies, does not know what foraging in the enemy's country means. Foraging parties are usually joined by every servant and idler about the camps, who, in the various expeditions, scatter over the country, enter houses and strip the inmates of jewelry, and every thing valuable that they possess, and often commit violence of the grossest kind. Sherman's army formed no exception to this rule.

Says an officer, who commanded in the expedition, in speaking of these lawless hangers-on :—"In most instances, they burned down houses to cover their depredations, and in some cases, took the lives of their victims, as they would not reveal concealed treasures. These gangs spread like locusts over the country. In all cases where the foraging parties were under the command of a respectable officer, they acted with propriety, simply taking what provisions and necessaries they needed. They might as well have stripped the place, though, for soon came the bummers, and commenced a scene of ruin and pillage. Boxes were burst open; clothes dragged about; the finest silks, belonging to the planters' ladies, carried off to adorn some negro wenches around camp; pictures, books, furniture, all tossed about and torn in pieces. Though these wretches were acting against military orders, there was no one to complain. The planter and his family were thankful if they escaped with their lives."

When about to start, Sherman wrote to Admiral Porter, on the Atlantic coast, that he might be "looking out for him about Christmas, from Hilton Head to Savannah," and to his wife, "this is my last letter from here; you will only hear of me hereafter through rebel sources."

The four Corps, as before stated, were divided into two wings—the right, consisting of the Fifteenth and Seventeenth, was commanded by Howard; and the left, composed of the Fourteenth and Twentieth, by Slocum. There was no general train of supplies for the army, but each Corps had its own, distributed among the brigades and regiments, the whole amounting to about two thousand wagons.

The march, when practicable, was to be by four parallel roads, to commence every morning at seven o'clock, and to average fifteen miles a day. Howard, with the right wing, was to follow the Georgia Central railroad, running in a south-westerly direction, through Macon and Milledgeville, to Savannah; while Slocum, with the left wing, would march along the railroad running due east to Augusta—both roads to be destroyed as the armies advanced. Two divisions of cavalry, under Kilpatrick, covered the flanks of the columns. It was a hundred and seventy miles to Augusta, by the railroad along which Slocum marched, and two hundred and ninety-one to Savannah, by that which Howard took.

Slocum, moving out on different roads, and destroying the rail track as he advanced, pushed on through Decatur, Stone Mountain, Social Circle, Rutledge, and Madison—filling the inhabitants with consternation, especially at the latter place. While the depot and railroad track were being destroyed here, together with two hundred bales of cotton, the stragglers entered the place and pillaged unchecked. Stores were burst open—houses entered, and plates and valuables carried off, while mirrors and pianos were ruthlessly smashed. Wine-cellars were broken into, and the liquors drank till soldiers were seen reeling along the streets. All the stores were gutted and the contents scattered around; even a milliner's shop was entered and sacked, and the ribbons and flowers put in the caps of the soldiers.

This disgraceful scene continued until the head of Slocum's column entered the place, when it was quickly brought to a close, and a guard placed over what was left of the town.

From Madison, the division of Geary marched on the Oconee River, while a body of cavalry crossed it and advanced to Greenboro', sixty-four miles from Augusta. From this place, however, it turned directly south toward Milledgeville. The Fourteenth Corps wheeled in the same direction before it reached the town, marching toward the same point, and last, Geary, farther to the east, took the same direction, moving down the west bank of the Oconee.

On the 21st, Slocum entered Milledgeville, the State Capital, one day ahead of Howard. The latter moved directly on Macon, covered by Kilpatrick's cavalry. Some three thousand militia were found at Lovejoy's, but a single charge of Kilpatrick served to scatter them. At Bear Creek, he encountered Wheeler's cavalry and forced it back to Macon. Howard followed leisurely, destroying the railroad behind him, until he arrived within a few miles of the place. A large army was concentrated here, defended by breastworks, well mounted with artillery, for the enemy never doubted that Sherman intended to lay siege to this place. He however had no such intention. He had apparently forgotten the old, well-established military maxim, "never to leave a fortified place of the enemy in your rear," and designed to pass it without halting.

Wishing to get across the Ocmulgee without opposition, and strike the railroad again beyond the town, he sent Kilpatrick over the river with a large force of cavalry, who came down on the place from the east—driving in the rebel pickets, and charging up to the very earthworks of the enemy. His daring and vigorous movements kept the garrison in a state of constant alarm, and while the rebel army was listening to the sound of his bugles, Howard quietly slipped across the river to Griswoldville, ten miles beyond. Leaving here a part of the Fifteenth Corps to protect his rear, the latter pushed on to Milledgeville, which, as we have said, he reached the next day after Howard entered it. Sherman took up his head-quarters in the Governor's house, but found it completely stripped of furniture. This, however, was of little consequence to one who had often made the earth his couch, and spreading a couple of blankets on the floor, slept in State.

The Georgia Legislature was in session when the news of the approach of our army was received, and at once adjourned in great terror. The soldiers took possession of the State House, and organized a Legislature of their own—winding up their hilarious proceedings by having a soldier appear at the door, shouting "the Yankees are coming," when the uproarious, laughing crowd rushed at once for the door.

In the meantime the rebel leaders at Macon, enraged at finding themselves so completely outwitted, made a furious attack with three brigades of militia, on the force left at Griswoldville, but were repulsed with a loss of a thousand men.

Having rested his now united army at Milledgeville, and stored forty days' rations in his wagons, Sherman once more turned the head of his columns toward the sea. At Sandersville, Wheeler made a stand, but after a brief action fell back to Waynesboro, only thirty miles south of Augusta, whither Kilpatrick followed him. Wheeler now attacked in turn, but was repulsed with a loss of two hundred men. The inhabitants of Augusta were alarmed at the near approach of Kilpatrick to the city, and entertained no doubt, that it was the point aimed at by Sherman. But while the cavalry swarmed the country in its vicinity, concealing the movements of the army, the latter was marching rapidly on Millen, located on the railroad that connects Augusta and Savannah. Here Sherman again halted for several days, while the cavalry scoured the country in every direction. Whether he intended to march north on Augusta, or south on Savannah, the rebel commanders could not tell, and hence the forces at these places remained separate.

From this position Sherman looked back in his track, and saw the Georgia railroad destroyed for a hundred miles, and the Georgia road for more than sixty.

He had hitherto completely deceived the enemy as to the point he was aiming at, but concealment was now no longer possible. Sherman, however, felt no vacillation as to his course, and when his columns were well closed up, and sufficient provisions stored in his wagons, he on the 2nd of December, swung his noble army on Millen as on a pivot, and in six grand columns by as many different roads, swept down on Savannah, leaving Augusta as he had Macon, far in his rear.

The face of the country, through which his line of march now lay, was totally different from the one he had hitherto traversed. Through richly cultivated fields and plantations, and past thriving towns, and peaceful country villages, where every luxury abounded, the army had for weeks been marching, but now it entered on long stretches of pine forests, whose dark green branches swayed with a ceaseless murmur over the soldiers' heads. A river on either side rolled its flood toward the Atlantic, whither the heads of his columns were pressing, protecting both his flanks—thus performing the duty which had hitherto devolved on Kilpatrick's cavalry. This force now marched in front and rear, awakening the echoes of the pine forest with their bugle calls, and lighting up its green arcades with the flashing weapons of the bold riders. It was a strange, yet magnificent spectacle, this mighty army moving unmolested through a hostile country, its bands making the woods resonant with their thrilling strains, and the gay battalions streaking them with the long lines of light from their camp-fires by night.

Thus, day after day, the army swept on for more than eighty miles to Savannah. About ten miles from the city, the left wing struck the Charleston railroad, when it came upon the skirmishers of Hardee, who was in command of the troops that held the place. As the right wing approached the outer line of the enemy's works, Sherman heard the deep, heavy thunder of cannon booming over the swamps and forests from Ossabaw Sound, where our fleet lay; and knew them to be signal guns for him, should he be approaching the coast. On the 9th he answered them by sending Colonel Duncan down the Ogeechee, who, three days after, stepped on board one of Dahlgren's vessels, and thus put the army once more in communication with the outer world.

Sherman now began to close gradually but steadily in upon the city. But he had no siege guns, for only field artillery could be taken in the long and difficult march across the State of Georgia. The former he must get up from the fleet in Ossabaw Sound, or the city could not be taken. But Fort McAllister, that had twice repulsed an attack by our iron-clads, commanded the entrance of the Ogeechee River, effectually preventing the ascent of our vessels. Its capture, therefore was indispensable to success. It is singular that the enemy did not see this and strengthen its garrison and defenses landward. But thinking the great danger was from the fleet, they left a garrison of less than three hundred men to hold it.

Sherman, aware of this, resolved by one bold stroke to seize it, and the gallant Hazen was selected with his tried division to carry it by assault. This division, the second, was Sherman's old division of the Fifteenth Corps, which was the corps he spoke so proudly of after the battle of Missionary Ridge. When he sent word to this old favorite division that he expected them to take Fort McAllister, they were as delighted, says an officer, as though "he had sent them a wagon load of brandy."

On the 12th Sherman sent for Hazen, and told him what he wanted him to do. In a half-hour this gallant officer was off with his division, and by night reached King's bridge, ten miles from the fort. The next morning he kept on till within a mile of it, when he halted. Selecting nine regiments with which to make the assault, he moved them forward to within six hundred yards of the works. The fort stood on the right bank of the Ogeechee, just where the firm land and sea-marsh join. Between him and it, stretched an open space more than a third of a mile wide, planted thick with torpedoes, and swept by artillery, across which in broad daylight, the storming force must march before they could reach the ramparts. These were surrounded by a heavy abattis, and beyond it was a deep ditch, along which were driven high, strong palisades. Sherman was well aware of the desperate nature of the undertaking, and designed to have the fleet co-operate in the attack, so as to draw off a part of the hostile force from Hazen. He had gone down the river with Howard, and was at this time standing on the top of a rice-mill, three miles off, on the opposite side of the stream, anxiously watching for the appearance of the expected gunboat, for he had not heard from the fleet since Colonel Duncan set off to communicate with it. At length he saw the smoke of a steamer seaward and exclaimed, "See, Howard, there is the gunboat." In a short time its signal waved, "Is fort McAllister ours?" "No," was the answering signal from the rice-mill. "Can you assist?" "Yes," was the reply, "what shall we do?" The thunder of guns from the fort announcing that the struggle had commenced, rendered a reply unnecessary.

Hazen had sent forward some sharp-shooters to within two hundred yards of the fort to clear the parapets, while he got his lines in position. This was attended with a good deal of difficulty on the right, where the marsh was soft, and crossed by a lagoon, and caused Hazen much solicitude. He saw this signal flying from the top of the rice-mill, three miles away, "*The fort must be taken at all hazards, to-night!*" and yet the sun was then almost touching the rim of the western horizon. He knew that Sherman and Howard were both watching him through their glasses, that Savannah was the stake at issue, and hence could not but feel the fearful responsibility under which he was to fight the coming battle. His anxiety was depicted on his grave countenance, yet every lineament was fixed and stern as fate itself. At length he saw his line in position, when he called the nearest bugler to him, and ordered him to sound the "Attention." The prolonged warning notes swept along the waiting line, and died in faint echoes over the sea. "Sound it again," he exclaimed, and again the well known strain stirred every heart, and called the foe to the ramparts. "Sound it again," cried Hazen in sterner accents, and for the third time the appealing notes swept in soft cadences over the plain, making each soldier clutch his musket with a firmer grasp. Now, shouted Hazen, in tones that made the bugler start, "*Sound the forward.*"

The shrill, rapid notes shook the excited line as a sudden wind-gust the tree-tops, and the next moment, with a loud and ringing cheer, it bounded forward. In an instant, the guns of the fort opened, sweeping all the level space the brave fellows must traverse, with a horrible fire. Breasting this without flinching, they came upon torpedoes, buried in the sand, that exploded to their tread, sending men, mangled and torn, into the air. Heedless of these, as of the fire in front, they kept unhesitatingly on their terrible way, moving on the double-quick, until, at length, they reached the abattis. Pulling this apart by main strength, they stormed through it and reached the ditch. Seizing the strong palisades here, they wrenched them fiercely out, and making a gap, poured through it with loud shouts, and mounted the parapets.

Sherman stood on the rice-mill watching all this, through his glass, with emotions that can but faintly be imagined. As the blue line swept steadily onward, he exclaimed "How grandly they advance! not a waver!" With his eye still glued to that unwavering line, he, in a few seconds, again exclaimed, "Look, Howard! see that flag in the advance; how steadily it moves! not a man falters. Grand, grand!" After a short pause, he cried, "The flag still goes forward; there is no flinching there." But in a few seconds, he said, in an altered tone, "Look, it has halted! They waver." But as the smoke lifted a moment, he almost shouted, "No, it's the parapet. There they go, again, right over it! See, there is a flag on the works! another! another! It's ours! The fort is ours."

The firing ceased; the rebel flag came down; the Stars and Stripes went up; the glass dropped, and a smile lighted up his features, for he well knew what a shout was going up from those smoking, bloody ramparts—and exclaiming, "Savannah is ours," he seized a slip of paper, and wrote a dispatch to the Government, closing with, "I regard Savannah as already gained." Calling one of his aids, he said, "Captain, have a boat ready, I must go over there." Swift rowers were soon pulling him across the river, and, just at dark, he walked into the fort—his face aglow with enthusiasm—and seizing Hazen by the hand, overwhelmed him with praises, as well he might, for Hazen had captured Savannah for him, and thus made his Georgia campaign the decisive movement of the war.

Sherman now communicated with the fleet, and going on board the Admiral's flag-ship—the Harvest Moon—arranged with General Foster to send some siege ordnance from Hilton Head. After consulting with Dahlgren he returned to his lines at Savannah.

The reports of the division Commanders on the condition of things, made him determine, the moment the siege guns arrived from Port Royal, to assault the enemy's works. A number of thirty-pounder Parrott guns having reached King's bridge, he, on the 17th, sent in a formal demand for the surrender of the city, which Hardee rejected. He now made further reconnoissances, and ordered Slocum to get in position siege guns, and make every thing ready for the final assault at the earliest moment. He also established a division of troops, under Foster, on the neck between the Coosawhatchie and Tullifinney Rivers, where his artillery could reach the railroad, and then started for Port Royal, in person, to get reinforcements for him, so that he could assault and carry the railroad, and thus obtain possession of the Union Causeway, from the direction of Port Royal. This was the plank road on the South Carolina shore, which once occupied, would complete the "investment of Savannah."

He put to sea on the night of the 20th, but a gale of wind arising, it was deemed impossible to get over the Ossabaw Bar, and the vessel (the Harvest Moon) ran into the Tybee to make the passage through the inland channel into Warsaw Sound, and thence through Romney Marsh. But the ship, caught in the ebb-tide, could not make the passage, and Dahlgren took him in his tug toward Vernon River. To his surprise, Sherman received, on the way, a message from his Adjutant, Captain Dayton, stating that Savannah was evacuated, and our troops already in possession of the enemy's lines. He immediately hurried back, and on the morning of the 22nd, rode into the City of Savannah.

The surrender of the place was made to Geary, who was placed in command of the city. Sherman sent the following terse dispatch to the President:—"I beg to present you, as a Christmas gift, the City of Savannah, with one hundred and fifty guns, and plenty of ammunition, and about twenty-five thousand bales of cotton." There proved to be thirty-eight thousand bales. Three steamers were also captured, besides locomotives, cars, &c., and eight hundred prisoners.

Thus ended this wonderful campaign, the success of which very few believed in. With an army of sixty or seventy thousand men, to swing entirely loose from his base, and move, for weeks, through a hostile country, depending solely on forage for supplies, was one of the boldest movements in military history.

The Southern press said, scornfully, that he was marching to the "paradise of fools," and the European journals, almost without exception, predicted a total failure.

At the North, his success was considered very doubtful. Even Grant, in reply to Sherman's request to be allowed to undertake the enterprise, said, "If you were to cut loose, I do not believe you would meet Hood's army, but would be bushwhacked by all the old men, little boys, and such railroad guards as are still left at home."

That march could not have been made through one of the Northern States, but slavery, which the South boasted was an element of strength in war, because it allowed all the whites to enter the army and yet secured the cultivation of the soil, was found, in an invasion, to be an element of fatal weakness. The working population, in a free State, would have hung around the flanks of such an invading army "like lightning around the edge of a thunder-cloud," but in the South, that population was all on the side of the invaders—in short, an element of strength to us.

CHAPTER XXXVIII.

NOVEMBER–DECEMBER, 1864.

EXPEDITION FROM VICKSBURG—GRIERSON'S EXPEDITION—BRECKENRIDGE IN EAST TENNESSEE—STONEMAN SENT AGAINST HIM—ROUT OF THE ENEMY—DESTRUCTION OF WYTHEVILLE AND THE SALT WORKS AT SALTVILLE—HOOD ADVANCES AGAINST NASHVILLE—SCHOFIELD FALLS BACK BEFORE HIM—BATTLE OF FRANKLIN—SIEGE OF NASHVILLE—IMPATIENCE OF GRANT—BATTLE OF NASHVILLE—RETREAT OF HOOD—OPERATIONS AROUND MURFREESBORO'—CLOSE OF THE CAMPAIGN—EVENTS EAST—PLOT TO BURN THE CITY OF NEW YORK—ARREST AND EXECUTION OF REBEL OFFICERS—WARREN'S EXPEDITION—FIRST ATTEMPT TO CAPTURE FORT FISHER—CO-OPERATIVE MOVEMENT FROM PLYMOUTH—LOSS OF THE OTSEGO.

BUT while, during the months of November and December, Sherman's army was leisurely making its way toward Savannah, "two expeditions, one from Baton Rouge, Louisiana, and one from Vicksburg, Mississippi, were started by General Canby to cut the enemy's line of communication with Mobile and detain troops in that field. General Foster, commanding Department of the South, also sent an expedition, *via* Broad River, to destroy the railroad between Charleston and Savannah. The expedition from Vicksburg, under command of Brevet Brigadier-General E. D. Osband, (Colonel of Third United States colored cavalry,) captured, on the 27th of November, and destroyed the Mississippi Central railroad bridge and trestle-work over the Big Black River, near Canton, thirty miles of the road, and two locomotives, besides large amounts of stores. The expedition from Baton Rouge was without favorable results.

"A cavalry expedition, under Brevet Major-General Grierson, started from Memphis on the 21st of December. On the 25th, he surprised and captured Forrest's dismounted camp at Verona, Mississippi, on the Mobile and Ohio railroad; destroyed the railroad, sixteen cars loaded with wagons and pontoons for Hood's army, four thousand new English carbines, and large amounts of public stores. On the morning of the 28th, he attacked and captured a force of the enemy at Egypt, and destroyed a train of fourteen cars; thence turning to the south-west, he struck the Mississippi Central railroad at Winona, destroyed the factories and large amounts of stores at Bankston, and the machine-shops and public property at Grenada, arriving at Vicksburg January 5th.

"During these operations in Middle Tennessee, the enemy with a force under General Breckenridge, entered East Tennessee. On the 13th of November, he attacked General Gillem, near Morristown, capturing his artillery and several hundred prisoners. Gillem, with what was left of his command, retreated to Knoxville. Following up his success, Breckenridge moved to near Knoxville, but withdrew on the 18th, followed by General Ammen. Under the directions of General Thomas, General Stoneman concentrated the commands of Generals Burbridge and Gillem near Bean's Station, to operate against Breckenridge and destroy or drive him into Virginia, destroy the salt works at Saltville, and the railroad into Virginia, as far as he could go without endangering his command.

"On the 12th of December he commenced his movement, capturing and dispersing the enemy's forces wherever he met them. On the 16th he struck the enemy, under Vaughn, at Marion, completely routing and pursuing him to Wytheville, capturing all his artillery, trains, and one hundred and ninety-eight prisoners; and destroyed Wytheville, with its stores and supplies, and the extensive lead works near there. Returning to Marion, he met a force, under Breckenridge, consisting, among other troops, of the garrison of Saltville, that had started in pursuit. He at once made arrangements to attack it the next morning; but morning found Breckenridge gone. He then moved directly to Saltville, and destroyed the extensive salt works at that place, a large amount of stores, and captured eight pieces of artillery. Having thus successfully executed his instructions, he returned General Burbridge to Lexington, and General Gillem to Knoxville."

These, however, were minor movements—the great interest centered around Hood's army, which Sherman had left behind him. When the former found himself north of the Tennessee, and his pursuer back to Atlanta, his surprise was complete. He knew that it would be useless to turn about and attempt to overtake him, and so he determined to advance north and attack Nashville.

Schofield, with the Fourth and Twenty-third Corps, was directed to keep the field and check, as much as possible, his advance, so as to give Thomas time to concentrate his troops. Steedman, at this time, held Chattanooga, Bridgeport, and that line of railroad.

After Hood crossed the Tennessee River, Schofield fell back across Duck River, where he made a stand, but the former pressed him so severely that he had to retreat. Setting fire to his own pontoon bridge, he marched swiftly for Franklin, eighteen miles from Nashville, for he knew if he did not cross Harpeth River first, his army would be hopelessly cut off. Hood was aware of this, and strained every nerve to reach the river before him.

Schofield's immense train crippled him sadly, and at one time it was doubtful if he could save it. It was a life and death race, but he won it nobly. Once over the river, where, if defeated, he could fall back on Nashville, he resolved to deal his powerful adversary one blow before retreating farther; and hastily throwing up breastworks, he calmly awaited his approach. Hood, confident of success, boldly advanced to the attack, on the last day of November, and the battle of Franklin commenced. Throwing himself, with his accustomed impetuosity, on the centre of Schofield's position, he carried it, and Wagner, who commanded here, was forced back, losing two guns. He, however, rallied his men, and charging back, re-took his guns, and captured a whole brigade.

In spite of Cox, Wagner, Opdyke, and Stanley, Hood, at last, got possession of the first line of works, though at a terrible sacrifice of life. But just at sunset, when Cox and Stanley, with their re-formed lines, advanced to drive back the enemy, the struggle became terrible, and assumed a savage ferocity. The rebels, though the canister and grape of the close batteries cut frightful lanes through their ranks, refused to yield an inch of the ground they had so gallantly won, and a gladiatorial contest followed, in which the combatants stood face to face, thrusting their bayonets into each other's bosoms—and with clubbed muskets, and demoniacal yells, fought in the deepening twilight, more like savages than civilized men.

Darkness, at length, closed on this strange battle, and Hood was at last compelled to give it up and retire from the captured works—to mourn over the loss of over six thousand men, and six general officers killed, six wounded, and one captured. Our loss was only twenty-three hundred, yet Schofield having done all that he intended to do—dealt his adversary a blow that severely crippled him—fell back that night to Nashville, leaving him in possession of the battle field.

On the same day that Schofield reached Nashville, A. J. Smith, with his command, arrived in transports from St. Louis, together with Steedman. with five thousand men and a brigade of colored troops from Chattanooga. The latter barely got through, for after the battle of Franklin, Hood at once advanced his lines around the city, and effectually cut off all communications south.

The rebel army occupied a series of hills, some four or five miles out of Nashville, while Thomas lay behind defensive works, erected on a similar range of hills near the city. Hood's only chance of success was in a sudden assault; but the moment he sat down before the place, in a regular siege, his doom was sealed.

The people were at once set to work on the fortifications, and two lines of works, exterior and interior, were constructed at a distance from the city, varying from one to two miles, with forts, redoubts, and rifle-pits, at every available point, until the range of hills, occupied by our forces, was a perfect net-work of fortifications.

Early in December, Thomas opened on the enemy with artillery, but designed to act only on the defensive until his preparations were complete. In the meantime, eight gunboats, with the iron-clad Neosho, came up the Cumberland, and were quite able to take care of the rebel batteries in that direction. Hood evidently designed to isolate Nashville as Sherman did Atlanta, by cutting its communications, yet it was not so clear how this was to be done with our gunboats patrolling the river.

Thomas was at length ready to take the field, but expecting to defeat his adversary, he wanted a cavalry force with which to follow up his victory, and make an utter end of him, and so telegraphed to the Secretary of War. The latter immediately directed Wilson, the chief of cavalry, to seize and impress all serviceable horses that could be found in Tennessee and Kentucky.

In the meantime, Grant became nervous over Thomas' delay, and telegraphed to him to move at once. The latter replied that he was not ready, and requested Grant, if he was dissatisfied with his course, to appoint a Commander in his place, and he would cheerfully serve under him. Grant sent back word that he had more confidence in him than in any other man, and that he might take his own time—still, he wanted to know the reasons of his delay.

Thomas not thinking it prudent to give them, lest they should leak out on the way, kept silent. This did not tend to lessen Grant's solicitude, and he says,—

"I grew very impatient over, as it appeared to me, the unnecessary delay. This impatience was increased, upon learning that the enemy had sent a force of cavalry across the Cumberland into Kentucky. I feared Hood would cross his whole army, and give us great trouble there. After urging upon General Thomas the necessity of immediately assuming the offensive, I started West to superintend matters there in person. Reaching Washington City, I received General Thomas' dispatch, announcing his attack upon the enemy, and the result, as far as the battle had progressed. I was delighted. All fears and apprehensions were dispelled."

It was strange that Grant did not feel that it was perfectly safe to let Thomas have his own way, as Sherman did when he placed his reputation in his keeping, and turned his back on Atlanta.

Near the middle of December, Thomas finding that he had all the cavalry that he could expect, though not all he wanted, resolved to attack Hood behind his works. But just then came a cold snap, glazing the hills with ice, so that neither men nor animals could keep upon their feet, and the advance was delayed until there should come a thaw. In a day or two the weather changed, and on the night of the 14th, Thomas gave orders to be ready to attack at daylight next morning. His plan was to make a feint on Hood's right flank, and then fall with sudden, overwhelming power on his left, and roll it back on the centre. A. J. Smith was stationed on the right, with the Sixteenth Corps, and at day-break moved forward—Wilson's cavalry keeping on *his* right along the river shore, while Wood, with the Fourth Corps, closed in on his left. Schofield, with the Twenty-third Corps, came in on Wood's left as a reserve. Three Corps were thus concentrated on the rebel left.

Far away, on our left, Steedman, commanding a mixed body of troops, was directed to push out a heavy force of skirmishers before daylight, and threaten the rebel right. He did so, and driving in the enemy's pickets, followed close on their heels, until he came upon a battery, planted behind a deep railroad cut, which the troops could not get over, and hence were forced to retire. Hood, aroused at early dawn by the heavy firing on his extreme right, called to horse, but before he had time to ascertain the true state of things there, down on his left came the two Corps of Smith and Wood.

So sudden and awful was the onset, that only a feeble resistance could be offered, and the rebel line crumbled swiftly before it, and in a twinkling the left was hurled, in confusion, back on the centre. "This let the cavalry loose, and now Wilson swept round and past the right like a thunderbolt, and hung like an avenging cloud on the flank and rear of the rebels, as they fell suddenly back on their centre."

Aroused to the imminent peril that threatened him, Hood now ordered over troops from his right to stay the reversed tide of battle—and from all the heights around Nashville, could be seen the hurrying lines of infantry and artillery sweeping to the rescue.

But though his left was gone, the position he held in the centre was a strong one; high hills—covered with breastworks, lined with rifle-pits, and fringed with abattis, beyond which frowned heavy batteries—commanded all the open country below. Smith paused before this formidable barrier, and began to reconnoitre. Wood and Schofield now came up, and all day long, Hood's intrenchments were swept by a fierce artillery fire, while here and there the infantry attempted to find a weak spot in his lines. But no impression was made on the strong position which the enemy occupied, and no particular advantage gained, except the possession of a battery, which was carried by a gallant rush. Still, the results of the whole day footed up well—two thousand prisoners captured, with sixteen pieces of artillery.

As the day declined, and darkness began to creep over the landscape, Thomas, who saw that no more could be done that night, ordered the firing to cease, and turning his horse's head, rode off to Nashville to telegraph his success to Washington.

Just as he was leaving the field he remarked to an officer, in his quiet way, "So far I think we have done pretty well. Unless Hood decamps to-night, to-morrow Steedman will double up his right, Wood will hold his centre, Smith and Schofield again strike his left, while the cavalry work away at his rear."

That night Hood took up a new and strong position, two miles in rear of his first, by which his lines were shortened from six miles to three. Thomas, carrying out his original plan, ordered Steedman to move at daylight against the enemy's right as before, while Wood advanced over the deserted works straight on the centre. Their orders, however, were merely to feel the hostile line and wait till Smith and Schofield broke with the thunder-crash of the day before on the rebel left. But the latter, too, were directed simply to hold their ground, until the cavalry which had been sent in a wide circuit to the rear, could be heard from.

Hood had again committed the mistake that he did at Atlanta, when he sent off all his cavalry to cut Sherman's communications, leaving that Commander to place his army where his own would be effectually destroyed. He possessed a fine body of cavalry, under Forrest, superior in number to that of Thomas, but he had sent it down the Cumberland after our transports, and back to Murfreesboro', to waste its energies in dashing against our strong defenses. Thomas was aware of this, and hence had no fear that it would interfere with his movements.

It was a long time, however, before our cavalry was heard from. It had made a wide detour to prevent the movement from being detected, so that noon came without any thing of importance being done. There had been heavy artillery firing all the forenoon, and Hood was evidently momentarily expecting an attack. Smith and Schofield chafed under the inaction, and sent to Thomas for permission to assault, but he firmly refused. The short winter's day wore on, and night threatened to come before any thing was accomplished. But Thomas remained imperturbable as ever, amid all the impatience and excitement around him. At length, about four o'clock, a prolonged fire of rifles and carbines, that swept around the rebel flank, and crept up along Hood's rear, told him that the hour had come. His blue eye flashed with sudden inspiration, and turning to his aids, he said, "Now tell Generals Schofield and Smith to advance."

The aids dashed off to deliver the order, but before they reached these impatient Generals, the latter were already advancing. With leveled bayonets and loud, defiant shouts, the columns moved straight on and over the rebel works. Wood, in the centre, at once advanced and came upon a strong fort which commanded the Franklin pike, and aided by Steedman on the left, with his colored troops, attempted to carry it. At first, the assaulting columns were repulsed with fearful slaughter, but the troops rallied when they heard the shouts of Wood's and Schofield's battalions, as, storming over the hostile batteries, they scaled the bald hill in their front, and again moved with loud cheers against the fort, and captured it, with nine pieces of artillery.

A gentle rain was falling, and not a breeze stirred the leafless branches of the dripping trees, while this whirlwind of death was sweeping the heights. Borne back at every point, the enemy abandoned their batteries, and throwing away every thing that could impede their flight, sped in dismay over the country.

Said a captured Brigadier-General, in speaking of the last charge, "Why, Sir, it was the most wonderful thing I ever witnessed. I saw your men coming and held my fire—a full brigade, too—until they were in close range, could almost see the whites of their eyes, and then poured my volley right into their faces. I supposed, of course, that when the smoke lifted, your line would be broken and your men gone. But it is surprising, Sir, it never even staggered them. Why, they did not even come forward on a run. But right along, cool as fate, your line swung up the hill, and your men walked right up to and over my works and around my brigade, before we knew that they were upon us. It was astonishing, Sir, such fighting."

Over five thousand prisoners, one Major-General, three Brigadiers, and more than two hundred commissioned officers were captured, not to mention the killed and wounded. Forty pieces of artillery were taken, with any quantity of small arms, battle-flags, &c.

Thus, in two days, Thomas had taken some eight thousand prisoners, and between fifty and sixty pieces of artillery.

As on the day before, so now, night put an end to the

conflict, and our army bivouacked on the field, while the demoralized rebel army retreated through the darkness to Harpeth River. At daylight, the next morning, the Fourth Corps, with the cavalry, commenced the pursuit. On the night of the 19th, Hood crossed Duck River and took up the bridge.

Thomas, in his report, says, "the pontoon train coming up to Rutherford's Creek about noon, of the 21st, a bridge was laid during the afternoon, and General Smith's troops were able to cross. The weather had changed from dismal rain to bitter cold, very materially retarding the work in laying the bridge, as the regiment of colored trops, to whom the duty was intrusted, seemed unmanned by the cold, and totally unequal to the occasion."

This caused a serious delay, but a whole day was lost in a manner not mentioned in any report. The pontoon train took the wrong road, when it left Nashville, and had been gone a part of a day before the mistake was discovered. At Columbia, Forrest's cavalry, that had been operating against Murfreesboro', joined the army, and formed a strong rear-guard for it.

Hood now saw the folly of dividing his forces, for Bates' division of Cheatham's Corps, with which Forrest had been sent against Murfreesboro', was repulsed in its attack on the first block house five miles north of the place, and afterward with another division, and twenty-five hundred of Forrest's cavalry, was driven from before Fort Rosecrans, which was under the command of Rousseau. Attacked in their position by Milroy with seven regiments, the rebels were defeated, with a loss of over four hundred men. Although Buford, with his cavalry, entered the town the same day, he was speedily driven out, so that Hood had weakened his army to no purpose—and now the whole, once more united, fled back toward Alabama.

Thomas kept up the pursuit, though the roads were terrible; but he succeeded in inflicting only slight loss on the enemy.

On the last of the month, Hood crossed the Tennessee, when it was abandoned, and the campaign ended.

This virtually closed the war in the Valley of the Mississippi. Thomas had done his work well and thoroughly, and vindicated the high opinion of Sherman, and nobly fulfilled the trust that had been imposed on him.

But while the months of November and December brought such glorious victories to our armies West and South, the Army of the Potomac won only the laurels due to patient endurance.

Among the minor events of November, was the attempt to burn the City of New York. The diabolical plot originated in Canada, among the rebel refugees there, and was attempted to be put in execution on the night of the 25th of the month. Intrusted to bungling hands, it failed of success, though the fires were started in various buildings. Captain Robert A. Kennedy, of the rebel service, was afterward arrested, at the West, for complicity in it, and tried and executed at Fort Lafayette the following Spring.

Beall, the rebel officer, who in September destroyed two steamboats on the Lakes, was arrested in December, near Suspension Bridge, for attempting to throw a train of cars off the railroad track, and in February was also hung on Governor's Island.

On the 20th of the month, the country was startled by a Proclamation of the President, calling for three hundred thousand more troops. Up to this time, two and a half millions of men had been called for, either for permanent or temporary service, though nothing like this number ever entered the field.

Although the army around Petersburg was engaged in no

battles while such stirring events were transpiring West and South, it was not idle. On the 7th of December, General Warren, with twenty thousand men, moved south toward Hatcher's Run, and in two days reached Bellefield Station, on the Meherrin River, forty miles from Petersburg, where he destroyed the rebel works, depot, &c. The next day he commenced his return march, destroying every thing in his line of march, and twenty miles of the Weldon railroad.

The most important event, however, of the month, connected with the Army of the Potomac, was the attempt to capture Fort Fisher, which commanded the entrance to Cape Fear River.

Wilmington, at this time, was the most important seaport left to the South, for through it she got most of her supplies, and from which she sent out blockade-runners, loaded with cotton and other products. The blockade had been only partially maintained here, and it was deemed very important by the Navy Department that it should be taken. Besides, it was a point of great strategic importance.

As there has been much dispute respecting the cause of the failure of the first attempt to capture the fort, and a direct issue made between the Commanders of the naval and land forces, on questions of fact, we prefer to let General Grant give the history of the affair himself.

"To secure the possession of this land required the co-operation of a land force, which I agreed to furnish. Immediately commenced the assemblage in Hampton Roads, under Admiral D. D. Porter, of the most formidable armada ever collected for concentration upon one given point. This necessarily attracted the attention of the enemy, as well as that of the loyal North; and through the imprudence of the public press, and very likely of officers of both branches of service, the exact object of the expedition became a subject of common discussion in the newspapers both North and

South. The enemy, thus warned prepared to meet it. This caused a postponement of the expedition until the latter part of November, when, being again called upon by Hon. G. V. Fox, Assistant Secretary of the Navy, I agreed to furnish the men required at once, and went myself, in company with Major-General Butler, to Hampton Roads, where we had a conference with Admiral Porter as to the force required and the time of starting. A force of six thousand, five hundred men was regarded as sufficient. The time of starting was not definitely arranged, but it was thought all would be ready by the 6th of December, if not before. Learning on the 30th of November that Bragg had gone to Georgia, taking with him most of the forces about Wilmington, I deemed it of the utmost importance that the expedition should reach its destination before the return of Bragg, and directed General Butler to make all arrangements for the departure of Major-General Weitzel, who had been designated to command the land forces, so that the navy might not be detained one moment.

"On the 6th of December the following instructions were given:

"City Point, Va., Dec. 6, 1864.

"General:—The first object of the expedition under General Weitzel is to close to the enemy the port of Wilmington. If successful in this, the second will be to capture Wilmington itself. There are reasonable grounds to hope for success, if advantage can be taken of the absence of the greater part of the enemy's forces now looking after Sherman in Georgia. The directions you have given for the numbers and equipment of the expedition are all right except in the unimportant matter of where they embark, and the amount of intrenching tools to be taken. The object of the expedition will be gained by effecting a landing on the main land between Cape Fear River and the Atlantic, north of the north entrance to the river. Should such landing be effected whilst the enemy still holds Fort Fisher and the batteries guarding the entrance to the river, then the troops should intrench themselves, and, by co-operating with the navy, effect the reduction and capture of those places. These in our hands, the navy could enter the harbor, and the port of Wilmington would be sealed. Should Fort Fisher and the point of land on which it is built fall into the hands of our troops immediately on landing, then it will be worth the attempt to capture Wilmington by a forced march and surprise. If time is consumed in gaining the first object of the expedition, the second will become a matter of after consideration.

"The details for execution are intrusted to you and the officer immediately in command of the troops.

"Should the troops under General Weitzel fail to effect a landing at or near Fort Fisher they will be returned to the armies operating against Richmond without delay.

U. S. GRANT, Lieutenant General.

Major General B. F. Butler.

"General Butler commanding the army from which the troops were taken for this enterprise, and the territory within which they were to operate, military courtesy required that all orders and instructions should go through him. They were so sent; but General Weitzel has since officially informed me that he never received the foregoing instructions, nor was he aware of their existence until he read General Butler's published official report of the Fort Fisher failure, with my endorsement and papers accompanying it. I had no idea of General Butler's accompanying the expedition until the evening before it got off from Bermuda Hundred, and then did not dream but that General Weitzel had received all the instructions, and would be in command. I rather formed the idea that General Butler was actuated by a desire to witness the effect of the explosion of the powder-boat. The expedition was detained several days at Hampton Roads, awaiting the loading of the powder-boat.

"The importance of getting the Wilmington expedition off without any delay, with or without the powder-boat, had been urged upon General Butler, and he advised to so notify Admiral Porter.

"The expedition finally got off on the 13th of December, and arrived at the place of rendezvous, off New Inlet, near Fort Fisher, on the evening of the 15th. Admiral Porter arrived on the evening of the 18th, having put in at Beaufort to get ammunition for the monitors. The sea becoming rough, making it difficult to land troops, and the supply of water and coal being about exhausted, the transport fleet put back to Beaufort to replenish; this, with the state of the weather, delayed the return to the place of rendezvous until the 24th. The powder-boat was exploded on the morning of the 24th, before the return of General Butler from Beaufort; but it would seem from the notice taken of it in the Southern newspapers, that the enemy were never enlightened as to the object of the explosion until they were informed by the Northern press.

"On the 25th a landing was effected without opposition, and a reconnoissance, under Brevet Brigadier General Curtis, pushed up toward the Fort. But before receiving a full report of the result of this reconnoissance, General Butler, in direct violation of the instructions given, ordered the re-embarkation of the troops and the return of the expedition.

"The re-embarkation was accomplished by the morning of the 27th."

The powder-boat was Butler's device, he having read of the effects of the explosion of a large amount of powder in England. It was placed under the command of Commander A. C. Rhind, who, with Lieutenant S. W. Preston, Engineer A. T. E. Mullen, and Acting Master's Mate Paul Boyden, and seven men undertook the perilous task of towing it in. Having anchored it within four hundred yards of the fort, he set fire to the fuse that was to explode it, and, hastening back to the Wilderness, steamed away twelve miles to avoid the effects of the explosion. The whole fleet lay off at this safe distance. The object was to explode the magazine of the fort, and blow it and the garrison together into the air. It proved however quite a harmless affair, but the bombardment that followed was one of the most terrific ever witnessed.

The fleet of Porter consisted of seventy-three vessels, carrying in all six hundred and fifty-five guns, some of them of the largest calibre. For two days it was kept up, completely silencing the fort, which Porter insists could easily have been taken by a man of any enterprise.

There is one short sentence in Grant's report, which for keen sarcasm, and quiet humor cannot be surpassed. In speaking of his ignorance that Butler was to command the expedition he says, "*I had rather formed the idea that General Butler was actuated by a desire to witness the effect of the explosion of the powder-boat.*"

This ended the extraordinary military career of General Butler, for soon after he was superseded by Ord.

As a co-operative movement in this expedition, General Palmer sent off a force from Plymouth, which proceeded up the Roanoke River beyond Jamestown, but not being sustained by the gunboats that were kept back by the torpedoes in the river, it effected nothing of importance. In the fore part of the month the gunboat Otsego was sunk in the river by one of these torpedoes.

CHAPTER XXXIX.

JANUARY, 1865.

GUERRILLAS—PEACE RUMORS—RELIEF FOR THE DESTITUTE IN SAVANNAH—GRANT PLANS A SECOND EXPEDITION AGAINST FORT FISHER—TERRY COMMANDS IT—THE BOMBARDMENT—THE ASSAULT AND VICTORY—EVACUATION OF OTHER FORTS IN THE VICINITY—THOMAS' ARMY BROKEN UP—SMITH'S COMMAND SENT TO JOIN CANBY—SCHOFIELD'S CORPS ORDERED EAST—NORTH CAROLINA MADE A SEPARATE MILITARY DEPARTMENT—NARROW ESCAPE OF THE ARMY OF THE POTOMAC—PEACE COMMISSIONERS APPOINTED BY DAVIS—THEIR INTERVIEW WITH THE PRESIDENT AND SECRETARY OF STATE—EXCHANGE OF PRISONERS—SOUTHERN PRISON LIFE—INHUMANITY OF THE SOUTH—ANDERSONVILLE PRISON—CAPTAIN WIRZ, THE COMMANDANT, TRIED AT WASHINGTON AND HUNG.

THE beginning of the year 1865 exhibited no active military movements in any part of the country. Guerrillas still swarmed in Kentucky, and other border States—the steamer Venango was burned by them, on the Mississippi, and the more desperate the cause of the Confederacy became, the more vindictive and ferocious seemed their conduct.

Peace rumors were afloat, which acquired importance from the repeated visits of Francis P. Blair, Senior, to Richmond.

The destitution of the people of Savannah, called forth the sympathies of the citizens of New York, and provisions and supplies, of various kinds, were furnished for their relief.

But under all this apparent quietness, the most important preparations were going on. Not only was Sherman getting ready for his northern march, but Grant, indignant at the failure of the expedition against Fort Fisher, was quietly preparing for a second and more serious attempt to capture it. His movements were all so secretly made, that the public journals got no hint of his intentions until his work was accomplished.

Still, we must confess that we cannot see the wisdom of this second expedition. When Sherman reached Savannah, Grant directed him to place his army on transports and join him at City Point, in order to aid him in his projected operations against Richmond. But after the defeat of Hood by Thomas, he changed his plans, and wrote to Sherman, asking him what, under the circumstances, he thought it best to do. The latter replied, that he would, at once, come to him by sea if he desired, but that he had expected to march to Columbia, South Carolina, and thence to Raleigh, where he would report to him.

Grant says:—"The confidence he manifested in this letter of being able to march up and join me, pleased me, and, without waiting for a reply to my letter of the 18th, I directed him, on the 28th of December, to make preparations to start, as he proposed, without delay, to break up the railroads in North and South Carolina, and join the armies operating against Richmond as soon as he could."

Now, this order was sent the day after the re-embarkation of the troops that, under the first expedition, were to assault Fort Fisher. Hence, Grant was perfectly aware of Sherman's plan to march north to Raleigh, and was so confident of its practicability that he approved of it. But he also knew that if Sherman succeeded in carrying out that plan, Fort Fisher and Wilmington would fall of themselves. No one knew better than he, that the enemy could no more hold Wilmington, with Sherman marching on Raleigh or Goldsboro', than he could Charleston, with him marching on Columbia.

Before he reached even Fayetteville, these places would

be evacuated, or the garrisons hopelessly cut off; hence, to our apprehension, it would have been just as wise to have sacrificed the lives of our soldiers in an attack on Charleston, at this time, as on Wilmington. A glance at the map will make this plain, and any one will see that nothing between Sherman's line of march and the sea could be held by the rebels.

The original plan of attempting to capture Fort Fisher was not Grant's, but it having failed, he determined that it should be carried out. Taking the same troops that Butler had, with the addition of only a small brigade numbering about fifteen hundred men, he placed them under General Terry, also a civilian Commander, with orders similar to those which he had given to the former, or rather to Weitzel. In neither case did he direct that an assault on the fort should be made—he left this entirely "to the discretion of the commanding officer."

The expedition sailed from Fortress Monroe on the 6th of January, "arriving on the rendezvous off Beaufort on the 8th, where, owing to the difficulties of the weather, it lay until the morning of the 12th, when it got under way, and reached its destination that evening." The next morning, the disembarkation of the troops commenced, and by three o'clock was completed without loss. The next day a reconnoissance was made to within five hundred yards of the fort, "and a small advance work taken possession of, and turned into a defensive line against any attempt that might be made from the fort."

The third day, Sunday, was fixed upon for the assault, but, in the meantime, the fleet had kept up a terrible fire upon the fort. It attacked in three columns. The first, led by the Brooklyn, numbered one hundred and sixteen guns; the second, by the Minnesota, one hundred and seventy-six guns; while the third, composed of gunboats, numbered one hundred and twenty-three—in all, over four hundred guns, that played with fearful precision on the hostile works. When the firing was most rapid, shells fell at the rate of four every second.

Under this horrible fire, guns were dismounted, embrasures blown open, and traverses disappeared with amazing rapidity.

A force of marines and sailors, numbering about two thousand, was to assault from the sea-side, at the same time that the columns of Terry advanced from the land-side. For three hours previous to the assault, the four hundred guns of the fleet were worked to their utmost capacity, till the ponderous shells fell thick as hailstones from heaven, on the doomed fort—driving the garrison to the casemates. The parapets were twenty-five feet thick, and twenty feet high, and surrounded by a strong palisade. About two hundred yards in advance of this, was strung a line of torpedoes, eighty-five feet apart—each one containing a hundred pounds of powder, and all connected by wires. Fortunately, the shells from the fleet had cut the wires leading to those that lay in the path of the assaulting columns. The shells, also, broke down a part of the palisade, so that they had almost a clear sweep to the ramparts—though in some places they had to be cut away or beaten down.

At length, every thing being ready, at three o'clock the signal was given, and the three brigades—the first led by Curtis, the second by Pennypacker, and the third by Bell—dashed forward, following one another about three hundred yards apart, making, in their final rush, for the west end on the land-side. As they started, Porter ran up his signal which set all the steam-whistles shrieking. This was the signal to change the fire of the fleet from the fort, and concentrate it on the batteries to the left and above, to avoid hitting our own troops. The smoke hanging over the mighty armada, out of which arose the shriek of countless steam-whistles, and came incessant explosions too quick to count—the volcano that opened from the fort, as with loud cheers those gallant brigades drove on, combined to make that Sabbath afternoon one of the most terrific the earth ever witnessed. On the sea-side, the marines and sailors dashed gallantly forward, but were swept like chaff before the wind, from the ramparts. Terry's troops, however, boldly mounted those in their front, when a fearful hand to hand conflict followed. Soon the high parapets swallowed up the combatants, but the work of death went on within. Shouts and curses, mingled with volleys of musketry, made the interior of that fort a pandemonium—but our troops, bent on victory, won their way steadily from traverse to traverse in spite of the desperate opposition of the enemy.

The wintry sun went down on the strange scene, and darkness closed around the combatants. Fighting in the fitful light of the flashes of musketry, and of the flaming shells streaking the sky above them, they drove the garrison back step by step, until at last, at half past nine the fort was cleared. A long, loud shout arose from the bosom of the bloody and trampled works, and then Terry's signal torches flamed from the summit, announcing to Porter that the place was won. The firing ceased, and rockets were immediately sent up from the flagship, signaling to the fleet the glorious news, when cheer after cheer rung over the water, ship answering ship in the darkness—the shouts being echoed back from the fort, till land and sea shook with the wild huzzas. About midnight, General Whitney, and Colonel Lamb, the Commanders, with the garrison, eighteen hundred in number, surrendered. Seventy-three guns fell into our hands, besides the camp equipage and stores.

Our loss was six hundred and forty-six in killed and wounded, while that of the enemy was only four hundred.

Unfortunately, in the morning the magazine blew up, killing and wounding several hundred more. Among our officers who fell in the assault were Colonels Bell and Moore, and Lieutenant Colonel Lyman, killed, and Colonels Curtis, Pennypacker and Lieutenant Colonel Coan, wounded. In the fleet the loss of which in the assault was about two hundred, Lieutenants Preston and Porter were killed, and Lamson and Bache, wounded. The other forts in the vicinity, one after another, with eighty-three cannon now fell into our hands, the garrisons retiring to Wilmington.

In the meantime Thomas' army being no longer needed in Tennessee, was broken up ; and A. J. Smith's command, with a division of cavalry, ordered to report to General Canby, while Schofield's Corps was brought east and sent to Fort Fisher, and Newbern. North Carolina was created a separate military department, and placed under the latter, with orders to report to General Sherman.

But while we were rejoicing in our victories on the Cape Fear River, a disaster came very near befalling the Army of the Potomac, that would speedily have wiped out its remembrance. Knowing that our war vessels were nearly all away at the former place, the rebels on the night of the 24th sent four iron-clads down the James River, with the intention of severing the armies on the two sides of the stream, and, reaching City Point to destroy the communications of the army. A heavy rebel force in the meantime, was massed north of the James, to fall on our army there the moment success was announced. The signal of this was to be the burning of a high tower at City Point, erected by us for the purpose of overlooking the enemy's lines. The iron-clads broke through the obstructions at Dutch Gap canal—passed Fort Brady—drove back the only vessel we had stationed in the river, and bid fair to reach City Point. The utmost consternation prevailed along our lines, and officers were seen galloping off in every direction. Fortunately the vessels grounded and one of them was blown up, and the other destroyed—so that the well-laid scheme totally failed.

In the Court of Inquiry summoned to investigate this affair, every officer but General Grant that was examined as a witness, testified, that had the rebel iron-clads reached City Point, the siege of Petersburg and Richmond would have been raised, as not another pound of provisions could have been got to the army. Grant, on the contrary, said he had provisions enough on hand, that with great economy might last two weeks, and he thought in that time the Government would have succeeded in re-opening his communications. Thus it will be seen even on Grant's testimony, that his salvation would have depended alone on outside help, and not on any thing that he could do. The country never dreamed how narrow was our escape, and how much depended on a few, more or less inches of water.

The close of the month was made memorable by the arrival at Fortress Monroe of Alexander H. Stevens, Vice President of the Confederacy, R. M. T. Hunter, of Virginia and J. A. Campbell, of Alabama, as Peace Commissioners from Jefferson Davis. President Lincoln and Secretary Seward met them two or three days after, on board a steamer, and had an informal interview. The rebel commissioners wished a postponement of the question of sepation, and proposed a cessation of hostilities and the resumption of intercourse between the two sections, to see what time and the subsidence of passion might effect. But Mr. Lincoln mildly yet firmly insisted on a complete restoration of the national authority every where, as the first condition to a cessation of hostilities, and hence the interview broke up without any beneficial results.

Nothing awakened more indignation at the North in the progress of the war than the treatment of our prisoners by the South, which during this Winter reached its climax. As stated in the previous volume, for more than a year after the war commenced we would consent to no cartel with the rebels, as it recognized them as belligerents—but finally, in the Summer of 1862 one was agreed upon, in which it was stipulated that prisoners should be exchanged man for man, and the excess, on either side, be paroled until regularly exchanged.

At that time the balance was greatly against us, and hence the cartel worked in our favor. But the introduction of colored regiments into our army, the soldiers of which the rebel authorities refused to place on the same footing as white ones, brought on an acrimonious correspondence between the Commissioners, Meredith and Ould; the latter insisting that the provisions of the original cartel should be carried out, and exchanges resumed, and the other refusing to consent to any exchange unless stipulations were made in regard to the colored soldiers. Besides, the prisoners captured at Vicksburg and Port Hudson, had turned the balance in our favor by nearly thirty thousand, whom we were afraid to release on parole, having no confidence in the good faith of the Confederate Government. Hence, no regular system of exchanges could be agreed upon. General Butler endeavored, while commanding at Fortress Montroe, to establish one, but failed.

At length, the whole subject assumed a character disgraceful to both Governments. The rebel Government had so treated Union prisoners that they were utterly worthless for active service, if exchanged, while it was sadly in need of soldiers for its rapidly diminishing army, and hence proposed to exchange officer for officer, and man for man, as far as it could be done. To this proposition, our Commissioner refused to accede, giving various reasons for his refusal, but they failed to satisfy the people who were becoming clamorous on the subject.

The real fact was, the Secretary of War saw that while we could raise an indefinite number of men, the South was exhausted, and he had no idea of reinforcing its armies with thirty or forty thousand able-bodied men, and getting in return the same number of emaciated, half-starved, enfeebled soldiers, that would not be fit for duty till the war was over, if ever. His motives, unquestionably, were right, and he thought that he was doing his country a service by keeping the rebel army reduced in this way. Doubtless, too, he thought this course would be a saving of life in the end, but it was cruel as the grave.

There are certain things to be done and to be left undone, without regard to consequences. A ruler may think it the quickest way to end a war, to massacre all the young men fit to bear arms, that he can capture, but the end sought to be obtained can never justify the use of such means. A powerful nation, in war with a weaker one, might think that the shortest way to end the struggle, would be to hoist the black flag and give no quarter, and judge rightly, too; but the whole civilized world would cry out against the barbarous act. And yet these measures have their excuses, but no course can be justified, that, for a probable good, allows brave soldiers, who have nobly struggled to sustain their Government, to languish and die in prison.

There is no class of men, whose interests and welfare should be so dear to the Government, as its soldiers captured in battle. So the country felt, and the pressure became at length so great on the Administration, that it was compelled to turn over the whole matter to General Grant. With his strong, practical common sense, and his love of the soldier, he did not long hesitate respecting the course he ought to adopt.

Not the injustice and wickedness of the South, nor the advantages that might accrue to it, could deter him from acting humanely to our own soldiers, and exchanging man for man as long as it could be done.

The exchange of prisoners, under his wise administration, became very active, and as the emaciated, dying, half-idiotic forms of humanity, that had once been brave American soldiers, reached our lines, the barbaric, diabolical system practised in Southern prisons became painfully apparent. It was vain for the rebel authorities to say that their own soldiers lacked food, and that the inhabitants were starving, and that our prisoners only shared the common fate. Making all due allowance for the scarcity of provisions in the South, the treatment of our prisoners indicated a depth of moral degradation and a savage hate, that will be a disgrace to Southern civilization as long as time endures. If such inhumanity and fiendish cruelty were the result of Slavery, it would need no deeper damnation.

We cannot go over the sickening details of Southern prison-life. Men left to perish with the scurvy—slowly eaten up with maggots—shot without excuse, and tortured, apparently, for mere love of cruelty, make up a picture from which the heart of any but a Fejee would turn with loathing and abhorrence.

The principal prisons, South, were Andersonville and Millen, Georgia; Columbia, Florence, and Charleston, South Carolina; Tyler, Texas; Salisbury, North Carolina; Cahawba, Alabama; Danville, Virginia; and Libby, Pemberton, Castle Thunder, and Belle Isle, Richmond. Of these, Millen, Andersonville, and the Richmond prisons, were preeminent for infamous barbarity.

It is impossible to tell how many perished in these various

prisons during the war, but some have put them as high as seventy thousand. Over ten thousand perished in Andersonville prison alone. In the latter, although the camp was located in the immediate neighborhood of large forests, the captives were allowed no shelter, and the sick groaned out their lives on the bare ground. The treatment was not the same at every period during the war, nor the same in all the prisons, but at Andersonville, the record of every day and month was one of horrors. Here some twenty acres were inclosed by a stockade, with a swamp in the centre, where, at times, thirty thousand Union prisoners were confined. This space was dotted with holes dug by the prisoners to obtain a place of shelter. American soldiers and citizens were here compelled by their former fellow-citizens, to burrow like wild animals in the earth.

The horrors and sufferings of this mundane hell were such that some went mad and roamed about in helpless idiocy; others deliberately walked across the dead-line, as it was called, to be shot, and so get rid of their misery. Those who attempted to escape were hunted with blood-hounds or shot down. Many of the efforts put forth by these men to keep up their spirits, and brace them to endure their sufferings, were most pitiful.

The rebel officers sought to take advantage of their sufferings and make them enlist in the Confederate army, but in most cases without success. The brave fellows, though utterly prostrated in strength and spirits, still refused to betray the flag under which they had fought—and so died, unknown and unsung, yet noble martyrs for their country. The rebel surgeons were, in most cases, humane, and remonstrated with the authorities against the cruelties perpetrated on Union prisoners.

Those who wish to read the heart-rending details of Southern prison-life, will find them at length in the account of the trial of Captain Wirz, who was in immediate command of Andersonville prison. This wretch, who, we are glad to know, was not born in this country, was arraigned soon after the close of the war, before a military commission in Washington, tried, convicted and hung.

There is no language too strong to express the enormity of the guilt of the Southern authorities. On the other hand, there can be no justification of a policy, on our part, that would permit tens of thousands of brave soldiers to perish under untold sufferings, when they might have been saved. If the principle, laid down by Mr. Lincoln, and given on a former page, had been carried out, a greater part of this misery might have been prevented.

CHAPTER XL.

JANUARY–FEBRUARY, 1865.

THE RIGHT WING OF SHERMAN'S ARMY THREATENS CHARLESTON—THE LEFT AUGUSTA—THE ARMY DELAYED BY HEAVY FLOODS—KILPATRICK'S CAVALRY—FORCING OF THE SALKEHATCHIE—THE ENEMY DECEIVED, AND THEIR FORCES HOPELESSLY SEPARATED—DESTRUCTION OF THE CHARLESTON AND AUGUSTA RAILROAD—CAPTURE OF ORANGEBURG—CROSSING THE EDISTO—CAPTURE OF COLUMBIA—BURNING OF THE CITY—DISTRESS OF THE INHABITANTS—BURNING OF WINNSBORO'—CHARLOTTE, N. C., THREATENED—SHERMAN SUDDENLY STRIKES EAST FOR FAYETTEVILLE—CAPTURE OF CHERAW—FALL OF CHARLESTON—JUNCTION OF THE TWO WINGS—CAPTURE OF FAYETTEVILLE—COMMUNICATIONS OPENED WITH SCHOFIELD AND TERRY—BATTLE OF AVERYSBORO'—BATTLE OF BENTONVILLE—OCCUPATION OF GOLDSBORO'—END OF THE CAMPAIGN—SHERMAN VISITS GRANT AT CITY POINT—SPEEDY REFITTING OF THE ARMY.

CAMPAIGN OF THE CAROLINAS.

SHERMAN, having rested his army at Savannah and completed his plans, began, in the middle of January, to send off a part of his troops, in transports, to Beaufort, preparatory to the commencement of his campaign through the Carolinas. But his army was not in motion until the first of February. It numbered about sixty-five thousand men, and was divided into four Corps, with a train of four thousand five hundred vehicles, of all kinds, which, if stretched in a single line, in marching order, would have extended forty-five miles. Each Corps, however, had its own train, which occupied a separate road so as to avoid crowding or delay.

The news of his departure from Savannah filled the South with alarm, and the North with solicitude The question was in every one's mouth, "Where next will this extraordinary man go?" Some thought that he would first strike Augusta, others, Charleston. But he had a grander object in view than the immediate capture of either of these places. Standing in Savannah, he cast his eyes north five hundred miles to Goldsboro', and determined to carry his gallant army thither, right through the heart of two hostile States. One standing by his side and looking forward on the route the brave Chieftain had marked out for his columns, must have been amazed at the mighty enterprise on which he was about to enter.

One rebel army lay at Charleston, on his right, another at Augusta, on his left—North Carolina swarmed with troops, while every step he advanced took him nearer to Lee's gathered forces at Richmond. Large rivers were to be crossed, swamps traversed, and battles fought, before he could reach the goal of his wishes.

In organizing this campaign, Sherman resolved to make Columbia his first objective point. To do this, without being compelled to fight heavy battles, it was necessary to keep the rebel armies at Charleston and Augusta divided. United they could make the rivers successive lines of defense, which could not be carried without severe loss. He, therefore, determined to threaten both places at the same time, and thus keep the enemy at each in a state of suspense and anxiety, and afraid to move in any direction. In carrying out this plan, he directed Slocum, with the left wing and Kilpatrick's cavalry, to move up the Savannah River and threaten Augusta, while Howard advancing from the sea-coast, was to threaten Charleston.

By this adroit management he prevented the enemy from doing the only thing that promised success—viz., the concentration of his forces on the line of the swampy Salkehatchie. Had this been done, and both Charleston and Augusta abandoned, Sherman would have had great trouble in carrying out his plans—for supposing that he could, with his superior strength, have forced this line, still the rebels, by the central position they would occupy, could have fallen back toward Columbia and made another stand on the Edisto. If, on the other hand, he had attempted to outflank, as he did, on the way from Chattanooga to Atlanta, his flanks and trains would have been greatly exposed while crossing the rivers. By trying to save too much, the rebel Commanders lost every thing, and that too without even the honor of fighting for it.

The supplies for the right wing were completed at Pocataligo, and those for the left at Sister's Ferry. At the latter place, Slocum and Kilpatrick were detained a long time by a heavy flood in the river, which, overflowing its banks, covered all the surrounding country with water, so that the inundated lowlands made the stream, at this point, three miles wide.

It was an extraordinary flood, and as Slocum looked at the spreading sea, and thought of his urgent orders to advance without delay, he was filled with great anxiety, and impatiently waited for the waters to subside. As soon, however, as the crossing could be commenced with any degree of safety, he put his army in motion, and the columns, half-waist deep in the water, moved rapidly over the inundated fields.

When he reached solid ground, in order to make up for lost time, he marched eighteen miles a day, though he was constantly compelled to halt and re-bridge streams, and remove trees that the enemy had felled across the road, while the wintry rains made the march heavy, and the night encampment cold and gloomy.

Kilpatrick in the meantime pushed on toward Augusta, and by his daring advance caused all the rebel troops in the vicinity to be concentrated there for its defense, leaving no enemy for Slocum to encounter.

Howard moved from Pocataligo on the last day of the month, leaving Hatch's division behind, in order to keep up the appearance of marching on Charleston by the railroad bridge over the Salkehatchie at that point. He found in his march the roads obstructed by trees felled across it, and the bridges over the swollen streams burned, but the pioneer battalion removed the one, and rebuilt the other so quickly, that the columns were scarcely compelled to halt.

A railroad runs across the state from Charleston to Augusta, and half way between the two stands Midway Station, lying due south from Columbia. Toward this point Howard directed his columns. But he had first to cross the Salkehatchie, which the rebels held in force, "having infantry and artillery intrenched at River and Beaufort bridges." The Seventeenth Corps was ordered to carry River bridge, and the Fifteenth Corps Beaufort bridge. Mower and Giles A. Smith, with their divisions promptly carried the former on the 3d of February "by crossing the swamp, nearly three miles wide, with water varying from knee to shoulder deep." Although the weather was bitter cold, those two gallant Commanders led their divisions on foot, wading the deep, chilly water side by side with the soldiers, and making a lodgment below the bridge, drove the rebel brigade that guarded it in terror toward Branchville. Our loss in this bold and brilliant movement was little less than ninety.

The line of the Salkehatchie being thus broken, the rebels could make no stand until they reached the Edisto at Branchville, a place lying some sixty miles out from Charleston. The army then pushed rapidly for the railroad at Midway, which it reached on the 7th, and at once began to tear it up. The left wing under Slocum struck it farther up toward Augusta, and also commenced the work of destruction. The rebel forces at Aiken and Augusta, on the one hand, and those at Branchville and Charleston on the other, were now hopelessly divided, and unable to act in concert.

Leaving the left wing still at work destroying the railroad, Sherman with the right moved north on Orangeburg. The Seventeenth Corps crossed the South Fork of the Edisto, at Binnaker's bridge, and marched straight on the place, while the Fifteenth Corps crossed at Holman's bridge and moved to Poplar Springs in support.

The rebel Commander had so long thought of nothing, and labored for nothing, but to save Charleston, that he could not be persuaded that *it* was not the chief object of Sherman's desires, and continued to lie behind his fortifications at Branchville, to protect it. Still, he had caused the bridge over the Edisto to be burned, and stationed a force at the spot to oppose the passage of our army. Ford, with the advance division, as he approached the burned bridge, was saluted with a heavy fire of artillery, which arrested his progress. Lower down, however, by wading to the armpits, and often swimming, the men succeeded in launching four pontoon boats into the water, and just as the moon was rising, the division was got across, which, pouncing upon the astonished rebels in flank, scattered them in confusion through the moonlit woods. For fifteeen miles along this river the spread-out army made demonstrations at different points, so that the scattered enemy could do very little in opposing the passage, except by skirmishing.

The rebel force in Orangeburg now fled north to Columbia, and this place, with a population of three thousand, fell into our hands. A conflagration, however, was raging at the time, which the soldiers, under the orders of Howard and Sherman, labored hard to extinguish. The place was set on fire by a Jew, in revenge for fifty bales of cotton belonging to him, and destroyed by the rebels. The negro pioneers here ran riot among the ornamented grounds of the wealthy citizens. Sherman says: "Blair was ordered to destroy the railroad effectually up to Lewisville, and to push the enemy across the Congaree, and force him to burn the bridges, which he did on the 14th, and, without wasting time or labor on Branchville or Charleston, which I knew the enemy could no longer hold, I turned all the columns straight on Columbia." The left wing swept on in the same direction, farther to the west, over the Edisto, and across swamps and streams; straight through the heart of the proud, rebellious State, the mighty columns moved with resistless power, till on the 16th, Howard drew up on the banks of the Saluda, in front of Columbia. An hour later the head of the advance column of the left wing appeared on the shore of the same stream, farther to the west, and the Capital of South Carolina lay under our guns. The Mayor surrendered the city, and Sherman, in anticipation of it, says: "I had made written orders to General Howard, touching the conduct of the troops. These were to destroy absolutely all arsenals and public property not needed for our own use, as well as all railroads, depots, and machinery useful in war to an enemy, but to spare all dwellings, colleges, schools, asylums, and harmless private property. I was the first to cross the pontoon bridge, and in company with General Howard, rode into the city. The day was clear, but a perfect tempest of wind was raging. The brigade of Colonel Stone was already in the city, and properly posted. Citizens and soldiers were on the streets and general good order prevailed. General Wade Hampton, who commanded the Confederate rear-guard of cavalry, had in anticipation of our capture of Columbia, ordered that all cotton, public and private, should be moved into the streets and fired, to prevent our making use of it. Bales were piled every where, the rope and bagging cut, and tufts of cotton were blown about in the wind, lodged in the trees and against houses, so as to resemble a snow storm. Some of these piles of cotton were burning, especially one in the very heart of the city, near the Court-House, but the fire was partially subdued by the labor of our soldiers." It must be remembered that the army did not enter Columbia. The Fifteenth Corps alone marched through, and encamped beyond on the Camden road. The Seventeenth did not enter the place at all, while the entire left wing and cavalry did not come within two miles of it. A single brigade was placed within it on duty. Sherman says: "Before one single public building had been fired by order, the smouldering fires set by Hampton's order were rekindled by the wind, and communicated to the buildings around. About dark they began to spread, and got beyond the control of the brigade on duty within the city. The whole of Wood's division was brought in, but it was found impossible to check the flames, which by midnight had become unmanagable, and raged until about four A. M., when, the wind subsiding, they were got under control. I was up nearly all night, and saw Generals Howard, Logan and Wood, and others, laboring to save houses and to protect families, thus suddenly deprived of shelter, and of bedding, and wearing apparel. I disclaim on the part of my army, any agency in this fire, but, on the contrary, claim that we saved what of Columbia remains unconsumed." He acknowledges, what any one acquainted with armies, would know must be inevitable—that, while the officers and men worked hard to extinguish the flames, "others not on duty, including the officers who had long been imprisoned there, rescued by me, may have assisted in spreading the fire, after it had begun, and may have indulged in unconcealed joy to see the ruin of the Capital of South Carolina."

All know what soldiers and released prisoners will do in a burning city, whether set on fire by friend or foe. The lawless and vindictive, and mercenary, will help to swell the conflagration, and add plunder and cruelty to the destruction caused by the flames. Hence those familiar with the history of invading armies will be prepared for the following description of an officer who was an eye-witness:

"Pillaging gangs soon fired the heart of the town, then entered the houses, in many instances carrying off articles of value. The flame soon burst out in all parts of the city, and the streets were quickly crowded with helpless women and children, some in their night-clothes. Agonized mothers, seeking their children, all affrighted and terrified, were rushing, on all sides, from the raging flames and falling houses. Invalids had to be dragged from their beds, and lay exposed to the flames and smoke that swept the streets, or to the cold of the open air in back yards.

"The scene at the convent was a sad one indeed. The flames were fast encompassing the convent, and the sisters and about sixty terrified young ladies huddled together on the streets. Some of these had come from the North, previous to the war, for their education, and were not able to return. The superioress of the convent had educated General Sherman's daughter, Minnie. He had assigned them a special guard of six men; so they felt secure, and were totally unprepared for the dreadful scene that ensued. Some Christian people formed a guard around this agonized group of ladies, and conducted them to the Park.

"I trust I shall never witness such a scene again—drunken soldiers, rushing from house to house, emptying them of their valuables, and then firing them; negroes carrying off piles of booty, and grinning at the good chance, and exulting, like so many demons; officers and men reveling on the wines and liquors, until the burning houses buried them in their drunken orgies.

"I was fired at for trying to save an unfortunate man from being murdered.

"The scene of desolation the city presented next morning was fearful. That long street of rich stores, the fine hotels, the court-houses, the extensive convent buildings, and last the old Capitol, where the order of secession was passed, with its fine library and State archives, were all in one heap of unsightly ruins and rubbish. Splendid private residences, lovely cottages, with their beautiful gardens, and the stately rows of shade trees, were all withered into ashes.

"The ruins alone, without the evidences of human misery that every-where met the view, were enough to inspire one with feelings of deep melancholy.

"Here was desolation heightened by the agonized misery of human sufferings.

"There lay the city wrapped in her own shroud—the tall chimneys and blackened trunks of trees looking like so many sepulchral monuments, and the woe-stricken people, that listlessly wandered about the street, her pallid mourners.

"Old and young moved about seemingly without a purpose. Some mournfully contemplated the piles of rubbish, the only remains of their late happy homesteads.

"Old men, women, and children were grouped together. Some had piles of bedding and furniture which they saved from the wreck; others, who were wealthy the night previous, had not now a loaf of bread to break their fast.

"Children were crying with fright and hunger; mothers were weeping; strong men, who could not help either them or themselves, sat bowed down, with their heads buried between their hands.

"The yards and offices of the Lunatic Asylum were crowded with people who had fled there for protection the night previous. Its wards, too, had received new subjects, for several had gone crazy from terror, or from having lost their children or friends in the flames." *

Having finished his work, and leaving behind enough provisions to sustain, for some time, the homeless population of the place, Sherman marched north toward Charlotte, followed by a horde of negroes and refugees. The army being spread out as much as possible, to obtain forage, it moved over the fertile country like the locusts of Egypt. "A garden was before them, a desert behind them." The steady, on-pouring columns, with their long trains, filled the inhabitants with unbounded terror, and well they might, for throughout the army, there reigned a feeling of intense hatred against this traitorous, rebellious, little State—and though plundering and violence were forbidden, in an army spread over such a vast extent of country they could not be prevented, and no soldier felt inclined to inform against even a reckless camp-follower, for firing a South Carolinian's house.

Says an officer:—"In Georgia few houses were burned; here, few escaped; and the country was converted into one vast bonfire. The pine forests were fired, the resin factories were fired, the public builings and private dwellings were fired. The middle of the finest day looked black and gloomy, for a dense smoke arose on all sides, clouding the very heavens. At night the tall, pine trees seemed so many huge pillars of fire. The flames hissed and screeched, as they fed on the fat resin and dry branches, imparting to the forests a most fearful appearance.

"Vandalism of this kind, though not encouraged, was seldom punished. True, where every one is guilty alike, there will be no informers; therefore the Generals knew little of what was going on.

* Captain Conyngham.

"The ruined homesteads of the Palmetto State will long be remembered. The army might safely march the darkest night; the crackling pine woods shooting up their columns of flame and the burning houses along the way would light it on, while the dark clouds and pillars of smoke would safely cover its rear."

Slocum, with the left wing, and Kilpatrick's cavalry covering his left flank, moved to Winnsboro', lying north-west of Columbia, which the foragers set on fire before he could arrive with his columns to prevent it.

Beauregard had fallen back on Charlotte from Columbia, thinking that it would be the next place on which Sherman would move. Cheatham's Corps, of Hood's old army, was striving to make a junction with him at this place—having marched all the way from Augusta almost parallel with Kilpatrick's cavalry.

A heavy rain storm now set in, making the roads almost impassable, yet Sherman, for two days, pushed on toward Charlotte—but on the 23rd the army suddenly made a grand right-wheel, and facing the rising sun, left this place, as it had Augusta and Charleston, far in the rear. Breasting the pitiless storm, this noble army pushed forward toward Fayetteville—the line of march cutting the swollen rivers that a hundred years before so obstructed Cornwallis in his pursuit of Greene.

Kilpatrick, in the meantime, covered this movement as long as he could, in order to enable the army to get across these formidable rivers without opposition. But when it was discovered that Sherman was actually crossing the country to Fayetteville, Hampton and Wheeler, with the rebel cavalry, attempted to reach the place first, on which Hardee, in his retreat from Charleston, was marching. In endeavoring to prevent this junction, Kilpatrick undertook to hold three roads, over any one of which he thought the enemy might

ENTRANCE OF THE FIFTY FIFTH MASSACHUSETTS (COLORED) REGIMENT INTO CHARLESTON,

FEB. 21 1865

pass. On one of them, with a small force, he lay one night, when his camp was suddenly surprised by Hampton, and swept like a whirlwind.

His head-quarters were carried in a twinkling, and all his artillery captured, while he and his bold troopers were driven into a swamp. His case now seemed hopeless, but looking out from his hiding place, he saw that the rebels were wholly taken up with plundering his camp, when rallying his remaining men, he charged them so suddenly and fiercely that they were driven back in confusion. Instantly turning the artillery on them he completed their discomfiture, and seized with panic they fled, leaving all the captured prisoners and artillery in his possession.

Crossing the Catawba without loss, Sherman struck for the Pedee, at Cheraw, where the rebels made a feeble stand, but were swept away with a single blow, leaving twenty-five pieces of artillery in our hands.

In the meantime the news reached the army that Charleston was evacuated, and the Union flag once more flying over Fort Sumter.

The troops, under Hardee, commenced leaving the place on the night of the 16th, and by next night were all gone. At midnight, some soldiers fired the upper part of the city, destroying the railroad depots, in which were two hundred kegs of powder, and a vast amount of cotton. The half-starved poor of the city rushed into the burning buildings to snatch from the flames some of the rice stored in them, when the powder exploded killing a hundred or more.

At daylight, the rebel rams in the harbor blew up with a terrific explosion.

The next morning, the 18th, the Mayor surrendered the city to Gillmore, with all the surrounding forts, and the National flag floated once more over what had been the emporium of the South—now a heap of blackened ruins. Here rebellion had been hatched for the purpose of degrading that flag, and at the same time preventing all interference with the servile condition of the black man—and behold the result! A colored regiment, with well-set ranks, wearing the National uniform and bearing above them that glorious flag, marched into its streets as conquerors. Human history can scarcely present another such a contrast, produced in the short space of four years.

Gillmore reported four hundred and fifty pieces of cannon captured in the various defenses of the place, before which he had sat down in siege, five hundred and eighty-five days before. For five hundred and forty days the city had been under fire.

Only some ten thousand inhabitants, of the lower classes, remained after its evacuation. Its overthrow was hailed with unbounded delight at the North, and scarce a sigh was heaved over its wide-spread desolation.

At Cheraw, the right and left wings of Sherman's army met for the first time since leaving Savannah, and now, together, marched on Fayetteville, which the advance columns reached on the 12th of March.

In anticipation of his arrival, he had sent trusty scouts to Wilmington, nearly a hundred miles distant, to announce his near approach. Our troops had entered this place about a fortnight before. Schofield, in conjunction with Porter, of the Navy, moved his forces up both sides of the Cape Fear River, and advanced against Fort Anderson—the enemy's main defense on the west bank of the river—which the garrison at once evacuated. During the following two days, some fighting occurred, but on the 22nd of February, our troops had possession of the place.

On the arrival of the scouts, the United States steam-tug Davidson was started up the river, and reached Fayetteville on the same day that Sherman's columns approached it, and was hailed by the latter with loud cheers.

A few hours later she returned with dispatches from Sherman to Terry, in command at Wilmington, and to Schofield who had transferred his Corps to Newbern, directing them to move at once on Goldsboro, and join him there, where he himself expected to be in five days. He knew that he would soon need these columns, that had been planted on the seaboard, on purpose to aid him, for he could no longer prevent the concentration of the enemy's forces. He was aware that Cheatham had effected a junction with Beauregard, and that both were marching on Raleigh, and that Hardee, who had evacuated Fayetteville at his approach, was falling back in the same direction. These, joined by Johnston and Hoke, with the forces from Wilmington and Newbern would make a formidable army.

Schofield, however, had some difficulty in making his way inland, for he was attacked on the 8th at Wise's Forks, and driven back with severe loss. Two days after, the enemy following up his success, attacked his intrenched position, but was repulsed with such a heavy loss that he was compelled to retreat. On the 14th Schofield crossed the Neuse and occupied Kinston.

The next day after this success, Sherman put his columns in motion up the Cape Fear River, as though his objective point was Raleigh instead of Goldsboro on the Neuse, up which Schofield was to march.

Hardee in his retreat from Fayetteville, had halted on a narrow, swampy neck of land between Cape Fear and South Rivers, near Averysboro, and with twenty thousand men now occupied an intrenched position. Here Kilpatrick found him and sent back word to Slocum. The latter, after getting his forces well up, began to feel the enemy's lines. The ground was so swampy that horses mired at every step, and it was difficult for the infantry to operate ; but it was necessary that this position should be carried—and amid torrents of rain, and fearful gusts of wind he advanced to the attack and drove the enemy in confusion from their works. Our loss in the engagement was about six hundred. The rebels retreated in the night during a frightful storm, leaving one hundred and eight dead on the field.

The next day Slocum ceased his movement on Raleigh, and wheeling to the right, crossed South River, swollen by the rains, and took the road to Goldsboro, whither Howard farther to the east was marching, "wallowing along the miry roads."

On the 18th both wings were within a few miles of the place, and Sherman, thinking there would be no more opposition to his advance, left Slocum and started across the country to see Howard. But he had gone scarcely six miles when he was startled by the sudden, angry roar of artillery behind him, evidently coming from the spot where Slocum's army lay. While listening to the heavy explosions, wondering what they could mean, a staff-officer galloped up, and quieted his anxiety by saying that it was merely an affair between Carlin's division and the rebel cavalry, and that the latter were in full retreat. In a few moments however, other officers arrived, who, to his surprise informed him that Slocum had suddenly found himself confronted by the whole of Johnston's army near Bentonville. Comprehending at once the new and dangerous position of affairs, he sent back word to Slocum to stand solely on the defensive until he could hurry up troops to his relief. Officers immediately dashed off over the country, bearing dispatches—one to Blair, to make a night march with his Corps, to Falling Creek Church, and with three divisions of the Fifteenth Corps to come up in Johnston's rear from the direction of Cox's bridge—another to Howard, to move, minus his wagon guard, at daylight on Bentonville.

While thus engaged in dispatching his orders, other couriers arrived, from Schofield and Terry. Ordering the former to march on Goldsboro, and the latter to move to Cox's bridge ten miles above, and establish a crossing there, he once more gave his undivided attention to Slocum, and the unexpected battle thus suddenly thrown upon him.

The latter, however, seemed to feel no uneasiness, and choosing an admirable position, placed his artillery so as to sweep his entire front. He then sent on Morgan's division to establish another line about a half a mile in advance. Against this Johnston advanced in overwhelming numbers, and hurled it in confusion back, capturing three guns and caissons. Slocum, seeing the heavy force opposed to him, at once deployed the two divisions of the Fourteenth Corps, General Davis, and hurried forward at their utmost speed the two divisions of the Twentieth Corps, General Williams. A line of barricades was hastily prepared, and the whole force put strictly on the defensive. In the meantime Kilpatrick aroused by the thunder of artillery, came dashing down the roads and massed his squadrons on the left. It was now four o'clock in the afternoon, and Slocum had hardly got every thing ready when the enemy came on in one of their dashing, impetuous charges. In three massive columns, they swept up to his frail barricades, and threatened by mere weight of numbers to carry every thing before them. Mowed down by our batteries, and the deliberate deadly volleys of the infantry, the first column recoiled, when the second, undaunted by the repulse of the first, charged with a cheer. But right in its path stood Davis' Corps—that won such immortal honor on the bloody field of Chickamauga—and stopped it with one terrible blow. The whole fury of the attack spent itself in less than an hour, and yet in that time the enemy had made six successive assaults, and in the last charge broke Slocum's line, but it quickly rallied, and charging in turn, drove him back. So close and desperate was the combat that many of the rebel dead lay within our lines, and even around the head-quarters of the Generals.

That night Slocum got up his wagon train, with its guard of two divisions, and the gallant Hazen's division, with which reinforcements he felt able to hold his ground, although Johnston, with Hoke's, Cheatham's and Hardee's Corps, greatly outnumbered him. The next day, Howard came up and connected with his left. Sherman now had his invincible army well in hand and presenting a strong line of battle in front of the enemy's intrenched position. Johnston had concentrated his forces rapidly, intending to catch the army divided, and break it up in detail. Instead of that, he suddenly found it all together, and boldly confronting him in his works. It was not, however, Sherman's wish to bring on a battle here, unless every thing was in his favor, and so he contented himself with pressing forward the skirmishers, and playing with his batteries on the woods in which the enemy lay, and threatening his strongly protected flanks.

This was the state of things on the 21st of March; on which day Schofield entered Goldsboro', and Terry got possession of the Neuse River at Cox's bridge, ten miles above, with a pontoon bridge across, and one brigade over. It was a stormy day, and the rain fell in torrents, yet during it Mower managed to work well around the enemy's flank, to the right, and nearly reached Mill Creek bridge—the only line of his retreat. "A noisy battle," as Sherman termed it, followed, and in the night Johnston retreated. Our total loss was sixteen hundred and forty-six.

Directing Howard, with the cavalry, to remain next day on the field and bury the dead, he gave orders for the troops to move to the various camps assigned them around Goldsboro'. After visiting Terry, at Cox's bridge, he rode into the town, where he found Schofield already arrived.

The campaign was now ended, for he had reached the point for which he had started the Autumn before. But what an astonishing march it had been! A desolate tract of country, forty miles wide, and between two and three hundred miles long, across the State of Georgia, and one equally wide, and far more desolate, for nearly five hundred miles, from Savannah to the heart of North Carolina, marked its line of progress.

Sherman now turned over his army to Schofield, and hastened to City Point to consult with Grant respecting the next move to be made. Here he also met the President, who welcomed him with great cordiality.

In the meantime, Quarter-master Meigs came down, and in a fortnight supplied twenty thousand men with shoes, and one hundred thousand with clothing, and every thing necessary for entering on another campaign.

CHAPTER XLI.

FEBRUARY—APRIL, 1865.

INTERVIEW BETWEEN GRANT AND SHERMAN—REVIEW OF THE MILITARY FIELD—CANBY'S PREPARATIONS AGAINST MOBILE—STONEMAN'S ADVANCE FROM EAST TENNESSEE—CAVALRY RAID FROM VICKSBURG—ANOTHER FROM EASTPORT, MISSISSIPPI—SHERIDAN'S RAID UP THE SHENANDOAH VALLEY AND ROUND RICHMOND TO THE WHITE HOUSE—HE REACHES THE ARMY OF THE POTOMAC THE SAME DAY AS SHERMAN—GRANT'S PLAN TO MOVE AROUND THE REBEL RIGHT FLANK—REBEL ATTACK ON FORT STEADMAN—SHERMAN RETURNS TO HIS ARMY—GRANT BEGINS HIS MOVEMENT—UNEXPECTED SUCCESS—BATTLE OF FIVE FORKS—GRAND ASSAULT OF THE ENEMY'S LINES—EVACUATION OF PETERSBURG AND RICHMOND—LEE RETREATS TOWARD DANVILLE—THE PURSUIT—LINCOLN AND DAVIS ON THE DAY OF THE BATTLE—WEITZEL ENTERS RICHMOND—THE CITY FIRED BY THE REBELS—LEE HARD PRESSED—HIS RETREAT CUT OFF—GRANT DEMANDS HIS SURRENDER—THE CORRESPONDENCE—THE CAPITULATION—SURRENDER OF THE TROOPS OF NORTHERN VIRGINIA—JOY OF THE NORTH OVER THE VICTORY.

THE interview between Grant and Sherman was one of intense interest. The subject of the consultation was no less than the manner in which the death blow should be given to the rebellion, for the final, decisive hour both believed to be near at hand. Still, a mistake on their part at this juncture might prove fatal—while a wise move in the right direction would bring complete triumph. The stake for which they were to throw, was this Great Republic, and they might well ponder on the threshold of such a momentous event.

Sherman from the 1st of February had been locked up in the heart of the enemy's country, and hence knew but imperfectly, either what Grant had done, or intended to do;

but now the military map was spread out before him, and the field of operations, both past and present, unfolded and explained.

First, as he was starting from Savannah, Grant had directed Thomas to send General Stoneman from East Tennessee, down into South Carolina, with a cavalry force to destroy the railroads, and military resources of the country. But before he could get away, Sherman was well-nigh across the State doing that work himself. Grant, therefore, on the last of February, ordered Thomas to send him, instead, with four or five thousand cavalry east, to destroy the railroad toward Lynchburg, in which work he was now engaged. At this time Canby was preparing a movement from Mobile Bay against Mobile, and Thomas was directed, in order to make a diversion in his favor, to send a cavalry force, ten thousand strong, from Eastport, Mississippi, deep into Alabama. In the meantime another body, seven or eight thousand strong, was to move east from Vicksburg for the same purpose. These movements, Grant thought, with the work done in South Carolina, were "all that would be wanted to leave nothing for the rebellion to stand on."

Sheridan, in the meantime had completed his raid from the Shenandoah Valley. On the 20th of February, Grant telegraphed to him to take a cavalry force as soon as the roads could be traveled and advance on Lynchburg, and after destroying the railroad and canal near it, to push on if practicable, and join Sherman who was inferior to the enemy in cavalry, and might be in great need of reinforcements to this arm.

On the 27th of the month, with two divisions of cavalry—in all ten thousand men—he left Winchester, and by a rapid movement succeeded, two days after, in securing the bridge across the middle fork of the Shenandoah at Mount Crawford, and the next day entered Staunton. The rebel troops in the Valley as before stated, had mostly been withdrawn to reinforce Lee at Richmond, yet Early was still here with a moderate force, and on the approach of Sheridan fell back to Waynesboro and intrenched. The latter pushed rapidly on after him, and arriving in front of his works, without waiting even for a reconnoissance, ordered the bugles to sound the charge. With a rush and a hurrah the bold riders dashed over every obstacle and carried the position like a whirlwind, capturing sixteen hundred prisoners, eleven pieces of artillery, with horses and caissons complete, two hundred loaded wagons and teams, and seventeen battle flags.

Sending the prisoners back under an escort to Winchester, he moved on to Charlottesville, destroying the railroad and bridges as he advanced. Reaching this place on the 3d, he halted two days to break up the railroad and bridges toward Lynchburg and Richmond, and to wait for the arrival of his trains. This delay gave the enemy at Lynchburg time to prepare for his approach, and he abandoned the design of capturing it.

On the 6th, he again put his force in motion, dividing it into two columns; one of which marched to Scottsville, from whence it moved up the James River to New Market, destroying the locks, and in many places the banks of the canal. From this point a force was sent out to secure a bridge across the river at Duiguidsville, but the enemy, apprised of the movement, burned it.

The other column moved down the railroad, toward Lynchburg, and destroyed it to within sixteen miles of the place.

Unfortunately the spring floods had so swelled the river that the pontoons which Sheridan had brought along would not reach across the river, and the enemy having burned the bridges, he was unable to get over and move south as he intended, and join Sherman. Of course, nothing was now left him to do, but either to retrace his steps, or, advancing down the river, sweep around Richmond to the north, and put himself in communication with Grant's army by reaching a new base at the White House. He chose the latter course, and keeping on toward the rebel Capital, destroying the railroad as he advanced, at length on the 10th concentrated his forces at Columbia. Here he rested one day, and sent off trusty scouts to Grant, informing him of his plans, and asking that supplies be sent to him at the White House. Two days after, these scouts were brought into the Lieutenant General's presence, who immediately on receiving Sheridan's message, dispatched an infantry force to hold the White House.

Sheridan, in the meantime, marched forward toward Richmond, sending consternation into the rebel Capital. A strong column was at once sent out to cut him off, but wheeling to the left, he crossed the North and South Anna Rivers—burning the bridges behind him—and moving down the north bank of the Pamunkey, reached the White House on the 19th. Halting here to rest and refit, he marched across to James River, and on the 27th, the very day of Sherman's arrival, joined the Army of the Potomac.

Grant now determined to send him around the rebel left, and reach, if possible, the South-side and Danville railroads. As this would be the line of Lee's retreat, should he evacuate Richmond and attempt to join Johnston, who was operating against Sherman's army, it was of vital importance that it should be destroyed. The movement was to commence on the 29th—two Corps being directed to advance in the same direction to support him, and, if possible, turn the rebel position at Petersburg. But two days before it was to take place, the rebels carried by sudden assault Fort

Steadman, in front of the Ninth Corps, and brought on an unexpected battle.

Whether Lee designed this as a movement to cover his own retreat, or hoped to break through our lines, and suddenly wheeling to the left, take our batteries in reserve, and keeping on, cut our communications, and thus raise the siege of Richmond, we cannot tell. At all events, it was a bold movement, and was made so suddenly that the fort was carried with a single bound, and its guns turned on us. Three mortar batteries adjoining it were also taken. But the troops on either flank held their ground, while Hartranft's division advanced to aid Wilcox in driving the enemy out of the captured works.

In the meantime our surrounding artillery was brought to bear upon Fort Steadman, the fire of which became so hot that the victors had to abandon their prize; and many of them, afraid to recross the intervening space to their own lines, surrendered. Our loss was nine hundred and nineteen, while we took nineteen hundred prisoners. Meade at once ordered the other Corps to advance and feel the enemy's line in their front. They did so, and captured and held the rebel picket line in front of the Second and Sixth Corps, taking eight hundred and thirty-four prisoners. Thus the transient success of the enemy proved a sad reverse to him.

Two days after this, as we have seen, Sherman reached Grant, to hold the interview mentioned in the commencement of the chapter.

The events above narrated, covered the whole military field, and Sherman when put in possession of them, comprehended the exact state of things.

It was plain to both Commanders, as before remarked, that the time for the last, great, decided movement had come. Even Davis could see that the crisis of the Confederacy was fast approaching. The year before, the prospect looked gloomy enough, and in its terror, the rebel Congress had prevailed on him to make Lee Commander-in-Chief of all the rebel forces. But that did not increase the army, and to do this, it was resolved to enroll the slaves. But this measure, if ever practicable, was adopted too late. The march of events was too rapid. Lee's new power gave him no new confidence. The heavens were gathering black as midnight above him, and the thunder was muttering angrily around the entire horizon. Look which way he would, the rebel Chieftain saw the lightning's flash. The hand-writing was being traced on the wall.

After full deliberation on the state of affairs, and the probable movements of the enemy, it was agreed that Sherman should return to his army, and making a feint, as if to move up the Neuse to Raleigh, march rapidly north to the line of the Roanoke. This would be closing the last door on Lee, and Grant knew that the moment Sherman approached this river, the former would evacuate Richmond.

It seems strange that Lee remained in the rebel Capital so long as he did. But knowing how closely he was watched by Grant, he may have feared to leave his fortifications—for desertions having become so fearfully great, the moment he retreated, they might and probably would be so increased as to leave him but the remnant of an army, and, therefore, he thought it the wisest course to wait and see if Johnston could not stop Sherman's northward march. Grant, however, felt very uneasy, and spent many an anxious night, fearing that the morning light would reveal Petersburg and Richmond evacuated, and the rebel army well on the road to Danville, to effect a junction with Johnston. He knew if he succeeded in doing this, new combinations would have to be formed, and a new campaign organized. He, therefore, determined to carry out his original plan, adopted before the attack on Fort Steadman, and before the arrival of Sherman.

He did not expect this to be the decided movement it turned out to be. But he said, "by moving out, I would put the army in better condition for pursuit, and would, at least, by the destruction of the Danville road, retard the concentration of the two armies of Lee and Johnston, and cause the enemy to abandon much material that he might otherwise save."

He, therefore, on the night of the 27th—the very day Sherman reached him—dispatched two divisions of Ord's Corps, under General Gibbon, and one division of the Twenty-fifth Corps, commanded by Birney, and McKenzie's cavalry, to a position near Hatcher's Run, the scene of so many bitter conflicts.

Thus it will be seen, that Grant was to repeat over again the unsuccessful experiment so often tried, of getting around the enemy's right flank.

The whole scope, and plan and object of this movement, is given so much more clearly by Grant, in the following letter of instructions to Sheridan, than any language of ours can do, that we quote it:–

"City Point, Va., March 28, 1865.

General:—The Fifth Army Corps will move by the Vaughn road, at three, A. M., to-morrow morning. The Second moves at about nine, A. M., having but about three miles to march to reach the point designated for it to take on the right of the Fifth Corps, after the latter reaching Dinwiddie Court-House. Move your cavalry at as early an hour as you can, and without being confined to any particular road or roads. You may go out by the nearest roads in rear of the Fifth Corps, pass by its left, and passing near to, or through Dinwiddie, reach the right and rear of the enemy as soon as you can. It is not the intention to attack the enemy in his intrenched position, but to force him out, if possible. Should he come out and attack us, or get himself where he can be attacked, move in with your entire force in your own way, and with the full reliance that the army will engage or follow, as circumstances will dictate. I shall be on the field, and will probably be able to communicate with you. Should I not do so, and you find that the enemy keeps within his main, intrenched line, you may cut loose and push for the Danville road. If you find it practicable, I would like you to cross the South-side road, between Petersburg and Burkesville, and destroy it to some extent. I would not advise much detention, however, until you reach the Danville road, which I would like you to strike as near to the Appomattox as possible. Make your destruction, on that road, as complete as possible. You can then pass on to the South-side road, west of Burkesville, and destroy that in like manner.

After having accomplished the destruction of the two railroads, which are now the only avenues of supply to Lee's army, you may return to this army, selecting your road further south, or you may go on into North Carolina and join General Sherman. Should you select the latter course, get the information to me as early as possible, so that I may send orders to meet you at Goldsboro'.

U. S. GRANT, Lieutenant-General."

On the morning of the 29th, the movement commenced, and Sheridan, sweeping around the extreme rebel right, pushed on toward Dinwiddie Court-House, which he reached that night, while the left of the infantry line had extended nearly to the junction of the Quaker and Boydton plank road.

Sheridan, as we have seen, was on our extreme left—next to him came Warren, then Humphreys, Ord, Wright, and Parke. It looked now as if Grant would succeed in getting well on the rebel flank, and he, therefore, sent word to Sheridan not to cut loose to operate against the railroads, saying, "I now feel like ending the matter, if it is possible to do so, before going back. We will all act together as one army here, until it is seen what can be done with the enemy."

The next day the rain fell in torrents, turning the roads into such beds of mud that neither artillery nor trains could be moved. Sheridan, however, advanced toward the Five Forks, while Warren pushed on toward the White Oak road, where he found the enemy in force.

Finding the enemy confronting his line, no matter how far he extended it, Grant determined to give Sheridan a Corps of infantry, and let him cut loose from the army, and swing independently around the rebel flank, and when this was done, advance with the other Corps sternly to the assault in front.

On the morning of the 31st, Sheridan moving forward, got possession of the Five Forks, while Warren advanced to seize the White Oak road. The enemy, at first, retired before the latter, but suddenly rallying, fell with such fury on Ayers' division, which had the advance, that it was driven back in confusion. Following up his success, he kept on, and striking Crawford next, bore him back also on the Third division, under Bell, where the onset was checked. A division of the Second Corps being now sent to Warren's support, he re-formed his broken lines, and charging in turn, drove the enemy back with heavy loss, and gained possession of the White Oak road.

The transient success, however, of the enemy enabled him to send a heavy force against Sheridan, which drove him out of the Five Forks back to Dinwiddie Court-House.

"Here," says Grant, "General Sheridan displayed great generalship. Instead of retreating with his whole command on the main army, to tell the story of superior forces encountered, he deployed his cavalry on foot, leaving only mounted men enough to take charge of the horses. This compelled the enemy to deploy over a vast extent of woods and broken country, and made his progress slow. At this juncture, he dispatched to me what had taken place, and that he was dropping back slowly on Dinwiddie Court-House. General McKenzie's cavalry and one division of the Fifth Corps, were immediately ordered to his assistance. Soon after receiving a report from General Meade that Humphreys could hold our position on the Boydton road, and that the other two divisions of the Fifth Corps could go to Sheridan, they were so ordered at once."

At midnight, the Fifth Corps joined him, and feeling strong enough to resume the offensive, he, in the morning, again advanced to the Five Forks—so called because here five roads meet—three of them leading directly back to the South-side railroad.

Driving the enemy into his intrenchments, he ordered a general attack, which he thus describes:—

"The Fifth Corps, on reaching the White Oak road, made a left wheel, and burst on the enemy's left flank and rear like a tornado, and pushed rapidly on; orders having been given that if the enemy was routed, there should be no halt to re-form broken lines. As stated before, the firing of the Fifth Corps was the signal to General Merritt to assault, which was promptly responded to, and the works of the enemy were soon carried at several points by our brave cavalrymen. The enemy were driven from their strong line of works, and completely routed; the Fifth Corps doubling up their left flank in confusion, and the cavalry of General Merritt dashing on to the White Oak road, capturing their artillery and turning it upon them, and riding into their broken ranks, so demoralized them, that they made no serious stand after their line was carried, but took to flight in disorder. Between five and six thousand prisoners fell into our hands, and the fugitives were driven westward, and were pursued until long after dark by Merritt's and McKenzie's cavalry, for a distance of six miles."

From some unexplained cause, right in the moment of victory, while Warren was in the front with his shouting troops, Sheridan removed him from the command of the Corps, and put Griffin in his place.

The report of this brilliant victory reached Grant just after dark, and knowing the importance of the position gained by Sheridan, he feared that the enemy would concentrate a heavy force against him and drive him out, in order to open the way of retreat, and he at once ordered Miles' division of Humphreys' Corps to march rapidly to reinforce him, and at the same time directed a heavy bombardment of the enemy's lines to be kept up all night.

At four o'clock next morning, he ordered a general assault, and the mighty army swept forward like the in-rolling tide of the sea. Wright forced the lines in his front, and passing through with his whole Corps, carried every thing before him, capturing a large number of guns and several thousand prisoners. Keeping on, followed by two divisions of Ord, he at length met the remaining divisions of the latter that had forced the rebel lines at Hatcher's Run, when the two corps swung together to the right, closing the enemy on that side of them in Petersburg. Humphreys then advanced with two divisions and joined Wright on the left; Parke carried the enemy's main line in his front, but could not penetrate the second, while a portion of Gibbon's Corps by a gallant charge, captured two strong works south of Petersburg. These successes enabled Grant to shorten his lines materially, and thus strengthen them. The battle now raged from right to left, and the Sabbath of the 2d of April was evidently to see the beginning of the end of the war.

The rebels fought behind their intrenchments with desperate determination—especially Hill's Corps, in their efforts to retain possession of Fort Mahone, mounting fourteen guns. Here Hill was killed. But now Sheridan came sweeping in from the west on the rebel flank and rear, when the enemy gave it up and fled in confusion, leaving in our hands his guns and a great number of prisoners. That night both Petersburg and Richmond were evacuated.

During the battle President Lincoln was at Grant's headquarters before Petersburg, anxiously awaiting the issue of the great contest. A few miles from him, in Richmond, Davis at the same time was attending church, and in the midst of the services, an orderly splashed with mud, strode up the aisle and handed him a paper. Glancing at its contents, he saw that all was over, and a few hours after, he had left behind him his Capital forever, and was fleeing toward Danville.

As soon as it was known that Lee had retreated, Sheridan wheeled about and pushed for the Danville road, followed by Meade with the Second and Sixth Corps, while Ord, keeping near the Appomattox, moved rapidly toward Burkesville, along the South-side railroad. Lee, north of the Appomattox was moving toward the same point, and it became a race of life and death to him. It was fifty-three miles from Petersburg to Burkesville, where the South-side and Danville railroads intersect. The condition of the roads, and of the troops after two days' fighting, made this one of the most fatiguing marches of the war. In the meantime, on Monday morning, Weitzel, with that portion of the Army of the James left under his command north of the James River, composed in part of colored troops, marched into Richmond with bands playing, and colors flying. The rebels had fired the city and plundered many of the stores and shops while evacuating. All the business part of Main Street was destroyed, together with all the bridges over the river. Weitzel took a thousand prisoners, and found some five hundred pieces of artillery left behind.

The two armies continued to stretch forward toward Burke's Station, but Grant this time had the inside track, and reached it first. Sheridan, pushing forward with his accustomed energy, struck the Danville road near Jettersville, more than half way up from Burkesville to Amelia Court-House, where Lee was with his shattered army. The next night Ord reached Burkesville below him. A glance at the map will show how desperate Lee's position had now become.

On the 6th, Sheridan ascertained that Lee, finding that he could not advance by the railroad, was attempting to swing around him to the west, and instantly moved out with his cavalry to strike him in flank, followed by the Sixth Corps.

The Second and Fifth Corps were in Lee's rear, pressing him so close that he had to abandon wagons and artillery.

Ord pushed forward north-west, toward Farmville, where Lee evidently expected to strike the railroad again. Two regiments of infantry in the lightest marching order, and a squadron of cavalry, were hurried on in advance to destroy the bridges there, and detain the enemy. These were placed under General Theodore Read, who, meeting near the place, the head of Lee's columns, gallantly attacked it, and held it in check until he was killed and his little force overpowered.

But in the meantime Ord with the rest of the Corps arrived, when the enemy began to intrench himself.

On the same afternoon Sheridan struck the enemy farther back, capturing sixteen pieces of artillery, and four hundred wagons, and detained him until the Second Corps came up, when a general attack was ordered, resulting in the capture of six or seven thousand prisoners, and among them Generals Ewell and Custis. Lee now moving off to the west, the pursuit was kept up till it became evident to all that his escape was hopeless. Grant having arrived at Farmville addressed a note to him which we give below, with the correspondence that followed.

"April 7, 1865.

General:—The result of the last week must convince you of the hopelessness of further resistance on the part of the Army of Northern Virginia in this struggle. I feel that it is so, and regard it as my duty to shift from myself the responsibility of any further effusion of blood by asking of you the surrender of that portion of the Confederate States Army known as the Army of Northern Virginia.

U. S. GRANT, Lieutenant-General.

General R. E. Lee.

"Early on the morning of the 8th, before leaving, I received at Farmville, the following:

General:—I have received your note of this date. Though not entertaining the opinion you express on the hopelessness of further resistance on the part of the Army of Northern Virginia, I reciprocate your desire to avoid useless effusion of blood, and therefore, before considering your proposition, ask the terms you will offer on condition of its surrender.

R. E. LEE, General.

Lieutenant-General U. S. GRANT.

"To this I immediately replied:—

April 8, 1865.

GENERAL:—Your note of last evening, in reply to mine of same date, asking the condition on which I will accept the surrender of the Army of Northern Virginia, is just received. In reply, I would say that *peace* being my great desire, there is but one condition I would insist upon, namely; that the men and officers surrendered should be disqualified for taking up arms again against the Government of the United States until properly exchanged. I will meet you or will designate officers to meet any officers you may name for the same purpose, at any point agreeable to you for the purpose of arranging definitely the terms upon which the surrender of the Army of Northern Virginia will be received.

U. S. GRANT, Lieutenant-General.

General R. E. LEE.

"Early on the morning of the 8th, the pursuit was resumed. General Meade followed north of the Appomattox, and General Sheridan, with all the cavalry, pushed straight for Appomattox Station, followed by General Ord's command and the Fifth Corps. During the day General Meade's advance had considerable fighting with the enemy's rear-guard, but was unable to bring on a general engagement. Late in the evening, General Sheridan struck the railroad at Appomattox Station, drove the enemy from there, and captured twenty-five pieces of artillery, a hospital train, and four trains of cars loaded with supplies for Lee's army. During this day, I accompanied General Meade's column, and about midnight received the following communication from General Lee:—

April 8, 1865.

GENERAL:—I received at a late hour your note of to-day. In mine of yesterday I did not intend to propose the surrender of the Army of Northern Virginia, but to ask the terms of your proposition. To be frank, I do not think the emergency has arisen to call for the surrender of this army, but as the restoration of peace should be the sole object of all, I desired to know whether your proposals would lead to that end. I cannot, therefore, meet you with a view to surrender the Army of Northern Virginia, but as far as your proposal may affect the Confederate States forces under my command, and tend to the restoration of peace I should be pleased to meet you at ten A. M. to-morrow, on the old stage road to Richmond, between the picket lines of the two armies.

R. E. LEE, General.

Lieutenant-General U. S. GRANT.

"Early on the morning of the 9th I returned him an answer as follows, and immediately started to join the column south of the Appomattox:—

April 9, 1865.

GENERAL:—Your note of yesterday is received. I have no authority to treat on the subject of peace; the meeting proposed for ten, A. M., to-day, could lead to no good. I will state, however, General, that I am equally anxious for peace with yourself, and the whole North entertains the same feeling. The terms upon which peace can be had are well understood. By the South laying down their arms, they will hasten that most desirable event, save thousands of human lives, and hundreds of millions of property not yet destroyed. Seriously hoping that all our difficulties may be settled without the loss of another life, I subscribe myself, &c.

U. S. GRANT, Lieutenant-General.

General R. E. LEE.

"On the morning of the 9th, General Ord's command and the Fifth Corps reached Appomattox Station just as the enemy was making a desperate effort to break through our cavalry. The infantry was at once thrown in. Soon after a white flag was received, requesting a suspension of hostilities pending negotiations for a surrender.

"Before reaching General Sheridan's head-quarters, I received the following from General Lee:—

April 9, 1865.

GENERAL:—I received your note of this morning, on the picket line, whither I had come to meet you, and ascertain definitely what terms were embraced in your proposal of yesterday, with reference to the surrender of this army. I now ask an interview in accordance with the offer contained in your letter of yesterday for that purpose.

R. E. LEE, General.

Lieutenant-General U. S. GRANT.

"The interview was held at Appomattox Court-House,

the result of which is set forth in the following correspondence:—

APPOMATTOX COURT-HOUSE, Va., April 9, 1865.

GENERAL:—In accordance with the substance of my letter to you, of the 8th instant, I propose to receive the surrender of the Army of Northern Virginia on the following terms, to wit: Rolls of all the officers and men to be made in duplicate, one copy to be given to an officer to be designated by me, the other to be retained by such officer or officers as you may designate. The officers to give their individual paroles not to take up arms against the Government of the United States until properly exchanged; and each company or regimental Commander sign a like parole for the men of their commands. The arms, artillery, and public property to be parked and stacked, and turned over to the officers appointed by me to receive them. This will not embrace the side-arms of the officers, nor their private horses or baggage. This done, each officer and man will be allowed to return to his home, not to be disturbed by United States authority so long as they observe their paroles, and the laws in force where they may reside.

U. S. GRANT, Lieutenant-General.

General R. E. LEE.

HEAD-QUARTERS ARMY OF NORTHERN VIRGINIA,
April 9, 1865.

GENERAL:—I received your letter of this date, containing the terms of the surrender of the Army of Northern Virginia as proposed by you. As they are substantially the same as those expressed in your letter of the 8th instant, they are accepted. I will proceed to designate the proper officers to carry the stipulations into effect.

R. E. LEE, General.

Lieutenant-General U. S. GRANT."

On the reception of the last letter, Grant hastened to the front, where Lee was awaiting him. They met in the parlor of a neighboring farm-house and saluted each other with dignified courtesy. In former years they had fought side by side, under the same flag, but for the last year, backed by two as fine armies as ever trod a battle-field, they had confronted each other as enemies. Well matched, neither had been able to obtain any decided success over the other. As they now stood face to face, what memories must have crowded on them, and what a different future spread out before them!

Lee acknowledged that the terms dictated by Grant were

more lenient than he had a right to expect. In killed, wounded, and prisoners, the rebel army had been reduced, in the last few days, full thirty thousand men, besides the vast number that had straggled off to their homes, so that less than twenty thousand were left to surrender.

When the news of the capitulation reached the army, loud cheers arose on every side, which lasted for hours. There was some disappointment, however, among the soldiers that, after their toils and hardships, they were not allowed to pass through the enemy's lines and witness their surrender. But Grant, magnanimous as he is great, wishing to abate as much as possible all ill-feeling between men, hereafter to be citizens of the same Government, allowed the rebel troops to return to their homes without further humiliation, on giving their parole not to take up arms against the Government, until properly exchanged.

By a singular coincidence, as the grand assault on the enemy's works at Petersburg took place on Sunday, so now on Sunday, and Palm Sunday too, the capitulation was signed.

The surrender of Lee's army was followed by that of most of the troops in the Shenandoah Valley. Mosby surrendered his command on the 17th. Hancock, who had succeeded Sheridan, when the latter started on his last great raid for Lynchburg, commanded here at this time.

With Lee's immediate army, were captured one hundred and seventy pieces of artillery, which number was of course swelled by the surrender of the other forces in Northern Virginia.

The joy of the North was unbounded over this great victory. Bonfires, illuminations, and the firing of cannon, attested the universal delight, while Grant became the idol of the Nation.

CHAPTER XLII.

APRIL–MAY, 1865.

SHERMAN REJOINS HIS ARMY—RECEIVES THE NEWS OF THE FALL OF PETERSBURG AND RICHMOND—HE MOVES ON RALEIGH—THE ARMY RECEIVES THE NEWS OF LEE'S SURRENDER—INTERVIEW WITH JOHNSTON—THE ARMISTICE—INJUSTICE OF THE SECRETARY OF WAR AND HALLECK—STONEMAN'S RAID—ASSASSINATION OF THE PRESIDENT—HIS LAST ORDER—HIS CHARACTER—FUNERAL OBSEQUIES—THE CONSPIRACY—ARREST, TRIAL, AND EXECUTION OF THE PRISONERS—REWARDS OFFERED FOR THE CAPTURE OF DAVIS AND OTHERS—THE MOVEMENT AGAINST MOBILE—ITS CAPTURE—WILSON'S CAVALRY EXPEDITION—RAISING THE FLAG AT FORT SUMTER—GRAND REVIEW OF THE ARMIES OF GRANT AND SHERMAN AT WASHINGTON—CLOSING SCENES—NATIONAL DEBT.

SHERMAN, when he hastened back to Goldsboro', from his interview with Grant, at once made preparations to move. He had said that he could not get ready before the 10th of April. This, it will be noticed, was one day after Lee surrendered.

Wholly ignorant of this great event, he, on the 10th, was about putting his columns in motion for the Roanoke, when he received the news of the fall of Petersburg and Richmond. This, of course, caused a change in his plans, for with the tidings came a dispatch from Grant, dated April 5th, in which he stated the hopeless condition of Lee's army, and added, "if you can possibly do so, push on from where you are, and let us see if we cannot finish the job with Lee's and Johnston's armies." Sherman at once wheeled his columns toward Raleigh, forcing the enemy back and destroying the bridges on the way.

On the 3rd day of the march, the news of the surrender

of Lee's entire force reached the army. It spread like wildfire, from regiment to regiment, and division to division, till one long, loud hurrah from the mighty host rent the heavens. When tired with cheering, the soldiers began to yell, till it seemed as if pandemonium had broke loose. Sherman seemed as much excited as the rest, and exclaimed in exulting accents, "Glory to God and our glorious Country." That night the elated army encamped within fourteen miles of Raleigh. The next day, Sherman entered the place, assuring the citizens that their property should be protected.

The following day, the 15th, Johnston, who was also informed of the overthrow of Lee, sent a letter to him, asking if some arrangement could not be made to save further effusion of blood. Sherman replied that he was ready to listen to any terms that he wished to propose. Johnston then requested a personal interview, and the next day, at noon, the two met upon the road, and shaking hands with apparent cordiality, adjourned to a neighboring farm-house for consultation. Johnston asked for four days' armistice, which Sherman refused to grant, and a meeting for arranging the terms of surrender was agreed upon for the next day.

They met at the same hour, attended by their splendidly mounted Staffs, and courteously lifting their hats to each other, shook hands, and then dismounted and walked together to the farm-house. Breckenridge, the rebel Secretary of War, was present at this interview, and though the terms of surrender that were granted to Lee, Johnston regarded as satisfactory, he thought that it would be for the interest of all if some basis of peace was adopted. A memorandum, looking to this, was signed by both parties, and a suspension of hostilities was agreed upon, until it could be submitted to the Government for its ratification or rejection.

Both armies were to remain in *statu quo* until a reply could be received.

The following is the memorandum:—

"FIRST. The contending armies now in the field to maintain their *statu quo*, until notice is given by the commanding General of either one to its opponent, and reasonable time—say forty-eight hours—allowed.

SECOND. The Confederate armies, now in existence, to be disbanded and conducted to their several State Capitals, there to deposit their arms and public property in the State arsenals, and each officer and man to execute and file an agreement to cease from acts of war, and abide action of both State and Federal authority. The number of arms and munitions of war to be reported to the Chief of Ordnance at Washington City, subject to future action of the Congress of the United States; in the meantime, to be used solely to maintain peace and order within the borders of the States respectively.

THIRD. The recognition by the Executive of the United States of several State Governments, in their Officers and Legislatures, taking oath prescribed by the Constitution of the United States, and where conflicting State Governments have resulted from the war, the legitimacy of all shall be submitted to the Supreme Court of the United States.

FOURTH. The re-establishment of all Federal Courts in the several States, with powers as defined by the Constitution and laws of Congress.

FIFTH. The people and inhabitants of all States to be guaranteed, so far as the Executive can, their political rights and franchise, as well as their rights of person and property, as defined by the Constitution of the United States and of States respectively.

SIXTH. The Executive authority of the Government of the United States not to disturb any of the people by reason of the late war, so long as they live in peace and quiet, and abstain from acts of armed hostility, and obey laws in existence at any place of their residence.

In general terms, war to cease; a general amnesty, so far as the Executive power of the United States can command, or on condition of disbandment of the Confederate armies, and the distribution of arms, and resumption of peaceful pursuits by officers and men as hitherto composing the said armies; not being fully empowered by our respective principals to fullfil these terms, we individually and officially pledge ourselves to promptly obtain necessary authority, and to carry out the above programme.

W. T. SHERMAN,
Major-General Commanding the Army of the United States in N. C.

J. E. JOHNSTON,
General Commanding Confederate States Army in North Carolina."

This memorandum was rejected by the President and Cabinet, and Sherman was directed to resume hostilities at once, unless Johnston should accept the terms which had been granted to Lee. Grant, in the meantime, was sent down to take charge of affairs.

Thus far every thing was quite natural and proper. An armistice granted for a few hours, by a General in the field, until proposed terms of surrender by an enemy could be submitted to the Supreme Authority, was nothing strange; and in this case, when all the advantages of delay were with us, perfectly right and reasonable.

The refusal of the Government to accede to the proffered basis of agreement, on the other hand, was not only justifiable, but clearly its duty, if it thought such an agreement prejudicial to the interests of the country.

There the matter should have ended. It was a very simple, ordinary affair altogether, and would scarcely have excited a remark, but for the absurd fuss made over it by the Secretary of War. He should have been content with sending a messenger down to Sherman with the decision of the Government. But instead of pursuing this simple, dignified course, he came out in the public newspapers with nine different reasons why the terms were inadmissible. The first reason was, that Sherman, as well as Johnston, knew that he had no right to make them. This was simply false. Every Commander in the field has a right to submit proffered terms of peace to his Government, unless he has special instructions to the contrary.

After this extraordinary explosion of patriotism it seemed to have dawned on the Secretary's mind, that his first grand reason would not be accepted by any sensible man, and so he gave to the public a telegram, which Mr. Lincoln had formerly sent to Grant, for his guidance, in any negotiations that he might make with Lee—implying that Sherman had seen this telegram, and had deliberately acted in direct violation of it.

Sherman, in reply to this implication, says:—"Now I was not in possession of it, and I have reason to know that Mr. Stanton *knew I was not in possession of it.*" This is a guarded way of making one of the severest accusations that can be brought against a man.

Halleck caught the spirit of the Secretary, and, as Chief of Staff, immediately sent dispatches to different Commanders in Sherman's department, with directions to pay no attention to him, but to resume hostilities at once. When he did this he knew perfectly well that the government dispatches, ordering Sherman to resume hostilities, would reach the latter before his own would those Commanders, and hence were unnecessary, except on the supposition that Sherman would turn traitor, and refuse to obey his Government. Indeed, the conduct of both him and Stanton can be accounted for only on the ground, that for some reason or other they wished to take advantage of the mere circumstances of this armistice of a few hours, to injure the character of Sherman.

In speaking of Halleck's impertinent interference with his command, he says: "This is too much; and I turn from the subject with feelings too strong for words." The pretext of the Secretary of War, that the armistice would allow Davis to get off with his fabulous amount of treasure, did well enough while the country was lashed into the intensest excitement by the murder of the President; but viewed from this more quiet point of view, it only awakens a smile of ridicule. Sherman says, "if the Secretary of War wanted Davis caught, why not order it, instead of, by publishing in the newspapers, putting him on his guard to hide away and escape? No orders or instructions to catch Davis or his stolen treasure ever came to me; but, on the contrary, I was led to believe that the Secretary of War rather preferred he should effect an escape from the country, if made 'unknown' to him."

There never was an instance, when, without any provocation, a man who for long years had been periling his life on the battle field for his country, lifting it by his genius to the highest pinnacle of military glory, and bearing it on to a glorious peace, was so bitterly assailed by those who should have been the first to protect him. The whole account of this disgraceful transaction is given in Sherman's Report, and in all future time it will furnish a chapter in our history, that some of the characters who figure in it will wish could be expunged.

Johnston, when informed of the decision of our Government, surrendered his immediate command on the same terms as those granted to Lee, together with all the rebel forces between him and the Chattahoochee.

A great many soldiers had gone off during the armistice, so that when on the 26th of the month, the surrender took place, only about twenty-seven thousand men laid down their arms. One hundred and eight pieces of artillery were given up. Johnston's army at the time of the surrender, though nearly fifty miles from Sherman, was in a most perilous position. Stoneman, who, as we have noticed had been sent east from Knoxville on the 20th of March, marched rapidly by way of Boone, North Carolina, and struck the railroad at Wytheville, Chambersburg and Big Lick. The portion of the column striking it at the latter place, pushed on to within a few miles of Lynchburg, destroying the bridges on the way, while the main force, after breaking up the road between New River, and Big Lick, turned off to Greensboro, on the North Carolina railroad, burning the bridges between that place and Danville, and between it and the Yadkin River, together with depots of supplies, and capturing four hundred prisoners. Crossing the river, Stoneman advanced on Salisbury, near which he attacked and defeated General Gardiner, capturing fourteen pieces of artillery, and one thousand, three hundred and sixty four prisoners. He was now but a little over a hundred miles west of Raleigh, and on the line by which Johnston received his supplies, and by which he must retreat. Burning rebel army stores here, he destroyed fifteen miles of railroad toward Charlotte, and then retired on Statesville. Thus it will be seen how comprehensive and complete Grant's plan was, to make this campaign a conclusive one.

But while these great victories were being achieved, and the mighty Confederacy that had attracted the gaze of the world was dissolving like a tower of mist, and the Nation, elate with hope was just lifting its head from out the bloody waves of revolution, an event occurred that thrilled the land with an excitement which, for a time made all other things sink into insignificance. "The President of the United States has been assassinated in the Capital," flew on wings of lightning over the North, making every face turn pale with horror. The man whose inauguration had been the signal for revolt, and who for four years had watched and waited, and labored, and prayed for a restored Union, was ruthlessly shot down by an assassin, just as the mountain was being lifted from his heart and the smile of joy was chasing away the look of care that had so long darkened his countenance. Anxious to take the first step toward peace, he on the 13th of April, caused the Secretary of War to issue the following bulletin:—

"WAR DEPARTMENT, WASHINGTON, April 13, 1865—6 P. M.

This Department, after mature consideration, and consultation with the Lieutenant-General upon the results of the recent campaigns, has come to the following determinations, which will be carried into effect by appropriate orders, to be immediately issued:

FIRST. To stop all drafting and recruiting in the loyal States.

SECOND. To curtail purchases for arms, ammunition, quartermaster and commissary supplies, and reduce the expenses of the military establishment in its several branches.

THIRD. To reduce the number of general and staff officers to the actual necessities of the service.

FOURTH. To remove all military restrictions upon trade and commerce, so far as may be consistent with public safety.

As soon as these measures can be put in operation, it will be made known by public orders.

EDWIN M. STANTON, *Secretary of War*."

The next night, while the President was at Ford's theatre with his wife, seeking a little relaxation, a play actor by the name of John Wilkes Booth shot him in the back of the head, then leaping on the stage and brandishing a dagger, he shouted "*Sic semper tyrannis*," and fled through a side door into the street. His plans were well laid, as far as human foresight could do it, to escape; but the mute flag of his country, hanging over the President's box, caught his spur as he leaped, flinging him heavily on the stage, and crippling him so that his flight was retarded, and he was eventually overtaken and shot while refusing to surrender.

In consequence of the intense excitement the country was in, just previous to the murder—the victim being the President of the United States, and a man possessing one of the kindliest and most forgiving hearts that ever beat in a human bosom—this assassination produced the profoundest sensation that ever shook a nation to its center.

It was altogether an extraordinary murder. There were men South who had not only been ruined in property by the war, but whose sons had been slain in battle or died in prison, and whose wives and daughters had been outraged by Federal soldiers, till they had gone mad with despair and the desire of revenge, of whom such an act might be expected. But the assassin had not been injured in a single interest, and could give no shadow of excuse for the hellish deed.

Mr. Lincoln committed some grave errors of policy, for

he was not infallible—he had faults, for he was not perfect, but as a man who, to use his own words, "felt malice toward none, and had charity for all," whose highest ambition was to do right, whose strongest desire was the peace and prosperity of his country, and "all whose faults leaned to virtue's side," he stands without a peer since Washington. His simple, honest, kindly nature, notwithstanding the bitter animosities that prevailed, had taken a deep hold of the National heart, and from enemies as well as friends, there arose a cry of horror and of grief at the "deep damnation of his taking off."

With but slender education, and no remarkable intellectual endowments, he had shown how wisely, in the stormiest times, and amid the greatest embarrassments and difficulties, an honest heart may cause a ruler to act. Indeed, a careful analysis of his life will show that nearly all his mistakes arose from not following his own judgment, but from yielding to the crooked, selfish policy of others.

The funeral obsequies were celebrated in the Executive Mansion on the 19th of April, when the body was taken to the Capitol, where it lay in state until the 21st, and then was borne back to its former home, in Springfield, Illinois. The tolling of bells, and the draping of the land in mourning, all along the line of the road over which the body was transported, and the crowds that thronged around the funeral car, attested how deep and universal was the grief.

On the same night of his murder, Mr. Seward, Secretary of State, was attacked in his sick bed, by an accomplice of Booth, and dangerously wounded, before the assassin could be driven off.

On May 10th, David E. Harrold, George A. Atzeroth, Lewis Payne, Michael O'Laughlin, Edward Spangler, Samuel Arnold, Mary E. Surratt, and Samuel A. Mudd, who had been arrested on suspicion, as accomplices of Booth, were arraigned before a military tribunal, as principals or accessories to the murder. After a trial of nearly two months, in the progress of which, the existence of a plot to murder not only Mr. Lincoln and Mr. Seward, but Vice President Johnson, General Grant, and others, was developed, Harrold, Payne, Mrs. Surratt, and Atzeroth, were found guilty of murder, and hung in Washington on the 7th of July; Mudd, Arnold, and O'Laughlin were sentenced to imprisonment for life, and Spangler to six years' imprisonment at hard labor.

In a few hours after the death of Mr. Lincoln, Andrew Johnson, Vice President, was installed into office—and so far as the affairs of the Government were concerned, every thing went on as though nothing had happened. While European powers looked for a new outbreak, or an attempted assumption of military power, or at least a sudden arrest of the wheels of Government, they saw, with amazement, that a Republic could not only put forth the greatest efforts, but stand, unmoved, the heaviest shocks, and the most sudden changes, of any Government on earth.

Owing to the excited state of the public mind, every fact bearing on the assassination of Mr. Lincoln, became magnified, and it was believed that Booth was only a tool in the hands of Jefferson Davis, and other prominent men of the South; hence heavy rewards were offered by the new President for their arrest—one hundred thousand dollars for Davis; twenty-five thousand dollars for Clement C. Clay, Jacob Thompson, George N. Sanders, and Beverly Tucker; and ten thousand dollars for William C. Cleary, clerk of Clay. In the meantime, Davis had fled into Georgia.

But little more remains to be told of military movements. With the surrender of Lee and Johnston, the rebellion was ended. But while the closing scenes were being enacted on the Atlantic Coast, events were transpiring on the Gulf of Mexico which, under ordinary circumstances, would have awakened the keenest interest. Grant designed that the expedition against Mobile should keep a large, rebel force in Alabama, which otherwise would reinforce Lee. Hence, as we have seen, Canby commenced his movements against it the 20th of March, or just as Sherman was reaching Goldsboro.

In the meantime, vessels, drawing but little water, had been gathered in Mobile Bay, so that the navy could co-operate with the army in the attack. A. J. Smith took his command from Fort Gaines to Fish River, by water, where he was joined by Granger, with the Thirteenth Corps, who moved from Fort Morgan. In the meantime, General Steele, with his command, struck across the country from Pensacola, and cutting the railroad leading from Tensas to Montgomery, effected a juncture with the former.

Thus, it will be seen that the army moved up on the east side of the bay. Two main forts prevented the passage of the gunboats up to Mobile—the Spanish Fort, as it was called, and Fort Blakely. It was determined to take the first of these by a combined attack of the army and navy—the latter to engage the water-batteries, while the land forces should assail the works in the rear. Siege guns were brought up, and on the 4th of April a tremendous bombardment was opened on the fort.

On the 8th, another was ordered—to be followed by a general assault, at five o'clock in the evening. The fire was terrific and crushing, and for three hours it was kept up with fearful effect, when two brigades of Carr's division moved gallantly to the assault. Mounting the ramparts with loud cheers, they carried some three hundred yards of the works, when they made themselves secure, to wait for daylight to complete the conquest, but at one o'clock in the morning—the same Sunday that Lee surrendered to Grant—the garrison capitulated.

On this day, also, so bright in our calendar, Steele assaulted Fort Blakely, in his front. This was situated some four miles north of the former, and twelve miles from Mobile. With the reading of the orders for the assault, to the troops, was read also a dispatch announcing the fall of Richmond and Petersburg, and the flight of Lee. Loud shouts rent the air at the glorious news, and gaily as though going to a banquet, the brave fellows moved forward. Garrard's division bore the brunt of the fight. For a whole hour the soldiers worked away at the obstructions, while a desolating fire swept them, and torpedoes were almost momentarily bursting under their feet.

At last they were cleared, and with a yell they jumped into the ditch and scaled the works. Colonel Rinneken's and General Gilbert's brigade turned the right of the fort and entered it at the same time. The colored troops on the right, under General Hawkins, behaved with great gallantry, charging like veterans through the fire. At seven o'clock, our flag was waving from the ramparts. Our loss in this gallant assault, was about one thousand, while that of the enemy was not over five hundred. Three thousand three hundred prisoners, four thousand stand of arms, and thirty-two pieces of artillery were captured. This secured the fall of Mobile.

Monday and Tuesday were spent in pushing forward reconnoissances, and in the removing of torpedoes from the river, by the navy, so that it could approach the city. The latter was hazardous work, for the bed of the stream was sown thick with them, while the batteries on shore kept up a steady fire on the vessels engaged in it.

On the 12th, our columns were already in motion to complete the investment of the place, when the signal came that the enemy had evacuated it.

Our total loss before the place was two thousand soldiers, and fifty seamen. We lost, besides two heavy iron-clads, two tin-clads, and one transport—all destroyed by torpedoes.

Admiral Thatcher commanded the naval force, and reported the amount of artillery captured at four hundred pieces.

We mentioned in connection with the movement of Canby on Mobile, the raid of Wilson east from Vicksburg. "The expedition, consisting of twelve thousand five hundred mounted men, was delayed by rains until March 22, when it moved from Chickasaw, Alabama. On the 1st of April, General Wilson encountered the enemy in force under Forrest, near Ebenezer Church, drove him in confusion, captured three hundred prisoners and three guns, and destroyed the central bridge over the Cahawba River. On the 2d he attacked and captured the fortified city of Selma, defended by Forrest with seven thousand men and thirty-two guns, destroyed the arsenal, armory, naval foundry, machine shops, vast quantities of stores, and captured three thousand prisoners. On the 4th he captured and destroyed Tuscaloosa. On the 10th he crossed the Alabama River, and after sending information of his operations to General Canby, marched on Montgomery, which place he occupied on the 14th, the enemy having abandoned it. At this place many stores and five steamboats fell into our hands. Thence a force marched direct on Columbus, and another on West Point, both of which places were assaulted and captured on the 16th. At the former place we got fifteen hundred prisoners and fifty-two field guns, destroyed two gunboats, the navy-yard, foundries, arsenal, many factories, and much other public property. At the latter place we got three hundred prisoners, four guns, and destroyed nineteen locomotives and three hundred cars. On the 20th he took possession of Macon,

Georgia, with sixty field-guns, twelve hundred militia, and five Generals, surrendered by General Howell Cobb." *

This was one of the most remarkable raids of the war; but its success and results not being known until after the surrender of Lee and Johnston, it excited but little interest. Three days after the fall of Macon, Davis started in his flight to Georgia, accompanied by his family. General Wilson at the former place, hearing of it, immediately scattered his cavalry over the country, and at length, on the morning of the 11th of May, succeeded in capturing him at Irwinsville. Colonel Pritchard, of the Fourth Michigan cavalry came suddenly upon his encampment, when the rebel President attempted to make his escape, disguised as a woman. Being detected by the heavy boots under his female apparel, he was seized, together with Reagan his Post Master General, and conveyed seventy miles distant to Macon, from whence he was transferred to Fortress Monroe to await his trial for treason.

Previous to this, the Government dispatched a steamer, with General Anderson to Fort Sumter, to raise the same flag which just four years before, he had been compelled to haul down at the bidding of traitors. With his own hands he sent it aloft, amid the cheers of the spectators.

In looking over the events of this Spring, one is struck with the remarkable unity of action, and the unvaried success of our armies in different parts of the widely extended military field. Indeed it is seldom that a single month is crowded with such momentous events as that of April, 1865. Selma, Montgomery, Macon, Mobile, and Columbus, Ga., all fell during the month—the two armies of Lee and Johnston surrendered, and the President of the United States was assassinated. It saw the culmination and overthrow of the Confederacy, and all that followed was but the mere picking up of the fragments.

* General Grant's Report.

"On the 4th day of May, General Dick Taylor surrendered to General Canby all the remaining rebel forces east of the Mississippi.

"A force sufficient to insure an easy triumph over the enemy under Kirby Smith, west of the Mississippi, was immediately put in motion for Texas, and Major-General Sheridan designated for its immediate command; but on the 26th day of May, and before they reached their destination, General Kirby Smith surrendered his entire command to Major-General Canby. This surrender did not take place, however, until after the capture of the rebel President and Vice President; and the bad faith was exhibited of first disbanding most of his army, and permitting an indiscriminate plunder of public property." *

Thus on sea and land, all resistance disappeared, with the exception of the pirate Shenandoah, which cruised all Summer in the Pacific Ocean, capturing our vessels. Her career did not close till November, when she surrendered to an English man of war in the Mersey.

As a fitting close to this long and terrible struggle which the country had passed through, a grand review of the two armies of Grant and Sherman took place in the National Capital on the 23d and 24th, of May in the presence of the President and Cabinet, and foreign Ministers. As the bronzed and proud veterans marched up Pennsylvania Avenue, the heavens resounded with the acclamations of the multitude, and the air was filled with bouquets of flowers that were rained on the noble leaders. The Duke of Wellington said, when 50,000 troops were reviewed in the Champs Elysèes, after the occupation of Paris by the Allies, that it was "a sight but once seen in a life time;" but here nearly two hundred thousand marched in an apparently endless stream past the Presidential mansion, not conscripts forced

* General Grant's Report.

into the ranks, but citizens, who had voluntarily taken up arms to defend not a monarch's rights, but their own.

Yet, sublime as was this spectacle, it sunk into insignificance before the grandeur of the one presented a few days after, when this army, strong enough to conquer a hemisphere, melted suddenly away into the mass of the people and was seen no more. Its deeds of renown had filled the civilized world, and European statesmen looked on and wondered what disposition could be made of it, and where it would choose to go, or what it would do. It was one of the grandest armies that ever bore on its bayonet points the destinies of a king or a nation—a consolidation and embodiment of power seldom witnessed; and yet, while the gaze of the world was fixed upon it, it disappeared like a vision, and when one looked for it he saw only peaceful citizens engaged in their usual occupations. The Major-General whose martial achievements had been repeated in almost every language under the sun, was seen amid his papers in his old law office, which he had left at the call of his country—the brave Colonel, who had led many a gallant charge, was in his counting house, acting as though he had been absent only a few days on business, while the veterans of the rank and file, whose battle shout had rung over scores of bloody fields, could only be found by name as one bent over his saw and plane, and another swung his scythe in the harvest field, or plied his humble toil along the streets. It was a marvelous sight, the grandest the world ever saw. It had been the people's war—the people had carried it on, and having finished their own work, quietly laid aside the instruments with which they had accomplished it, and again took up those of peaceful industry. Never did a Government on earth exhibit such stability, and assert its superiority over all other forms, as did this republican government of ours, in the way its armies disappeared when the struggle was over.

The war being ended, there now remain for the country the great work of reconstruction and the management of the National debt. After the disbanding of the armies, the sale of governmental vessels and the vast amount of army stores and supplies of every kind, and settling up the most important claims against the National Treasury, our public debt, on the 1st of February, 1866, was two thousand seven hundred and sixteen millions, eight hundred and ninety-eight thousand, one hundred and fifty-two dollars. The following is a condensed summary of it at that time:—

PUBLIC DEBT OF THE UNITED STATES, FEBRUARY 1, 1866.

Original 5-20 Bonds, 1862,	$514,780,500
New 5-20 Bonds, 1864,	100,000,000
New 5-20 Bonds, 1865,	50,590,300
Six per cent. Bonds, 1881,	282,648,250
Five per cent. 10-40 Bonds,	172,769,100
Old six per cents.,	19,339,592
Old five per cents.,	27,022,000
Total gold-bearing Bonds,	$1,167,149,742
Seven-thirty per cent. Treasury Notes,	$830,000,000
Compound Legal Tenders,	180,012,141
Five per cent. Legal Tenders,	8,536,900
Six per cent. Certificates,	60,637,000
Deposits on Interest,	114,755,840
Six per cent. to Pacific Railroad,	3,354,000
Total Currency Interest,	$1,197,295,881
Greenbacks,	$423,902,223
Gold Certificates,	8,391,080
Fractional Currency,	26,553,244
Total free of Interest,	$458,846,547
Less Treasury balances,	*107,493,348
Total,	$351,353,199
Past due debt,	1,099,330
Grand total of all debt,	$2,716,898,152
*On hand in Coin,	$51,443,162
*On hand in Currency,	56,050,186
Total as above,	$107,493,348

The principal changes in the statement since January 1st, are:—

Increase of Currency Deposits from,		$97,257,194
To 1st of February,		114,755,840
Increase,		$17,498,646
Increase of Gold Certificates,		1,102,940
Total increase of Deposits,		$18,601,586
Nearly balanced by increase of Cash on hand,		16,764,467
Difference,		$1,837,119
Add increase Pacific railroad Bonds,	$352,000	
Increase of Fractional Currency,	552,824—	904,824
Difference,		$2,741,943
Deduct Greenbacks reduced,	$2,329,107	
Other Items reduced,	96.220—	2,425,327
Net increase of Public Debt,		$316,616
Total, January 1, 1866,		$2,716,581,536
Total, February 1, 1866,		2,716,898,152
Difference as above,		$316,616

The Public Debt reached its maximum on the schedule of the 31st of August last, when the total stood,

The Public Debt reached its maximum on the schedule of the 31st of August last, when the total stood,	$2,757,781,190
Present total,	2,716,898,152
Net reduction in five months,	$40,883,038

The Public Debt stood, on the 1st of October last, at the close of the first Quarter of the current fiscal year,	$2,745,061,844
As against February 1, 1866,	2,716,898,152
Decrease since October 1, 1865,	$28,163,692

www.ingramcontent.com/pod-product-compliance
Lightning Source LLC
LaVergne TN
LVHW021100110826
845150LV00001B/126

* 9 7 8 1 4 2 5 5 6 6 3 7 1 *